THE CAMBRIDGE COMPANION TO
WOMEN AND ISLAM

The Cambridge Companion to Women and Islam provides a comprehensive overview of a timely topic that encompasses the fields of Islamic feminist scholarship, anthropology, history, and sociology. Divided into three parts, it makes several key contributions. The volume offers a detailed analysis of textual debates on gender and Islam, highlighting the logic of classical reasoning and its enduring appeal, while emphasizing alternative readings proposed by Islamic feminists. It considers the agency that Muslim women exhibit in relation to their faith as reflected in women's piety movements. Moreover, the volume documents how Muslim women shape sociopolitical life, presenting real-world examples from across the Muslim world and diaspora communities. Written by an international team of scholars, the Companion also explores theoretical and methodological advances in the field, providing guidance for future research. Surveying Muslim women's experiences across time and place, it also presents debates on gender norms across various genres of Islamic scholarship.

Masooda Bano is Professor of Development Studies at the University of Oxford and a Senior Golding Fellow at Brasenose College, Oxford. She has held numerous prestigious research awards, including European Research Council Starting and Advance grants. Bano is the author of *Female Islamic Education Movements: The Re-Democratisation of Islamic Knowledge* (2017) and has edited several volumes on Islamic educational institutions in Muslim-majority countries as well as in the West.

CAMBRIDGE COMPANIONS TO RELIGION

This is a series of companions to major topics and key figures in theology and religious studies. Each volume contains specially commissioned chapters by international scholars, which provide an accessible and stimulating introduction to the subject for new readers and nonspecialists.

Other Titles in the Series

AMERICAN CATHOLICISM Edited by Margaret M. McGuinness and Thomas F. Rzeznik
AMERICAN ISLAM Edited by Juliane Hammer and Omid Safi
AMERICAN JUDAISM Edited by Dana Evan Kaplan
AMERICAN METHODISM Edited by Jason E. Vickers
AMERICAN PROTESTANTISM Edited by Jason E. Vickers and Jennifer Woodruff Tait
ANCIENT MEDITERRANEAN RELIGIONS Edited by Barbette Stanley Spaeth
APOCALYPTIC LITERATURE Edited by Colin McAllister
APOSTOLIC FATHERS Edited by Michael F. Bird and Scott Harrower
AUGUSTINE'S CITY OF GOD Edited by David Vincent Meconi
AUGUSTINE'S 'CONFESSIONS' Edited by Tarmo Toom
KARL BARTH Edited by John Webster
THE BIBLE, 2nd edition Edited by Bruce Chilton
THE BIBLE AND LITERATURE Edited by Calum Carmichael
BIBLICAL INTERPRETATION Edited by John Barton
BIBLICAL NARRATIVE Edited by Keith Bodner
BIBLICAL WISDOM LITERATURE Edited by Katharine J. Dell, Suzanna R. Millar, and Arthur Jan Keefer
BLACK THEOLOGY Edited by Dwight N. Hopkins and Edward P. Antonio
DIETRICH BONHOEFFER Edited by John de Gruchy
THE BOOK OF ISAIAH Edited by Christopher B. Hays
JOHN CALVIN Edited by Donald K. McKim
CHRISTIAN DOCTRINE Edited by Colin Gunton
CHRISTIAN ETHICS Edited by Robin Gill
CHRISTIAN MYSTICISM Edited by Amy Hollywood and Patricia Z. Beckman
CHRISTIAN PHILOSOPHICAL THEOLOGY Edited by Charles Taliaferro and Chad V. Meister
CHRISTIAN POLITICAL THEOLOGY Edited by Craig Hovey and Elizabeth Phillips
CHRISTIANITY AND THE ENVIRONMENT Edited by Alexander J. B. Hampton and Douglas Hedley

(continued after index)

THE CAMBRIDGE COMPANION TO
WOMEN AND ISLAM

Edited by

Masooda Bano
University of Oxford

Shaftesbury Road, Cambridge CB2 8EA, United Kingdom

One Liberty Plaza, 20th Floor, New York, NY 10006, USA

477 Williamstown Road, Port Melbourne, VIC 3207, Australia

314–321, 3rd Floor, Plot 3, Splendor Forum, Jasola District Centre, New Delhi – 110025, India

103 Penang Road, #05–06/07, Visioncrest Commercial, Singapore 238467

Cambridge University Press is part of Cambridge University Press & Assessment, a department of the University of Cambridge.

We share the University's mission to contribute to society through the pursuit of education, learning and research at the highest international levels of excellence.

www.cambridge.org
Information on this title: www.cambridge.org/9781009206716

DOI: 10.1017/9781009206587

© Cambridge University Press & Assessment 2025

This publication is in copyright. Subject to statutory exception and to the provisions of relevant collective licensing agreements, no reproduction of any part may take place without the written permission of Cambridge University Press & Assessment.

When citing this work, please include a reference to the DOI 10.1017/9781009206587

First published 2025

A catalogue record for this publication is available from the British Library

Library of Congress Cataloging-in-Publication Data
NAMES: Bano, Masooda, editor.
TITLE: The Cambridge companion to women and Islam / edited by Masooda Bano.
DESCRIPTION: Cambridge, United Kingdom : Cambridge University Press, 2025. | Series: Cambridge companions to religion | Includes bibliographical references and index.
IDENTIFIERS: LCCN 2024037711 | ISBN 9781009206716 (hardback) | ISBN 9781009206563 (paperback)
SUBJECTS: LCSH: Women in Islam. | Feminism – Religious aspects – Islam. | Muslim women – Social conditions. | Muslim women – Conduct of life. | Women in the Hadith.
CLASSIFICATION: LCC BP173.4 .C352 2025 | DDC 297.082–dc23/eng/20241015
LC record available at https://lccn.loc.gov/2024037711

ISBN 978-1-009-20671-6 Hardback
ISBN 978-1-009-20656-3 Paperback

Cambridge University Press & Assessment has no responsibility for the persistence or accuracy of URLs for external or third-party internet websites referred to in this publication and does not guarantee that any content on such websites is, or will remain, accurate or appropriate.

Contents

List of Contributors *page* vii
Preface xi
A Note on Foreign-Language Words xiv

Introduction 1
MASOODA BANO

Part I *Logic of Classical Reasoning* 33

1 Women in the Qur'an 41
   KAREN BAUER

2 Women's Inheritance 64
   SOHAIL HANIF

3 Veiling and Restrictions on Sexual Liberty 85
   KATERINA NORDIN

4 Muhammad: The Ideal Man 106
   FARAZ A. KHAN

5 Prophet's Wives: "Mothers of the Believers" 124
   MAHJABEEN DHALA

Part II *Asserting Agency in Faith* 145

6 Becoming Salafi 151
   ARNDT EMMERICH AND ALYAA EBBIARY

7 Joining Political Islam 174
   LIV TØNNESSEN

8 Conversions to Islam 195
   VANESSA VROON-NAJEM

9 Islamic Feminists' Approaches 214
   NINA NURMILA

10 Women's Mosques in China 234
    MARIA JASCHOK

Part III *Asserting Agency in Socio-Political Life* 259

11 Patrons of Art, Architecture, and the Urban Environment 267
D. FAIRCHILD RUGGLES

12 Women and Political Authority 296
SHAHLA HAERI

13 Women as Social Activists 315
NELLY VAN DOORN-HARDER

14 Poets and Writers 338
ZUZANNA OLSZEWSKA

15 'Feminist Spirituality' as Lived Religion 359
ZILKA SPAHIĆ ŠILJAK

Volume Bibliography 380

Index 392

Contributors

Masooda Bano is Professor of Development Studies at the University of Oxford and a Senior Golding Fellow at Brasenose College, Oxford. She specializes in the comparative study of Muslim societies and leads large-scale, multidisciplinary projects. Among other themes, she has explored the conditions fostering the emergence of female religious engagement with Islamic knowledge acquisition and dissemination across the Muslim world and in diaspora communities in recent years. She has published many books, including *Female Islamic Education Movements: The Re-Democratisation of Islamic Knowledge* (2017), and has edited several volumes on Islamic educational institutions in Muslim-majority countries as well as in the West. Professor Bano has also held numerous prestigious research awards, including European Research Council Starting and Advance grants.

Karen Bauer is Associate Professor at the Institute of Ismaili Studies, London. Her books include *Women, Households and the Hereafter in the Qur'an: A Patronage of Piety* (with Feras Hamza), *Gender Hierarchy in the Qur'an: Medieval Interpretations, Modern Responses*, and *An Anthology of Qur'anic Commentaries: On Women* (with Feras Hamza). In addition to her work on women in the Qur'an and in Muslim tradition, Dr Bauer has written several articles on emotions in the Qur'an and in early Islam.

Mahjabeen Dhala is Assistant Professor of Islamic Studies and Chair of the Women's Studies in Religion program at the Graduate Theological Union in Berkeley, California. Her work focuses on reviving premodern Muslim women's contributions to Islamic theology, exegesis, and activism. Her recent book, *Feminist Theology and Social Justice in Islam: A Study on the Sermon of Fatima*, explores the seventh-century protest of the Prophet Muhammad's daughter against the government's confiscation of her lands and denial of her inheritance rights. Her current research project examines early African Muslim women's role in shaping Islamic thought and institutions.

Nelly van Doorn-Harder teaches Religious Studies at Wake Forest University (USA) and at the Center for Islamic Theology (CIT) at Vrije Universiteit Amsterdam. Her research explores Islam in Indonesia and Coptic Christianity in Egypt, with a focus on leadership, gender, freedom of religion, and interfaith dialogue. Currently, she is working on a book about the Indonesian National Commission for Women's Rights (Komnas Perempuan), analyzing Komnas' efforts to combat violence against women, including domestic violence and child marriage. She is the author of *Women Shaping Islam: Reading the Qur'an in Indonesia* (2006).

Alyaa Ebbiary is Lecturer in Religion, Society, and Politics at Lancaster University. Prior to this, she held a postdoctoral position in the Department of Anthropology at Durham University, where she worked on the cross-European Encounters project. She completed her PhD in Social Anthropology and Islamic Studies at the School of Oriental and African Studies (SOAS), focusing on Islamic higher education in the UK. Her research particularly delved into pedagogy, religious authority, and female scholarship. Beyond her academic pursuits, Alyaa has been actively involved as a teacher, community organizer, and interfaith trainer.

Arndt Emmerich is Lecturer in Sociology at the University of Hertfordshire, a guest researcher at the Max Planck Institute for the Study of Religious and Ethnic Diversity, and an honorary research fellow at the Department of Psychosocial Studies at Birkbeck, University of London. He specializes in conducting in-depth ethnographic fieldwork, particularly with Muslim youth communities. Emmerich's research has resulted in numerous journal articles, and his work has been featured by major media outlets, including the BBC. His doctoral thesis was published as *Islamic Movements in India: Moderation and Its Discontents* (2020).

Shahla Haeri is Professor of Anthropology and a former director of the Women's Studies Program (2001–10) at Boston University. A pioneer in Iranian anthropology, she is the author of *Law of Desire: Temporary Marriage in Shi'i Iran* (1989, and translated into Arabic). Her other books include *No Shame for the Sun: Lives of Professional Pakistani Women* (2002) and *The Unforgettable Queens of Islam: Succession, Authority, Gender* (2020). Professor Haeri has also produced and directed the video documentary *Mrs President: Women and Political Leadership in Iran* (2002), which focuses on six women presidential contenders during the Iranian presidential election of 2001. She has received numerous grants and fellowships.

Sohail Hanif began his journey with traditional Islamic Studies in Jordan before completing his doctoral thesis at Oxford, focusing on Hanafi jurisprudence. His research is especially centred on its development between the fifth and eighth Islamic centuries. Through his thesis, Hanif delves into the foundational ideas of this legal system and their role in interpreting classical legal commentaries. Hanif is an experienced teacher in various settings, both formal and informal. Recently, he accepted the position of director at the National Zakat Foundation in the UK. Previously, he was a faculty member at Cambridge Muslim College and continues to contribute as an associate lecturer.

Maria Jaschok is Senior Research Associate in Contemporary China Studies at the Oxford School of Global and Area Studies, as well as a supervisor and tutor for the MSt in Women's, Gender, and Sexuality Studies at the University of Oxford. From 2019 to 2021 she held the position of director at the International Gender Studies Centre at Lady Margaret Hall. Her research primarily focuses on gendered constructions of memory, feminist and aural ethnography, innovative research methodologies, and the application of oral history in documenting the history of

Muslim women in Asia, with a particular emphasis on China. Jaschok is actively involved in numerous international academic and professional organizations, contributing to steering committees, editorial boards, and advisory panels.

Faraz A. Khan is a lecturer and senior research fellow at Zaytuna College in Berkeley, California, where he specializes in teaching Kalam (Islamic philosophical theology) and ethics. He completed his classical Islamic scholarship in Jordan, where he studied a broad range of religious sciences, including Ash'ari and Maturidi scholastic theology, Hanafi jurisprudence, Prophetic narration (sira and hadith), and logic with renowned scholars. He received scholarly authorization (ijazah) to teach these subjects. His most recent work, *An Introduction to Islamic Theology: Imam Nūr al-Dīn al-Ṣābūnī's Al-Bidāyah fī Uṣūl al-Dīn*, was published in 2020. His current projects include a translation of a text in logic by al-Ghazali.

Katerina Nordin holds an MPhil in Islamic Studies and History from the University of Oxford and a History BA from the School of Oriental and African Studies (SOAS). Her research interests lie in education in Islamic communities, with a focus on female-led spaces. She has been involved in various research projects focused on the Muslim world and Muslims in the European context. Notably, she possesses a deep understanding of the Islamic educational landscape in the UK, focusing on how young Muslim women strive to carve out their own spaces in a manner that honors tradition.

Nina Nurmila serves as the Dean of the Faculty of Education at Universitas Islam Internasional Indonesia (UIII) and is Professor of Gender and Islamic Studies at the State Islamic University (UIN SGD) Bandung. She is author of *Women, Islam, and Everyday Life: Renegotiating Polygamy in Indonesia* (2009). As a self-identified Muslim feminist, Nurmila is an active participant in both the Indonesian academic community and activist networks. She is dedicated to promoting Islamic feminist scholarship in Indonesia and connecting it with women's rights activism.

Zuzanna Olszewska is Associate Professor in the Social Anthropology of the Middle East at the University of Oxford and a Fellow of St John's College, Oxford. She is author of the award-winning *The Pearl of Dari: Poetry and Personhood among Young Afghans in Iran* (2015) and numerous articles on Afghan literature and culture. She is also a translator of Persian-language Afghan poetry.

D. Fairchild Ruggles holds the Presidential Chair in the Humanities and Social Sciences at the University of Illinois, Urbana-Champaign, where she directs the Unit for Criticism and Interpretive Theory and teaches in the Department of Landscape Architecture and the School of Architecture. She serves as the art and architecture field editor for the *Encyclopedia of Islam*. In addition to her book publications on Islamic architecture, landscape, and environmental history, she has edited two volumes on the cultural patronage of women in the Islamic world and South Asia, and is the author of the award-winning *Tree of Pearls: The Extraordinary Architectural Patronage of the 13th-Century Egyptian Slave-Queen Shajar al-Durr* (2020).

Zilka Spahić Šiljak is Associate Professor in Gender Studies and serves as the Academic Director of the Gender Resource Center at the University of Sarajevo. She is also Director of the TPO Foundation (Transcultural Psychosocial Educational Foundation), which champions gender equality, dialogue, and peace through collaborations among civil society, academic institutions, and government. Her efforts are particularly concentrated on promoting gender mainstreaming in Bosnia's higher education, and she is a co-founder of the Balkans' first online school on Feminism and Religion.

Liv Tønnessen is Senior Researcher at the Chr. Michelsen Institute (CMI) and director of the Center on Law and Social Transformation. A political scientist specializing in gender and politics, Tønnessen has been involved in long-term academic collaborations with local researchers and institutions in Sudan. Tønnessen has published extensively on women's rights and Islam.

Vanessa Vroon-Najem is an anthropologist affiliated with the University of Amsterdam, where she also earned her PhD. Her main research interest lies in the study of conversion experiences to Islam in the Netherlands, on which she has published extensively. She has curated three museum exhibitions based on her research and created a documentary entitled *Marrying before Allah – Personal Stories of Converts* with visual anthropologist Wendy van Wilgenburg. Additionally, she works as an educator at the Amsterdam Museum and serves on the board of editors of the Amsterdam Museum journal.

Preface

As scholars, our disciplinary backgrounds inevitably shape our perceptions of significant questions within our field and the methods deemed suitable for their exploration. A notable entry point for research on women and Islam within Western academia centres on textual reinterpretation. This approach is particularly understandable for Muslim women scholars situated in Gender Studies or Feminist Studies departments, highlighting a clear avenue for the feminist reinterpretation of Islamic texts. Recent years have seen the emergence of compelling scholarship in this domain, to which this volume offers exposure. Drawing from my expertise as a social scientist with a focus on ethnographic studies, I have, however, increasingly come to emphasize the importance of studying lived experiences of Muslim women. Having held multiple substantial comparative research grants has afforded me the opportunity to conduct extensive fieldwork across various Muslim-majority countries and within Muslim diasporas in the West. Throughout my interactions with Muslim women, I have observed a steadfast defence of Islam, noting their profound devotional love for God, the strength derived from their spiritual connections, and the sense of beauty, happiness, and confidence these relationships foster – aiding them in maximizing life's joys and navigating its challenges.

Furthermore, I have documented their justifications for Islamic gender norms, as elucidated by classical Islamic scholarship, which continues to influence religious practices in Muslim societies. These women also critique the perceived limitations of Western feminism, arguing that it renders women more vulnerable than their own positions. I might be one of the few scholars to have documented this evidence across multiple fieldwork sites, but, as we will see in this volume, the growing number of ethnographic studies involving Muslim women is showing that these observations are no longer unique. Beginning with Lila Abu-Lughod's groundbreaking research in the 1980s, which highlighted the agency of even impoverished Bedouin women in Egypt, and significantly advanced by the 2005 publication of Saba Mahmood's *The Politics of Piety*, focusing on the pietistic agency of mosque-going Muslim women, we have witnessed a consistent increase in studies documenting the agency of Muslim women. These studies explore not only how Muslim women navigate daily life but also their engagement with faith. The beliefs of these women, and the reasons behind these beliefs, are seen as the result of dynamic, reflective processes, rather than merely products of socialization or false consciousness.

This Companion volume aims, on the one hand, to faithfully capture the dynamic intellectual agency of female scholars, most of whom are of Muslim origin, in providing a feminist interpretation of foundational Islamic texts, namely the Qur'an and hadith (sayings of the Prophet Muhammad), as well as the broader body of classical Islamic scholarship. On the other hand, it places equal emphasis on highlighting the necessity of understanding Muslim women's experiences by first appreciating why traditional Islamic interpretations of gender norms, which offer a distinct logic of equality different from that demanded by the Western liberal feminist framework, continue to resonate with the majority of Muslim women. We must recognize that for many believing women, particularly those from well-educated and economically affluent backgrounds, this acceptance is not the result of patriarchal structures, but a conscious choice driven by conviction in the logic of an alternative worldview. In this worldview, the spiritual aspect of human life is significant, and gender complementarity – rather than equality, in recognition of biological differences between genders – is seen as logically appealing. This perspective is something Western feminist theory, with its focus on socialization over biology as the primary cause of gender division in societies, is currently reluctant to consider.

In my experience, many educated Muslim women draw on scientific evidence of gender differences to defend the logic behind the Islamic proposed division of labour between genders. This perspective is also shared by prominent Islamic scholars in the West, such as Tim Winter and Hamza Yusuf, who have a strong following among young, university-going Muslim men and women. Recognizing these divisions is not seen as inherently limiting female agency, as it is argued that Islam allows for considerable scope for negotiation between couples to develop a balance that suits them best. Therefore, when evaluating the fairness of Islamic dictates on gender norms against Western feminist ideals, we must be open to allowing space for the critique of those ideals themselves, based on one's initial assumptions about what constitutes the most important human values. This volume introduces the reader to cutting-edge scholarship on women and Islam, in the hope that it will inspire both graduate and undergraduate students to engage more actively with this field. It aims to help early career researchers identify the most intellectually and socially relevant questions for future research, serve as a useful resource for senior scholars teaching about this subject, and enable ordinary readers to appreciate the richness of Muslim women's experiences. It highlights their energy and dynamism and shows how, for many, their faith in Islam is a fundamental source of strength.

I would like to take this opportunity to express my gratitude to Beatrice Rehl, my editor at Cambridge, for inviting me to consider this project. Initially hesitant to embrace this significant commitment, given the predictable challenge of engaging established and like-minded scholars, I recognized the value of undertaking such an assignment to reach a broader audience. Recruiting authors capable of providing insights into the reasonings presented in classical texts posed a specific challenge, as this work is typically undertaken by scholars trained in the Islamic educational tradition. The emergence of two young but notable Islamic seminaries in the West, Zaytuna College in Berkeley, USA – the first American Islamic liberal arts college – and Cambridge Muslim College in the UK, both of which encourage students to pursue classical Islamic sciences while engaging with Western scholarship, facilitated the identification of two significant contributors to Part I. I am also deeply thankful to Holger Zellentin, a distinguished academic in comparative religion and a dear friend, and Celene Ibrahim, for their support with this project. Additionally, I would like to thank Zora Kostadinova for her indispensable assistance and enthusiasm for this project, and Christopher Jackson for his exceptional copyediting expertise, which went a long way in ensuring stylistic consistency across the text.

This volume would not exist without the contributions of the fifteen authors who recognized the value of joining this endeavour and have condensed years of their research into concise chapters. It is as much their effort as it is mine.

A Note on Foreign-Language Words

Each chapter in this volume is designed to stand alone, with foreign-language terms translated upon their first occurrence. Should the same term reappear after a significant interval, its translation is provided again to facilitate smooth reading. For terms used in a single chapter, we adhere to the author's preferred transliteration style. However, for Arabic terms recurring across chapters, we employ a simplified transliteration approach. To enhance clarity, diacritical marks are generally omitted, except for the apostrophe (') used to denote the Arabic letters *ayn* (') and *hamza* ('). When pluralizing Arabic words, we typically add an 's' to the singular form, except for 'ulama', which remains an exception. Names are presented without diacritical marks, except in rare instances where their inclusion is crucial for accurately identifying the individual. Bibliographical references, however, retain full transliterations as per the original publication or preference of the author.

Introduction
MASOODA BANO

The scholarship on women and Islam is at a significant turning point, characterized by its depth, diversity, and energy. This volume brings together voices and perspectives that highlight the richness of this field, reflecting on its recent achievements while highlighting promising areas of future research. Despite prevalent media narratives and policies, such as France's ban on the hijab and *abaya* (Islamic robe-like dress) in public schools, which often depict Muslim women as uniformly oppressed by Islamic principles, these oversimplified views no longer dominate academic debates. The era of Orientalist portrayals of Muslim women in Western academia, with its focus on harems and female submission, which began facing significant critique starting in the 1970s, has decidedly ended. This shift, however, is quite new. As recently as 2002, Lila Abu-Lughod's seminal work "Do Muslim Women Really Need Saving?,"[1] published in *American Anthropologist*, challenged the implicit biases in the portrayal of Muslim women in public policy but also within academic discourses. Writing in the wake of the US decision to invade Afghanistan after the events of September 11, 2001 – an action that was partly justified as an effort to free Afghan women from Taliban oppression – she presented a persuasive critique. She illustrated how these biased perceptions not only serve to further Western imperialistic goals but also inform Western liberal scholarship, including feminist narratives. These discourses consistently fail to recognize the autonomy and agency of Muslim women.

Today, these assumptions are in no need of exposition, as the expansive scholarship that has emerged in the two past decades, to which this volume aims to introduce the reader, has made earlier simplistic claims about the limited agency of Muslim women, and Islam as a religion,

---

[1] Lila Abu-Lughod, "Do Muslim Women Really Need Saving? Anthropological Reflections on Cultural Relativism and Its Others," *American Anthropologist* 104, no. 3 (2002): 783–790.

untenable. On one hand, a growing generation of scholars and their resulting publications argue persuasively, through close study of the Qur'an and hadith (the sayings of the Prophet Muhammad) – the two pivotal sources that shape religious debates in Muslim societies – that Islamic legal and moral ethics emphasize equality regardless of gender. Concurrently, there is a steady stream of anthropological studies showcasing how a majority of Muslim women voluntarily adhere to classical readings of Islamic gender norms and experience a sense of empowerment and exhibit agency, which they find more empowering than ideals associated with Western feminism. Has the field reached its peak if all of this has already been accomplished? The answer is unequivocally no. The proliferation and analytical breadth of publications over the past two decades have not only corrected foundational assumptions but also established a robust framework. This development is allowing researchers to now shift their focus towards posing more specialized questions, which will contribute to the field's maturation. A process of fine-tuning and refinement has commenced. Should this work continue for another decade or two, the field will fully mature, with its theories beginning to influence other areas of study.

The expanding interest in women and Islam is due to several factors, a key one being the expansion in the geographical spread of Muslim communities across the globe. Islam and Muslim women are no longer viewed merely as exotic, foreign subjects onto which various assumptions are projected. Despite the significant diversity among Muslim countries and the large global Muslim population, the increased visibility and vocal presence of Muslims in the Western world have notably influenced academic scholarship in this area. The notion of a "clash of civilizations" has limited utility in societies where multiple faith traditions must coexist under a democratic framework. This mixing has led to a heightened interest in moving beyond simplistic stereotypes to achieve a deeper understanding of others. The growth of Muslim communities in Western countries, such as Europe and the US, has thus triggered research studies exploring why Muslim women adhere to their faith even when exposed to secular environments. The interest in this subject is also mirrored by the growth of faculty positions in American academia that support Islamic feminist scholarship. The work of many scholars occupying these positions is referenced in this volume. Additionally, there is an increasing body of work on Muslims living as religious minorities in non-Western countries like India, China, and Russia. This includes scholarship on Muslim women's dynamic engagement with their faith and the broader society, even in contexts where their faith may face hostility.

As the editor of this volume, my objectives are twofold. First, I endeavor to offer a comprehensive resource for academics at all levels, from seasoned scholars to undergraduate students venturing into this field for the first time. This resource is designed to navigate the intricacies of existing scholarship while spotlighting the most vibrant areas of current research. The scholarly vigor in this domain is dynamic, characterized by recent contributions that not only refine our understanding but also set the stage for promising future explorations. Secondly, my goal is to also make this work accessible to any curious reader, not just those who are students of this field, who is interested in gaining a deeper understanding of Islam and the experiences of Muslim women. My intention is to present a nuanced view that reveals the complexity and diversity of these experiences, moving beyond the reductive narratives of pervasive oppression frequently portrayed in mainstream media. Such an effort also has relevance for policymakers and can potentially generate reflection on why evidence-based academic insights have limited impact on shaping public perceptions and policy discussions in the West regarding Islam and Muslim women. A reflection that is much needed.

The titling of this Companion volume as *Women and Islam*, rather than *Islam and Women*, is reflective of these ongoing developments in the field. While grammatically similar, the choice of word order subtly alters the emphasis and nuance, foregrounding the experiences and perspectives of women in the context of Islam. Both phrasings suggest a focus on women actively involved in Islamic religious or cultural practices, their experiences within Islamic communities, or their depiction in Islamic literature and art. However, the sequence of words hints at differing levels of women's agency. Positioning Islam at the forefront places the religion as the main focus, potentially reinforcing the perception, as critiqued in Orientalist literature, of Islamic texts as overly prescriptive and dominating. Conversely, leading with "women" shifts the focus to them as the primary subjects, highlighting their engagement with Islamic texts and their deliberate choice to embrace specific teachings. This approach challenges the assumption that their faith is merely the result of indoctrination, instead emphasizing their informed and voluntary commitment to Islam.

Within this framework, our analysis extends beyond examining the agency of Muslim women in advocating for or transforming women's rights within Muslim societies. We also emphasize the importance of recognizing that the relationship between Muslim women and their faith is fundamentally an expression of human agency. This perspective acknowledges that spiritual identity, along with moral and ethical commitments, not only significantly influences an individual's self-conception and their place within a social collective but also shapes their understanding of a fulfilling life. Moreover, this agency is expressed in various, sometimes conflicting, manners, influenced by such factors as socio-economic status and educational backgrounds. This diversity underlines the multiplicity inherent in any religious tradition, including Islam, and accounts for the wide range of experiences among Muslim women across different periods and locations. Throughout this volume, we will observe that Islam, characterized by its unique belief system regarding gender norms, plays a crucial role in the decisions of devout Muslim women. However, the interpretation and application of specific gender-related rulings significantly vary, influenced by each woman's socio-economic background, family history, and dedication to religious devotion.

Additionally, these practices are influenced by the broader socio-political and economic conditions prevailing in their respective communities. Adopting diverse positions does not, however, entail the rejection of core principles that might conflict with Western notions of agency – a stance taken by some Islamic feminists. Rather, it involves interpreting these principles in a manner that aligns with their contemporary realities, making the rulings relevant and applicable to their current lives. Throughout history, we observe Muslim women from specific socio-economic backgrounds exercising significant agency in shaping their expressions of piety, as well as influencing broader societal outcomes as activists, political leaders, writers, patrons, and peacemakers, but equally in their role as revered mothers. Simultaneously, as societies experience socio-economic modernization, interpretations that allow women increased participation in the public sphere – while adhering to fundamental Islamic principles – become more popular, even in traditionally conservative societies. The recent social transformations in Saudi Arabia, which I have observed first-hand, serve as a compelling example of this trend.[2]

Acknowledging the diversity within Islamic tradition and the varied experiences and rationales of Muslim women across classes and societies should not distract us from recognizing that Islam, as observable in lived faith traditions and a dominant belief system, proposes an alternative model of gender equality. This model, grounded in classical Islamic scholarship with the Qur'an and hadith as its foundation, presents

---

[2] Masooda Bano, *Saudi Social Awakening: What Explains the Rapid Change in Social Norms* (forthcoming).

a unique perspective on gender norms that contrasts sharply with the principles of equality that underpin liberal feminist thought. Unlike Western feminist ideologies, which often view the family as a patriarchal unit, champion sexual liberty, and advocate for absolute equality without considering biological differences, the classical Islamic view emphasizes the significance of family, sexual restraint, and biological distinctions. These different starting assumptions, as well as desired end goals, result in very different reasoning as to what constitutes a fair distribution of rights and responsibilities between men and women.

Islamic feminists have largely sought to highlight Islam's liberating potential by re-reading the traditional texts through a feminist lens. What sets this Companion volume apart is its focus on explaining the concepts and rationale behind gender norms as outlined in classical Islamic scholarship and its resonance with Muslim women from diverse backgrounds, while also recognizing the contributions of Islamic feminists. As we will see in this volume, the two cater to quite different audiences. Understanding why Muslim women make certain choices, such as wearing the hijab or abstaining from sex outside marriage – the latter expectation also applying to Muslim men – requires an appreciation of the traditional logic. True respect for the choices of Muslim women extends beyond merely recognizing their agency: it entails a concerted effort to understand the value they find in traditional teachings. Without this understanding, merely acknowledging their agency can inadvertently reinforce Western biases, suggesting that their faith compels them to settle for less-than-optimal life choices.

This volume is organized into fifteen chapters, divided into three sections. Part I invites readers to explore the rationale behind classical Islamic teachings on gender norms and presents a concept of women's well-being and gender equality that significantly diverges from Western feminist ideologies. In Part II, the focus shifts to specific examples of women exercising their agency in the quest for piety by adhering to the classical interpretations of gender norms, as well as those engaging in reinterpretations of the texts. These chapters illustrate that pious agency is not merely passive compliance with the most stringent religious laws. Rather, they highlight how women actively engage with and adapt Islamic teachings to their daily lives, a flexibility that is central to Islamic legal tradition without compromising its fundamental principles. Part III expands the discussion of Muslim women's agency beyond personal piety and family life, acknowledging the historical and ongoing significant contributions of Muslim women to the development and shaping of states and societies. This section examines expressions of agency that align more closely with the traditional Western feminist framework. To truly grasp the sophistication of current scholarship, it is crucial to explore the evolution of both textual and ethnographic scholarship, with a special focus on advancements made over the past two decades and areas ripe for future exploration. This comprehensive approach allows for a deeper appreciation of Muslim women's roles and the dynamic interplay between faith, agency, and societal conditions.

REDEEMING ISLAM: RE-READING THE TEXTS

In her pioneering 1975 study, *Beyond the Veil: Male–Female Dynamics in a Modern Muslim Society*,[3] Fatima Mernissi – a Moroccan sociologist and a foundational figure in the field of Islamic feminism, as explored in this volume – adopted a method known as multiple critique. Through this approach, she eloquently critiqued both the disempowering portrayals of Muslim women prevalent in Western scholarship and the patriarchal dynamics within Muslim societies. This early sociological work laid the foundation for her subsequent efforts to reinterpret Islamic texts from a feminist perspective. Mernissi's scholarship made a decisive contribution to the core argument of Islamic feminist scholarship: that Muslim women's disempowerment, contrary to Orientalist portrayals, is not rooted in Islamic principles but rather in patriarchal control over the production of classical Islamic scholarship. This endeavor to defend Islamic interpretations – while critiquing both Western viewpoints and traditional Islamic exegesis – has given rise to a vibrant area of scholarship commonly known as Islamic feminism. Like any feminist movement, scholars grouped as Islamic feminist diverge in their methodologies and points of departure – some even try to avoid the label due to its Western connotation.[4] Yet, as a body of scholarship the field is today quite visible and distinct.

Notable figures in the field, following Mernissi's lead, include Leila Ahmed, Asma Barlas, and Amina Wadud, who contributed significant foundational texts in the 1980s and 1990s. While Nina Nurmila showcases the diverse and rich landscape of Islamic feminist scholarship and the foundational contributions of these early scholars in Chapter 9, their influence also becomes apparent to the reader through frequent

[3] Fatima Mernissi, *Beyond the Veil: Male–Female Dynamics in a Modern Muslim Society* (Bloomington: Indiana University Press, 1975).
[4] Margot Bardan, *Feminism in Islam: Secular and Religious Convergences* (Oxford: Oneworld Publications, 2009).

references to their work across numerous chapters. Together, these scholars have scrutinized gender-related rulings in Islam affecting women in various spheres, including religious practices, domestic roles focusing on marital duties and obligations, and participation in the public arena, ranging from mosque leadership to political authority. In their analyses, they have primarily engaged with the two central sources of Islamic scholarship: the Qur'an and hadith. Their engagement with the Qur'an encompasses both direct interpretations and the study of *tafsir* (Qur'anic exegesis). When examining hadith, their focus has predominantly been on assessing the authenticity of these traditions and their coherence with Qur'anic interpretations. A related method employed by these scholars involves examining gender norms through studying the life and actions of the Prophet Muhammad (*sira*), not solely through the study of hadith but by examining his actions and interactions with women in his life, whether as a husband, father, or leader within the community of female believers. An associated focus has been on the lives of Muhammad's wives, who hold esteemed positions for being addressed in the Qur'an as the "mothers of the believers" (Q. 33:6) and exemplars of faith. By studying their actions and roles, scholars aim to challenge, and question established norms, offering insights into the lived realities and potential interpretative flexibility within Islamic traditions.

Over the last two decades, the foundational work of these scholars in the field of Islamic feminist scholarship has seen significant growth and diversification. This period has been marked by a deepening of inquiry, with questions becoming more nuanced and detailed analyses emerging. This surge in scholarly activity has enriched the discipline, expanding the range of topics and perspectives explored. Kecia Ali, representing what could be considered the second generation of scholars in this domain, has made a notable impact. She engages with texts within the Islamic legal tradition from an Islamic feminist perspective. In her book, *Sexual Ethics and Islam: Feminist Reflections on Qur'an, Hadith, and Jurisprudence*,[5] Ali navigates the intricate debates on sexual ethics in Islam, addressing such sensitive topics as marital obligations, divorce, homosexuality, and extramarital relations. As an Islamic feminist scholar, Kecia Ali delves into the criteria for lawful and ethical sexual conduct in Islam, broadening the scope of inquiry by incorporating diverse readings across different periods and disciplines. Similarly, in

---

[5] Kecia Ali, *Sexual Ethics and Islam: Feminist Reflections on Qur'an, Hadith, and Jurisprudence* (Oxford: Oneworld Publications, 2006).

Marriage and Slavery in Early Islam,[6] Ali notes that early jurists from the Maliki, Hanafi, and Shafi'i schools of Islamic law likened marriage to a purchase transaction and divorce to manumission, sparking rigorous debates. These deliberations sought to harmonize scriptural mandates, historical precedents, and societal norms with the imperative for logical coherence. Over time, this discourse subtly shifted towards an analogy that positioned husbands in a role akin to masters, and wives comparable to slaves, reflecting the complex interplay between legal theory and social practice within Islamic jurisprudence.

Kecia Ali's work exemplifies the refinement of inquiries within legalistic analysis in Islamic feminist scholarship. Simultaneously, the field has broadened its analytical horizons by incorporating additional genres of Islamic scholarship beyond the Qur'an, *tafsir* (Qur'anic exegesis), hadith, and *sira* (biography of the Prophet). Notably, there has been growing interest in exploring gender dynamics within Islam through the lens of mystical tradition associated with the field of Sufism. In *Sufi Narratives of Intimacy: Ibn 'Arabī, Gender, and Sexuality*,[7] Sa'diyya Shaikh, for example, engages with the work of the thirteenth-century Sufi poet and scholar Muhyi al-Din ibn al-Arabi. By engaging with his mystical ideals, as compared with the stricter readings offered by the legal jurists, Shaikh's approach sheds light on Ibn al-Arabi's nuanced understanding of gender as it relates to human existence and moral considerations, illustrating the diverse ways in which Islamic thought can engage with contemporary discussions on gender. This analysis delves into the potential of Sufi metaphysics and theology, as interpreted by the author, to enact significant shifts in Islamic gender ethics and legal practices. It addresses contemporary concerns such as women's rights within marriage, the practice of veiling, and the possibility of women leading prayers. By challenging the conventional separation between the spiritual and political spheres, the author aims to make a meaningful contribution to both Islamic feminism and feminist ethics. This is achieved by re-evaluating notions of selfhood, spirituality, and social justice within the Islamic tradition. The work stands out for critiquing traditional approaches not by directly reinterpreting Qur'anic verses or questioning the validity of hadith, but rather by engaging with the writings of a mystical scholar. These mystical perspectives are presented as offering more inclusive and moderate approaches to gender

---

[6] Kecia Ali, *Marriage and Slavery in Early Islam* (Cambridge, MA: Harvard University Press, 2010).

[7] Sa'diyya Shaikh, *Sufi Narratives of Intimacy: Ibn 'Arabī, Gender, and Sexuality* (Chapel Hill: University of North Carolina Press, 2012).

issues in Islam, showcasing an innovative pathway for reconciling religious tradition with contemporary feminist values.

Similarly, Zahra Ayubi's *Gendered Morality: Classical Islamic Ethics of the Self, Family, and Society*[8] has garnered notable attention for its innovative approach to rethinking Islamic philosophical ethics through a feminist critical lens. As opposed to engaging with the legalistic or mystical writings, Ayubi advocates for a philosophical shift in the analysis of gender within Islam, highlighting the potential for gender equality found within feminist engagements with Islamic ethical traditions. By examining the works of three prominent Islamic philosophers, Abu Hamid Muhammad al-Ghazali, Nasir ad-Din Tusi, and Jalal ad-Din Davani, Ayubi critiques their conceptualization of masculinity and femininity. She points out that their definitions often position the ethical human as an elite male, thereby marginalizing women and slaves. Arguing that these philosophical ethicists have acknowledged women's equality in the moral domain but argue for women's natural and ontological inferiority in this world, she delves into the conceptualization, definition, and justification of gender identity and differences at the most fundamental level of existence, significantly shaping views on gender roles, equality, and hierarchy in Muslim contexts. She argues that Muslim ethicists' gendered perceptions of existence and metaphysics have led them to formulate virtue ethics entrenched in inequality, thereby rendering these ethical frameworks incompatible with the ideals of equality inherent in their own philosophical traditions. Ayubi observes that despite their hierarchical perspectives, these ethicists offer insights into ethical conduct that reveal more intricate understandings of gender and human relationships, challenging their own established hierarchies. By arguing for noting an egalitarian thread within Islamic philosophy she questions the patriarchal readings, arguing for that philosophy's inherent compatibility with principles of gender justice and human flourishing.

These scholarly endeavors underscore the vibrant dynamism within the field, characterized by conceptual expansions, methodological innovations, and challenges to traditional narratives. However, despite their pioneering nature and cross-disciplinary approaches, these works are not immune to critique. A persistent critique, common throughout the evolution of this discourse, concerns their practical impact. While these scholarly debates have broadened in scope and even catalyzed a few

---

[8] Zahra Ayubi, *Gendered Morality: Classical Islamic Ethics of the Self, Family, and Society* (New York: Columbia University Press, 2019).

national or transnational movements under the banner of "gender jihad," as discussed by Nelly van Doorn-Harder in the context of Indonesia in Chapter 13, they have yet to significantly influence societal behavior or alter religious practices at a broader scale. This disconnect between academic discourse and tangible societal change highlights the complex interplay between scholarly innovation and real-world application, pointing to an ongoing challenge within the field of Islamic feminist scholarship. There are indications that the relevance of this scholarship is slowly increasing among young, university-going Muslim women in the US, as suggested by some of the authors in this field. However, concrete shifts in attitudes or practices aligned with these progressive interpretations remain limited. Initiatives such as women leading mixed-gender prayers, a practice championed by Amina Wadud based on her reinterpretation of classical views on who can serve as an imam, have resonated with only a small segment of the community, even in the US.[9] Consequently, since its inception, the field has faced scrutiny regarding its reach and the demographic it engages. This ongoing dialogue reflects the nuanced challenge of bridging scholarly innovation with widespread community acceptance and practice.

Relatedly the field is perceived to have arisen in response to the demands of the Western audience and the desire of a few Muslim women scholars to engage with it, whether motivated by the aim to shield Islam from prejudiced views or by genuine discontent with the inequalities observed within their religious teachings. Such motivations are thought to delineate the boundaries of discourse, positioning Western feminism as the benchmark for optimal gender equality and prompting the re-examination and reinterpretation of Islamic texts to align with these ideals. This critique, consistently refuted by Islamic feminists, nonetheless persists as a valid point of discussion. In contrast, as we see in the next section, ethnographic accounts reveal a swift proliferation of Islamic networks that adhere to traditional Islamic teachings on gender norms, as evident in the doctrines of these groups.[10] This observation is not meant to undermine the value of the field in question but rather to provide readers with a broader perspective. While focusing solely on texts that highlight Islam's liberal potential might illuminate one aspect of the religion for readers, it does not fully

---

[9] Masooda Bano and Hilary Kalmbach, eds. *Women, Leadership, and Mosques: Changes in Contemporary Islamic Authority* (Leiden, Boston: Brill, 2012); Juliane Hammer, Kecia Ali, and Laury Silvers, eds., *A Jihad for Justice: Honoring the Work and Life of Amina Wadud* (ebook, 2012), http://unc.academia.edu/JulianeHammer.

[10] Bano and Kalmbach, eds., *Women, Leadership, and Mosques.*

capture the essence of Islam's enduring appeal. This appeal is highlighted by its remarkable resilience in terms of adherence, as evidenced by consecutive rounds of the World Values Survey, which measure levels of religiosity across different faith traditions globally.[11] This juxtaposition aims to deepen the reader's understanding of the complex and multifaceted nature of Islamic faith and practice.

The claim that traditional interpretations of Islam, instrumental in shaping gender norms within Muslim societies, have persisted solely due to patriarchal frameworks not only oversimplifies the richness of classical Islamic scholarship but also undermines the agency of Muslim women. This viewpoint posits that adherence to these gender norms stems from a lack of critical reflection among Muslim women – an assumption increasingly contested by a growing body of ethnographic studies. As these investigations reveal, the lived experiences and conscientious engagements of Muslim women with their faith demonstrate that such a presumption is unsustainable. These studies provide a nuanced understanding of the dynamic interplay between religious interpretation, societal structures, and individual agency in how Muslim women relate to the teachings of their faith.

This identifies an area requiring attention within the field, and there are indications that such introspection is underway. The influence of the audience on the nature and scope of analysis, as well as on which questions are prioritized, is a universal phenomenon in scholarship. A roundtable at the 2022 International Qur'anic Studies Association (IQSA) conference held in Italy highlighted this challenge for the field of Islamic feminism. Celene Ibrahim, whose 2020 publication *Women and Gender in the Qur'an*[12] has received much attention, presented the most honest assessment of the challenges Muslim women scholars face navigating the field of Qur'anic Studies amidst secular academic environments. Ibrahim outlines the two choices available to them based on personal experience: "Get the Bulse, Lose the Pulse" suggests winning academic favor and precarious job security at the cost of disconnecting from everyday religious communities.[13] Alternatively, "Better a Jester" suggests embracing the applied aspects of one's work, risking academic marginalization but engaging more directly with the public. This

---

[11] Ronald F. Inglehart, *Religion's Sudden Decline: What's Causing It, and What Comes Next?* (New York: Oxford University Press, 2021).

[12] Celene Ibrahim, *Women and Gender in the Qur'an* (New York: Oxford University Press, 2020).

[13] Celene Ibrahim, "Of Poets and Jesters: Methodologies and Reception Politics in Qur'anic Studies," *Journal of Feminist Studies in Religion* 39, no. 2 (2023): 79–81.

exploration of navigating intellectual decolonization and choosing a scholarly path highlights the intricate interplay between authority, relevance, and community engagement in Qur'anic Studies. Navigating both worlds, she advocates for a progressive methodology which she refers to as *tafsir tawhidi* – a methodology that adopts a holistic perspective, incorporating practical, analytical, literary, historical, and theoretical discussions equally confidently.

Mahjabeen Dhala, another scholar who has recently published (*Feminist Theology and Social Justice in Islam: A Study on the Sermon of Fatima*,[14] demonstrating the socio-political agency exercised by the Prophet Muhammad's daughter) and was also a participant at this roundtable, shared related concerns about the limits that a Western academic framework puts on what is viewed as legitimate critique.[15] She noted that many secular (nonreligious) scholars don't fully appreciate different ways of studying and learning, especially from an Islamic point of view. They often find these methods not "critical" enough because they're used to a different style that comes from a background focused on Christianity. In Islam, questioning and exploring ideas deeply is important, and Muslims often discuss various aspects of their faith, such as what God is like or how to understand the Qur'an. This variety in thoughts is valued. She identifies a list of important questions if the field is to allow for more authentic scholarship from the Islamic perspective: Should the way of thinking that came from Europe a long time ago be the only way to judge all scholarship, especially studies about Islam or from non-Western cultures? When studying the Qur'an in Western places, should these studies have to fit into the usual Western ways of thinking to be taken seriously? How much freedom do women who study the Qur'an from a feminist point of view have in Western academia? And what about the opinions of women scholars from these cultures, who are often not taken as seriously and seen as "traditional"?

While this acknowledgment might appear to underscore concerns about the borrowed nature of Islamic feminist scholarship, shaped by the frameworks of Western academic priorities, it also signifies the field's maturation. We are witnessing the emergence of a cohort of scholars who possess the capability and confidence to address these critical questions, marking a significant phase of growth and self-reflection. This reflection is crucial for the analytical and methodological innovations that Islamic

---

[14] Mahjabeen Dhala, *Feminist Theology and Social Justice in Islam: A Study on the Sermon of Fatima* (Cambridge: Cambridge University Press, 2024).

[15] Mahjabeen Dhala, "Muslim Feminist Exegetes, Not 'Handmaidens of Empire'," *Journal of Feminist Studies in Religion* 39, no. 2 (2023): 83–85.

feminist scholars introduce, enhancing the legitimacy of this scholarship within Muslim communities. Currently, much of Islamic feminist scholarship examines the works of early scholars in a piecemeal fashion, reflecting a limited understanding of classical Islamic scholarship as a whole. Consequently, while these studies gain recognition among Western scholars, they fail to fully convince those familiar with the complexity of Islamic scholarly tradition. As a scholar engaged in both ethnographic fieldwork and the study of classical Islamic traditions on gender norms, I find, for instance, Zahra Ayubi's analysis of Ghazali's work on ethics[16] to be overly literal and detached from the depth of Ghazali's contributions. He authored over seventy books and his work is foundational to the teaching of traditional Islamic scholarly institutions such as al-Azhar University in Egypt. His scholarship acts as a bulwark against radical interpretations associated with conservative Islamic groups, such as Saudi Salafism or the South Asian Deobandi tradition, and is pivotal to the revival of Islamic philosophical and mystical movements in the West.[17] Ayubi begins her chapter "Ethics of Marriage and the Domestic Economy" by asserting that marriage ethics, in view of the scholars studied, have little to do with love – a perspective starkly at odds with the narratives from my respondents, who often view marriage ethics, precisely those aspects Ayubi criticizes for neglecting women's needs, as foundational to genuine love. This highlights a significant critique of feminist methodology when engaging with classical Islamic scholarship: its tendency towards a fragmentary approach that either cherry-picks quotations to portray these texts and their authors as patriarchal or, at best, engages with a full-length text, as Ayubi does.

To fully understand the intellectual ideas of any writer or scholar, it's crucial to place their work within the broader scholarly landscape. This includes considering the methodological expectations of their field, the stances of their contemporaries, and the societal debates of their era. Marilyn Booth's work, *The Career and Communities of Zaynab Fawwaz: Feminist Thinking in Fin-de-Siècle Egypt*,[18] exemplifies a holistic approach to comprehending another individual's thoughts and ideas through their texts. In this intellectual biography of an early

---

[16] Ayubi, *Gendered Morality*.
[17] Masooda Bano, *The Revival of Islamic Rationalism: Logic, Metaphysics and Mysticism in Modern Muslim Societies* (Cambridge: Cambridge University Press, 2019).
[18] Marilyn Booth, *The Career and Communities of Zaynab Fawwaz: Feminist Thinking in Fin-de-Siècle Egypt* (New York: Oxford University Press, 2021).

Egyptian feminist, Booth not only analyzes Fawwaz's writings but also situates them within the broader dialogues of her time, including those she directly or indirectly responded to. As Booth articulates, "Deep listening must be wide listening. To understand Fawwaz's writings and her lexicon locally means hearing them within communities of discourse. While this book focuses on Fawwaz, it is a collective study in that it addresses the gender-political writings and approaches of others with whom she was in dialogue."[19] Looking forward, adopting this comprehensive approach in Islamic feminist scholarship – especially when studying a specific scholar or text – could greatly enhance the credibility of their work among modern, educated, believing Muslims.

The need for these areas of future refinement by engaging more holistically with Islamic scholarly tradition is being acknowledged by numerous scholars. In her review of Sa'diyya Shaikh's *Sufi Narratives of Intimacy*,[20] Dilyana Mincheva addresses the historical sidelining of works that, despite their liberating potential for women, were marginalized by the dominant theological discourses of their era. Mincheva points out that these progressive insights, even when recognized for their emancipatory possibilities, struggle to shift mainstream Islamic discourse today, which often remains wary of concepts perceived as Western imports, such as hermeneutics and feminism. Furthermore, Mincheva critiques the approach of integrating the egalitarian views of a thirteenth-century mystic into modern Muslim thought, arguing that it risks overshadowing the understanding that principles of emancipation are not the static legacy of a singular thinker but rather the result of ongoing collective human endeavor and interpretation. She emphasizes that a believer's grasp of ideals like equality, social justice, and freedom evolves not merely through engaging with a text under the guidance of a single scholar but through a dynamic, dialogic process. This interaction between the reader and the texts, a reciprocal relationship that shapes meaning, underscores the ethnographic studies of Islamic movements that are explored in the subsequent section.

Karen Bauer's *Gender Hierarchy in the Qur'an: Medieval Interpretations, Modern Responses*,[21] published in 2015, stands out for its distinct contribution to enriching our understanding of the internal logic of Islamic gender norms from within the classical lens. An established scholar in the field of Qur'anic Studies, Bauer diverges from the

---

[19] Ibid., 17.
[20] Shaikh, *Sufi Narratives of Intimacy*.
[21] Karen Bauer, *Gender Hierarchy in the Qur'an: Medieval Interpretations, Modern Responses* (Cambridge: Cambridge University Press, 2015), 3.

paths commonly taken by other scholars; she does not aim to reinterpret Qur'anic verses through a feminist lens, nor does she share the primary objective of many Muslim feminists to redeem Islam within a liberal framework. Bauer's primary interest is in understanding the Qur'an on its own terms, interpreting gender-related verses not in isolation but within the broader moral framework of the Qur'an. Having deeply engaged with classical *tafsir* texts, in *Gender Hierarchy in the Qur'an* Bauer observes how classical scholars, even while accepting the premise of hierarchy, do not depict a husband's control as unbounded, unconditional, or absolute. She notes that, despite some scholars providing extreme interpretations, the scholarly community as a whole always developed a moderate consensus. As she notes, "there is room for many conflicting views, but not every view is tolerated; respected works by respected scholars are read across the boundaries of legal schools; and the correct interpretation is bounded by common practice, common understanding, and ideas of right and wrong."[22] Her analysis reveals the Qur'an's internal logic of gender norms as an integral part of its moral framework, emphasizing spiritual equality and the worldly well-being of both genders. Presented in Chapter 1, this analysis offers an excellent introduction to the logic of Islamic gender norms as understood by believing Muslims. It explains why, despite their apparent discrimination against women, the majority of Muslims are convinced of their fairness.

In Chapter 2, we explore the subject through the perspective of one of the four main Sunni schools of law (*madhhab*). Sohail Hanif, trained in the classical Islamic jurisprudence of the Hanafi school and having completed a doctoral thesis at Oxford University on the comprehensive thought system of Abu Hanifa – encompassing its unique theological premises, its conception of tradition, its understanding of the human mind's role in interpreting God's law, and its framing of the roles of *fiqh* (jurisprudence) and *fuqaha'* (jurisprudents) in society – illustrates the intricate debates and detailed concerns addressed in discussions on each topic, specifically women's inheritance in this instance. He elucidates the complexity of the Islamic inheritance system, clarifying that it does not uniformly grant women less than men, and highlights how the framework of inheritance can only be fully understood when considering Islam's overall model of financial responsibility.

Building on the discussion in Chapter 2, Chapter 3 by Katerina Nordin explores the consensus across different Islamic schools of

[22] Ibid.

thought, including the Shi'a–Sunni divide, on the rules regarding women's covering and sexual restraint outside marriage. This chapter also highlights the role of vernacular Islamic scholarship in making complex jurisprudential texts accessible to the lay public, most of whom do not engage directly with these detailed works. In Chapter 4, Faraz Khan leverages his background in classical Islamic sciences to craft a biography of the Prophet Muhammad, examining how he is perceived within the tradition. The analysis of his interactions with the female members of his family demonstrates how his life serves as a model, persuading Muslim women that Islamic gender norms can support an empowered and fulfilling female life. Mahjabeen Dhala takes this further, emphasizing the significance of the lived experiences during the Prophet's time as crucial for understanding Muslims' perspectives on appropriate behavior, including gender relations. She elaborates on the dynamic agency of the Prophet's wives, who chose to adhere to the lofty moral expectations as the mothers of the believers. With her Islamic feminist perspective, Dhala seeks to show that their agency was more significant and expressed in more revolutionary ways than is traditionally acknowledged by classical scholars.

These chapters collectively provide readers with a comprehensive exploration of five major domains in classical Islamic scholarship: Qur'an/*tafsir*, *fiqh*, rich vernacular Islamic literature that adapts foundational texts to local languages and contexts, *sira*, and the historical roles of female figures, notably the wives of the Prophet, as moral exemplars. Over centuries, these streams have shaped ordinary Muslims' understanding of the Islamic moral framework, including gender norms. The depth of analysis presented will reveal to readers why, for many, the persuasive power of classical reasoning negates the need for reinterpretation.

REDEEMING AGENCY OF BELIEVING WOMEN: STUDYING LIVED EXPERIENCES

In 2008, I began researching Islamiyya schools in Kano, the most populous state in northern Nigeria and a key representative of North African and West African Islamic traditions, particularly the Maliki school of thought. These institutions, which originated in the 1970s, distinguish themselves from the region's older Qur'anic schools by welcoming students of all ages, ranging from young girls to married women with children, and even women in their eighties. Women, notably, constituted the majority of the student body. Despite the low enrollment rates in state schools within the region, these Islamic or Qur'anic schools attracted nearly universal attendance. They primarily focused on basic Islamic rituals and moral teachings derived from Maliki *fiqh*, utilizing vernacular Islamic literature in Hausa. Additionally, informal study sessions of Qur'anic learning took place in the homes of elite families' women. My interest in Islamiyya schools was notably heightened by my prior experiences with female madrasas in Pakistan. From 2006 to 2008, I conducted fieldwork across Sunni and Shi'i madrasa networks in Pakistan, where I observed a similar emergence and rapid expansion of female madrasas since the late 1970s.[23] Women from elite families in Pakistan were also participating in private-study circles, notably within the al-Huda network. Initially functioning as weekly educational gatherings in the halls of upscale hotels, al-Huda has now become a formal institute. Primarily, it focuses on imparting the teachings of Hanafi *fiqh*, disseminated through vernacular Islamic scholarship in Urdu.

Navigating through these diverse contexts, my research unfolded against the backdrop of Saba Mahmood's seminal work, *The Politics of Piety: The Islamic Revival and the Feminist Subject*,[24] which has cast a long-lasting influence on the study of female participation in mosque- and madrasa-based Islamic educational networks. These networks have gained popularity among women in Muslim-majority countries and diaspora communities.[25] My inquiry extended to pre–civil war Syria, where, in 2010, I conducted fieldwork with women participating in study circles led by the Qubasiyyat and those attending Islamic lessons in mosques. The focus in Syria leaned towards Hanafi and Shafi'i *fiqh*. Despite Arabic being the native tongue, much of the instruction relied on simplified texts by contemporary scholars, rather than the foundational *fiqh* texts.

Organizational differences notwithstanding, a commonality was evident in the approach to teaching gender norms, rooted in a fundamental interpretation of Islamic precepts.[26] Throughout my research, I frequently encountered references to similar Qur'anic verses and hadith by these women and their instructors, to justify traditional interpretations of the texts. For instance, the discourse on veiling

---

[23] Masooda Bano, *The Rational Believer: Choices and Decisions in Madrasas of Pakistan* (Ithaca: Cornell University Press, 2012).

[24] Saba Mahmood, *The Politics of Piety: The Islamic Revival and the Feminist Subject* (Princeton: Princeton University Press, 2005).

[25] Bano and Kalmbach, eds., *Women, Leadership, and Mosques*; Mirjam Künkler and Devin J. Stewart, eds., *Female Religious Authority in Shi'i Islam: Past and Present* (Edinburgh: Edinburgh University Press, 2021).

[26] Masooda Bano, *Female Islamic Education Movements: The Re-democratisation of Islamic Knowledge* (Cambridge: Cambridge University Press, 2017).

commonly cited verse Q. 33:59 from *Sura al-Ahzab*, emphasizing modesty. This was often used to argue that, following the example of the Prophet's wives, modesty is incumbent upon all Muslim women. However, there was also a perspective, albeit less common, suggesting that such injunctions were specific to the Prophet's wives and not universally applicable.

The references to the Prophet's wives, particularly Aisha bint Abi Bakr, and Khadija bint Khuwaylid, were pervasive across all three research contexts. These references were used to illustrate how Islam, contrary to some Western feminist critiques, grants women significant freedoms. Khadija's role as a businesswoman and Aisha's contributions as a hadith scholar and leader in battle were frequently cited examples. Moreover, the Prophet's affection and respect for his wives, especially Aisha and Khadija, were highlighted as exemplary of how, within Islamic teachings, the prescribed leadership role for men in the household, when understood in the context of the Prophet Muhammad's life, fosters a mutually supportive relationship.

In all three contexts I studied, including Syria, women's primary motivation for attending study circles was to master the proper recitation of the Qur'an, with many focusing on *tajweed* (the art of Qur'anic recitation).[27] The preachers usually lectured on everyday issues, such as performing daily rituals or adhering to moral conduct, particularly concerning responsibilities towards family members. However, in the question-and-answer sessions, a distinct disparity became apparent between the queries posed in study circles attended by women from low-income households and those frequented by women from affluent families. The former group often inquired about issues related to managing relationships with husbands and mothers-in-law, as well as the moral upbringing of children, reflecting their daily realities. Conversely, discussions in elite circles delved into topics like women traveling alone, participating in co-ed studies and mixed-gender workplaces, and balancing religious obligations with everyday practical needs.

Particularly within the latter group, there was lively debate, with women exchanging their interpretations and understandings of various issues among themselves and with the preacher. The overarching consensus leaned towards adopting practical solutions that adhered to individual realities, as long as they did not breach fundamental Islamic principles. The insights gained from these discussions were influenced as much by the women's socio-economic

[27] Ibid.

and educational backgrounds and their level of religious commitment as they were by the preacher's teachings or the specific texts underpinning their viewpoints. Overall, these women championed the Islamic perspective on gender norms and frequently criticized Western feminism for imposing extra burdens on women while concurrently undermining the family structure – a critique also captured by Lila Abu-Lughod.[28]

Saba Mahmood's influential work on women's participation in mosque movements in Egypt[29] garnered significant attention within the field primarily for its theoretical contribution. By examining women's voluntary adherence to Islamic teachings as a conscious pursuit of piety, Mahmood challenged the conventional feminist notion that agency is solely manifested through resistance to structures of power. Instead, she posited that cultivating a pious disposition is, in itself, an expression of agency. Through her engagement with these women, Mahmood demonstrated the active effort they invested in adhering to the high pietistic standards of modesty (*haya'*) they had set for themselves. While her ethnography was relatively focused, involving in-depth interactions with a limited number of women, it nonetheless had a profound impact by spotlighting this area as a valuable empirical field of study.

Subsequent research has extensively explored the question why, in an era marked by modernity, educated Muslim women continue to seek traditional Islamic knowledge. This expanding body of scholarship, including my own work, has built upon Mahmood's arguments, shedding light on the dynamic nature of agency among women involved in these movements. These studies are showing that while some may aspire to fully embody a highly restrictive form of female piety, akin to Mahmood's respondents, the majority navigate a delicate balance. They carefully weigh their beliefs against their practical considerations, striving to reconcile worldly concerns with their faith without transgressing the boundaries defined by classical Islamic scholarship as constituting core Islamic principles. This nuanced approach highlights the complex interplay between personal convictions and everyday realities, further enriching our understanding of agency within the context of Islamic female piety.

---

[28] Lila Abu-Lughod, "Do Muslim Women Really Need Saving? Anthropological Reflections on Cultural Relativism and Its Others," *American Anthropologist* 104, no. 3 (2002): 783–790.

[29] Mahmood, *Politics of Piety*.

The burgeoning interest in exploring the allure of traditional Islamic networks for women extends beyond those participating in study circles in mosques, madrasas, or elite gatherings. It also encompasses a growing body of research on women's involvement in Salafi networks and political Islam movements. These studies highlight the intricate internal negotiations these women engage in to strike a balance between their religious commitments and worldly aspirations, aiming for an optimal personal well-being. Alessandra Bonci, in her examination of women joining Salafi networks in Tunisia, cautions against simplifying quietist Salafism into a monolithic ideology or set of practices.[30] Similarly, Anabel Inge's ethnographic work on Salafi women in the UK[31] delves into their journeys towards Salafism, their integration within Salafi communities, and the practical application of Salafi principles in everyday life. This includes navigating challenges related to marriage and societal expectations. Despite the inherent tensions between Salafi ideals and social realities, particularly for women, Inge's book[32] reveals that these women manage such conflicts by occasionally choosing less favored options from the Salafi viewpoint. This flexibility is due to the diversity of interpretations even within Salafism itself, allowing for creative adaptations that align their lifestyles with their faith amidst the roles and expectations of being wives and mothers. Inge's insights shed light on how her subjects reconcile these tensions, demonstrating a nuanced prioritization of religious dictates that accommodates the complexities of their lives.

Research on women's participation in political Islam movements consistently records a similar trend whereby there is focus on adhering to core Islamic rulings, universally acknowledged in classical Islamic scholarship, while actively seeking ways to adapt daily *fiqh* (Islamic jurisprudence) rulings to their specific circumstances. Omayma Abdel-Latif's 2008 study[33] records how women within Egypt's Muslim Brotherhood, traditionally assigned subordinate roles, have advocated for increased representation without departing from the gender norms established in classical Islamic texts. Their demands for more significant roles in decision-making processes are interpreted not as a challenge to

---

[30] Alessandra Bonci, "*Ilmi* Salafi Women in Tunisia after the Revolution: What Kind of Quietism?," *Contemporary Islam* 17, no. 2 (2023): 243–262, 250.

[31] Anabel Inge, *The Making of a Salafi Muslim Woman: Paths to Conversion* (Oxford: Oxford University Press, 2016).

[32] Ibid.

[33] Omayma Abdel-Latif, "In the Shadow of the Brothers: The Women of the Egyptian Muslim Brotherhood," *Policy Commons: Carnegie Papers*, Carnegie Endowment for International Peace: United States of America, 2008.

the established order but as a natural part of the movement's evolution. Mhajne and Brandt[34] similarly observed that in the aftermath of the revolutions in Egypt and Tunisia starting in late 2010, Islamist movements and parties, including the Egyptian Muslim Sisterhood and Tunisia's Ennahda, have emerged as formidable political entities. This shift has opened new opportunities for activism and political engagement for both men and women, without necessitating a reinterpretation of classical texts to justify their increased political involvement as the conditions allowed. Elora Shehabuddin's 2008 study[35] on the female members of Jamaat-i-Islami in Bangladesh similarly highlighted how the leadership of this prominent South Asian political Islam party broadened the scope of women's participation in the educational and political spheres. This expansion was achieved by adjusting, rather than abandoning, the party's foundational philosophy on gender norms. These examples underscore a nuanced approach to engaging with traditional Islamic teachings while navigating the complexities of contemporary political and social realities.

Simultaneously, growing research on Western female converts to Islam reveals trends consistent with previous findings. The female converts are drawn to Islam's traditional understanding of gender roles, which they perceive as more appealing than the freedoms associated with Western feminism. Studies indicate that, upon integrating into their new faith, these women, similar to those mentioned earlier, begin to value the diverse interpretations of everyday matters. This flexibility allows them to conform to their religious obligations while remaining engaged with broader society. Karin van Nieuwkerk's work,[36] examining the factors that attract Western women to Islam by analyzing gender discourses among Dutch converts, highlights an initial attraction to the coherent framework of Islamic gender norms. She records how many converts are motivated by the Islamic principle of "gender equity," or complementary roles for men and women, as opposed to the Western notion of "gender equality." They also appreciate Islam's stringent moral and ethical guidelines, especially when contrasted with their prior

---

[34] Anwar Mhajne and Rasmus Brandt, "Rights, Democracy, and Islamist Women's Activism in Tunisia and Egypt," *Politics and Religion* 14, no. 4 (December 2021): 577–608.

[35] Elora Shehabuddin, "Jamaat-i-Islami in Bangladesh: Women, Democracy and the Transformation of Islamist Politics," *Modern Asian Studies* 42, nos. 2–3 (March 2008): 577–603.

[36] Karin van Nieuwkerk, "Introduction: Gender and Conversion to Islam in the West," in *Women Embracing Islam: Gender and Conversion in the West*, ed. Karin van Nieuwkerk (Austin, TX: University of Texas Press, 2006), 1–16.

experiences of sexual liberty and the "objectification of the female body." The high esteem Islam places on motherhood, family, and community, along with the logical coherence of its theology, are also cited as attractive aspects. Over time, van Nieuwkerk observes, these converts gradually shift their spiritual quest from a focus on Islamic rules and regulations to a more embodied and personal expression of faith, leading to the development of a "conservative-feminist" gender discourse that evolves over time. Similarly, Lana Sirri's study[37] on White Christian German women in Berlin who convert to Islam illustrates how these converts navigate the stages of conversion, eventually finding ways to blend "Western" ideals of gender relations with Islamic principles. She notes the importance of examining the reflective processes through which these women forge a new identity.

The growth in these studies has illuminated the intrinsic allure of classical Islamic perspectives on gender norms for many women. This attraction to Islam does not hinge on reinterpretations of classical texts through a feminist lens, although such reinterpretations remain a valid approach for those who find the traditional Islamic views on gender restrictive. The chapters in Part II delve deeper in these debates. In Chapter 6, Arndt Emmerich and Alyaa Ebbiary critically examine the literature on Salafi movements, highlighting how recent research challenges previous assumptions by acknowledging the autonomy of women who, over time, tailor religious edicts to their personal experiences and insights, all the while adhering to the principles of Salafism. Following this, Liv Tønnessen offers an insightful analysis in the subsequent chapter on women's participation in Islamic political parties with the case study of Sudan. She explores how women engaging with political Islam manage to uphold conventional interpretations while also making concessions on amendable matters. This includes advocating for legislation to establish a minimum marriage age, even as they support the concept of *qawama* (male guardianship), which they argue offers substantial protections for women.

In Chapter 8, Vanessa Vroon-Najem presents a fascinating study of Dutch converts to Islam from various ethnic and social backgrounds, finding that they are drawn by the traditional Islamic rationale on gender norms as a counterpoint to Western feminist ideals, as the Islamic perspective emphasizes sexual restraint and the roles of wives and mothers. Over time, as these converts gain confidence in their understanding of Islam, they seek to find, and often succeed in finding, an optimal balance.

---

[37] Lana Sirri, "Identification and Belonging: A Case Study of White German Women Converts to Islam," *Feminist Theology* 30, no. 1 (2021): 104–119.

They respect foundational principles while making necessary adjustments to harmonize their Islamic identity with their Western lifestyles, enhancing their comfort and integration.

The discussion proceeds with an analysis of how Islamic feminist scholars, within a specific context, have sparked a grassroots movement. This movement aims to reconcile foundational Islamic teachings with contemporary understandings of gender equality. In Chapter 9, Nina Nurmila, a distinguished Indonesian Islamic feminist with a background in traditional Islamic education and a doctorate in Gender Studies from Australia, illustrates the impact of scholars from traditional Islamic academies on Islamic feminist discourse in Indonesia. She observes a burgeoning of vernacular Islamic literature that weaves feminist ideals into the fabric of traditional Islamic debates. This integration indicates that the ideals championed by Islamic feminist scholars in Western universities are likely to reach a broader audience only after being embraced and incorporated by traditional scholars within vernacular scholarship.

The concluding chapter expands the analysis by placing these discussions within contexts where Islam or Muslim communities encounter broader social pressures. These circumstances may prompt Muslim women either to reconsider their faith or to critically question traditional gender norms. Maria Jaschok, leveraging her extensive research on women mosques and female imams (*ahong*) in Hui Muslim communities of central China, reveals how these women adeptly navigate the secular state's scrutiny of male religious authority to establish a niche for themselves. Importantly, while they exploit the broader opportunities available in their surroundings, they largely adhere to the classical interpretations of fundamental Islamic principles governing gender norms. This chapter underscores the resilience and adaptability of Muslim women and classical Islamic teachings in the face of challenges, as they strive to maintain their faith and its teachings amidst challenging societal landscapes.

Throughout the chapters, it becomes evident that Muslim women, even those involved with ostensibly more conservative movements, do not adhere to their faith uncritically. Their commitment stems from a conviction in the superiority of norms as delineated in classical Islamic scholarship. These women do not limit themselves to the doctrines of a single scholar. Rather, they thoughtfully select from the array of arguments within the classical tradition communicated to them largely through vernacular Islamic scholarship, always mindful of upholding the foundational principles. This approach demonstrates a nuanced engagement with their faith, balancing respect for tradition with an active, discerning participation in its interpretation.

WOMEN IN MUSLIM SOCIETIES

The foregoing discussion sets the stage for the concluding section of the volume, illustrating the multifaceted influence of religion on the lives of Muslim women. It becomes evident that there is no singular experience among them. While some women face challenging circumstances, others ascend to the highest echelons of power, mirroring the diversity of experiences found in all societal contexts. This segment thus connects with studies that have endeavored to document the lives and contributions of women in Muslim societies, spanning both historical and contemporary perspectives. With women increasingly gaining access to education and the workforce, research has shifted towards exploring evolving gender dynamics. This includes examining women's representation in parliament, their involvement in politics, economic participation rates, and educational achievements. This area of study, less theoretical or methodologically focused than the previous two discussed, is crucial to explore. It highlights that Muslim women's identities extend beyond mere categorizations as liberal or religious; they are dynamic participants in their communities and societies. While, for some, Islam may be a source of inspiration, for others, it may not play a central role. This broad spectrum of experiences underscores the complexity and richness of Muslim women's lives and their contributions to their societies.

Muslim women have historically played important roles, starting with the examples found in the lives of the Prophet Muhammad's wives. In Chapter 5, Mahjabeen Dhala shows the social and political activism of Zaynab bint Jahsh and Umm Salama, the latter being particularly influential in Shi'i tradition. Aisha bint Abi Bakr, who was the daughter of the Prophet's companion, Abu Bakr, and to whom the Prophet was particularly affectionate, and on whom much has been written, was one of the most important early Islamic scholars, especially in the hadith tradition. Her contributions were crucial to the development of Islamic jurisprudence and the interpretation of the Qur'an. Known for her intelligence and memory, she is credited with narrating over 2,200 hadith, covering various aspects of life, making her the third-most prolific contributor to the collection of hadith. After the death of Muhammad, Aisha played a significant role in the political and social life of the Muslim community. She was involved in several important events, including the Battle of the Camel (656 CE), which was part of the early Islamic civil wars.

The tradition of powerful Muslim women who played a role in shaping social political domains of Muslim communal life is thus as old as the origin of Islam. Fatima al-Fihri is a remarkable figure in Islamic history, particularly noted for her significant contributions to education. Born in the early ninth century in the city of Qayrawan (in present-day Tunisia), Fatima moved with her family to Fez, Morocco, where she later made her indelible mark. Her major contribution to education and Islamic culture is the founding of al-Qarawiyyin Mosque and University in Fez, Morocco, in 859 CE. Al-Qarawiyyin University is considered by many historians and scholars the oldest continually operating educational institution in the world and is recognized as such by UNESCO and the Guinness World Records. Fatima al-Fihri's vision was to create a center of learning that was accessible to a broad segment of society, and that would contribute to the intellectual and spiritual development of the Muslim community. Her endowment to the university ensured its operational continuity, allowing it to become a key intellectual center during the medieval period. Al-Qarawiyyin University played a crucial role in the cultural and academic exchanges between the Islamic world and Europe, influencing the development of universities in the medieval period.

Nana Asma'u, a princess, poet, and teacher, and a daughter of the founder of the Sokoto caliphate, Usman dan Fodio, is a prominent figure in West African history for her contributions as an educationist, women's rights activist, and social reformer. Living from 1793 to 1864, she had a profound impact on the education and status of Muslim women in the region, and her work showcases her commitment to Islamic education and social reform. She continues to be a prominent figure in the imagination of Muslims in northern Nigeria, as I have found during my fieldwork on Islamiyya schools in Kano, demonstrating the liberating potential of classical Islamic teachings.[38] She established a system of education that reached women of all social classes, empowering them with knowledge of the Qur'an, Islamic law, and the principles of the Sokoto caliphate. This educational movement, known as the *Yan Taru* (the Associates), was a network of itinerant teachers, trained by Nana Asma'u, who traveled across the caliphate to educate other women. These efforts significantly improved literacy rates among women in the region and ensured that Islamic education was accessible to all, regardless of gender.

Nana Asma'u advocated for the rights of women within the framework of Islamic teachings. Her work challenged the prevailing norms that restricted women's access to education and their roles in society. By

---

[38] Bano, *Female Islamic Education Movements*.

promoting literacy and knowledge among women, she provided them with the tools to understand their rights within Islam and to question practices that were culturally oppressive but not Islamic. Her advocacy for women's education was revolutionary, laying the foundation for a more informed and equitable society. Beyond her focus on women's education and rights, Nana Asma'u's influence extended to broader social reforms within the Sokoto caliphate. Her poetry and writings served as a medium to communicate ethical teachings and the values of the caliphate, promoting unity, social justice, and adherence to Islamic principles. Through her educational initiatives, she also helped to stabilize the caliphate by integrating diverse ethnic and social groups into a cohesive community united by faith and shared values.

The contributions of dynamic women through history are vast and varied, with many, such as those mentioned previously, becoming the subject of scholarly research. A notable area of interest has been their support for the arts and architecture. Among numerous works on the subject, Patricia Blessing's analysis highlights the architectural patronage of Mahperi Khatun, mother of the Seljuk sultan Ghiyath al-Din Kaykhusraw II (who reigned from 1237 to 1246), in thirteenth- and early fourteenth-century Anatolia.[39] The study compares her patronage style with that of other female benefactors active in Anatolia during the Seljuk and Ilkhanid periods, often commemorated in foundation inscriptions. Furthermore, literature exists on women who assumed political leadership roles. An extensive biography of Sultan Jahan, the Begam of Bhopal (reigned 1901–26) in central India, illustrates her exceptional oratory and organizational skills, alongside her generous support for education and healthcare.[40] She established schools for girls, hospitals, maternal–child health centers, and numerous women's organizations, both within her domain and beyond in India, adeptly navigating between tradition and modernity.

Yet, the narrative is not confined to women from elite backgrounds. Particularly from the nineteenth century onward, amidst modernization, the spread of education, and the socio-political shifts resulting from Western colonization and the subsequent decolonization of Muslim societies, a robust tradition of grassroots female activism emerged. Influential activists and social reformers, such as the Egyptian advocates Zaynab Fawwaz and Zaynab al-Ghazali, rose from ordinary families. Part III

---

[39] Patricia Blessing, "Women Patrons in Medieval Anatolia and a Discussion of Māhbarī Khātūn's Mosque Complex in Kayseri," *Belleten* 78, no. 282 (2014): 475–526.

[40] Siobhan Lambert-Hurley, *Muslim Women, Reform and Princely Patronage: Nawab Sultan Jahan Begam of Bhopal* (London, New York: Routledge, 2007).

aims to introduce readers to the socio-political engagement of these remarkable women, spanning from community activists to those from elite circles, illuminating their enduring legacy in shaping contemporary society.

In Chapter 11, D. Fairchild Ruggles provides insights into the role of women as patrons of art and architecture, highlighting that, unlike their Christian counterparts, they had the ability to inherit property. In Chapter 12, Shahla Haeri examines their involvement in politics, challenging the scholarly debates that have historically argued against women's capability for political leadership. By employing an Islamic feminist perspective, she critiques earlier interpretations, arguing that the exclusion of women from political roles was more a modern phenomenon, reflecting a politicized use of religion by those with vested interests, rather than a historical truth.

In Chapter 13, Nelly van Doorn-Harder enhances the analysis from Nina Nurmila's chapter on Indonesian Islamic feminism by exploring the catalysts for the development of an Islamic feminist grassroots movement in Indonesia. She demonstrates the considerable impact of traditional women's social activism, rooted in both secular and religious foundations, on the narrative of Indonesian Islamic feminism. Issues such as gender roles, polygamy, child marriage, and basic gender human rights are shown to be central concerns that do not inherently conflict with one another. From my readings of these two chapters, it becomes clear that the success of Islamic scholars in Indonesia in contextualizing Islamic feminist discourse within local Islamic conversations, and connecting it to the local context, has been crucial for its widespread acceptance and growth.

In the following chapter, Zuzanna Olszewska explores the roles of Muslim women as dynamic writers and poets, channeling deep emotions and expressing creative visions and imaginations. Their works range from those adhering to Islamic principles to those that do not, encompassing both written texts and oral poetry. Notably, oral poetry emerges as a powerful medium for expressing protest and articulating alternative aspirations.

The concluding chapter shifts focus from women categorized as philanthropists, writers, poets, activists, or political leaders to the everyday lives of ordinary women. These women, not necessarily involved in devout movements or leading Western-inspired feminist NGOs, are nevertheless dedicated to asserting their right to choose their own paths and to pressing for socio-political and economic institutions to be attuned to their needs. Through a lens of "feminist spirituality" and extensive interviews with her subjects, Zilka Spahić Šiljak records how Islam – particularly its mystical traditions – retains a profound spiritual significance even for relatively secular Muslim women who may not adhere to institutionalized religion. The deep Sufi underpinnings of Bosnian Islam, with its focus on *taqwa* (God-consciousness), *adab* (etiquette), and *khidma* (service), act as a powerful influence. These principles guide women, raised in socialist and post-socialist contexts, to pursue a feminist agenda in everyday life that champions equality in the workplace and in the socio-political sphere.

Zilka's research, though set in a distinct context, underscores the influential role of the mystical dimension of Islam, particularly within the Sufi tradition, and highlights women's central role in this domain, as observed by Annemarie Schimmel.[41] Schimmel's work on women in the Sufi tradition emphasized their contribution to fostering a mystical way of life and the spread of love not only for the afterlife but in this world as well. The metaphor of the woman-soul, representing the ultimate aspiration of the seeker after God, has been notably prevalent in the Sufi tradition, especially in the Indo-Pakistani context. She noted how, as mothers, women with mystical inclinations have had a profound impact on their sons, who often grew up to be eminent Sufi masters, owing much to their early spiritual education. The contribution of women to the spread of mystically infused Islamic thought, particularly in rural areas and among all social strata, is immense. They have been pivotal in preserving and disseminating mystical knowledge and in promoting a simple, sincere faith in God and the Prophet.

The chapters in this section effectively illustrate that there is no singular experience for Muslim women: religion shapes the experiences of each Muslim woman uniquely. Yet, for many, Islam provides a comprehensive framework – whether through its detailed legal tradition or its profound mystical teachings – that is perceived as both equitable and empowering. This framework empowers them to lead dynamic and fulfilling lives in the contemporary world, manifesting a form of agency that resonates with feminist principles.

STYLE AND SCOPE

The selection of regions covered acknowledges the impossibility of encompassing all areas. Muslim-majority regions are diverse, with each country exhibiting its own variations. Additionally, Muslims in the West form an expanding group with distinct characteristics across Europe and

---

[41] Annemarie Schimmel, "Women in Mystical Islam," *Women's Studies International Forum, Special Issue: Women and Islam* 5, no. 2 (January 1982): 145–151.

North America. Minority Muslim contexts also vary widely, from longstanding communities in India, China, and Russia to more recent mid twentieth-century groups in Latin America. While the primary evidence originates from majority-Muslim contexts and the Middle East, efforts were made to ensure representation from other areas. For instance, Chinese Muslims offer a compelling study within minority contexts. Indonesia serves as a notable example of core versus borderland dynamics in principal Muslim regions. Furthermore, specific countries may be examined more than once to highlight conceptual points in greater detail. This approach aims to showcase a broad spectrum of experiences and examples across all conceptual categories, rather than adhering to a country-by-country checklist, which would be unfeasible. In the realm of textual analysis, where possible Part I includes considerations of all Sunni schools, ensuring a comprehensive and diverse representation.

The distinction between Shi'i and Sunni Islam is a recurring concern, primarily because most scholarly work tends to focus on Sunni Islam unless specifically dedicated to exploring Shi'i perspectives. Given the significant legalistic and authoritative differences between the two traditions, adequately addressing them would require separate discussions for each theme, rendering such a comprehensive approach impractical for a single volume. Furthermore, focusing equally on both traditions might not be justified unless the goal is a comparative analysis, especially considering that Sunnis constitute the majority of the Muslim population, with Shi'is estimated to represent 15–20 per cent. Conducting a systematic comparison within each chapter is challenging due to these differences, and it is rare to find scholars with expertise in both the textual or spiritual traditions and sociological aspects of both Shi'i and Sunni Islam. Scholars engaged in comparative research on Muslim societies, myself included, typically exercise caution when making comparative claims. My comparative research, for instance, concentrates entirely on Sunni Islam and the countries where it predominates. Despite these constraints, which are common to the field, this volume makes a concerted effort to incorporate Shi'i perspectives where feasible, such as the discussion on veiling and sexuality in Chapter 3. In Chapter 5, which emphasizes the significant roles played by the Prophet's wives, a deliberate choice was made to include Umm Salama, a figure of great importance in Shi'i theology, rather than focusing on Khadija and Aisha, who are more prominently featured in the Sunni tradition and are extensively studied. This approach reflects a commitment to providing a broader understanding of Islamic tradition, within the limits of the volume's scope.

In crafting this volume, a deliberate emphasis has been placed on respecting each author's unique style and agency. Feminist scholarship has traditionally valued the expression of personal motives and experiences over the conventional social science objective of maintaining neutrality. Many contributors have a deep personal connection to their topics, often driven by their own experiences and initial positions. As the editor, my approach has been to allow contributors the freedom to explore their subjects in their own way, rather than imposing a singular vision upon them, while ensuring coherence across the volume.

To bridge the individual contributions without enforcing a uniform style – particularly the conventional start with a literature review – I have opted to write a concise introduction to each of the three parts of this volume to better situate each chapter within the relevant scholarly debates. This allows readers to dive directly into the distinctive narratives and methodologies of each author. The main analytical contributions of each chapter are highlighted in these introductions, facilitating a seamless integration into the volume's overarching framework. I hope this structure will not only enhance the reader's engagement with each unique perspective but also clarify how each argument contributes to the collective understanding.

SELECT BIBLIOGRAPHY

Abu-Lughod, Lila. *Do Muslim Women Need Saving?* Cambridge, MA: Harvard University Press, 2013.
Ali, Kecia. *Sexual Ethics and Islam: Feminist Reflections on Qur'an, Hadith, and Jurisprudence*, Oxford: Oneworld Publications, 2006.
Bano, Masooda. *Female Islamic Education Movements: The Re-democratisation of Islamic Knowledge*. Cambridge: Cambridge University Press, 2017.
  The Revival of Islamic Rationalism: Logic, Metaphysics and Mysticism in Modern Muslim Societies. Cambridge: Cambridge University Press, 2019.
Bano, Masooda and Kalmbach, Hilary E., eds. *Women, Leadership, and Mosques: Changes in Contemporary Islamic Authority*. Leiden, Boston: Brill, 2012.
Bardan, Margot. *Feminism in Islam: Secular and Religious Convergences*. Oxford: Oneworld Publications, 2009.
Bauer, Karen. *Gender Hierarchy in the Qur'an: Medieval Interpretations, Modern Responses*. Cambridge: Cambridge University Press, 2015.
Booth, Marilyn. *The Career and Communities of Zaynab Fawwaz: Feminist Thinking in Fin-de-Siècle Egypt*. New York: Oxford University Press, 2021.
Dhala, Mahjabeen. "Muslim Feminist Exegetes, Not 'Handmaidens of Empire'." *Journal of Feminist Studies in Religion* 39, no. 2 (2023): 83–85.
Ibrahim, Celene. "Of Poets and Jesters: Methodologies and Reception Politics in Qur'anic Studies."*Journal of Feminist Studies in Religion* 39, no. 2 (2023): 79–81.

Inge, Anabel. *The Making of a Salafi Muslim Woman: Paths to Conversion.* Oxford: Oxford University Press, 2016.
Künkler, Mirjam and Stewart, Devin J., eds. *Female Religious Authority in Shi'i Islam: Past and Present.* Edinburgh: Edinburgh University Press, 2021.
Mahmood, Saba. *The Politics of Piety: The Islamic Revival and the Feminist Subject.* Princeton: Princeton University Press, 2005.
Mernissi, Fatima. *Beyond the Veil: Male–Female Dynamics in a Modern Muslim Society.* Bloomington: Indiana University Press, 1975.
Schimmel, Annemarie. "Women in Mystical Islam." *Women's Studies International Forum, Special Issue Women and Islam* 5, no. 2 (January 1982): 145–151.

Part I
Logic of Classical Reasoning

Hierarchy and complementarity are key concepts highlighted by proponents of the view that Islamic perspectives on gender norms embody a coherent rationale for fairness, despite assigning distinct and differentiated roles to each gender. This stands in contrast to Western feminist ideologies, which advocate for absolute equality and dismiss biological differences as grounds for varied roles between men and women. Advocates for Islamic gender norms contend that Islam promotes equity, rather than the equality emphasized by Western feminism. The chapters in this section examine the principles of gender norms in classical Islamic scholarship, which continue to influence gender norms in Muslim societies and diaspora communities today. They aim to elucidate the underlying logic provided by the Qur'an and hadith (sayings of the Prophet) regarding gender norms, asserting that, although these norms may appear unfair from a Western standpoint, they are underpinned by a consistent principle of fairness, contingent upon recognizing the paramountcy of the spiritual self. Additionally, these chapters highlight the significance of interpretative flexibility, as demonstrated through diverse readings by classical scholars, legal jurists, and lay believers, in understanding the enduring strong adherence to Islamic gender norms in practice. The opening chapter of this section delves into the topic through the lens of the Qur'an and the *tafsir* tradition. The second chapter examines the subject from the perspective of the Hanafi school within Islamic law. The third chapter explores the discussion through examples from vernacular Islamic literature, which demystifies classical texts for the general public. The fourth chapter is informed by the *sira*, the biography of the Prophet, while the final chapter highlights the exemplary role models of the Prophet's wives, revered in the Qur'an as the "mothers of the believers." Collectively, these chapters provide a comprehensive insight from various scholarly disciplines within Islam, illustrating how the bedrock of these beliefs is rooted in a multifaceted array of discussions.

Starting with the Qur'an, in Chapter 1 Karen Bauer delves into the complex moral framework of the Qur'an in its approach to gender dynamics. A highly respected scholar in the field of Qur'anic Studies, in her contribution Bauer notes how the Qur'anic text's treatment of women is often seen to pose contradictions due to verses advocating for equal spiritual worth among the sexes, such as Q. 33:35, which espouses equal piety, and those that seem to enshrine a hierarchical order favoring men, exemplified by Q. 4:3. Bauer's analysis, however, reveals a harmonious moral logic underpinning these verses when examined through four pivotal considerations: the Qur'an's overarching emphasis on spiritual equality, the societal role of decorum and ethical conduct, the protection afforded to society's vulnerable, and the autonomy the Qur'an grants women in navigating personal relationships. Central to the Qur'anic ethos, as Bauer expertly articulates, is the concept of moral agency afforded to every individual, irrespective of gender. This agency underscores the ability to make moral decisions, pivotal for one's spiritual journey, which transcends earthly social hierarchies. In this divine narrative, the ultimate measure of a person is not their temporal status but their spiritual trajectory towards the afterlife, a journey equally accessible to men and women (Q. 16:97–98).

Further, Bauer contextualizes the Qur'anic directives within the socio-political milieu of seventh-century Arabia. This setting, characterized by tribal affiliations and a lack of centralized governance, significantly shaped the Qur'anic moral discourse. The Qur'an's approach to the societal frameworks of the time, particularly those governing household and community interactions, was not one of outright revolution but of moral reorientation. By advocating for ethical conduct and compassion towards the weak, the Qur'an checked many of the male privileges in that society, giving protections to women. The commands that appear repressive by modern standards, Bauer argues, were not rigid laws but guidelines aimed at minimizing harm and maximizing goodness. These verses served protective functions, safeguarding women's property and their social standing against potential exploitation.

Equally, the Qur'anic discourse on modesty and public morality, often misconstrued as gender-specific, is in fact applicable to both men and women. This universal call to ethical behavior is emblematic of the broader Qur'anic vision for a morally upright community, wherein public decorum becomes a manifestation of individual piety. Equally importantly, Bauer's analysis highlights that the Qur'an does not depict women as subjugated or controlled by men. Instead, it presents instances of women acting independently, demonstrating that within the Qur'anic narrative women are recognized as autonomous moral agents. This evaluation of Qur'anic verses, through Bauer's scholarly lens, affirms the text's deep-rooted commitment to moral equality and spiritual dignity for all individuals.

Adopting a similar approach to taking a comprehensive view of gender logic within the Islamic tradition, Sohail Hanif elucidates the complex debates and meticulous details discussed in each dimension of gender norms in the classical Islamic legal tradition. Drawing on his training in traditional Islamic sciences and doctoral research in the Hanafi school of law, Hanif aims to demonstrate this complexity. He specifically focuses on the dimension of inheritance law within the Hanafi *madhhab* (school of law), considering it one of the issues perceived as overtly discriminatory, since women inherit half of what men do. Hanif delves into the nuanced dynamics of women's inheritance rights within Islamic law, providing a thorough analysis that deepens our understanding of the financial obligations and maintenance (*nafaqa*) detailed in Islamic legal texts. Similarly to Bauer's analysis of Qur'anic verses, he situates the discussion of inheritance rules within the Hanafi school in a broader socio-legal framework highlighting the tension between hierarchical and egalitarian worldviews. This tension he notes is emblematic of the broader clash between pre-modern perspectives, which envisaged society within a cosmic hierarchy extending from the divine to earthly relations, and modern enlightenment ideals that champion equality and reject hierarchical structures.

Hanif argues that imposing modern notions of equality on societies that did not share these ideals can obscure our understanding of their perceptions of justice and social values. By dissecting the legal framework governing financial maintenance, he reveals how Islamic legal theory does not prioritize equality as a virtue in the same manner as contemporary frameworks. Instead, it constructs a complex interplay of rights and duties that vary based on one's position within the social hierarchy, including gender distinctions. These legal principles are not shaped by the individual variations among men and women in terms of physical strength, intellect, or emotional capacity, but rather on a generalized view of gender roles. This generalization forms the basis for assigning financial and protective duties predominantly to men, while positioning women primarily in roles related to childcare and domestic responsibilities. Notably, the chapter emphasizes that while Islamic law assigns to women the role of childcare, it frames this responsibility as a right, affording women the opportunity to fulfill this role if they choose. He further illustrates how the Islamic legal system manages financial responsibilities between genders, so that what women might ostensibly lose in inheritance is compensated for by their entitlement to maintenance.

In Chapter 3, Katarina Nordin draws on a variety of specialist as well as more accessible popular sources used by ordinary Muslims to demonstrate the markedly different approach Muslim women have to the subjects of veiling and sexual freedom compared with what is perceived as an essential right in Western feminist thought. She elucidates the legal and spiritual rationale behind sexual restrictions and veiling within Islam, highlighting the balanced responsibility shared by both genders.

The hijab (headscarf) emerges not merely as a piece of cloth but as a profound symbol of a woman's devotion and commitment to a set of deeply held spiritual and moral convictions concerning the soul, salvation, and life on earth. This symbol reinforces the idea of spiritual equality before God, as mentioned in Q. 4:124. Nordin sheds light on how veiling relates to the concept of *haya'*, a term deeply embedded in the Islamic moral compass, denoting modesty, shame, and a heightened awareness of God. This concept underscores the importance of communal obligations and self-refinement, with its roots traced back to the story of Adam and Eve. Drawing on ethnographic studies, she also explains how Muslim women articulate and defend the practice of veiling as an expression of spiritual dedication, despite the challenges it may entail. Through this voluntary act, they exercise their agency, affirming their faith and personal convictions.

Her exploration into Islamic sexuality underscores the often overlooked point that sexual restrictions apply equally to both men and women. The prohibition of *zina* (fornication) is framed not only as a religious mandate but also as a measure to safeguard societal and individual dignity, emphasizing the significant social repercussions of such actions, including implications for lineage and inheritance rights. The sanctity of marriage is portrayed as a cornerstone of Islamic social and spiritual life, celebrated as a means of fulfillment, protection, and joy. Within this institution, Islam promotes a sex-positive attitude, encouraging pleasure and intimacy between spouses. This contrasts sharply with the strictures against fornication, illustrating the nuanced balance Islam seeks to maintain between individual desires and societal welfare. Nordin's paper also touches on the evolving interpretation of Islamic law, acknowledging the growing discourse within the Muslim community on sexual ethics, women's pleasure, and the dynamics of marital relations. The recent emergence of publications like *The Muslimah Sex Manual* signifies a shift towards a more open discussion on sexuality from an Islamic perspective, challenging traditional norms while upholding the faith's core values. This evolving dialogue underscores the historical emphasis on adaptation and reinterpretation within the Muslim community, reflecting a commitment to both religious principles and the realities of contemporary life.

In Chapter 4, Faraz Khan adeptly utilizes classical Islamic sources to emphasize that appreciating the Prophet's exemplary treatment of women does not require a reinterpretation of the texts. My extensive fieldwork with women in Muslim societies across various countries has reaffirmed this insight. The model of gender relations exemplified by the

Prophet's life is highly idealized. Trained in classical Islamic sciences, Faraz elucidates how the theological, legal, and mystical frameworks within Islam universally recognize the Prophet Muhammad as the epitome of virtue in the tangible realm of human existence. His life is a beacon of virtues, compassion, and wisdom. His teachings and actions serve as a blueprint for ethical conduct, spiritual growth, and communal harmony, encapsulating the essence of Islamic doctrine and its application through the ages. Unlike Plato, who envisioned ideals as intangible, eternal forms, Islamic tradition positions Muhammad himself as the embodiment of truth, beauty, and goodness. According to Muslim scholars, virtue's essence is not captured through abstract concepts like justice or compassion but through the personalized qualities of Muhammad: his form of justice, his bravery, his empathy. This personification of virtue through the Prophet's life and actions offers Muslims a direct pathway to understanding and embodying these virtues. This exploration is deeply anchored in the hadith tradition, which chronicles the Prophet's sayings and actions, providing a comprehensive view of his character as the Ideal Man.

Khan illustrates how Muhammad's life exemplified a deep commitment to empowering women, both spiritually and socially. Among the Prophet's wives, Aisha stands out as a key figure of this empowerment. Recognized as both a scholar and a significant figure in early Islamic history, Aisha's contributions to hadith scholarship and her roles in education and politics underscore Muhammad's support for women's intellectual and ethical growth. Her expertise and eloquence in interpreting hadith highlight the Prophet's dedication to creating an environment conducive to women's intellectual and spiritual flourishing. Muhammad is also noted for his gentle and affectionate demeanor towards his wives. For example, when Safiyya, his non-Arab wife, felt marginalized by his other wives, Muhammad encouraged her to embrace her Jewish heritage, thereby empowering her and showcasing the inclusive nature of his teachings. His interactions with his daughters show profound paternal love, characterized by acts of kindness and significant gestures that reflect his compassion and care. Muhammad's approach to fatherhood, extending to his role as a grandfather and his concern for orphans, emphasizes Islam's high spiritual value on caring for the vulnerable. His leadership in the community, defined by compassion and wisdom, and his family life, centered on the remembrance of God, charity, and compassion, serve as exemplars of his gentle and generous character. Khan provides insight into how Muhammad's life and his treatment of women serve as a model, demonstrating that Islamic gender norms are inherently supportive of protecting women's interests.

As Bauer discusses in Chapter 1, the presence of a gender hierarchy in Islam does not negate women's agency. Women have the capacity to make choices and decisions, a fact vividly exemplified by the lives of the Prophet's wives, who are referred to in the Qur'an as the mothers of the believers. Despite often being depicted controversially in Orientalist literature, these wives serve as important role models for Muslim women on how to excel in piety and assertiveness in daily life. Khadijah, the Prophet's first wife, was a successful merchant fifteen years his senior. Aisha, who has garnered significant attention in Islamic literature, played a crucial role in recording hadith and influencing politics after the Prophet's demise. These women are cited by Muslim women as evidence that Islam empowered women at a time when the West did not.

In the final chapter of Part I, Mahjabeen Dhala demonstrates the strong personalities of Zaynab bint Jahsh and Umm Salama, with the latter notably revered in the Shi'i tradition. Dhala argues that these women were not only exemplars of piety and traditional roles but also agents of social and political reform. They were offered the choice of living in the Prophet's household in accordance with divine ethics or leaving freely. Choosing to stay, these women exemplify agency, as seen in Zaynab's marriage to the Prophet Muhammad, which challenged societal norms and customs, and in Umm Salama's advocacy for Ali's leadership and defense of Fatima, the Prophet's daughter.

Dhala's research resonates with Islamic feminist frameworks. She offers a fresh perspective on the agency of these women, criticizing earlier works for limiting their roles to traditional spheres. Introducing the idea of "non-normative mothering," Dhala contends that, as in many cultures, classical Islamic scholarship has typically interpreted women's agency within the confines of conventional roles, overlooking their contributions in various other areas. Despite adopting a scholarly approach distinct from the four previous scholars, her chapter, like the others, helps illuminate the same point: the need to appreciate the depth and complexity of Islamic debates on gender norms and their focus on establishing a fair gender balance.

MASOODA BANO

1 Women in the Qur'an

KAREN BAUER

Women's status in the Qur'an is a highly debated topic.[1] Scholars over time have debated the extent to which the Qur'an granted women rights in seventh-century Arabia. More recently, the focus has been on the seeming inconsistency between verses that are clearly egalitarian because they propose equal piety for the sexes (e.g., Q. 33:35), and those that are clearly hierarchical because they seem to grant men privileges over women (e.g., Q. 4:3). This chapter does not propose to rehash existing debates, which are well documented.[2] Rather, it seeks to explain the Qur'an's own moral logic with regard to its treatment of women. To understand the Qur'an's attitude towards women, it is important to recognize the way that the Qur'an's moral trajectory is situated in relation to its social milieu. The fundamental purpose of this life, in the Qur'anic view, is as a moral test, the results of which will determine one's fate in the afterlife. It is not only that this life is transient and temporary and the afterlife permanent and everlasting, but also that this life is construed as a testing-ground, rather than an end in itself (Q. 67:2). God judges humans on their deeds: He weighs and measures human actions and pays the 'wage' (*ajr*) for those actions in the afterlife: the word 'wage' appears more than 100 times in the text. Both men and women have an equal opportunity to earn their wage for the afterlife,

---

[1] This chapter is based on Karen Bauer and Feras Hamza, *Women, Households, and the Hereafter in the Qur'an: A Patronage of Piety* (Oxford: Oxford University Press, 2023), and 'Qur'anic Morality as Qur'anic Law', forthcoming in *Regulative Verses of the Qur'an: From Historical Trends to Contemporary Trajectories*, ed. Karen Bauer, Mohammed Fatemi, Robert Gleave, and Devin Stewart. Though I have written this chapter, in an important sense this could be considered as a co-authored piece.

[2] For instance, Kecia Ali, *Sexual Ethics and Islam: Feminist Reflections on the Qur'an, Hadith, and Jurisprudence* (Oxford: Oneworld Publications, 2006); Ayesha S. Chaudhry, *Domestic Violence and the Islamic Tradition: Ethics, Law, and the Muslim Discourse on Gender* (Oxford: Oxford University Press, 2013); Aysha Hidayatullah, *Feminist Edges of the Qur'an* (Oxford: Oxford University Press, 2014); Celene Ibrahim, *Women and Gender in the Qur'an* (Oxford: Oxford University Press, 2020).

regardless of their social status in this life (Q. 16:97–8). This morality is predicated on the idea that a person's social status cannot determine their ultimate spiritual fate, and this has important consequences for how the Qur'an treated existing social structures.

The Qur'an emerged in seventh-century Arabia, in a tribal society without a centralized state, and this fundamentally shaped Qur'anic morality. Without state structures, the care of the vulnerable had to occur through social structures of patronage and kinship, within households. Since at least classical antiquity, the male head of household, the *pater familias*, had been expected to act as protector and patron for vulnerable members of society, which included women themselves, and others such as 'orphans', a term used in the Qur'an to designate children without parents and others in need of protection, such as adult women. Kinship was created in households, both through the birth of children and through marriage ties that would connect lineages together. Thus, the household was not only a primary structuring force for social bonds, but also for social and political power. The Qur'an did not completely overturn the hierarchical social structures of households and patronage. Rather, it assured its audience that moral action in these spheres would assure their salvation: social morality and care of the vulnerable became matters on which God judged individuals as worthy of salvation or damnation. Moreover, the vulnerable themselves had opportunities for pious action both within households and outside them. Qur'anic piety can be described as quotidian piety, enacted in everyday spaces of households and marketplaces.

One aspect of the Qur'an's quotidian piety is that decorum, sexual morality, and the treatment of women became defining features of the Qur'anic community of believers. Sexual morality distinguished the Qur'anic community from the pagans, who were deemed sexually licentious in the Qur'an, and sexual morality also showed the Qur'anic community's closeness to the norms of other monotheists (Jews and Christians). Moreover, the protection of women served as a clear demonstration of the Qur'an's morality towards the vulnerable. In this morality, not every person had the same social status, but every person, no matter what their gender or social status, could earn salvation through correct belief and righteous action.

Although men were generally assumed to be heads of household and patrons of the vulnerable, women in the Qur'an are seen to have an active social role, and to have an equal opportunity for pious action. The crucial point to be made here is that women are not portrayed as being ultimately under the domination or control of men. As shall be described in the following pages, women are able, for instance, to leave their unbelieving husbands without those husbands' permission and join the believers, or vice versa (Q. 60). There are examples of women in the Qur'an who undertake actions entirely independently of their kin or husbands: in one Qur'anic sura, a woman meets alone with the Prophet to complain about her husband, and God takes the woman's side in the dispute (Q. 58); even the wives of prophets could go astray, while the wives of unbelievers could be exemplary believers (Q. 66:10–12). Believing women are expected to undertake the same pious actions as men, such as feeding the poor, giving alms, fasting, praying, and believing in God (Q. 33:35), and women and men are both told that they should command decency and forbid indecency in the public realm (Q. 9:71). Needless to say, wealthy women would have been patrons of the poor in their own right.[3] Thus, women in the Qur'an lived within social hierarchies, but they were not controlled by their male kin or husbands. To assume such a degree of male control is to misread the way that the household structure is assumed in the Qur'an.

The remainder of this chapter explains these points in more detail. It is divided into four parts: a. The Qur'anic moral worldview of spiritual equality: narratives of piety and impiety; b. Communal identity as expressed through decorum, modesty, and sexual ethics; c. Household morality and quotidian piety in marriage and divorce; and d. Women's moral agency and their social agency: does the Qur'an put men in control over women?

THE QUR'ANIC MORAL WORLDVIEW OF SPIRITUAL EQUALITY: NARRATIVES OF PIETY AND IMPIETY

The Qur'an's doctrine of spiritual equality and moral agency runs through its commands and its narratives. As noted in the introduction to this chapter, in the Qur'an every person, male or female, has moral agency, which is the ability to understand morality and to make moral choices.[4] This is why the Qur'an repeatedly emphasizes that God has created human with eyes to see, ears to hear, and hearts (Q. 67:23; 76:2); the heart is, in this text, considered to be the locus of both feeling and

---

[3] Emran Iqbal el-Badawi, *Queens and Prophets: How Arabian Noblewomen and Holy Men Shaped Paganism, Christianity, and Islam* (London: Oneworld Publications, 2022).

[4] On the debate between predestination and free will in Islamic thought, see Maria de Cillis, *Free Will and Predestination in Islamic Thought: Theoretical Compromises in the Work of Avicenna, al-Ghazālī and Ibn ʿArabī* (Abingdon: Routledge, 2013).

understanding. Humans are admonished to train their senses to see God's signs, reflect, and understand them (Q. 22:46). God created the world full of inequalities, and with many sorts of temptations, and humans were created with desire for worldly power and goods (Q. 3:14). This is the nature of the fundamental moral test: will they fall prey to the temptation of their own arrogance and greed, ignoring God's signs and disobeying His commands, or will they act as His righteous servants, distributing their own wealth to the poor, controlling their base desires, responding to aggression in the best way (Q. 23:96), and humbly enacting the rites of prayer, fasting, and remembrance of God?

The equal moral agency of all people, including men and women, is stated outright in several Qur'anic verses. This is the import of Q. 33:35, which states that there shall be a heavenly reward for men and women who embrace certain qualities and actions, including submission, belief, devout obedience, humility, fasting, praying, enduring hardship, guarding their private parts, giving in charity, being truthful, and remembering God. This list, which includes both male and female adjectives to describe every action, makes the point that both men and women are moral agents who are responsible for their own salvation. Such verses are crucial to understanding the moral trajectory of the text, in which a person's social status does not avail them in the afterlife. Rather, their good deeds will determine their ultimate fate. Every human has the ability to act in a pious manner, but not everyone does: the Qur'an says repeatedly that most people do not listen and do not obey.[5] The Qur'an presents itself as moral guidance, and salvation can be achieved by humble obedience to God's commands or through sincere repentance after error. Those who have seen and been warned, and who continue in wrongdoing, are damned.

The moral trajectory of salvation or damnation is illustrated through the stories of male and female characters. These characters' stories can be imagined as a plot, which is enacted by the characters and can be enacted by believers. Although crucial elements of characters' stories hinge on their gender – Mary could not have been male – their overall plotlines pertain to the salvation of the soul and are ungendered. There are three common plotlines in the Qur'an: the plotline of error and repentance; the plotline of obedience to God's command and reward through closeness to God; and the plotline of continued error and

---

[5] In the Qur'an this is often presented as God leading people astray, hardening their hearts, and so forth. But the Qur'an also says that God only leads astray those who are already transgressing (Q. 2:26), and that God judges everyone on the basis of their deeds. See Bauer and Hamza, *Women, Households, and the Hereafter*, 20–6.

damnation. These plotlines can be considered as typological: the same character can develop over time, enacting more than one plot, and this is a model for believers who may err at one time in their lives, and who may be patient and enduring through hardship at another.[6] While the gender of Qur'anic characters often matters for the lives they live and the way their stories are told, the crucial point in Qur'anic terms is that all of these characters have moral agency, and it is their moral choices that determine whether they are saved or damned. This is one example of the way that the fundamental Qur'anic message of salvation transcends gender. From the Qur'anic perspective, the most important aspect of the human predicament is a person's spiritual trajectory in whatever social circumstances they find themselves.

Characters who err and repent include Adam and Eve, Moses, Abraham, the Queen of Sheba, and the officer's wife (called Zulaykha in Islamic tradition) who attempts to seduce Joseph. The paradigmatic instance is Adam and Eve, who are told by God not to eat of one of the trees of the garden, but they are tempted by Satan to eat from the forbidden tree. Subsequently, they realize their nakedness – which is both physical and metaphorical, representing their spiritual divestment from God's protection – seek forgiveness, and are guided by God. Unlike in the Biblical version, in the Qur'an both the male and the female characters are tempted by Satan; however, in some of the Qur'anic versions only Adam is named as repenting. This should not be taken to indicate that only he repents, however, for Eve is implicated in all parts of the story (see the use of the dual in Q. 7:22–3, for instance). Other examples of error and repentance by prophets include Abraham, who worshipped a star, the moon, and the sun before realizing that he should be worshipping the creator of all of those things (Q. 6:76–9); and Moses, who killed a man and realized his error (Q. 28:15–16). These stories of prophets' errors are echoed in the stories of female characters who also err and repent. Like Abraham, the Queen of Sheba worships the sun; then she realizes the error of her ways and repents (Q. 27:44). In the story of Joseph and Zulaykha, told in Q. 12 (*Sura Yusuf*), Zulaykha is a wealthy woman who, along with her husband, has taken in the young

---

[6] On Prophetic typology, see Nora K. Schmid, 'Lot's Wife: Late Antique Paradigms of Sense and the Qur'ān', in *Qur'ānic Studies Today*, ed. Angelika Neuwirth and Michael Sells (Abingdon: Routledge, 2016), 52–81; Devin J. Stewart, 'Understanding the Quran in English: Notes on Translation, Form, and Prophetic Typology', in *Diversity in Language: Contrastive Studies in Arabic and English Theoretical and Applied Linguistics*, ed. Zeinab M. Ibrahim, Sabiha T. Aydelott, and Nagwa Kassabgy (Cairo: American University in Cairo Press, 2000), 31–48; Roberto Tottoli, *Biblical Prophets in the Qur'ān and Muslim Literature* (Richmond: Routledge Curzon, 2002).

Joseph. But she finds herself attracted to him and attempts to seduce him. He, too, is tempted, but he refuses her temptation, and so she persecutes him, imprisoning him for several years. She eventually realizes that she has erred and accepts responsibility for her error, imploring God to forgive her (Q. 12:53).

These stories illustrate crucial messages about what it means to live a decent and moral life, and sometimes this is emphasized in the text around the stories. Adam and Eve realize that they must obey God and follow Him, even when they do not understand His commands fully; they also realize that they must maintain modesty and decorum, which entails donning clothes physically and donning the metaphorical clothing of piety (Q. 7:26). The Queen of Sheba, Abraham, and Moses all show that people who are innately good and wise can fall into grievous error, harming others and themselves, by not following God's path. They realize that they are prone to error and need God's guidance.[7] Ultimately, by worshipping the wrong thing, or by harming someone else, they harm their own chance for salvation. In the next life, harm done to others does not harm the innocent victim: it harms the perpetrator. Therefore, although all these stories have important aspects other than plot, it is the prospect of salvation that frames them and gives them an overall purpose in the text.

Characters who obey God's command, enduring through hardship, and who are rewarded through closeness to God include Abraham, Moses, Noah, Joseph, Mary, and Moses' mother. Both Moses and Abraham develop as characters, moving from wrongdoing to obedience to God's command. So, for instance, after Abraham begins to worship God rather than the sun, moon, or stars, he is tested by God, who asks him to sacrifice his own son. The son is willing and compliant; but as Abraham is about to sacrifice him, God stops him, tells him this was a test, gives him greetings of peace, and distinguishes him as one of the virtuous (*muhsinun*) (Q. 37:100–113). Moses kills a man, repents, and goes on to lead his people out of Egypt. Joseph's story is a classic illustration of endurance: despite being oppressed, he is still able to exercise moral agency by resisting his attraction to Zulaykha and choosing to be imprisoned rather than to engage in illicit sexual relations. These characters illustrate the crucial moral message of trusting God and behaving righteously through all manner of tests and hardship.

Female characters also endure God's tests. God asks Moses' mother to give Moses up, which she does not want to do; when she nearly despairs of

---

[7] For a fuller analysis of these stories, see Bauer and Hamza, *Women, Households, and the Hereafter*, 105–59.

him, God brings him back to her, so that she might be comforted (Q. 28:13). Mary is miraculously impregnated and withdraws from her household to give birth. In the throes of labour, she calls out to God, who provides her with comfort. It is God who enables Jesus to speak from the cradle, defending her when she returns with him to her people, who revile her (Q. 19:16–33). Her story shows the danger of slander: she was innocently following God's wish, but her people doubted her. The protagonists of these stories are rewarded for their obedience to God's command and for their attitude of humility and acceptance. They serve as a model for ordinary believers, who are repeatedly told to endure (practise *sabr*) through hardship. The quality of endurance and gratitude to God through both good and bad times, and through events that cannot be immediately comprehended, is central to the spiritual progress of Qur'anic protagonists.

The moral trajectory of damnation is also a plot enacted by both male and female characters. The prototypical example of this is Pharaoh, who was warned many times and invited to become a believer, but who continued oppressing people. At the moment before his death Pharaoh repents, but too late: he has been judged on the deeds he committed in his lifetime (Q. 10:90–1). By harming others, he harmed his own soul. Two female characters are mentioned as being damned: the wives of the prophets Noah and Lot (Q. 66:10). Their stories are not told in detail, but the Qur'an specifies that Noah's and Lot's wife were 'under' (*taht*) God's righteous servants: this refers to the women being in their husbands' household, and it is telling that this term is used to convey their dependent status. Yet their social status as dependants does not have any effect on their spiritual trajectory: they are damned despite being married to prophets. Q. 66:11–12 gives the counterexamples: Mary and the wife of Pharaoh, who are cited as exemplary for believers; Pharaoh's wife exemplifies the situation of a believing woman in an unbelieving household. Therefore, the women in Q. 66 exemplify the moral agency held by every person, no matter where they sit in the social hierarchy. This is a fundamental indicator of the spiritual equality and moral agency of all humans as a basic tenet of Qur'anic theology, and it shows that pious women can be models for all believers, not just for female believers.

COMMUNAL IDENTITY AS EXPRESSED THROUGH DECORUM, MODESTY, AND SEXUAL ETHICS

The Qur'an includes many rulings that mention women specifically. Aside from those rulings that pertain to general matters of piety such as prayer and fasting, the rulings that mention women centre on two spheres of activity: decorum, including sexual ethics and modesty; and women's rights (particularly their financial rights) in marriage, divorce, and inheritance. This section and the following section treat each of these subjects in turn; but it is worth first saying a few words about the nature of Qur'anic law itself. For some modern readers, the overall purpose of Qur'anic law is unclear, and the Qur'an's commands on women may seem to be nonsensical or unethical. In fact, it is common for modern readers to separate the Qur'an into a legal sphere and an ethical sphere that either goes beyond the 'law' or that even is opposed to it.[8] According to that perspective, the 'law' imposes a basic set of regulations or requirements, whereas the sphere of morality is behaviour that is more ethical, or beyond the law. Because the Qur'an's rulings pertain specifically to the social structures of seventh-century Arabia, some scholars assert that the 'law' pertains to a specific time and place, but morality transcends time and place. One issue with this perspective is that it separates law from morality. Indeed, in secular societies, law can be separate from morality. However, law that is considered to be divine, such as Qur'anic law, may follow a different logic.

Qur'anic law is not a binary matter of simple obedience or disobedience, and its focus is not only the prevention of harm, but also doing good. Therefore, Qur'anic commands can be graded along a moral scale, the minimum being the prevention of serious harm, and the maximum being the maximum good one can do. Some laws enable behaviour that is not ideal, to prevent an even more serious harm; but better behaviour is always possible. It could be argued that the spirit of these laws is not opposed to morality or separate from it. Instead, Qur'anic rulings serve to define the conduct fitting to believers on an ever-increasing scale of goodness, which is connected to moral purity and which, if followed, will help them attain salvation in the afterlife. Thus 'law' may be a misleading term for Qur'anic commands. Rather, the Qur'an's rulings serve to establish a boundary around the Qur'anic community of believers and to establish a moral rule in that community, even if that morality is not obvious to readers today.

Many of the Qur'an's rulings on sexual ethics, modesty, and decorum elaborate on points that are made in a general way in Qur'anic narratives, which shows a clear connection between 'law' and general morality. For instance, the narrative of Adam and Eve – in which their nakedness becomes apparent to them as a physical need to clothe

---

[8] See, for instance, Fazlur Rahman, *Major Themes of the Qur'an* (Chicago: University of Chicago Press, 1980); repr. with an intro. by Ibrahim Moosa, 2009, 47.

themselves and a spiritual need to follow God's command – acts as a precursor to the Qur'an's rulings on the modesty and decorum for the current believing community. Public morality and decorum for both men and women are outward signs of piety through which believers behave in ways that are befitting of monotheists in late antiquity, so these become integral to the identity of the nascent Muslim community.

According to the Qur'an, both men and women should maintain decorum in public: the Prophet is described as 'cloaked' and 'enwrapped' (Q. 73, 74), and both men and women are expected to lower their gazes from temptation and to cover their private parts to maintain moral purity (Q. 24:30–1). It is in this larger context that women are told to cover their cleavage with their wraps, and not to display their hidden adornment or stamp their feet to call attention to themselves (Q. 24:31). The modesty that characterizes the Muslim community is in contrast to the Qur'an's depiction of pagan behaviour.[9] According to the Qur'an, the pagans were sexually licentious (Q. 7:28), and pagan women used to flaunt themselves (Q. 33:33). Such behaviour, which is considered in the Qur'anic perspective to be immoral, is a symptom of the pagans' moral ignorance. In the Qur'an, the wives of the Prophet are put in direct contrast with pagan women; they are told to stay in their houses and not flaunt themselves as the pagans did (Q. 33:33). This command should not be understood as a restriction of women's movements outside the house. Rather, it is an assertion that whereas pagan women were sexually libertine, Muslim women observe due propriety precisely by not going out to flaunt themselves; moreover, this command of staying in the houses may relate to their elevated social status. It is, however, clear that Muslim women are not actually confined to their houses, because they are told to draw their cloaks around themselves when they go out (Q. 33:59).

Sexual propriety is key to the Qur'anic story of Joseph. As noted earlier in this chapter, in the Joseph story the character of the officer's wife, Zulaykha, is overcome with lust for her ward, Joseph. She attempts to seduce him, and he is likewise tempted; when he resists her advances, she invites her friends to see him and experience his beauty for themselves. They too are overcome, and Joseph begs God to imprison him rather than give in to what they wish from him (Q. 12:33). He secludes himself from their temptation, staying protected in prison, and subsequently Zulaykha repents of her misdeeds. In prison, Joseph acquires

[9] See Holger Michael Zellentin, *The Qur'ān's Legal Culture: The Didascalia Apostolorum as a Point of Departure* (Tübingen: Mohr Siebeck, 2013); Holger Michael Zellentin, *Law beyond Israel: From the Bible to the Qur'an* (Oxford: Oxford University Press, 2022).

a closeness to God, which is shown when he acquires the ability to interpret dreams in prison, which he was unable to do at the beginning of the sura (Q. 12:5–6). In the late antique milieu, where dreams were often considered visions from God, the ability to interpret dreams and therefore to see the future would have been clearly understood as a sign of Joseph's special status with God. This story is a clear illustration of the importance of sexual propriety: Joseph is rewarded for maintaining sexual decorum and propriety, and equally Zulaykha realizes the error of her ways, repents of her misdeeds, and begs God's forgiveness. Social class and gender are both important for the narrative tension in this story: Joseph is a vulnerable individual with low social status who must resist the advances of Zulaykha, a wealthy, high-status individual who has power over him. The Qur'anic point is that, no matter what their social status or gender, and no matter what the power dynamics between them, neither is absolved of their own individual responsibility to obey the rules of sexual decorum and decency. In the end, both come to understand this lesson.

Sexual morality is a major theme in two Qur'anic suras, *al-Nur* (Q. 24) and *al-Ahzab* (Q. 33). A careful reading of these suras shows how their rulings have as a theme not only the equal moral responsibility of men and women, but also the protection of women. *Al-Nur* begins with the rules of punishment for fornication (*zina*): 100 lashes for both the male and the female, and after this the guilty parties may not marry believers, but only other fornicators or polytheists (Q. 24:2–3). The Qur'an goes on to say that someone who accuses an innocent woman and who does not bring four witnesses should face a punishment that is very nearly equal to the punishment for the act itself: eighty lashes (Q. 24:4). If a husband has no witnesses, he may swear four times that his wife is guilty, and a fifth time to invoke God's curse on him if he is lying; but his wife may also perform the same procedure, and if she does so, her word is accepted, and she averts the punishment from herself (Q. 24:6–9). It is significant that in the Qur'an the punishment for adultery is equal for men and women, that there is such a high standard of proof for wrongdoing (four witnesses), that a woman's word is accepted as equal to her husband's, that the punishment for slander is so close to that for fornication itself, and that the guilty parties are not killed but only punished. It seems that these measures are intended to protect women, perhaps in a society in which women alone had been punished for sexual misadventure, and in which the punishment was unduly harsh. Indeed, it is noteworthy that Islamic law (*fiqh*) came to prescribe stoning to death for adultery, and that today it is common in Muslim-majority countries for women to be killed for so-called crimes of honour. Such practices directly contradict the Qur'an.

Another aspect of sexual propriety is that a boundary is maintained around private spaces and private matters. This is the import of requiring four witnesses to fornication; the high burden of proof makes it almost impossible to say that it has actually occurred, and in that case, it is best to say nothing. Maintaining propriety is the upshot of many Qur'anic verses that in the modern period may not make much sense; for instance, believers are warned to approach houses by the front door (Q. 2:189) and to announce their presence (Q. 24:27, 24:61), not to go into uninhabited houses unless one's own possessions are inside (Q. 24:28–29), and not to call out from behind houses to the occupants inside (Q. 49:4). Moreover, even slaves and children have to ask permission to enter private chambers at certain times of day (Q. 24:58). These measures would protect the inhabitants from outsiders intruding on private matters by seeing or hearing anything that they shouldn't.

This sphere of protection around private matters extends to speaking about matters that should not be aired, with a particular focus on slander. The Qur'anic rules on slander hark back to the slander Mary herself encountered from her people, a connection that is made in Q. 4 (Q. 4:156, cf. Q. 24:16). A major theme in *Sura al-Nur* is the danger posed to the whole community by those who slander chaste women and who do not think the best of each other (Q. 24:11–20). This sort of behaviour is 'following in the footsteps of Satan' (Q. 24:21). Slander not only harms the innocent women in question, it also harms the cohesion of the whole community. This is one example of how communal morality is construed around the protection of vulnerable individuals and the maintenance of public decorum.

Taken as a whole, it becomes clear that visible, public piety and private piety within households are concomitant, and that public and private morality combine with decorum to create communal cohesion. The community is visibly pious through the public decorum of its members. Believers' decorum is also maintained by not prying into private matters and not engaging in gossip. Yet it is not to be imagined that God ignores matters that occur in private; on the contrary, as described in the following section, the Qur'an repeatedly states that God is watching people's conduct in private just as much as in public.

HOUSEHOLD MORALITY AND QUOTIDIAN PIETY IN MARRIAGE AND DIVORCE

It is important to note that what might be construed as the 'private sphere' in the Qur'anic context is not necessarily the same as today's 'private sphere'. The Qur'an presumes a household structure that was in itself not strictly 'private': houses or private chambers (*bayt, buyut*) can be seen to be hubs of communal activity where meals are shared (Q. 24:61, 33:53) and where patronage occurs, through the number of people that such households may have supported (Q. 24:31). Households were home not only to a nuclear family but also to others such as slaves, servants, orphans, and other individuals in need of protection. Households were large, but houses themselves were likely to have been simple structures that may not have enabled true privacy in the modern sense. Parts of houses may have been open to the air, without secure windows: hence the prohibition against calling to the Prophet over the walls of his house. Moreover, in Medina, archaeological evidence indicates that the Prophet's wives' chambers were adjoined to the mosque.[10] To be a wife in a large household would have been a position of great social status, and to be a slave woman who ascended to the position of wife, even in a poor household, would have been a significant leap in status. The social status of 'wife' is key to the Qur'an's attitude to marriage and divorce.

Whereas many of the Qur'anic commands on marriage and divorce might, today, seem as though they are granting men power over women, in the context of seventh-century Arabia those commands place controls on men, precisely so that they do not have unlimited power.[11] Verses that seem to disempower women from today's perspective in that context served as guarantees that they could maintain their own property and social status. Such safeguards were necessary because in a large and wealthy household, the *pater familias* – the male head of household – would have had responsibility for many different types of dependants. The problem that emerges is the case in which that *pater familias* is himself immoral and prone to abuse his power. The Qur'an has a primary interest in protecting the rights of vulnerable individuals, and particularly in protecting their financial rights, from any such abuse.

One might say that the point hiding in plain sight in many of the Qur'an's 'problematic' verses is that the upstanding, moral members of the community probably would not have needed these instructions. Rather, many of the verses on marriage and divorce are warnings given to men who had a propensity to transgress and to abuse their position of power in the household. The ultimate message being given is that if the

---

[10] Essam S. Ayyad, 'The "House of the Prophet" or the "Mosque of the Prophet"?' *Journal of Islamic Studies* 24, no. 3 (2013): 273–344.

[11] Asma Barlas, *Believing Women in Islam: Unreading Patriarchal Interpretations of the Qur'an* (Austin, TX: University of Texas Press, 2002).

powerful in society maltreat the vulnerable, this is an act of impiety and will affect their own salvation. They might feel that they are getting away with it, but God serves as a final reckoner and will avenge those vulnerable individuals in the afterlife. This perspective sheds light on verses that might otherwise seem entirely unethical to a modern reader, such as whether the Qur'an endorses men having multiple wives, slave concubinage, or marital abuse.

Two examples of the way in which the Qur'an seeks to protect the rights of the vulnerable, and particularly their financial rights, are found in passages on marriage and divorce in Q. 4 (*al-Nisa'*) and Q. 2 (*al-Baqara*). At the beginning of Q. 4, a sura entitled *al-Nisa'* ('the women'), the Qur'an lays out some limits on the *pater familias*' power. The sura begins by reminding all people of their connection to one another through their creation from a single soul (usually understood in the tradition to be Adam), and the creation from the same substance of that soul's mate. The single soul and its mate in this instance act as a primordial precursor to all humans. Humans are here reminded to be wary of God and of their kinship ties, the 'wombs' (*arham*). This sets up one of the major themes of the sura, which is the care of the vulnerable, such as orphans, women, and those who are legally incompetent (*sufaha'*), all of whom might have been in the protection of prominent households. It is in this larger context that Q. 4:2–4 warn the audience, which here is presumably the male heads of household, not to consume the property of the orphans in their care as though it were their own. They are told that if they fear they may not deal equitably with the orphans, they may marry the women, two or three or four of them. The women here are presumably the female orphans in their care, who were not necessarily children but rather women without another protector (see also Q. 4:127). However, the *pater familias* must give those women their dowries, and if they fear that they will not deal equitably with them, then they must marry only one:

> Give the orphans what belongs to them, exchanging not what is wholesome for what is vile, and do not consume what belongs to them with what is yours, for that is a dreadful sin. And if you fear that you will not be just [*qist*] towards the orphans, then marry the women as you see fit, two, three, or four. But if you fear that you will not be equitable ['*adl*], then just one or what your right hand owns, lest you become unable to provide for them. Give the women their

bridal payment as a gift, so if they themselves give you any good from it, then consume it beneficially and wholesomely. (Q. 4:2–4)

Verses that, read from a modern context, may seem to grant men the power to marry several women, were, in their own context, a warning to men that if they abused the people in their protection, they would face retribution in the afterlife. In a tribal milieu where multiple marriages were apparently common, and where the *pater familias* had the power to take advantage of those in his care, these verses set up limits and permit him to marry them in order to prevent a much worse harm: consuming their property, potentially taking advantage of them in other ways, and leaving them destitute. In Q. 4:10 the warning is repeated: those who consume the property of orphans unjustly 'only consume fire in their bellies'. The focus on protecting the financial rights of the vulnerable continues through the rulings on inheritance in Q. 4:11–12, which gives a share to women, children, and other relatives.

The overall import of Q. 4:3, which over time has been read to grant men permission for multiple marriages, is that instead of being left destitute, vulnerable women could be married and thereby achieve status, a bridal payment, and the sole right of disposal over their property. The husband is, moreover, warned that he is only allowed to take more than one wife if he is able to be equitable among them and to provide for them; in a later verse, he is told that he will never manage to be equitable (Q. 4:129). This is a tacit recognition that, despite his overt right to take more than one of his wards as a wife, it is morally preferable to marry one woman and to treat her well. It is also a tacit recognition that some men might wish to marry many women as a means of showing their own wealth and status.

From a modern perspective, the arrangement described in Q. 4:2–4 can be considered unfair, unjust, or simply not right, because these verses imply that the ultimate control of marriage is in the husband's hands, because they grant the possibility of polygamy, and because they presume a society in which there were slaves. For those who seek to understand how the Qur'an could be considered an ethical text in its own time and still include such provisions, it is important to remember that in late antiquity there was no notion of social equality: slavery was common, and slave women had few, if any, rights. Furthermore, marriages were often primarily formed on the basis of practical considerations such as allegiances between families and lineages. In such a social context, it is significant that the Qur'an encourages believing men to marry believing slave women and to give them a dowry (Q. 2:221, 4:25), and it tells them not to compel their female slaves into sexual acts (Q. 24:33).

A prominent example of a stipulation that contradicts modern norms and notions of morality is that if the wife rises up (presumably to commit a breach of the marital bond), her husband is permitted to undertake a three-step process, which begins with admonishment and culminates in striking her. He is told that if the wife obeys, he must not seek any way against her (Q. 4:34). For his own rising up against the marital bond, the couple is advised to reconcile (Q. 4:128). These verses have naturally generated a great deal of controversy over time, particularly over their ethical implications and the question of whether husbands have the right to beat their wives. Although it is impossible to fully explore or explain these verses here, it is possible to say that in late antiquity it was probably considered natural for husbands to have a duty of control over the spousal relationship, and rather than granting permission to beat, Q. 4:34 would probably have been understood as a radical limitation on a husband's unlimited right to beat his wife. Yet even in that tribal context, this measure is presented as a last resort, something that was considered less bad than the breach that might result from the rupture of their relationship. Needless to say, Q. 4:34 does not grant permission for spousal abuse; rather, it indicates that in seventh-century Arabia the husband's rights over his wife needed to be controlled and curtailed. This may be why the families are brought to help resolve the conflict, according to Q. 4:35, a provision that indicates how marriage at the time was not merely a bond between two people, but an alliance between households; that may be one reason why divorce is considered such a serious matter.

The Qur'an's verses on divorce may be considered another example of a curtailment of men's rights and a protection for their wives: many of the Qur'an's verses on divorce serve to ensure that women have some financial and social stability. The divorce passage in *al-Baqara*, from Q. 2:226–42, in combination with the verses on divorce in Q. 65:1–7, stipulate various protections for women. The term commonly translated as 'divorce', *talaq*, has a dual meaning. It refers to a period of separation between the couple which ends in the choice to separate or to remain together (Q. 2:228, 2:231, 2:232), and it also refers to the final, permanent separation (Q. 2:230, 2:236, 2:237, 2:241, 65:1).

The period of separation (*talaq*) must only happen twice (Q. 2:229). This period, during which separation has been effected but not finalized (the *'idda*), lasts three menstrual cycles, or three months, and must be calculated precisely according to Q. 65:1. In that time, the husband has a 'greater right' to take his wife back if they desire to reconcile (Q. 2:228), meaning that he has a greater right to resume the relationship than another person can have to start a new one. The Qur'an emphasizes men's responsibilities towards their wives during the period of separation. During this period, the husband must support his wife, feeding and clothing her according to his own standard of living, and he must not turn her out of her house unless she has committed a sexual transgression; if she is found to be pregnant, she is to be maintained until she delivers the baby and paid maintenance whilst breastfeeding (Q. 65:1–7). For her part, she must not move out of her own accord, and she must not conceal it if she is pregnant (Q. 2:228, 65:1). In Q. 2:235 it becomes clear that in the waiting period after a woman is widowed, but also possibly if she has been divorced, a woman may come to an arrangement to marry a new husband, but this must not be formalized until after the waiting period has finished. Q. 2:236–7 treat the case where separation occurs before the marriage has been consummated, and even in this case the husband owes the betrothed some financial recompense; this is also confirmed in Q. 33:49. Thus, men are bound to any promises they may have made to women, presumably because of the social and financial ramifications for the women themselves of any broken promises.

At the conclusion of any period of separation, the husband must settle his wife's legal status conclusively by deciding whether to take her back as his wife, or to release her from the marriage (Q. 2:229, 2:231, 65:2). If he releases her and hence effects a more permanent separation (what we might term a 'divorce'), he must not take anything that he has given to her, he must not thwart her from marrying someone else (Q. 2:232), and he must bring two just witnesses to the act of separation (Q. 65:2). All of this indicates that the decision to separate after the waiting period renders her free of any hold he once had over her as her husband. According to Q. 2:230, if the husband has invoked the separation, he may not take his wife back until she has married someone else.[12] These stipulations serve to deter men from leaving their wives destitute if they do decide on a permanent separation. Husbands are

---

[12] There are alternative readings of this complicated passage, in which Q. 2:230 stipulates that if he divorces her (permanently) she must marry someone else before he can take her back, and Q. 2:232 says that if he has released her, she must not be thwarted from (another) marriage. Q. 2:230 is generally interpreted to mean that she must marry someone else if he invokes a *third* separation after the first two permitted separations. An alternative reading is that the stipulation for the wife to marry someone else might come into effect any time the husband decides on a permanent separation, even after the first or second waiting period. Marianna Klar has questioned whether Q. 2:230 refers to a third divorce, since the Qur'an specifies that 'divorce is twice' ('*Fa-ayna*

expressly told that if they take their wives back to cause them harm, this is making a mockery of God's signs, and God will punish them for it (Q. 2:231). Everything that both parties do in this period is watched by God and has an impact on their standing in the afterlife, but the focus is mostly on the husband's conduct. The wife is warned to be wary of God only once, at Q. 2:228; both parties are warned in Q. 2:229; and the husband is warned – sometimes quite starkly – to treat his wife decently in Q. 2:229, 2:231, 2:232, 2:233, 2:235, 2:241, 65:1, 65:2, 65:4, 65:5, 65:6; and he is also reassured that he has God's support for good conduct in 65:2, 65:3, and 65:7.

Overall, the picture that emerges is that marrying and staying married are preferable, particularly when the alliance is between believers who obey the moral codes that bind the community. Thus, adulterers can only marry each other or pagans (Q. 24:3), and 'impure women are for impure men, and impure men are for impure women, and good women are for good men, and good men are for good women' (Q. 24:26). Marriage to the 'people of the book' is permitted (Q. 5:5). The preference is for marriage to a Qur'anic believer of any social status, even a slave; for according to Q. 2:221, marriage to a believing slave is preferable to marrying a pagan, and believers are permitted to marry believing slave girls if they cannot afford to marry a free woman; slave women are also owed a dowry (Q. 4:25). Presumably, the formation of believing households will make it more likely that morality is observed both in those households and in the community.

The Qur'an's practical approach and its heavy focus on men's duties do not mean that women's wishes were not considered, and do not preclude the possibility of attraction and affection between the spouses. On the contrary, it seems that women's preferences were taken for granted. For instance, Q. 2:232 describes a situation where a woman and man come to an arrangement of marriage by mutual consent. Q. 33:50–1 describe a situation in which believing women offer themselves in marriage to the Prophet; he is permitted to accept those whom he wishes, because that will bring them comfort, and it means that they will not grieve. Presumably, women in the Prophet's household had great status, and in this case their own choice and happiness are a primary consideration in whether he will marry them. Moreover, the Qur'an says that the couple might find love and mercy between them (Q. 30:21) and describes the spouses as 'garments' for one another (Q. 2:187). On the

l-thālithah? Qur'anic Divorce in the Context of Roman, Rabbinic, and Sasanian Law', forthcoming).

whole, households seem to be a place of comfort. However, sometimes affection is wanting, and this might explain why the husband is admonished that marriage is a solemn covenant (Q. 4:21), and that although he might hate his wife he should still look after her, for 'perhaps you hate a thing in which God has put much good' (Q. 4:19). The implication here is that God sees the wives' moral worth even when their husbands cannot. It is also important to note that men are warned repeatedly against turning women out and taking their bridal payment, and against other measures that might deprive women of their due inheritance, such as marrying the women their fathers had married (Q. 4:22). Women's unequal share in inheritance should be read in view of the duty men had to provide for the women in their care; in this milieu, it was crucial that women were granted an allotted share in inheritance and could not be left destitute. Ultimately, passages that may be read from today's perspective as limiting women's rights were in their own context a curtailment of men's rights over women, and women's own inherent status is the backdrop to this curtailment of their husbands' rights.

WOMEN'S MORAL AGENCY AND THEIR SOCIAL AGENCY: DOES THE QUR'AN PUT MEN IN CONTROL OVER WOMEN?

The notion of social equality was alien to seventh-century Arabia; but this does not mean that men had control over women. Women in the Qur'an are always empowered to make their own choices about the matters that were the most important in the Qur'an's own moral worldview: whether to become believers and how to enact that belief. This moral empowerment leads to a degree of social empowerment that might be surprising to modern readers, who might expect that the Qur'an echoes the positions that were adopted in Islamic law (*fiqh*). Islamic law granted men a high degree of control over women. Yet a close reading of the Qur'an shows that men were not 'in charge' of women in the ways that might be imagined by a modern audience. The following paragraphs describe some of what we can know about women's social empowerment in early Islamic Arabia from the hints that we have in the Qur'an.

It is worth beginning with the moral status of slave women, who would have been on the lowest rung of the social hierarchy. There is not much information about slave women in the Qur'an, but it seems that men were assumed to have sexual rights over their female slaves. Yet, according to Q. 24:33, if a slave woman wished to remain chaste (probably through marriage to someone else) her owner should not compel her into sexual activity.¹³ This means that even slave women were not mere objects: ideally, their decision to be believers and to remain chaste was respected (see also Q. 4:25; 24:33). This is one example of the ways in which women's moral choices – even the moral choices of the most disenfranchised members of society – translate into a certain degree of social agency. The community was supposed to support believing slave women's moral progress, enabling them to marry and form their own believing households.

Unsurprisingly, the Qur'an has more hints about free women's social agency than about slave women's. *Al-Mujadila* (Q. 58) describes a scene in which a woman has come to the Prophet to complain about the conduct of her husband. It seems that the husband had divorced her using a pre-Islamic formula, which is to liken her to his mother's back (called *zihar*). God takes the wife's side, saying that He has heard her complaint (Q. 58:1), and outlawing *zihar* (Q. 58:2–5). It is clear that this woman was speaking alone with the Prophet, because the dual grammatical form in Arabic is used to describe their exchange. Yet the point being made here is not that the Prophet and this woman should not have been alone together. Rather, it is that there is no conversation that is truly private from God, who hears everything. From this, we may conclude not only that women went out on their own, without their husbands, but also that a woman would have been permitted to have a private conversation with a man who was not her husband.

Al-Mumtahana (Q. 60) describes the situation of believers in marriages and other close relations with unbelievers. The final verses of this short sura deal with the question of believing women who come from the unbelieving community, and of unbelieving women who are married to believers. The believers are told to test the women who come claiming to be believers (Q. 60:10), and if these women are found to be believers, they are not to be sent back to the unbelievers. Rather, the believers will pay the unbelievers what the unbelievers had paid as a bridal payment, and then the women may join a believing household by marrying a believing man, who must pay her bridal payment to her directly. Likewise, if believers are married to unbelieving women, those women may leave

---

13   The term *bigha'* in Q. 24:33 is almost universally translated as 'prostitution', which gives the meaning that slave owners should not compel their female slaves into prostitution if the slaves wish to remain chaste. This common reading implies that, if the slave agreed, it would be legal for a man to prostitute her. A more accurate reading of Q. 24:33 is that if slave women wish to remain chaste, their owner has no right to compel them into sexual acts (*bigha'*): the root b-gh-y as used elsewhere in the Qur'an means simply to be unchaste (Q. 19:20, 19:28).

to join the unbelieving community, and the believers may ask from the unbelievers the bridal payment they had made. Finally, the Prophet is given the pledge that the newly believing women must take in order to be in the believing community (Q. 60:12). Though a financial negotiation occurs between male believers and unbelievers, the women alone are responsible for deciding which community to join. They are tested without any male relative being present, and no hint of a guardian. Women's husbands seem to have no say in whether they stay or go.

Women's freedom to leave their marriages is epitomized by the wives of the Prophet, who are addressed directly in two suras and told that they may choose to stay with the Prophet and obey God and the Prophet, or to leave him. To modern readers, this choice seems quite stark, and, taken out of context, it seems to revolve around obedience to the Prophet himself as their husband:

> O Prophet! Tell your wives, 'If you should desire the life of this world and its ornament, come, and I shall grant you that enjoyment, and I shall release you in a virtuous way. But should you desire God and His Messenger, and the abode of the Hereafter, assuredly God has prepared for those of you who are virtuous a tremendous reward [...] The one among you who obeys God and His messenger with devotion, and does good works, to her We shall give the reward twice, and We shall prepare for her in addition a noble provision. (Q. 33:28–29, 31)

The choice here is clear: the Prophet's wives may choose to stay with him and obey him and God, do good works, and receive a reward, or they may choose to leave him, and he will let them go freely. The implication is that they will face a consequence in the afterlife. Taken out of context, this seems to imply that the Prophet's wives owe him personal obedience, *as wives*. But in reality, the Prophet's wives are simply emblematic of all believers, who are told repeatedly to obey God and the Prophet or to be considered as unbelievers, with consequences in the afterlife (e.g., Q. 24:54). Therefore, it is not that the Prophet's wives must obey him solely in his capacity as their husband. Rather, he is insisting that his household be a place where God's law is obeyed, and his wives must be mindful of God's bounds if they choose to stay with him. In the Qur'anic worldview, the Prophet's house becomes a sphere of moral protection for his wives and for himself, a sphere in which God's commands are enacted.

Significantly, the Prophet himself will let his wives go freely if the wives choose to go; the language used echoes the language with which husbands are commanded to let their divorced wives go freely, once they have decided on a permanent separation. There can be little doubt that in the late antique milieu the *pater familias* was expected to have some control over the household along with his responsibility for it, and this is what is reflected in the phrase 'if they obey you, seek not a way against them' from Q. 4:34. However, there is no hint that a husband can control his wife in any ultimate sense. The Prophet is told repeatedly throughout the Qur'an that he cannot control people, only warn them (Q. 38:65); people's fate is ultimately determined by their own actions. In this larger context, the Prophet's wives are a prominent, symbolically important example of the way in which moral agency works in the Qur'an.

One of the important Qur'anic passages on women's moral agency and their social agency is where believing men and believing women are described as those who 'command right and forbid wrong' in Q. 9:71. In later Islamic law, this was often construed as men's duty alone;[14] but in the Qur'an there is no differentiation between the genders. Rather, this passage comes amid the larger struggle between believers and unbelievers, in which it becomes clear that male and female believers must act as allies to one another, just as the hypocrites do (Q. 9:67–71; see also Q. 48:5–6). These instances show how the Qur'an portrays the believing community as one in which both men and women play an important part.

It is the true believers who do good works, both male and female, who will end up together in the afterlife, according to the Qur'an. It is well documented that the Qur'anic image of women in the afterlife develops over time, from the early mentions of houris, who are sensual companions presented as a reward for male believers in some of the earliest suras, to the fully fledged promise of believing women present in the afterlife in the Medinan suras.[15] The culmination of this progression can be found in *Sura al-Hadid* (Q. 57), where the believing men and women are described in the afterlife with their light 'flowing before them and by their right hands' (Q. 57:12). The male and female hypocrites, meanwhile, will be asking them for some of their light; but it is not possible to pass on this light (Q. 57:13). That is because the light has been earned by the good deeds that the believers have undertaken in their lives. The image of these radiant believers in the afterlife, male and female together, is, in the Qur'anic perspective, the ultimate vindication of their spiritual equality.

---

[14] See Michael Cook, *Commanding Right and Forbidding Wrong in Islamic Thought* (Cambridge: Cambridge University Press, 2000).

[15] See now Ana Davitashvili, 'The Inner-Qur'ānic Development of the Images of Women in Paradise: From the *ḥūr 'īn* to Believing Women', *Journal of the International Qur'anic Studies Association* 7 (2022): 27–54.

CONCLUSION

The social morality proposed by the Qur'an sits in the context of late antiquity, in a milieu in which the dominant piety was Christian asceticism. In late antique Christianity in the Near East, the pious exemplars were often celibate, whether living as solitary ascetics or monks in monasteries. Ascetics were hardly removed from the world: ascetic holy men and monasteries played a key function in society, and affectionate bonds among monks were important; but worship was largely enacted in spaces dedicated to that function, such as churches, and sensual pleasure was considered to be sinful. In the Qur'an, by contrast, the ideal of piety is neither celibate nor removed from family life: piety takes place primarily in households, by men and women, and believers are encouraged in a temperate enjoyment of this world's pleasures. They are commanded to enjoy the good things of God's bounty, while still maintaining God's bounds (Q. 2:172, 5:4–5, 23:51). What emerges strongly from the Qur'anic text is that, on the one hand, the protection of women is of paramount importance, and that, on the other, there is no separate sphere of the 'sacred' from the 'profane'. Qur'anic piety is quotidian piety, and this has important ramifications for women's status.

The fact that in both antiquity and late antiquity households were presumed to have a *pater familias*, who was supposed to act as patron and protector for all those in the household and even for the vulnerable outside it, shapes Qur'anic morality in ways that are only now being understood fully. Importantly, although the Qur'an presumes male-headed households, that does not equate with the subsequent tradition of interpretation, which granted men a high degree of control over women. Rather, in the Qur'an, it is the physical protection of women, and the moral protection of the entire community, that is paramount. Ultimately, women are empowered to make their own moral choices, and it is their piety that will determine their ultimate rank in the afterlife, when, according to the Qur'an, all worldly hierarchies will be overturned and replaced with a just hierarchy based on a person's deeds, rather than any accident of their birth.

SELECT BIBLIOGRAPHY

Ali, Kecia. *Sexual Ethics and Islam: Feminist Reflections on the Qur'an, Hadith, and Jurisprudence*. Oxford: Oneworld Publications, 2006.

Ayyad, Essam S. 'The "House of the Prophet" or the "Mosque of the Prophet"?' *Journal of Islamic Studies* 24, no. 3 (2013): 273–344.

el-Badawi, Emran Iqbal. *Queens and Prophets: How Arabian Noblewomen and Holy Men Shaped Paganism, Christianity, and Islam*. London: Oneworld Publications, 2022.

Barlas, Asma. *Believing Women in Islam: Unreading Patriarchal Interpretations of the Qur'an*. Austin, TX: University of Texas Press, 2002.

Bauer, Karen and Feras, Hamza. 'Qur'anic Morality as Qur'anic Law (What Is Qur'anic Law?)', forthcoming in *Regulative Verses of the Qur'an: From Historical Trends to Contemporary Trajectories*, ed. Karen Bauer, Mohammed Fatemi, Robert Gleave, and Devin Stewart.

Women, Households, and the Hereafter in the Qur'an: A Patronage of Piety. Oxford: Oxford University Press, 2023.

Chaudhry, Ayesha S. *Domestic Violence and the Islamic Tradition: Ethics, Law, and the Muslim Discourse on Gender*. Oxford: Oxford University Press, 2013.

Cook, Michael. *Commanding Right and Forbidding Wrong in Islamic Thought*. Cambridge: Cambridge University Press, 2000.

Davitashvili, Ana. 'The Inner-Qur'ānic Development of the Images of Women in Paradise: From the ḥūr 'īn to Believing Women'. *Journal of the International Qur'anic Studies Association* 7 (2022): 27–54.

de Cillis, Maria. *Free Will and Predestination in Islamic Thought: Theoretical Compromises in the Work of Avicenna, al-Ghazālī and Ibn 'Arabī*. Abingdon: Routledge, 2013.

Hidayatullah, Aysha. *Feminist Edges of the Qur'an*. Oxford: Oxford University Press, 2014.

Ibrahim, Celene. *Women and Gender in the Qur'an*. Oxford: Oxford University Press, 2020.

Rahman, Fazlur. *Major Themes of the Qur'an*. Chicago: University of Chicago Press, 1980; repr. with an intro. by Ibrahim Moosa, 2009.

Schmid, Nora K. 'Lot's Wife: Late Antique Paradigms of Sense and the Qur'ān'. In *Qur'ānic Studies Today*, ed. Angelika Neuwirth and Michael Sells, 52–81. Abingdon: Routledge, 2016.

Stewart, Devin J. 'Understanding the Quran in English: Notes on Translation, Form, and Prophetic Typology'. In *Diversity in Language: Contrastive Studies in Arabic and English Theoretical and Applied Linguistics*, ed. Zeinab M. Ibrahim, Sabiha T. Aydelott, and Nagwa Kassabgy, 31–48. Cairo: American University in Cairo Press, 2000.

Tottoli, Roberto. *Biblical Prophets in the Qur'ān and Muslim Literature*. Richmond: Routledge Curzon, 2002.

Zellentin, Holger Michael. *Law beyond Israel: From the Bible to the Qur'an*. Oxford: Oxford University Press, 2022.

The Qur'ān's Legal Culture: The Didascalia Apostolorum as a Point of Departure. Tübingen: Mohr Siebeck, 2013.

2 Women's Inheritance

SOHAIL HANIF

A lot has been written on the question of women's inheritance in Islamic law. A large number of academic contributions to 'inheritance' in Index Islamicus pertain directly or indirectly to the question of women's inheritance in Islam. Clearly, there is a perceived problem here. The problem in the question of women's inheritance stems from the fact that, in several cases, women inherit only half of what their male counterparts do – as per the teachings of the Holy Qur'an, thereby raising concerns about fairness. Many authors point out that this unequal division is offset by the greater financial responsibility borne by men in Islamic law. This chapter contributes to the literature on women's inheritance in Islam by providing a more granular assessment of the rules of financial maintenance in works of Islamic law, and thereby offers a more detailed assessment of how the rules of inheritance fit into the larger social and legal imagination of Muslim jurists. Most of the legal discussions in this article draw from a single school of law (*madhhab*), namely, the Hanafi school. This is because the focus of this article is not comparative law, but to reveal what can be learnt from a more detailed engagement with the rules of financial maintenance, and this detailed engagement is facilitated by studying the interrelated rules from a single legal tradition.

The backdrop to this topic and to our problematizing the inheritance division of the Qur'an is a conflict between two world-views, one maintaining hierarchy, the other promoting equality. The question of hierarchy versus equality, still being negotiated in many areas of modern life, sums up the clash between the premodern and the modern.[1] Premodern civilizations built their conception of this world, and the role of the human being, within a cosmic hierarchy, starting from a godhead, and

---

[1] For example, consider the literature on the clash between hierarchy and equality in the workplace, where equality is often presented as a moral ideal, while hierarchy is typically linked to operational efficiency. An example of this is Alexander Motchoulski's article, 'Equality, Efficiency and Hierarchy in the Workplace', *Economics and Philosophy* (2024): 1–20.

coming down to this world. This cosmic hierarchy was reflected in a perceived social hierarchy – and differentiating between the roles of men and women is an extension of this hierarchical world-view. The modern project of the Enlightenment, on the other hand, was grounded in a rejection of hierarchy. In cosmology, there developed a rejection of a higher hierarchy of being on which the observed order is dependent, leading to the diminished significance of religion and religious institutions. Socially, there grew a questioning and removal of hierarchical values and structures. Equality and freedom were the highest ideals of this movement that shaped our modern world. Hasan Spiker offers an excellent contrast between the two world-views and argues, amongst other points, that the rejection of hierarchy led to the inability of modern thinkers to offer a definitive foundation for human morality.[2]

I do not mean by the preceding observation that premodern societies had no interest in equality, or that modern societies lack a notion of hierarchy. However, there is a stark difference in emphasis and ideals that we must bear in mind. Implicit in all engagements with the topic of women's inheritance is the premise that inequality between the genders is unjust. If we impose our own ideal of equality on a world that did not strive towards such a notion of equality as our own, we will fail to understand their own conception of ideal social values and of justice. This is why a granular study of related topics of the law sheds light on the vision for organizing society into which the rules of inheritance were embedded.

In the current chapter, we reflect first on the gendered underpinning of Islamic law. This is followed by highlighting the parts of inheritance law where women receive unequal shares, and then presenting and analysing a detailed summary of the rules of financial maintenance (nafaqa). We then reflect on how the fact of gender was to be identified according to Muslim jurists. Finally, we reflect on how this topic might come into conversation with a modernity that does not reflect the hierarchical structure of Islamic law.

THE GENDERED UNIVERSE OF ISLAMIC LAW

Islamic sacred law, at its core, is a discourse on rights and duties. One's rights and duties reflect one's position in a legal hierarchy. Examples of legal hierarchies include slaves and free individuals, leaders and

---

[2] Hasan Spiker, *Hierarchy and Freedom: An Examination of Some Classical Metaphysical and Post-Enlightenment Accounts of Human Autonomy* (Dublin: New Andalus Press, 2023).

followers, rich and poor, sane and insane, adults and children. I apply the notion of hierarchy to the relationship between men and women in Islamic law. This is not a simple hierarchy, as one gender is not absolutely above the other, and each has different duties towards the other. However, Islamic legal literature provides more detailed accounts of men's duties to women, as this chapter will show, reflecting a greater duty of care that men have towards women. This fits broadly into a larger hierarchical narrative in Islamic law, where men are seen as carers.

Islamic law is, therefore, gendered. A person's gender informs their rights and duties. Now, we all know that individual men and women vary greatly in physical, rational, social and emotional traits. Many women are physically stronger than many men, for example. However, a gendered law ignores the specifics of individuals and applies a general assumption of traits to the genders. Ignoring individual variations is typical of legal systems. Not all instances of speeding or crossing red lights are dangerous, for example, but generally they are. This generalizing nature of the law is indicated by the Islamic legal maxim: 'Consideration is given to the predominant and widespread, not to the rare.'[3] To help us explore the assumed traits of the genders, we can coin the terms 'legal-man' and 'legal-woman' – as opposed to individual men and women, who each vary greatly in their respective characteristics.

The general rule in Islamic law is that legal-man carries financial and protective duties. Financially, he is responsible for dependants. The rules of financial duties are expressed in greatest detail in the *Book of Maintenance* (*Kitab al-Nafaqat*), and we will explore this further below. Legal-man's protective duty is most expressed in his military duties in the *Book of War* (*Kitab al-Jihad*). Men are expected to join the military effort if required. Women do not bear this duty, except in the case where the enemy has penetrated the settlement, in which case all adults must join the war effort.[4] This last case illustrates that these rules have exceptions, even in areas of well-known gender distinction.

Legal-woman is financially and militarily dependent. As we will see below, a rich wife and mother has no duty to spend on herself or her children. The poor husband is bound before the law to earn and spend on his rich wife and child. Legal-woman is assumed to have domestic

---

[3] Muhammad Mustafa al-Zuhayli, *Kitab al-Qawa'id al-fiqhiyya wa-tatbiquha fi al-madhahib al-arba'a*, 2 vols. (Damascus: Dar al-Fikr, 2006), vol. I, 325.
[4] al-Mawsili, *al-Ikhtiyar li-ta'lil al-Mukhtar*, ed. Bashshar Bakri 'Urabi, 2 vols. (Damascus: al-Maktaba al-'Umariyya, n.d.), vol. II, 341–2.

responsibilities, but, perhaps surprisingly, she bears few domestic *duties* in the law.⁵

Here are some examples from the chapters of law to illustrate these basic distinctions. Friday prayer is a duty on all free men healthy enough to make it to the mosque. Women are not obliged to attend, though, if they do attend, the prayer is valid and replaces the ordinary noon prayer. A common reason given for this distinction in legal commentaries is that women are busy with serving their husbands (*khidmat al-zawj*).⁶ Now, not all women have husbands, and domestic service is seldom a duty according to the law, so why assume this busy-ness for the entire gender? A possible answer is that there is a clear social detriment if all adults of a settlement are duty-bound to attend the mosque at the same time, as households – and the children, the sick, and the elderly they might contain – could suffer from lack of attention. So, in this hierarchical legal system, an easily defined human trait – gender – is summoned to cover this social exposure, by excusing a gender from the duty, on the grounds of domestic service, while accepting the ritual prayer from them if they attend.

Another good illustration of gendered norms is in the chapter on childcare (*hadana*).⁷ Young children are in need of care. Islamic law is categoric in declaring that legal-woman is best suited to offer this care. Yet, fascinatingly, it is not a *duty* on a woman to care for a child; rather, it is her *right*, and she must be offered the chance to exercise this right. In the case of marital dispute or divorce, the closest female relative is offered to exercise the right to care for the child; if she refuses, the next closest female relative is asked. This right to care for a child is first offered to the child's mother, then the females from her family, and then to females of the father's family – the closest unmarried female relation to the child has the greatest right to care for the child. The law states that the mother's side of the family has a greater right to care than the father's side. The law also states that the father is not offered the chance to care for the child if these female relatives exist, yet the father must bear the financial costs of the childcare. When children are older – past seven years for boys and past nine years or puberty for girls – they transfer to the direct care of the father or his closest male relative, as the need of boys is for discipline (*ta'addub*) and acquiring the character of

---

⁵ Various historical attempts to theorize women's domestic duties by Muslim jurists, and the generally light list of domestic duties, is studied in Marion Katz, *Wives and Work: Islamic Law and Ethics before Modernity* (New York: Columbia University Press, 2022).

⁶ al-Mawsili, *al-Ikhtiyar*, vol. I, 124.

⁷ Ibid., vol. II, 226–9.

men, and the need of girls is to be protected and guarded (*hifz wa-siyana*). This topic is remarkable for the firm assumptions made about the genders (which gender is better suited for care and which is better suited for discipline and guarding), about the man's undisputed duty of financial care for his children, and even that relatives on the mother's side are better at caring for a child than relatives on the father's side.[8]

INHERITANCE AND MAINTENANCE

In this section, we review the divisions of inheritance amongst the genders, and then contextualize the divisions by reviewing the basic rules of financial maintenance. The goal of this section is to see a more complete picture of financial rights and duties within which to understand the rules of inheritance.

Inheritance

Inheritance is one of the few topics of the law that has been detailed in the Holy Qur'an.[9] Most other injunctions – including the number and manner of daily prayers – are only described in detail in the teachings of the Prophet. The most common explanation for this extra focus on inheritance rules is that disputes about inheritance can destroy families, so the rules were preserved in the Qur'an so as not to leave any doubt as to the correct way to divide up a person's estate.

These rules of inheritance are further detailed in books of Islamic law, and also within their own genre called *'ilm al-fara'id* or *'ilm al-mawarith*. In Islamic inheritance, there are two types of inheritor: some inherit through fixed fractions – called *ashab al-furud* – and others inherit by taking what remains after fixed fractions have been given out – called *'asabat*. Men and women are not given the same amount. It is incorrect to say that men are always favoured in inheritance. Women inherit more than men in many scenarios. A simple illustration is when a person leaves behind a mother, father, and daughter: the daughter takes half, the mother one-sixth, the father one-third; daughters here are favoured over fathers. There are more complicated scenarios, such as those in which a granddaughter inherits, although, if she were replaced

---

[8] Modern studies confirm the phenomenon of a matrilineal advantage – that children tend to have closer relations to the mother's side of the family. See, for example, Chiara Dello Joio, 'Why Dad's Side of the Family Tends to Miss Out', *The Atlantic*, 12 May 2023, www.theatlantic.com/family/archive/2023/05/mother-kinkeeping-roles-women-family-network/674039/.

[9] This is over three verses in *Sura al-Nisa'* (Chapter of Women): Q. 4:11, 12, 176.

by a grandson, he would not inherit; and similarly, a grandmother might inherit in scenarios where, if she were replaced by a grandfather, he would not inherit.[10]

However, there are scenarios where it is undeniable that men are favoured over women in inheritance. A man receives double the share of a woman in the following scenarios: (1) where the deceased is survived by sons and daughters, each son has a double share of each daughter; (2) where the deceased is not survived by a son or father but by full or paternal brothers and sisters, each brother's share is double each sister's share; and (3) where the deceased is survived by a mother and father with no children or siblings, the father's share is double the mother's. In addition, a husband is awarded a half-fraction[11] of his wife's wealth when she dies without children, while she inherits a quarter-fraction of his wealth in this case; and if there are children, then he inherits a quarter-fraction from her, while she would inherit an eighth-fraction from him if he dies. When discussing inequality between men and women in Islamic inheritance, it is these particular relations and scenarios to which we refer.

So how to understand the difference between the genders in these scenarios? The general answer given to this question is that in this gendered moral code, men bear more financial duties, and therefore are awarded a greater share of the inheritance from which to discharge these duties.[12] In order to assess the accuracy of this explanation, we turn now to a more detailed assessment of the rules of maintenance (*nafaqa*). To facilitate a detailed review of these rules, I will present them from the legal texts of one particular legal school as an illustrative presentation. The school for this survey is the Hanafi school.

Below, I present in list form the basic rules of maintenance presented in the *Kitab al-Nafaqat* in the foundational Hanafi legal digest (*mukhtasar*) of Ahmad ibn Muhammad al-Quduri (d. AH 428/1037 CE),[13] adding key notes from 'Abd Allah ibn Mahmud al-Mawsili's (d. AH 683/1284 CE) digest

---

[10] A good overview and breakdown of the different gendered scenarios in inheritance can be found in an article on the Egyptian Dar al-Ifta website: 'Do Women Take Unequal Shares of Inheritance in Islam?', www.dar-alifta.org/en/article/details/120/do-women-take-unequal-shares-of-inheritance-in-islam.

[11] I use 'half-fraction', and not simply 'half', because once the shares of other inheritors are taken into account, the husband's half might become less than half of the estate.

[12] See Haifaa Jawad, *The Rights of Women in Islam: An Authentic Approach* (London: Palgrave Macmillan, 1998), 65–9. Jawad further adds, in the case of marriage, that a woman already receives a marriage-payment (*mahr*) from the husband, so the disparity accounts for this prior payment.

[13] The *K. al-Nafaqat* of al-Quduri's *Mukhtasar* is translated from al-Maydani's commentary: al-Maydani, *al-Lubab fi sharh al-Kitab*, ed. 'Abd al-Hamid al-Halabi, 2 vols. (Beirut: Dar al-Ma'rifa, 1998), vol. II, 87–95.

al-Mukhtar and commentary *al-Ikhtiyar*.[14] The following is an abridged translation, in list format for ease of reference.

i Wives

    a The husband must pay maintenance to the wife – Muslim or non-Muslim – if she surrenders herself (*sallamat nafsaha*) to his home. He must cover food, clothing, and shelter. The amount of maintenance is dependent on both their social standings (i.e., if the woman is from a rich family and the husband from a poor family, she must be maintained at a medium standard, between that of both families).

    b If she refuses to surrender herself unless he pays her full marriage payment (*mahr*), she still deserves maintenance.

    c If she deserts the marital home without permission (*nashazat*),[15] then she does not deserve maintenance until she returns home.

    d He must provide the maintenance of her servant (*khadim*) if he can afford it (*musir*); he does not have to maintain more than one servant.

    e He must provide her with residence in a home where none of his family or children from another marriage are present, unless she chooses to forgo this right.

    f If he cannot afford to maintain her, the judge does not dissolve the marriage. Rather, he instructs her to borrow money in the husband's name (i.e., to put the husband into debt to cover the maintenance).

    g If the man is absent and has left wealth with a person, the judge will ensure that the husband's wealth is given to the woman in accordance with the required maintenance payments. Similarly, the judge will apportion maintenance from that wealth for the absent man's young children and parents if they need it.

    h If the judge determines a lower maintenance amount due to the husband's being of little means (*muʿsir*), and then the husband becomes richer (*musir*), and she takes him to court, the judge will raise the maintenance level to reflect his richer status.

    i If a time passes in which the husband does not give maintenance to the wife, the wife is not entitled to demand missed payments (i.e., it is not a debt that compounds), unless the judge had fixed

---

[14] al-Mawsili, *al-Ikhtiyar*, vol. II, 222–4.

[15] *Nushuz* is explained by al-Maydani as the wife leaving the marital home without the husband's permission and without any right, even if he has travelled: al-Maydani, *al-Lubab*, vol. II, 88.

the maintenance payments, or they had reached a formal settlement (*sulh*) on maintenance amounts.
    j   If the husband gives a year's maintenance in advance, but then dies, none of it is taken back from the wife.
    k   If a slave marries a freewoman, her maintenance is a debt on him for which he is sold.[16]

ii Ex-wives
    a   If a man divorces his wife, she is entitled to maintenance and residence during her waiting period (*'idda* – the length of three menstrual cycles, or three months, or a pregnancy, based on the circumstance).
    b   If the separation was caused by an act of the wife – for example, by her leaving Islam, or her kissing the husband's son with desire[17] – then she has no maintenance.

iii Widows
    a   There is no maintenance for the one whose husband has died (as the husband is dead, and her maintenance is not a responsibility of the inheritors).

iv Children
    a   The maintenance of young (prepubescent) children is on the father; no one else shares this responsibility with him.
    b   If the child is wet-nursing, it is not a duty on the mother to wet-nurse the child. If she refuses, the father must hire the services of a wet-nurse who can give milk to the child in the residence of the mother.
    c   A man may not pay the mother of the child for this service if she is his wife or in a waiting period (*'idda*) after a divorce from him. He can pay her if she is no longer his wife. In such a case, he may not hire someone else if the mother wishes to be hired for wet-nursing her child, as long as she is not charging more than the usual market rate.

---

[16] The slave would marry with the permission of the master, and then the master would need to pay the maintenance to the wife, or sell the slave and pay the maintenance of the wife from the payment, and so he would be sold master-to-master to cover the maintenance of his wife. See ibid., vol. II, 93.

[17] Touching the son with desire would render her marriage to the child's father invalid in Hanafi law.

    d   The father must maintain the young child, even if of a different religion, just as he must do for the wife.

v   Parents

    a   The maintenance of parents and grandparents – if they are poor – is on their male and female children. (*Al-Ikhtiyar*: It is a duty on the sons and daughters in equal share according to one narration, and this is the chosen position, as both sons and daughters are equal in the cause of this duty (*'illa*) and in the divine injunction of care for parents (*khitab*). It has also been said that the duty is apportioned in accordance with inheritance (i.e., sons bearing twice the cost of daughters).)[18]

vi   Relatives (*dhu al-rahim*)

    a   The maintenance of relatives other than children and parents is in accordance with inheritance portions (i.e., those who inherit more bear more of the cost of the maintenance).

    b   Maintenance is only due for male relatives if they are (1) poor and (2) unable to earn due to physical inability. (*Al-Ikhtiyar*: because a person is rich through his ability to earn, not so a person's (poor) parents, whom he must maintain even if they are able to earn, since it leads to their tiredness and exhaustion, and a son/daughter is ordered to ward off harm from them.)

    c   Maintenance is due for females who are poor (i.e., they do not need to demonstrate earning ability, unlike their male counterparts).

    d   Maintenance is also due for those who lack the skill to earn, or who are of a class that does not work to earn (*buyutat*), or are seekers of sacred knowledge.

vii   Other relations

    a   The stepmother: her maintenance is on her stepson.

    b   The daughter-in-law: her maintenance is on her father-in-law if her husband is young and poor, or if he is disabled.

viii   Miscellaneous rules

    a   If the father is poor and the mother rich, she spends on the child and then reclaims her expenditure from the father when he becomes able to afford it.

---

[18] al-Mawsili, *al-Ikhtiyar*, vol. II, 222.

b   If the father is poor but has a rich brother, the brother is ordered by the judge to spend on the child and then reclaim the expenditure from the father. Likewise, if a wife has a poor husband but a rich son from a previous marriage or a rich brother, then the son or brother is ordered to spend on her and then reclaim from the husband. The judge will imprison the son or brother if they refuse to pay.

c   If a poor person has both a rich father and rich son, then the maintenance is on the son.

d   The maintenance amongst ancestors and descendants (*qarabat wilad*) is on the nearest, without regard to whether they would inherit. The maintenance of other blood relatives (*dhu rahim mahram*) is due only if the person would be an inheritor; and if there are several of such description, then maintenance duty is divided amongst them in accordance with their inheritance shares. Illustrative examples – if a poor person has:[19]

    i   a daughter and son: both share the maintenance equally

    ii   a daughter and brother: maintenance is on the daughter, as she is closer

    iii a daughter-of-a-daughter, a son-of-a-son, and a brother: the maintenance is shared by the two grandchildren (the brother is cancelled by the grandson, as is the case in inheritance; the daughter-of-a-daughter is not an inheritor but bears the burden of maintenance, as per viii d, above

    iv   a full-brother and full-sister: the maintenance is shared by them in accordance with their inheritance (i.e., the brother bears two-thirds and the sister bears one-third of expenditure)

    v   a sister and paternal uncle: maintenance is shared equally (in accordance with the inheritance division)

    vi   a mother and paternal grandfather: mother bears one-third and grandfather two-thirds (in accordance with the inheritance division); in another narration, the grandfather bears it all

    vii a mother, grandfather, and brother: the mother bears one-third, the grandfather the rest (in accordance with the inheritance division), according to Abu Hanifa (while the

---

[19] The following cases are from ibid., vol. II, 224.

remainder is shared equally by grandfather and brother, in the opinion of Abu Hanifa's two students)

viii a maternal uncle and paternal uncle: maintenance is all on the paternal uncle (in accordance with the inheritance division), and

ix a maternal aunt and paternal aunt: two-thirds on the paternal aunt and one-third on the maternal aunt (neither would inherit, but in the spirit of inheritance the paternal relative is given a greater burden).

Analysis

I have present a detailed summary of the rules of maintenance from the *Mukhtasar* of al-Quduri and the *Ikhtiyar* of al-Mawsili, so we can assess how the rules of inheritance fit within a wider system of legally enforceable financial responsibilities. There is much that can be deduced from this set of rules. The following are the key insights from the doctrine presented above.

i The rules of maintenance follow a clear, gender-based hierarchy, where men typically take greater or exclusive responsibility for maintenance.

ii The system of maintenance is legally enforceable by the shari'a judge (*qadi*). The judge makes a number of interventions: (1) determining the amount of a maintenance payment in the case of a dispute; (2) threatening imprisonment (*habs*) if a person withholds maintenance; (3) authorizing debts to be taken in the name of the party that owes maintenance; (4) authorizing maintenance payments to be taken directly from the wealth of the party owing maintenance if that party is absent; and (5) facilitating the reclaiming of maintenance expenditure if paid by other than the responsible party.

iii The maintenance due to the wife is peculiar to the nature of the marital contract. The woman deserves maintenance by virtue of her 'surrendering herself' to the home her husband provides. He must maintain her, even if he can't afford it; and she may demand this maintenance through a court, even if she is rich and in no need of his support. This marital maintenance is a unique case, arising out of a contract, unlike the other cases of maintenance, which arise out of blood ties.

iv The maintenance that arises out of family ties is closely connected to, but not always identical with, the divisions of inheritance. It appears that the underlying assumption of Muslim jurists was that all maintenance was to be in accordance with inheritance divisions unless overridden by a stronger consideration. We can summarize the relevant considerations as follows:

a *Support of parents* Parents were treated exceptionally by most Hanafi jurists. They divided the maintenance equally amongst sons and daughters, contrary to the inheritance division.[20] This is because they saw this as the most appropriate response to the frequent Qur'anic injunctions of good treatment of parents, injunctions that do not differentiate between sons and daughters. Furthermore, they held that poor parents must be supported even if they are able to work. We saw above that there is another narration of Hanafi doctrine, weaker according to the school, that does divide maintenance between sons and daughters according to inheritance divisions, with each son bearing double the maintenance cost of each daughter. Grandparents are treated similarly to parents.

b *Support of children* The support of children is exclusively on the father. The mother has no duty of maintenance: if she pays, she can reclaim the payment from the father. This is contrary to inheritance rules, as both parents inherit from a child. Here, Hanafi jurists went against inheritance divisions due to the clear Qur'anic injunction of fathers maintaining children and their wetnurses,[21] and the various hadith about the peculiar financial connection between a father and his children, such as 'You and your wealth are your father's.'[22]

c *Support of the remaining blood relatives* The rules for the remaining blood relatives are generally identical to inheritance divisions, as in most cases in viii, d above. In a few cases, jurists debated whether an alternative to inheritance division made more sense, as in viii, d, vi and viii, d, vii. In one case, they derived a rule from the spirit of inheritance division for relatives who otherwise have no share of inheritance: viii, d, ix.

We can conclude that there is great harmony – though not perfect equivalence – between inheritance rules and legally enforceable rules of maintenance payments. A question that arises is whether inheritance

---

[20] In the absence of sons and daughters, they similarly equated between grandsons and granddaughters, even granddaughters who don't inherit, as in viii, d, iii, above.
[21] Q. 2:233.
[22] al-Mawsili, *al-Ikhtiyar*, vol. II, 222.

laws were made to fit into this maintenance system, or whether the maintenance system was constructed to be harmonious with inheritance divisions. Considering the clear Qur'anic precedence for inheritance divisions, and considering the debates surrounding key points of maintenance doctrine, we must conclude that the maintenance system presented by Muslim jurists was developed to fit harmoniously with the divisions of Islamic inheritance. Of course, there would be Prophetic precedent for key points of maintenance, but jurists were tasked to develop the system in the light of Qur'anic and Prophetic precedent with less explicit guidance than the revelatory precedent for inheritance divisions. This insight – that inheritance rules informed maintenance rules for the juristic community – is fascinating.

The rules of inheritance should therefore not be seen as merely fractions for how the wealth of a dead person is divided up amongst their relatives. Rather, these rules laid the foundation for a social imagination. It is this social imagination that Muslim jurists fleshed out – informed by this inheritance blueprint – in the various chapters of social responsibilities, and especially in the chapter of maintenance. At the heart of this inheritance-informed social imagination was the necessity of a financial safety net for women, the poor, and those unable to work.

A question that arises is to what extent this social imagination was realized: were judges actually imprisoning husbands for withholding maintenance payments, and were wives really empowered to drive their husbands into debt by borrowing money to live at a standard their husbands were unable to maintain? Surprisingly, the answer appears to be yes. Yossef Rapoport provides an impressive and detailed array of case studies on how marriage and maintenance were managed through courts in medieval Cairo. The picture his case studies present – a picture completely in line with the preceding legal doctrine – is one of empowered, economically secure women and of husbands often struggling under the law to maintain marital households.[23]

In our modern context, it is normal for complicated legal proceedings to occur after the dissolution of a marriage, as assets and custodies are apportioned. But a legal dispute *within* a marriage to arrange maintenance is unthinkable. The picture from Islamic law is the complete opposite: legal disputes are expected within marriage, and not after the expiry of a woman's waiting period (*'idda*), at which point the man and woman are legally strangers. This complete inversion in the relationship

---

[23] Yossef Rapoport, *Marriage, Money and Divorce in Medieval Islamic Society* (Cambridge: Cambridge University Press, 2005).

between legal courts and marriage is because modern marriage does not consider a hierarchy of rights. Modern law sees both husband and wife as equally free from financial duties towards the other, so there are few rights for the law to enforce within marriage. Reading Rapoport's many case studies, one can see that the hierarchical framing of rights and duties in Islamic marriage brings a legally enforced financial security to women. This financial security was part of a larger nexus of financial duties constructed upon the blueprint of responsibilities indicated by the division of Islamic inheritance.

WHAT DETERMINES GENDER?

We have emphasized the centrality of gender to the nexus of rights and duties in Islamic law, but have not addressed the identification of gender. In our modern climate, we entertain a distinction between gender and biological sex, as we entertain the possibility of human determination of a person's gender. How do classical Muslim jurists identify gender in their gendered legal universe?

In their treatment of the hermaphrodite (*khuntha*), Muslim jurists display their concern for establishing gender and the extreme physicality of this determination. There is a chapter in classical *fiqh* manuals called *Kitab al-Khuntha*, the Book of the Hermaphrodite. Below is a translation of the first half of this chapter from al-Quduri's *Mukhtasar*,[24] followed by a summary of the rest of the chapter.

i   If a newborn has a vagina and penis, then it is a hermaphrodite (*khuntha*).
ii If the newborn urinates through the penis, then it is a male. And if it urinates through the vagina, then it is a female.
iii If the newborn urinates through both, but the urine comes first through one, then the gender is attributed to the genital through which urine comes first.
iv If the urine comes at the same time from both genitals, then there is no consideration to quantity according to Abu Hanifa. Abu Yusuf and Muhammad say the [child's gender] is based on the genital through which most urine exits.
v   If the hermaphrodite comes of age and grows a beard or is physically able to have intercourse with women, then the person is a man. And if the person grows breasts like those of a woman or produces milk in their breasts or menstruates or becomes pregnant or is able to

[24] Translated from al-Maydani, *al-Lubab*, vol. I, 361–3.

have sexual intercourse in the vagina, then the person is a woman. If none of these signs shows, then it is a Perplexing Hermaphrodite (*khuntha mushkil*).

The remainder of the chapter presents how key gendered points of law can be implemented by the Perplexing Hermaphrodite, of whose gender determination we are uncertain – points of law such as where to stand in group prayer, how to be circumcised, and how inheritance is to be divided. In each case, jurists came up with creative answers that would account for the possibility of either gender. For example, in prayer they are to stand in their own line between men and women, as they can't pray next to men in case they are in reality women, and can't pray next to women in case they are in reality men (in Hanafi law, a man's prayer is invalidated if he is standing next to a woman in group prayer).[25] In inheritance, Abu Hanifa treated them as women, out of precaution, so as not to unfairly give them someone else's share. His two companions – Muhammad ibn al-Hasan and Abu Yusuf – gave them a fraction between the fraction given to men and women at their respective inheritance level.

The chapter demonstrates two points very clearly. The first is that in a gendered legal system the determination of gender is of extreme importance. Without such a determination, the appropriate set of rights and duties cannot be applied. The second noteworthy point is the extreme physicality of this determination. There is no scenario where they entertained the exercising of choice in this matter. In rare cases where there was no physical recourse to determine gender, Hanafi jurists produced a unique set of rules that were based on the precautious assumption of the possibility of both genders in these individuals.

This approach is understandable. In a gendered legal code, a person should not be able to choose their gender, just as with other legal categories such as being a parent or child, master or slave, guardian or ward, rich or poor. Throughout, legal hierarchies must reflect stable objective phenomena. There is no possibility of a choice that would instantly shift one's legal rights and duties, as that would lead to an unstable and inoperable legal code.

MODERN REFLECTIONS

It has been shown above that the rules of Islamic inheritance gave rise to a system of gendered financial responsibility that was enforced by courts.

---

[25] Ibid., vol. I, 66.

This system of financial responsibility ensured that rights, duties, and needs were addressed in a way harmonious with how estates were to be divided upon death. What a woman might lose out on in an inheritance division she would be able to gain from a perceived right to maintenance generated by that 'loss'. This is perhaps similar to the loss of wealth through taxation being offset by perceived social benefits maintained by taxed wealth. But what if there is disharmony? What if a loss in inheritance shares is not offset by a greater right to maintenance?

This disharmony describes the modern predicament. Modern legal codes do not present such a gendered division of rights and duties. Marriage is now akin to a partnership, where neither partner bears a greater financial duty within the marriage. Furthermore, individuals facing poverty are expected to turn to the state or public charities for support; there is typically no enforcing of familial financial responsibility, and no attempted ordering of how familial responsibility would be apportioned among family members. In such a context, what do we make of Islamic inheritance?

It is not the objective of the current chapter to offer a solution, but to present the problem. It would appear that a community keen to uphold both the rules and the social vision of the Islamic legal tradition is faced with two options: to change the world or change the rules. Both options are fraught with risks and challenges.

Option one is to change the world. This would be by clarifying to people the details of this gendered vision of financial responsibilities that reflect the values of Islamic inheritance divisions, and then, the harder task, of finding a way to enforce this vision. Where Muslims form a minority, enforcement would be limited to the coercive powers of community-based shari'a arbitration councils. Such councils exist and have focused on recording *nikah* (marriage) contracts and facilitating *talaq* (divorce) proceedings – especially in cases where husbands refuse to offer the *talaq*. Their activity would need to be extended to teaching an Islamic system of financial responsibilities and finding ways to exert communal pressure where these financial duties are unfulfilled. Social pressure would be the only recourse for a community unable to enforce such a vision formally through courts. In a Muslim-majority setting, changing the world would entail political campaigning to bring about enforcement of these maintenance rules. Depending on the country, this could be a very tall order of business.

Option two is to change the rules. This would be by employing the appropriate Islamic legal mechanisms for legal change – mechanisms such as change in custom (*'urf*), necessity (*darura*), the corruption of the times (*fasad al-zaman*), widespread affliction (*'umum al-balwa*) or others. There are numerous examples across the schools of law where such principles have been employed to bring about substantial legal change to ultimately ensure a form of harmony between the law and the world in which people lived the law.[26]

Perhaps the most notable attempt in recent times at changing the rules was the move to change inheritance legislation in Tunisia. In 2017, President Beji Caid Essebsi established the Committee on Individual Liberties and Equality (COLIBE) to review the compatibility of particular laws, including inheritance, with the constitution and international conventions. A report was produced on the basis of which Essebsi put forward to parliament a proposal of inheritance reforms that would equalize inheritance between men and women. A lively debate ensued – in parliament, in public, and across the Muslim world. Sari Hanafi and Azzam Tomeh provide a helpful analysis of the range of arguments that were made for and against these reforms.[27]

COLIBE's report employed several forms of argument, summoning Islamic jurisprudence, sociology, and secular law. Regarding Islamic jurisprudence, the committee argued that 'The Qur'an emphasized the equality of men and women in numerous verses. However, they traditionally had different rulings with their differing social roles. Since they have the same social roles now, they should have the same rulings, affirming original equality.'[28] Another argument was that '[i]nheritance does not fall under ritualistic acts of worship [*'ibadat*]. It is a worldly matter systematized by religion [*mu'amalat*], and thus should be subject to worldly reconsiderations.'[29] This distinction between ritual law and the law of social dealings is employed here to open the door to legal change, as the law for worldly dealings (*mu'amalat*) must consider prevalent social circumstances. Sociologically, they cited a clear shift from the premodern roles of women by highlighting the prominence of

---

[26] For the employment of these mechanisms in Hanafi commentaries, see chapter 4 in Sohail Hanif, 'A Theory of Early Classical Ḥanafism: Authority, Rationality and Tradition in the *Hidāyah* of Burhān al-Dīn 'Alī ibn Abī Bakr al-Marghīnānī (d. 593/1197)' (DPhil diss., University of Oxford, 2017). There are several monographs dedicated to legal change within the broader system of Islamic law. See, for example, Baber Johansen, *Contingency in a Sacred Law: Legal and Ethical Norms in the Muslim Fiqh* (Leiden: Brill, 1999) and Wael Hallaq, *Authority, Continuity, and Change in Islamic Law* (Cambridge: Cambridge University Press, 2004).

[27] Sari Hanafi and Azzam Tomeh, 'Gender Equality in the Inheritance Debate in Tunisia and the Formation of Non-Authoritarian Reasoning', *Journal of Islamic Ethics* 3 (2019): 207–32.

[28] Ibid., 216.

[29] Ibid., 217.

women in higher education and as breadwinners. Finally, they argued that this change would be more in line with the nation's constitution.

As stated, this proposal led to large public debate. Ultimately, the law did not pass parliament, and the following president, Kais Saied, has stated his disapproval of this reform plan. This Tunisian example illustrates both possible arguments for legal change regarding inheritance divisions, but also the extreme challenge of convincing a Muslim public to accept such a change to rules laid out so clearly in the Qur'an.

A final angle that has been pursued for bringing greater harmony between inheritance divisions and financial responsibilities is to employ a creative application of Islamic legal rules to circumvent the fact of unequal division of inheritance while not explicitly violating the rules of inheritance. These creative solutions are a form of legal stratagem (*hila*). Islamic law, and Hanafi law in particular, has a long history of the application of such stratagems to provide practical solutions to people without technically violating the law.[30]

One common method in this regard is to advise people to divide their estate in their lifetime, so that it is not technically a division of inheritance. This leads to the commonly asked question: are there any restrictions on gifts made to children during a person's life? General answers offered for this are that a person should divide gifts fairly amongst children, some scholars making this an obligation and others a recommendation. Most scholars explain 'fairness' here as equality amongst children, though some explain that fairness in gifts during one's lifetime is to make them in accordance with inheritance divisions, giving sons double the share of daughters, though the latter is a minority view.[31]

Another method that has been employed is to utilize the provision in the shari'a for the *wasiyya* (bequest), whereby a person may add to their will a gift of up to one-third of their estate. The established position across the well-known schools of law is that this final bequest cannot be made to an inheritor – as that would lead to an undermining of the inheritance divisions of the Qur'an, unless the inheritors after the death of the person agree to a bequest to an inheritor having effect. Some scholars have allowed this provisional gift to be given to an inheritor.[32] According to

---

[30] On the *hila*, see Satoe Horii, 'Reconsideration of Legal Devices (Ḥiyal) in Islamic Jurisprudence: The Ḥanafīs and Their "Exits" (*Makhārij*)', *Islamic Law and Society* 9, no. 3 (2002): 312–57.

[31] See for example islamweb.net/ar/fatwa/6242/بعض-بعضهم-على-وتفضيل-الأولاد-لبعض-الهبة-حكم.

[32] This is the position of the Dar al-Ifta' al-Misriyya: 'Ali Jumu'a, 'Hukm al-wasiyya al-maktuba ghayr al-muwaththaqa lil-warith wa-li-ghayrihi wa-tawzi' tarika', 30 July 2008, fatwa no. 6786, accessed from dar-alifta.org/ar.

this minority position, a person might use the bequest to promote greater equality in the division of their estate. This was apparently one solution that was offered by the Hanafi *mufti* Habib Belkhouja, who was consulted on the proposed Tunisian inheritance reforms: Belkhouja rejected the reforms on the grounds they violated Qur'anic law, and suggested the *wasiyya* be used to create a more equal division.

In this section I have suggested some possibilities for what is meant by changing the world or changing the rules. Can people do neither? Doing neither would suggest that people are not seeking to be true either to the rules or the larger vision for society drawn from those rules, as there is an evident tension between the rules and the many contexts where they are currently being applied.

CONCLUSION

This chapter highlights the fact that it is not possible to explain a part of a legal code without considering the interrelated parts of that code. The implicit question behind research into women's inheritance in Islam is, 'Is it fair?' To answer this, we need to first reflect critically on the assumptions within our own judgement of fairness, and, secondly, understand the wider social and economic vision of Islamic law, to then understand whether a standard of fairness is at play that is alternative to our own modern standard. I have argued above that, indeed, an alternative standard of fairness is evident.

This alternative standard is understandable through the framework of a gendered and hierarchical view of rights and duties. The assumptions within this framework are as follows:

- Men are obliged to exert the effort necessary to support themselves, their wives, and their children. Furthermore, they must bear the bulk of maintenance contributions to poor relatives – apart from parents, who are maintained equally by sons and daughters. A man will be threatened with imprisonment by a Muslim judge for withholding maintenance payments.
- Women do not have a legal duty to work to earn a living. If an adult woman has financial needs, her relatives must support her – and she can seek the help of the Muslim judge to ensure this support reaches her. She may seek this support even if she is able to work. A woman with surplus wealth still has no obligation of financial care to her husband or to her children. A rich woman does, however, have a duty of care towards her other relatives. For maintaining parents, she shares this

burden equally with her brothers. Towards other relatives she typically has a lower burden than her male counterparts, in accordance with inheritance divisions.

We saw in the preceding discussions that inheritance divisions informed the creation of a vast system of maintenance rules that offered a secure safety net for women that the law could enforce. To enforce these maintenance payments, a woman would raise her case before a judge (qadi), who had broad powers to determine, enforce, and even imprison, so that the maintenance payments would be made. This gendered and family-based safety net was not just a theory: it was enforced historically.

These rules of maintenance show a vision for social security not powered by taxation and not framed by the ever-present bureaucracy of a state structure. Instead, it was a safety net that was based in a strong theory of family. It reinforced family values, reminding people of the great duty and spiritual virtue of spending on one's kin and fulfilling the rights of wealth. It was a system grounded in personal responsibility, and duty to God through duty to family and dependants. These are values we are not easily able to summon in our modern societies. And some would argue that that is to our detriment.

SELECT BIBLIOGRAPHY

Baderin, Mashood A. 'Law of inheritance'. In Baderin, *Islamic Law: A Very Short Introduction*. Oxford: Oxford Academic, 2021.

Bishin, Benjamin G. and Cherif, Feryal M. 'Women, Property Rights, and Islam'. *Comparative Politics* 49, no. 4 (2017): 501–20.

Chowdhury, Safiah, Alkiek, Tesneem, and Khan, Nazir. 'Women in Islamic Law: Examining Five Prevalent Myths'. Yaqeeninstitute.org, 24 July 2019, https://yaqeeninstitute.org/read/paper/women-in-islamic-law-examining-five-prevalent-myths.

Hallaq, Wael. *Authority, Continuity, and Change in Islamic Law*. Cambridge: Cambridge University Press, 2004.

Hanafi, Sari and Tomeh, Azzam. 'Gender Equality in the Inheritance Debate in Tunisia and the Formation of Non-Authoritarian Reasoning'. *Journal of Islamic Ethics* 3 (2019): 207–32.

Hanif, Sohail. 'A Theory of Early Classical Ḥanafism: Authority, Rationality and Tradition in the *Hidāyah* of Burhān al-Dīn 'Alī ibn Abī Bakr al-Marghīnānī (d. 593/1197)'. DPhil diss., University of Oxford, 2017.

Horii, Satoe. 'Reconsideration of Legal Devices (Ḥiyal) in Islamic Jurisprudence: The Ḥanafīs and Their "Exits" (Makhārij)'. *Islamic Law and Society* 9, no. 3 (2002): 312–57.

Jawad, Haifaa. *The Rights of Women in Islam: An Authentic Approach*. London: Palgrave Macmillan, 1998.

Johansen, Baber. *Contingency in a Sacred Law: Legal and Ethical Norms in the Muslim Fiqh*. Leiden: Brill, 1999.

Katz, Marion. *Wives and Work: Islamic Law and Ethics before Modernity*. New York: Columbia University Press, 2022.

al-Nagar, Samia El and Tønnessen, Liv. "Family Law Reform in Sudan: Competing Claims for Gender Justice between Sharia and Women's Human Rights." *CMI Report* no. 5, December 2017.

Quraishi, Asifa. 'What If Sharia Weren't the Enemy? Rethinking International Women's Rights Advocacy on Islamic Law'. *Columbia Journal of Gender and Law* 22, no. 1 (2011).

Rapoport, Yossef. *Marriage, Money and Divorce in Medieval Islamic Society*. Cambridge: Cambridge University Press, 2005.

Spiker, Hasan. *Hierarchy and Freedom: An Examination of Some Classical Metaphysical and Post-Enlightenment Accounts of Human Autonomy*. Dublin: New Andalus Press, 2023.

Welchman, Lynn. *Women's Rights and Islamic Family Law: Perspectives on Reform*. London: Zed Books, 2004.

3 Veiling and Restrictions on Sexual Liberty
KATERINA NORDIN

The topic of veiling and sexual liberty has been at the forefront of popular and academic discussions regarding women and Islam for decades, and it is a conversation that does not seem to be abating. Despite an overwhelming amount of criticism, the decision to veil and avoid extramarital sexual relations continues to be actively chosen by many Muslim women. When looking at the contentious topics of veiling, sexual restriction, and women in Islam it is crucial to understand the hierarchy of priorities and subtleties of belief held by believing women and what drives their 'pietistic agency'.[1] The hijab is, among other things, a sign of a woman's devotion. This devotion is built on a complex set of beliefs about the soul, salvation, and corporeal life (*dunya*). Recent ethnographic studies have done well in delineating the many reasons for which a woman may choose to cover.[2]

This chapter will review the normative, majority Islamic *fiqh* positions of sexuality and veiling and look at them against the relevant Islamic spiritual concepts. Rather than offering a feminist examination, it will present to the reader the internal logic understood, defended, and acted upon by believing women. In doing so, it will demonstrate the

---

[1] Saba Mahmood, *The Politics of Piety: The Islamic Revival and the Feminist Subject* (Princeton: Princeton University Press, 2011).
[2] Irene Zempi, '"It's a Part of Me, I Feel Naked without It": Choice, Agency and Identity for Muslim Women Who Wear the Niqab', *Ethnic and Racial Studies* 39, no. 10 (2016): 1738–54; Jameelah Medina, 'This Battlefield Called My Body: Warring over the Muslim Female', *Religions (Basel, Switzerland)* 5, no. 3 (2014): 876–85;Asifa Siraj, 'Meanings of Modesty and the Hijab amongst Muslim Women in Glasgow, Scotland', *Gender, Place and Culture: A Journal of Feminist Geography* 18, no. 6 (2011): 716–31;Tabassum F. Ruby, 'Listening to the Voices of Hijab', *Women's Studies International Forum* 29, no. 1 (2006): 54–66;Viola Thimm, *(Re-)Claiming Bodies through Fashion and Style: Gendered Configurations in Muslim Contexts* (Cham, Switzerland: Springer International Publishing AG, 2021);Nuray Karaman and Michelle Christian, '"Should I Wear a Headscarf to Be a Good Muslim Woman?": Situated Meanings of the Hijab among Muslim College Women in America', *Sociological Inquiry* 92, no. 1 (2022): 225–43.

relative flexibility of the interpretation of Islamic law in different contexts. This chapter focuses on the parameters of heterosexual relations and the cisgender male–female binary, as this is what is predominantly addressed in classical Islamic law.

GENDER AND THE SOUL

'Anyone, male or female, who does good deeds and is a believer, will enter Paradise and will not be wronged by as much as the dip in a date stone' (Q. 4:124).[3] Islamic belief teaches people that the soul is the entity which separates humans from other living creation and is the subject of guidance, nurture, judgement, and treatment in the afterlife. The corporeal form of the body is temporary and, like this mortal plane, is both a blessing and test for believers. It is the vehicle from which physical acts of worship and obedience that transcend to the ethereal are performed. The above Qur'anic verse describes how those who believe in Islamic *tawhid* (monotheism) will be held to account for their deeds fairly and justly. Both male and female souls, created as a cosmic pairing, are equally independent and accountable for their actions without one being preferred over the other. This metaphysical justice is repeated throughout the Qur'an, such as in Q. 99, 'Whoever has done an atom's-weight of good will see it, but whoever has done an atom's-weight of evil will see that', and in numerous hadith where the intricate issue of judgement, the remit of which belongs to Allah, will be meted out to men and women the same.

The creation of souls themselves is considered a unique sign from Allah, which has informed Muslims about human nature: 'And of all things We created pairs, that perhaps you may be mindful' (Q. 51:49). This verse, as understood in both Sunni and Shi'i *tafsir* (Qur'anic exegesis), emphasizes the dependence that creation has on God-created binaries – male and female, night and day, hot and cold, evil and good – in contrast to God's eternal Oneness.[4] The emphasis on contrasting pairs implies an expectation that male and female would have differences

---

[3] All Qur'anic quotations will be cited from M. A. S. Abdel Haleem, trans., *The Qur'an*, (Oxford: Oxford University Press, 2004).

[4] *Tafsir al-Qurtubi* (17/53); *Kashf al-Asrar*. All the translated hadith cited here have been taken from the online database of Islamic texts set up by the University of Southern California Muslim Student Association (USC-MSA). They have been accessed through the site https://sunnah.com/Compendium_of_Muslim_Texts. The translated *tafsir* words have been taken from the online database of Qur'anic *tafsir*: www.altafsir.com/Tafasir.asp?tMadhNo=0&tTafsirNo=0&tSoraNo=1&tAyahNo=1&tDisplay=no&LanguageID=2.

despite deriving from the same source. The soul in Islam is one of innate purity, unburdened by any concept of original sin or taking on the sins of others, and within which the belief in God is intrinsic. This is defined by the Qur'anic concept of *al-fitra*, which is the belief that humankind is born with the pure inclination towards worshipping God, which Muslims strive to retain and return to throughout their lives.[5]

Given the equal consideration of male and female souls, the question of a gendered difference between humankind is raised with Qur'anic verses such as in *Sura al-Baqara*. When outlining the rights pertaining to both parties in a divorce, it states that 'Wives have [rights] similar to their [obligations], according to what is recognized to be fair, and husbands have a degree [of right] over them: [both should remember that] God is almighty and wise' (Q. 2:228). In the classical *tafsir* of Ibn Kathir he states, 'this *ayah* [verse] indicates that men are in a more advantageous position than women physically as well as in their mannerism, status, obedience (of women to them), spending, taking care of the affairs and in general, in this life and in the Hereafter'.[6] The responsibility bestowed on them is based on physical advantages. Aisha Abdul Rahman (d. 1998), also known as Bint al-Shati, was an Egyptian author whose work includes a *sira* (biography) of the Prophet and a *tafsir* of the Qur'an. She argued against the imposition of Western thought on Egyptian society and derived the concept of equality as a God-given right from the Qur'an. She argued that the guardianship that men have been bestowed with the verse Q. 2:228 was conditional upon them fulfilling those obligations[7] and was not a given. This is also echoed in Shi'i *tafsir*,[8] which highlights the social responsibility men are held to. The differentiation between men and women here, then, is understood not as one soul being better than the other but that physical differences and circumstances in this *world* dictate the roles and responsibilities given to different members of humankind.

The role of man's increased public responsibility has led to abuse of this material advantage and fed the assumption that Islam is inherently

---

[5] Ṣaḥīḥ al-Bukhari 4775: Book 65, Hadith 297.
[6] Ibn Kathīr, Ismā'īl ibn 'Umar, and Ṣafi al-Raḥmān Mubārakfūrī, *Al-Miṣbāḥ al-Munīr fī Tahdhīb Tafsīr Ibn Kathīr = Tafsir Ibn Kathir (Abridged)*, 1st ed. (Riyadh: Darussalam, 2000), vol. I, 634.
[7] Aisha Abdul Rahman, 'The Islamic Conception of Women's Liberation', *Al-Raida* 125 (1970): 37–43, 41.
[8] Sayyid Kamal Faqih Imani (Sayyid Abbas Sadr-'Ameli, trans.), 'An Enlightening Commentary on the Holy Quran volume 2', *Al-Islam*, www.al-islam.org/enlightening-commentary-light-holy-quran-vol-2/section-28-regulation-about-divorce#:~:text=228.,(in)%20the%20Last%20Day.

misogynistic. In more recent works, harnessing the idea of binaries, the complementarity of the genders has been acknowledged as the Islamic approach that answers the pressing question of gender equality. Through this complementarity, women are to have a fair chance of worship and devotion without any physical or societal constraints, and it emphasizes that their natures can even be advantageous in spiritual pursuits over men's natures. Bint al-Shati asserted the concept of complementarity between the sexes. She argued that:

> We, as modern liberated women, believe that man and woman perfect each other and need each other to realize their full existence. Husband and wife are founding partners of one social cell, and companions in the journey of life. Their joint life is united in pulse, harmony, and conformity. It does not fall apart by a conflict over power and authority.[9]

Similarly, British academic and Islamic scholar Abdal Hakim Murad explains the complementarity through spiritual and biological bases. In his work 'Boys Will Be Boys: Gender Identity Issues'[10] he aligns Islam's approach to gender difference with Germaine Greer's difference feminism. He protests against the wholesale adoption of Western secular values as deficient ideas that do not fit reality. He proposes a form of equity that considers the genders' particular attributes and strengths. This is echoed, amongst other schools of thought, with publications of fatwas on the Salafi website *Islam Question & Answer* confirming the equal accountability of the sexes, but also the bespoke responsibilities given to both.[11] Shaykh Muhammad Akram Nadwi, a renowned scholar who has compiled a vast biographical dictionary on women hadith transmitters, questions the paradigm from which the question of gender equality and agency is even considered. He argues that 'Undue emphasis on agency (being able to do) as a measure of dignity and liberty is an error of more serious import. In the believers' perspective, the best of what we do is worship and, especially, prayer.'[12]

The alignment to a different set of prioritizations – the devotional – means that there is an equal expectation to worship, do virtuous deeds, and abide by Islamic law, but with certain corporeal nuances. For example,

---

[9] Abdul Rahman, 'The Islamic Conception of Women's Liberation', 40.
[10] Abdal Hakim Murad, 'Boys Will Be Boys: Gender Identity Issues', *About Islam*, https://aboutislam.net/shariah/contemporary-issues/boys-will-boys/.
[11] 'Are Women Equal with Men in Reward and Punishment?' *Islam Question & Answer*, https://islamqa.info/en/answers/12840/are-women-equal-with-men-in-reward-and-punishment.
[12] Muḥammad Akram Nadwi, *Al-Muḥaddithāt: The Women Scholars in Islam* (Oxford: Interface Publications, 2007), 16.

women are to pray five times a day and fast the compulsory and voluntary fasts just like men are. They are not, however, expected to do this during menstruation or postpartum bleeding, when they are temporarily relieved of this duty. The precise social demarcation of these gender norms outside of worship is not as clear-cut. This vagueness could lead, and indeed *has* led, to an exploitation of these open-ended generalizations. However, looking at this from another angle, the shari'a offers a form of flexibility of what is deemed 'masculine' or 'feminine' according to different contexts and cultures. It is expected that Muslims find examples and precedent within the Prophetic tradition or *sunna*, the diversity of the exemplars of the 'mothers of the believers', and the early Muslim communities. *'Urf* (custom) is to assist in governing these demarcations too, but also is to be challenged if they transgress the rights outlined within Islam. The understanding that practising Muslim women have of their direct responsibility for their soul and relationship with their creator drives the impulse to obey and practise the laws of Islam.

RESTRICTIONS ON SEXUAL LIBERTY

Sexuality in Islam is socially conservative. It calls for no premarital sex, no extra-marital sex, heightened consent with regards to touch, and a restricting interaction between men and women. Criticism comes from the notion that women bear the greater burden in managing these relationships and have less agency in navigating the field than men, and that their satisfaction is deprioritized. An exploration of the Islamic approach and its appeal reveals a subtle and complex balance aimed at preserving the individual's dignity, safety, and spiritual salvation. Movements within Muslim communities to redress any existing cultural imbalance of sexual ethics and assert the existing benefits of the Islamic approach to sex have proven there is growth towards what Kecia Ali calls for as a 'a more viable and equitable ethics of sex'.[13]

Fornication: Equal Restraint, Equal Responsibility

Zina (fornication) within Islam is any type of extra-marital sexual relationship, the prohibition of which applies to both men and women equally. Although no longer applicable in contemporary times, the exception to this was for men who were able to have sex with any bondswomen they owned. Kecia Ali, in *Sexual Ethics and Islam: Feminist Reflections*

---

[13] Kecia Ali, *Sexual Ethics and Islam: Feminist Reflections on Qur'an, Hadith, and Jurisprudence* (Oxford: Oneworld Publications, 2006), 72.

on *Qur'an, Hadith, and Jurisprudence*,[14] examines this issue in great depth. The accountability and punishment for extra-marital relations (not including rape) is equal between the sexes. The only differences between the punishments are related to the degree of fornication (premarital, extra-marital) and whether the individuals involved are free or slaves. Premarital sex is treated with less severity than extra-marital sex due to the transgression of rights and a contract involved in the latter.

Sura al-Nur, Q. 24, is regarded in Sunni *tafsir* as a Medinan chapter revealed at the time of the false accusation against Aisha (the wife of the Prophet) of adultery. This sura encapsulates the command. The verses demand equal sexual restraint between the sexes: 'O Prophet! Tell the believing men to lower their gaze and guard their chastity. That is purer for them. Surely Allah is All-Aware of what they do. And tell the believing women to lower their gaze and guard their chastity, and not to reveal their adornments except what normally appears' (Q. 24:30–1). The mirroring responsibility for avoiding the sin of *zina* shows the equal benefit to guarding oneself and the equal degrading impact this sin would have on a believer's soul. Ibn Kathir's *tafsir* of this verse utilizes several hadith that emphasize the importance of lowering the gaze, and more broadly maintaining a respectful distance from non-related members of the opposite sex. These hadith show this deed is on a par with other important deeds, such as trustworthiness and telling the truth, showing the way it fits into a tapestry of moral behaviour all aimed at reducing harm to other people and oneself.

Although rarely applied, the punishments for *zina* are demarcated as part of the *hudud* laws, which are known commonly as the strict shari'a laws with extreme physical consequences. They are defined as punishments for encroaching on the limits set by God. Muslims have argued, however, that the creation of these laws acted more as a deterrent to the act. The requirements to prove adultery in a court are either four male witnesses to the very details of the act (Sunni law) or two female witnesses for every one male, but there must be at least one male (Shi'i law). Contemporary apologetics argue the requirements are so detailed and unlikely that it could hardly be followed through. Judith Tucker's survey of these laws throughout history argues that the performance of punishments for fornication was rare and was phased out by the late nineteenth and early twentieth centuries.[15]

Zina is considered, like other sins, to have a negative impact not only on the soul but also on the social fabric of society. Ranking as one of the

[14] Ibid.
[15] Judith E. Tucker, *Women, Family, and Gender in Islamic Law*, Themes in Islamic Law (Cambridge: Cambridge University Press, 2008), 204.

major sins in Islam, one of the ill-effects of the act of *zina* is the potential of having a child whose lineage is denied or is unknown, and to leave a woman bearing the responsibility of raising a child with no support. Lineage is deemed a right upon an individual in Islam, not only to understand where their ties of kinship lie and grant them familial security, but also to gain access to what is legally theirs – inheritance, their right to maintenance, and knowledge of who they can and cannot marry.

There are also gradations of fornication besides intercourse. The ideal within Islam is to avoid anything to do with it altogether: 'do not go anywhere near adultery: it is an outrage, and an evil path' (Q. 17:32). An oft-cited hadith on the seriousness of *zina* and free-mixing is as follows:

> Abu Huraira reported Allah's Messenger as saying: 'Allah fixed the very portion of adultery which a man will indulge in. There would be no escape from it. The adultery of the eye is the lustful look and the adultery of the ears is listening to voluptuous (song or talk) and the adultery of the tongue is licentious speech and the adultery of the hand is the lustful grip (embrace) and the adultery of the feet is to walk (to the place) where he intends to commit adultery and the heart yearns and desires that which he may or may not put into effect.'[16]

Sayyid Muhammad Rizvi, a prominent Twelver Shi'i scholar (that is, representative of a normative Shi'i opinion), likens the command to lower the gaze to the Christian teaching when Jesus said, 'whosoever looks on a woman to lust after her has committed adultery with her already in his heart'.[17]

The practical implementation of these dire warnings is evident in the *fiqh* and *sunna*. For example, in one hadith, a woman approaches the Prophet Muhammad to ask him a question about the Hajj. His cousin, Al-Fadl ibn Abbas, is sitting with him and the Prophet, noticing that Al-Fadl is staring at her, took his cousin's chin to turn it away from her.[18] The Prophet here did not reprimand the woman or blame her for tempting his cousin, but rather rectified the man's behaviour.

Certain *fiqh* rulings compound the distancing from this type of interaction. For example, within Shafi'i *fiqh*, an individual is to perform *wudu* (ritual ablution) if they touch a member of the opposite sex even if unintentionally. Other *madhhabs*, apart from the Hanafi *madhhab*,

[16] Ṣaḥīḥ Muslim 2658.
[17] Sayyid Muhammad Rizvi, *Hijab, the Muslim Women's Dress, Islamic or Cultural?* (Toronto: Jafari Islamic Centre, 1997).
[18] Ṣaḥīḥ al-Bukhari 1442; Ṣaḥīḥ Muslim 1334.

argue that *wudu* should only be performed when the touching is with desire. In Twelver Shi'ism too it is forbidden to touch a non-related male's hand. Similarly, men and women alike are recommended to occupy preferred positions in congregational prayer to avoid distraction from the opposite sex during worship. These are just some of the moral and spiritual ways in which a distancing between the sexes is encouraged and ordered within day-to-day life. The rules have a particular emphasis on the rupturing of the purity of worship.

The spiritual emphasis and responsibility on the individual require a sense of discipline, restraint, and self-regulation that is found throughout Islamic practice, such as fasting, praying, and giving alms. Accountability to the self and to Allah is central to Islamic practice, and the navigation of sexual boundaries between men and women here is no different.

Marriage and Sex-Positivity
To contrast with the dire warnings against fornication, the social and spiritual institution of marriage is exalted within Islam for both men and women as a source of worship, protection, joy, and satisfaction. The institution is part of the Prophetic *sunna* and is recommended as a deterrent to sin and to create the foundation of a stable society. In its plainest form, marriage within Islam is a contract (*nikah*) that allows legitimate sexual intercourse. The basic *fiqh* requirements involve both parties being eligible for marriage, the dowry being paid to the bride, the consent of both parties and the contract being signed in front of witnesses. Once in a marriage, both parties are protected by contractual rights. The spiritual benefits of marriage are weighty. The hadith '[n]arrated by Anas ibn Malik, Allah's Messenger (peace be upon him), said, "When a man marries, he has fulfilled half of the *'deen'* [religion]; so, let him fear Allah regarding the remaining half."'[19] Not only is this because it helps avoid the sin of fornication but, as Abu Hamid al-Ghazali (d. 1111) argues in his *Book on the Etiquette of Marriage*, it is also an arena of disciplining oneself. The tasks of being patient with one another, meeting each other's rights and responsibilities, and raising dependants sees marriage as a platform for improving character.[20] Within Shi'i law the institution of *mut'ah* is also allowed. These are known as temporary marriages and serve as a legally sound way for

[19] al-Tirmidhi 3096.
[20] Ghazzālī and Farah Madelain, *Marriage and Sexuality in Islam: A Translation of al-Ghazālī's Book on the Etiquette of Marriage from the Iḥyā'* (Salt Lake City: University of Utah Press, 1984), 67–70.

couples to have intimate relationships for a defined period. These were phased out in Sunni law but remain a way in which intimate relationships can be sanctified and rights fulfilled.

Within marriage, Islam is seen as sex-positive, encouraging sexual relations and pleasure between husband and wife beyond procreation. In the Qur'an and hadith, the topics of gratification are spoken about sensitively but explicitly, and the companions would approach the Prophet about such matters. Ali observes that although Islam does encourage mutual gratification, the responsibility for the woman to please her husband is greater than that of the man. Current publications and movements within the Muslim community point to a communal shift away from this attitude, reinforcing the heightened awareness of a woman's pleasure and the ethics of sexuality that Islamic tradition had upheld. Writing under a nom de plume, Umm Muladhat published *The Muslimah Sex Manual: A Halal Guide to Mind-Blowing Sex*,[21] which, although shocking to more prudish members of the community, is important in the application of Islam's sex-positive approach being harnessed by women outside of works of jurisprudence and guides that read like law manuals. The eagerness to please partners for peace, blessings on the marriage, and the pleasure of Allah can be viewed as exercising pietistic agency, displayed in Mariam Khan and Fatima Seedat's study on Muslim women in South Africa.[22] More refined and improved scholarship also shows a shift away from the original interpretation of the hadith that says a woman is cursed by the angels if she refuses her husband sex. On the *Seekers Guidance* website, an online Islamic Studies academy popular in the West, Shaykh Abdul-Rahim Reasat clarifies the meaning of the hadith. He argues that linguistic subtleties were lost in original interpretations and that it was a deterrent against wives manipulating their husbands by withdrawing sexual proximity. As this was not something that could be taken before a law court – unlike, say, if a husband withdrew financial support from his wife – 'the deterrent is purely religious'.[23]

Movements that incorporate ethical and Islamic standards to serve the Muslim community include charities such as FACE (Facing Abuse in

[21] Umm Muladhat, *The Muslimah Sex Manual: A Halal Guide to Mind-Blowing Sex* (Opensource, 2017).
[22] Mariam B. Khan and Fatima Seedat, 'Secure between God and Man: Peace, Tranquillity and Sexuality through the Pietistic Aspirations of Believing Women', *Journal for the Study of Religion* 30, no. 1 (2017): 137–60.
[23] Shaykh Abdul-Rahim Reasat, 'Explaining Misunderstood Hadith about Women', *Seekers Guidance*, 17 August 2018, https://seekersguidance.org/answers/general-counsel/im-fearful-islam-causing-depression-can/.

Community Environments) and the Hurma Project, led by Ingrid Mattson. From a protective and ethical standpoint, these charities actively work to redress abuses within the Muslim community and provide education and resources to the community on ethical sexual practices and protection. Sameera Qureishi is a psychologist who, under the name 'Sexual Health for Muslims'[24] on social media, educates Muslims about mental, sexual, and spiritual health. Angelica Lindsey-Ali, known as 'the Village Auntie', is a sexual health educator, and does this through an Islamic lens, teaching women about womanhood and pleasure in an ethical and fair way.[25] Muslim women are confronting difficult topics and problems in the community and are steering a shift towards an ethical Islamic framework. They do so within the Islamic legal boundaries that they proactively abide by.

A more complicated aspect is the institution of polygyny. Islam allows men to marry up to four wives, whereas women are limited to one marriage at a time. Many Muslim treatises justify this ruling through its revealed context. The *asbab al-nuzul* of verse Q. 4:3 was after the Battle of 'Uhud, when many men were killed, leaving many widows vulnerable. Hadia Mubarak argues that the scholars engaged with these texts were not inherently misogynistic, despite working within a patriarchal framework. These laws were protective of women's legal rights, which at the time were being exploited through the trend of men marrying multiple women for their money and exploiting their positions.[26] Traditional scholars also emphasize the almost impossible standards that polygamy requires, which are a risk to one's standing on the Day of Judgement. For example, Imam al-Shafi'i said, 'I prefer a man to limit himself to one wife, even though it is permissible for him to marry more, due to the saying of Allah Almighty: If you fear you will not be just, then only one.'[27] This subject is one that Muslim jurists throughout the ages have treated with caution.

Some female Muslim figures have gone as far as to provide a logic to and praise for the institution, akin to some of the contemporary arguments for polyamory. The Muslim writer Zaynab bint Younus, a Canadian Muslim who used to blog under the nom de plume 'The

---

[24] Sameera Qureishi, *Sexual Health for Muslims*, https://sexualhealthformuslims.com/.
[25] 'Village Auntie', *Linktree*, https://linktr.ee/villageauntie.
[26] Hadia Mubarak, 'Classical Qur'anic Exegesis and Women', in *The Routledge Handbook of Islam and Gender*, ed. Justine Howe, 1st ed. (London: Routledge, 2020), 23–42.
[27] Yaḥya Ibn Abi al-Khayr 'Imrānī and Nūrī Qāsim, *Al-Bayān fī Madhhab al-Imām al-Shāfi'ī*, al-Tab'ah 1 (Jiddah: Dār Al-Minhāj, 2000), 189.

Salafi Feminist', approaches the topic with a vocabulary imbued with both sexual ethics and Islamic standards. She emphasizes the full consent, understanding, and mettle that participants in the relationship need. She also fights against the insidious practice adopted by some men who have secret wives. She extols the benefits of polygamy and promotes an online hashtag, #positivepoly, citing such benefits of the arrangement as the fact that it provides security, freedom, and sexual gratification without pressure, and being able to have alone time to pursue studies and personal interests.[28]

The confines of sexual restrictions are clearly being navigated willingly by practising Muslim women in a way that takes their soul and accountability seriously into account. By using Islamic boundaries to their advantage, they are drivers in redressing any imbalance that has been produced from cultural (both Western and Muslim) norms. The range of approaches shows the diversity in lived experience, but all hold the same undercurrent of priorities.

VEILING

The term 'veiling' is one that is loaded with Orientalist and Islamophobic implications. The veil has been represented by current discourse as a mystery, a confrontation, an empowerment, and an oppression all at once. The focus on veiling has been disproportionate, compared with the vastness of Islamic practice. Academic examinations of veiling have ranged from feminist critique, legal questions, historic surveys, and ethnographic studies. The practice has seen a growth over the last few decades, and the modest-fashion industry has seen exponential growth since the events of 9/11. Veiling has been defined as a form of protest, a cultural practice, a means for protection, religious embodiment, and a recourse to social mobility.[29] Here I will focus on the religious aspects, although the other elements are often intertwined.

For want of a better phrase, both the hijab (covering of the hair and chest) as well as broader *jilbab* (covering of the entire body) will both be referred to here as 'veiling', to correspond with the Arabic term *khimar*.

[28] Zaynab bint Younus, '(Almost) Everything You Want to Know about Polygamy', *Muslim Matters*, 16 June 2022, https://muslimmatters.org/2022/06/16/polygamy-frequently-asked-questions-2/; Zaynab bint Younus, 'What to Expect When You're Expecting ... Polygamy', *Muslim Matters*, 17 November 2021, https://muslimmatters.org/2021/11/17/what-to-expect-when-youre-expectingpolygamy/.

[29] Katherine Bullock, *Rethinking Muslim Women and the Veil: Challenging Historical and Modern Stereotypes*, 2nd ed. (London: International Institute of Islamic Thought, 2007).

Veiling in modern times relates mostly to the garments used for personal covering and monitoring of behaviour, which is what this chapter will look at, and which differs according to school of thought and cultural setting. The meaning in premodern societies included levels of physical seclusion, particularly amongst women from the urban elite. As Tucker delineates, veiling and seclusion were a part of local law and custom, and had been left to communities to manage themselves. Veiling became one of the main discursive projects of asserting Islamic identities in the face of Western pressures.[30]

The choice to cover and the acceptance of the command to do so has been actively asserted, practised, and defended by Muslim women throughout the world to various degrees as a unique spiritual obligation bestowed on women and an extension of sexual restriction. This part of the chapter will examine the undercurrent within ideal Islamic behaviour that ties sexual restraint and veiling together and how exactly Muslim believers, particularly women, respond to and absorb critiques of and misconceptions about veiling.

Haya'

Before we dive into veiling proper, the overarching Islamic concept of *haya'* will be looked at. Within the Islamic worldview the characteristic of *haya'* is an important, and almost central, sensibility. *Haya'* comes from the same Arabic root as the word 'life' and can be defined as 'shame, diffidence, bashfulness, shyness'.[31] Scholars have added that its deeper meanings also include God-consciousness as well as modesty. The role of *haya'* has the implications of communal obligation and benefit alongside self-refinement. One hadith tradition even defined *haya'* as a branch of faith.[32] It was after Adam and Eve's expulsion from paradise that they became aware of their nakedness, and the feeling of *haya'* led them to cover themselves.

It is an attribute impressed upon both genders. In Sunni Islam, the Caliph al-Rashidun Uthman ibn Affan was revered for his modesty. The Prophet Muhammad stated, 'Modesty is part of faith, and the most modest of my nation is Uthman.'[33] Various hadith show the degree to which Uthman upheld the standards of modesty even in private. There

---

[30] Tucker, *Women, Family, and Gender*, 203.
[31] Hans Wehr and J. Milton Cowan, *A Dictionary of Modern Written Arabic (Arabic–English), Considerably Enlarged and Amended by the Author*, 4th ed. (Urbana, IL: Spoken Languages Service, 1994), 256.
[32] Ṣaḥīḥ Muslim, 35a.
[33] Tārīkh Dimashq, 39916.

are also several aspects to *haya'* that relate specifically to men and do not apply to women. The wearing of extremely long robes, silk, and gold is forbidden to men, as a deterrent against ostentation and excessive luxury. The modesty demanded of men, especially amongst those in leadership, shows a challenge to the status quo of the time and the tailored commands for what is considered men's nature. In some communities, such as among the Tuareg, the men are expected to veil completely. Navigating the terrain of life modestly, with correct deportment and God-consciousness, is a priority for both believing men and women.

Veiling

If we understand it as a prioritisation of modesty and a way of regulating sexual proximity, the practice of veiling seems an appropriate fit. The following verses of the Qur'an serve as the foundational jurisprudential sources for the command:

> And tell the believing women to lower their gaze and guard their chastity, and not to reveal their adornments, except what normally appears. Let them draw their veils over their chests, and not reveal their hidden adornments except to their husbands, their fathers, their fathers-in-law, their sons, their stepsons, their brothers, their brothers' sons or sisters' sons, their fellow women, those bondwomen in their possession, male attendants with no desire, or children who are still unaware of women's nakedness. Let them not stomp their feet, drawing attention to their hidden adornments. Turn to Allah in repentance all together, O believers, so that you may be successful. Q. 24:31

This verse is known as the verse of *khimar*, and the following is referred to as the verse of *jilbab*: 'O Prophet! Ask your wives, daughters, and believing women to draw their cloaks over their bodies. In this way it is more likely that they will be recognized as virtuous and not be harassed. And Allah is All-Forgiving, Most Merciful' (Q. 33:59).

Among the dominant schools of law there is *'ijma* (consensus) regarding the meaning of veiling and its general implementation. In relation to Q. 24:31, Al-Tabari specifies that 'Abu Al-Aliyah said: 'Every *ayah* of the Qur'an in which protecting the private parts is mentioned means protecting them from *zina*, except for this *ayah* – *and protect their private parts* – which means protecting them from being seen by anybody.'³⁴ Within Shi'ism, the verse even holds a metaphysical importance for women, whereby repeated recitation of it protects from adultery.³⁵

Veiling in Islamic law is usually demarcated in *fiqh* works with regards to appropriate dress for worship which carries through to everyday life.³⁶ As a Qur'anic command, jurists delineated that the *'illa* (*ratio legis*) of veiling was a woman's coming of age,³⁷ and within Shi'ism this is after nine lunar years. The schools of law differ on the definition of *'awra* (private parts), which varies according to who the observer is. In front of non-related men, the Hanafi *madhhab* defines everything as *'awra* except the face, hands, and feet; the Shafi'i and Maliki position includes the feet; and the Hanbali stance is that everything is *'awra*, including a woman's face. It is interesting to note that the spectrum of covering is inversely reflected in traditional positions on women's access to the mosque.³⁸ Within Shi'i Islam, the hands and face should be covered too if there is the risk of someone looking at them with lust.³⁹ Different rules apply if the onlooker is a woman. The style of veiling is left to the individual, although the material should be opaque, and there are some recommendations based on the *sunna* of the colours worn. Debates about the niqab (face-covering) continue over time and context. Compulsory veiling, which is imposed on women by some regimes, lies outside of this study, which looks only at the practice among women who have the freedom of choice to do so.

For some believing Muslim women, the *'ijma* concerning veiling is enough for them to adopt the practice. Their faith in Allah as the All-Wise and All-Knowing, and trust in the Muslim generations before them, gives them confidence in adopting this rule. Feminist and academic critiques of veiling hinge partly on the historical argument of whether veiling was just an extension of pre-existing Arab custom or the adoption

---

[34] Ibn Kathīr, Ismā'īl ibn 'Umar, and Ṣafī al-Raḥmān Mubārakfūrī, *Al-Miṣbāḥ al-Munīr*, vol. VII, 68.

[35] Sayyid Kamal Faqih Imani, 'An Enlightening Commentary'.

[36] Aḥmad Ibn Lu'lu' ibn al-Naqīb and Noah Ha Mim Keller, *Reliance of the Traveller: The Classic Manual of Islamic Sacred Law*, rev. ed. (Beltsville, MA: Amana Publications, 1994).

[37] Marzuqa Karima, 'On the Hermeneutics of the Qur'ānic Verse of khimār', *Medium*, https://medium.com/@marzuqa.karima/on-the-hermeneutics-of-the-qur%CA%BE%C4%81nic-verse-of-khim%C4%81r-73f7a43665f1, last modified 23 August 2021.

[38] Christopher Melchert, *Whether to Keep Women out of the Mosque: A Survey of Medieval Islamic Law* (Oxford: Oxford University Research Archive, 2006). Available online: https://ora.ox.ac.uk/objects/uuid:a3a2d845-1b22-4e36-96bc-b3d0566b1c5b.

[39] Rizvi, 'Hijab'.

of Byzantine custom. Some argue that the rulings are applicable only to the mothers of the believers on account of the wording 'so that you may be known' in the verse, and that it took on a more spatial meaning.

Muslim adherents argue against this logic. Understanding that Islamic commands were born from a place of either complete communal shift or adaptation of existing custom, Muslim scholars agree that veiling was a custom that was abided by in various degrees during the *jahiliyya* (Age of Ignorance and Injustice). The knowledge of this is how early scholars understood nuances within the commands. For example, Ibn Kathir states that the verse 'let them draw their veils over their chests' means that they should wear the outer garment in such a way as to cover their chests and ribs, so 'that they will be different from the women of the *jahiliyya*, who did not do that but would pass in front of men with their chests completely uncovered, and with their necks, forelocks, hair, and earrings uncovered. So, Allah commanded the believing women to cover themselves.'[40]

Further, Muslims have argued that the command went beyond the obligation of the mothers of the believers at the time. A popular US-based Islamic institution, the Yaqeen Institute, which is run by Imam Omar Suleiman, produced an article 'Is Hijab religious or cultural?',[41] which cites a hadith of Aisha in which she relates that the *ansar*[42] women tore their waist-wraps and covered themselves with them as soon as they heard the revelation to cover.[43] Anse Tamara Grey, the founder of the Rabata Institute, which focuses on Muslim women's education, has penned a manifesto entitled 'Lean In: Our Feminist Manifesto' that puts a Muslim slant on Sheryl Sandberg's 'lean in', which encourages women to proactively stake their roles in society. Grey writes about the aforementioned hadith:

> They tore this fabric and covered themselves with it. It is akin to the Muslims throwing their alcohol in the streets when the verse forbidding alcohol was revealed. No one ran around looking for a man to ask permission of, nor did they question their own interpretations of the verse. They understood. They followed through. They leaned in.

---

[40] Tesneem Alkiek, 'Is Hijab Religious or Cultural? How Islamic Rulings Are Formed', Yaqeen Institute, https://yaqeeninstitute.org/read/paper/is-hijab-religious-or-cultural-how-islamic-rulings-are-formed, last modified 20 September 2023.
[41] Ibid.
[42] The *ansar* women, or 'Helpers', refers to the community in Medina who welcomed the Prophet Muhammad and his followers when they emigrated to Medina from Mecca.
[43] Saḥīḥ al-Bukhārī, *Kitāb al-tafsīr*, no. 4758.

And we follow in their footsteps when we too lean in and embrace this flag of our religion, this hijab.[44]

The mothers of the believers and the Prophet's companions, being positioned as norm-setters for Muslim women,[45] in this instance show a complete submission to God's command. This has been interpreted as a subversive and emboldening act against contemporary norms. This echoes the argument against foreign colonialism in Abu al-Ala al-Mawdudi's *The Hijab*.[46]

A main critique of veiling is the imbalance of the responsibility that women must bear in the pursuit for societal harmony. Further, the connotation that women are considered a *'fitna'* (here meaning the temptation that could lead to strife) puts the blame on women for any wrongdoing. This perception has been both endorsed and fought against by the Muslim community. The command is often tied to the distancing from any type of *zina*. Some women actively accept that even though they are not responsible for a man's actions, they have a social responsibility to act appropriately and to create stability within society.[47] Similarly, some might wear the hijab based on cultural expectations grounded in these ideas. And so, while in Islam the sin is pinned solely on the individual who committed it, the communal understanding to 'Order what is right and forbid what is wrong' (Q. 3:110) sees individuals acting selflessly for what they perceive is the greater good. A prioritization of the spiritual over the material is a common trend throughout Muslim belief.

Scholars have also tried to show that the task owned by women should be regarded as a privilege and manifestation of the sacred. In a 2013 interview, Abdul Hakim Murad explained that:

> Allah (*subḥānahu wa taʿālā*) has created this world as an expression of His beauty and He has placed the greatest and most miraculous concentration of His beauty in His creation in the beauty of women ... of course that is to be celebrated but in the Semitic tradition not everyone has the right to gaze at intense concentrations of holiness ... the hijab isn't a sign that something is unworthy or

---

[44] Anse Tamara Gray, 'Lean in – Our Feminist Manifesto', Rabata Institute, www.rabata.org/lean-in-our-feminist-manifesto/.

[45] Barbara Stowasser, 'The Mothers of the Believers in the "Hadith"', *The Muslim World* (Hartford) 82, nos. 1–2 (1992): 1.

[46] Barbara Stowasser, *Women in the Qur'an, Traditions, and Interpretation* (New York: Oxford University Press, 1994), 128.

[47] Masooda Bano, *Female Islamic Education Movements: The Re-Democratisation of Islamic Knowledge* (Cambridge: Cambridge University Press, 2017), 124.

impure or dangerous, rather it's an expression of the presence of holiness.[48]

But it could be argued, despite this lofty shift to the metaphysical realm, that it still objectifies a woman's being by likening her physicality to the sanctity of holy objects. Common analogies of women being diamonds that need protecting, or a lollipop without a wrapper that attracts unwanted flies, have been balked at by many Muslim women and writers.[49] They have articulated frustration at the rhetoric used on their behalf to justify veiling. In an article on a popular Muslim web magazine, 'The Purpose of Hijab: Reclaiming the Narrative',[50] the author acknowledges the authenticity of the hadith 'I have not left behind me a *fitna* (trial) more injurious to men than women.'[51] She argues that the greater responsibility is on men, and not women, to restrain themselves. Using a recent scientific study from Princeton University which showed that men's impulse control and their ability to see women as agents rather than objects significantly decreases when women are dressed immodestly, she argues that it is for men to accept this inherent flaw and remedy themselves. The line, then, between the Islamic social responsibility to protect one another from sin is a symbiotic one which relies on the full efforts of men to restrain themselves, and which many Muslim women are taking differing levels of responsibility for.

Muslim women have themselves defended and defined veiling as a particular spiritual obligation unique to women.[52] A participant in Irene Zempi's study on veiling with the niqab says, 'For me it is very much about expressing my love of my God. It is a way of coming closer to Allah. It's like me saying "Look, I am doing this to show you how much I love you and what my faith means to me."'[53] The difficulty and sacrifice of veiling are felt but it is done out of pious motivations. Muslim women continually assert their pietistic agency through this choice.

[48] Abdal Hakim Murad, 'Women, Modesty, and Hijab in Islam (an Interview with Sheikh Abdal Hakim Murad)', video blog, 2:18, 17 April 2013, www.youtube.com/watch?v=GXO6b3oMHzU.
[49] Nuriddeen Knight, 'Double Standards: Stop Comparing Hijabis to Lollipops and Pears', *Muslim Matters*, 26 June 2015, https://mvslim.com/double-standards-stop-comparing-hijabis-to-lollipops-and-pearls/.
[50] Um Talhah Sadaf Syed, 'The Purpose of Hijab: Reclaiming the Narrative', *Muslim Matters*, 10 March 2022, https://muslimmatters.org/2022/03/10/the-purpose-of-hijab-reclaiming-the-narrative/.
[51] Muslim 2740, USC-MSA web (English) reference: Book 36, Hadith 6603.
[52] Roohi Tahir, 'Hijab: Spotlighting Servitude to God', *Yaqeen Institute*, 25 March 2023, https://yaqeeninstitute.org/read/paper/hijab-spotlighting-servitude-to-god.
[53] Zempi, 'It's a Part of Me', 1742.

The shaping of this discourse has continued strongly in recent years. The anthologies *It's Not about the Burqa: Muslim Women on Faith, Feminism, Sexuality and Race*,[54] edited by Mariam Khan, and *Cut from the Same Cloth*,[55] edited by Sabeena Akhtar, are more recent examples of intelligent, diverse essays written by Muslim women. They range from the failings of Western feminism, employment, and race, to spirituality. The online magazine *Amaliah*[56] takes different and riskier angles regarding the topic of veiling. Rather than being subjected to critique, they proactively challenge the shortcomings of the societies that criticize them and harness debate on a level that uses the vocabulary and concepts used to condemn them.

The assumption from strands of secularism and feminism that veiling is oppressive is being fought against by Muslim women's actual experience. Harnessing the language of Islam and feminism, Muslim women highlight the veil's role in subverting the male gaze. Studies that engage Muslim women who choose to veil find that they often assert that veiling gives them the feeling of taking ownership of their own bodies and controlling how people have access to them. One participant said, 'I wear [the hijab] in obedience to my Creator and because my body is my own business.'[57] The hijab grants the ability to take unwanted attention away in public and not subscribe to cultural standards of beauty. The control that women enjoy over their bodies with regards the male gaze and opting out of social norms also grants empowerment through their ability to transcend societal expectations. Further, the way in which women juxtapose modern beauty standards and Islamic dress codes to varying degrees shows a self-awareness of their agency, as does the way in which they use this as a form of protest or assimilation.

The 2004 hijab ban and 2023 *abaya* ban in French schools serve as a case study that epitomizes the elements at play in the conversation about veiling, as well as the assertive agency performed by French Muslim women against the moving goalposts of secularism. The 'veil ban' came under a broader ban on larger religious symbols, and it highlighted several important points. Firstly, the idea that the *'illa* of veiling was its ability to protect the wearer is clearly negated, as in cases such as these it singles Muslim women out. If anything, it is only a tangential

---

[54] Mariam B. Khan, ed., *It's Not about the Burqa: Muslim Women on Faith, Feminism, Sexuality and Race* (London: Picador, 2020).
[55] Sabeena Akhtar, ed., *Cut from the Same Cloth* (London: Unbound, 2020).
[56] *Amaliah*, www.amaliah.com/.
[57] Madinah, 'This Battlefield Called My Body', 880.

benefit.⁵⁸ Secondly, the juristic reaction, which Tucker assesses in detail, is a microcosm of the various stances and shows how the interpretation of Islamic law is contextual. For example, Muhammad Sayyid Tantawi, the Grand Imam of Al-Azhar, announced that although veiling was a divine obligation, since France was a secular country, one would not be disobeying the commands of the religion if women were forced not to wear the hijab.⁵⁹ The Conseil Français du Culte Musulman (CFCM) argued that it is an obligation to wear it, but that students should not give up their education in order to do so. The Comité de Coordination des Musulmans Turcs de France (CCMTF) argued that it is a cultural tradition, not an obligation, to wear it, whereas the European Council for Fatwa and Research argued that it is a religious matter and a means of worship.⁶⁰ Muslim students continued to wear the hijab, despite fatwas alleviating them of this duty. The protests that ensued and the challenging of the state showed the assertive agency that Muslim women have and the manifestation of the veil's 'situated practice'.

The more recent ban on anything resembling an *abaya* in schools (September 2023) has put France's position more squarely on the political far-right. The vagueness of the law means that authority figures can discriminate as to what they deem acceptable fashion, forcing Muslim communities to discern further between culture and religion. The CFCM states that the *abaya* is a traditional cultural and not a religious symbol.⁶¹ Students and teachers in one school in Seine-Saint-Denis went on strike to protest the measures.⁶² The recognition that this law is now encroaching on human rights has been picked up by Amnesty International, who argue that the *abaya* ban can lead to discrimination and abuse.⁶³ It questions many of the theoretical debates about freedoms and feminism. The ability of Muslim women to firmly hold on to their practice amidst this maelstrom shows a focus, dedication, and embodied

---

58 Karima, 'On the Hermeneutics'.
59 'Tantawi: France Has Right to Ban Hijab', *Al-Jazeera*, 31 December 2003, www.aljazeera.com/news/2003/12/31/tantawi-france-has-right-to-ban-hijab.
60 Tucker, *Women, Family, and Gender*, 209–12.
61 'L'abaya n'est pas un signe religieux musulman pour le Conseil français du culte musulman', *West France*, 12 June 2023, www.ouest-france.fr/societe/religions/labaya-nest-pas-un-signe-religieux-musulman-pour-le-conseil-francais-du-culte-musulman-5cb22280-090f-11ee-ba55-0a72f336f6ba.
62 '"Islamophobic Policy": French High School Goes on Strike over Abaya Ban', *Al-Jazeera*, 7 September 2023, www.aljazeera.com/news/2023/9/7/islamophobic-policy-french-high-school-goes-on-strike-over-abaya-ban.
63 Amnesty International, 'France: Authorities Must Repeal Discriminatory Ban on the Wearing of Abaya in Public Schools' (3 October 2023, Index Number: EUR 21/7280/2023).

protest. The prioritization shown by women of obedience to Islamic laws, rather than state laws, embodies the believers' worldview.

CONCLUSION

This chapter has attempted to lead the reader through the Islamic legal and spiritual logic behind sexual restriction and veiling, and show the equal responsibility placed on male and female believers. The debates and conversations that exist are far too vast to include in so short a chapter, but by providing a snapshot of how Muslim women are protecting and nurturing Islamic practices, rather than discarding them because they have faced criticism or because of cultural imbalances, we see the priorities that are important for Muslim women and the agency with which they practise. By shaping the discourse themselves, they are focusing on what matters to them, in line with Islamic tradition. The intense focus on these topics politically and academically has demanded a flexibility and growing sophistication in Islamic thought that have been met in both scholarly and lay circles.

REFERENCES

Abdul Rahman, Aisha. 'The Islamic Conception of Women's Liberation'. *Al-Raida* (1970): 37–43.

Akhtar, Sabeena, ed. *Cut from the Same Cloth*. London: Unbound, 2020.

Ali, Kecia. *Sexual Ethics and Islam: Feminist Reflections on Qur'an, Hadith, and Jurisprudence*. Oxford: Oneworld Publications, 2006.

Bullock, Katherine. *Rethinking Muslim Women and the Veil: Challenging Historical and Modern Stereotypes*. 2nd ed. London: International Institute of Islamic Thought, 2007.

Karaman, Nuray and Christian, Michelle. '"Should I Wear a Headscarf to Be a Good Muslim Woman?": Situated Meanings of the Hijab among Muslim College Women in America'. *Sociological Inquiry* 92, no. 1 (2022): 225–43.

Karima, Marzuqa. 'On the Hermeneutics of the Qur'ānic Verse of *khimār*', *Medium*, https://medium.com/@marzuqa.karima/on-the-hermeneutics-of-the-qur%CA%BE%C4%81nic-verse-of-khim%C4%81r-73f7a43665f1, last modified 23 August 2021.

Mahmood, Saba. *The Politics of Piety: The Islamic Revival and the Feminist Subject*. Princeton: Princeton University Press, 2011.

Medina, Jameelah. 'This Battlefield Called My Body: Warring over the Muslim Female'. *Religions (Basel, Switzerland)* 5, no. 3 (2014): 876–85.

Mubarak, Hadia. 'Classical Qur'anic Exegesis and Women'. In *The Routledge Handbook of Islam and Gender*, ed. Justine Howe, 23–42. Milton: Taylor & Francis Group, 2020.

Ruby, Tabassum F. 'Listening to the Voices of Hijab'. *Women's Studies International Forum* 29, no. 1 (2006): 54–66.
Siraj, Asifa. 'Meanings of Modesty and the Hijab amongst Muslim Women in Glasgow, Scotland'. *Gender, Place and Culture: A Journal of Feminist Geography* 18, no. 6 (2011): 716–31.
Stowasser, Barbara. 'The Mothers of the Believers in the "Hadith"'. *The Muslim World (Hartford)* 82, nos. 1–2 (1992): 1–36.
Thimm, Viola. *(Re-)Claiming Bodies through Fashion and Style: Gendered Configurations in Muslim Contexts*. Cham, Switzerland: Springer International Publishing AG, 2021.
Tucker, Judith E. *Women, Family, and Gender in Islamic Law*. Themes in Islamic Law. Cambridge: Cambridge University Press, 2008.
Zempi, Irene. '"It's a Part of Me, I Feel Naked without It": Choice, Agency and Identity for Muslim Women Who Wear the Niqab'. *Ethnic and Racial Studies* 39, no. 10 (2016): 1738–54.

4 Muhammad: The Ideal Man
FARAZ A. KHAN

THE "IDEAL" IN ISLAM

Characteristic of Islam's theological, legal, and mystical discourses is the centrality of the Prophet Muhammad, who represents for believers the manifestation of every virtue in the concrete world of lived, earthly experience. While Plato had identified the perfect ideals as immaterial and eternal Forms, Muslim scholars generally concurred that the model of truth, beauty, and goodness was Muhammad himself, and that the most direct method of apprehending and comprehending the virtues was by carefully examining the behavior of the Prophet. Although he is not eternal but, rather, created by God, it could be said that his character represents *the one* (the archetypal or universal *good* of morality) and that Muslims seeking to inculcate virtue constitute *the many*, each of whom, imperfectly and to varying degrees, approximates the Muhammadan ethos of perfection. (The contrast with Plato, and the related terms *one* and *many*, are deployed here in the context of ethics, not metaphysics.) Indeed, for Muslims, to describe the Prophet as ideal might be regarded as nearly tautological.

Thus, his personal traits (*akhlaq*) served as the point of departure for Muslim ethical contemplation, as evidenced in the early *Shama'il* genre, the contents of which were not abstracted values like "justice," "courage," "compassion" and the like, but rather personalized qualities ascribed to him: "his justice," "his courage," and "his compassion." Here, we note a significant paradigm shift from the epistemology most common in philosophical ethics: virtues are not derived as pure concepts inferred solely by ratiocination and divorced from the complex nexus of human emotions, relationships, and a myriad of social realities; they are inferred from an inductive survey of the actions of a human being living in the world and interacting with real people in real time, as both emissary of God and simultaneously a husband, father, preacher, teacher, mentor, reformer, army general, or head of state. The results of that induction and inference – the conduct and comportment of Muhammad – signify for Muslims the fullness and entification of all virtue (*kamal*). As such, it is somewhat unavoidable to explore how Muslims have regarded the Prophet as the Ideal Man without a detailed survey of the hadith tradition (which will comprise much of this chapter).

Yet, given some of modernity's more contentious conceptions of supremacy, the notion of "ideal" in this context requires clarification. Praised in the Qur'an with the proclamation, "Verily, you are upon a tremendous mighty character" (68:4), the Prophet was no Nietzschean Übermensch who was *beyond* good and evil; Dostoevsky's Raskolnikov made this error in *Crime and Punishment*, deeming Muhammad to be, like Napoleon, an example of the character's flawed thesis of extraordinary men who may rightfully transgress moral boundaries to pursue their extraordinary aims. Nor was he a harbinger of a weak "slave morality" born of cynicism and *ressentiment* against human "masters" who carry out their whims of self-actualization and thereby "create" their own values. Rather, for Muslims, the Prophet was a man who, while certainly supreme and exceptional, represents the very *criterion* and delineation of good, much like the Islamic scripture itself (one of its names being *al-Furqan*, "the Ultimate Criterion").

In the words of Aisha, "His character was the Qur'an,"[1] and as a human reflection of the scripture, he demonstrated to his followers the essence of sincerity to the divine prerogative and preference. Here we do not find underlying motives informed by a worldly Will to Power. His concerns were but celestial, and hence, with respect to motives, the power of his noble self towards which he directed his will was that of loving surrender and slavehood to the Divine, a power nonetheless so forceful ("a tremendous mighty character") as to generate an ethical, legal, and mystical precedent that would constitute the bedrock of an entire civilization.

Muhammad's role as exemplar to a multitude of nations, cultures, and generations likewise warrants brief deliberation. The Qur'an makes it clear that he was in the line of Abraham, Moses, and Jesus and thus part of a continuum of prophets and emissaries sent by God: "Say: I am not unprecedented among the messengers" (Q. 46:9). Earlier religious communities could easily recognize Muhammad and his teachings; the analogs were in their books. Hence, for Muslims, the Qur'an represents the

---

[1] Aḥmad ibn Ḥanbal, *al-Musnad*, 52 vols. (Beirut: Mu'assasat al-Risāla, 2008), vol. XLIII, 15, no. 25813.

Final Testament, and Islam constitutes the culmination of the teachings of Judaism and Christianity. However, Islamic doctrine also affirms his historical uniqueness: he is the final messenger, sent to all mankind until the eschaton; he is therefore the final model of the ethical life and final archetype of mystical ascent. His uniqueness is further underscored considering Arabian society of the seventh century and before, immersed as it was in a *jahiliyya* ("Age of Ignorance and Injustice") characterized by pagan idolatry, tribal warfare, the abuse of the poor and weak, and widespread depravity. While "not unprecedented among the messengers," he was entirely unprecedented for his times and society; and even among the messengers of past, he was entirely unique in his universality and finality. From both vantages, his emergence marks a categorical distinction in history; the Prophet cannot be reduced to a Hegelian dialectic unfolding out of a nebulous *Geist*. As the Catholic theologian Hans Küng notes:

> Muhammad is discontinuity in person, an ultimately irreducible figure, who cannot be simply derived from what preceded him, but stands radically apart from it as he, with the Qur'an, establishes permanent new standards. In that respect, Muhammad and the Qur'an represent a decisive break, a departure from the past, a shift toward a new future.[2]

Nonetheless, Küng makes his insightful remark in his discussion exploring how Jews and Christians might, from a Biblical standpoint, consider Muhammad to have fulfilled a prophetic role, largely based on the similarities between Muhammad and the prophets of Israel. Of course, Islam emphasizes the oneness of the creedal and ethical teaching of all messengers, and (recalling the principle of *entified virtue* mentioned above) Islamic prophetology holds "infallibility" (*'isma*) to be an intrinsic quality of all prophets in history. As an emissary of God, a prophet was necessarily free from vice and hence the exemplar of virtue for his community or nation.[3] Some Muslim sages identified this earthly manifestation of perfection, along with the spiritual journey of believers to approximate it, as the very telos of the world's existence, whereby the descent of Adam from Eden represents not a demotion but a special honor and opportunity (somewhat akin to the notion of the "fortunate fall" that has been inferred from Book XII of *Paradise Lost*, where

---

[2] Hans Küng, *Christianity and the World Religions: Paths to Dialogue with Islam, Hinduism, and Buddhism* (Garden City, NY: Doubleday, 1986), 24–28.

[3] Muḥammad ibn Yūsuf al-Sanūsī, *Matn al-Sanūsiyya* (Cairo: Muṣṭafā al-bābī al-Ḥalabī, 1934), 5.

Milton's Adam proclaims, regarding mankind's forthcoming good, "O goodness infinite, goodness immense!").[4] In Islam, were it not for the descent, prophetic and saintly perfection would have remained latent. The nineteenth-century rector of al-Azhar Mustafa al-Arusi expressed this fortune as "the existence of the Perfect Man [al-insan al-kamil] and supreme blessing, namely, the Muhammadan Reality [haqīqa muhammadiyya], along with all other messengers of God."[5]

Arguably the Islamic tradition's most salient articulation of this principle is found in the thought of Ibn Arabi, whose Sufi metaphysics[6] centers on the notion of the Perfect Man and Muhammadan Reality. While early Sufis like Hakim al-Tirmidhi and Sahl al-Tustari had invoked similar concepts in their exegesis, Ibn Arabi systematized them[7] (and related mystical doctrines) into a comprehensive theosophy that would permanently shift the trajectory of Muslim scholastic and spiritual discourse (predominantly with reverential acceptance, yet not without controversy). For them and adherents to their "school" of mysticism, the prophet of Islam was both "a beautiful exemplar" (Q. 33:21) and the manifestation of a primordial light (nur muhammadi) that was God's first creation and the ontological archetype of truth, beauty, and goodness in the cosmos. His spirit was created but ancient and luminous; and whereas Adam was granted the divine names by God (Q. 2:31), Muhammad was bestowed with *their meanings* (or, *words*),[8] which comprise the basis of theophany in the world of multiplicity. In this doctrine, because Muhammad was the site of the manifestation of the divine name Allah, which is the greatest name that encompasses all the divine names, all theophanies in the world that disclose the divine names are mediated through the Muhammadan Reality. As the Shaykh al-Akbar states, "Thus, he [Muhammad] was the first indicator of his Lord, for he was granted the *words of supreme totality* [jawami 'al-kalim], that is, the referents of the names given to Adam." Dawud al-Qaysari comments:

> Given that the Muhammadan Spirit was the most perfect of this species [humanity], he was the first indicator of his Lord, because the

---

[4] See Arthur O. Lovejoy, "Milton and the Paradox of the Fortunate Fall," *ELH* 4, no. 3 (September 1937): 161–179.
[5] Muṣṭafā al-'Arūsī, *Natā'ij al-afkār al-qudsiyya fī bayān ma'ānī sharḥ al-risāla al-Qushayriyya*, 4 vols. (Cairo: Būlāq, 1873), vol. III, 33.
[6] "Sufi metaphysics" is Nettler's preferred term. See Ronald L. Nettler, *Sufi Metaphysics and Qur'ānic Prophets: Ibn 'Arabī's Thought and Method in the Fuṣūṣ al-Ḥikam* (Cambridge: Islamic Texts Society, 2003).
[7] See, e.g., Michel Chodkiewicz, *Seal of the Saints: Prophethood and Sainthood in the Doctrine of Ibn 'Arabi* (Cambridge: Islamic Texts Society, 1993), 60–73.
[8] Yūsuf al-Nabahānī, *al-Ḥaqīqa al-Muḥammadiyya 'inda aqṭāb al-sādah al-ṣūfiyya* (Beirut: Kitāb Nāshirūn, 2012), 18–19.

Lord is manifest only through His slave and site of manifestation ... and he [Muhammad] was given the *words of supreme totality*, which are the sources of the divine realities [i.e., the disclosure of divine names] and [the sources] of the cosmic realities that entail all particulars in the world. This is what is meant by the referents of the names given to Adam.[9]

Of course, these mystical doctrines are well beyond the requisites of the foundational Muslim creed. But they signify the depth of Muslim discourse on Prophetic perfection, and even scholars who did not subscribe to such mysticism concurred that Muhammad, like all emissaries before him, was *al-insan al-kamil* and, in the context of his dealings with the women of his family and community, the Ideal Man.

THE CHIVALROUS PROPHET

Perhaps the most comprehensive category of the Prophetic virtues is *futuwwa*, a form of spiritual chivalry that Muslim sages described in myriad ways. According to the Persian Sufi Abu Ali al-Daqqaq, its essence is altruism rooted in selflessness: "The basis of *futuwwa* is for the servant to always be concerned with the welfare of others." His student, al-Qushayri, includes in his list of its definitions: overlooking faults, defending those in need, spending from one's time and resources, and "to not flee when someone approaches you for help."[10] Thus, Anas relates that the Prophet was once walking with some of his companions on a street in Medina, when an unnamed woman stopped him and said, "God's messenger, I need your help." Without hesitation he replied, "Mother of so-and-so, choose any nearby sidestreet, and I will sit down with you to discuss the matter." Anas says that he sat with her for as long as it took to fulfill her need.[11] In another report of this incident, Anas adds that the woman had a partial mental disability. Of course, that detail only underscores the Prophetic chivalry exemplified here.[12]

---

[9] Dāwūd al-Qayṣarī, *Maṭlaʿ khuṣūṣ al-kalim fī maʿānī fuṣūṣ al-ḥikam* (Beirut: Dār al-Kutub al-ʿIlmiyya, 2012), 730.

[10] Abū al-Qāsim al-Qushayrī, *Al-Risāla al-Qushayriyya* (Beirut: Dar al-Minhāj, 2017), 506–508.

[11] Abū Dāwūd al-Sijistānī, *Kitāb al-sunan*, 6 vols. (Beirut: Muʾassasat al-Rayyān, 2004), vol. V, 282, no. 4818.

[12] Ṣaḥīḥ Muslim no. 2326. See al-Qāḍī ʿIyāḍ ibn Mūsā, *Ikmāl al-muʿlim bi-fawāʾid Muslim*, 9 vols. (Mansoura: Dār al-Wafāʾ, 2004), vol. VII, 290. (The chapter employs a classical style of referencing hadith. Readers unfamiliar with this system can find relevant information at https://sunnah.com.)

When he proposed to Umm Salama for marriage, she expressed her concerns at not being a suitable match: she was no longer young, she was sensitive and perhaps given to jealousy, and she had young children now orphaned. The Prophet responded that he was even older, he would pray that God protect her from jealousy, and "As for thy orphaned children, God and His messenger will take care of them." In the spirit of *futuwwa*, he not only alleviated her trepidation but specifically took upon himself the financial responsibility of her four young children.[13]

At times, his chivalrous support of the distressed was more subtle. When his non-Arab wife, Safiyya, complained that some of the wives had boasted that they were dearer to the Prophet than her because they were from his tribe of Quraysh, the Prophet empowered her to defend herself by taking pride in her Jewish heritage: "Next time, respond to them and say, *In what way are you better than me, when my husband is Muhammad, my father is Aaron, and my uncle is Moses?*"[14]

Years after the passing of Khadija, he still honored her and demonstrated his love for her. Anas, the young lad who served the Prophet for ten years, remarked, "Whenever the Prophet was gifted any food, he would instruct me: *Take it to so-and-so, for she was a friend of Khadija.*" In a more detailed report, Aisha relates that the Prophet would frequently mention Khadija; that often when he slaughtered a sheep, he would make portions of the meat and have them distributed to the friends of Khadija; and that if Aisha expressed slight frustration at this fond recollection of his deceased wife, he responded by listing Khadija's virtues, one after another, ending with, "And, she bore my children." Sometimes Aisha's objection was firmer, with her explicitly stating the name, "Khadija?", to which the Prophet would reply, "Love of her was placed in me," underscoring that the source of that deep love was God Himself.

The divine basis of the Prophet's love for his household at times manifested itself in a more direct manner. Early in his married life, the Archangel Gabriel – whose descent to earth signified only the most momentous occasions, such as the revelation of scripture, support of the Prophet in military conflict, defending his life against assassins, or the like – once visited the Prophet and said, "O God's messenger,

---

[13] 'Alī ibn Balbān, *Ṣaḥīḥ Ibn Ḥibbān*, 18 vols. (Beirut: Mu'assasat al-Risāla, 1997), vol. IX, 372, no. 4065; Ibn Sayyid al-Nās, *'Uyūn al-athar fī funūn al-maghāzī wa al-shamā'il wa al-siyar*, 2 vols. (Damascus: Dār Ibn Kathīr, n.d.), vol. II, 397–398.

[14] Abū 'Īsā al-Tirmidhī, *al-Sunan* (Riyadh: Dār al-Ḥaḍāra, 2015), 737, no. 3892.

Khadija is approaching, bringing a container with some food and drink. When she arrives, convey to her the greetings of peace from her Lord, and from me similar greetings, and give her glad tidings of a pearl house in Paradise that is free of any shouting or exhaustion." (Evident here is Khadija's unparalleled spiritual rank, the context of which is her virtue. As Ideal Woman, she never once raised her voice to the Prophet, never angered him, and was never rude to him. She supported him when society abused him, and she provided him immense comfort during tribulation.)[15]

One day, Khadija's sister, Hala bint Khuwaylid, visited the house and sought permission to enter. Aisha noted how the Prophet recognized the similarity of Hala's voice to Khadija's and recalled how Khadija would enter the room, and that he was visibly startled by this, remarking, "O God, Hala." In another report, Aisha highlights that the Prophet married no other woman while Khadija was his wife, but only after her death married more than one woman. Indeed, on more than one occasion the Prophet said that the best women between heaven and earth were Mary (the mother of Jesus) and Khadija; and in a more sublime description, that the supreme women of Paradise are four: Mary (the mother of Jesus), his daughter Fatima, Khadija, and Asiya (the wife of Pharoah).[16]

A particularly telling example of his *futuwwa* is his treatment of Hind bint Utba, who for years displayed unparalleled animosity towards the Prophet, to the extent of her goading the hired mercenary Wahshi to kill the Prophet's uncle Hamza at the Battle of Uhud and, after the battle, viciously mutilating Hamza's body and eating from his liver. (Some companions remarked that the Prophet never saw anything more painful to his heart than the sight of Hamza's disfigured body.)[17] Several years later, at the Conquest of Mecca, she embraced Islam. The Prophet not only pardoned her and welcomed her conversion, but also patiently sat with her to answer her legal questions regarding marriage and the financial responsibilities of a husband towards his wife.[18]

[15] Aḥmad Zaynī Daḥlan, *al-Sīra al-nabawiyya wa al-āthār al-Muḥammadiyya*, in the margin of ʿAlī ibn Burhān al-Dīn al-Ḥalabī, *al-Sīra al-Ḥalabiyya: Insān al-ʿuyūn fī sīrat al-Amīn al-Maʾmūn*, 3 vols. (Beirut: Dār Iḥyāʾ al-Turāth al-ʿArabī, n.d.), vol. I, 169.

[16] Muhammad Abdullah al-Aʿẓamī, *al-Jāmiʿ al-kāmil fī al-ḥadīth al-ṣaḥīḥ al-shāmil*, 12 vols. (Riyadh: Dār al-Salām, 2016), vol. IX, 285–288, citing Ṣaḥīḥ al-Bukhārī, Ṣaḥīḥ Muslim, Ṣaḥīḥ Ibn Ḥibbān, Musnad Aḥmad, and others.

[17] Ibn al-Athīr, *Usud al-ghāba fī maʿrifat al-ṣaḥāba* (Beirut: Dār Ibn Ḥazm, 2012),299.

[18] Ṣaḥīḥ al-Bukhārī no. 7161; Ṣaḥīḥ Muslim no. 1714. See Ibn Ḥajar al-ʿAsqalānī, *Fatḥ al-Bārī sharḥ ṣaḥīḥ al-Bukhārī*, 13 vols. (Beirut: Dār al-Fikr, n.d.), vol. XIII, 138–140; al-Qāḍī ʿIyāḍ, *Ikmāl al-muʿlim*, vol. V, 564–567; Ibn Kathīr, *al-Bidāya wa al-nihāya*, 15 vols. (Beirut: Maktabat al-Maarif, 1990), vol. IV, 319.

THE IDEAL HUSBAND AND FAMILY LIFE

After revelation commenced, the foundation of Muhammad's family life was the remembrance of God. Khadija was "the first of mankind to believe in him," and when Gabriel taught him the ritual ablution and prayer, the Prophet immediately went to Khadija to teach what he had learned, and together they performed the first obligatory prayer in Islam.[19] This spiritual anchor proved immutable; years later, when Aisha was asked about his domestic life, she remarked, "He would spend time in the service of his family, but when the time for prayer came, he immediately left to pray."[20]

After the prayer, perhaps the devotional act he emphasized most to his household was charity, which was often a teaching opportunity of metaphysical truths. Aisha reports that one day they slaughtered a sheep; when the Prophet came home, he asked, "What remains of it?", the implication being that they had donated the bulk of it to the needy. She answered, "Nothing remains save its shoulder." He said, "Rather, *all of it* remains save its shoulder."[21] From the vantage of the afterlife, charity *remains*, as reward and the divine pleasure, whereas that which one consumes is forever lost. Another time, a destitute woman with two baby daughters came to the home, and Aisha gave them three dates. The mother gave one to each girl and kept one for herself, yet when the two ate theirs, they gazed at their mother, longing for more. To Aisha's amazement, the mother split her date and gave each daughter a half. When God's emissary came home and Aisha told him what happened, he said, "Are you amazed at that? Indeed, because of her mercy to her babies, God has shown her mercy," signifying that she was a woman of Paradise.[22] The principle taught here (and in countless other incidents in the Prophet's life) would constitute the basis of an entire system of metaphysics and ethics: to the extent a believer inculcates virtues that mirror the divine names, she will ascend in sainthood and attain divine love. (Ghazali delineated the method of applying this system in his *Al-Maqsad al-asna*.)[23]

---

[19] Ibn Sayyid al-Nās, *'Uyūn al-athar*, vol. I, 177–178.
[20] Ṣaḥīḥ al-Bukhārī no. 676. See al-'Asqalānī, *Fatḥ al-Bārī*, vol. II, 162.
[21] al-Tirmidhī, *al-Sunan*, 486, no. 2470.
[22] al-Ḥākim al-Nīsāpūrī, *al-Mustadrak 'alā al-ṣaḥīḥayn*, 5 vols. (Cairo: al-Fārūq al-Ḥadīthiyya, n.d.), vol. IV, 177; Ṣaḥīḥ Muslim no. 2630. See al-Qāḍī 'Iyāḍ, *Ikmāl al-mu'lim*, vol. VIII, 110.
[23] Abū Ḥāmid al-Ghazālī, *The Ninety-Nine Beautiful Names of God: Al-Maqsad al-asnā fī sharḥ asmā' Allāh al-ḥusnā*, trans. David B. Burrell and Nazih Daher (Cambridge: Islamic Texts Society, 1999).

In light of the aforementioned testimony of Aisha, "His character was the Qur'an," Muslims find in the Qur'anic discourse on spouses a window into the Prophet's comportment with his wives. The Qur'anic supplication regarding family is to be the "delight of the eyes" for one another (Q. 25:74), its description of the spousal relationship is one predicated on love and mercy (Q. 30:21), and its imperative is to "live with them in virtue" (Q. 4:19). Qurtubi's exegesis of the latter verse emphasizes both the financial duties of the husband and courtesies owed to the wife, the latter including "not frowning in her face in the absence of any wrongdoing; being pleasant in speech and never rude or harsh; and not displaying to her an inclination to anyone else." He also cites the precedent of two early pious figures: Ibn Abbas once said, "Verily, I love to dress up for my wife just as I love that she dress up for me"; and when Muhammad ibn al-Hanafiyya left his house one day, wearing a red cloak and his beard dripping with perfume, and was asked about his appearance, he replied, "This cloak was gifted to me by my wife, and she oiled my beard with perfume. Indeed, women desire from us what we desire from them."[24] Certainly, Muslims regard the wisdom of such sages as rays emanating from the lamp of the Prophet's example; the legal tradition is no exception. The master jurist Malik ibn Anas taught that courtesy to one's wife secures the pleasure of one's Lord, deepens love in the family, increases one's wealth and extends one's life. His students described Malik as "among the best in character to his wife and children" and cited him as instructing that "It is obligatory on a man to continue making himself beloved to his household, until he is the most beloved of all people to them."[25]

Indeed, the Prophet had explicitly taught, "The best of you are the best to their families, and of all men with their families, I am the best to my family."[26] Aisha provides numerous corroborating reports. Once, when asked what God's emissary was like when alone with his family, she said, "He was the gentlest of people and the most generous of people. He was a man like other men [with similar daily chores of living], except that he was always cheerful and smiling."[27] Other times she described how he would always choose the easier of two options, so long as neither was sinful,[28] and that he never once struck a woman, a servant, or even

---

[24] Muhammad ibn Aḥmad al-Qurṭubī, *al-Jāmiʿ li aḥkām al-Qurʾān*, 24 vols. (Beirut: Muʾassasat al-Risāla, 2006), vol. VI, 159–160.
[25] al-Qāḍī ʿIyāḍ ibn Mūsā, *Bughyat al-rāʾid fī mā fī ḥadīth Umm Zarʿ min al-fawāʾid* (Beirut: Dār al-Kutub al-ʿIlmiyya, 2003), 33.
[26] al-Tirmidhī, *Al-Sunan*, 737, no. 3895.
[27] Muḥammad ibn Saʿd, *al-Ṭabaqāt al-kubrā*, 9 vols. (Beirut: Dār Ṣādir, 1985), vol. I, 365.
[28] Ṣaḥīḥ al-Bukhārī no. 3560. See al-ʿAsqalānī, *Fatḥ al-Bārī*, vol. VI, 566.

an object.²⁹ Beyond domestic peace, courtesy, and ease, even play and merriment were features of the Ideal Man's family life. Aisha once prepared a meat stew and brought it to Sawda and the Prophet, who was seated between the two ladies. When Sawda declined Aisha's request to eat, she replied with a playful threat that she would rub Sawda's face with it. Sawda stood firm, and Aisha carried out the warning. The Prophet laughed and told Sawda to retaliate in kind, which she did, to their amusement.³⁰ Aisha also relates that her husband twice challenged her to a race, the first when she was young and more agile, the second when she was older. She won the first race but lost the second, and to ensure she felt no sadness at losing, the Prophet said lightheartedly, "This one was for that first one."³¹ There also exists precedent in his family life for appreciating literature. In a famous report, Aisha recounted from memory a mirthful tale of eleven women who once gathered and made a pact that each would fully disclose the qualities of her husband: five husbands proved awful, and five proved noble. The eleventh description, by Umm Zar' of her husband Abu Zar', was the longest and most praising of his virtue and kindness, although the man ended up divorcing her. After listening attentively, without frustration or interruption, the Prophet responded in chivalrous fashion, "I am to you like Abu Zar' was to Umm Zar', except that he divorced her, but I will not divorce you." (In his treatise on this hadith, al-Qadi 'Iyad devotes roughly two-thirds of the book to linguistic, grammatical, and rhetorical analysis of the eleven descriptions.)³²

THE IDEAL FATHER

The well-being of daughters constituted a distinct and sacred concern for the Ideal Man, whose society before revelation had sanctioned the tyranny of burying female infants alive. Speaking to converts leaving such corruption, he taught, "Whoever has a daughter and does not bury her, does not demean her, and does not show preference to his son over her, shall be granted Paradise by God." He also taught, "Whoever rears three daughters, educates them, gets them married, and treats them with grace

---

[29] Muhammad ibn Māja, *al-Sunan*, 5 vols. (Beirut: al-Risāla al-'Ālamiyya, 2009), vol. III, 152, no. 1984.
[30] Aḥmad ibn 'Alī al-Tamīmī, *Musnad Abī Ya'lā al-Mawṣilī*, 16 vols. (Damascus: Dār al-Ma'mūn li al-Turāth, 1989), vol. VII, 449, no. 4476.
[31] Abū Dāwūd, *Kitāb al-sunan*, vol. III, 250, no. 2578; 'Abdullāh Sirāj al-Dīn, *Sayyidunā Muḥammad Rasūl Allāh* (Aleppo: Maktabat Dār al-Falāḥ, n.d.), 194–195.
[32] al-Qāḍī 'Iyāḍ, *Bughyat al-rā'id*, 13–26, citing Ṣaḥīḥ al-Bukhārī, Ṣaḥīḥ Muslim, and others. For linguistic commentary, see 40–150.

and courtesy, shall attain Paradise"; according to another version of this report, he said "three sisters, two sisters, three daughters, or two daughters."[33] The Prophet himself was the father of four daughters. Regarding the eldest daughter, Zaynab, biographers noted how "he loved her dearly" and that her daughter, Umama, was the one who, as a baby girl, the Prophet would sometimes carry on his shoulder during ritual prayer, place her on the ground during prostration, and lift her again when standing. Ruqayya was his second daughter, and for her sake the Prophet instructed her husband, Uthman ibn Affan, to remain in Medina and tend to her in her severe illness rather than take part in the Battle of Badr; upon the Prophet's return from that victory, he received the tragic news of her death. His third daughter, Umm Kulthum, was later married to Uthman by the command of God, for which, according to a narration, the Archangel Gabriel descended; for Muslims, such was heaven's reflection of her father's love for her. The fourth daughter, Fatima, was the only child of his who outlived him, and her marriage to Ali ibn Abi Talib carried perennial significance for the community. In addition to being praised by her father as one of the supreme women of Paradise, she was honored to be described by him as "a portion of me." (One narration even noted how her walk resembled his walk.) In his final illness, a distinct concern of his was informing Fatima of his approaching death, for which she immediately wept, and then of her near reunion with him, for which she expressed joy. (She would die six months later.) The daughter of God's emissary had no longing in her heart that matched the longing to be with her father.[34]

The Ideal Man as father was no less ideal as grandfather. He often supplicated for his two grandsons, Hasan and Husayn, asking God to love them because of his own love for them; in one report, he did so while seating them in his lap. Once, when asked who in his household was most beloved to him, he said, "Hasan and Husayn"; another time, he described them as "the two liege lords of the people of Paradise." In a tender family moment, the two young boys were wrestling in the presence of the Prophet, who started cheering for Hasan. Their mother, Fatima, playfully complained, "O God's emissary, you support the older brother against the younger one?" He replied, "Here is Gabriel cheering for Husayn against Hasan."[35] Another tender moment occurred earlier in their life when they first started walking. Dressed in long red shirts, the

[33] Abū Dāwūd, Kitāb al-sunan, vol. V, 413, nos. 5146–5148.
[34] Mu'min al-Shablanjī, Nūr al-abṣār fī manāqib āl bayt al-nabī al-mukhtār (Cairo: Muṣṭafā al-bābī al-Ḥalabī, 1948), 49–52.
[35] Ibid., 126, 139, citing Ṣaḥīḥ Muslim, Sunan al-Tirmidhī, and Ja'far al-Ṣādiq.

two boys entered the mosque while the Prophet was delivering a sermon. When they began to stumble on the ends of their shirts, he interrupted the sermon to descend the pulpit and pick them up and then ascended the pulpit to resume.[36] In addition to the subject of the sermon, the congregation learned a lesson in the Ideal Man's compassion for children, even when in public.

The lesson was reinforced in different contexts. When one of his grandsons was in the last moments of life and was placed in the arms of his grandfather, the Prophet's eyes welled up with tears. His companion Sa'd became confused at the notion of God's emissary, who was fully resigned to the divine decree, displaying emotion. When questioned by him, the Prophet responded, "This is but mercy, which God has placed in the hearts of His servants, and God shows mercy only to the merciful among His servants."[37] A similar exchange occurred with the death of his son, Ibrahim, who lived only to the age of sixteen months. While the boy was in his final illness, the Prophet entered the room and began to weep. This time, his companion, Abd al-Rahman b. 'Awf, expressed confusion, and the Prophet responded, "O son of 'Awf, it is but mercy." He then wept again, saying, "The eye weeps, and the heart grieves, but we say only what pleases our Lord. Indeed, O Ibrahim, we are saddened at your departure."[38]

The connection between love of children and divine mercy proved salient in his teaching. The Prophet once kissed Hasan while a visitor from Bani Tamim was in his presence. The man found it strange and objected, saying, "I myself have ten kids, but I have never kissed a single one of them!" The Prophet simply looked at him and remarked, "He who does not show mercy is not granted mercy." In another report, an unnamed Bedouin complained to the Prophet, "Verily, you all kiss your kids, but we never kiss ours." The Prophet replied, "Can I do anything for you if God Himself has removed mercy from your heart?"[39]

THE IDEAL COMMUNITY LEADER

The Ideal Man's compassion extended far beyond domestic life. As community leader, he was a refuge for the indigent of society. Anas relates, "Verily, any young slavegirl of Medina would take the Prophet by the

---

[36] al-Nasā'ī, *al-Sunan*, 9 vols. (Beirut: Dār al-Bashā'ir al-Islāmiyya, 1994), vol. III, 108, no. 1413.
[37] Ṣaḥīḥ al-Bukhārī no. 7377. See al-'Asqalānī, *Fatḥ al-Bārī*, vol. XIII, 358.
[38] Ṣaḥīḥ al-Bukhārī no. 1303. See al-'Asqalānī, *Fatḥ al-Bārī*, vol. III, 172–174.
[39] Ṣaḥīḥ al-Bukhārī no. 5997, 5998. See al-'Asqalānī, *Fatḥ al-Bārī*, vol. X, 426.

hand and go forth with him wherever she wanted," that is, as another report clarifies, "to fulfill her needs," such as buying food and basic commodities, even if outside the city.[40] Other companions confirm such acts of service as his inveterate habit: according to one testimony, the Prophet would regularly visit the poor, particularly when they were ill, and he would be present at their funeral prayers; and in another testimony, "The Prophet was never too haughty or scornful to walk with widows, the indigent, or slaves, until he fulfilled their needs."[41]

Orphans were of a particular concern for him, and the concern echoed the dictates of the revelation: "So, do not be harsh with the orphan" (Q. 93:9). He left no doubt in the minds of his companions regarding the spiritual rank of one who tends to their needs: "I and the caretaker of an orphan shall be in Paradise like this," whereupon he indicated proximity by holding up his index and middle fingers together.[42] On another occasion, he made a similar remark and gesture, to emphasize proximity with him in Paradise, regarding widows who, despite their beauty and social status, remain unmarried in order to tend to their young orphaned children until they reach adulthood; in the narration, he was sensitive to the pains and personal sacrifice such a woman endures, describing her as "a woman with cheeks turned ashy in color," meaning who cannot focus on her own beauty, and one who "imprisons herself for the sake of her young children."[43] In this context, his teaching offered practical solutions for orphans who might otherwise be neglected, abused, or outright homeless. Nonetheless, his program of social support did not forsake such spiritually luminous women; according to numerous reports, he said, "The one who strives to look after widows and the destitute is like a warrior who fights in the path of God and is like one who prays at night and fasts in the day."[44]

His support for the womenfolk of the community was not limited to material means but included, and centered around, matters spiritual. Thus, Jamra bint Abdullah relates that when she was a young girl, her father took her to the Prophet with the request, "O God's emissary, pray to God that He bless this daughter of mine with special grace [*baraka*]." In the testimony of Jamrah, "So, the

[40] Ṣaḥīḥ al-Bukhārī no. 6072. See al-'Asqalānī, *Fatḥ al-Bārī*, vol. X, 489–490.
[41] Muhammad 'Abd al-Ra'ūf al-Munāwī, *Fayḍ al-Qadīr*, 6 vols. (Cairo: Maktabat Miṣr, 2003), vol. V, 252, 314, citing Abū Ya'lā, Ṭabarānī, and Ḥākim for the first hadith and al-Nasā'ī and Ḥākim for the second.
[42] Abū Dāwūd, *Kitāb al-sunan*, vol. V, 414, no. 5150.
[43] Ibid., vol. V, 413–414, no. 5149.
[44] Ṣaḥīḥ al-Bukhārī no. 6006; Ibn Māja no. 2140. See al-'Asqalānī, *Fatḥ al-Bārī*, vol. X, 437; Ibn Māja, *al-Sunan*, vol. III, 273.

Prophet sat me in his lap, placed his hand on my head, and supplicated for me that I receive special grace." Other times, the spiritual support he provided addressed more immediate or even existential concerns. Moreover, that support proved so tremendous and salient that subsequent generations would venerate its recipient as a true legend of nobility and of proximity to the Divine. Ata b. Abi Rabah relates that his teacher, Ibn Abbas, once said to him, "Shall I not show you a woman of the people of Paradise?" He replied, "Of course." He then pointed out a tall Ethiopian woman named Su'ayra Umm Zufar and described how she once approached the Prophet and complained of epileptic seizures, due to which her clothes would move and reveal parts of her body, so she requested a prayer. The Prophet replied, "If you wish, you can be patient, and Paradise shall be yours; or if you wish, I can pray to God that He heal you." She said, "I choose patience. But my body still gets exposed, so pray to God that I remain covered [during my seizures]," and he made that prayer.

At times, the revelation would directly address the needs of women in the community, such that spiritual support would be manifested with material solutions rooted in the sacred law. Aisha relates,

> All praise be to God whose hearing encompasses all voices. Khawlah bint Tha'labah once visited God's emissary and complained about her husband. I could not hear their conversation, but God (Mighty and Majestic) revealed: *God has heard the words of the woman who disputed with you [O Prophet] about her husband and who complained to God. God heard what you both had to say. Verily God is All-hearing, All-seeing.* Q. 58:1

In Khawla's own testimony of what transpired,

> Regarding me, by God, and regarding Aws ibn Ṣāmit did God (Mighty and Majestic) reveal the opening of *The Chapter of the Disputing Woman* [Q. 58]. I was his wife, and he was then an irritable old man whose character had worsened. He entered one day, and I talked back to him about something, at which he got angry and said, "You are to me like the back of my mother [an Arabic idiom implying unlawfulness for intimacy]" and walked out. After spending some time in the sitting area of his clan, he returned and desired intimacy with me, but I said, "By no means, by the One in whose grasp is Khawla's soul, will you be intimate with me after you said what you said! Not until God and His messenger give their judgment regarding us." He [proceeded anyway and] jumped on me, but I refused. I overpowered him the way a woman can

overpower a weak old man, and I threw him off me. I immediately went to a female neighbor of mine and borrowed some clothes, and then I set out to God's messenger. [When I arrived] I sat in front of him and told him everything that had transpired, and I started complaining to him of my husband's bad character. God's messenger started saying, "O Khuwayla [dear Khawla], your husband is an old man, so fear God with respect to him." By God, at once some verses of the Qur'an were revealed regarding me, and God's messenger was overcome by what overcame him [during revelation]. When it subsided, he said, "O Khuwayla, God has sent revelation regarding you and your companion" and then recited to me: *God has heard the words of the woman who disputed with you [O Prophet] about her husband and who complained to God. God heard what you both had to say. Verily God is All-hearing, All-seeing,* until His statement *and for the disbelievers there is a painful punishment* [Q. 58:1–4].

Then God's messenger said, "Tell him to free a slave." I said, "By God, O God's messenger, he owns no slaves." He instructed, "Then, let him fast two consecutive months." I said, "By God, O God's messenger, he is but an old man, unable to fast." He said, "Then, let him feed sixty poor people a large portion of dates." I said, "By God, O God's messenger, he doesn't own even that [amount of wealth]." God's messenger replied, "In that case, we shall aid him with a portion of dates." I asked, "And I too, God's messenger, shall I aid him with another portion of dates?" He said, "You hit the mark, and you certainly did well. Go forth, and donate on his behalf, and then treat your husband well." And I did just that.

In this telling account, the Ideal Man's community leadership is predicated on compassion, even in the context of meting out the divinely sanctioned penalty for a husband's ill-treatment of his wife; moreover, fully confident in that compassion, she had showed no hesitation in seeking the Prophet's counsel and complaining to him directly of the exigencies of her marital life. Aisha, for example, was not consulted; she could not even hear the conversation. His leadership was also predicated on a penetrating wisdom, as the distressed woman left his presence with a renewed commitment to empathy and moral excellence, to the extent of volunteering, in emulation of the Prophet, to give charity to the very husband whose lapse in character had precipitated the entire ordeal.[45]

[45] Aḥmad ibn Ḥanbal, *al-Musnad*, vol. XL, 228, no. 24195, and vol. XLV, 300–302, no. 27319; Abū Dāwūd, *Kitāb al-Sunan*, vol. III, 82–83, no. 2214.

The political and social empowerment of women was also a critical feature of Muhammad's leadership. Aisha's distinction as a scholar (and political figure, such as at the Battle of the Camel) is well known. Of all the companions, she was the fourth-most prolific narrator of hadith[46] and therefore preeminent in education, arguably the societal function that denoted the very essence of the nascent civilization.[47] The Ideal Man had edified Aisha to intellectual mastery: she was described as the most eloquent of the companions, and whenever they found difficulty understanding a hadith and consulted her, she proved knowledgeable of its meaning. And, corresponding to the Prophetic teaching, her erudition was not disconnected from the ethical imperative; Gabriel himself once descended to convey to her his greetings of peace, of which the Prophet informed her.[48]

An example of explicit political empowerment relates to conferring security on adversaries. At the Conquest of Mecca, whereas the Meccans in general were granted asylum so long as they surrendered, a handful were exempted due to past war crimes. When Ali was fighting one of them, his sister, Umm Hani', granted the man security, and when the matter was raised with the Prophet, he confirmed her political right to do so,[49] thus establishing a legal precedent that any of his followers, male or female, could grant security to enemies even in wartime. Other examples relate to the battlefield itself; Nusayba bint Ka'b attended the Battle of Uhud to provide water to the wounded. When the battle was at its fiercest, and fewer than ten companions were with the Prophet (the sole target of the Meccan enemies and thus the point of greatest danger), she shielded him with a valor that earned her his praise and and a legendary status; suffering a dozen wounds that day, one of which she nursed for a year, she would be described by biographers as "the noble warrior woman." Years later at Yamama, she suffered another dozen wounds, including the loss of her hand. Moreover, her political presence was not limited to the military; she was also present at the momentous origin of Medinan alliance with the Prophet that prefaced his emigration there: the 'Aqaba pledge.[50]

---

[46] Muhammad Zubayr Siddiqi, *Hadith Literature: Its Origin, Development and Special Features* (Cambridge: Islamic Texts Society, 1993), 18.
[47] See, e.g., Franz Rosenthal, *Knowledge Triumphant: The Concept of Knowledge in Medieval Islam* (Leiden: Brill, 2007).
[48] al-Tirmidhī, *al-Sunan*, 735, no. 3882–3884.
[49] Ṣaḥīḥ al-Bukhārī no. 357, Ṣaḥīḥ Ibn Ḥibbān no. 1188. See al-'Asqalānī, *Fatḥ al-Bārī*, vol. I, 469; 'Alī ibn Balbān, *Ṣaḥīḥ Ibn Ḥibbān*, vol. III, 460–461.
[50] Muhammad ibn Aḥmad al-Dhahabī, *Siyar a'lām al-nubalā'*, 28 vols. (Beirut: Mu'assasat al-Risāla, 2001), vol. II, 278–282.

THE HONOR OF WOMEN

In the sermon of his farewell pilgrimage, in which he delineated the critical priorities of the faith, the Prophet stressed the rights of women and the imperative to treat them with kindness,[51] but the message was not new. Once when a man asked, "To whom is owed my best companionship and courtesy?" the Prophet replied, "Your mother." When the question was repeated, he gave the same reply, and again a third time, until the fourth time, when he answered, "Your father."[52] In other reports, he clarified that the basis of the hierarchical distinction was her sanctified receptacle. "The womb is attached to the Throne [of God], and it proclaims: *God shall connect with whoever connects with me and shall cut off whoever cuts me off.*"[53] This celestial anchor of family and society was in fact named after the divine benevolence: "God, the Exalted, states: I am the All-merciful [*al-Rahman*], and she [the womb] is *rahim*. From My name did I derive hers. I shall connect with whoever connects with her, and I shall cut off whoever cuts her off."[54]

Other reports underscore the relation between the mother's compassion for the child and the divine compassion that envelops creation. In one of the more striking metaphors, the Prophet describes God's mercy as having a hundred parts, one of which God apportioned to this life and is the source of all mercy between creatures. "By it, the mother has tender love for her child." Yet the remaining ninety-nine parts are reserved for Judgment Day, with everlasting significance.[55] And it is perhaps the woman's denotation of God's everlasting mercy that explains the Ideal Man's mention of women in his statement: "Of this world, women and perfume were made dear to me, and the delight of my eye was placed in the prayer."[56]

SELECT BIBLIOGRAPHY

Armstrong, Karen. *Muhammad: A Prophet for Our Time*. San Francisco: HarperOne, 2007.

Brown, Jonathan A. C. *Muhammad: A Very Short Introduction*. Oxford, New York: Oxford University Press, 2011.

[51] 'Abd al-Malik ibn Hishām, *al-Sīra al-nabawiyya*, 4 vols. (Beirut: Dār al-Kitāb al-'Arabī, 1990), vol. IV, 249.
[52] Ṣaḥīḥ al-Bukhārī no. 5971; Ṣaḥīḥ Muslim no. 2548. See al-'Asqalānī, *Fatḥ al-Bārī*, vol. X, 401; al-Qāḍī 'Iyāḍ, *Ikmāl al-mu'lim*, vol. VIII, 5.
[53] Ṣaḥīḥ Muslim no. 2555. See al-Qāḍī 'Iyāḍ, *Ikmāl al-mu'lim*, vol. VIII, 19–20.
[54] Abū Dāwūd, *Kitāb al-sunan*, vol. II, 387–388, no. 1694.
[55] Ibn Māja, *al-Sunan*, vol. V, 352–353, nos. 4293, 4294.
[56] al-Nasā'ī, *al-Sunan*, vol. VII, 61, no. 3939.

al-Ghazālī, Abū Ḥāmid. *The Book of Prophetic Ethics and the Courtesies of Living.* Trans. Adi Setia. Louisville: Fons Vitae, 2019.

Haylamaz, Resit and Harpci, Fatih. *The Sultan of Hearts: Prophet Muhammad.* Clifton, NJ: Tughra Books, 2020.

Ibn Hishām, 'Abd al-Mālik. *The Life of Muhammad.* Trans. Alfred Guillaume. Karachi: Oxford University Press, 2011.

Ibn Musa al-Yahsubi, Qadi 'Iyad. *Muhammad, Messenger of Allah: Ash-Shifa of Qadi 'Iyad.* Trans. Aisha Bewley. Bolton: Madinah Press, 2014.

Ibn Sayyid an-Nās, Abū'l-Fatḥ Muḥammad. *Nūr al-'Uyūn: The Light of the Eyes.* London: Turath Publishing, 2016.

Khalidi, Tarif. *Images of Muhammad: Narratives of the Prophet in Islam across the Centuries.* New York, London: Doubleday, 2009.

Lings, Martin. *Muhammad: His Life Based on the Earliest Sources.* Rochester: Inner Traditions, 2006.

Nadwi, Abul Hasan Ali. *Prophet of Mercy* [Nabiyy-i Rahmat]. London: Turath Publishing, 2014.

Safi, Omid. *Memories of Muhammad: Why the Prophet Matters.* New York: HarperCollins, 2010.

Schimmel, Annemarie. *And Muhammad Is His Messenger: The Veneration of the Prophet in Islamic Piety.* Chapel Hill: University of North Carolina Press, 1985.

Sirajuddin, 'Abdallah. *Our Master Muhammad, The Messenger of Allah.* Trans. Khalid Williams. 2 vols. Rotterdam: Sunni Publications, 2008.

at-Tirmidhī, Muḥammad ibn 'Īsā. *A Portrait of the Prophet: As Seen by His Contemporaries.* Trans. Muhtar Holland. Louisville: Fons Vitae, 2017.

Yamani, Muhammad Abduh. *Our Lady Fāṭima al-Zahrā'.* Trans. Khalid Williams. Alburtis, PA: Ihya Publishing, 2024.

5 Prophet's Wives: "Mothers of the Believers"
MAHJABEEN DHALA

Biographical literature on the Prophet's life (*sira*) is a crucial resource in the development of Qur'anic exegesis, Islamic jurisprudential thought, and virtue ethics. Alongside the Qur'an, the Prophetic tradition (*sunna*) plays a key role in shaping Islamic doctrine, practice, and the Muslim identity and society. While Muslims unanimously believe the Qur'an to be the unadulterated word of God, the voluminous genre of *sira* and *sunna* is open to critique as it was compiled by Muslim historians nearly a hundred years after the Prophet died in AH 11/632 CE. Prominent classical scholarship on *sira* ranges between Ibn Ishaq's (d. 761 CE) *Sira al-Nabawiyya* and Ibn Kathir's (d. 1373 CE) work with the same title. As accounts of the formative period of Islam and Muslims were primarily transmitted through oral tradition for the first century of the post-Prophetic period, they inevitably carried the narrators' cultural, social, political, and sectarian biases and preferences.

In this chapter, I draw on Qur'anic exegesis to explore the exemplary position of the Prophet's wives as "unlike any other women" (Q. 33:32) and the "mothers of the faithful" (Q. 33:6). Among other *tafsir* (Qur'anic exegetical) works, I engage with Muhammad ibn Jarir al-Tabari's (d. 923 CE) *Jaame Al-Bayan an Ta'wil Aayae al-Qur'an* and Naser Makarim Shirazi's *Tafsir Namuna* to include classical and contemporary interpretations from Shi'i and Sunni exegesis. Additionally, I draw on contemporary constructive and critical readings of the historical narratives of the Prophet's wives to ask: What sets these women apart? How might the term "mother" be understood in their context when considering that, among his wives, only Khadija bint Khuwaylid, his first wife, was the biological mother of the Prophet's children?[1] How does their "mothering" continue to be of relevance and value to contemporary Muslim women, Muslim societies, and the Islamic ethos of social

---
[1] The Prophet had another child, with Maria the Copt; however, since she is referred to as a concubine in classical literature, I have refrained from mentioning her.

justice? Deploying Andrea O'Reilly's idea of "non-normative mothering" and "it's real power to bring about a true and enduring cultural revolution," I portray the Prophet's wives as embodying a form of motherhood that transcends conventional definitions, through their contributions to establishing a paradigm of piety, social reform, and activism. O'Reilly suggests that within the field of motherhood studies, the conventional view of motherhood is largely a patriarchal construct, shaped and perpetuated by ideological beliefs that emphasize the biological aspects of motherhood and the experience of nurturing. Concepts of non-normative mothering question the ideological foundations of patriarchal constructs, broadening the scope to encompass alternative viewpoints. These perspectives help in appreciating the "nurturing roles"[2] that the Prophet's wives have played within the Muslim community, both historically and in contemporary times.

MOTHERS UNDER THE GAZE OF CLASSICAL AND CONTEMPORARY SCHOLARSHIP

The Prophet's house was a center for divine revelations, his life serving as a human manifestation of the Qur'anic teachings. The circumstances of these revelations (asbab al-nuzul) play a crucial role in the interpretation of the Qur'an. Sira literature, which chronicles the Prophet's life, similarly enhances our understanding of the Qur'an by detailing how he exemplified and propagated divine instructions. His interactions with family members, allies, and adversaries were extensively recorded in the ninth century, resulting in the production of early texts in Islamic history and sunna. Over the centuries, these texts, broadly referred to as hadith, became an essential resource, second only to the Qur'an, in shaping Islamic doctrine, law, and ethics.[3] Emerging in an era characterized by shifting political regimes, entrenched patriarchal standards, and intense sectarian debates, the sira and sunna naturally reflect the biases

---

[2] Margaret Aziza Pappano and Dana M. Olwan, *Muslim Mothering: Local and Global Histories, Theories, and Practices* (Bradford: Demeter Press, 2016), 5.

[3] The hadith corpus is copious, including six Sunni collections (*Sihāh al-Sitta*) compiled between 870 and 915 CE, and four Shi'i collections (*Kutub al-Arba'a*) compiled between 864 and 1067 CE. *Sihāh al-Sitta* refer to Imam al-Bukhari's *Sahih al-Bukhari* (7,275 hadith), Muslim al-Hallaj's *Sahih Muslim* (9,200 hadith), Abu Dawood's *Sunan Abi Dawood* (4,800 hadith), Al-Tirmidhi's *Jami' al-Tirmidhi* (3,956 hadith), Al-Nisaee's *Sunan al-Sughra* (5,270 hadith), and Imam Malik's *Muwatta al-Malik* (1,720 hadith). *Kutub al-Arbi'a*) refer to Al-Kulayni's *Al-Kafi* (16,199 hadith), Sheikh Saduq's *Man Laa Yahdhuruh al-Faqih* (9,044 hadith), and Sheikh Tusi's *Tahdhib al-Ahkam* (13,590 hadith) and *Al-Istibsar* (5,511 hadith).

and inclinations of their authors. In this analysis, I explore how these predispositions have shaped portrayals of the Prophet's wives, thereby influencing the concept of female piety in Islam.

While the Qur'an generally refers to them as a collective, exegetes and historians from the formative period of Islamic thought presented some wives as more prominent than others. In Sunni traditions, Aisha and Khadija are particularly highlighted, while Shi'i traditions accord special reverence to Umm Salama. Both classical and modern Western studies extensively explore the roles of these wives. By examining the Qur'anic references to the Prophet's wives as "unlike other women" and the "mothers of the believers," I advocate for an approach that transcends patriarchal, sectarian, and secular prejudices. This perspective allows for an appreciation of their inspirational and symbolic contributions to fostering a paradigm of piety and social reform, which is motivating for both female and male believers. Contemporary research into alternative forms of mothering sheds light on indigenous concepts of motherhood. This includes recounting tales of ancestral mothers to challenge and reframe the experiences of minority cultures and traditions from a decolonial perspective.[4] Jennifer Brant's edited collection, *Mothers, Mothering and Motherhood across Cultural Differences*, brings together chapters that explore varied conceptions of motherhood from Aboriginal, African American, South Asian, Korean, Latina, and other immigrant viewpoints. Together, these chapters counter white, Western, and patriarchal norms of motherhood by presenting alternative voices.[5] O'Reilly argues that normative mothering is defined by a set of assumptions that mirror the dominant cultures,[6] while non-normative mothering critiques the patriarchal understanding of motherhood, which restricts the identity of mothers to bodily accomplishments and household success judged by way of pleasing the male members of the family and the community.[7]

In the context of Muslims living in the Global North, normative mothering would be defined by a white, male, and Christian, if not secular, culture. Similarly, for Muslims living in the Global South, motherhood norms would be defined by patriarchy and gender-restricting socio-economic norms, and religiously burdening

---

[4] Jennifer Brant, "Aboriginal Mothering: Honouring the Past, Nurturing the Future," in *Mothers, Mothering and Motherhood across Cultural Differences: A Reader*, ed. Andrea O'Reilly (Bradford: Demeter Press, 2014), 7–40.
[5] Andrea O'Reilly, "African American Mothering: 'Home Is Where the Revolution Is'," in *Mothers, Mothering and Motherhood*, ed. O'Reilly, 93–118.
[6] Ibid., 2.
[7] Ibid., 4, 5.

women with parenting tasks that might not be divinely ordained for them. In the following sections, I build on contemporary non-normative ideas of mothering to interpret the Prophet's wives' Qur'anic identity as the mothers of the believers from the framework of ancestral mothers whose empowering mothering continues to guide believers through their challenges. I illustrate how they can be seen as a collective of mothers who exercised their agency to embrace a distinguished position, making them eternal exemplars who fostered a legacy of spirituality and activism.

MOTHERING FROM A POSITION OF AGENCY

Q. 33:6 states, "The Prophet has a greater right (authority) over the faithful than they have over their own selves, and his wives are their mothers." While the first part of this verse is interpreted as the Prophet's judicial authority as a state leader,[8] hadith literature also alludes to his authority on the personal matters of Muslims.[9] Since they were not mothers in the biological sense (except Khadija) how might the term "mothers" be interpreted from this verse? Is "mother" a reference to the impermissibility of their marriage to anyone after the death of the Prophet or the annulment of their marriage by divorce? Or does "mother" allude to their reverential status as the Prophet's consorts?

Being affiliated with a Prophet divinely vested with political, judicial, personal, and spiritual authority came with a unique set of privileges and restrictions. One such restriction, which does not apply to any other Muslim women, was the jurisprudential impasse of not being able to remarry after the Prophet.[10] According to al-Qastalani (d. 1517), the Qur'an refers to the Prophet's wives as "mothers" solely because of this impermissibility of their remarriage. He states that this was not a reverential status because of their affiliation with the Prophet, because, if that had been the case, the Prophet would have said something about

---

[8] Q. 33:36 states: "A faithful man or woman may not, when Allah and His Apostle have decided on a matter, have any option in their matter, and whoever disobeys Allah and His Apostle has certainly strayed into manifest error."

[9] In his exegesis *Fi Zilāl al-Qur'an*, Sayyid Qutb narrates that the Prophet said: "I swear by the One who holds my soul, none among you will attain faith until I am dearer to them than themselves, their wealth, their children, and all humanity." Quoting Sahih Bukhari, Sayyid Qutb contends that the Prophet's authority over the believers extends beyond this world into the hereafter. The verse then designates the Prophet's wives as "mothers" of the faithful. See Sayyidd Qutb, *Fi Zilāl al-Qur'an*, trans. Syed Maruf Shah Shirazi (Lahore: Reza Printers, 1997), vol. V, 334, 335.

[10] Q. 33:53 states: "You may not torment the Apostle of Allah, nor may you ever marry his wives after him. Indeed, that would be a grave [matter] with Allah."

his daughters as sisters of the believers, which he did not.[11] Al-Tabarsi (d. 1153) echoes this remark by arguing that reverence does not emerge by family affiliation, as the Prophet did not bestow on his sisters and brothers the titles of aunts and uncles of the believers.[12] Their designation as mothers is solely a jurisprudential issue regarding marriage: believers would neither inherit from them as they would inherit from their biological mothers, nor would they be in their unveiled presence.

Furthermore, al-Tabari suggests that labelling them "mothers" and forbidding their remarriage was to protect them from the vice of men. He reports men saying, "He marries our widows, and we don't get to marry his? By God, when he dies, we will marry his women."[13] The social popularity of these women made them attractive to Muslims in a way that was not always positive. Shirazi remarks that the verse on the prohibition on marrying the Prophet's wives begins with "you may not torment the Apostle of Allah" (Q. 33:53), which suggests that some individuals intended to hurt the Prophet's reverential memory by marrying women who had been intimately connected to him. By forbidding his wives' remarriage, the Qur'an essentially protects the status and reverence of the Prophet. Also, as women who had lived at the site of divine revelation, they were privy to first-hand accounts of sacred texts and their application in the Prophet's life, and as such they would go on to play a vital role in how the religion would be interpreted and applied in Muslim life. These women's remarriages would not only make their bodies a dominion of power but also the experiences and knowledge they embodied. Thus, to protect their bodies and the body of literature that would serve as a witness to divine teachings from power-seeking contenders, the Qur'an forbade their remarriage, awarding them with the honorific title of the mothers of the believers.[14]

Alongside their jurisprudential impasse (*tahrim*) and their reverential status (*ta'zim*), Q. 33:32 also posits the Prophet's wives as "unlike any other women if you are God-wary." Reading this verse as a continuum of the preceding and proceeding verses, I posit their being "unlike any other women" as comprising a fusion of distinction, agency, and responsibility. Q. 33:28–31 states:

[11] Ahmad ibn Muhammad al-Qastalani, *Al-Mawāhib al-Ladunniya bil Minah al-Muhammadiyya*, trans. Muhammad Siddique Hazarawi (Lahore: Farid Book Stall, 2012), vol. II, 384.
[12] Fadhl ibn al-Hasan al-Tabarsi, *Majma al-Bayan fi Tafsir al-Qur'an* (Beirut: Dar Al-Murtaza, 2006), vol. VIII, 93.
[13] Muhammad ibn Jarir al-Tabari, *Jaame Al-Bayan an Ta'wil Aayae al-Qur'an* (Cairo: Dar Hijr, 2001), vol. XIX, 169.
[14] Makarim Shirazi, *Tafsir Namuna* (Lahore: Misbah Qur'an Trust, 1989), vol. XVII, 335.

> O Prophet! Say to your wives, "If you desire the life of the world and its glitter, come, I will provide for you and release you in a graceful manner. But if you desire Allah and His Apostle and the abode of the Hereafter, then Allah has indeed prepared for the virtuous among you a great reward." O wives of the Prophet, whoever of you commits a gross indecency, her punishment shall be doubled, and that is easy for Allah. But whoever of you is obedient to Allah and His Apostle and acts righteously, We shall give her a twofold reward, and We hold a noble provision in store for her.

Shirazi states that the Prophet had acquired much wealth because of successful military expeditions. Consequently, his wives demanded servants, robes, and other favors from him. Considering the plight of the many underprivileged Muslim families in Medina, the Prophet did not comply with their demands, and many of his wives separated themselves from him.[15] As a result, the above verses were revealed, offering them the choice either of staying with the Prophet and embracing a modest lifestyle, or leaving him in pursuit of worldly comforts.

While the Islamic tradition encourages Muslims to make things easier for their families, this rigorous modest conduct for the Prophet's household might be attributed to the Prophet's political and spiritual leadership. How could the Prophet avail himself of riches while unhoused Muslims still lived in the mosque's courtyard and depended on charity for their survival? Nonetheless, it is essential to note that his wives were given the choice of following in his footsteps. Q. 33:28 and Q. 33:29 repeatedly reference this agency, using such phrases as "if you desire ... ." Their crucial choices would have distinct consequences: double reward or penalty (Q. 33:31–32). The twofold consequence of their choices is indicative of the two-dimensional aspect of their identity: a personal aspect, insofar as their choices would affect their spirituality as believing women in their own rights, and a public aspect, which would inevitably affect norms of social piety, given their status as wives of the Prophet of Islam and role models for Muslims. The Qur'an hails the Prophet as a good exemplar (Q. 33:21), and his family would have been expected to demonstrate model conduct.

The women are being offered the choice between the pursuit of worldly extravagance, and the pleasure of God and His Messenger and the bliss of the hereafter, setting a standard for doctrinal piety as understood in the Islamic tradition. The verses also iterate that mere doctrinal testimony would not benefit them unless accompanied by obedient

---

[15] Ibid., 238.

practice. While these directives are addressed to the Prophet's wives, they apply to all believers. Q. 33:28–29 do not coerce these women into adopting the doctrine and practice but rather incentivize their choice by stating that should they "desire Allah and His Apostle and the abode of the Hereafter," they would be entitled to "a great reward" (ajran azima), and should they "desire the life of the world and its glitter," they would be released from any obligation "in a graceful manner" (sarahan jamila). Not only does their privilege of being rewarded twofold and their restriction of remarriage and simple lifestyle set them apart as "unlike any other women," but it is also the unique opportunity to embody the Qur'anic paradigm of piety and justice by exercising their agency, earning the position of being role models to Muslim women and men.

MOTHERING A QUR'ANIC PIETISTIC PARADIGM

Living in a home that was a divine site constituted spiritual currency that would attract the admiration of early and future generations of Muslims. This lofty distinction would inevitably entail being bound by a list of unique responsibilities, further depicting the Prophet's wives as "unlike any other women." While these responsibilities are often understood as pertaining to female pious conduct, prescribed solely for Muslim women, the core message of these verses (Q. 33:32–34) is relevant to all believers, regardless of gender.[16] By embodying pious conduct with agency and not passively, these women were mothering the Qur'anic paradigm of doctrinal and ethical piety, and serving as ancestral model mothers guiding Muslims through their spiritual challenges. Addressing the Prophet's wives, the Qur'an states:

> O wives of the Prophet, you are unlike any other women: if you are wary [of Allah], then do not be complaisant in your speech ... and speak honorable words. Stay in your houses and do not display your finery with the display of the former [days of] ignorance ... Maintain the prayer and pay the zakat and obey Allah and His Apostle. And remember what is recited in your homes of the signs of Allah and wisdom. Indeed, Allah is all-Attentive, all-Aware. Q. 33:32–34

---

[16] While the jurisprudential distinction might apply solely to male Muslims, the reverential address as "mother" might be for all believers regardless of gender. Al-Alusi (d. AH 1270 / 1854 CE) narrates that when a woman addressed Aisha as mother, she replied: "I am the mother of your men and not your women." He also narrates that another wife of the Prophet, Umm Salama, said, "I am the mother of your men and women." See Mahmud ibn Abdullah Al-Alusi, *Rul al-Ma'ani fi Tafsir al-Qur'an al-Azim wa Sab'a al-Mathani* (Beirut: Al-Resalah Publishing House, 2010), vol. XXI, 199.

These verses delineate six commandments for the Prophet's wives. First, prescribing both style and content of speech, they are told not to be submissive in their speech (*la takhda'na bi-l-qawl*) but rather to speak honorable words (*qawlan ma'rufa*). Most exegetes have interpreted this verse as female modesty in talking with their male counterparts. Submissive (*takhda'na*) speech here is read as suggestive speech, a style that sexually arouses the listener, hence the phrase, "lest he in whose heart is a sickness should aspire." Regarding the content of their speech, the verse states, "Speak honorable words [*qawlan ma'rufa*]." Ma'ruf (honorable) can be widely interpreted to mean well-known good, including pious, formidable, truthful, wise, and respectful speech. Both these aspects of speaking formidably in style and content can be applied to believing women and men.

The second ordinance is "stay in your houses." Al-Tabari suggests that *qarna* can either be a derivation of *qarara* (to stay) or from *waqara* (to respect).[17] Thus, it has been interpreted as "stay in your houses" and "respect lies in your houses," which has informed the common Muslim understanding that the most respectable place for a pious Muslim woman is in her house, even when it comes to offering prayers in a mosque.[18] The physical seclusion and pietistic concealment of the Prophet's wives are repeated elsewhere in the Qur'an:

> O you who have faith! Do not enter the Prophet's houses unless permission is granted you for a meal, without waiting for it to be readied. But enter when you are invited, and disperse when you have taken your meal, without settling down to chat. Indeed, such conduct torments the Prophet, and he is ashamed of [asking] you [to leave]; but

---

[17] al-Tabari, *Jaame Al-Bayan*, vol. XIX, 96.

[18] Islamic social media platforms serve as a site for public scholars to respond to questions raised by the Muslim laity. With regards to questions about the implications of the verse "stay in your houses," responses vary from conservative, to moderate, to more liberal. The *Islam Question & Answer* website, https://islamqa.info/en/8868, states that: "women must be protected and concealed from men." On *Islam Question & Answer* https://islamqa.org/?p=42803, a female scholar (*ustadha*) states:

> Traditionally, Muslim women were encouraged to stay at home in order to create a peaceful, loving environment for their families. There is also the need to protect women from being exposed to negative influences and harassment outside the home ... it is permitted for a woman to go to the mosque particularly when she goes to seek knowledge or enjoy the fellowship of her Muslim sisters.

Another website, *AboutIslam*, https://aboutislam.net/counseling/ask-about-islam/muslim-women-stay-houses/, notes: "The wives of the Prophet, who were directly referenced ('Oh wives of the Prophet ...') did not take these verses literally and lived their normal lives, inside and outside the house."

Allah is not ashamed of [expressing] the truth. And when you ask anything of [his] womenfolk, ask it from them from behind a curtain. That is more chaste for your hearts and their hearts. You may not torment the Apostle of Allah, nor may you ever marry his wives after him. Indeed, that would be a grave [matter] with Allah. Q. 33:53

The jurisprudential restriction on remarrying the Prophet's wives, which appears at the end of this verse, has already been discussed in the previous section of this chapter. The first part of this verse will be explored in the following section, when we delve into the matter of the Prophet's marriage to Zaynab bint Jahsh. The part relevant to our discussion here is "when you ask anything of [his] womenfolk, ask it from them from behind a curtain." It was common practice among the Medinan society for neighbors to borrow basic household items from each other. Still, in the case of the Prophet's wives, the Qur'an directs Muslims to ask for things from behind the hijab. While the contemporary use of the word "hijab" implies Muslim women's head covering, in this verse it refers to a barrier[19] that is exclusively ordained for these women and not understood to be incumbent on other Muslim women, then or now.[20] Once again, the nuanced motherhood of these women is iterated as being distinct from that of biological mothers.[21]

Al-Tabari implies that the concealment verse was revealed when Umar suggested to the Prophet that his women be secluded and not permitted to meet visitors freely.[22] His commentary on this verse includes traditions that suggest a policing of these women's piety and mobility by Umar. In one instance, he commanded Zaynab to stay behind a curtain. She replied, "Will you adjudicate (with jealousy) while divine verses descend in our home?" The hijab verse was revealed at this time.[23] In another instance, when Sauda left her house for something she needed, Umar called out, "You are not hidden from me. I see you. You should be mindful of leaving the house." She returned to the Prophet and asked if she was in the wrong. He affirmed that there was no problem with her leaving the house for her needs.[24] Reports such as these

---

[19] For example, it is written in Q. 42:5: "It is not [possible] for any human that Allah should speak to him except through revelation or from behind a curtain [hijab] or send a messenger who reveals by His permission whatever He wishes."
[20] Shirazi, *Tafsir Namuna*, vol. XVII, 333.
[21] Islamic piety does not require conversing with biological mothers from behind a curtain.
[22] al-Tabari, *Jaame Al-Bayan*, vol. XIX, 164.
[23] Ibid., 165.
[24] Ibid., 168.

infuse a gendered hierarchy perceived by early hadith and exegetical literature, and obstruct an ethical reading of the text, which might, as stated in the previous section, be a command to protect the bodies and sanctity of women perceived as "mothers." Perhaps the commandment "Do not trouble the Prophet" might be indicative of such an adjudication of his women by the Muslim men of his time and, by establishing such behavior as authoritative, legitimize the policing of future generations of Muslim women and their bodies.

Hadith restricting women's mobility and agency continue to misconstrue the Prophetic teachings as oppressive, hindering Muslim women from relating to a lifestyle that the Prophet's wives chose for themselves. Stowasser remarks that, after the Prophet's demise, Umar forbade the Prophet's wives from performing Umra (Lesser Hajj) and Hajj. After decades of pleading, they were allowed to travel to Mecca under escort.[25] Aisha Geissenger suggests that the pietistic seclusion of the Prophet's wives was constructed by early male authorities and augmented by classical exegetes and hadith scholars. As elite women, their status was not just that of honorific mothers but also informed a social order of privilege, insofar as access to these women was selective.[26] Similarly, the abode of the Prophet's wives remained under the gaze of Muslim exegetes and historians who authored the *sunna* to reflect the cultural, social, and religious norms constructed by the cultural patriarchy of their time, arguing for their "gendered hierarchical constructions as divinely ordained."[27]

The third, fourth, and fifth injunctions are to "maintain prayer," "pay the zakat," and "obey Allah and His Apostle." Together, these three directives represent Islamic practice and ethics. While *salat* and zakat refer to foundational ritual practice, "obey Allah and His Apostle" indicates an Islamic ethical lifestyle emulated by the Prophet. Despite being addressed to the Prophet's wives, these three injunctions pertain to all believers, women and men.[28]

Finally, the Qur'an directs the Prophet's wives to "remember what is recited in your homes of the signs of Allah and wisdom." Exegetes have widely interpreted "the signs of Allah" (*ayat*) as the universe's way of

---

[25] Barbara Stowasser, "The Mothers of the Believers in the 'Hadith'," *The Muslim World* (Hartford) 82, nos. 1–2 (1992): 1–36, https://onlinelibrary.wiley.com/doi/10.1111/j.1478-1913.1992.tb03539.x

[26] Aisha Geissinger, *Gender and Muslim Constructions of Exegetical Authority: A Rereading of the Classical Genre of Qur'ān Commentary* (Leiden: Brill, 2015), 229.

[27] Ibid., 40.

[28] Shirazi, *Tafsir Namuna*, vol. XVII, 248.

pointing towards its Creator. In this verse, however, *ayat* refers to Qur'anic verses. In the same way, "wisdom" (*hikma*) has been understood as a virtue, but in this verse it refers to divine revelation.[29] Whenever *ayat* and *hikma* appear together in a verse, the former has been understood as the literal word of the sacred text. The latter has, at times, been interpreted as the esoteric meanings of the word and, at others, a reference to the Prophetic *sunna*, which constitutes a crucial resource in understanding the context and application of the word. Q. 33:34 implores the Prophet's wives to be mindful of the responsibility that comes with the privilege of inhabiting the home where divine revelation (*ayat*) and wisdom (*hikma*) descend.

The wives had the privilege of living at the location of revelation and the beacon of education and reform from where divine teachings emanated and spread across space and time. Qur'anic teachings spread far and wide, and the accounts of the Prophetic home became an essential resource for understanding and interpreting Qur'anic verses. Their proximity to this nexus of revelation would attract the curiosity of knowledge-seekers, and every aspect of their lives would be scrutinized to unravel deeper understandings of *ayat* and *hikma*, as they would continue to affect the lived experiences of Muslims for centuries beyond the women's lifespans.

While Q. 33:32–34 addresses the Prophet's wives, the doctrinal, ritual, and ethical injunctions apply to all Muslims. Ninth-century classical exegetes and hadith scholars interpreted these verses as injunctions of female piety and prescribed them to Muslim women, constructing a social order where pious Muslim women were confined to their homes and the pleasure of their husbands determined their eternal abode in the hereafter. In their effort to authoritatively justify their cultural norms, they presented the Prophet's wives paradoxically: as role models when they endorsed hadith advancing gendered hierarchies, and as competitive wives overpowered by women's nature, when traits such as jealousy and conspiring are arguably part of human nature. Reading their narratives from a perspective of empowerment, however, depicts them as women trying to do what was humanly possible to live a pious life, braving the unjust norms of seventh-century Arabian society. They are role models for all human believers endeavoring to live by a divine code. These women mothered an inspiring pietistic paradigm, if not a perfect lifestyle.

[29] "Signs" and "wisdom" have appeared together elsewhere in the Qur'an. For example, Q. 2:231: "and remember Allah's blessing upon you, and what He has sent down to you of the Book and wisdom, to advise you therewith," and Q. 3:113: "Allah has sent down to you the Book and wisdom."

MOTHERING SOCIAL REFORM

In this section, I explore the narrative of the Prophet's marriage to Zaynab bint Jahsh, which did not only agitate the social norms of seventh-century Arabia: its telling by ninth-century classical hadith scholars and exegetes and its retellings by Orientalists and contemporary scholars have also negatively affected the integrity of the Prophet's character. Drawing on classical and contemporary engagements with Q. 33:36–40, I argue that Zaynab worked as a divine agent, supporting the Prophetic mission of pushing back against class discrimination and advancing social reform, even if it rocked her personal life and jeopardized her public image. The Qur'an documents her marriage(s) as follows:

> A faithful man or woman may not, when Allah and His Apostle have decided on a matter, have any option in their matter, and whoever disobeys Allah and His Apostle has certainly strayed into manifest error. When you said to him whom Allah had blessed, and whom you [too] had blessed, "Retain your wife for yourself, and be wary of Allah," and you had hidden in your heart what Allah was to divulge, and you feared the people though Allah is worthier that you should fear Him, so when Zayd had got through with her, We wedded her to you, so that there may be no blame on the faithful in respect of the wives of their adopted sons, when the latter have got through with them, and Allah's command is bound to be fulfilled. There is no blame on the Prophet in respect of that which Allah has made lawful for him. Allah's precedent with those who passed away earlier – and Allah's commands are ordained by a precise ordaining – such as deliver the messages of Allah and fear Him, and fear no one except Allah, and Allah suffices as reckoner. Muhammad is not the father of any man among you, but he is the Apostle of Allah and the Seal of the Prophets, and Allah has knowledge of all things. Q. 33:36–40

Exegetes and historians posit the context of the revelation of these verses (*asbab al-nuzul*) as the saga of Zaynab's marriage to Zaid, which ended in divorce, and her subsequent marriage to the Prophet.[30] The episode became a sensitive issue, perking the imaginations of early Muslims and sparking controversies among *sira* authors. Zaid was Khadija's slave, and after she married the Prophet, he came to live with them. The Prophet freed Zaid and allowed him to return to his tribe, but he chose to continue living with Khadija and the Prophet. So, the couple

---

[30] al-Tabari, *Jaame Al-Bayan*, vol. XIX, 113, 114.

adopted him as their son. When the Prophet proclaimed Islam, Zaid was among his early followers.

As guardian of his adopted son, the Prophet proposed that Zaid be married to Zaynab. Her family disapproved of the marriage, because they believed they were higher in status. In the spirit of Qur'anic teachings' challenging unjust societal norms, Q. 33:36 was revealed, reminding Zaynab's family of their commitment to the faith. Class discrimination was a feature of pre-Islamic Arabian society, and, as the family of the Prophet, they had a duty to emulate the Qur'anic reforms. While marriage cannot be coerced on any woman or man in the Islamic tradition, this was a unique case, divinely orchestrated to demonstrate the Prophet's authority over the Muslims, albeit in advancing a reformative praxis. In this case, "the matter" decided by "Allah and His Apostle" is interpreted as the marriage of Zaid to Zaynab, leaving Zaynab and her family with "no option" but to submit, or else they would "certainly [have] stray[ed] into manifest error." Zaynab's situation was "unlike [that of] any other women," and her compliance with God's plan makes her a mother of social reform.

The marriage, however, was turbulent. Q. 33:37 alludes to several mediations by the Prophet, counselling Zaid to pursue ways of holding on to his wife and "be wary of Allah." While historians have not documented details, the couple's incompatibility is generally attributed to differences in their social statuses and personal dispositions. Nonetheless, despite the Prophet's counsel, their marriage ended in divorce. Up until this point, Zaynab's narrative appears to be fraught with social and cultural stigmas: marriage to someone lower in status, justified as being "decided" by God and mediated by the Prophet, and finally ending in divorce. The saga took on a new oddity when Q. 33:37 commanded the Prophet to marry Zaynab as another divine command, stating, "We [God] wedded her to you."

Even though the verse goes on to explain the reason behind the divine injunction of the Prophet's marriage to Zaynab as "so that there may be no blame on the faithful in respect of the wives of their adopted sons, when the latter have got through with [divorced] them," *sira* authors presented another, romanticized version of the saga. Al-Tabari recounts an event where, as the Prophet was walking by Zaid's residence, a gust of wind lifted the curtain, allowing him a brief view of Zaynab. This incident awakened feelings of desire within him. Upon hearing Zaid's inclination towards divorce, the Prophet concealed his emotions and advised Zaid to reconsider and keep his marriage intact. Al-Tabari's account suggests that the verse "you had hidden in your heart what Allah was to divulge, and you feared the people though Allah is worthier that you should fear Him" relates to the Prophet's hidden feelings for Zaynab. These feelings, if exposed, might have subjected him to public mockery. However, Allah was cognizant of the Prophet's desires, and, following the conclusion of Zaynab's marriage to Zaid, divinely instructed the Prophet to marry her.

Contemporary Muslim scholars have responded to this alternate narrative in different ways. Despite its being recorded by early hadith scholars, Muhammad Ali Qutb blames Orientalists for conjuring up such fabrications "to diminish the status of the prophethood."[31] Calling it "the lovestruck narrative," Hasan Ashraf examines the authenticity of early traditional scholarship on the matter, deeming it "logically unfeasible" and iterating that the sole purpose of the marriage was to bring about social reform.[32] Bint al-Shati acknowledges that reports about the Prophet's desire for Zaynab were written by Muslim traditionalists a long time before the Orientalists and missionaries, but offers an interesting twist, stating that this episode depicts the Prophet as a person who never "pretended to be free from human sentiments and whims." He demonstrated "chastity, self-control, and restraint," despite his attraction to Zaynab while she was still married to Zaid.[33]

In contrast to the romanticized *sira* literature, Q. 33:38–40 provide a straightforward premise for Zaynab's saga – the Prophet must "deliver the message[s]" and "fear no one except Allah," because even though Arabian culture deemed marrying the divorced wife of an adopted son as taboo, the Islamic reform made it clear to them that "Muhammad is not the father of any man." The verses emphasize to the Prophet the duty of conveying divine messages, regardless of how unsettling or transformative they may seem. It's crucial to recognize that the implementation of these significant social reforms was a joint effort with Zaynab. Her participation was indispensable; without it, these profound changes could not have been achieved. Overlooking her contribution diminishes the narrative of a woman who embraced the divine decree, leading a life that boldly challenged pre-Islamic social and class hierarchy. This highlights the profound shifts advocated by Islamic theology and legal principles.

[31] Muhammad Ali Qutb, *Women around the Messenger*, trans. Abdur-Rafi' Adewale Imam (Riyadh: International Islamic Publishing House, 2007), 97.
[32] Hasan Ashraf, *The Prophet's Marriage to Zaynab bint Jahsh: A Reexamination from a Historiographic Perspective*, Yaqeen Institute, March 2, 2022, https://yaqeeninstitute.org/read/paper/the-prophets-marriage-to-zaynab-bint-jahsh.
[33] Bint al-Shati, *Wives of the Prophet*, trans. Matti Moosa (New Jersey: Gorgias Press, 2006), 149.

The marriage was so instrumental in challenging Arab culture that the wedding feast is also elaborated upon in the Qur'an. As mentioned in the previous section, the first part of Q. 33:53 is in the context of Zaynab's wedding feast. Al-Tabari reports that the Prophet sent Anas ibn Malik to invite everyone to the wedding feast. Guests arrived before the set time and stayed well after the feast. The Prophet tried respectful ways of letting them know that it was time for them to leave. They remained inattentive, so the Prophet left and returned after some time to find these individuals still lingering at his house. At this point, Anas states, "the verse was revealed, commanding the guests to leave."[34] Shirazi notes that Zaynab's wedding feast was a significant social occasion, and the Prophet intentionally organized it as such to underscore the reformative impact it had on transforming pre-Islamic social and cultural norms.[35] Despite the social ridicule and cultural frustrations her marriage invoked, Zaynab remained grateful that she was the only woman whose marriage to the Prophet was decreed in the Qur'an.[36]

Verses 33:36 and 33:37 challenged two prevailing norms of pre-Islamic Arabia, eroding the distinctions in class hierarchies and clearly differentiating between the legal and social statuses of biological and adopted sons. Arabs took pride in their tribal superiorities and looked down upon enslaved people; by arranging Zaynab's marriage to Zaid, the Prophet was demonstrating class equality. Similarly, the Arabs deemed that the wife of an adopted son held the same position as the wife of a biological son, such that it would be a social taboo to marry the divorcee of an adopted son. The Prophet's marriage to Zaynab was a radical clarification of the jurisprudential distinction between adopted and biological children. The embodiment of these two social reforms disrupted the cultural norms of Arabia and consequently placed the Prophet in a vulnerable position. Overshadowed by the narratives of early Muslim biographers, which were later reinterpreted by Orientalists as "lovestruck" stories, and the efforts of contemporary Muslim scholars to shift the emphasis towards the Prophet's human qualities – though notably pious – is the courageous role of a woman who aligned herself with a divine purpose. Her experience as a woman married to a formerly enslaved person, then divorced, then remarried to the Prophet to mother social reform put her in a vulnerable situation, not just during her life but also amidst the retelling of her story through the biased gaze of early Muslim scholars.

[34] al-Tabari, *Jaame Al-Bayan*, vol. XIX, 164, 165.
[35] Shirazi, *Tafsir Namuna*, vol. XVII, 330, 331.
[36] al-Tabari, *Jaame Al-Bayan*, vol. XIX, 118.

MOTHERING ACTIVISM

Another social activist among the Prophet's wives is Umm Salama. While much has been recorded about her in early and contemporary scholarship, in this section I will highlight her role in supporting Fatima, the Prophet's daughter, in her stand against Abu Bakr, in Sunni tradition known as the first Rightly Guided Caliph, for her inheritance rights. For publicly defending Fatima against the caliph, she was denied her stipend for that year.[37] Umm Salama is revered for being among the early Muslims and having migrated both to Abyssinia and Medina.[38] While Shi'i and Sunni historians have included her among authentic narrators of hadith, she enjoys a unique position in the Shi'i tradition because of her proximity to Fatima and Ali. She oversaw Fatima's wedding feast and helped raise her children, al-Hasan and al-Hussain. Muhammad Baqir Al-Majlisi (d. AH 1111/1699 CE) narrates that she became the custodian of the legacies, including books and weapons for Ali, al-Hasan, and al-Hussain. When Ali traveled to Iraq, he left them with her to hand over to his successor, al-Hasan, who charged her with guarding them for al-Hussain. When al-Hussain left for Karbala, he left the items with her to hand over to his son, al-Sajjad, who would survive the massacre of Ashura and return to Medina.[39]

Umm Salama's standing among Shi'i historians as second to that of Khadija is due to the many narrations she transmitted about Ali's succession to the Prophet and her counselling Aisha against leaving her home to rise against Ali in the Battle of Jamal.[40] Recent scholarship by Christopher Clohessy and Yasmin Amin suggests that she also played a crucial role in the Karbala narrative and served as a religious authority authenticating the position of the Imams. In his *Angels Hastening: The Karbala Dreams*, Clohessy elaborates on her mystical encounters regarding the Karbala narrative. It is important to note that hadith literature includes narratives of the Prophet's wives' miraculous experiences and abilities.[41] Clohessy draws on Umm Salama's witnessing of the Prophet miraculously receiving the news of his grandson, Hussain's, killing

---

[37] Dhabih Mahallati, *Rayahin al-Shari'ah* (Tehran: Dar Kutub al-Islamiyyah, 2010), vol. II, 25.
[38] Nahleh Gharavi Naeeni, *Shi'ah Women Transmitters of Hadith* (Qum: Ansariyan Publication, 2011), 91.
[39] Muhammad Baqir al-Majlisi, *Bihar al-Anwar* (Beirut: Dar Ihya al-Turath al-Arabiyya, 2000), vol. XXII, 223.
[40] Sayyed Murtaza, *Rasa'il al-Sharif al-Murtaza* (Qum: Manshurat al-Qur'an al-Karim, 1989), vol. IV, 67.
[41] Stowasser, "The Mothers of the Believers," 16.

during the Umayyid reign in Karbala, Iraq. Ibn Hanbal narrates that the angel also delivered the dust from Karbala along with the news.[42] The Prophet placed the dust in a vial. On his death bed, the Prophet entrusted the vial to Umm Salama, stating that the day the dust turned to blood would be the day that al-Hussain was killed in Karbala.[43] Analyzing Shi'i and Sunni renditions of this hadith, known as *hadith al-qarura* (the tradition of the glass vial), Clohessy states:

> It is, [however], within the precincts of Umm Salama's own house that the most salient angelic encounters occur, transforming her family home into the locus of divine activity and embedding her deeply into the Karbala event … It is through a crack in that door that Umm Salama will herself be an eyewitness to an angelic visitation … It is here too, in her own residence, that Umm Salama will receive the dust of Karbala, secreting it in a simple glass vial which becomes the central feature of the narrative.[44]

Furthermore, the Prophet entrusted her with a unique book that would serve as documentary evidence, consolidating the authority of the twelve holy Imams in Fatima's progeny. Shi'i theologians hail Umm Salama as the bearer of critical textual proof of the authority of Imams in the Twelver Shi'i tradition. In Islamic theology, *nass* is one of the fundamental proofs of imamate and comprises textual designations by the Qur'an and hadith.[45] Muhammad ibn al-Hasan al-Saffar (d. 903 CE) narrates that Umm Salama said, "The Prophet sat with Ali in my house and asked for a sheepskin. He dictated, and Ali wrote till the entire sheepskin was covered, even the margins. The Prophet then entrusted the writing to me, saying, 'Give it to the person bearing such-and-such signs who comes seeking it after my demise.'" Umm Salama held on to it and waited as Abu Bakr came to power, then Umar, and then Uthman, but none of them came to her seeking it. When Ali became caliph, he came to Umm Salama and retrieved it. She handed it over to Ali and advised her son never to leave his side, as no one after the Prophet is more fit to be an Imam.[46] Yasmin Amin delves

---

[42] Imam Ibn Hanbal, *Kitab Fadha'il al-Sahaba* (Jeddah: Dar al-Ilm li-Tiba'at wa-Nashr, 1983), vol. II, 770.

[43] Shaikh al-Mufid, *Al-Irshad fi Mar'rifat Hujaj Allah ala al-Ibad* (Beirut: Mu'assassat Aal al-Bayt, 2008), vol. II, 130, 131.

[44] Christopher Paul Clohessy, *Angels Hastening: The Karbala Dreams* (New Jersey: Gorgias Press, 2021), 99.

[45] Muhammad bin Jarir bin Rustam al-Tabari, *Dala'il al-Imama* (Qum: Mu'assassat al-Bi'tha, 1992), 18.

[46] Muhammad ibn al-Hasan al-Saffar, *Basa'ir al-Darajat* (Beirut: Sharikat al-A'lamiyy li-al-Matbu'at, 2010), 198–199.

deeper into Umm Salama's role as the *hafizat al-nass* (keeper of the *nass*) as an example of female religious authority within the Shi'i tradition.[47]

For this chapter, I want to highlight Umm Salama's social activism in supporting Fatima's stand against Caliph Abu Bakr. Soon after the Prophet's demise, Abu Bakr confiscated Fatima's lands in Fadak. When she demanded an explanation, she was asked to produce proof of ownership. Fatima rallied amongst Muslims to testify on her behalf. While prominent men like Ma'az bin Jabal declined to support her, fearing the consequences of agitating political authorities, two women responded to her call: Umm Ayman, the woman who had raised the infant Prophet, and Asma bint Umays, who was married to Abu Bakr at the time. Asma's support for Fatima provoked not just the political leader but also threatened her social status as the caliph's wife.[48] Despite the courageous stand of these women, their testimonies were denied.

Fatima then asked for Fadak as her inheritance. At this point, Abu Bakr said that he heard the Prophet say that prophets do not leave inheritances, and their assets become state properties. In response to the attribution of this hadith to her father, Fatima delivered a public protest in the mosque, which is referred to as the *Khutba al-Fadakiyya* or sermon of Fatima.[49] Fatima drew on five Qur'anic verses to critique the hadith produced by Abu Bakr, boldly putting forth her question, "Is it in the Book that you [Abu Bakr] may inherit from your father and I cannot inherit from mine? You have certainly come up with an odd thing!" (Q. 19:27).[50]

Umm Salama's opportunity to join Fatima's stand emerged when she heard Fatima delivering her sermon in the Prophet's Mosque. It was rare for women to publicly address a male-dominated audience. The eleventh-century historian al-Tabari al-Saghir[51] narrates that when

[47] Yasmin Amin, "Umm Salama: A Female Authority Legitimating the Authorities," in *Female Religious Authority in Shi'i Islam: Past and Present*, ed. Mirjam Künkler and Devin J. Stewart (Edinburgh: Edinburgh University Press, 2021), 74.

[48] Mahjabeen Dhala, *Feminist Theology and Social Justice in Islam: A Study on the Sermon of Fatima* (Cambridge: Cambridge University Press, 2024), 89.

[49] For more details on this sermon, see ibid. and Alyssa Gabbay, "Heiress to the Prophet: Fatima's Khutba as an Early Case of Female Religious Authority in Islam," in *Female Religious Authority*, ed. Künkler and Stewart, 78–104.

[50] Ahmad Ibn Tayfur, *Balaaghat al-Nisa'* (Qum: Intesharat Maktab al-Haideriyya, 1999), 25.

[51] Muhammad bin Jarir bin Rustam al-Tabari, who was a contemporary of Shaykh al-Tusi (d. 1067), is a Shi'i historian and is referred to as al-Tabari al-Saghir so as not to be confused with the popular Sunni historian and exegete, Muhammad bin Jarir bin Yazid al-Tabari. Al-Tabari al-Saghir's *Dala'il al-Imama* is sometimes attributed to another Shi'i scholar by the same name who lived a century earlier. The original manuscript is missing the first few pages, which makes it difficult to ascertain the precise date of death of the author. See Afzal Sumar, review of *Fatima, Daughter of*

Umm Salama heard Fatima imploring the Muslims for justice, she appeared from behind the curtain and said:

> Are the likes of Fatima addressing the crowds, for she is a houri among humans and a human among souls, raised in the lap of prophets, attended to by the hands of angels, brought up in pure thresholds, originated from the best origin, and educated by the best pedagogue?! Are you alleging that God's Messenger would deny her inheritance rights without informing her, while the Qur'an states, "And warn [O Prophet] your nearest relations" (Q. 26:214). Will you reprimand her for raising her claim? At the same time, she is the best of women, the mother of the chiefs of paradise [Hasan and Hussain], the like of Maryam, daughter of Imran, wife of the lion among his contemporaries?! Through her father, God completed His messages. By God! He [the Prophet] stood by her in the heat and the cold, leaning on her from his right and covering her with his left. Tread carefully, for God's Messenger witnesses your transgression, and you will undoubtedly return to God. Woe be to you! You will soon know the consequence of your act.[52]

Much like Umm Ayman and Asma, Umm Salam's interjection was dismissed by the caliph. Fatima returned home, having lost her inheritance, and Umm Salama was denied her stipend for that year. In this narration, Umm Salama emerges as a mother of social activism, setting a precedent for supporting Muslim women arguing for their rights from a religious perspective.

CONCLUSION

Early biographical accounts of the Prophet's wives are deeply influenced by the works of classical exegetes and hadith scholars. These scholars, predominantly male, compiled their narratives around a century after the Prophet's death. As a result, their writings reflect the cultural, social, political, and sectarian predispositions of their time, despite being indispensable for understanding Islamic law, Qur'anic interpretation, and moral principles. The Qur'an praises the Prophet's wives as exceptional and as the mothers of the believers. However, early Islamic literature often interprets these accolades to

---

Muhammad, by Christopher Clohessy, *Journal of Shi'a Islamic Studies* 8, no. 1 (winter 2015): 97.
[52] al-Tabari, *Dala'il al-Imama*, 124.

support patriarchal values, which seems at odds with the Qur'anic principle of justice. In response, modern feminist scholarship critiques these early texts, advocating for a re-evaluation of the Prophet's wives beyond their traditional roles to recognize their contributions to piety, social change, and activism. This chapter argues for employing contemporary insights on "non-normative mothering" to appreciate their influence in fostering a devout community, driving societal reforms, and inspiring activism. Far from being merely rivals for the Prophet's attention, they emerge as a powerful group whose legacy continues to inspire and empower, addressing complex issues in today's Muslim world.

SELECT BIBLIOGRAPHY

Ali, Kecia. "A Beautiful Example: The Prophet Muhammad as a Model for Muslim Husbands." *Islamic Studies* 43, no. 2 (summer 2004): 273–291.

Amin, Yasmin. "Umm Salama: A Female Authority Legitimating the Authorities." In *Female Religious Authority in Shi'i Islam: Past and Present*, ed. Mirjam Künkler and Devin J. Stewart, 47–77. Edinburgh: Edinburgh University Press, 2021.

Ascha, Ghassan. "The 'Mothers of the Believers': Stereotypes of the Prophet Muhammad's Wives." In *Female Stereotypes in Religious Traditions*, ed. Ria Kloppenborg and Wouter J. Hanegraaff, 89–107. Leiden: Brill, 1995.

Ashraf, Hasan. *The Prophet's Marriage to Zaynab bint Jahsh: A Reexamination from a Historiographic Perspective*, Yaqeen Institute. March 2, 2022. Updated: November 24, 2023 https://yaqeeninstitute.org/read/paper/the-prophets-marriage-to-zaynab-bint-jahsh

Bint al-Shati, *Wives of the Prophet*. Trans. Matti Moosa. New Jersey: Gorgias Press, 2006.

Brant, Jennifer. "Aboriginal Mothering: Honouring the Past, Nurturing the Future." In *Mothers, Mothering and Motherhood across Cultural Differences: A Reader*, ed. Andrea O'Reilly, 7–40. Bradford: Demeter Press, 2014.

Clohessy, Christopher Paul. *Angels Hastening: The Karbala Dreams*. New Jersey: Gorgias Press, 2021.

Dhala, Mahjabeen. *Feminist Theology and Social Justice in Islam: A Study on the Sermon of Fatima*. Cambridge: Cambridge University Press, 2024.

Gabbay, Alyssa. "Heiress to the Prophet: Fatima's Khutba as an Early Case of Female Religious Authority in Islam." In *Female Religious Authority in Shi'i Islam: Past and Present*, ed. Mirjam Künkler and Devin J. Stewart, 78–104. Edinburgh: Edinburgh University Press, 2021.

Geissinger, Aisha. *Gender and Muslim Constructions of Exegetical Authority: A Rereading of the Classical Genre of Qur'an Commentary*. Leiden: Brill, 2015.

O'Reilly, Andrea. "African American Mothering: 'Home Is Where the Revolution Is'." In *Mothers, Mothering and Motherhood across Cultural Differences*, ed. Andrea O'Reilly, 93–118. Bradford: Demeter Press, 2014.

Pappano, Margaret Aziza and Olwan, Dana M. *Muslim Mothering: Local and Global Histories, Theories, and Practices*. Bradford: Demeter Press, 2016.

Qutb, Muhammad Ali. *Women around the Messenger*. Trans. Abdur-Rafi' Adewale Imam. Riyadh: International Islamic Publishing House, 2007.

Roded, Ruth. "Bint al-Shati's 'Wives of the Prophet': Feminist or Feminine?" *British Journal of Middle Eastern Studies* 33, no. 1 (May 2006): 51–66.

Stowasser, Barbara. "The Mothers of the Believers in the 'Hadith'." *The Muslim World (Hartford)* 82, nos. 1–2 (January–April 1992): 1–36, https://onlinelibrary.wiley.com/doi/10.1111/j.1478-1913.1992.tb03539.x.

Part II

Asserting Agency in Faith

In the opening part of this volume, readers are introduced to the dynamic and expanding field of research on female mosque movements, notably pioneered by Saba Mahmood's seminal work, *The Politics of Piety*. This discourse has been enriched further by various scholars, including my contributions. The research has evolved from an initial focus on acknowledging the agency of Muslim women in cultivating an ethical self, to a broader understanding that pursuing piety need not exclude worldly pursuits and desires. We see how believing women exercise significant agency in their faith engagement, skillfully merging study and contemplation to align the fundamental teachings of their religion with everyday life. This includes a balance between adherence to essential beliefs and adaptability in practices of secondary importance. The chapters in Part II highlight the inherent flexibility within Islamic scholarly tradition, allowing for discussion and varying interpretations on a range of issues, yet upholding a consistent set of core principles.

The chapters in this part present extensive insights from numerous ethnographic studies on Muslim women's active involvement with Islamic teachings, showcasing their adeptness at navigating and adjusting religious directives. This includes making pragmatic adjustments in areas open to negotiation – such as working in mixed-gender settings or distributing responsibilities within partnerships – while steadfastly upholding key tenets like the prohibition on extramarital sexual relations.

Chapter 6 delves into Salafism, known for its conservative, literal approach to Islam, which is closely associated with the Saudi Wahhabi tradition. This branch is particularly noted for its stringent views on female autonomy and mobility. Some practices, like full facial veiling, are viewed by many in the larger Muslim community as excessively conservative. In this chapter, Arndt Emmerich and Alyaa Ebbiary examine the burgeoning research on female Salafis, seeking to understand how they navigate their lives within the confines of strict Islamic principles while still asserting their autonomy. They organize the literature into three phases of research: initial Salafi-phobia, characterized by perceptions of Salafi women as passive victims; a subsequent shift towards philo-Salafi perspectives that focus on the women's intrinsic motivations and their internalized sense of empowerment; and a current trend that looks at new understandings of female Salafi agency. This progression from viewing Salafi women through a lens of victimhood to recognizing their active participation and autonomy reflects a significant shift, moving away from simplistic portrayals towards an appreciation of the nuanced roles these women occupy within the Salafi movement.

The latest development in Salafism research introduces a nuanced, longitudinal approach, spotlighting the evolving and multifaceted identities and agencies of female Salafis. This approach critiques both external and internal perspectives that have historically pigeonholed Salafi women within simplistic narratives of victimization or bottom-up agency. The authors illustrate that recent studies unveil the sophisticated decision-making processes of Salafi women, highlighting the malleability of their association with Salafism over time. They record that while Salafism may initially offer empowerment, its influence can wane, prompting some women to critically reassess Salafi gender norms, particularly after life-changing events like marriage or childbirth. Nonetheless, these individuals often navigate a complex path to understanding Salafi gender discourses independently, without renouncing their Salafi identity. This body of work documents their deep engagement with theological discourse and the nuanced negotiation of personal beliefs in their everyday lives.

A parallel discussion emerges in Chapter 7, by Liv Tønnessen, regarding women in political Islam movements. Tønnessen examines the significant roles women play within Islamic political parties, especially those influenced by the Muslim Brotherhood in the Middle East and North Africa. With a focus on movements such as Ennahda in Tunisia and various Islamist factions in Sudan and Egypt, she investigates how these groups interpret and apply gender ideologies. Echoing classical Islamic scholarship on gender norms, Tønnessen points out that these ideologies rest on the concept of complementarity, advocating distinct, biologically based roles and responsibilities for men and women as prescribed by Islam. Her analysis sheds light on how women within these movements actively engage with and influence ongoing religious debates on gender roles, moving beyond reductive portrayals of them as mere passive recipients of patriarchal dictates.

Tønnessen further explores the inclusion–moderation hypothesis, which posits that Islamic political parties may enhance women's roles purely for strategic reasons. Yet, contemporary scholarship challenges this view, arguing it overlooks the complex agency of women. Through her extensive research with women in Islamist political parties in Sudan, Tønnessen reveals how these women skillfully negotiate and challenge established gender norms while still embracing the Islamic principles of gender complementarity and justice. This chapter counters the argument that shifts in ideological stances regarding women's roles are solely strategic, underlining the critical role of women's agency in the ideological transformation and integration process. It questions the stark dichotomies often drawn between Islamic and secular frameworks, advocating for a deeper appreciation of Muslim women's agency.

Tønnessen notably addresses the activism of Islamist women in opposing gender-biased laws and practices. She illustrates how women associated with the Muslim Brotherhood in Egypt and Islamist movements in Sudan have advocated for reforms in line with Islamic tenets of gender equity, challenging patriarchal interpretations and practices in the process. In Sudan, she points out how, over three decades, Islamist governance has shifted towards a more inclusive view of women's empowerment, progressively adopting interpretations of Islam that support broader rights for women under the banner of gender equity and complementarity. These women have been at the forefront of advocating for legal reforms, such as establishing a minimum marriage age, through an Islamic legal framework that harmonizes these reforms with sharia law.

In Chapter 8, Vanessa Vroon-Najem explores the complex motivations behind Western women's conversion to Islam, particularly in the Netherlands, challenging the oversimplified notion that marriage is the foremost reason. She reveals that the initial curiosity about Islam among these women frequently arises from existential inquiries and positive encounters with Muslims, including immigrants to the Netherlands and their descendants. Despite their initial interactions with born Muslims, who may find it challenging to express the principles of their faith, women interested in conversion actively seek a deeper understanding through various channels, such as literature, digital platforms, and women-only groups.

Contrary to common assumptions, the study underscores that personal belief is a significant factor in women's conversion to Islam, with many converting while single, thus reframing misconceptions about women's autonomy in their conversion journey. Invoking Saba Mahmood's work, Vroon-Najem critiques the traditional feminist view of agency as merely the ability to resist societal norms. This interpretation often overlooks the nuanced agency of women converting to Islam, perceiving their decision through a prejudiced lens that associates conversion with the forsaking of women's rights.

The chapter also sheds light on the gender-specific and experiential aspects of converting to Islam, emphasizing the transformations in daily life and self-perception that accompany this spiritual path. Converts maintain their ethnic or national identities, yet their sense of

"Dutchness" is frequently scrutinized. In seeking knowledge and community, they engage with or establish Dutch-speaking Muslim women's groups. These grassroots efforts provide a platform to address the familial and societal challenges linked to their new Muslim identity and foster discussions among women from diverse backgrounds on practicing Islam. These communities, often spearheaded by volunteers known as "knowledgeable women," play a pivotal role in easing the converts' transitions by offering advice, organizing workshops, and creating online forums and social networks focused on Islamic sisterhood. This environment encourages women from various backgrounds to connect with and support each other in their active and creative journey of embracing Islam and living as Muslims.

In Chapter 9, Nina Nurmila offers an engaging overview of how Islamic feminist scholarship has reached a broader audience beyond Western academic circles in Indonesia, particularly through the efforts of a dynamic group of Indonesian scholars. These scholars, who have roots in traditional madrasas (Islamic schools) before advancing to university studies, include Nurmila herself, who has contributed to the discourse with her analysis of polygyny in the Qur'an. She outlines the pioneering methodological approaches of early Islamic feminists like Fatima Mernissi, Amina Wadud, and Asma Barlas, setting the stage for a deeper exploration. Nurmila highlights how, from the mid 1990s, the translation and increased accessibility of works by these international scholars, coupled with the Pusat Studi Wanita (Women's Studies Center) initiatives to hold gender-training sessions on Indonesian campuses, were instrumental in spreading these feminist interpretations among a new generation of Indonesian scholars in Islamic and women's studies.

The chapter details a surge in gender-focused Islamic scholarship within Indonesia, significantly featured in publications managed by the Center for the Study of Gender and Children (PSGA). This blossoming of scholarly work has been pivotal in the rise of Indonesian Islamic feminists who champion gender justice in Muslim families and societies. Their contributions to transnational movements, such as Musawah, founded by Malaysian feminist Zainah Anwar, and their establishment of critical institutions and platforms in Indonesia, underscore their relentless pursuit of equality and justice. Nurmila introduces readers to the influential work of both male and female Indonesian scholars, trained in traditional Islamic settings, who advocate for gender equality by reinterpreting religious texts, particularly on issues intersecting with fundamental human rights. The chapter not only acquaints the reader with the reinterpretative strategies of early Islamic feminists, but also illustrates how these discussions permeate wider society through the engagement of traditional religious academies. By leveraging argumentation and reasoning intrinsic to vernacular Islamic literature, these debates have found a resonant audience, marking a significant chapter in the dialogue on gender and Islam.

The final chapter in Part II explores the experiences of Muslim women in China, highlighting the contrast between the austere Islamic gender norms in borderland Muslim communities, where women's mosques are historically absent, and the vibrant tradition of women's mosques in other parts of Chinese Muslim society, especially in central China. Maria Jaschok, drawing on her extensive research with Chinese Muslim women, situates these communities within a "diaspora" framework, emphasizing their connection to the global Muslim community (*ummah*) and how they have leveraged secular state pressures, particularly the Chinese Communist Party's reforms in education and women's rights, to their advantage. This has particularly benefited older generations of female religious leaders in the Hui communities, allowing for strategic negotiations for equality and legitimate access to religious and material resources.

The chapter also discusses intra-Muslim community dynamics, where the concept of equality is viewed through gender complementarity, emphasizing mutual respect and the historical solidarity between men and women in central China's Muslim communities. This tradition of gender complementarity has been crucial in the evolution of women's Qur'anic schools and mosques, marking them as an integral part of local Muslim culture. Furthermore, sustained solidarity has been essential for engaging with political, administrative, and civil society groups, ensuring the survival and relevance of mosques in a non-Muslim society. This interdependence between women's and men's mosques, shaped by realpolitik, allows for negotiation and a degree of independence for women's religious spaces.

In Zhengzhou, Henan Province, the improved education and material status of younger generations of female religious leaders have facilitated greater religious and social mobility. This revival of the expressive culture of women's mosques has also sparked debates and criticisms regarding the "feminization" of Islamic life in central China, pointing to the complex and evolving nature of gender dynamics within these communities.

MASOODA BANO

6 Becoming Salafi

ARNDT EMMERICH AND ALYAA EBBIARY

In December 2022, one of the authors of this chapter received a text message from a long-standing Salafi interlocutor in Germany during the football World Cup in Qatar. The content entailed a link to the article 'Moroccan players prefer to celebrate with their mothers after winning: What are the roots of this all-encompassing motherly love?' The activist was happy that the national, centre-left newspaper *Süddeutsche Zeitung* had published such a 'well-balanced' and 'positive' article, including authentic citations from the Qur'an, reflecting the high status of mothers and women in Islam. One week later, one of Germany's most recognizable Salafi preachers, Pierre Vogel, addressed the World Cup in relation to the role of women in Islam during an online seminar 'Lessons from the World Cup in Qatar'. With an emotional intonation, Vogel recalled:

> when the Moroccan players ran to their mothers, even the kuffar were impressed! Normally they [Western football players] go to their super-model girlfriends, while the Moroccans go straight to their mothers, who all wear headscarves, *Subhan Allah* [Praise be to God]. What an amazing message! Usually, the world thinks women wearing a veil are backward, but now these mothers of football celebrities are wearing a veil. One of them was even wearing a niqab, *Subhan Allah*. These are [beautiful] images. In Germany, a woman with a veil is still perceived as uneducated and oppressed, who has nothing to say and has no value [in the public eye]. During the World Cup, however, during the Moroccan games, everyone saw the value of a women [in Islam]. Such images, I believe, achieve more than a thousand words.

These vignettes capture some of the themes which this chapter seeks to address, namely the contested debates of passive victimhood, agency, and the difference of external and internal accounts regarding Salafi women. Salafism is seen to be a particularly conservative form of Islam that is associated with the Saudi Wahhabi tradition, is very literal in its interpretations, and is particularly restrictive of female agency and basic mobility.[1] The choices exercised by some women members of Salafi movements, such as full facial coverage, are viewed as extreme by the majority of Muslim women. This chapter focuses on female Salafis to understand how these women rationalize living by a particularly conservative mode of Islam, while also showing that they constitute a minority and express agency. The chapter will draw from scholarship regarding the quietist form of Salafi movements, which focuses on imparting Islamic knowledge but also introduces the sensitive issue of radicalization among Muslim women, especially as witnessed in the case of ISIS (Islamic State of Iraq and Syria), which claims to be Salafi in creed. Contemporary Salafis have been characterized most prominently by Wiktorowicz[2] as: quietist (those who focus on daily practice and *da'wa* (call to Islam), and accept secular governments); politicos (those who advocate for political action to establish an Islamic state); and jihadis (those who excommunicate deviants and propagate political violence). Debates on the fluidity and validity of these categories and hybrid identities are ongoing.[3] Bonci recently added a (long-overdue) gender perspective to the extensive critique of Salafi labels: 'despite the uncompromising textual injunctions about how Salafi women should behave and perform their piousness, the Salafi trends are more internally divided and incoherent than Wiktorowicz's categorization shows.'[4]

By bringing together the academic literature on quietist, political, and Salafi jihadi women, the authors critically discuss three overlapping research phases: (1) Salafi-phobia, (2) philo-Salafi perspectives, and

---

[1] Salafism is frequently associated with the Islamic reformists (modernists) Jamal al-Din al-Afghani (d. 1897) and Muhammad 'Abduh (1849–1905) in the nineteenth century, as well as contemporary Sunni reform movements – influenced by the religious establishment of Saudi Arabia and vocally opposed to other Islamic traditions. Salafis, in the latter understanding as contemporary Sunni reformists, promote a return to the practice and reading of the Qur'an and Sunna (literature that prescribes Islamic customs and practices of the Islamic community) that follows a continuous chain of narrations and Islamic practice, which can be traced to the first three generations of the Prophet Muhammad's companions (*sahaba*). Because of their exclusive claim to authenticity, Salafis frequently stress that only the Salafi *'aqida* (creed) offers exemption from divine punishment.

[2] Quintan Wictorowicz, 'Anatomy of the Salafi Movement', *Studies in Conflict and Terrorism* 29, no. 3 (2006): 207–39.

[3] Joas Wagemakers, 'Revisiting Wiktorowicz: Categorising and Defining the Branches of Salafism', in *Salafism after the Arab Awakening: Contending with People's Power*, ed. Francesco Cavatorta (New York: Oxford University Press, 2017), 7–24.

[4] Alessandra Bonci, '*Ilmi* Salafi Women in Tunisia after the Revolution: What Kind of Quietism?', *Contemporary Islam* 17, no. 2 (2023): 243–62, 250.

(3) new trends in the study of female Salafi agencies. First, we argue that notions of Salafi women were initially dominated by external, academic, and media accounts defined by essentialist and static views of false consciousness, passive female victimhood, grooming, and manipulation – a phase we refer to as Salafi-phobia. In these descriptions, Salafi women mainly play an instrumental role within a movement defined by men. The second development, we show, can be understood as a response to these passive and essentializing portrayals of Salafi women in relation to security concerns and moral panics. This emerging internal perspective has been established through detailed qualitative and ethnographic research endeavours, painstakingly investigating the inside worlds and intrinsic motivations of Salafi women. Notions of agency, autonomy, and empowerment obtained through the Salafi creed, a heightened sense of belonging, the appeal of alternative lifestyles, and counterculture featured prominently in this literature on quietist, political, and Salafi jihadi women. We refer to this phase as philo-Salafi.

Third, we introduce a new development within contemporary research on Salafi women that stresses the importance of long-term social processes and identity formations, which highlights the complex nature of theological and pragmatic agencies, and thereby aims to generate a non-essentialist Salafi perspective. This latest phase points out that both external and internal Salafi perspectives reduced Salafi women to certain monolithic narratives and trajectories between dominant discourses of passive victimhood and agency from below. This has led to the third phase in the study of Salafism, namely a processual and long-term research framework that focuses on dynamic boundary processes, negotiations, and ambivalences with uncertain outcomes regarding female Salafi identities and agencies.

Drawing on insights from a vast number of empirical studies from Asia, the Middle East, Africa, and Europe, we argue that these developments and discussions are taking place across all Salafi categories in the Global South and North and within Muslim-minority and Muslim-majority situations, without however sidelining the geographical nuances and variations at the micro and macro levels, which will be addressed throughout the chapter. Salafism has developed local roots with contextual understandings and pragmatic applications of the Salafi method (*manhaj*) to the everyday challenges of young Muslims in minority and majority contexts.[5] Against this backdrop the present chapter speaks to

---

[5] Masooda Bano, *Modern Islamic Authority and Social Change, Volume I: Evolving Debates in Muslim Majority Countries* (Edinburgh: Edinburgh University Press,

the recent scholarship on Salafism that stresses the importance of parallel and entangled histories, polycentrism, regional variations, and multiple theological, cultural, and socio-economic factors which explain the heterodox manifestations of the movement across the world.[6]

LACK OF RESEARCH ON SALAFI WOMEN

Negotiating access and building rapport within securitized and comparatively insular Salafi communities are recurring challenges for field researchers.[7] In this difficult context, academic projects on Salafism have predominately focused on men, due to a specific Salafi belief separating the private and public spheres along rigid gender boundaries. Such symbolic demarcations have impeded the production and circulation of teaching material, books, and recorded presentations by female activists that could be studied.[8] They also created difficulties for researchers to gain access to female spaces and respondents, especially since most of the research on the subject has been conducted by men.[9] Unsurprisingly, histories, organisational developments, attempts at institutionalization, internal conflicts, and schisms, but also the everyday realities, negotiations, and challenges of Salafi movements across the world, have been predominantly written from a male Salafi perspective.[10]

2018); Arndt Emmerich, 'Salafi Youth Activism in Britain: A Social Movement Perspective', *Journal of Muslims in Europe* 9, no. 3 (2020): 3–34; Anabel Inge, *The Making of a Salafi Muslim Woman: Paths to Conversion* (New York: Oxford University Press, 2016).

[6] Phillip Bruckmayr and Jan-Peter Hartung, 'Introduction: Challenges from "The Periphery"? Salafi Islam outside the Arab World: Spotlights on Wider Asia', *Die Welt des Islams* 60, nos. 2–3 (2020): 137–69.

[7] Sabine Damir-Geilsdorf and Mira Menzfeld, '"Looking at the Life of the Prophet and How He Dealt with All These Issues": Self-Positioning, Demarcations and Belongingness of German Salafis from an Emic Perspective', *Contemporary Islam* 10 (2016): 433–54; Emmerich, 'Salafi Youth Activism in Britain'.

[8] Inge, *The Making of a Salafi Muslim Woman*.

[9] Iman Dawood, 'Reworking the Common Sense of British Muslims: Salafism, Culture, and Politics within London's Muslim Community', PhD diss., London School of Economics, 2021; Inge, *The Making of a Salafi Muslim Woman*; Sara Silvestri, 'Faith Intersections and Muslim Women in the European Microcosm: Notes towards the Study of Non-Organized Islam', *Ethnic and Racial Studies* 34, no. 7 (2011): 1230–47; Joas Wagemakers, *Salafism in Jordan: Political Islam in a Quietist Community* (Cambridge: Cambridge University Press, 2016).

[10] M. J. M. de Koning, *Changing Worldviews and Friendship: An Exploration of the Life Stories of Two Female Salafists in the Netherlands* (Oxford: Oxford University Press, 2009); Jonathan Laurence, *The Emancipation of Europe's Muslims* (Princeton: Princeton University Press, 2011); Richard A. Nielsen, 'Women's Authority in Patriarchal Social Movements: The Case of Female Salafi Preachers', *American*

This gender bias seems to multiply for empirical investigations into Salafi–jihadi groups, which have neglected the experiences of women.[11] After 9/11 in particular, scholarly attention has largely focused on male Salafi activism, due to security concerns and relations with violent extremism, in which women were not understood as active agents[12] but as part of the wider pyramid and support structure. This inattention to female Salafi activists in the literature of the Global South and North reflects a larger issue within the study of women in Islamic movements, who are often only mentioned as 'an appendix of men's religious authorities'[13] resulting 'from their perceived lack of relevance in the study of power and resistance'.[14]

Notwithstanding the persistent overrepresentation of male voices within academia, a small but growing body of scholarship with an analytical focus on Salafi women from different analytical angles has been emerging. This includes studies on everyday practices, negotiations, the conversion processes of female Salafis in different European contexts,[15] Asia,[16] and the Middle East,[17] and the changing role of female preachers

Journal of Political Science 64, no. 1 (2020): 52–66; Meijer Roel, *Global Salafism: Islam's New Religious Movement* (London: Hurst, 2009).

[11] Kathrine Elmose Jørgensen and Henriette Frees Esholdt, '"She Is a Woman, She Is an Unbeliever – You Should Not Meet with Her": An Ethnographic Account of Accessing Salafi-Jihadist Environments as Non-Muslim Female Researchers', *Journal of Qualitative Criminal Justice and Criminology* 10, no. 3 (2021): 1; Michael Kenny, *The Islamic State in Britain: Radicalization and Resilience in an Activist Network* (New York: Cambridge University Press, 2018); Hamoon Khelghat-Doost, 'The Strategic Logic of Women in Jihadi Organizations', *Studies in Conflict and Terrorism* 42, no. 10 (2019): 853–77; Elizabeth Pearson and Emily Winterbotham, 'Women, Gender and Daesh Radicalisation: A Milieu Approach', *The RUSI Journal* 162, no. 3 (2017): 60–72.

[12] Inge, *The Making of a Salafi Muslim Woman*; de Koning, *Changing Worldviews and Friendship*.

[13] Eva F. Nisa, 'Embodied Faith: Agency and Obedience among Face-Veiled University Students in Indonesia', *Asia Pacific Journal of Anthropology* 13, no. 4 (2012): 366–81.

[14] Laila Makboul, 'Beyond Preaching Women: Saudi Dāʿiyāt and Their Engagement in the Public Sphere', *Die Welt des Islams* 57, nos. 3–4 (2017): 303–28.

[15] Dawood, 'Reworking the Common Sense of British Muslims'; Inge, *The Making of a Salafi Muslim Woman*; Martijn de Koning, 'The Moral Maze: Dutch Salafis and the Construction of a Moral Community of the Faithful', *Contemporary Islam* 7 (2013): 71–83; de Koning, *Changing Worldviews and Friendship*; Esra Özyürek, *Being German, Becoming Muslim: Race, Religion, and Conversion in the New Europe* (Princeton: Princeton University Press, 2014); Ineke Roex, 'Should We Be Scared of All Salafists in Europe? A Dutch Case Study', *Perspectives on Terrorism* 8, no. 3 (2014): 51–63.

[16] Nisa, 'Embodied Faith'; Eva F. Nisa, 'Women and Islamic Movements', in *Handbook of Islamic Sects and Movements*, ed. Muhammad Afzal Upal and Carole M. Cusack (Leiden: Brill, 2021), 151–75, 151.

[17] Bonci, '*Ilmi* Salafi Women in Tunisia'.

and influencers in Saudi Arabia, in particular through social media,[18] as well as female jihadi Salafis who support Daesh (ISIS).[19] Methodologically, recent scholarship has addressed the impact of the different positionalities of those researchers setting out to study and access different female Salafi milieus.[20] To better understand the lifeworlds of Salafi women, a wide range of theoretical concepts, beyond grievance explanations, have been applied, including moral community and relationality frameworks,[21] social movement theories,[22] concepts of new religious movements,[23] counterhegemony within commonsense behaviour,[24] and feminist theories of gender as socially constructed.[25] Informed by these vast empirical debates and theoretical applications, we will now sketch out three significant developments in the study of Salafi women over the last twenty years.

SALAFI-PHOBIA AND THE NOTION OF PASSIVE SALAFI WOMEN

Ideas of female Salafis have been dominated by academic and media accounts and perspectives defined by essentialist and static notions of passive female victimhood, grooming, and manipulation, where women played mainly an instrumental role within a movement defined by men.[26] Public perceptions of Salafi women have consequently been

---

[18] Makboul, 'Beyond Preaching Women'; Nielsen, 'Women's Authority'; Amélie le Renard, 'From Qur'ānic Circles to the Internet: Gender Segregation and the Rise of Female Preachers in Saudi Arabia', in *Women, Leadership, and Mosques: Changes in Contemporary Islamic Authority*, ed. Masooda Bano and Hilary Kalmbach (Leiden: Brill, 2012), 105–26.

[19] Jørgensen and Esholdt, 'She Is a Woman'; Pearson and Winterbotham, 'Women, Gender and Daesh Radicalisation'.

[20] Martijn de Koning, Annelies Moors, and Aysha Navest, 'On Speaking, Remaining Silent and Being Heard: Framing Research, Positionality and Publics in the Jihadi Field', in *Jihadi Audiovisuality and Its Entanglements: Meanings, Aesthetics, Appropriations*, ed. Christof Günther and Simone Pfeifer (Edinburgh: Edinburgh University Press 2021), 27–50.

[21] de Koning, 'The Moral Maze'.

[22] Nina Wiedl, *Zeitgenössische Rufe zum Islam: Salafitische Da'wa in Deutschland, 2002–2011* (Baden-Baden: Nomos Verlag, 2017).

[23] Inge, *The Making of a Salafi Muslim Woman*.

[24] Dawood, 'Reworking the Common Sense of British Muslims'.

[25] Sara Jul Jacobsen, 'Calling on Women', *Perspectives on Terrorism* 13, no. 4 (2019): 14–26.

[26] Madawi Al-Rasheed, *A Most Masculine State: Gender, Politics and Religion in Saudi Arabia* (New York: Cambridge University Press, 2013); Irene Zempi and Neil Chakraborti, *Islamophobia, Victimisation and the Veil* (London: Palgrave Macmillan, 2014).

dominated by images of passive victimhood within the patriarchal structures of Salafism, which has provoked critical responses from (Islamic) feminists and secularists across political spectrums.

These perceptions have been influenced by grievance explanations within social movement theory: 'whether defined by cultural [and religious] alienation or political and economic deprivation, the rise of Islamic [and specifically Salafi] activism is typically portrayed as a collective protest against the abject conditions' in Muslim-majority and -minority contexts.[27] Muslim women and converts – so the rationale goes – are drawn to the rigid Salafi creed and lifestyle owing to their marginalized position with their own ethnocultural family milieus and wider experiences of alienation and rejection in society.[28] This assumed vulnerability makes Muslim women open to and tempted by the gendered discourses of male Salafi authorities,[29] offering a way out 'for young Muslims who are unable or unwilling to adjust'[30] to mainstream society.

Especially after the Arab Spring that began in the winter of 2010, when, in some instances, Salafi actors gained access to government power, concerns over deteriorating women's rights as a result of an anti-women agenda were expressed at the national and international level. Those women who adopted a Salafi lifestyle and attire in the public domain were framed as passive victims and linked to notions of 'sexual jihad in Syria'.[31] Such framing of passive Salafi women can also be seen in political strategies dealing with the prevention of violent extremism. Female Salafis are often seen as either less policy-relevant or as a first component towards radicalization.[32] In the UK, for example, the Home Office's Counter-Extremism Strategy categorizes quietist Salafis as non-violent extremists, who provide indirect assistance to violent Salafi–jihadi groups. The rationale for this can be found within so-called 'pyramid explanations' used by security agencies, which see

---

[27] Carrie Rosefsky Wickham, 'The Muslim Brotherhood in (Egypt's) Transition', in her *The Muslim Brotherhood: Evolution of an Islamist Movement* (Princeton: Princeton University Press, 2015), 247–88.
[28] Olivier Roy, *The Failure of Political Islam* (Cambridge, MA: Harvard University Press, 1994); Olivier Roy, *Globalized Islam: The Search for a New Ummah* (New York: Columbia University Press, 2004).
[29] Salman Sayyid, *A Fundamental Fear: Eurocentrism and the Emergence of Islamism* (London: Zed Books, 2015).
[30] Mohamed-Ali Adraoui, 'Salafism in France: Ideology, Practices and Contradictions', in *Global Salafism*, ed. Roel, 364–83.
[31] Iris Kolman, *Gender Activism in Salafism: A Case Study of Salafi Women in Tunis* (Oxford: Oxford University Press, 2017).
[32] Roex, 'Should We Be Scared of All Salafists in Europe?'

violent jihadis 'as the apex of a pyramid' built on sympathizers and bystanders 'who share their beliefs and feelings'. According to this logic, non-violent extremists such as female Salafis within this security framework are seen as ideological supporters who constitute the 'conveyor belt' for violent extremism.[33] Hence, although women have been important in supporting jihadi networks such as al-Qa'ida, if mostly in non-violent ways, security agencies and researchers on counterextremism were frequently 'bias[ed] against considering women, even when they are embedded in the roots of terrorist organisations'.[34] However, this has changed with the emergence of the Salafi–jihadi group Daesh/ISIS since 2012 and the subsequent recruitment of thousands of young women, mainly from the Middle East and North Africa, but also from Europe, South Asia, and other parts of the world. Daesh reached out to women as new citizens to help create a territorial Islamic state through marriage, child-rearing, online recruitment, and administrative tasks. In media and political debates women who supported or joined Daesh were portrayed as 'naïve' 'jihadi brides' being 'groomed' by male activists.[35]

Moreover, female participants of Salafi organizations are described as 'pawns in a grand patriarchal plan',[36] in which female behaviour and sexuality are monitored and sanctioned to enforce ideas of Islamic piety and modesty in relation to dress codes, traditional gender roles, and in particular motherhood. For Salafi movements and their male leaders, the protection of female piety and other gender boundaries constitute important mobilizing strategies for their own constituents and to discredit opponents. The idea of women as moral guardians, according to Mosse,[37] is manifested in the 'virtue to be exerted in a passive way, protecting the continuity and the immutability of the nation [or in this case religious community] and its morality'. The rationale for the 'grand patriarchal plan' can then be understood as giving women a certain degree of authority within patriarchal movements when it is politically useful, such as during election campaigns,[38] as maintained within the

[33] Emmerich, 'Salafi Youth Activism in Britain'.
[34] Pearson and Winterbotham, 'Women, Gender and Daesh Radicalisation'.
[35] Ibid.
[36] Saba Mahmood, *The Politics of Piety: The Islamic Revival and the Feminist Subject* (Princeton: Princeton University Press, 2005).
[37] George L. Mosse, *Nationalism and Sexuality: Middle-Class Morality and Sexual Norms in Modern Europe* (Madison: University of Wisconsin Press, 2020).
[38] Sarah Sunn Bush and Eleanor Gao, 'Small Tribes, Big Gains: The Strategic Uses of Gender Quotas in the Middle East', *Comparative Politics* 49, no. 2 (2017): 149–67; Nielsen, 'Women's Authority'.

moderation thesis. Wickham[39] argued in her study on political moderation processes in Egypt after the Arab Spring that Islamist groups have changed their political outlook and started to see that a departure from such 'illiberal features' as the shari'a, violence, and anti-democratic agendas, as well as a drive towards participation and gender equality, are viable organizational strategies. Women 'are helpful to patriarchal movements' as they can put forward 'persuasive arguments supporting patriarchy that men cannot', defend conservative gender norms, and 'draw in new audiences'.[40] However, doubts about the lasting effects and female agency remain, because critics contend that these reforms are mainly instrumental and superficial, as women are pressured to adopt the official narratives and policies of male-centric Salafi authority structures, without tangible results regarding gender equality.[41]

PHILO-SALAFI RESEARCH PERSPECTIVES

The second development that we introduce has occurred as a response to these largely negative and passive portrayals of Salafi women. An ambitious normative agenda within this internal Salafi perspective motivated these researchers from Islamic Studies and the social sciences more broadly to spotlight the lack of academic accounts of Salafism outside the purview of security studies, international relations, and radicalization frameworks.

The 'conveyor-belt' thesis has been criticized in this context for ignoring structural explanations and non-linear trajectories towards radicalization. Social milieu and media studies that focused on women joining Salafi–jihadi groups, for instance, showed that their motives 'to take part in jihad are complex and without clear patterns'.[42] Pearson and Winterbotham[43] summarized manifold motivations and reasons among women joining Salafi–jihadi groups, including the 'rejection of Western feminism; online contact with recruiters who offer marriage and adventure; the influence of peers or family; adherence to the ideology and politics of Islamic state; naïvety and romantic optimism; and the chance to be part of something new, exciting, and illicit'. In fact, non-violent Salafis rarely share the same social spaces with jihadi Salafis, who are opposed to each other. The majority of Salafi women have nothing to do

[39] Wickham, 'The Muslim Brotherhood'.
[40] Nielsen, 'Women's Authority'.
[41] al-Rasheed, *A Most Masculine State*; Nielsen, 'Women's Authority'.
[42] Jacobsen, 'Calling on Women'.
[43] Pearson and Winterbotham, 'Women, Gender and Daesh Radicalisation', 62.

with either political or jihadi groups or street and online *da'wa* activism, but tend to live privately.[44] Hence, researchers have increasingly criticized those grievance-based explanations and passive, grooming accounts of women joining Salafism, which pathologize women and deny their agency.[45] In her research on Dutch Salafis, including jihadis, Roex[46] was unable to find a 'connection between the Salafi movement and the violation of women's autonomy'. The prevalent male-centric and passive-grooming explanations, according to the dominant trend in the study of Salafism, are unable to create meaningful insights as to why women decide to become Salafi in the first place, which from a liberal perspective goes against their self-interest. Instead, these explanations leave many questions unanswered, which has motivated a new generation of scholars, committed to qualitative and ethnographic research methods, to explore the internal lifeworlds of female Salafis, and how they articulate their own ideas of Salafism in majority and minority contexts.

This rich empirical work from an internal Salafi perspective has employed an agency-from-below framework, in which Salafi women negotiate, reflect, and exert agency, which may (or may not) question and influence the Islamic authority structures. The agency approach within the study of female Salafis has been influenced by Saba Mahmood's pioneering work[47] on the role and impact of women in patriarchal *da'wa* and mosque movements in Egypt, in which she has shifted the debate on the veil and Islam away from the dominant discourse of resistance and repression. In doing so, her research has questioned Western feminist assumptions that women, if imbued with agency, would resist the (submissive) ideals, virtues, and moralities of patriarchal movements. Instead, she analysed female agency through the notions of modesty and piety, which had previously been associated with internalized oppressive dispositions by the victims of patriarchy. For instance, the veil is either worn functionally to get by in daily life or as resistance to the hegemony of secular norms. The deliberate choice of a pious life by Muslim women had rarely been accepted in public and academic discourse around the time Mahmood was writing. This Salafi perspective's conscious effort to study the everyday life-choices of

[44] Inge, *The Making of a Salafi Muslim Woman*; Emmerich, 'Salafi Youth Activism in Britain'.
[45] Quintan Wiktorowicz, *Islamic Activism: A Social Movement Theory Approach* (Bloomington: Indiana University Press, 2004).
[46] Roex, 'Should We Be Scared of All Salafists in Europe?', 59.
[47] Mahmood, *Politics of Piety*, 15–16.

female Salafis thus mirrors Mahmood's re-framing of Muslim women as empowered agents, who may choose to support patriarchal movements and ideologies. With this agency perspective in mind, a new research question has emerged, namely, if women can freely choose from the vast Islamic education market without external pressure, why do they opt for Salafism in its different manifestations, which ostensibly restricts and isolates them more than other Islamic schools of thought?

WHY IS SALAFISM SO APPEALING TO SOME WOMEN?

Although Salafism as a creed does not encourage female agency and autonomy from a Western feminist perspective, according to Roex's research[48] in the Netherlands Muslim women have turned to Salafism 'to achieve autonomy from their parents, family members or partners, and to break with traditions, like forced marriages, that hinder them in their personal development'. Within the internal Salafi perspective exists a consensus that the notion of female agency is linked to the importance of Salafi literalism, the rejection of cultural traditions, an emphasis on individual choices in studying and learning about Islam, a logical and rules-based pathway to achieve salvation, a strong focus on *tawhid* (the oneness of God) through which hardships (for being a Salafi) are interpreted as a divine challenge, a strong conviction of being part of a sect whose members are saved, and an empowering countercultural identity, and non-conformism towards other Muslim and non-Muslim groups.[49]

This agency and empowerment thesis is substantiated by the tendency of Salafi mosques and groups to be overall more welcoming to women and children, compared with other, in particular ethnic, mosque traditions. Özyürek has argued[50] that 'Salafi mosques are the only Muslim spaces in Germany where piety matters more than ethnic, [gender] or national background.' In 2021, 95 per cent of Salafi mosques in the UK had a women's section, in contrast to only 49 per cent in Deobandi mosques.[51] Similarly, the amount of female voices and participation on Salafi-run websites appears to be higher compared with websites of other Islamic traditions.[52] In addition, countries like Saudi

---

[48] Roex, 'Should We Be Scared of All Salafists in Europe?', 59.
[49] Inge, *The Making of a Salafi Muslim Woman*; de Koning, 'The Moral Maze'; de Koning, *Changing Worldviews and Friendship*; Özyürek, *Being German, Becoming Muslim*.
[50] Özyürek, *Being German, Becoming Muslim*.
[51] Dawood, 'Reworking the Common Sense of British Muslims'.
[52] Nielsen, 'Women's Authority'.

Arabia have witnessed a sharp rise in female Salafi preachers, initially in women-only spaces, but more recently in mixed online spaces. Some of these female Salafi influencers have more than a million followers on X, reaching mixed-gender audiences.[53] The rise of these newly emerging female Salafi authorities can partially be explained by the recent moves towards social liberation in Saudi Arabia, but also through their embeddedness within the local context, increasing levels of female education, and agency in navigating these traditional, male-dominated spaces.

Moreover, Salafism appeals to women of diverse ethnic, cultural, and religious backgrounds owing to its culturally neutral and post-ethnic understanding of Islam,[54] which reflects the lifeworlds of super-diverse and ethnically mixed European societies. Özyürek[55] describes the feeling of one of her Salafi respondents in a Salafi mosque in Berlin, enjoying the youthful and relaxed atmosphere. In Turkish mosques, her female interlocuter 'felt oppressed by older Turkish women, who seemed too serious'. Hence, Özyürek argues that 'certain characteristics of Salafism, particularly its conversionism [religious awakening], literalism, and anticulturalist, antinationalist stance, make it appealing to many Europeans of diverse backgrounds'. Salafism may thereby solve the identity crisis of young Muslims by mediating the tension arising from the competing demands of host country, family, and transnational expectations.

In this context, scholars such as Inge[56] have studied the empowering process of what it means to 'become Salafi' by looking at the long-standing scholarship on religious conversion[57] for women who have already been born into Islam and those who have just converted. This is important, given that a significant increase in conversions to Islam in Europe has coincided with the emergence of Salafism. Özyürek has shown[58] that female converts and Salafis in Germany are united in their 'call for a culture- and tradition-free Islam that speaks directly to

---

[53] Makboul, 'Beyond Preaching Women'; Nielsen, 'Women's Authority'; le Renard, 'From Qurʾānic Circles', 105–26; Amélie le Renard, *A Society of Young Women: Opportunities of Place, Power, and Reform in Saudi Arabia* (Stanford: Stanford University Press, 2014).

[54] Roy, *Globalized Islam*.

[55] Özyürek, *Being German, Becoming Muslim*, 128.

[56] Inge, *The Making of a Salafi Muslim Woman*.

[57] John Lofland and Rodney Stark, 'Becoming a World-Saver: A Theory of Conversion to a Deviant Perspective', *American Sociological Review* 30, no. 6 (1965): 862–75; Lewis Ray Rambo, *Understanding Religious Conversion* (New Haven: Yale University Press, 1993).

[58] Özyürek, *Being German, Becoming Muslim*, 5.

the rational individual'. Inge has also demonstrated[59] that those in her diverse sample of female Salafi respondents within London's Brixton mosque 'reached the conclusion that Salafism was the only correct approach to Islam [and ...] had all undergone more or less radical conversions'. De Koning[60] comprehends conversion to Salafism as a 'process of revitalisation', 'self-realisation', and 'symbolic transformation of a personal crisis' through the Salafi creed and networks. This newfound meaning and network help new adherents 'to rewrite their own life stories and to construct their sense of self as strong women'. His findings illustrate that the 'choices [of Salafi women] based upon free will and authenticity are valued above choices that are forced upon them by their parents'. Similarly, Inge[61] drew on McGuire's work[62] on conversion and the 'transformation of one's self', which implies consequential 'cognitive and behavioural changes'. Such self-transformations may result in a stricter form of dress sense and the sacrifice of many former habits and pleasures, as well as future opportunities, through gender and religious segregation. However, her data also suggest that becoming Salafi lacks 'uniformity and linearity, and often revealed the process of becoming Salafi to be interrupted and intermittent'.

Similar agency-led conversion and empowerment narratives can be found in the existing scholarship on Salafi women in Muslim-majority contexts such as Indonesia, Sudan, or Tunisia. In post–Arab Spring Tunisia, Kolman showed[63] how Salafi women reflected on the systemic relegation of Islam to the private sphere and police harassment under the secular authoritarian regime ('It was like hell with Ben Ali'). After the revolution, her female respondents 'experienced a sense of liberation'. The emotions of these young female Salafis in Tunisia mirror the personal accounts by Salafi women in Europe regarding self-transformation and a desire to 'reaffiliate with their religion' through 'a gradual process' influenced by micro- and macro-factors such as individual motivations, peer groups, and the political context.

However, becoming a Salafi woman within Muslim-majority contexts goes beyond its self-transforming and empowering potential. In fact, Salafism can become a form of political agency to defend gender

---

[59] Inge, *The Making of a Salafi Muslim Woman*, 6.
[60] de Koning, *Changing Worldviews and Friendship*.
[61] Inge, *The Making of a Salafi Muslim Woman*, 6–7.
[62] Meredith B. McGuire, *Religion: The Social Context* (Long Grove, IL: Waveland Press, 2008).
[63] Kolman, *Gender Activism in Salafism*.

segregation in the public sphere against political secularism in Sudan or Indonesia.[64] In Tunisia, Salafism has been linked to the hope of female political inclusion during the post-revolutionary process, given women's otherwise marginalized position in society. Kolman shows[65] that Salafi women 'believed their male counterparts to be the true protectors of the revolution and wish to participate in the project of turning Tunisia into a pristine Islamic society'. In other words, 'Salafism has become a vehicle through which part of the Tunisian youth remains protagonists of a revolution they see being hijacked by a generation of old politicians.'[66] One of Kolman's female respondents remarked in this context that 'You can't just sit around and let everything happen.' This echoes Shitrit's findings[67] of women activists in patriarchal movements, developing 'discursive framing tools to justify and promote forms of political [and social] participation that diverge from the gender ideology upheld by the [male leadership of the] movement'.

Moreover, the narratives of conversion, agency, and self-transformation are resonating with existing scholarship on Salafi women who joined or sympathized with ISIS. Scholars have shown that they 'reject gender equality'[68] while portraying themselves as empowered individuals, deliberately advancing ISIS's cause. In their milieu-based qualitative study in the UK, Canada, France, Germany, and the Netherlands,[69] Pearson and Winterbotham challenge the view of women who support Salafi–jihadi groups as 'innately peaceful', 'relatively innocent', 'lured', or 'coerced.' Such reductive counterterrorism and security-related narratives have 'reinforced gender stereotypes, such as the notion of the groomed and naive "jihadi bride"'. Similar to studies on quietist and political Salafi women that we reviewed earlier, these critical security-study scholars further stress the notion of female

---

[64] Nisa, 'Women and Islamic Movements', 151; Liv Tønnessen, 'Ansar Al-Sunna and Women's Agency in Sudan: A Salafi Approach to Empowerment through Gender Segregation', *Frontiers: A Journal of Women Studies* 37, no. 3 (2016): 92–124.

[65] Kolman, *Gender Activism in Salafism*, 190.

[66] Fabio Merone, Francesco Cavatorta, and Nouri Gana, 'The Rise of Salafism and the Future of Democratization', in *The Making of the Tunisian Revolution: Contexts, Architects, Prospects*, ed. Nouri Gana (Edinburgh: Edinburgh University Press, 2013), 258.

[67] Lihi Ben Shitrit, *Righteous Transgressions: Women's Activism on the Israeli and Palestinian Religious Right* (Princeton: Princeton University Press, 2015), 61.

[68] Esholdt, 'The Attractions of Salafi–Jihadism as a Gendered Counterculture: Propaganda Narratives from the Swedish Online "Sisters in Deen"', in *Salafi-Jihadism and Digital Media*, ed. Magnus Ranstorp, Linda Ahlerup, and Filip Ahlin (London: Routledge, 2022), 66–91.

[69] Pearson and Winterbotham, 'Women, Gender and Daesh Radicalisation'.

empowerment to understand the phenomenon of Salafi–jihadism. In the constrained societal and political contexts faced by Muslim minorities (e.g., during the French ban of the niqab) in particular, but also in the pre- and post-revolutionary contexts of North Africa and the Middle East, the opportunity for living an unrestricted religious life in a Daesh-controlled Islamic state has been perceived as empowering for some women. Hence, Pearson and Winterbotham's respondents[70] felt a heightened sense of agency by 'deliberately seeking to challenge both traditional and Western-imposed gender norms, [and] by seeking a new identity for themselves'.

This mirrors Esholdt's social media analysis[71] of the Swedish Salafi–jihadi group 'sisters in deen', which projects a self-image of 'strong, free, and empowered individuals – who wish to submit themselves to traditional gender roles' while promoting a 'gendered counterculture' against 'the Western world's "defeminisation" (and "demasculinisation") of the genders in late-modern society'. Hence these jihadi messages are 'rearticulating the records of tradition and history (e.g., by uploading stories of charismatic female fighters from the Prophet Muhammad's time and appealing to modern Muslim women to emulate their example) into emotions and aspects specific for contemporary Muslim western women'. In this context, 'Jihadi–Salafism becomes an important source not only of authenticity but also of strong self-identity and (em)power(ment).'[72]

While there is the common theme in the literature, whereby the Salafi creed may provide a route to self-realization and female empowerment at the individual level, in certain scenarios Salafism can also become a powerful resource for social and political recognition and – in rare cases – a specific form of empowerment conducive to condoning violent action, which reflects the messy and hybrid nature of (female) agency.

Contradictions, Pragmatism, and Compromises

According to the philo-Salafi perspective, the widely held assumption of Salafi women striving for total isolation and gender segregation through their assumed quest for doctrinal purity, as suggested in media portrayals and earlier studies,[73] has been debunked by empirical investigations into

---

[70] Ibid.
[71] Esholdt, 'The Attractions of Salafi–Jihadism', 83.
[72] Jacobsen, 'Calling on Women', 15.
[73] Adraoui, 'Salafism in France'; Sadek Hamid, 'The Attraction of "Authentic Islam": Salafism and British Muslim Youth', in *Global Salafism*, ed. Roel, 364–83.

the everyday realities of these women. In fact, the empowering process of becoming a Salafi woman – accompanied by increased autonomy and self-determination in relation to societal expectations and specific ethnic and cultural milieus – inevitably leads to contradictions and pragmatic compromises in both Muslim-minority and -majority contexts.[74] In his research on Salafis in Western Europe, de Koning[75] follows Schielke's critique[76] of Mahmood's work,[77] which overemphasized the search for moral perfection among Muslim women without sufficient attention to the daily struggles and ambiguities they face in their everyday lives, resulting in deviations from the Salafi ideal. However, it is precisely this tension between the ideal doctrine and messy reality that constitutes the 'incentive [for Salafi women] to continuously work on self-improvement and [...] fulfil their desire for moral perfection. It is in the effort of trying to achieve moral perfection that many Salafi Muslims take pride and feel empowered.'[78] For de Koning, Salafi women 'differentiate between unbelief and unbeliever – through that they can reject certain notions of practices but not the practitioners', such as friends, co-workers, or family members. Such everyday pragmatism is also manifested in adjustments of Islamic attire, language and behaviour, depending on the different macro and micro contexts (e.g., not wearing a full niqab in school or with parents, but during Salafi mosque or seminar visits). These findings on Salafi women mirror earlier studies on urban religions and lived religion, working out an everyday coherence through individual agency, navigation, and compromise,[79] which we will come back to in the conclusion.

Towards a Comprehensive Understanding of Female Salafi Agency

The agency-from-below agenda within the internal Salafi perspective has produced many insightful results regarding the study of Salafi women. However, this scholarship has failed to analyse the manifold internal negotiations of and resistance to the Salafi creed by Salafi women beyond pragmatic considerations, compromises, and adaptations, due to local

---

[74] Yunus Dumbe and Abdulkader Tayob, 'Salafis in Cape Town in Search of Purity, Certainty and Social Impact', *Die Welt des Islams* 51, no. 2 (2011): 188–209; Inge, *The Making of a Salafi Muslim Woman*; Kolman, *Gender Activism in Salafism*.

[75] de Koning, 'The Moral Maze'.

[76] Samuli Schielke, 'Being Good in Ramadan: Ambivalence, Fragmentation, and the Moral Self in the Lives of Young Egyptians', *Journal of the Royal Anthropological Institute* 15 (2009): 24–40.

[77] Mahmood, *Politics of Piety*.

[78] Koning, 'The Moral Maze', 79.

[79] McGuire, *Religion*.

constraints. In other words, the internal Salafi perspective has partially perpetuated the assumption that Salafi women would always aspire to achieve doctrinal purity and perfection within an ideal social scenario – thereby denying these women an all-encompassing understanding of agency capable of negotiating, criticizing, and amending the doctrine itself.

This omission is partially a result of the scholarly agenda to empower and return agency to Salafi women, thereby seeking to demonstrate 'normality' within everyday Salafism. In its attempt to prove the empowering potential of Salafism, the internal Salafi perspective, however, denied Salafi women certain aspects of their agency, in particular the ability to 'evaluat[e] Salafi viewpoints'.[80] For instance, Inge,[81] who acknowledges the practical constraints of local contexts, nonetheless stresses the overarching power of the Salafi creed. Provided that her female Salafi respondents 'accepted the authorities on which Salafism rests, they tend to internalize fully the Salafi system of reward and punishment'. For de Koning,[82] 'the ethics of pragmatism', however, 'remains firmly rooted in the ethics of duty that emanate from the Salafi understanding of the ambition to become a pious Muslim'. Similarly, Kolman argued[83] that for all Salafi women 'their religious and political identity as well as their ideology is based on a strict interpretation of the Qur'an and the Sunna [...] [while] their motivations, goals, and activities can all be placed within this conservative Islamic [Salafi] framework'. Scholars within the field of security studies have also adopted an agency approach, with often extreme interpretations, in which Salafism is seen as an escapist, all-encompassing model around rigid gender hierarchies, which draws women in, freeing them from decision-making burdens and self-doubts, while giving them a subjective sense of self- and status-improvement.[84]

Dawood has warned against such unidimensional agency frameworks that 'often stem from researchers' determination to counter existing essentialist discourses about "submissive Muslim women"'. Their eagerness to prove that 'women have willingly gravitated towards Salafism' as a response to the manifold victimhood accounts in security-related

---

[80] Sabine Damir-Geilsdorf and Mira Menzfeld, 'Who Are "the" Salafis? Insights into Lifeworlds of Persons Connected to Salafis(m) in North Rhine-Westphalia, Germany', *Journal of Muslims in Europe* 6, no. 1 (2017): 22–51.
[81] Inge, *The Making of a Salafi Muslim Woman*.
[82] Martijn de Koning, 'Between the Prophet and Paradise: The Salafi Struggle in the Netherlands', *Canadian Journal of Netherlandic Studies* 33, no. 2 (2012): 34.
[83] Kolman, *Gender Activism in Salafism*, 202.
[84] Ahmed Toprak and Gerrit Weizel, *Salafismus in Deutschland: Jugendkulturelle Aspekte, pädagogische Perspektiven* (Wiesbaden: Springer Verlag, 2017); Wiktorowicz, *Islamic Activism*.

studies can partially be explained by the academic legacy of Mahmood's understanding[85] of female agency: not through resisting conservative Islamic norms, but by choosing to live by them. However, this analytical lens on agency assumes that female Salafis 'will always be fully and firmly convinced that these discourses are the "Truth"'. Roex[86] has already addressed the 'pluriformity' within Dutch Salafism, namely the diversity in Salafi interpretations and practices of a seemingly unchangeable doctrine. She has further noted that Salafi interpretations, commitments, and practices are always in flux, due to their 'frequently non-binding, diverse, contradictory and temporary' characteristics. In this context, she recorded examples where Salafis 'form mixed groups, in which they combine Salafi ideas with those from Sufism or from the Maliki school'. These findings regarding the agency of Salafi women in engaging with Salafism in a complex and multidirectional manner has foreshadowed Dawood's extensive critique[87] of the existing agency-from-below approaches. These groundbreaking, yet narrowly conceptualized studies run 'the risk of further essentializing Muslim women and overemphasizing the role of Salafism [...] in these women's lives'. She points out that existing research tends to analyse Salafism through 'molecular phases' focusing on the empowering nature of the 'initial conversion' which sidelined the long-term aspects of 'women's experiences', including the life trajectories of children who grow up in Salafi families.

Through a historically grounded and life-history methodology, Dawood is able to capture common-sense decision-making strategies of Salafi women in the UK over a long period of time, demonstrating the ways her respondents 'at one point identify with certain elements of Salafism, but at a later point in their lives find these same elements, or other elements, to be impractical or problematic'. Her findings show that 'while Salafism (or certain Salafi discourses) may work to empower women [...], it can [also] stop having this same impact'. Using these long-term and complex experiences within different Salafi milieus, some of her respondents questioned Salafi gender norms, for instance after marriage or after having children. However, 'even in cases where women have found elements of Salafism to be problematic' Dawood convincingly demonstrates that the women 'themselves have come to this understanding on their own [...] critically examin[ing] Salafi gender

[85] Mahmood, *Politics of Piety*.
[86] Roex, 'Should We Be Scared of All Salafists in Europe?'
[87] Dawood, 'Reworking the Common Sense of British Muslims', 170.

discourses. This [self-reflexive] process [...] has in some cases involved a critical application of Salafi common sense such as ideas about the dangers of blind following. These women have thus not needed "saving" or completely abandoned Salafism.' Similarly, quietist female Salafis in the Muslim-majority context of Tunisia, according to Bonci,[88] are perfectly capable of 'engag[ing] in theoretical debates and negotiat[ing] their own derogations to the rule'. Through long-term fieldwork, she shows how women 'dare to discuss the Salafi principle of al-wala' wa-l-bara' in their daily lives,' while 'opening a debate on what entails being a Salafi woman entrepreneur'. Bonci, however, refrains from interpreting the findings as 'evidence of women's empowerment' but argues that 'context, traditions, and personal preferences influence the literal understanding of sacred texts'.

Dawood's and Bonci's studies mirror Emmerich's ethnographic findings[89] from within the quietist group Salafi Publications, near Birmingham, UK, in which activists reflected on their everyday navigations and compromises, for example when they prayed with Shi'a friends or in Deobandi mosques, visited seminars led by the Sufi scholar Timothy Winter, watched lectures by Zakir Naik on Peace TV (both were deemed deviant authorities by Salafi Publications), and exposed their children to Deobandi teachings or sent them to local nurseries. Other members expressed dissatisfaction with the weekly study circles and late-night seminar trips to Birmingham, describing them as 'not practical' and 'exhausting'. These narratives indicate the fluidity of everyday decision-making among Salafis, one activist noting 'We are all just normal people who try to practise our religion with authenticity, but otherwise we get on with our life like anyone else', implying the necessity for everyday compromises without striving for doctrinal perfection or attaining the best model of Islam.

These new research trends around a broader understanding of female agency speak directly to the latest academic discussion and the local turn in the study of Salafism, which employs processual approaches and shuns neatly categorizing Salafi behaviour and interpretations. Bruckmayr and Hartung,[90] for instance, question the notion of coherent Salafi actors as 'consistent representatives of clear-cut doctrinal camps' and instead focus on their changing, and often incoherent, positions within regionally (rather than transnationally) embedded Salafi (and non-Salafi) networks

---

[88] Bonci, '*Ilmi* Salafi Women in Tunisia'.
[89] Emmerich, 'Salafi Youth Activism in Britain'.
[90] Bruckmayr and Jan-Peter Hartung, 'Introduction', 139.

and opportunity structures. 'The assumption that the boundaries between the academic categories of Salafis [...] are rather impermeable' is misleading, according to Damir-Geilsdorf and Menzfeld,[91] who demonstrate that Salafi beliefs, practices, and theological commitments 'are deeply processual and not general, depending on how justified they are by scholars of a respective *manhaj* [...] or how certain guidelines seem to be proven by textual evidence'.

CONCLUSION

This chapter started with a vignette on external and internal perceptions of female Salafis during the 2022 World Cup in Qatar. Salafi activists in this context voiced reservations about the media portrayal of Muslim women as 'uneducated and oppressed' while juxtaposing the behaviour of pious mothers, hugging and kissing their sons after the football matches, as an example of female agency and self-determination. Subsequently, the chapter discussed the existing tension between scholarly accounts of passive victimhood and agency-driven choice-making among different types of Salafi women, drawing on the existing literature regarding quietist, political, and jihadi strands of Salafism in the Global South and North. These interrelated external and internal perspectives have recently led to new developments in the study of Salafi women. This could be seen in the re-conceptualization of a more comprehensive understanding of female agency, beyond the dominant frames of oppression, resistance, and piety, in which women question, modify, or reject (aspects of) the Salafi ideal within local, everyday life situations, and on their own terms.

Such re-conceptualization of female agency is important, as it shows that Salafi women, similar to other faith practitioners, do not always strive towards and adhere to the Salafi ideal under unrestricted socio-political conditions, as implied by internal Salafi perspectives in the past. Having engaged with these established and emerging debates for the study of Salafi women, the remaining part of the chapter will briefly outline some future analytical trajectories within this dynamic field. In particular, the recent proposal for the application of processual approaches and historically grounded methodologies for the study of Salafi women,[92] with its emphasis on temporality and complex negotiations over practice, doctrine, and the creed itself, is noteworthy and opens a new array of research

---

[91] Damir-Geilsdorf and Menzfeld, 'Looking at the Life of the Prophet', 452.
[92] Dawood, 'Reworking the Common Sense of British Muslims'.

avenues. In this context, upcoming research on Salafi women may benefit from the literature on urban religious networks and post-secular landscapes[93] in which Salafi women are embedded. According to Kuppinger,[94] 'religious transformation[s] do not occur apart from other urban processes, but are both reflective and constitutive of the former'. Hence, by employing the analytical framework of urban religions, future studies on Salafi women may be better equipped to unpack the existing tension between superimposed categories and doctrines, temporality and fluidity, and the participation and navigation of Salafi women in local urban contexts. Such a processual neighbourhood and milieu analysis thereby speaks to notions of post-Salafism and how Salafi ideas and lifestyles are disseminating across other Muslim groups and societies around the world, as it will inevitably include not only self-identifying Salafis, but the wider social and spiritual landscapes of which Salafi women are a part. For instance, similar to the intergenerational religious transmission of ultra-orthodox Jewish communities in the United States, neighbourhood encounters between Salafis and non-Salafis are happening and may not necessarily result in a decline in Salafism.[95] Such an application of a processual research perspective to female Salafi jihadi milieus may also add analytical value to the recent debate on female agency. Existing studies on female Salafi jihadis have predominantly focused on the negative dialectic of empowerment narratives through certain Salafi–jihadi doctrines and male-dominated networks, thereby depriving women of their full agency through time-sensitive questioning, internal negotiations, and reflections regarding theory and practice.

More recently, scholars have investigated how formally inward-looking Salafi actors have started to demonstrate knowledge of legal and human rights discourses and legal advocacy, owing to generational changes and shifting opportunity structures.[96] Themes of gender and women (e.g., defending the right to wear the niqab through court cases) play an important role in mobilizing supporters, building bridges with

---

[93] Paul Cloke and Justin Beaumont, 'Geographies of Postsecular Rapprochement in the City', *Progress in Human Geography* 37, no. 1 (2013): 27–51; Kim Knott, *The Location of Religion: A Spatial Analysis* (London: Routledge, 2015); Ceri Peach and Richard Gale, 'Muslims, Hindus, and Sikhs in the New Religious Landscape of England', *Geographical Review* 93, no. 4 (2003): 469–90.

[94] Petra Kuppinger, 'One Mosque and the Negotiation of German Islam', *Culture and Religion* 15, no. 3 (2014): 313–33.

[95] Inge, *The Making of a Salafi Muslim Woman*.

[96] Dawood, 'Reworking the Common Sense of British Muslims'; Arndt Emmerich, 'Arrival of Legal Salafism and Struggle for Recognition in Germany: Reflection and Adaptation Processes within the German *Da'wa* Movement between 2001 and 2022', *Politics and Religion* 16, no. 3 (2023): 416–34.

other conservative groups, and discrediting opponents. Future research thus needs to understand the role and impact of female Salafi activists, lawyers, and teachers on these new organizational developments of legal Salafism. Such analytical inclusion enhances our understanding of female involvement in the institutional development and other structural dimensions of past and contemporary Salafi movements. In sum, new lines of research are currently emerging that have the potential to reduce the current exceptionalism and sensationalism relating to Salafi women, thereby making them comparable to other social and religious phenomena and communities, and contributing to the emerging research field of post-Salafism.

SELECT BIBLIOGRAPHY

Bonci, Alessandra. '*Ilmi* Salafi Women in Tunisia after the Revolution: What Kind of Quietism?', *Contemporary Islam* 17, no. 2 (2023): 243–62.

de Koning, M. J. M. *Changing Worldviews and Friendship: An Exploration of the Life Stories of Two Female Salafists in the Netherlands*. Oxford: Oxford University Press, 2009.

Esholdt, Henriette Frees. 'The Attractions of Salafi-Jihadism as a Gendered Counterculture: Propaganda Narratives from the Swedish Online "Sisters in Deen"'. In *Salafi-Jihadism and Digital Media*, ed. Magnus Ranstorp, Linda Ahlerup, and Filip Ahlin, 66–91. London: Routledge, 2022.

Inge, Anabel. *The Making of a Salafi Muslim Woman: Paths to Conversion*. New York: Oxford University Press, 2016.

Jacobsen, Sara Jul. 'Calling on Women'. *Perspectives on Terrorism* 13, no. 4 (2019): 14–26.

Jørgensen, Kathrine Elmose and Frees Esholdt, Henriette. '"She Is a Woman, She Is an Unbeliever – You Should Not Meet with Her": An Ethnographic Account of Accessing Salafi-Jihadist Environments as Non-Muslim Female Researchers'. *Journal of Qualitative Criminal Justice and Criminology* 10, no. 3 (2021): 1.

Khelghat-Doost, Hamoon. 'The Strategic Logic of Women in Jihadi Organizations'. *Studies in Conflict and Terrorism* 42, no. 10 (2019): 853–77.

Kolman, Iris. *Gender Activism in Salafism: A Case Study of Salafi Women in Tunis*. Oxford: Oxford University Press, 2017.

le Renard, Amélie. *A Society of Young Women: Opportunities of Place, Power, and Reform in Saudi Arabia*. Stanford: Stanford University Press, 2014.

Makboul, Laila. 'Beyond Preaching Women: Saudi Dā'iyāt and Their Engagement in the Public Sphere'. *Die Welt des Islams* 57, nos. 3–4 (2017): 303–28.

Nielsen, Richard A. 'Women's Authority in Patriarchal Social Movements: The Case of Female Salafi Preachers'. *American Journal of Political Science* 64, no. 1 (2020): 52–66.

Nisa, Eva F. 'Women and Islamic Movements'. In *Handbook of Islamic Sects and Movements*, ed. Muhammad Afzal Upal and Carole M. Cusack, 151–75. Leiden: Brill, 2021.

Özyürek, Esra. *Being German, Becoming Muslim: Race, Religion, and Conversion in the New Europe*. Princeton: Princeton University Press, 2014.

Pearson, Elizabeth and Winterbotham, Emily. 'Women, Gender and Daesh Radicalisation: A Milieu Approach'. *The RUSI Journal* 162, no. 3 (2017): 60–72.

Tønnessen, Liv. 'Ansar Al-Sunna and Women's Agency in Sudan: A Salafi Approach to Empowerment through Gender Segregation'. *Frontiers: A Journal of Women Studies* 37, no. 3 (2016): 92–124.

7 Joining Political Islam

LIV TØNNESSEN

Women are active members of political Islamic movements.[1] This chapter will explore women's agency and their roles within these movements, and how these roles are justified within the framework of Islam. It will delve into the gender ideology of political Islam movements, which typically rely on the principle of complementarity: the idea that men and women have different rights and obligations due to their biological differences. A specific focus will be on the experiences of women participants in Muslim Brotherhood–inspired movements across the Middle East and Northern Africa. It will examine variations among these movements, from those affiliated with Ennahda in Tunisia to Islamist movements in Sudan, as well as the experiences of women activists in Egypt. The chapter will demonstrate how the gender norms idealized by women in these movements, legitimized within Islam, do not prevent them from being politically and socially active or even from challenging gender dogmas.

This chapter is divided into three main sections. The first section elaborates on gender complementarity and its interpretation by Islamists, how these interpretations have varied across different contexts, and how women themselves have actively participated in these evolving religious debates. The second section focuses on the inclusion–moderation literature, examining political pragmatism, and taking a critical look at the instrumental view of women's political participation. It demonstrates that the political context matters, but women find ways to navigate even under challenging political conditions. However, this literature has been criticized for overlooking women's agency. Therefore, the third section provides an overview of the literature that places women's political agency at the forefront. The chapter also includes a case study from

---

[1] Political Islam and Islamism are used interchangeably in this chapter to denote religious-political movements that employ Islamic symbols, draw on Islamic doctrine and tradition, and advocate for Islamic law to be part of the political system. The aims and objectives of Islamist movements vary widely, and so do their interpretations of Islam.

Sudan, based on original interviews, aiming to show how Islamist women are challenging gender dogmas while remaining committed to Islamist principles of gender complementarity and gender justice.

IDEOLOGICAL OUTLOOK: GENDER COMPLEMENTARITY

Islamic movements, similar to other religious and conservative groups and political parties, propose a gender ideology that is rooted in the biological differences between the sexes.[2] These movements advocate for the concept of complementarity rather than equality between men and women.[3] According to Islamist perspectives, this complementarity is based on the belief that men and women possess different, innate biological capacities and dispositions, which are seen as divinely ordained. As a result, women's role in reproduction is particularly emphasized, reinforcing the traditional division between private and public spheres of life.[4] Islamists argue that highlighting the complementary roles of men and women is crucial for maintaining Islamic piety. While their views on gender differences may preclude women from certain roles or activities, it is argued that men and women are of equal moral worth. This means that, from an ontological standpoint (concerning the nature of being), women are considered equal to men. However, they are seen as having different functions or roles due to their biological differences.

The term "complementarity" was heatedly debated in the wake of the Arab Spring in Tunisia (where it started in January 2011). During the debate on the first constitutional draft in August 2012, article 28 of the constitution aimed for complementarity (*yatakamul* in Arabic) rather than equality; it was later dropped after massive protests.[5] Complementarity is a concept often employed by Islamists to say that women and men have different rights and obligations within the family, society, and state.[6] In the words of Seesemann:

---

[2] Margot Badran, "Political Islam and Gender," in *The Oxford Handbook of Islam and Politics*, ed. John L. Esposito and Emad el-Din Shahin (Oxford: Oxford University Press, 2013), 112–124.
[3] Erika Biagini, "Islamist Women's Activism under Morsi's Government (2011–2013): Political Inclusion, Gender and Discourse," *Égypte/Monde arabe* 21 (2020): 37–55.
[4] Badran, "Political Islam and Gender."
[5] Mounira Charrad and Amina Zarrugh, "Equal or Complementary? Women in the New Tunisian Constitution after the Arab Spring," *Journal of North African Studies* 19, no. 2 (2014): 230–243.
[6] Loes Debuysere, "Tunisian Women at the Crossroads: Antagonism and Agonism between Secular and Islamist Women's Rights Movements in Tunisia," *Mediterranean Politics* 21, no. 2 (2016): 226–245.

Each sex has its own task to accomplish, on the family level as well as on the national level, and up to the level of the Muslim umma. If one of the two complementary partners fails to fulfill his assigned role, the functioning of society as a whole is called into question.[7]

Complementarity is placed within a paradigm of gender equity (*insaf*) often constructed as "modern" or "authentic Islam," which is juxtaposed both with traditional interpretations of Islam and "Western" notions of gender equality.[8] It can be traced back to Hassan al-Banna, the first leader of the Muslim Brotherhood in Egypt, who, in an article published in 1940 entitled *Risalah al Mar'a al Muslima*, wrote that "the difference between man and woman in rights is attributable to their different natures and in accordance with the different roles assigned to each".[9] Al-Banna's views have been echoed by many Islamists.[10] Although the term "equity" was first used by male Islamist leaders, it has been actively debated also by female Islamists. In the words of Suad al-Fatih al-Badawi, a leader of the Islamist movement in Sudan, "there is no equality in Islam in the Western sense, but there is equity [*Insaf*]. There is balance [...] men and women complete and perfect each other."[11]

The interpretations of complementarity vary between Islamic movements and across time periods, including how it mitigates women's role in political activism. However, there is wide agreement that complementarity entails different rights and obligations for women and men within the family sphere.[12] Within the private sphere, complementarity becomes closely entangled with *qawama*, which can loosely be translated as male guardianship.[13] It projects an ideal Muslim family where men are the guardians of and providers for the family and women the main carers. Therefore, women can only play a role in public life, including politics, if their primary responsibilities within the family are

---

[7] Rudiger Seesemann, "Islamism and the Paradox of Secularization: The Case of Islamist Ideas on Women in the Sudan," *Sociologus* 55, no. 1 (2005): 102.

[8] Liv Tønnessen, "Feminist Interlegalities and Gender Justice in Sudan: The Debate on CEDAW and Islam," *Religion & Human Rights* 6, no. 1 (2011): 25–39.

[9] Quoted in Mariz Tadros, "The Muslim Brotherhood's Gender Agenda: Reformed or Reframed?," *IDS Bulletin* 42, no. 1 (2011): 91.

[10] Eva F. Nisa, "Women and Islamic Movements," in *Handbook of Islamic Sects and Movements*, ed. Muhammad Afzal Upal and Carole M. Cusack (Leiden: Brill, 2021), 151–175.

[11] Interview with Suad al-Fatih al-Badawi, Khartoum, 2008.

[12] Badran, "Political Islam and Gender."

[13] Asma Abdel Halim, "A Home for Obedience: Masculinity in Personal Status for Muslims Law," *Hawwa* 9, no. 1 (2011): 194–214.

fulfilled and upon the consent or permission of the male guardian. This creates a tension between women's role in politics and their subordination to men within the family sphere. In contexts like Sudan, where the Islamists ruled the country for three decades (1989–2019), it was codified into law that women needed the permission of their male guardian to work outside of the home.[14] Thus, although the constitution granted women political rights, including the presidency, their constitutional political right was contingent on securing the permission of male guardians.[15]

Some Islamists have interpreted complementarity to exclude or restrict women's role in politics and public life more generally, thereby limiting women's role to the domestic sphere and family life.[16] For example, in Kuwait, male Islamist parliamentarians have repeatedly voted down proposals to grant women political rights in the country. In 2005, the enfranchisement of women was eventually passed in parliament, despite the continued opposition of Islamist.[17] The Muslim Brotherhood in Egypt issued its first statement on women as voters and candidates in 1994, declaring that women could run as candidates.[18] Meanwhile in Sudan, the first Islamist woman ran as a candidate for parliament, albeit with objections from conservative members of the Muslim Brotherhood, already in 1964.[19] The representation of women in the political structures and leadership of Islamist movements has thereby varied extensively across states.[20] Scholarship does suggest that the presence of women in political arenas is bearing positive results in terms of pushing women's rights onto the agenda; even in contexts like Kuwait, male Islamists and Salafists have become "reluctant feminists."[21]

[14] Samia al-Nagar and Liv Tønnessen, "Family Law Reform in Sudan: Competing Claims for Gender Justice between Sharia and Women's Human Rights," *CMI Report* no. 5 (December 2017): 1–27.
[15] Ibid.
[16] Badran, "Political Islam and Gender."
[17] Meriem Aissa, "Kuwait: Why Did Women's Suffrage Take So Long?," in *The Palgrave Handbook of Women's Political Rights*, ed. Susan Franceschet et al. (London: Palgrave Macmillan, 2019), 201–212.
[18] Anwar Mhajne and Rasmus Brandt, "Rights, Democracy, and Islamist Women's Activism in Tunisia and Egypt," *Politics and Religion* 14, no. 4 (2020): 577–608.
[19] Liv Tønnessen, "An Increasing Number of Muslim Women in Politics: A Step towards Complementarity, Not Equality," *CMI Brief* no. 3 (2018): 1–5.
[20] Katarina Škrabáková, "Islamist Women as Candidates in Elections: A Comparison of the Party of Justice and Development in Morocco and the Muslim Brotherhood in Egypt," *Die Welt Des Islams* 57, nos. 3–4 (2017): 329–359.
[21] Rania Maktabi, "Reluctant Feminists? Islamist MPs and the Representation of Women in Kuwait after 2005," *Die Welt des Islams* 57, nos. 3–4 (2017): 429–457.

However, the advocacy for a more active role for women in politics became evident in most mainstream Islamist movements well before the Arab Spring.[22] Islamist women took an active part in these debates in ways in which Azza Karam has described as Islamist feminism.[23] Different interpretations emerged which justified women's public participation, including in political activism.[24] However, the ways that female Islamists have entered the political arena, through politicization of motherhood and biological essentialisms, have limited and restricted the ways in which they *can* exercise political agency, according to a range of scholars within the field.[25] In the words of Biagini, it "limits their participation in the public sphere to areas that reflect such a gender complementarity and are considered non-threatening to men's status and leadership."[26] In the draft political program presented by the Muslim Brotherhood in Egypt in 2007, it was explicitly stated that it is not desirable for a woman to be president, because the head of state will also be the leader in war, something that is not in harmony with female nature.[27] Even in areas where women have equal rights and constitutional access, their roles are often framed and recognized primarily within the context of "the family" as the central unit of productivity and the domain where women are considered to excel.[28]

Another restriction or limitation is related to women's mobility in the public arena. Since most Islamist movements regard public spaces as "masculine", restrictions are put on women by advocating for gender segregation, as in the case of Hamas[29] or the Salafi movement in Sudan.[30] This is to avoid the dangers of gender-mixing between unrelated men and

---

[22] Bjørn Olav Utvik, "What Role for the Sisters? Islamist Movements between Authenticity and Equality," *Religions* 13, no. 3 (2022): 1–10.

[23] Azza Karam, *Women, Islamisms and the State: Contemporary Feminisms in Egypt* (Basingstoke: Macmillan, 1998).

[24] See, for example, Rashid al-Ghannoushi, *Al-Huriyyat al-Amma fi al-Dawla al-Islamiyya* (Beirut: Markaz Dirasat al-Wahda al-Arabiyya, 1993).

[25] Lihi Ben Shitrit, "Authenticating Representation, Women's Quotas and Islamist Parties," *Politics & Gender* 12, no. 4 (2016): 781–806; Biagini, "Islamist Women's Activism"; Tønnessen, "An Increasing Number of Muslim Women in Politics."

[26] Biagini, "Islamist Women's Activism," 37.

[27] Utvik, "What Role for the Sisters?," 1–10.

[28] Liv Tønnessen, "The Many Faces of Political Islam in Sudan: Muslim Women's Activism for and against the State," PhD diss., University of Bergen, 2011.

[29] Sara Ababneh, "The Palestinian Women's Movement versus Hamas: Attempting to Understand Women's Empowerment outside a Feminist Framework," *Journal of International Women's Studies* 15, no. 1 (2014): 35–53.

[30] Liv Tønnessen, "Ansar al-Sunna and Women's Agency in Sudan: A Salafi Approach to Empowerment through Gender Segregation," *Frontiers: A Journal of Women Studies* 37, no. 3 (2016): 92–124.

women, including within the political sphere.³¹ Some Islamists in Kuwait, for example, used arguments related to the dangers of gender-mixing within parliament as justification for voting against new legislation granting women's political rights.³² However, there is a diversity of opinions and interpretations. Rashid al-Ghannoushi, the ideologue of the Tunisian Ennahda movement, and along with him many women activists within Islamist movements across the region, have declared that gender segregation is foreign to Islam.³³

Hassan al-Banna articulated the danger of gender-mixing in 1940 in these words: "This fascistic mingling of sexes among us in schools, institutes ... all of this is foreign goods which have absolutely no relation to Islam and has had the worst effects in our social life."³⁴ Often, improper women's dress or inappropriate gender-mixing are framed not only as against Islamic doctrine, but also as an import from the West.³⁵ Taraki explains that the Jordanian Muslim Brotherhood has spent a lot of effort campaigning against gender-mixing, or what they call *ikhtilat*.³⁶ Meanwhile, the Islamists in Sudan have never advocated for segregation, but instead introduced public morality regulations, including the mandatory wearing of the hijab and modest dress, restrictions on movement after dark, and restrictions on travel.³⁷ Such regulations have been regarded by the Islamists themselves not as a means to oppress women, but as an "entry ticket" to public spaces.³⁸ Faribah Adelkhah makes a similar argument based on the Iranian case.³⁹ However, it is important to note that some women have taken leadership in pushing back against such interpretations. For example, Farida Banani of Morocco argued "that the practices of veiling and seclusion were only designed for the wives of the Prophet" and thereby rejected conservative Islamists' stance on gender-mixing and veiling.⁴⁰

[31] Ibid.
[32] Bjørn Olav Utvik, "The Ikhwanization of the *Salafis*: Piety in the Politics of Egypt and Kuwait," *Middle East Critique* 23, no. 1 (2014): 5–27.
[33] Muhammad Mahmoud, "The Discourse of the Ikhwan of Sudan and Secularism," *Women Living under Muslim Laws* 19 (1997): 75–80.
[34] Quoted in Tadros, "The Muslim Brotherhood's Gender Agenda," 91.
[35] Giorgia Baldi, "Re-thinking Islam and Islamism: Hamas Women between Religion, Secularism and Neo-Liberalism," *Middle East Critique* 31, no. 3 (2022): 241–261.
[36] Lisa Taraki, "Jordanian Islamists and the Agenda for Women: Between Discourse and Practice," *Middle Eastern Studies* 32, no. 1 (1996): 140–158.
[37] The Salafi movement, on the other hand, *has* advocated for gender segregation: Tønnessen, "Ansar al-Sunna and Women's Agency in Sudan."
[38] Tønnessen, "The Many Faces of Political Islam in Sudan."
[39] Faribah Adelkhah, *La révolution sous le voile: Femmes islamiques* (Paris: Karthala, 1991).
[40] Mervat Hatem, "Gender and Islamism in the 1990s," *Middle East Report* 222 (2002): 46.

Such arguments have been regarded as an impediment to women's political activism by, for example, pushing them into women's branches or informal networks outside of the formal power structures of the Islamist movements.[41] However, there is a growing scholarship suggesting that Islamist women mobilize and maneuver in ways which ultimately politically empower them, even under circumstances of gender segregation and political oppression.[42] They do this by challenging the public–private dichotomy upon which ideologies of complementarity build.[43]

Research from Sudan both illustrates shifting interpretations of complementarity over different political periods and shows how ideologies of complementarity can limit women's political agency.[44] When women's right to vote and stand for election made it to the national political agenda during the 1950s, on the brink of the country's independence, prominent members of the Sudanese Muslim Brotherhood were ideologically against granting women political rights.[45] Many members of the Muslim Brotherhood were hesitant to nominate a woman as a candidate in the 1965 election, stating that women have no place in politics. This caused a split in the Sudan Women's Union at the time, and the Muslim Sisters exited the organization because they were ideologically against fighting for women's political rights.[46]

This position was justified by the principle of complementarity and by reference to a hadith that appears in Sahih al-Bukhari, one of six major

---

[41] Biagini, "The Egyptian Muslim Sisterhood between Violence, Activism and Leadership," *Mediterranean Politics* 22, no. 1 (2017): 35–53.

[42] Tønnessen, "Ansar al-Sunna and Women's Agency in Sudan"; Biagini, "The Egyptian Muslim Sisterhood"; Ababneh, "The Palestinian Women's Movement versus Hamas."

[43] Stacey Philbrick-Yadav, "Segmented Publics and Islamist Women in Yemen: Rethinking Space and Activism," *Journal of Middle East Women's Studies* 6, no. 2 (2010): 1–30.

[44] Sara Abbas, "The Sudanese Women's Movement and the Mobilisation for the 2008 Legislative Quota and Its Aftermath," *IDS Bulletin* 41, no. 5 (2010): 100–108; Liv Tønnessen and Samia al-Nagar, "The Women's Quota in Conflict-Ridden Sudan: Ideological Battles for and against Gender Equality," *Women's Studies International Forum* 41, no. 2 (2013): 122–131; Tønnessen, "An Increasing Number of Muslim Women in Politics."

[45] Nagwa Mohamed Ali al-Bashir, "Women in Public Life: The Experience of al-Akhwat al-Muslimat (Muslim Sisters): A Case from Sudan," MA thesis, University of Khartoum, 1996.

[46] Samia al-Nagar and Liv Tønnessen, "Women's Rights and the Women's Movement in Sudan (1952–2014)," in *Women's Activism in Africa: Struggles for Rights and Representation*, ed. Balghis Badri and Aili Marie Tripp (London: Zed Books, 2017), 121–155.

hadith collections in Sunni Islam: "those who entrust their affairs to a woman will never know prosperity."[47] Suad al-Fatih al-Badawi, a prominent female Islamist and later member of parliament and presidential advisor, was outspoken against women's political rights at the time, although she did not argue for women's seclusion from public life. She and others were nonetheless active within the Muslim Brotherhood organization and even formed a Muslim Sisters branch.[48] In other words, they were very much active in politics. When the Muslim Brotherhood developed into a political party in 1964, the formal party line on women's political involvement slowly started to change, and female Islamists actively took part in this development. The work of a male ideologue of the Islamist movement, Hasan al-Turabi, was foundational and has been a reference point for female Islamists in the country.[49] In 1973, Hasan al-Turabi published a pamphlet with the title *Al-mar'a bayna ta'alim al-din wa taqalid al-mujtama*, advocating strongly for women's political rights.[50] He noted that during the Prophetic era, for example, women were allowed to participate in congregational prayer, and they took an active role in military expeditions. He argued that Muslim women participated actively in the community's economic life and acquired education. When the opinions of Muslims were sought to decide on a caliph after the assassination of Umar Ibn al-Khattab, women were included in the consultation process. Female leaders and thinkers within the Islamist movement engaged with this debate and pushed for expanding women's political role. One of the active female figures has been Suad Abu Qashawa, who explained in an interview with the author how Islamist women reinterpret Islam to further the political rights of women:

> We try to find a link between the time of Prophet Muhammad and the role given to women then and in today's society. We work hard to make the decision makers realize that it is important for women to participate in politics. It is part of the religion [...] a woman can be head of state. Some refer to a hadith saying that a woman cannot

---

[47] Mernissi writes that it is almost impossible to discuss women's political rights in Islam without debating this hadith. Fatima Mernissi, *The Veil and the Male Elite: A Feminist Interpretation of Women's Rights in Islam* (Reading, MA: Addison-Wesley, 1991).
[48] al-Bashir, "Women in Public Life."
[49] Tønnessen, "The Many Faces of Political Islam in Sudan."
[50] Hasan al-Turabi, *Women between the Teachings of Religion and the Customs of Society (Al-Mar'a bayna Ta'alim al-Din wa Taqlid al-Mujta'ma)* (Khartoum: Al-Dar al-Su'udiya li al-Nashr wa al-Tawzi', 1973).

have the top position. But I do not find any definite saying in the Qur'an.[51]

The changed ideological position on women's political rights included a debate about women's leadership of the state, but also the military and the religious sphere. Many prominent female Islamists came down in favor of women exercising political rights and thereby rejected male conservative positions which excluded women from those positions based on arguments of biology and religion. Among those women was Lubaba al-Fadl, who asserted:

> Women can lead prayer. If a woman can lead a country like Balqis, the king of Saba, then why is the prayer difficult? It is difficult to lead a society, not to lead prayer. I went to *umra*. I insisted on praying with the men. "It is a house of God, not your house," I told the men who refused to let me pray with them. "I'm here with my God," I said to them. I'm a lecturer in any place at any time. Men and women are in heaven together. There is no separate hell and heaven for men and women so why should we be separated here on earth?[52]

A new interpretation of complementarity emerged: one that allows for women's inclusion within politics, first formally and equally to men, and later in 2008 through affirmative action.[53] Against the backdrop of an Islamist state (1989–2019) Sudan enacted a new National Election Law in 2008 which included 25 per cent of seats reserved for women in national and subnational legislative assemblies.[54] Beyond arguments rooted in religion, it was argued that women have a different and complementary perspective to men in the political debates that is essential to making sound political decisions. Women bring on board their experiences in the role of carer for children and family into the political arena.[55] And, in order to create a balance in political decision-making, then the perspective of women is needed equally to that of men. According to Asma Turabi, the daughter of Hasan al-Turabi and an active female politician, "Women are better at mercy and justice. Men do not consider the issues in the same way. Men do not consider the weak, the children, and the disabled. Women are the most skilled to help and represent these groups."[56]

---

[51] Interview with Suad Abu Qashawa, Khartoum, 2008.
[52] Interview with Lubaba al-Fadl, Khartoum, 2009.
[53] Tønnessen, "An Increasing Number of Muslim Women in Politics."
[54] Abbas, "The Sudanese Women's Movement"; Tønnessen and al-Nagar, "The Women's Quota in Conflict-Ridden Sudan."
[55] Tønnessen "An Increasing Number of Muslim Women in Politics."
[56] Interview with Asma Turabi, Khartoum, 2012.

Their position is that positive discrimination, such as a gender quota, is evidence of equity (*insaf*) or justice, and is not along the lines of principles of equality. The reason it is important to include women in politics is not only because Islam dictates it, but because it brings a woman's touch into political decision-making. It is argued that women have a different perspective from men in political debates, and that women bring on board their experiences in the role as a carer for children and family into politics. In this sense the "public" and the "private" are not separate spheres, but a continuum.

The underlying reasoning behind women's inclusion in the public sphere, and particularly political decision-making, is therefore that, because of their biological make-up, they represent different values, experiences, and interests from men.[57] And in order to create balance in political decision-making, then, the perspective of women is needed equally to that of men. Meanwhile, women represent "soft" political issues like education and children's well-being, whereas men represent "hard" political issues like the military and finance; both are considered important, but in practice women's roles become highly gendered and limited to certain political issues.[58]

As the Islamists took control of the state through a coup in 1989 and stayed in power for over three decades, the public role of women, including in politics, became an important symbol of "modern" or "authentic" Islam. The shift from the exclusion to the inclusion of women in politics eventually transformed the ways in which the Islamist movement thought about itself and differentiated itself from other Islamist movements and sectarian political parties in Sudan and in the region more generally. The inclusion of women in politics was described as not only important for making sound political decisions, but was talked about with pride as the ultimate symbol of "modern" Islam.[59] Although the Muslim Brotherhood in the beginning rejected women's political rights, it is important to note that the Muslim Sisters have been active members and leaders in the organization from early on. They exercised political agency even at the time when they themselves rejected the adoption of women's suffrage and right to stand for election.

---

[57] Tønnessen "An Increasing Number of Muslim Women in Politics."
[58] Ibid.
[59] Tønnessen, "The Many Faces of Political Islam in Sudan."

WOMEN'S INCLUSION/EXCLUSION: A RESULT OF POLITICAL PRAGMATISM OR WOMEN'S ACTIVISM?

The literature is broadly divided between those who regard the inclusion of women in political Islamic movements and political parties as a result of pragmatic or strategic decisions by male party leaders versus those who focus on women's agency and mobilization. This section will give an overview of the literature. The inclusion of women in Islamist movements and political parties is often regarded as a "moderation of ideology," or "ideological moderation."[60] Ideological moderation is seen as a result or effect of cross-ideological cooperation, whereby the groups holding extreme political positions will be forced to moderate their ideological positions if they are included in the governance's institutions, even in authoritarian settings.[61] Inclusion in political institutions thereby creates incentives for cross-ideological collaboration which are simply not possible in an entirely exclusive political system.[62] Not only is this cross-ideological cooperation beneficial for women's rights and their inclusion in the political sphere, but it is also a stepping-stone for larger democratization processes.[63]

In some of the scholarship, the ideological position on women's participation in politics is moderated as result of strategic choices, for example to counter competition from leftist political parties[64] or to gather support during elections.[65] Based on case studies of Islah in Yemen and IAF (Islamic Action Front) in Jordan, Clark and Schwedler argue that strategic considerations, such as gaining votes and internal debates between moderates and hardliners, strongly influenced Islamist parties' decision to incorporate women candidates.[66] The evolution in Islamist thinking on women's political participation, therefore, happened on account of Islamists' strategic adaptation to their political environment.[67]

---

[60] Biagini, "The Egyptian Muslim Sisterhood."
[61] Jillian Schwedler, "Can Islamists Become Moderates? Rethinking the Inclusion–Moderation Hypothesis," *World Politics* 63, no. 2 (2011): 347–376.
[62] Jillian Schwedler, "Islamists in Power? Inclusion, Moderation, and the Arab Uprisings," *Middle East Development Journal* 5, no. 1 (2013): 1–18.
[63] Janine Clark, "The Conditions of Islamist Moderation: Unpacking Cross-Ideological Cooperation in Jordan," *International Journal of Middle East Studies* 38, no. 4 (2006): 539–560.
[64] Islah Jad, "Islamist Women of Hamas: Between Feminism and Nationalism," *Inter-Asia Cultural Studies* 12, no. 2 (2011): 176–201.
[65] Omayma Abdellatif and Marina Ottaway, "Women in Islamist Movements: Toward an Islamist Model of Women Activism," *Carnegie Endowment for International Peace* no. 2 (June 2007); Carrie Roosefsky Wickham, *The Muslim Brotherhood: Evolution of an Islamist Movement* (Princeton: Princeton University Press, 2013).
[66] Janine Clark and Jillian Schwedler, "Who Opened the Window? Women's Activism in Islamist Parties," *Comparative Politics* 35, no. 3 (2003): 293–312.
[67] Ibid.

However, there is a difference in opinion as to whether shifting ideological positions can be viewed as purely instrumental or whether they represent a genuine willingness to include women in these movements. The way that women's agency is viewed differs substantially between these different strands of literature. In their studies on the Muslim Brotherhood in Egypt, Tadros and Wickham come to completely different conclusions. According to Tadros, the Muslim Brotherhood has gone through a reframing, rather than a change of its ideological position on women's rights.[68] Tadros claims that the gender ideology of the Muslim Brotherhood has largely remained steady, with an emphasis on complementarity rather than equality. She noted that the overall "ideological foundation of the Muslim Brotherhood's contemporary stance on gender issues has not changed: women and men have strictly defined social roles based on their sex".[69] As such, she concludes that we can trace shifts in the Muslim Brotherhood's discourse on women, but that is a product of external pressures: the actual ideology has remained steady. Wickham originally argued that in the case of the Wasat Party in Egypt, moderation occurred as a result of strategic calculation.[70] Later on she claimed, in the context of the Muslim Brotherhood in Egypt, that shifting ideological positions may be a result of pragmatism, but that they eventually "metamorphosed into matters of principles" over time and that an instrumentalist approach was insufficient.[71]

This inclusion–moderation literature has come under stark critique, employing a range of different arguments. A primary concern is that women's agency was overshadowed by an instrumentalist approach, whereby their own agency in shaping the discourses within these parties has been ignored.

WOMEN'S AGENCY AND MOBILIZATION: CHALLENGING DOGMAS

A critique of the inclusion–moderation focused literature is that it denies women's agency in the process of their inclusion. Philbrick-Yadav articulates it in the following way: "Scholars addressing women and Islamism tend to write of women as the objects of (male)

---

[68] Mariz Tadros, *The Muslim Brotherhood in Contemporary Egypt: Democracy Redefined or Confined?* (New York: Routledge, 2012).
[69] Tadros, "The Muslim Brotherhood's Gender Agenda," 96.
[70] Carrie Roosefsky Wickham, "The Path to Moderation: Strategy and Learning in the Formation of Egypt's Wasat Party," *Comparative Politics* 36, no. 2 (2004): 205–228.
[71] Wickham, *The Muslim Brotherhood*, 219.

Islamist activism, rather than as agents in the transformation of polity and society."[72] There is scant research on women joining political Islam "free from orientalist and essentialist perspectives."[73] Women who participated in Islamist movements were often viewed as a pawn in men's political game. For decades, studies on women in the Middle East and Northern Africa primarily focused on women opposing patriarchal structures and norms, and thus, women who conformed to ideologies of gender complementarity and segregation were either ignored as "religious fundamentalists (...) incapable of agency,"[74] or labelled as suffering from "false consciousness" – "with the veil as a symbol *par excellence* of ideological deceit."[75] Women's active involvement in Islamist movements, therefore, was for a long time regarded as a puzzle and a paradox, since the gender ideologies underpinning these movements were considered overtly patriarchal.[76] But since then, scholarship has emerged challenging such stereotypes and further challenging Islamic-secular dichotomies[77] and Western assumptions about Muslim women's agency.[78] However, the ways in which women's agency has been approached theoretically have varied over time.[79]

A great bulk of the literature focused on Islamist women's agency and mobilization has portrayed and positioned it in *opposition* to secular women's rights activists forefronting the competing gender ideologies at play[80]; it has also shown how Islamist and secular women's groups build

---

[72] Philbrick-Yadav, "Segmented Publics and Islamist Women in Yemen," 2.
[73] Mhajne and Brandt, "Rights, Democracy," 605.
[74] Therese Saliba, "Introduction: Gender, Politics and Islam," in *Gender, Politics and Islam*, ed. Therese Saliba, Carolyn Allen, and Judith A. Howard (Chicago: University of Chicago Press, 2002), 2.
[75] Sarah Bracke, "Author(iz)ing Agency: Feminist Scholars Making Sense of Women's Involvement in Religious 'Fundamentalist' Movements," *European Journal of Women's Studies* 10, no. 3 (2003): 337.
[76] Hatem, "Gender and Islamism"; Sertac Sehlikoglu, "Revisited: Muslim Women's Agency and Feminist Anthropology of the Middle East," *Contemporary Islam* 12 (2018): 73–92.
[77] Zakia Salime, *Between Feminism and Islam: Human Rights and Sharia Law in Morocco* (Minneapolis: University of Minnesota Press, 2012).
[78] Saba Mahmood, *The Politics of Piety: The Islamic Revival and the Feminist Subject* (Princeton: Princeton University Press, 2005).
[79] Sehlikoglu, "Revisited: Muslim Women's Agency."
[80] See, for example, Jan Feldman, "Models of Feminism: Tunisia's Opportunity to Overcome the Secular/Islamist Binary," *Journal of Women of the Middle East* 13 (2015): 51–76; Doris Grey, "Tunisia after the Uprising: Islamist and Secular Quests for Women's Rights," *Mediterranean Politics* 17, no. 3 (2012): 285–302; Julie Elisabeth Pruzan-Jørgensen, "Islamic Women's Activism in the Arab World," *The Danish Institute for International Studies* 2 (2012): 1–82.

coalitions and oftentimes navigate the political domain using the same strategic toolbox.[81] In Tunisia, for example, Maro Youssef finds that conservative Islamist women align with liberal feminists when it is in their interest to do so.[82] Both so-called secularist and Islamist groups employ Islamic arguments and refer to international human rights depending on the political and discursive context within which they operate.[83]

For example, in her study of Muslim women's rights activism in Iran and Turkey, Tajali explores how women have negotiated to advance female political representation.[84] She finds that Islamist activists articulate their demands for political rights and representation strategically by framing it according to the opportunities presented by the discursive opportunity structure.[85] She adds, this strategic framing represents women's agency because they might choose discursive frames based on their effectiveness in achieving their goals rather than their resonance with their core ideology.[86] Tajali suggests, "many Islamic women's rights activists in Turkey strategically frame their demands for head scarfed-women's right to political representation in secular terms in an appeal to secular sectors of society, while also pressuring pro-religious elites."[87] In contrast, due to Iran's theocratic government, women's rights groups with different ideological leanings use religious terms to frame and support their demands for women's increased political participation.[88]

Another strand of research offers in-depth studies of women active in a broad range of religious movements ranging from charity and *da'wa* (call to Islam) groups to activist groups, and also political Islamic movements and parties, in ways which challenge Western notions of Islamic

---

[81] Maro Youssef, "Unlikely Feminist Coalitions: Islamist and Secularist Women's Organizing in Tunisia," *Social Politics: International Studies in Gender, State & Society* 30, no. 1 (2021): 1–21.

[82] Maro Youssef, "Strategic Choices: How Conservative Women Activists Remained Active throughout Tunisia's Democratic Transition," *Sociological Forum* 37, no. 3 (2022): 836–855.

[83] See, for example, Mona Tajali, "Islamic Women's Groups and the Quest for Political Representation in Turkey and Iran," *The Middle East Journal* 69, no. 4 (2015): 563–558; Mona Tajali, *Women's Political Representation in Iran and Turkey: Demanding a Seat at the Table* (Edinburgh: Edinburgh University Press, 2022); Tønnessen, "Feminist Interlegalities and Gender Justice in Sudan."

[84] Tajali, *Women's Political Representation in Iran and Turkey*.

[85] Ibid.

[86] Ibid.

[87] Tajali, "Islamic Women's Groups," 573.

[88] Ibid.

homogeneity.[89] This has sometimes been referred to as the piety turn in the research on Muslim women's agency.[90] This literature focuses on women's agency as a crucial factor to be taken into consideration in work on women's activism in Islamist organizations.[91] Albeit cognizant of how political changes internal or external to Islamic movements create opportunities for mobilization, this literature explores the trajectories of women active in different types of religious movement, including those identifying with Islamism. It puts an emphasis on women being able to seize political windows of opportunity because they already are influential activists within their own spaces[92] and already possess a desire to increase their voice and activities in Islamist movements and how their strategic interactions reshape political opportunities.[93] Tajali's work from Iran and Turkey highlights the role that prominent Islamist women have played in pressuring their male party leaders to address women's political underrepresentation in formal politics.[94] Gender norms related to gender complementarity, or even gender segregation, which are idealized by women in these movements, do not restrict them from being politically and socially active and even enable them to challenge gender dogmas within their movements.[95] In the words of Mhajne and Brandt: "Despite the various restrictions on their participation as Islamists and as women, these women strategically engaged with the political structure, asserting their agency and creating wider openings in the structure of the movement for their political participation."[96]

Scholars have shown how sex segregation within political Islamic movements and parties has pushed women into separate women's branches and informal networks, but also showcased how it can

[89] Youssef, "Strategic Choices"; Salime, *Between Feminism and Islam*; Sherine Hafez, *An Islam of Her Own: Reconsidering Religion and Secularism in Women's Islamic Movements* (New York: New York University Press, 2011).
[90] Sehlikoglu, "Revisited: Muslim Women's Agency."
[91] Mhajne and Brandt, "Rights, Democracy," 577–608.
[92] Philbrick-Yadav, "Segmented Publics and Islamist Women in Yemen," 1–30.
[93] Anwar Mhajne, "Political Opportunities for Islamist Women in Morocco and Egypt: Structure or Agency?," in *Double-Edged Politics on Women's Rights in the MENA Region*, ed. Hanane Darhour and Drude Dahlerup (London: Palgrave Macmillan, 2020), 179–205.
[94] Mona Tajali, "Protesting Gender Discrimination from Within: Women's Political Representation on Behalf of Islamic Parties," *British Journal of Middle Eastern Studies* 44, no. 2 (2017): 176–193.
[95] Tønnessen, "Ansar al-Sunna and Women's Agency in Sudan."
[96] Mhajne and Brandt, "Rights, Democracy," 583.

simultaneously be conducive to female leadership and political activism.⁹⁷ The exclusion of women from formal leadership positions within the Egyptian Muslim Brotherhood has pushed women into women-only groups, utilizing their informal networks, where they have gained valuable experience in leadership. As Biagini writes:

> Islamist informal networks can be conducive to female leadership under "negative" political circumstances. As the case of the Muslim Sisterhood demonstrates, the repression of Islamists following the coup favored the emergence of women's leadership, firstly within women-only movements and subsequently, as the very survival of the MB [Muslim Brotherhood] became increasingly compromised, in the MB movement as a whole.⁹⁸

Biagini goes on further to suggest that the exclusion of women from the political decision-making offices of the Muslim Brotherhood over an extended period led to the development of more radical feminist positions among some of the Muslim sisters.⁹⁹

Studies also show how women active in Islamist movements use their political agency to challenge gender-discriminatory laws and practices. Biagini's work demonstrates through ethnographic research not only how the revolutionary struggle in Egypt has created a new generation of Islamist activists who actively challenge patriarchal tendencies within the Muslim Brotherhood,¹⁰⁰ but also the desire for pluralism and the opening-up of spaces for women to express diverse identities and positions.¹⁰¹

SUDAN: ISLAMIST WOMEN PUSHING FOR REFORM FROM WITHIN

Islamists in Sudan were in power for three decades (1989–2019), and during this time they developed a view that promoted women's

---

[97] Tønnessen, "Ansar al-Sunna and Women's Agency in Sudan"; Ababneh, "The Palestinian Women's Movement versus Hamas"; Biagini, "The Egyptian Muslim Sisterhood."
[98] Biagini, "The Egyptian Muslim Sisterhood," 35.
[99] Erica Biagini, "A Revolution of Their Own: The Activism of the Egyptian Muslim Sisterhood and Its Evolution since the Arab Spring (1928–2014)," PhD diss., Dublin City University, 2017.
[100] Erika Biagini, "Islamist Women's Feminist Subjectivities in (R)evolution: The Egyptian Muslim Sisterhood in the Aftermath of the Arab Uprisings," *International Feminist Journal of Politics* 22, no. 3 (2020): 382–402.
[101] Erika Biagini, "Women and the Egyptian Muslim Brotherhood post-2013: Calls for Gender Reforms and Pluralism," *Middle East Law and Governance* 13, no. 2 (2021): 171–195.

empowerment within an Islamic frame. Within the ranks of Islamists there was an evolving discourse about what an Islamic approach to women's empowerment entailed, and it changed over the course of three decades of Islamist rule in the country. Increasingly, Islamist women challenge gender dogmas in ways which have expanded women's rights; however, they have remained loyal to the state and the overarching ideological principles of gender equity and complementarity.

Most Islamist women interviewed by the author claim to be active seekers of gender "equity" (*insaf*), not equality. Feminism was rejected as a foreign ideology not suitable for Sudan. Although boundaries were pushed and advocated for within an Islamic framework, women's international human rights also featured in their advocacy campaigns for the advancement of women's rights. However, CEDAW (the Convention on the Elimination of All Forms of Discrimination against Women) was rejected, especially article 16, which postulates equality within the family.[102]

As part of the pursuit for gender equity, Islamist women reconciled the expansion of women's political rights with maintaining a stance that supported male guardianship or *qawama* within the family and legitimized the latter with reference to *Sura al-Nisa'* 4:34.[103] According to female Islamists in Sudan, this should not be misunderstood as discrimination. In the view of Suad Abu Qashawa, who was a long-standing member of the political bureau of the Islamist movement in Sudan:

> Some people misunderstand *qawama* as oppression and discrimination of women. But this is wrong. *Qawama* obliges men to support and sustain the household financially. This is an advantage for Muslim women. It means women are treated as precious in Islam. It means that the woman is part of a unit. In the West, a woman is dealt with as an individual. In Islam, the family comes first.[104]

In the eyes of Sudanese Islamists, *qawama* is an advantage to Muslim women that Western women cannot enjoy because they insist on equality in rights.[105]

The Islamist understanding of *qawama* is especially apparent in central aspects of Sudan's family law codified by the Islamist regime in

---

[102] Tønnessen, "Feminist Interlegalities and Gender Justice in Sudan."
[103] al-Nagar and Tønnessen, "Family Law Reform in Sudan."
[104] Interview with Suad Abu Qashawa, Khartoum, 2008.
[105] Liv Tønnessen, "Women at Work in Sudan: Marital Privilege or Constitutional Right?," *Social Politics: International Studies in Gender, State & Society* 26, no. 2 (2019): 223–244.

1991. The 1991 law has been described as a backlash against women's rights activists, as it (among other things) legalizes child marriage, stipulates a wife's obedience to her husband, and denies wives the possibility of working outside of the home without their husbands' permission.[106] Regarding central aspects of the 1991 law, female Islamists have challenged its discriminatory aspects related to a) the marriage contract, b) obedience in marriage, and c) the minimum age for marriage. Although the law stipulates consent, a woman must take her male guardian to court to annul a marriage that she did not consent to. Further, it gives the male guardian the right to repeal a marriage contract signed without his permission. It also stipulates a woman's obedience (*ta'a*) to her husband. Qawama is commonly interpreted as the husband's obligation to support his family financially (*nafaqa*) in exchange for his wives' obedience, according to female Islamists in the country. Because the law stipulates obedience, a wife can be declared disobedient (*nashiz*) and lose her right to maintenance.[107]

Islamist women increasingly taking part in politics as members of parliament, in the state bureaucracy, and as ministers has entailed challenging certain aspects of this law while staying loyal to principles of equity and complementarity. For example, Islamist women suggested repealing articles 24 and 34 of the 1991 law, which gives a guardian the right not only to repeal a marriage contract that has been signed without his consent, but also to basically force women to accept the guardian's decision to contract her marriage without her permission or prior knowledge. According to a female Islamist central to suggesting Islamic reform of the 1991 law, Soad Abdel Aal, who took a prominent part in the National Committee for the Review of Women's Status in Laws (2009–12), it is important that the Sudanese codified law reflects societal realities and principles of justice. Although the law as it stands is in accordance with various established interpretations by the traditional law schools in Islam, there is a need for new interpretations to reflect societal changes. During an interview with me, she noted:

> We cannot take the Islamic law schools as the ultimate truth. It builds on the Qur'an, but it is a human interpretation at the end of the day. They interpreted Islam in a certain context. Society has

---

[106] Al-Nagar and Tønnessen, "Family Law Reform in Sudan."
[107] She loses that right if she (i) refuses to move to the matrimonial home, (ii) leaves the matrimonial home for no legitimate excuse, (iii) works outside the home. Al-Nagar and Tønnessen, "Family Law Reform in Sudan."

changed, and Islamic law has to change with it. We must build it on the Qur'an but interpret it in light of justice and the good life.[108]

Islamist reformists have also advocated for constitutional reform that guarantees a woman's consent to marriage, and proposed replacing "obedience" with "mutual respect," ensuring women's consent in marriage, and setting the minimum age of marriage at eighteen. Although they advocate within the framework of Islam, international human rights are also employed, especially as they apply to children's rights.[109] This shows that although the state has ideologically rejected international human rights, those rights have nonetheless featured in female Islamists' framing strategies for enhancing women's rights.

But new interpretations of Islam are also central to this process. Islamist female reformers who have pushed for setting eighteen years as the minimum age of marriage believe that this does not contradict Islam. According to the 1991 law, the age of marriage is the age of puberty (*baligh*), which is interpreted as ten years of age. They rely on a more progressive Islamic interpretation of maturity to argue that the change conforms to shari'a, as well as to the CRC (Convention on the Rights of the Child). Amira al-Fadil, the then minister of social development (2010–13) in Sudan, explained the reformists' reasoning in an interview with the author:

> Eighteen years as a minimum age for marriage does not contradict *shari'a* law. Muslim scholars have given us a fatwa that supports 18 as a minimum age of marriage [...] *Baligh* is an Islamic term that refers to a person who has reached maturity and has full responsibilities under the law. But maturity in Islam should not go hand in hand with physical signs of puberty (sexual maturity), but rather intellectual maturity. And there is no reason why intellectual maturity cannot be set at 18 years.[110]

Although few reforms materialized during the Bashir regime, there was an active debate internally on women's rights within shari'a law. Women took a leading role in expanding the boundaries of gender equity and complementarity and employed innovative new ways of interpreting Islam as the discussion related to 'maturity' showcases.

---

[108] Interview with Soad Abdel Aal, Khartoum, 2011.
[109] Ragnhild Muriaas, Liv Tønnessen, and Vibeke Wang, "Counter-Mobilization against Child Marriage Reform in Africa," *Political Studies* 66, no. 4 (2018): 851–868.
[110] Interview with Amira al-Fadil, Khartoum, 2013.

CONCLUSION

This chapter attempts to provide an overview of the literature within the field of women joining political Islam. For a long time women joining political Islam was seen as a "paradox," because the ideologies of Islamic movements were seen as hostile towards women. The shift from excluding to formally including women in politics was therefore interpreted as political pragmatism on the part of male Islamists to expand the membership base, and to gain votes and political positions. As such, it was argued, women became pawns in men's political game. However, this literature has been critiqued for ignoring women's agency. Although political context and opportunity structure clearly matter, the studies have come to acknowledge women's active involvement in pushing for political leadership.

Challenging what has been perceived as a liberal feminist bias, increasing numbers of studies have showcased the agency of women in these movements and thereby refuted reductionist representations of female Islamist politicians in particular and Muslim women more generally. Although women in political Islam movements might not adhere to Western feminist ideas of gender equality, they are clearly challenging gender dogmas within their movements in ways that enhance women's rights, status, and roles. However, there is also a diversity of positions among women who identify with or are active in Islamist movements and political parties. This diversity exists not only across different political contexts but also across classes and generations.

SELECT BIBLIOGRAPHY

Badran, Margot. "Political Islam and Gender." In *The Oxford Handbook of Islam and Politics*, ed. John L. Esposito and Emad el-Din Shahin, 112–124. Oxford: Oxford University Press, 2013.

Biagini, Erika. "The Egyptian Muslim Sisterhood between Violence, Activism and Leadership." *Mediterranean Politics* 22, no. 1 (2017): 35–53.

"Islamist Women's Activism under Morsi's Government (2011–2013): Political Inclusion, Gender and Discourse." *Égypte/Monde arabe* 21 (2020): 37–55.

Clark, Janine. "The Conditions of Islamist Moderation: Unpacking Cross-Ideological Cooperation in Jordan." *International Journal of Middle East Studies* 38, no. 4 (2006): 539–560.

Mhajne, Anwar and Brandt, Rasmus. "Rights, Democracy, and Islamist Women's Activism in Tunisia and Egypt." *Politics and Religion* 14, no. 4 (2020): 577–608.

Philbrick-Yadav, Stacey. "Segmented Publics and Islamist Women in Yemen: Rethinking Space and Activism." *Journal of Middle East Women's Studies* 6, no. 2 (2010): 1–30.

Salime, Zakia. *Between Feminism and Islam: Human Rights and Sharia Law in Morocco*. Minneapolis: University of Minnesota Press, 2012.

Schwedler, Jillian. "Islamists in Power? Inclusion, Moderation, and the Arab Uprisings." *Middle East Development Journal* 5, no. 1 (2013): 1–18.

Sehlikoglu, Sertac. "Revisited: Muslim Women's Agency and Feminist Anthropology of the Middle East." *Contemporary Islam* 12 (2018): 73–92.

Tadros, Mariz. *The Muslim Brotherhood in Contemporary Egypt: Democracy Redefined or Confined?* New York: Routledge, 2012.

Tajali, Mona. *Women's Political Representation in Iran and Turkey: Demanding a Seat at the Table*. Edinburgh: Edinburgh University Press, 2022.

Tønnessen, Liv. "Ansar al-Sunna and Women's Agency in Sudan: A Salafi Approach to Empowerment through Gender Segregation." *Frontiers: A Journal of Women Studies* 37, no. 3 (2016): 92–124.

Wickham, Carrie Roosefsky. *The Muslim Brotherhood: Evolution of an Islamist Movement*. Princeton: Princeton University Press, 2013.

Youssef, Maro. "Strategic Choices: How Conservative Women Activists Remained Active throughout Tunisia's Democratic Transition." *Sociological Forum* 37, no. 3 (2022): 836–855.

8 Conversions to Islam

VANESSA VROON-NAJEM

During the past couple of decades, women's conversion to Islam has become a popular subject of academic research.[1] Scholars agree that women's conversion is often met with surprise – something that can be connected to Islam's bad reputation in "the West," particularly in the field of women's rights. Surely, there are tensions that arise in the lives of Muslim converts of all genders.[2] This is related to the supposed incompatibility of "Western" values with Islamic values. In the media and politics, Islam is often stereotyped as monolithic and static, as "other," irrational, primitive, inferior, violent, aggressive, as a political and military ideology, as intolerant and without critical capacity, and as deserving of discriminatory practices towards Muslims.[3] But being *visibly* Muslim by means of wearing the hijab is a gendered practice, and its consequences therefore affect women to a greater extent. In this light, it is unsurprising that the question of *why* women convert to Islam has received much attention,[4] often in relation to questions of national belonging.[5]

Despite the strong association of Islam with oppression, a growing number of women in Western countries are becoming Muslim.[6] My research in this field took place in the Netherlands, and I found that

---

[1] Paul Mitchell, Jessica Mamone, and Halim Rane, "Gender, Identity and Conversion: A Comparison of Male and Female Converts to Islam in Australia," *Islam and Christian–Muslim Relations* 32, no. 3 (2021): 279–306.
[2] Conversion/convert are common labels for becoming/being Muslim amongst my interlocutors.
[3] Commission on British Muslims and Islamophobia, and Gordon Conway, *Islamophobia: A Challenge for Us All*, Report of the Runnymede Trust Commission on British Muslims and Islamophobia (London: Runnymede Trust, 1997).
[4] Karin van Nieuwkerk, ed., *Women Embracing Islam: Gender and Conversion in the West* (Austin, TX: University of Texas Press, 2006).
[5] Tina Jensen, "To Be 'Danish,' Becoming 'Muslim': Contestations of National Identity?," *Journal of Ethnic and Migration Studies* 34, no. 3 (2008): 389–409.
[6] There are no statistics available on how many women convert to Islam, but scholars agree that research indicates the number is growing.

my interlocutors' initial interest in Islam was usually sparked by a combination of existential questions and positive social contacts with Muslims. In most cases, these were Muslims who came to the Netherlands through migration during the past half-century, and/or their descendants. In the Netherlands, the biggest communities are Muslims with a Turkish or Moroccan background, who came to the Netherlands in the context of labor migration. Two smaller groups are from Surinam and Indonesia, who came to the Netherlands in the context of post-colonial migration. When questioned about Islam, the ability of these "born Muslims" to explain the tenets of their religion often proved to be limited. In other instances, ties with the born Muslims they had first met were severed because of a new job, the end of a relationship, or for other reasons. Women then began to search and socialize beyond this first Muslim circle, in books, or online through watching videos and visiting websites for people with an interest in Islam, and through going to lectures and meetings of Muslim women's groups. If organized at a mosque, these meetings and events were always gendered, but also when groups formed online, used spaces at community centers, or organized outdoor gatherings they were always "women-only."

In popular conceptions about women's conversion to Islam, it is usually assumed that marriage is the impetus. (In reality, most women follow personal convictions when choosing Islam, and many of them are single at the time of conversion.)[7] This points to a presumed lack of women's agency in the conversion process. Saba Mahmood argues that the notion of human agency in feminist scholarship, too, usually "seeks to locate the political and moral autonomy of the subject in the face of power."[8] In this form of analysis, agency "is understood as the capacity to realize one's own interests against the weight of custom, tradition, transcendental will, or other obstacles (whether individual or collective)."[9] Interestingly, this type of definition can create a paradox

---

[7] Vanessa Vroon-Najem, "Sisters in Islam: Women's Conversion and the Politics of Belonging: A Dutch Case Study," PhD diss., University of Amsterdam, 2014; Annelies Moors and Vanessa Vroon-Najem Moors, "When Islamic Marriage Travels to the Netherlands: Convert Muslim Women (Re)Signifying the Marriage Guardian and the Dower," in *Muslim Marriage and Non-Marriage: Where Religion and Politics Meet Intimate Life*, ed. Julie McBrien and Annelies Moors (Leuven: Leuven University Press, 2023), 223–247.

[8] Saba Mahmood, "Feminist Theory, Embodiment, and the Docile Agent: Some Reflections on the Egyptian Islamic Revival," *Cultural Anthropology* 16, no. 2 (2001): 202–236, 203.

[9] Ibid., 206.

in regard to women who convert to Islam. In respect to the popular view that Muslim women are oppressed by Muslim men and conversion equals a retreat from women's rights, female converts regularly find themselves defending their embrace of this religion. Therefore, changes in daily life that result from conversion to Islam fit the description of realizing one's own interests against the weight of customs. However, since these changes can cause, or be perceived to cause, women to move away from liberal thought, their choices are often not recognized as expressions of agency.[10]

Over the past two decades, women's involvement in conservative religions has been researched in new directions by scholars who have critically engaged with the assessment of this involvement as a form of "false consciousness." Nevertheless, the scholarly responses to such claims often focus solely on agency as a form of empowerment, as a means of subversion, or to further extra-religious ends. Contributions in the field of women's conversion to Islam in Europe that take these types of conceptualization of agency as their focal point tend either to privilege the voices of women who critically engage with the sacred texts, often glossed as Islamic-feminism, or depend on overly functionalistic analyses of conversion motives.[11]

In this chapter, I favor the approach of religious women's agency as put forward by Mahmood[12] and Avishai.[13] Their subject-centered conceptualization of agency as a form of performativity, of "doing religion," provides a framework for addressing women's choices for an accommodative stance towards religious conservatism, that is, those women who prefer to remain within the limits of established Islamic jurisprudence or favor literalist readings of the sacred texts. Agency, in this conception, is not so much tied to resistance and liberation as it is to Foucault's analysis of ethical formation: "the employment of practices, techniques, and discourses through which a subject transforms herself in order to

---

[10] Cf. Joan Wallach Scott, *The Politics of the Veil* (Princeton: Princeton University Press, 2010).

[11] See also Tina Jensen and Kate Ostergaard, "Conversion to Islam in Denmark," in *Islam in Denmark: The Challenges of Diversity*, ed. J. S. Nielsen (Plymouth: Lexington Books 2012), 161–172.

[12] Saba Mahmood, *The Politics of Piety: The Islamic Revival and the Feminist Subject* (Princeton: Princeton University Press, 2005).

[13] Orit Avishai, "'Doing Religion' in a Secular World: Women in Conservative Religions and the Question of Agency," *Gender & Society* 22 (2008): 409–433; see also Lieke Schrijvers, "Questioning the Conversion Paradox: Gender, Sexuality, and Belonging amongst Women Becoming Jewish, Christian, and Muslim in the Netherlands," PhD diss., Universiteit Utrecht, Universiteit Gent, 2022.

achieve a particular state of being, happiness, or truth."[14] This perspective allows consideration of conversion to Islam for religious reasons, conceptualized as a transformative project of existential reorientation.

To draw attention to conversion to Islam as a processual, gendered, and embodied trajectory, in this chapter I will address women's agency in light of the changes in their daily lives that preceded, accompanied, and followed their conversion to Islam. These changes engendered shifting boundaries of belonging. For instance, my interlocutors did not feel that they had abandoned their ethnic or national identities when becoming Muslim;[15] still, their *Dutchness* became questioned. But besides ethnic and national belonging, converts also look for religious belonging. Therefore, the second focus in this chapter is on how my interlocutors subsequently became part of the *ummah*, the world community of Muslims, as "sisters in Islam."

DOING ETHNOGRAPHY

This chapter is based on anthropological research among converts to Islam in the Netherlands. It is unknown how many Dutch converts there are, but circumstantial evidence suggests they may number in the tens of thousands. In the context of my doctoral dissertation, I conducted ethnographic fieldwork (2006–2011) among five Dutch-language Muslim women's groups in the Amsterdam metropolitan area. These groups were all founded by convert women but attracted visitors and volunteers with different ethnic backgrounds, comprised of born Muslims, as well as converts, and women with an interest in Islam. My research focused on changes in daily life when becoming Muslim, how converts form and become part of (new) communities, and how they try to differentiate between *culture* and *religion*. From 2014 till 2020, I continued this research, focusing on how Muslim converts find a partner and conclude their marriages.[16] In the course of these many years, I participated in hundreds of meetings, lectures, social and religious events, and was granted access by participants to their online activities as well. In addition to countless informal conversations,

---

[14] Mahmood, *Politics of Piety*, 28.
[15] Vanessa Vroon-Najem, "Muslim Converts in the Netherlands and the Quest for a 'Culture-Free' Islam," *Archives de Sciences Sociales des Religions* 186 (2019): 33–51.
[16] Together with Prof. Dr. Annelies Moors. Research for this project was funded by the ERC advanced grant on "Problematizing 'Muslim Marriages': Ambiguities and Contestations" (Grant number: 2013-AdG-324180).

I interviewed more than eighty women, many of them multiple times, in the form of topical life stories.[17]

In the last section of this chapter, I will provide some more details about the variety of women I met during my fieldwork, but they also had some characteristics in common. They all visited meetings of Muslim women's groups and, to various degrees, considered themselves practicing Muslims. Converts who do not participate in these types of women's groups were not included in this research. Another commonality is that they were all Sunni Muslims. In regard to differences between Islamic Schools of Law, generally, participants believed that following the Qur'an and *sunna* (Prophetic tradition) sufficed. Usually, they avoided theological debates about differences between various strands and sects and either followed the opinion of a few leading Muslim scholars, read books, asked the advice of women they trusted, often the volunteers of the women's groups, or relied on their common sense. Although my interlocutors differed in terms of age, social and ethnic background, how long ago the conversion occurred, or their preferred practice, they cannot be considered representative of all converts to Islam. Since there are no formal records, claiming a representative cross section of converts to Islam in the Netherlands would be questionable in any event, due to the absence of an overall picture.

EXISTENTIAL REORIENTATION

On the one hand, conversion to Islam is easy. It does not involve an elaborate ritual or extensive studies. It only entails saying the *shahada*, the declaration of faith. When said with sincerity, pronouncing the *shahada* is considered by Muslims to grant access to Paradise, and the convert should now be recognized by other Muslims as a "brother or sister in Islam."[18] By saying the *shahada* with the intention to convert, the person doing so indicates they are prepared to live by what Allah has decreed in the Qur'an, the divine revelation transmitted by the Prophet Muhammad, and the *sunna*, the normative practice of the Prophet.[19]

---

[17] Daniel Bertaux, "From the Life-History Approach to the Transformation of Sociological Practice," in *Biography and Society: The Life-History Approach in the Social Sciences*, ed. Daniel Bertaux (Beverly Hills/London: Sage Publications, 1981), 29–45.

[18] Yasin Dutton, "Conversion to Islam: The Qur'anic Paradigm," in *Religious Conversion: Contemporary Practices and Controversies*, ed. Christopher Lamb and Darroll Bryant (London: Cassell 1999), 151–166.

[19] This is the *Sunni* Muslim perspective, as all participants in my research were Sunni Muslims. To live by these decrees is a personal responsibility, both in theory, as

When the *shahada* was said by a new convert at one of the women's groups, it was usually mentioned that becoming Muslim involves acting upon the five pillars of Islam (the *shahada*, the five daily prayers, fasting during the month of Ramadan, the giving of alms, and a once-in-a-lifetime pilgrimage to Mecca), and the six pillars of faith (belief in God, angels, the prophets, the divinely revealed books, Judgment Day, and the concept of fate). These pillars of faith, too, were usually mentioned as central to being Muslim.

As conversion to Islam is so simple, many of the women in my research took the step to do so alone, by themselves. At the same time, conversion is also quite complex. In the Netherlands, as well as in other Western countries, it means adopting a minority religion that is under intense, often critical or hostile, scrutiny. This is amplified when gender is taken into account, as the "position of women in Islam" is often a focal point of the critical stance of Europeans towards Islam.[20] While the *option* to convert can be considered a consequence of the pluralism and individualization of the Western religious landscape, a woman's choice for Islam is usually not seen as personal agency. Despite the fact that "being yourself" and "finding your own path" has become the prevalent social–spiritual frame in the Netherlands, women choosing Islam are suspected of following their husbands, who are presumed to be Muslim. Although in the Netherlands, in general, decisions in regard to one's religious status and affiliation are considered a matter of personal choice,[21] to use this freedom to choose *Islam*, particularly for women, is considered puzzling at best and treasonable at worst.

This puzzlement is reflected in the near-universal assumption on the part of non-Muslim Dutch that conversion to Islam is not so much a personal, "authentic" choice, but occurs because of a romantic relationship. It seems that it is only then that conversion to Islam becomes imaginable and acceptable. However, marriage does not play the pivotal role in women's conversion that many assume. On the contrary, the women I met regarded their conversion as a personal, informed choice, whether they were married or not, and a considerable number of them were single at the time of their conversion. This points to a significant

Dutton argues by citing the Qur'anic verse "Have fear of Allah, as far as you are able" (Q. 64:16), and in practice, as personal responsibility was a common understanding among the women's groups in my research.

[20] Lila Abu-Lughod, "Do Muslim Women Really Need Saving? Anthropological Reflections on Cultural Relativism and Its Others," *American Anthropologist* 104, no. 3 (2002): 783–790.

[21] Thomas Luckmann, "The Religious Situation in Europe: The Background to Contemporary Conversions," *Social Compass* 46, no. 3 (1999): 251–258.

divergence in perception regarding the choice for Islam between converts and their non-Muslim environment.

A vital step in the trajectory to Islam, I found, is the occurrence of positive social contacts with Muslims. These contacts can vary in nature: boyfriends and husbands, but also girlfriends, neighbors, colleagues, classmates, or travel companions. All participants in my research also formed or became visitors of Muslim women's groups. These experiences, too, informed and shaped their conversion, as women could ask questions and learn from the experience of others.[22] Volunteers of the women's groups and attendants alike often warned new converts to start with the basics of prayer and fasting and not to bite off more than they could chew. For instance, it was often said that it was better to do something small and be consistent than to engage in too many new practices at once, only to have to abandon them because it was too much, too soon.[23]

As stated above, becoming Muslim is a simple, short ritual. All it takes is a sincere declaration of faith, the *shahada*, followed by a ritual washing called *ghusl*. However, to arrive at that point often took years of investigation and deliberation, which I conceptualized as a project of existential reorientation. Over time, women began to distance themselves from some of the common aspects of Dutch society such as freely mingling with the opposite sex or drinking alcohol. Conversion affected their choice of marriage partner, friendships, leisure activities, and sometimes their education or occupation. The selective rejection of certain aspects of Western life such as drinking culture or sexual morality is not exclusive to Muslims but part of many conservative religions. The often-employed dichotomy between "Islam and the West" seems to be the main reference point for the idea of conversion to Islam as a radical break with the past, even if converts express that they experience continuity.[24]

Why Islam became the preferred choice for some and not for others is difficult to answer. Push and pull factors are reviewed by several scholars of conversion to Islam and can be clustered around a few themes. One such theme is a dissatisfaction with secular ideologies and/or feelings of

---

[22] E.g., Nicole Bourque, "How Deborah Became Aisha: The Conversion Process and the Creation of the Female Muslim Identity," in *Women Embracing Islam*, ed. van Nieuwkerk, 233–249.

[23] Karen Turner, "Convertitis and the Struggle with Liminality for Female Converts to Islam in Australia," *Archives de Sciences Sociales des Religions* 186 (2019): 71–91.

[24] See also Anna Mansson McGinty, *Becoming Muslim: Western Women's Conversions to Islam* (New York: Palgrave Macmillan, 2006); Yafa Shanneik, "Conversion and Religious Habitus: The Experiences of Irish Women Converts to Islam in the Pre-Celtic Tiger Era," *Journal of Muslim Minority Affairs* 31, no. 4 (2011): 503–517.

emptiness because of the oversecularization of society.[25] Another often mentioned theme in academic literature is Western converts' appreciation of Islam over Christianity as a more "rational" religion. The difficulty of explaining the concept of the Holy Trinity is absent from Islam, as is the doctrine of original sin. Instead, the emphasis is on personal responsibility.[26] Another theme is converts' criticism of Western society, for instance citing pornography as humiliating to women.[27] Others focus on women's appreciation of Islam's clear guidelines for gender relations, contributing to clarity and stability in familial and marital life,[28] or mention the daily discipline and specific requirements of Islam as appealing.[29]

Some of these themes surfaced in my research, too, mostly regarding living life in a secularized society and the clear role of Islam in structuring daily life. For young converts, questions concerning life and death were frequently a starting point for exploring Islam. As teenagers, they asked the big existential questions: Who am I? What is the meaning of life? What is death? They often started with a broad search among several world religions. They read, used the internet, and asked friends about their religion. Often, Muslim friends were the only ones to come up with answers or provide a doctrine. Gender relations were not explicitly mentioned as an impetus to convert but gradually became more appreciated in the course of conversion. Instead of clear-cut reasons to explain why conversion happened, I found that the formation of new Muslim subjects, foremost, stemmed from the experimental practice of Islam. Considering becoming Muslim and the experimental practice of (some of) Islam's precepts proved difficult to untangle. For many participants, it was the practice of Islam that motivated them to think of becoming Muslim themselves, making it problematic to pinpoint the exact moment of their conversion.

[25] Beebe Bahrami, "A Door to Paradise: Converts, the New Age, Islam, and the Past in Granada, Spain," *City & Society* 10, no. 1 (1999): 121–132; Ali Köse, "The Journey from the Secular to the Sacred: Experiences of Native British Converts to Islam," *Social Compass* 46, no. 3 (1999): 301–312.

[26] E.g., Anne Sofie Roald, *New Muslims in the European Context: The Experience of Scandinavian Converts* (Leiden: Koninklijke Brill NV, 2004).

[27] Madeleine Sultán, "Choosing Islam: A Study of Swedish Converts," *Social Compass* 46, no. 3 (1999): 325–335.

[28] Karin van Nieuwkerk, "Gender, Conversion, and Islam: A Comparison of Online and Offline Conversion Narratives," in *Women Embracing Islam*, ed. van Nieuwkerk, 95–119.

[29] Yvonne Haddad, "The Quest for Peace in Submission: Reflections on the Journey of American Women Converts to Islam," in *Women Embracing Islam*, ed. van Nieuwkerk, 19–47.

In my research, in almost all cases, positive social contacts with Muslims played a pivotal role in regard to considering becoming Muslim oneself. Through these contacts, curiosity developed, questions could be asked, stereotypes countered, books on Islam or a Qur'an were provided, and company to go to lectures, meetings, or a mosque was secured. Through this process, the plausibility of Islam being "the truth" was contemplated, usually by trying it out through the experimental practice of Islamic precepts. Fasting, but also prayer, switching to *halal* meat, or the abandonment of pork or alcohol, often preceded the actual conversion. The experimental practice of Islam occurred for several reasons, for instance curiosity or solidarity in the case of fasting, but also because women wanted certainty that practicing Islam suited them, and it could be a choice for life.

Spiritually, conversion to Islam is considered to be a new beginning. It is believed that all prior transgressions are forgiven by God: the slate is wiped clean. As was often mentioned in the women's groups after a convert recited the *shahada*, she is now as free of sin as a newborn baby. In order to make full use of this extraordinary metaphysical purification, women sometimes held back on their conversion until they were certain they could pray five times a day or comply with other prescriptions. However, these experimental practices often included saying the *shahada*, for instance during prayer, and therefore obscured the exact moment of conversion. Some converts I talked to could not exactly remember when they converted. At least a dozen of them said the *shahada* more than once in the context of conversion, for instance once while alone and once at a mosque, the consulate, their friends' or a Muslim spouse's country of origin, or at one of the Muslim women's groups. When contemplating conversion, the idea of one's deeds being judged by God gained meaning, as did belief in the existence of an afterlife, to be spent in heaven or hell depending on the divine judgment. In the absence of guidance, young women in particular often postponed their *shahada*. They adopted many or most Islamic practices before declaring themselves Muslim. Sometimes, they only realized they had converted after the fact.

CHANGES IN DAILY LIFE

All the women in my research made changes to their wardrobe ahead of, or as a consequence of, their conversion. The nature of these changes varied, as there are different opinions among Muslim women considering what entails Islamic dress. There are Muslim women who do not find it necessary to wear a headscarf and are therefore not easily recognizable as Muslims.[30] Others consider modest styles of dressing the body, including covering their hair, a religious obligation, which they themselves may or may not practice.[31] Wearing the hijab, meaning modest dress that covers up, should, similar to conversion, be based on personal conviction and understanding. If not, it lacks religious value because the intention of an act is crucially important in relation to its religious value.[32] Therefore, from an Islamic, normative perspective the main function of the hijab is not that of a symbol expressing the religious affiliation of the person wearing it. Still, being recognizably Muslim was an important side effect for many of my interlocutors.

The popular perception that wearing the hijab is connected to the wish of or demand from a Muslim husband, similar to the perception of women's decision to convert, again points to a striking absence of Muslim women's agency in the eyes of non-Muslim Dutch. Some women suspected that wearing a headscarf because of a husband's demand would make covering more palatable to non-Muslims than considering it a woman's personal, informed choice. As Tarlo, in her book about the implications of being visibly Muslim in Britain, points out too, the subject of women's choice is of crucial importance. If veiled, "women are perceived to be submissive or dangerous, deluded or transgressive, oppressed or threatening, depending on whether their covering is thought to have been forced or chosen."[33] In the Netherlands this is closely linked to the headscarf as the opposite of Dutchness. As van Nieuwkerk found, too, "the self-image of the Dutch is that the Dutch, in contrast to Muslims, are very liberal and emancipated. The Dutch narratives on nationality or ethnicity are thus very much linked to the gender discourse."[34] In this discourse, a Dutch woman wearing a headscarf commits a grave transgression.

Another area of changes in daily life when converting to Islam is food and drink. Although changes in diet are more private than changes in dress, since eating and drinking are also social activities, adhering to Islamic restrictions in regard to alcohol and switching to the consumption of *halal* meat can cause tensions as well. The "publicness" of new

---

[30] See also Mikaela Rogozen-Soltar, "Striving toward Piety: Gendered Conversion to Islam in Catholic-Secular Spain," *Current Anthropology* 61, no. 2 (2020): 141–167.
[31] Annelies Moors, "Islamic Fashion in Europe: Religious Conviction, Aesthetic Style, and Creative Consumption," *Encounters* 1, no. 1 (2009): 175–201.
[32] Wasif Shadid and Sjoerd van Koningsveld, "Muslim Dress in Europe: Debates on the Headscarf," *Journal of Islamic Studies* 16, no. 1 (2005): 35–61; Moors, "Islamic Fashion in Europe."
[33] Emma Tarlo, *Visibly Muslim: Fashion, Politics, Faith* (New York: Berg, 2010), 4.
[34] van Nieuwkerk, "Gender, Conversion, and Islam," 106.

rules and restrictions, again, was most problematic. On a personal level, women converts' new, *halal* diet was usually considered healthier, and many participants were charmed by the emphasis in Islam on caring for one's body. In this respect, changes in diet were often part of a larger reevaluation of cleanliness and attitudes towards responsibility for one's health. For many participants, no more alcohol was one of their first steps on the path to Islam. Some abode by the strict rule that Muslims should not be present at a place where alcohol is sold or served; others just refrained from drinking it themselves. As with changes in dress, most participants slowly introduced new rules to their families, especially when living with their unconverted parents and siblings. Honoring one's parents is an important Islamic precept, and participants engaged in complex balancing acts when presented with instances of conflicting norms.

Another point of tension was that those who practiced according to strictly interpreted Islamic norms ceased to celebrate their birthday, arguing that doing so is *haram*, forbidden, in Islam. They lived by the rule that Muslims should only celebrate two holidays: *Eid al-Fitr*, to celebrate the end of the month of Ramadan, and *Eid al-Adha*, the remembrance of Abraham's obedience to God. They did not attend other people's birthdays either, although family ties could trump this prohibition.

Unlike dress, food, drink, and festivities, which, at least partly, take place in the public or social sphere, converts could express their new identity at home in an uncompromised fashion. This, however, was truer for women running their own household than for girls still living with their parents, or for women with husbands who did not share all of their new convictions. Converted girls, while living under their parents' roof, were often restrained in their practice, in particular when they kept their conversion a secret. Even when parents did know, if they did not approve, practicing Islam at home was often difficult.

Some changes at home were made by everyone, most notably those connected to cleanliness. Not wearing shoes inside the house or washing yourself because of ablutions in the context of prayer more often were frequently mentioned. Many participants decorated their homes with visible signs of being a Muslim, such as framed Qur'an verses or self-made murals, special clocks displaying the proper prayer times, and small tables designed to hold a Qur'an. Behavior in respect to handling the Qur'an also changed. Usually, participants had already bought a Qur'an, or borrowed one from the library, before conversion. Consequently, they treated it as any other book, reading it in bed or at the beach while on holiday. After becoming Muslim, this attitude changed. They would place the book in a safe place and perform a washing before touching it.

For some participants, a considerable change connected to conversion was the notion that listening to music, or playing musical instruments, is considered *haram*. Women who adopted this opinion stopped listening to music, with the exception of one type of drum. Other participants considered listening to or playing music allowed, provided that it did not transgress other norms, such as decency. Some participants completely abandoned displaying photographs, while others did not.

These changes in daily life as a result of conversion convey that becoming Muslim is not solely a spiritual, affectual, or intellectual endeavor, but is also embodied, in that it involves prayer and fasting, changes in dress, diet, and drinking habits, and in attitudes regarding cleanliness, joining in festivities, interior decoration, and leisure activities.[35] As Tarlo argues about being visibly Muslim in Britain, too, many of the difficulties that converts in the Netherlands experience lie in a mismatch between the message they want to convey and the interpretations of their actions by non-Muslim Dutch.

Largely, participants made changes for religious reasons.[36] As Zebiri found in the British context, too, when she asked converts about their purpose in life, "the vast majority answered along the lines of: 'To worship God to the best of my ability'."[37] However, given the contentious nature of the practice of veiling, many non-Muslims hold different views, regarding it as oppressive, unnecessary, and a retreat from women's liberation. This image is so strong that converts often no longer register as Dutch.[38] Unconverted parents, siblings, or children can feel embarrassed when seen with the convert in public. Being visibly Muslim can provoke violence and verbal abuse in the public domain, or it can hinder finding an internship or having a career. However, in line with the appreciation of conversion as a project of existential reorientation, when Islam became the focal point in the lives of my interlocutors, then following divine rule, even if it caused conflict, was often deemed most important, also in light of securing a favorable position in the afterlife.

---

[35] See also Kate Zebiri, *British Muslim Converts: Choosing Alternative Lives* (Oxford: Oneworld Publications, 2008).
[36] Conveying their Islamic identity was also frequently mentioned as a reason for being visibly Muslim.
[37] Zebiri, *British Muslim Converts*, 249.
[38] This occurs in other European countries, too.

During women's groups' lectures, the afterlife, *al-akhira*, was often discussed, and *taqwa*, awe or fear of Allah, was promoted as a virtue. Good deeds, attendants were told, result in *hasanaat*, divine blessings, that weigh positively in regard to spending the afterlife in heaven, or not. Another key concept in Islam, *sabr* (patience), helped participants to endure negative behavior, and most believed they would be rewarded for their patience in life on Judgment Day, resulting in a better chance of enjoying the afterlife in paradise. This religious discourse was often complemented with human rights discourse – for instance, women argued that, since they did not impinge on other people's freedoms, then why should their right to dress as they wished be denied to them? – or with the emancipatory discourse of a "woman's right to choose."

SISTERS IN ISLAM

Women not only engaged in personal transformation processes. Through conversion, they also became part of the *ummah*, the world *community* of Muslims, usually conceptualized as a symbolic family of brothers and sisters. This Islamic concept of sisterhood was a means to take part in and shape their (feelings of) religious belonging. Generally, the converts I met had formed and participated in multiethnic social networks, emanating from the work of a number of volunteers. In most cases, these volunteers were also converts who organized a variety of offline gatherings and events, and online meeting points such as forums, websites, and social media pages. Online and offline, these activities were centered around the common goal of learning about Islam and sharing experiences of being a (new) Muslim in the Netherlands. Coming together in the context of "gaining knowledge," as it was often phrased, combined with the opportunity to meet like-minded women, produced a pious sociality and ethical communality that informed and shaped women's belonging within the abstract notion of the *ummah*.

The five women's groups that were part of my research all had an established structure and volunteers who organized the workshops, meetings, and lectures. The groups met at regular intervals, ranging from twice a week to once every three months. The visitors varied widely. Some women were loyal participants, while others came only occasionally or once in a while. There were regularly women attending for the first time, both Muslim women who were raised as Muslims at home and converted women. Usually, there were also women attending who had not converted but wanted to know a little more about Islam.

Besides the regular meetings, there were also special meetings, for instance when a woman wanted to convert. Together, the women paid attention to the month of Ramadan and Islamic holidays. Before the summer break, there was usually a festive gathering or a picnic.

If women said the *shahada* at a mosque or at a meeting of one of the women's groups, the notion that conversion marked now being a "sister in Islam" was usually explained. Converts who converted alone often learned about such specific aspects of conversion after the fact. If women started attending these meetings after they already had become Muslim, the notion of sisterhood became implicitly clear, as women often addressed each other as "sister" face to face and used it when announcing "sister meetings" or "sister days." The title "sister" was also used in emails, on websites, forums and social media, and (lack of) sisterhood was frequently mentioned in lectures.

The ideal of sisterhood was usually summarized by participants with the *hadith* that states that, as a Muslim, one's faith is incomplete until you wish for the other what you wish for yourself.[39] Sisterhood embodied a range of positive attitudes towards each other. For instance, during an interactive exercise at a meeting of one of the women's groups, the young women who had gathered were asked to name a word that exemplified sisterhood. They came up with: love, friendship, affection, support, warmth, respect, understanding, helpfulness, and encouragement. This ideal included all Muslims but also induced a sense of responsibility towards other converts.

Mosques in the Netherlands tend to cater to the needs of the immigrant communities who established the mosque. Usually, the imam has the same ethnic background as the mosque visitors. During recent decades, however, converts, too, have increasingly been organizing events taking place at mosques. These range from small-scale lectures to large events such as the National Convert Day. During these events, often, non-Muslims take the opportunity to say the *shahada*. This means that for born Muslims conversion to Islam has become an increasingly familiar phenomenon. However, it does not mean that there is always a program in place that informs the role of the mosque. Although this has been changing in the more recent past as conversion has become a more familiar phenomenon at Dutch mosques, women who had experienced insufficient support after conversion often turned out to be motivated to help and guide others. Over the past few decades some of them

---

[39] Included in *hadith* collections such as Bukhari and Muslim, transmitted by Anas ibn Malik.

have become increasingly active in welcoming and mentoring new Muslims, offline as well as online. Social media and internet sites have become important means of communication in this regard. Converts sometimes live far apart, and the internet is helpful in bridging these distances. Even if they do live near each other, social media are a useful and frequently used means of keeping in touch, sharing information, and preparing for meetings.

My interlocutors came from all walks of life and converted at different ages. There was a greater number of women converting in their early twenties, but also women converting in their seventies, and everything in between. Also, in terms of religious background there was great variety. As a consequence of the rapid secularization of the Netherlands in the recent past, young women were often raised without religion. Some of the older women were raised Catholic or Protestant, but most of them had already left the church before becoming Muslim. Also, in regard to social class and education there was great variation, from women with a PhD to those with only a high-school diploma. An often-unmentioned aspect of differences between converts in the scholarly literature is ethnic background. Unsurprisingly, I met many white Dutch converts, but also converts with migrant backgrounds, as well as with multiple ethnic backgrounds. The concept of Islamic sisterhood did not negate all these differences, but it did provide women with an overarching discourse to communally work at what it means to live a Muslim life in the Netherlands.

Two currents were most influential among participants in the way women discussed and tried to implement Islamic tenets in their daily lives. These were the Islamic Revival, with its calls for a return to the high moral values of the first Muslim community, and an emphasis on Muslim women's rights. The latter encompasses what some researchers call an Islamic Feminist turn:[40] women who engage in reinterpretations of the Qur'an and *hadith*.[41] In the language of both currents, however, women regularly taught and discussed the various rights of women in Islam. The topic of Islamic marriage, for instance, was often discussed, and it was usually emphasized that it is a man's duty to be the family

[40] Cf. Margot Badran, "Feminism and Conversion: Comparing British, Dutch and South-African Life Stories," in *Women Embracing Islam*, ed. van Nieuwkerk, 192–232.

[41] Cf. Fatima Mernissi, *The Veil and the Male Elite: A Feminist Interpretation of Women's Rights in Islam* (Reading, MA: Addison-Wesley, 1991); Amina Wadud, *Qur'an and Woman: Rereading the Sacred Text from a Woman's Perspective* (New York: Oxford University Press 1999); Asma Barlas, *Believing Women in Islam: Unreading Patriarchal Interpretations of the Qur'an* (Austin, TX: University of Texas Press, 2002).

provider. The husband needs to take care of food, clothing, and shelter, and all other things that his wife and children, reasonably, need for their daily life. It was said, at all women's groups, that a Muslim woman has the right to work, but she does not *have to* work. In the case she chooses to work, her income is hers alone. Of course, she could spend it on her family but, Islamically speaking, she was not obliged to. In a similar vein, women who emphasized the importance of honoring one's parents or husband would always add that this, of course, did not apply to anything that would go against the teachings of Islam. For instance, the right to education, to work, or to choose or refuse a marriage partner could never be denied, as these were women's rights secured through Islam.

This challenge to the dominant discourse about Muslim women's lack of autonomy quite similarly exists elsewhere in Europe. For instance, as Jouili found in France, women who related to the discourse of the Islamic Revival rejected the dominant narrative of "a linear temporality of European progress with the liberation of women at its end" and favored another narrative, "an Islamic temporality, where ultimate progress is epitomized within the first Islamic state in Medina, during the lifetime of the Prophet."[42] One of the arguments frequently advanced by her respondents was that in France it was only in 1965 that women gained the right to dispose of their own goods without the authorization of their husbands, while Muslim women held that right for fourteen centuries, since the beginning of Islam.[43] The notion that "the religious sources provide complete gender justice and female dignity, plus all of the rights necessary for self-realization"[44] prevalent in Revival discourse was common amongst my interlocutors as well. That these rights often remain unrealized was also acknowledged. For instance, most married participants who were professionally employed were obliged to work, for various reasons.

Attiya Ahmad's research on conversion to Islam among domestic workers in Kuwait[45] shows that women coming together to communally work at becoming Muslim and practice Islam also exist in a Muslim-majority country. Despite stark differences in structural position, there are striking similarities between her interlocutors in Kuwait and the

---

[42] Jeanette Jouili, "Beyond Emancipation: Subjectivities and Ethics among Women in Europe's Islamic Revival Communities," *Feminist Review* 98 (2011): 51.
[43] In the Netherlands, women gained this right in 1956.
[44] Jouili, "Beyond Emancipation."
[45] Attiya Ahmad, "Explanation Is Not the Point: Domestic Work, Islamic *Da'wa* and Becoming Muslim in Kuwait," *Asia Pacific Journal of Anthropology* 11, nos. 3–4 (2010): 293–310.

women in my research in Amsterdam. Over the past decades, Ahmad found, tens of thousands of domestic workers from Asian countries working in Kuwait have converted to Islam. This occurred not because of their employers' wishes or desires but because of the development of an interest in Islam through social interaction with Muslims. At meetings of local women's groups about the practice of Islam, comprised of domestic workers and conducted in their native languages, women addressed the same tensions that my interlocutors discussed with each other. One of the women in Ahmad's research, for instance, shared a story that could have as easily been told within one of the women's groups in my research.

The woman in question shared with the others that she had called her parents in India and told them about her developing interest in Islam. Their response had been quite negative, and, at one point in the conversation, they had threatened to cut off all ties. She concluded her story to the other women by saying that although she did read the Qur'an and fasted during the month of Ramadan, she did not dare take the *shahada*, as she feared it would alienate her parents. Ahmad recounts how in the ensuing discussion several suggestions were offered regarding how to deal with this predicament. These suggestions were identical to the advice my interlocutors would have offered in such a circumstance. For instance, one of the women in Ahmad's study stated that parents often talk bigger than they are prepared to act; another suggested taking the *shahada* without telling her parents; and a third woman advised her to be patient, wait a while, and then broach the subject again.[46] These similarities between women in different positions but with comparable solutions to personal dilemmas arising in the context of conversion to Islam should not go unnoticed, as they point to interesting convergences between women converting to Islam in different parts of the world.

CONCLUSION

In his famous book *Orientalism*, Edward Said puts forward that Islam's negative reputation in Europe is not a recent phenomenon. For centuries, he argues, Islam has been "counterpoised imaginatively, geographically, and historically against Europe and the West."[47] This negative image is reflected in the tensions my interlocutors encountered when they considered conversion or decided to become Muslim. Although many of them, at first, kept their choice for Islam a secret from their non-

---

[46] Ibid., 303.
[47] Edward Said, *Orientalism* (London: Penguin Books 2003).

Muslim loved ones, practices they adopted in the course of their conversion, such as wearing the hijab, created a public visibility of their new identity. Many of them described this process as "coming out" and were highly aware that their choices were routinely attributed not to their personal agency but assigned to the presumed wishes or demands of a Muslim husband.

Contrary to this perception of women's conversion as a precondition for marriage, in the course of my research I met hundreds of women who made an informed, personal choice for Islam. Many of these women were single at the time of conversion, but also, if they did have Muslim boyfriends or spouses, their proficiency in answering women's questions when exploring Islam often proved limited. In their subsequent search for knowledge, they formed or visited Dutch-language Muslim women's groups. These grassroots initiatives helped them mitigate familial and societal challenges connected to their Muslimness and allowed women from different backgrounds to communally discuss and explore how to practice Islam.

These networks emanated from the work of a number of volunteers, who, although not scholars, through their status as "knowledgeable women" mediated many of the tensions that converts wrestled with in the form of advice, lectures, workshops, and other events, and online through forums, blogs, or Facebook communities. Within these groups, sociality was usually organized around the concept of Islamic sisterhood. This provided an opportunity to participate in the abstract notion of the *ummah*, as well as to help shape (feelings of) local belonging, allowing women from widely different backgrounds to find each other in the context of an active and creative process of becoming/being Muslim.

SELECT BIBLIOGRAPHY

Abu-Lughod, Lila. "Do Muslim Women Really Need Saving? Anthropological Reflections on Cultural Relativism and Its Others." *American Anthropologist* 104, no. 3 (2002): 783–790.

Ahmad, Attiya. "Explanation Is Not the Point: Domestic Work, Islamic *Da'wa* and Becoming Muslim in Kuwait." *The Asia Pacific Journal of Anthropology* 11, nos. 3–4 (2010): 293–310.

Avishai, Orit. "'Doing Religion' in a Secular World. Women in Conservative Religions and the Question of Agency." *Gender & Society* 22 (2008): 409–433.

Dutton, Yasin. "Conversion to Islam: The Qur'anic Paradigm." In *Religious Conversion: Contemporary Practices and Controversies*, ed. Christopher Lamb and Darroll Bryant, 151–166. London: Cassell, 1999.

Jouili, Jeanette. "Beyond Emancipation: Subjectivities and Ethics among Women in Europe's Islamic Revival Communities." *Feminist Review* 98 (2011): 47–64.

Mahmood, Saba. "Feminist Theory, Embodiment, and the Docile Agent: Some Reflections on the Egyptian Islamic Revival." *Cultural Anthropology* 16, no. 2 (2001): 202–236.

The Politics of Piety: The Islamic Revival and the Feminist Subject. Princeton: Princeton University Press, 2005.

McGinty, Anna Mansson. *Becoming Muslim: Western Women's Conversions to Islam*. New York: Palgrave Macmillan, 2006.

Moors, Annelies and Vroon-Najem, Vanessa. "When Islamic Marriage Travels to the Netherlands: Convert Muslim Women (Re)Signifying the Marriage Guardian and the Dower." In *Muslim Marriage and Non-Marriage: Where Religion and Politics Meet Intimate Life*, ed. Julie McBrien and Annelies Moors, 223–247. Leuven: Leuven University Press, 2023.

Nieuwkerk Karin van ed. *Women Embracing Islam: Gender and Conversion in the West*. Austin, TX: University of Texas Press, 2006.

Rogozen-Soltar, Mikaela. "Striving toward Piety: Gendered Conversion to Islam in Catholic-Secular Spain." *Current Anthropology* 61, no. 2 (2020):141–167.

Said, Edward. *Orientalism*. London: Penguin Books (2003).

Tarlo, Emma. *Visibly Muslim: Fashion, Politics, Faith*. New York: Berg, 2010.

Vroon-Najem, Vanessa. "Muslim Converts in the Netherlands and the Quest for a 'Culture-Free' Islam." *Archives de Sciences Sociales des Religions* 186 (2019): 33–51.

Zebiri, Kate. *British Muslim Converts: Choosing Alternative Lives*. Oxford: Oneworld Publications, 2008.

9 Islamic Feminists' Approaches
NINA NURMILA

The continuously expanding body of literature within Western academia often termed as Islamic feminism traces its origins to the mid to late 1970s.* Noteworthy authors from this period include the Egyptian scholar Nawal Saadawi,[1] the Moroccan thinker Fatima Mernissi, and Azizah al-Hibri, who made significant early contributions. As we will see in this chapter, these pioneering efforts paved the way for a subsequent wave of influential figures in the 1990s and early 2000s, including such prominent names as Amina Wadud, Asghar Ali Engineer, Riffat Hassan, and Asma Barlas. This chapter serves a dual purpose. First, it acquaints the reader with the fundamental methodological approaches developed by these initial two generations of authors, most of whom were affiliated with Western academic institutions. It delves into their arguments for the reinterpretation of Islamic texts from a feminist perspective, providing a detailed exploration of the methodological stances they advocated. References to various issues they addressed in their scholarship, such as polygamy, husband–wife relationships, and leadership within the family, are also included. Secondly, the chapter documents how the works of these writers influenced the discourse on Islamic feminism in Indonesia, particularly by shaping the perspectives of young men and women who encountered their scholarship, especially during their graduate studies.

The increased availability of translations of the works by these international scholars in Indonesia since the mid 1990s, coupled with the proactive role played by the *Pusat Studi Wanita* (Women's Studies Center) on Indonesian campuses in organizing gender training sessions, significantly facilitated the transmission of their ideas. This influence is vividly evident in the body of Indonesian Islamic feminist scholarship

---

* Please note that the majority of the translations from the Qur'an used in this chapter are based on that of Abdullah Yusuf Ali.
[1] N. Saadawi, *Memoirs of a Woman Doctor* (London: Saqi Books, 1988).

that has emerged since the late 1990s. The gender training sessions and translated publications authored by the aforementioned Islamic feminists, along with books penned by Indonesian feminists inspired by their work, have been actively studied by many lecturers and students within Islamic higher education institutions in Indonesia. This engagement has resulted in a substantial increase in publications addressing gender issues in Islam, featured in journals managed by *Pusat Studi Gender dan Anak* (PSGA) – the Center for the Study of Gender and Children, which has now adopted a new name, throughout Indonesia.

This systematic exchange of ideas across various levels, as discussed by Nelly van Doorn-Harder in Chapter 13 in this volume, on women's basic human rights in Indonesia has empowered some Indonesian Islamic feminists to take the lead in pioneering platforms aimed at promoting gender justice within Muslim families and societies. They have also joined transnational movements, such as Musawah, established by a Malaysian feminist, Zainah Anwar, with the goal of achieving justice and equality within the Muslim family. Additionally, they have played a pivotal role in establishing influential institutions within Indonesia focused on promoting gender justice, including the hosting of the Indonesian Women's Ulama Congress (KUPI) in 2017 and 2022.

I would like to emphasize that I personally prefer to refer to these scholars and activists in Indonesia who advocate for the reinterpretation of Islamic texts through a gendered lens as Muslim feminists. I make this distinction to highlight their approach, which differs from that of Muslim scholars who advocate for the defense of the traditional model of Islamic reasoning with an emphasis on gender differentiation.[2] However, since this volume primarily aims to capture the dominant debates within the field of scholarship, I use the term Islamic feminism, as it remains the prevailing terminology in established scholarship.

---

[2] I refer to Azza M. Karam's book in using the term "Muslim feminist" instead of "Islamic feminist": Azza M. Karam, *Women, Islamism and the State: Contemporary Feminisms in Egypt* (New York: St. Martin's Press, 1998). In this book, Karam differentiates Muslim feminists from Secular and Islamist feminists. Muslim feminists use Islam, mainly the Qur'an, to liberate women. These Muslim feminists argue that the Qur'an has been interpreted to justify women's subordination, and therefore to liberate women is to reinterpret the Qur'an from gender-equal perspectives. I use the term "Muslim feminist" in my other publications, even though I am aware that these Muslim feminists are normally referred to as "Islamic feminists," for example by Etin Anwar, *A Genealogy of Islamic Feminism: Pattern and Change in Indonesia* (London: Routledge, 2018), and Lana Sirri, *Islamic Feminism: Discourses on Gender and Sexuality in Contemporary Islam* (London: Routledge, 2022).

REINTERPRETING THE QUR'AN AND HADITH

It is important to begin by acknowledging that feminist methodology is rooted in the postpositivist paradigm[3] and asserts that research is inherently subjective and that knowledge is not devoid of values.[4] Scholars who engage in the re-examination of Islamic texts have adopted a similar approach, contending that the traditional understanding of gender norms in Muslim societies is a product of its time and influenced by male religious authorities who controlled the interpretation process. In this section, I will focus on how such scholars as Fatima Mernissi, Asghar Ali Engineer, Amina Wadud, and Asma Barlas, while working towards the shared goal of revealing Islam's egalitarian essence, use slightly different methodological approaches. First, I will briefly introduce each author before delving into their respective approaches to challenge historically dominant interpretations.

The late Fatima Mernissi stands out as one of the most influential Islamic feminists. Born in Fez in the 1940s, she pursued her higher education at Mohammed V University in Rabat. She furthered her academic journey with an MA in France and obtained her PhD from Brandeis University in the US. Proficient in English, Arabic, and French, she has been translated into numerous languages, including Indonesian. Mernissi's multifaceted career encompassed roles as a sociologist, writer, novelist, artist, and civil society advocate, making her an iconic figure in the field of Islamic feminism.[5] One of Mernissi's core concerns was centered on critically analyzing the authenticity of hadith (sayings attributed to the Prophet). To illustrate her methodological approach, I examine her treatment of a frequently cited hadith used to justify the notion that women cannot hold leadership positions: "Those who entrust their affairs to a woman will never know prosperity." This hadith is often accepted as authentic by many ordinary Muslims because it appears in Shahih Bukhari, a compilation of hadith considered authentic.[6] However, Mernissi raised doubts regarding the authenticity

---

[3] Sotirios Sarantakos, *Social Research* (Brisbane: Macmillan Education Australia, 1993).
[4] Ibid.
[5] Margalit Fox, "Fatema Mernissi, a Founder of Islamic Feminism, Dies at 75," *New York Times*, December 9, 2015, www.nytimes.com/2015/12/10/world/middleeast/fatema-mernissi-a-founder-of-islamic-feminism-dies-at-75.html; Fatima Sadiqi, "Biographical Sketch of Fatema Mernissi (1940–2015)," 2018, Middle East Studies Association (MESA): https://mesana.org/awards/category/fatema-mernissi-book-award/biographical-sketch-of-fatema-mernissi.
[6] The chapter employs a classical style of referencing hadith. Readers unfamiliar with this system can find relevant information at https://sunnah.com.

and validity of this hadith. She delved into *Fath al-Bari*, a work by Ibn Hajar al-'Asqalani (d. AH 852), one of the commentators on Shahih Bukhari.[7] Mernissi highlighted that the narrator of this hadith, Abu Bakra, relayed it twenty-five years after the Prophet's passing, during a tumultuous political period when the Muslim community had to choose between supporting Aisha, one of the Prophet's wives, who led the Battle of the Camel against Ali bin Abi Thalib, the fourth Caliph in Islam.

Mernissi further examined the character of Abu Bakra, building on Imam Malik Ibn Anas's emphasis on the importance of moral integrity in those who narrate hadith. Mernissi's research revealed that during the time of Caliph Umar bin Khattab, Abu Bakra had been punished with eighty lashes for making false accusations of adultery without being able to provide the required four witnesses. According to Imam Malik's criteria for morality, Mernissi argued that the hadith narrated by Abu Bakra should not be categorized as authentic (*shahih*), despite its inclusion in Shahih Bukhari.[8] Additionally, Mernissi demonstrated that not all early Muslim scholars accepted the prohibition of women assuming public leadership, even though this hadith is found in Shahih Bukhari. Prominent exegetes like al-Tabari opposed the content of the hadith, as they did not find sufficient grounds within it to deny women the right to exercise political authority.[9]

While Mernissi focused on scrutinizing the authenticity of contentious hadith, other scholars have often concentrated on reinterpreting the interpretations and explications of Qur'anic verses in contrast to traditional readings. Amina Wadud, whose work has wielded significant influence in this area, was born in Bethesda, Maryland, USA, in the early 1950s as a Methodist. She converted to Islam at the age of twenty. After completing her PhD in Arabic and Islamic Studies at the University of Michigan in 1988, she furthered her studies in Islamic sciences in Cairo. From 1989 to 1992 she taught at the International Islamic University, Malaysia, before returning to the US, where she held various teaching positions. During her time in Malaysia, Wadud engaged with women activists associated with Sisters in Islam, a platform dedicated to interpreting the Qur'an from a woman's perspective. Her book, *Qur'an and Woman*, was published in Malaysia in 1992[10] and, republished in 1999 in

---

[7] Fatima Mernissi, *Women and Islam: An Historical and Theological Enquiry* (Oxford: Blackwell, 1991), 3.
[8] Ibid., 49–61.
[9] Ibid., 61.
[10] Amina Wadud, *Qur'an and Woman* (Kuala Lumpur: Fajar Bakti SDN BHD, 1992).

New York under the longer title *Qur'an and Woman: Rereading the Sacred Text from a Woman's Perspective*,[11] garnered significant attention. Wadud is also renowned for her religious activism, such as leading a Friday congregational prayer involving both men and women in 2005 in New York, a role traditionally reserved for men. Wadud's approach to reinterpreting the Qur'an is heavily influenced by Fazlur Rahman's contextual approach, known as the "double movement." Wadud explicitly states that she utilizes Rahman's method in interpreting the Qur'an.[12] Rahman's double movement is an approach aimed at contextual understanding of the Qur'an by moving twice: first from the current era to the era of the Qur'anic revelation. This initial movement seeks to distil the general principles or intended message of the Qur'anic revelation. The second movement is a return to the current time, with the aim of applying the spirit of the Qur'an or the intended message derived from its historical context to conform to these general principles and values in the current context. To apply the spirit of the Qur'an to the contemporary situation, one must thoroughly understand the present circumstances.[13]

Adopting this approach to studying Qur'anic texts through a gendered lens, Wadud provides an example of how to extract the intended principles from the Qur'an regarding veiling and seclusion, especially in the context of wealthy and powerful tribes, as an indication of protection. In this context, the spirit or intended message of the Qur'an is not solely about the importance of veiling and seclusion for women, but rather emphasizes the significance of modesty, a virtue applicable to all women, regardless of their economic class. The practice of modesty and how it should be implemented to respect and safeguard women can be culturally defined and may vary within various societal contexts. In building her arguments, Wadud underscores the importance of understanding the intricacies of the Arabic language to make readers aware that the Qur'an is not exclusively directed at men but encompasses both men and women.

---

[11] Amina Wadud, *Qur'an and Woman: Rereading the Sacred Text from a Woman's Perspective* (New York: Oxford University Press, 1999). This is the edition referenced throughout the chapter.

[12] Ibid., 3–4.

[13] Fazlur Rahman, *Islam and Modernity: Transformation of an Intellectual Tradition* (Chicago: University of Chicago Press, 1982), 5–7.

In Arabic, the masculine plural form includes females, unless specific indicators exist to denote exclusively masculine plural forms, typically by adding the plural form for females.[14] Furthermore, she highlights the distinction between the text (the Qur'an) and its interpretation, emphasizing that interpretation is subjective and influenced by the backgrounds and interests of the interpreters, which she terms "prior text."[15] Following the publication of her book, Wadud often faced resistance from those who failed to differentiate between the text and its interpretation, accusing her of altering the Qur'an. Her proposed hermeneutical model for analyzing Qur'anic verses is thus fourfold: (1) within the context in which the text was originally produced; (2) in the context of discussions on similar topics within the Qur'an; (3) with reference to similar language and syntactical structures used elsewhere in the Qur'an; and (4) in relation to the overarching Qur'anic principles and within the framework of the Qur'anic worldview.[16]

The benefit of employing such a hermeneutical approach becomes evident when examining her reinterpretation of the nature of marital relationships in Islam. She makes four key analytical points. First, the context of the revelation in the Arabian Peninsula was patriarchal, characterized by a culture of male domination and female subordination, and featuring an androcentric bias where male experiences were considered the norm and women were positioned in relation to male interests, primarily in reproductive roles.[17] Second, two Qur'anic verses support the idea that marital relationships are meant to be equal and reciprocal. In Q. 2:187, the relationship between men and women is likened to garments for each other, and in Q. 30:21, the purpose of marriage is to foster love and mercy between husband and wife.[18] Third, in response to the prevailing patriarchal construct that expects women to be obedient to their husbands, Wadud analyzes the use of the term *qanitat*, often interpreted as implying that wives should obey their husbands. However, by referencing the use of *qanitat* in other Qur'anic verses like Q. 2:238, 3:17, and 33:35, she concludes that *qanitat* actually means "being cooperative with one another and subservient before Allah,"[19] emphasizing a reciprocal and equal relationship as worshippers of Allah. Obedience to other human beings is described as *ta'a*, not

---

[14] Wadud, *Qur'an and Woman*, 10.
[15] Ibid., 1–5.
[16] Ibid., 5.
[17] Ibid., 80–1.
[18] Ibid., 83.
[19] Ibid., 74.

qanitat. Finally, Wadud underscores key principles of human development within marital relationships, including justice, equity, harmony, moral responsibility, spiritual awareness, and development.[20] Applying these principles leads to a view of husband and wife as equal partners who cooperate in their efforts to submit to Allah. Such a relationship leaves no room for polygamous marriages, where a husband–father is divided between multiple families. According to her interpretation, Q. 4:3 is not about permitting polygamy but rather concerns justice in managing funds for orphans and providing for wives, as affirmed by Q. 4:129.[21]

Another scholar who has employed a similar methodological approach is Asghar Ali Engineer. Born in India and not affiliated with a professional academic institution, Engineer authored more than fifty books and articles. In his work *The Rights of Women in Islam*,[22] akin to Wadud, Engineer advocates for discerning the substance, norms, morality, and ethics contained within Qur'anic verses, recognizing that their application may vary in different contexts. Engineer also utilizes the same example as Wadud to illustrate this differentiation, focusing on the case of veiling, which he refers to as *purdah*. Similar to Wadud's perspective, Engineer contends that in the past, *purdah* was a means to safeguard women's chastity. However, it was misconstrued as synonymous with chastity, leading to the judgment that women not wearing the veil were deemed "immoral."[23] In contrast to this assumption, Engineer emphasizes that chastity represents the norm, while *purdah* serves as a contextual means to achieve that norm. Consequently, a woman can be considered chaste even without wearing a veil.[24] Consistent with Wadud's approach, Engineer also distinguishes Qur'anic verses into normative and contextual categories. To comprehend the norm prescribed by the Qur'an, it must be contextualized within concrete circumstances, rather than being considered an abstract concept. When circumstances change, the norm can be preserved but may take on a different form. Engineer cites Ibn Taymiyya's argument that the law can evolve with changing times.[25] Therefore, he suggests selecting what is transcendent from what the Prophet practiced while disregarding context-dependent aspects.[26]

---

[20] Ibid., 95.
[21] Ibid., 83.
[22] Asghar Ali Engineer, *The Rights of Women in Islam* (London: C. Hurst & Co., 1992).
[23] Ibid., 5.
[24] Ibid., 6.
[25] Ibid., 11.
[26] Ibid., 12.

I will illustrate how the approach used by Engineer informs his reinterpretation of Qur'anic verse 4:34. According to him, the Qur'an literally states that men have a slight edge and social superiority over women. However, he contends that this should be understood in a contextual or socio-theological context, rather than purely theological. Engineer believes that Q. 4:34 does not endorse sexual superiority or excellence but is a reflection of the societal roles of men as family breadwinners and economic providers at that particular time. He interprets Q. 4:34 as describing the social circumstances prevalent at the time of its revelation. It states that men "are *qawwam* [guardians]," not that men "should be *qawwam*." He emphasizes that Q. 4:34 is a contextual statement, not a normative one. It would be normative if the verse stated that men should always be *qawwam*, applicable universally and at all times, but the verse does not convey this directive. In response to feminist recognition of women's domestic contributions to the family, Engineer cites Q. 53:39, which acknowledges that each person will reap the consequences of their own actions: "That every person will get only the fruit of their own deeds." He also refers to Q. 45:22, which guarantees that each person will be treated justly: "Allah created the heavens and the earth for just ends, and in order that each soul may find the recompense of what it has earned, and none of them be wronged."[27] Engineer's reading of Q. 4:34 allows us to understand that social conditions in certain societies can change. In some cases, women may assume the role of family breadwinners and, as a result, they can be *qawwam*, a social function that either men or women can undertake. It is not binding exclusively for men in all eras and under all circumstances.

Similarly, Asma Barlas, a Pakistani-born American scholar who obtained her PhD in International Studies from the University of Denver and served as a professor of politics and director of the Center for the Study of Culture, Race, and Ethnicity at Ithaca College in New York, has advanced similar arguments advocating for a gender-based re-evaluation of the Qur'an in her book *Believing Women in Islam: Unreading Patriarchal Interpretations of the Qur'an*.[28] In this work, Barlas challenges the oppressive interpretations of the Qur'an and focuses on "recovering the liberating and egalitarian voice of Islam."[29] In the acknowledgments section of her book, the first name that Barlas mentions as a source of gratitude is Amina Wadud, highlighting

---

[27] Ibid., 45–46.
[28] Asma Barlas, *Believing Women in Islam: Unreading Patriarchal Interpretations of the Qur'an* (Austin, TX: University of Texas Press, 2002).
[29] Ibid., 4.

Wadud's profound influence on her work.³⁰ Like Wadud, Barlas criticizes the position of hadith, asserting that the Qur'an does not require the hadith, but rather the opposite: the hadith needs the Qur'an to be accepted as a source of Islamic teaching, because Muslims cannot accept hadith whose content contradicts the Qur'an. Furthermore, Barlas criticizes the politicization of Qur'anic access and interpretation, emphasizing the imposition of numerous requirements for engaging in *ijtihad* (independent scholarly interpretation). Consequently, the Qur'an has been positioned as inaccessible to many Muslims or has been displaced by patriarchal classical Islamic jurisprudence, which is often regarded as sacrosanct.

As someone who acknowledges being influenced by Wadud, who in turn drew inspiration from Rahman, Barlas employs a methodology for reinterpreting the Qur'an that aligns with that of Wadud and Rahman, albeit using distinct terminology. In her Qur'anic reevaluation, Barlas engages in three primary modes of reading: (1) *reading the Qur'an as a text*: this involves seeking to understand the intention of the text and discern what God may have intended in its verses,³¹ akin to Rahman's concept of distilling the intended message or the spirit of the Qur'an; (2) *reading behind the text*: here, Barlas endeavors to uncover the context of the Qur'anic revelations, delving into the circumstances and conditions surrounding its revelation;³² and (3) *reading in front of the text*: in this step, Barlas recontextualizes the Qur'anic text in light of contemporary needs, ensuring that the spirit of the Qur'an is applied to current situations.³³ Notably, she explicitly cites Rahman's approach, which advocates a double movement: first, moving from the present to the past (the time of revelation), and then back to the present. Additionally, Barlas references Wadud's perspective, emphasizing that considering the context of revelation during the interpretation process serves to distil the spirit or intended message of the Qur'an, thereby confirming its universality.

According to Barlas, patriarchal and oppressive interpretations of the Qur'an are a result of reading the Qur'an in a fragmented and decontextualized manner, such as giving precedence to specific words, phrases, or lines over the Qur'an's teachings as a whole. Additionally, this issue arises when less clear verses take precedence over those with fundamental meanings or when the Qur'an is not read in its entirety. She advocates

---

30   Ibid., xv.
31   Ibid., 21.
32   Ibid., 22.
33   Ibid., 23.

for a holistic reading of the Qur'an.[34] I will now demonstrate how Barlas applies this methodology to reinterpret Qur'anic verses pertaining to husband–wife relationships and the issue of polygyny. First, in reading the Qur'an as a text, Barlas contends that the Qur'an promotes ethical and egalitarian values and opposes patriarchy. She highlights the Qur'anic support for egalitarianism, citing Qur'anic verse 16:72, which asserts that God has created mates of "your own natures" and has crafted "helpmeets from yourselves" to enable tranquillity (sukun), love, and mercy, as expressed in Qur'anic verse 30:21. According to Barlas, this verse underscores the capacity of both men and women, created from the same nature, to love each other as husband and wife. It also suggests that they share the same ethical standards, as emphasized in Q. 24:30–31, which instructs both men and women to protect their chastity.[35] Barlas posits that the Qur'an can be seen as anti-patriarchal based on such examples as Abraham, who challenged his father's authority to obey God. Furthermore, she notes numerous Qur'anic verses that prohibit blindly following the ways of fathers.[36]

Secondly, when reading behind the text or delving into the context of the Qur'anic revelations, Barlas is acutely aware of the historical context and the plight of women during that era. At the time of revelation, women were not considered fully equal human beings, and they suffered from severe mistreatment within a deeply patriarchal culture. Misogyny was rampant in many societies, husbands being allowed to subject their wives to horrific abuses, including pulling out their hair, mutilating their ears, and smashing their teeth with burnt bricks. Polygyny was also prevalent without significant restrictions. In this context, Islam emerged with the aim of improving the status and condition of women.[37]

Thirdly, in reading in front of the text, or recontextualizing the text to address contemporary needs while upholding the spirit of the Qur'an, Barlas acknowledges the existence of controversial views on Islamic marriage. Some perceive it as oppressive and patriarchal, while others view it as elevating women's status.[38] Despite these differing perspectives, Barlas maintains that the Qur'anic concept of the family is rooted in egalitarianism and nurturing. She substantiates her argument by highlighting Qur'anic injunctions to prioritize the needs of women and children, considering the home as the central place for the family. Barlas

[34] Ibid., 168–169.
[35] Ibid., 183–184.
[36] Ibid., 173.
[37] Ibid., 169–170.
[38] Ibid., 200–201.

emphasizes that the Qur'an treats wives as independent agents with rights in marriage and divorce, and that marriage is founded on mutuality. She posits that Islamic marriage, characterized by rights and responsibilities, represents a structured and nonoppositional framework that is nonhierarchical, thereby fostering liberation for both men and women.[39]

In this context, Barlas asserts that the values of Islamic marriage applicable in the present day emphasize egalitarian, nurturing, and mutual relationships between men and women, encompassing their respective rights and responsibilities, all contributing to liberation. Within such a marital framework, there is no room for polygamy, and polygyny does not align with the Qur'anic ideals. Barlas maintains that Qur'anic verse 4:3, often cited to justify polygyny, is intended to ensure justice for female orphans. Disagreeing with polygyny, she underscores Qur'anic admonitions to marry only once, the Qur'an's recognition that men cannot treat women justly under polygamous conditions, and the concept of the oneness of the human heart.[40]

INDONESIAN FEMINISTS' RE-READING OF THE QUR'AN

The study of gender in Indonesia has been a burgeoning field since the early 1990s, fostering critical thinking among Indonesian Muslims. Translations into Indonesian of works by Fatima Mernissi, Amina Wadud, Asghar Ali Engineer, and Asma Barlas have played a pivotal role in this development. Consequently, numerous doctoral dissertations have been dedicated to the reinterpretation of the Qur'an, authored by established scholars including Nasaruddin Umar, Zaitunah Subhan, Nurjannah Ismail, and myself. Furthermore, several feminist scholars, such as Kiyai Husein Muhammad, Faqihuddin Abdul Kodir, Nur and Badriyah Fayumi, have made significant contributions by writing and publishing their own feminist reinterpretations of religious texts. This section will provide an overview of the profiles and approaches adopted by these scholars, with a particular focus on their perspectives regarding husband–wife relationships and family life.

Nasaruddin Umar, a prominent scholar who also serves as the high priest of the Istiqlal Mosque in Jakarta, the largest mosque in Southeast Asia and the sixth largest globally in terms of its congregational capacity, has played a pivotal role in advancing Gender Studies within Islamic scholarship in Indonesia. Previously, he held the position of vice

[39] Ibid., 202.
[40] Ibid., 190–192.

minister of religious affairs from 2011 to 2014. His academic journey included pursuing master's and doctoral degrees at the State Islamic University (UIN) in the 1990s. During that time, he was also a visiting student at various international universities, including McGill University in Canada (1993-4), Leiden University in the Netherlands (1994-5), and the University of Paris in France (1995). Additionally, he conducted library research at several universities around the world, spanning America, Japan, England, Belgium, Italy, Turkey, Sri Lanka, South Korea, Saudi Arabia, Egypt, Jordan, Palestine, the Philippines, and Malaysia.

One of his significant contributions to the field of Gender Studies in Islam in Indonesia is his book titled *Argumen Kesetaraan Jender: Perspektif al-Qur'an* [Gender Equality Argument in Qur'anic Perspective].[41] This book represents the published version of his doctoral dissertation. Within its pages, he underscores the theme of gender equality in the Qur'an, asserting that men and women are equal as God's servants, vicegerents on Earth, participants in the cosmic drama, and possessors of potential for achievement. A noteworthy contribution from his work is the differentiation he establishes between the terms "sex" and "gender" in Qur'anic terminology. He contends that the Qur'an employs *dzakar* (male) and *untsa* (female) to refer to biology, while *rijal*, *nisa'*, and *mar'ah* represent the concept of gender.[42]

This critical distinction holds significance when interpreting Qur'anic verse 4:34 concerning family leadership. Q. 4:34, as translated by Abdullah Yusuf Ali, states:

> Men are the protectors and maintainers of women, because Allah has given the one more (strength) than the other, and because they support them from their means. Therefore, the righteous women are devoutly obedient, and guard in (the husband's) absence what Allah would have them guard. As to those women on whose part ye fear disloyalty and ill-conduct, admonish them (first), (Next), refuse to share their beds, (And last) beat them (lightly); but if they return to obedience, seek not against them Means (of annoyance): For Allah is Most High, great (above you all).

While many Muslims interpret this verse literally to justify male-only family leadership, Umar's differentiation between sex and

---

[41] Nasaruddin Umar, *Argumen Kesetaraan Jender: Perspektif al-Qur'an* [Gender Equality Argument in Qur'anic Perspective] (Jakarta: Paramadina, 1999).
[42] Ibid.

gender in Qur'anic terms provides a more nuanced understanding. According to Umar, *rijal* denotes males with specific capacities, as not all males are inherently superior to women. This implies that females possessing certain capacities can assume leadership within the family as well. Q. 4:34 outlines two key qualifications for serving as the protector (leader) of the family: (1) having superiority over the spouse; and (2) providing financial support to the family. In the contemporary context, superiority may manifest in the form of higher educational levels and/or greater income. Consequently, anyone, whether male or female, who fulfils these two requirements can assume the role of family protector or leader.

Faqihuddin Abdul Kodir, a prominent Indonesian scholar born in Cirebon, West Java, in the early 1970s, has made significant contributions to the fields of Islamic Studies and gender justice. He received his education in Syria, earning two degrees from the Faculty of Dawah and the Faculty of Shari'a at Damascus University. Later, he pursued a master's degree in Islamic Revealed Knowledge and Human Sciences at the International Islamic University Malaysia, specializing in the development of *fiqh* of zakat (Islamic law on almsgiving). He completed his doctoral studies at the Indonesian Consortium for Religious Studies (ICRS) at Universitas Gadjah Mada, focusing on Abu Syuqqah's interpretation of hadith texts for empowering women's rights in Islam. Abdul Kodir serves as a lecturer at IAIN Cirebon and is an active advocate for religious tolerance and gender justice. He cofounded such organizations as Fahmina, Rahima, and Alimat, dedicated to promoting equality and justice in Muslim families.

He also played a key role in organizing KUPI I in 2017 and KUPI II in 2022. A prolific writer, his renowned work *Qirā'ah Mubādalah: Progressive Tafsir for Gender Justice in Islam*[43] introduces a method for reinterpreting religious texts, including the Qur'an and hadith, to foster a just understanding of these texts. This approach, inspired by Abd-al-Halim Muhammad Abu Shuqqa, seeks to engage women as active participants in the interpretation process and advocates for egalitarian gender relations (*musawah*) through a "hermeneutics of equality."[44]

---

[43] Faqihuddin Abdul Kodir, *Qirā'ah Mubādalah: Tafsir Progresif untuk Keadilan Gender dalam Islam* [Qirā'ah Mubādalah: Progressive Interpretation for Gender Justice in Islam] (Banguntapan, Yogyakarta: IRCiSoD, 2019). The volume has been reprinted six times in 2019, twice in 2020, in 2021, 2022, and 2023.

[44] Faqihuddin Abdul Kodir, "*Qirā'a Mubādala*: Reciprocal Reading of Hadith on Marital Relationships," in *Justice and Beauty in Muslim Marriage: Towards Egalitarian*

Abdul Kodir's *Qirā'ah Mubādalah* method advocates for equal cooperation between men and women in all aspects of social life, including family and society. This approach ensures that both sexes are considered equal subjects when interpreting religious texts, addressing kindness, and preventing wrongdoing. Regardless of whether a text is directed explicitly at men or women, its core message must apply to both sexes. Abdul Kodir emphasizes reading religious texts holistically, similar to Amina Wadud's approach in *Qur'an and Women*, instead of dissecting them piecemeal. He categorizes texts into three types: *al-mabadi'* (fundamental values), *al-qawa'id* (thematic principles), and *al-juz'iyyat* (contextual implementations). Verses mentioning men or women often fall into the last category (*al-juz'iyyat*), which can be reinterpreted to align with the broader principles of *al-mabadi'* and *al-qawa'id*. The steps of the *Qirā'ah Mubādalah* method involve identifying texts related to gender relations in either family or society, recognizing whether they mention men or women explicitly, and determining whether they convey principles or behaviors. Principles apply directly to the unstated subject, while behavioral texts require a deeper understanding of their general meanings regarding kindness and wrongdoing before being applied to both genders. This method promotes a balanced and cooperative approach to interpreting religious texts, emphasizing gender equality in all aspects of life.[45]

Abdul Kodir employs the *Qirā'ah Mubādalah* method to reinterpret hadith related to husband–wife relationships. He illustrates that hadith advising men to display good character, kindness, and responsibility towards their wives[46] are ethically applicable to women as well. These fundamental norms (*al-mabadi'*) become the foundation of marriage (*al-qawa'id*) binding both genders for mutual benefit. Abdul Kodir posits that the Prophet delivered partial hadith to men due to their societal roles, emphasizing the responsible use of authority for women's benefit, and discouraging authoritarianism or cruelty.

Another example of understanding hadith through *Qirā'ah Mubādalah* relates to statements targeting "a woman" or wife who shows ingratitude, fails to fulfill her husband's biological needs, or

Ethics and Laws, ed. Ziba Mir-Hosseini, Mulki al-Sharmani, Jana Rumminger, and Sarah Marsso (London: Oneworld Academic, 2022), 181–209.

[45] Ibid., 2022.
[46] "A woman" or a wife who is not grateful for the kindness of her husband will enter hell (Bukhari no. 305); "a woman" who cannot serve/fulfil her husband's biological need will be cursed by the angel (Bukhari no. 5248); and "a woman" who asks for a divorce without any crucial reason will not enter Paradise (Abu Dawud no. 2228).

seeks divorce without valid reasons. These texts only mention women as subjects and impose rewards or punishments without addressing men. Abdul Kodir rejects the idea that Islam exclusively addresses one gender. Instead, he seeks broader principles rooted in the Qur'an and hadith (*al-mabadi'*) that emphasize believers, good deeds, gratitude, service, and maintaining household unity for both men and women. Five principles (*al-qawa'id*) underpin husband–wife relationships: partnership, maintaining a strong marital bond, mutual kindness, consultation, and striving for each other's comfort. Using the concept of *mubādalah* (reciprocal reading), Abdul Kodir interprets these hadith as applicable to both spouses. Failure to reciprocate kindness, meet sexual needs, or seek divorce without substantial reasons can lead to exclusion from Paradise for either husbands or wives. Thus, the *mubādalah* approach ensures equal expectations and responsibilities for both partners in marital relationships.

Another prominent Indonesian scholar and activist is Nur Rofiah, who holds a doctoral degree in Qur'anic exegesis from Ankara University, Turkey. She is actively engaged in various Islamic organizations, including Fatayat (Nahdlatul Ulama's Young Women's Organization), Alimat (a movement advocating for equality and justice in Indonesian Muslim families), and Rahima (the Center of Information for Islam and Women's Reproductive Rights). Nur Rofiah has developed an approach she terms "women's substantive justice" (*keadilan hakiki perempuan*) for interpreting the Qur'an. The concept of substantive justice that she advocates rejects the idea of favoring the strong and dominant over the weak and vulnerable. Instead, this approach insists on considering women's unique biological experiences, such as menstruation, pregnancy, childbirth, and breastfeeding, along with their social realities when interpreting the Qur'an to achieve substantive justice. Nur Rofiah also emphasizes the importance of recognizing the diversity among women, avoiding the imposition of a single woman's experiences as a universal standard. Simultaneously, she underscores the equal status of men and women as servants of Allah.[47]

Similar to Abdul Kodir, Nur Rofiah categorizes Qur'anic verses into three hierarchical groups: (1) *the mission*: these verses aim to establish a life system that is a blessing for all, including women; (2) *moral foundations*: these verses encompass the fundamental values of Islam,

---

[47] Nur Rofiah, *Nalar Kritis Muslimah: Refleksi atas Keperempuanan, Kemanusiaan, dan Keislaman* [Muslimah's Critical Reasoning: Reflections on Women, Humanity, and Islam] (Bandung: Afkaruna, 2020).

such as monotheism (*tawhid*), belief (*iman*), *ihsan* (perfection), justice, humanity, benefit, safety, health, security, peace, sustainability, and other virtues that encourage the development of noble character, including noble treatment of women; and (3) *methods*: these verses provide practical guidance for transforming the concrete life system during the Qur'an's revelation into the idealized system of Islam. Nur Rofiah argues that this hierarchical categorization implies that lower-tier verses cannot contradict higher-tier ones. The mission and moral foundations are nonnegotiable and immutable in any system. In contrast, the verses related to methods not only can be negotiated but also should be adaptable to changing contexts if the textual interpretation leads in a direction that contradicts the attainment of the mission and moral foundations.[48]

Furthermore, Badriyah Fayumi, the leader of Alimat 2015–24 and one of the organizers of KUPI, stands out as a prominent activist and *pesantren* leader. Her notable contribution is the development of the *makruf* approach.[49] Fayumi highlights that the term *makruf* is mentioned thirty-two times in the Qur'an, with eighteen occurrences in verses related to marriage, the family, and husband–wife relationships. *Makruf* signifies what is "known" or "understood," and also conveys the meaning of "kindness" or "the truth" that is generally accepted, contrasting with *munkar*, which denotes something unacceptable or incomprehensible. Another exegetical definition of *makruf* is "anything considered right and good according to shari'a, reason, and social traits."[50] According to the Hanafi school of law, it is synonymous with *'urf*, signifying anything widely accepted due to its sound reasoning and positive community response. Building on these definitions, Fayumi defines *makruf* as "anything deemed right and good according to shari'a, reason, and social norms and can be accepted wholeheartedly."[51] To qualify as *makruf*, an action should align with the dialogue between universal values found in revelation and the local and specific social realities.[52] Based on this framework, Fayumi argues that polygamous marriage is not considered *makruf* if the existing wife cannot

---

[48] Nur Rofiah, "Tafsir Perspektif Keadilan Hakiki Perempuan [Interpretation of Women's Essential Justice Perspective]," https://ibihtafsir.id/2022/02/14/tafsir-perspektif-keadilan-hakiki-perempuan/.
[49] Badriyah Fayumi, "Konsep Makruf dalam Ayat-ayat Munakahat dan Kontekstualisasinya dalam Beberapa Masalah Perkawinan di Indonesia" [Makruf Concept in the Verses on Marriage and Its Contextualisation in Several Marital Problems in Indonesia], unpublished MA thesis, UIN Jakarta, 2008.
[50] Ibid., 40.
[51] Ibid., 43.
[52] Ibid., 57.

wholeheartedly accept it or if it has a detrimental impact on the existing marriage, despite its literal mention in the Qur'an. Fayumi supports Indonesian state laws, such as the 1974 Marriage Law and the 1991 Compilation of Islamic Law, which impose various requirements on polygamous marriages, including obtaining permission from the existing wife. She regards these legal restrictions as *makruf* and even suggests seeking the consent of the children, as they will also be affected by their father's additional marriage.[53]

In my scholarly work, I have also focused on the subject of polygamy, using Fazlur Rahman's double movement method. My educational journey began with secondary schooling at a *pesantren* in Central Java and culminated in a doctoral degree from the University of Melbourne. While many scholars generally concur on the need for restrictions on polygamy, I advocate for its outright prohibition, using Fazlur Rahman's double movement method. I categorize existing interpretations of polygamy into three groups. The first group interprets polygamy as permissible in Islam, relying on the Qur'anic verse 4:3, which states, "then marry other women of your choice – two, three, or four." The second group, while also citing Qur'anic verse 4:3, believes that polygamy is restricted in Islam, as the verse continues with "then marry other women of your choice – two, three, or four. But if you are afraid you will fail to maintain justice, then [content yourselves with] one." The third group, to which I belong, argues for the prohibition of polygamy by employing the double movement method. Instead of selectively quoting the verse, I base my argument on a comprehensive examination of Qur'anic verses 4:2–3 and 129 together.

The first movement in the double movement method is to move back to the time of revelation of the Qur'an to distil the intended message of the Qur'an. The context of the revelation of Q. 4:3 stems from the aftermath of the Muslims' defeat at the Battle of Uhud, which resulted in the death of seventy Muslim men who had left behind wives, children, and wealth. Some male guardians, entrusted with caring for the orphaned girls, misappropriated their wealth. Others expressed interest in marrying these orphaned girls for their beauty and wealth, but were unwilling to provide them with a proper marital gift (*mahr*). In response to the mistreatment of vulnerable orphaned girls by certain male guardians, verses 4:2–3 were revealed:

> Give orphans their wealth [when they reach maturity], and do not exchange your worthless possessions for their valuables, nor cheat

---

[53] Ibid., 153.

them by mixing their wealth with your own. For this would indeed be a great sin. (Q. 4:2)

If you fear you might fail to give orphan women their [due] rights [if you were to marry them], then marry other women of your choice – two, three, or four. But if you are afraid you will fail to maintain justice, then [content yourselves with] one or those [bondwomen] in your possession. This way you are less likely to commit injustice. (Q. 4:3)

Q. 4:2 reveals Allah's awareness of the male guardians' exploitation of orphaned girls and admonishes them to cease such dishonest practices. In Q. 4:3, God instructs these male guardians to marry women other than the orphaned girls, expecting that they will provide a proper *mahar*, fearing the consequences from the girls' fathers if they fail to do so. Examining this context of revelation clarifies that the Qur'an's intended message is not to promote polygamy. During the time of revelation, polygamous marriages were prevalent and unrestricted. Instead, the emphasis lies on the instruction to treat wives justly, particularly highlighting the importance of justice for vulnerable orphaned girls. These verses underscore the crucial role of justice in the treatment of multiple wives, a requirement mentioned repeatedly in the text. Notably, Q. 4:129 acknowledges that achieving perfect justice in such situations may be exceedingly challenging:

You will never be able to maintain justice between your wives – no matter how keen you are. So do not totally incline towards one leaving the other in suspense. And if you do what is right and are mindful ʾof Allahʾ, surely Allah is All-Forgiving, Most Merciful.

Hence, considering the context of the revelation and the relation between Q. 4:2–3 and 129, I have constructed a case for the prohibition of polygamy.[54]

CONCLUSION

The growing number of Islamic feminist scholars and activists is today playing a crucial role in challenging prevailing interpretations of religious texts in Indonesia that often subordinate women. Renowned

---

[54] Nina Nurmila, *Women, Islam and Everyday Life: Renegotiating Polygamy in Indonesia* (London, New York: Routledge, 2009), 44.

non-Indonesian Islamic feminists like Fatima Mernissi, Asghar Ali Engineer, Amina Wadud, and Asma Barlas have employed hermeneutical and contextual readings of the Qur'an. Their fresh perspectives have influenced Indonesian Muslim scholars to reinterpret religious texts through a gender-equal lens, addressing such issues as women's leadership, husband–wife relationships, and polygamy. All these Islamic feminists reject literal and fragmented Qur'anic interpretations, opting instead for holistic approaches.

Their methods yield interpretations supporting equal relations between men and women. These reinterpretations have inspired not only Indonesian but also Malaysian Islamic feminists like Zainah Anwar and Rozana Isa to establish Sisters in Islam in 1988 and, later, Musawah in 2009, a global movement advocating for equality and justice in Muslim families. In Indonesia, Alimat was founded in 2009 with a similar mission. These feminist movements bridge theory and practice, combining knowledge production and activism. Musawah and Alimat have published numerous books and articles authored by scholars within their movements, including such prominent figures as Amina Wadud, Ziba Mir Hussaini, Faqihuddin Abdul Kodir, and Kiayi Husain Muhammad, who champion gender justice. Additionally, both Musawah and Alimat offer grassroots support for women who are victims of violence, exemplified by initiatives like Sisters in Islam's Telenisa and the Women's Crisis Center/WCC Balqis, affiliated with Alimat. These endeavors underscore their commitment to advocating for women's access to justice.

SELECT BIBLIOGRAPHY

Abdul Kodir, Faqihuddin. *Hadith and Gender Justice: Understanding the Prophetic Traditions*. Cirebon: Fahmina Institute, 2007.

Anwar, Etin. *A Genealogy of Islamic Feminism: Pattern and Change in Indonesia*. London: Routledge, 2018.

Barlas, Asma. *Believing Women in Islam: Unreading Patriarchal Interpretations of the Qur'an*. Austin, TX: University of Texas Press, 2002.

Engineer, Asghar Ali. *The Rights of Women in Islam*. London: C. Hurst & Co, 1992.

Hibri, Azizah al-. *Women and Islam*. Oxford, Sydney: Pergamon Press, 1982.

Karam, Azza M. *Women, Islamism and the State: Contemporary Feminisms in Egypt*. New York: St. Martin Press, 1998.

Mernissi, Fatima. *Beyond the Veil: Male–Female Dynamics in Modern Muslim Society*. Bloomington: Indiana University Press, 1975.

  Dreams of Trespass: Tales of a Harem Girlhood. Reading, MA: Addison-Wesley, 1994.

The Forgotten Queens of Islam. Cambridge: Polity Press, 1993.
Women and Islam: An Historical and Theological Enquiry. Oxford: Blackwell, 1991.
Nurmila, Nina. "The Influence of Muslim Global Feminism on Indonesian Muslim Feminist Discourse." *Al-Jami'ah. Journal of Islamic Studies* 49, no. 1 (2011): 33–64.
"Qur'ān: Modern Interpretations: Indonesia." In *Encyclopedia of Women and Islamic Cultures*, gen. ed. Suad Joseph. Netherlands: Brill Online, 2012.
"The Spread of Muslim Feminist Ideas in Indonesia: Before and after the Digital Era." *Al-Jami'ah Journal of Islamic Studies* 59, no. 1 (2021): 97–126.
Women, Islam and Everyday Life: Renegotiating Polygamy in Indonesia. London, New York: Routledge, 2009.
Rahman, Fazlur. *Islam and Modernity: Transformation of an Intellectual Tradition*. Chicago: University of Chicago Press, 1982.
Sirri, Lana. *Islamic Feminism Discourses on Gender and Sexuality in Contemporary Islam*. London: Routledge, 2022.
Wadud, Amina. *Qur'an and Woman*. Kuala Lumpur: Fajar Bakti SDN BHD, 1992.
Qur'an and Woman: Rereading the Sacred Text from a Woman's Perspective. New York: Oxford University Press, 1999.

10 Women's Mosques in China
MARIA JASCHOK

This chapter explores female piety in the context of female-led Islamic institutions in China, arguing for an interpretation of piety as relational and diasporic. Such an approach entails a focus on locally situated, multilayered interdependencies between social space and relational agency, between mosque and mosque-centred communities, and between the leadership and congregation of Muslim women,[1] constitutive of the specific nature of the Islamic diaspora in central China (*zhongyuan diqu*). The term 'diaspora' is interpreted through the lens of female gendered history, and more specifically through Hui Muslim women's negotiations for meaningful forms of inclusion in mosque institutional life. I contend that the unique genealogy of Chinese female Islamic leaders and a long history of women's own sites that evolved in mainland China under the conditions of diaspora – although hard pressed to stay relevant to the lives of globally connected younger generations of Muslims – have much to contribute to international Islamic discourses, are enriching, and are potentially challenging enduring patriarchal orthodoxies on female mobility and authority, and female engagement in the public sphere.

---

[1] China's Muslim population, generally estimated to comprise about 25 million believers, is made up of ten ethnic nationalities (or 'minorities') among which the Hui nationality is the most numerous. The vast majority of China's Muslims are Sunni Muslims, mainly adhering to the Hanafi Maturidi Madhhab. A high percentage identify as *Gedimu*, an orthodox form of Islam, known for rejection of unorthodoxy and *bid'ah* (religious innovation). Islam is referred to as *xiaojiao* (minority religion) by non-Muslims. See Dru C. Gladney, *Muslim Chinese: Ethnic Nationalism in the People's Republic* (Cambridge, MA: Harvard University Press, 1991). It is among the Hui Muslims in central China that women's mosques first emerged, constituting an important part of the Islamic landscape until the present day; see Maria Jaschok and Shui Jingjun, *The History of Women's Mosques in Chinese Islam* (New York: Curzon/Routledge, 2000); in contrast, for women's religious education in Qur'anic schools elsewhere in China, see Francesca Rosati, 'Women's Qur'anic Schools in China's Little Mecca', in *Ethnographies of Islam in China*, ed. Rachel Harris, Guangtian Ha, and Maria Jaschok (Honolulu: University of Hawai'i Press, 2021).

Placing the women's mosque or *nüsi* (*qingzhen nüsi*, hereafter referred to as *nüsi*), guided by a female *ahong* (woman imam)[2] at the empirical core of this chapter, is to highlight the particular significance of this unique institution to the lives of Chinese Muslim women in the Hui Muslim communities of (predominantly) central China. Its history is a key to understanding the embeddedness of local women's piety as fundamentally shaped by Chinese Muslim diasporic culture, reinforced by an overlapping, mutually reinforcing gender regime of strict Confucian and Islamic injunctions which, so the argument in this chapter goes, forged an agential piety that has had lasting impact on the long evolution of the institution of the women's mosque. Ultimately, the priority was for women – burdened with fear over their religious ignorance and scriptural illiteracy – to gain legitimacy for claims to their own material and social resources, enabling acquisition of knowledge long denied in a strictly gender-segregated society.

During a time of crisis (the so-called 'era of adversity', *enan shidai*, during the sixteenth and seventeenth centuries)[3] for Chinese Muslims, the education of women of little or no religious knowledge became a priority for Hui educators and religious practitioners. The imperative instruction of women in rudimentary ritual and practical religious knowledge as a key to salvaging an Islamic way of life for all Muslims far from their spiritual home offered an historical opportunity for women.[4]

The history of religious piety among Chinese Hui Muslim women is a narrative of gender and spatial identity, a story of agential transformation of what in the late nineteenth century would become women's space of spiritual salvation. This female-centered institution, or *nüsi*, symbolizes, and is founded on, a relational piety of consequence both cultural and socio-political in its nature. Originating in Chinese Muslim women's dependence on learned women *ahong* for rudimentary scriptural and ritual knowledge, authoritative counsel on Muslim family life, and guided communal recitations of worship and prayer, a noteworthy history of over more than three centuries culminated in the professionalization of religious leadership and the institutionalization of

[2] *Ahong*, a generic title for female and male religious leaders in China who often supervise the religious affairs of mosques; a transliteration of the Persian *ākhūnd*, more common in Chinese Muslim discourse than the Arabic term 'imam'. See Maria Jaschok, 'Sources of Authority: Female *Ahong* and *Qingzhen Nüsi* (Women's Mosques) in China', in *Women, Leadership, and Mosques*, ed. Masooda Bano and Hilary Kalmbach (Leiden: Brill, 2012), 37–58.
[3] All dates in this chapter are CE.
[4] Jaschok and Shui, *The History of Women's Mosques*.

permanent sites for women's religious and social life. The gendered nature of circumscribed religious knowledge of what became the corpus of scriptural passages and selected hadith associated with women's mosque education, and the nature of its transmission, would only become a subject of critical debate, if limited in its terms of reference, during the recent Islamic resurgence in China.[5]

AN INTERPRETATION: PIETY AS A DIASPORIC, RELATIONAL CONSTRUCT

The case study of China verifies the importance of intersectional analysis[6] in the discussion of the importance of mosques and mosque leaders to the shaping of Chinese Hui Muslim women's piety. Factors of kinship and shared cultural and political influences, relevant ethno-religious policies, and, importantly, local translations of overarching religious values highlight the power of those in charge of the 'vernacularization'[7] of Islamic values and conduct, and a people's accommodation to a central political authority ideologically committed to the sinicization, if not complete assimilation, of all (foreign) religions as a prerequisite to the making of the modern Chinese nation-state. Linked to an intersectional approach, the notion of a relational agency serves an understanding of religious piety in the particularity of a Chinese context and the diasporic lives of Muslim women in a society ideologically committed to the triumph of secularism over all forms of religious practices.

The interpretation of Chinese Hui Muslim women as diasporic subjects, informing both their multi-faceted and relationally constructed identity, is indebted to the postcolonial intervention in diaspora studies. In an editorial introduction to *Diasporas Reimagined: Spaces, Practices*

---

[5] See ibid. for the origin and evolution of a highly gendered institution; the Islamic resurgence noted by numerous scholars of Islam in China has slowed down considerably since the Chinese state reasserted its absolute authority over all religious life. This makes the record of the female-centred sites of Islamic worship and learning that continue, if under changing and unpredictable conditions, all the more important. See Harris, Ha, and Jaschok, eds., *Ethnographies of Islam in China*; Guangtian Ha, *The Sound of Salvation: Voice, Gender, and the Sufi Mediascape in China* (New York: Columbia University Press, 2022).

[6] Kimberlé Crenshaw, Neil Gotanda, Gary Peller, and Kendall Thomas, eds., *Critical Race Theory: The Key Writings That Formed the Movement* (New York: The New Press, 1996).

[7] Peggy Levitt and Sally Engle Merrit, 'Vernacularization on the Ground: Local Uses of Global Women's Rights in Peru, China, India, and the United States', *Global Networks: A Journal of Transnational Affairs* 9, no. 4 (2009): 4–461.

and Belonging,⁸ the editors refer to the wide spectrum that encompasses meanings of diaspora, 'between emphasising group identity as the bounded object of institutional intervention, to understanding diasporic belonging and mobilisation in more fluid, dynamic and performative ways'.⁹ Whereas the conventional school of enquiry, harking back to the origin of diaspora as a Jewish narrative of migration or exile, is characterized by nostalgia and longing for the lost homeland – in the words of Dufoix, 'a centered, essentially political, version of diaspora',¹⁰ a more postmodern approach that understands diaspora as 'emancipatory, deterritorialised and cultural'.¹¹ Such an approach (most relevant to considerations of the gendered aspects of diasporic identity) privileges heterogeneity, as opposed to homogeneity, life as opposed to survival, and membership of transnational communities rather than membership tied to a territorially bounded homeland. This growing semantic diversity in interpretations of diaspora widens our field of investigation, allowing for cross-disciplinary, nuanced interpretations of fluid, complex, and sometimes seemingly paradoxical situations in which the members of a diaspora, however defined, find themselves.

The unique history of women-only mosques and the concomitant development over time of the institution of female imams in (largely) central China are all the more remarkable when considering women's near-exclusion from common sites of worship and learning elsewhere in China's nationwide Muslim settlements. The justification for such exclusion in interviews with male imams would frequently bring references to a near-mythological Islamic ancestry, an ancestry to which only men could lay claim (with their spiritual home, Arabia) as descendants of a patriline centred on cultural-religious identity, rather than factual historical origin. In conversations conducted for an earlier publication, male interlocutors stated that 'we [men] are all Arabs' (*women [nanren] dou shi alabo ren*),¹² reinforcing a diasporic identity with the commonly uttered phrase, 'we are all guests [in China]' (*dou shi keren*).¹³ Yet historically, the Islamization of the Chinese began with the conversion of local women when they were married to foreign Muslim settlers from Arabia

---

⁸ Nando Sigona, Alan Gamlen, Giulia Liberatore, and Hélène Neveu Kringelbach, eds., *Diasporas Reimagined: Spaces, Practices and Belonging* (Oxford: Oxford Diasporas Programme, 2015).
⁹ Ibid., xviii.
¹⁰ Stéphane Dufoix, 'The Loss and the Link: A Short History of the Long-Term Word "Diaspora"', in ibid., 8–12, 8.
¹¹ Ibid., 10.
¹² Jaschok and Shui, *The History of Women's Mosques*, 192.
¹³ Ibid.

and central Asia, who arrived in China as early as the seventh century, with the Islamic injunction demanding marriage to a spouse of faith, and the Confucian tradition calling for a wife's submission to the husband.[14] An enduring myth came about that resonates up to contemporary times. A dual discrimination of Chinese Muslim women, it may be argued, is underpinned by their membership of the Islamic faith in a society defined ideologically, since 1949, by the Chinese Communist Party government, and by their gender in a mosque-centred organizational structure where, despite the prolonged historical presence, ever contested, of women's mosques in central China's Muslim communities, a patriarchal myth continues to justify the exclusion of women from the religious, educational, and social facilities of mosque life elsewhere. In the words of a male *ahong* in a northeastern region of China where very few women's mosques can be found, 'women are after all outsiders' (*nüren jibenshang shi wairen*). As Jaschok and Shui noted:

> If [Chinese] Muslim men must negotiate their sense of belonging and of 'returning home' to one's ancestral home [Mecca], and final resting place (*guizhen*), where do women belong in this diaspora of disparate attachments and identifications, of disparate frameworks of reference and validation?[15]

Borrowing from Ian Burkitt's poststructuralist definition, relational agency entails an interdependence that makes people 'possessors of capacities that can only be practised in joint actions, and capable of sensitive responses to others and to the situations of interaction', and whereby 'agency emerges from our emotional relatedness to others as social relations unfold across time and space'.[16] The importance that Hui Muslim women in central China invest in belonging to mosque communities constituted of what are essentially non-kin ties reinforces recent challenges to received sociological assumptions about the primacy and dominance of family and kinship relations in our understanding of Chinese sociality.[17]

The dependence of largely illiterate Muslim women on everyday religious guidance and scriptural knowledge foregrounds the indispensable role of a female *ahong* in a gender-segregated society and, in turn,

---

[14] Ibid.
[15] Ibid., 194.
[16] Ian Burkitt, 'Relational Agency: Relational Sociology, Agency and Interaction', *European Journal of Social Theory* 19, no. 3 (2016): 322–39, 323.
[17] Jack Barbalet, 'The Analysis of Chinese Rural Society: Fei Xiaotong Revisited', *Modern China* 47 (2021): 355–82.

shines a light on the dependence of the *ahong* on members of her congregation for the legitimacy of her role as a religious leader of integrity and repute.[18] Gender and gender segregation (the dual impact of Confucian and Islamic injunctions that engendered female-led and female-centred mosque sociality and culture), as well as the diasporic subjectivities of believers distant from 'authentic' Muslimness,[19] create kin-like interdependency predicated on the faithful performance of leading religious roles, characteristic of familial relations (if without the closed nature of familial units). Yet non-kin relations retain a significant aspect of Confucian morality, 'an emphasis on the uniqueness of each person in the performance of the roles he or she occupies',[20] in contrast to an individualism associated with Western morality, whereby 'one's individuality derives from one's autonomy from prescribed positions in relationships'.[21] Respect is extended ultimately to all with a claim to religious authority – female and male – who occupy positions of vital importance in the context of Islam as a minority religion in an avowedly secularist Communist state.[22]

Diasporic subjectivity, informed by anxiety over the authentic performance of Muslimness and mandatory religious and ritual duties, shapes religious piety as fundamentally relational and interactive, the emotional foundation of closely knit female mosque congregations. Borrowing from relational sociology, piety may be understood as relationally constructed agency which 'is to do with people producing particular effects in the world and on each other through the relational connections and joint actions, whether or not those effects are reflexively produced'.[23] Piety is not an external force but an ever-present constituent part, and an all-pervasive part at that, of living. But that interdependence contains different kinds of interaction, where participants' specific roles and associated statuses inflect an individual's dominance, dependency, aspiration, and social resources, adding to the complexity of relationships the volitional compliance by women with the trusted authority of transmitters of knowledge, and thus of hope.

[18] Jaschok, 'Sources of Authority', 37–58.
[19] Maria Jaschok and Shui Jingjun, 'Chinese Hui Muslim Pilgrims – Back Home from Mecca: Negotiating Identity and Gender, Status and Afterlife'. In *The Changing World Religion Map: Sacred Places, Identities, Practices and Politics*, ed. Stanley D. Brunn (Dordrecht: Springer, 2015), 3169–3187.
[20] Jack Barbalet, 'The Analysis of Chinese Rural Society', 365.
[21] Ibid.
[22] See the changes that have taken place over time in state control over the training and certification of *ahong*, Jaschok, 'Sources of Authority'.
[23] Burkitt, 'Relational Agency', 323.

For women's mosques, group identities are cemented in emotional relations in which deference (to superior learning, perceived superior religiosity, and superior performance of Muslim duties) mingles with affection and close attachment. Particularly in women believers' relationship with their mosque *ahong*, reliance on the *ahong*'s religious guidance and scriptural knowledge is ever predicated on trust and the implicit trustworthiness of their *ahong*.[24] As Burkitt holds, 'Thus, people's relationships are always central to their reflexivity, rationalities and emotions',[25] allowing the researcher to understand something of the resilience of a relational piety as it connects with ties of affection and obligations that reach back not only into a distant past (connecting up with generations of women who went before them and their faith, and thus a salvation safeguarded by learned women and collective learning) but also the lived present, anchoring belonging equally in the overarching values of the Islamic belief system and the intimate sphere of intergenerational ties. Performing piety becomes a ritualized enactment of collective memory and commitment to women's historical legacy, to be treasured and kept alive for future generations.

MOSQUES AND 'HOME' IN DIASPORIC CONTEXTS

The application of concepts from postcolonial diaspora study to China's Muslims brings to the fore the relevance of two core conceptual elements of diaspora, 'the loss of "home" and the ongoing link to some notion of it'.[26] This asks us to consider 'home' as shaped by the historical experience of Chinese Hui Muslims, inviting references to the manifold political, demographic, geopolitical and cultural challenges faced historically by Chinese Muslims in a non-Muslim country. And, more difficult to ascertain, we are faced with the challenge of understanding diasporic subjectivities, a challenge which invites us to imagine the likely impact on believers 'in exile' of the sacred resources of Islam, with the opportunity for pilgrimage, Hajj, as a fundamental Muslim duty, accomplished only with difficulty and until recently, in the case of women, by relatively few.[27]

---

[24] It is important to note that the appointment of an *ahong* is conditional on rigorous appraisal of the character, professional track record, public standing, and (ideally) scriptural erudition of the candidate by the women's mosque management committee. Most commonly, members of the wider mosque congregation are kept informed and asked for feedback throughout the interview process; see Jaschok, 'Sources of Authority'.

[25] Burkitt, 'Relational Agency', 335.

[26] Nando et al., *Diasporas Reimagined*, xix.

[27] Jaschok and Shui, 'Chinese Hui Muslim Pilgrims'.

A key characteristic of diaspora is connection with a homeland through the preservation of ways of life and of cultural practices. These are enduring habits, rituals, and everyday practices that are collectively used to sustain and share a collective ethno-religious identity within a maelstrom of external forces threatening the precarious hold on identity and culture in diaspora. In this context, mosques occupy a vital dual function, sustaining communal memory, faith, and practices whilst at the same time mediating between Muslim communities and their host societies. Their powerful symbolism demarcates visible identity and presence in a non-Muslim host society and provides potent subtexts of political and cultural contestation in which cultural processes of belonging, adaptation, and transcendence are negotiated at the most local level. Barbara Metcalf[28] refers to mosques as 'borderlands' in which gender regime and women's rights contribute to emblems of inclusion and exclusion of the Other. The complexity of a social space such as the mosque, Amina Wadud[29] says, thus requires varied perspectives on the uses of space, the claims to space, and the conceptualization of its meaning (which is always gendered).

Moreover, an idea that carries significant implications for women's spatial claims concerns the 'portability'[30] of essential 'Islam' (the scriptures and images of the holy shrines of Islam). The significance of the mosque to believers is thus not predicated on fixed notions of unchanging, immovable qualities, and it may be reconstituted wherever essential conditions are fulfilled. In an expanding Muslim 'global sacred geography',[31] and moreover in an era of a growing assertion of variously constructed modern (religious) subjectivities,[32] Muslim women in a number of societies are claiming rights to 'their own mosque', whether

[28] Barbara D. Metcalf, ed., *Making Muslim Space in North America and Europe* (Berkeley: University of California Press, 2016).
[29] Amina Wadud, *Inside the Gender Jihad: Women's Reform in Islam* (Oxford: Oneworld Publications, 2006).
[30] Metcalf, *Making Muslim Space*.
[31] Pnina Werbner, *Imagined Diasporas among Manchester Muslims: The Public Performance of Pakistani Transnational Identity Politics – World Anthropology* (Oxford: James Currey, 2002).
[32] Saba Mahmood, 'Feminist Theory, Embodiment, and the Docile Agent: Some Reflections on the Egyptian Islamic Revival', *Cultural Anthropology* 16, no. 2 (2001): 202–36; Ding Hong (2008), 'Wenhua, xingbie yu huizu shehui', *Xibei minzu yanjiu* 3 (2008): 32–7; Fan Ruolan (2006), 'Wenming chongtu zhong de miansha', *Shijie jingji yu zhengzhi* 3 (2006): 32–8; Jaschok and Shui, 'The Study of Islam, Women, and Gender in China: Taking a Gender-Critical Turn', *A Journal of the Singapore Society of Asian Studies* 37 (August 2013): 1–14.

constituted in private homes, in unclaimed social spaces, or in cyberspace. The tension between conventional spatial segregation and the creation of new social spaces raises critical research issues on the changing nature of the 'mosque' and women's religiosity and agency.[33]

Comparative and interdisciplinary research has contributed important findings to help understand the potent matrix of gender norms, religio-cultural practices and their spatial inscriptions surrounding the notion of the 'mosque'.[34] Mosques are imbued, by the Muslim faithful and non-Muslim alike, with compelling meanings variously associated with religious tolerance or with alienating provocation in countries where Muslims are in the minority.[35] Whatever the interpretation of the role played by mosques in Muslim minority communities, whether as a site of worship and source of collective faith, as a site of 'cultural brokerage',[36] as an emblem of multi-faith tolerance or as a reminder of alienating Otherness, their centrality both in the eyes of Muslims and of mainstream society – contested, controversial, ever visible – is integral to understanding the lives of members of a given Muslim community, the status of women and prevalent gender regimes.

[33] Fazila Bhimji, 'Assalam u Alaikum: Brother, I Have a Right to My Opinion on This: British Islamic Women Assert Their Positions in Virtual Space', in *Gender and Language Use in Religious Identity*, ed. A. Jule (London: Palgrave Macmillan, 2005), 203–220; Anna Piela, 'Piety as a Concept Underpinning Muslim Women's Online Discussions of Marriage and Professional Career', *Contemporary Islam* 5, no. 3 (2011): 249–265; Anna J. Secor, 'The Veil and Urban Space in Istanbul: Women's Dress, Mobility and Islamic Knowledge', *Gender, Place and Culture: A Journal of Feminist Geography* 9, no. 1 (2002): 5–22.

[34] Doreen Massey, *Space, Place and Gender* (Minneapolis: University of Minnesota Press, 1994); Doreen Massey and P. Jess, eds., *A Place in the World?: Places, Cultures and Globalization* (Oxford: Oxford University Press, 1995); Kim Knott, *The Location of Religion: A Spatial Analysis* (London: Routledge, 2005); Shirley Ardener, ed., *Women and Space* (Oxford: Berg, 1993); Gary Bouma, *Mosques and Muslim Settlement in Australia* (Canberra: Australian Government Publishing Service, 1994); Ghazi-Walid Falah and Caroline Nagel, eds., *Geographies of Muslim Women: Gender, Religion and Space* (New York: Guilford Press, 2005); Samina Yasmeen, 'Muslim Women as Citizens in Australia: Diverse Notions and Practices', *The Australian Journal of Social Issues* 42, no. 1 (autumn 2007): 41–54.

[35] Ingrid Mattson, 'Women, Islam and Mosques', in *Encyclopaedia of Women and Religion in North America*, ed. R. S. Keller and R. R. Reuther (Bloomington: Indiana University Press, 2006), 615–19; Mohamed Elmastry, 'Women in Mosques', 29 May 2007, www.islamicity.org/3110/women-in-mosques/; Jamillah Karim, 'Negotiating Gender Lines: Women's Movement across Atlanta Mosques', 31 May 2010, https://southernspaces.org/2010/negotiating-gender-lines-womens-movement-across-atlanta-mosques/.

[36] Richard T. Antoun, *Muslim Preacher in the Modern World: A Jordanian Case Study in Comparative Perspective* (Princeton: Princeton University Press, 1989).

THE RELIGIOUS PIETY OF CHINESE HUI MUSLIM WOMEN AND MALE–FEMALE EQUALITY

Muslim women are the principal transmitters and transformers of cultural traditions and associated values.[37] As the keepers of Muslim cultural traditions at home, through their primary roles of wives and mothers, encoded in multiple patriarchal strictures and sanctions, and through their personal conduct and outer appearance in public, women are held to signify the essence of Islamic faith and the distinctiveness of their entire community. Nevertheless, in spite of their centrality to the symbolic and cultural identity of the community, this communal identity is predicated on women's public marginality, even invisibility, in the social spaces where interaction with non-Muslim society takes place. This contradiction between the value of women to the community and the community's fear – because of their value – of women's 'transgression' of paradigmatic conduct is at the core of many studies. Jaschok and Shui, Mernissi, Peteet, and Sabbah, among others,[38] have studied the indispensable contributions made by women to the preservation of Islam and Muslim identity in the face of the community's often punitive gender codes. A complicating factor arises from the status of women in contemporary Chinese society identified as members of religious organizations. The abiding symbiotic linkage between the revolutionary founding mythology of the Communist Party state and the accomplished factuality of 'women's liberation',[39] with the deliverance of women from

[37] Haleh Afshar, 'Muslim Women in West Yorkshire: Growing up with Real and Imaginary Values amidst Conflicting Views of Self and Society', in *The Dynamics of 'Race' and Gender: Some Feminist Interventions*, ed. Haleh Afshar and Mary Maynard (London: Taylor & Francis, 1994), 127–46; Gillian Tett, 'Guardian of the Faith: Gender and Religion in an (ex-)Soviet Tajik Village', in *Muslim Women's Choices*, ed. Camillia Fawzi el-Sohl (Oxford: Berg, 1994); Gina Buijs, ed., *Migrant Women: Crossing Boundaries and Changing Identities* (Oxford: Berg, 1993); Yvonne Haddad, 'Islam, Women and the Struggle for Identity in North America', in *Encyclopedia of Women and Religion in North America*, ed. Suad Joseph (Bloomington: Indiana University Press, 1999); Wadud, *Inside the Gender Jihad*; Ghassan Hage, 'At Home in the Entrails of the West: Multiculturalism, Ethnic Food, and Migrant Home-Building', in *Home/World: Space, Community, and Marginality in Sydney's West*, ed. Helen Grace et al. (London: Pluto Press, 1997).

[38] Jaschok and Shui, *The History of Women's Mosques*; Fatima Mernissi, *Beyond the Veil: Male–Female Dynamics in a Modern Muslim Society* (Cambridge, MA: Halsted Press, 1975); Julie Peteet, 'Authenticity and Gender: The Presentation of Culture', in *Arab Women: Old Boundaries, New Frontiers*, ed. Judith E. Tucker (Bloomington: Indiana University Press, 1993); Fatna A. Sabbah, *Woman in the Muslim Unconscious* (London: Pergamon Press, 1984).

[39] Wang Zheng, '"State Feminism?" Gender and Socialist State Formation in Maoist China', *Feminist Studies* 31, no. 3 (2005): 519–51.

regressive dependencies (among these the fetters of religion) as one of the central pillars of legitimation of the Communist Party's claim to political relevance, creates an entrenched, unsettling paradigm for the modern Chinese woman.

Previous writing by Jaschok, and by Jaschok and Shui,[40] considered the early record of the Chinese Communist Party's much-lauded legislative, social, and policy reforms of women's lives, particularly important in the field of education, and the specific impact on the older generation of female religious leaders of influential women's mosques in central China's Hui communities. These progressive measures, in the case of women religious leaders, were marred by punitive thought-reform campaigns, suffered often under conditions of internment and forced labor.[41] Nevertheless, such a deeply coercive political education of a now elderly generation of *ahong*, as they would themselves maintain in many interviews, can serve Hui Muslim women in different positive ways, as, for example, in strategic bargaining with Islamic patriarchy, when plentiful references are made to their legal status as Chinese women, for an acknowledgement of the equal status of elected female *ahong* and for the legitimate right of women's mosque communities to gain equal access to religious and material resources.

Frequently stated pride in the achievements of the raised legal and social status of *all* women under Communist Party rule, whatever their lived reality as women of marginalized status, may be interpreted as deeply felt patriotism and an assertion of a national identity that binds Chinese Muslim women to all Chinese women.[42] Yet there are nuances. The Chinese Communist Party's gender rhetoric on male–female equality (*nan-nü pingdeng*), has been applied by religious women leaders, as pointed out above, to conduct external negotiations for material and legal resources equal to those granted to men's mosques.[43] In relation

---

[40] Maria Jaschok, 'Violation and Resistance: Women, Religion and Chinese Statehood', *Violence against Women* 9, no. 6 (2003): 655–75; Jaschok and Shui, *The History of Women's Mosques*.

[41] Jaschok, 'Sources of Authority'; Jaschok, 'Violation and Resistance'.

[42] The relational construction of women's identity as a Muslim, as a woman, and as a member of an ethnic minority includes, importantly, identity as a Chinese citizen, if of marginalized status. For the women leaders interviewed, such an identity is a matter of pride, which serves as a basis for comparison with the perceived status of women in other Muslim contexts and is understood as buttressing their quest for strengthened religious knowledge as Chinese Hui Muslim women, and for improved status in their communities, rather than representing the intention to fit into a paradigmatic ideal of Chinese socialist womanhood 'unfettered' by religion. See Jaschok and Shui, 'Chinese Hui Muslim Pilgrims'.

[43] Jaschok and Shui, *The History of Women's Mosques*.

to intra-Muslim community interactions, however, the concept of equality is filtered through a lens of gender complementary (*xingbie hezuo*). That is, gender complementarity as defining of societal structures delineating the division of labor, spatial assignment, physical and cultural mobility, and gender-coded morality, is idealized as rooted in mutual respect and popularized in frequent references to the historical significance of solidarity between men and women for central China's Muslims. As will be described below, it is not therefore static or impervious to change. The evolution of women's Qur'anic schools and mosques, particular (if not exclusively so) to central China's Muslims, has become an integral part of the celebrated local Muslim culture as demonstrating a rich tradition of gender complementarity.

Such interdependence characterizes not only relationships among members of a given mosque congregation, at its centre the relationship of the congregation with their *ahong*, but also relationships among women's mosques in the region. Collectively sustained solidarity enables engagement with political, administrative, and civil society groups through which mosques negotiate and sustain survival and relevance in a non-Muslim host society. In this light, pressure for survival makes cooperation and the nurturing of harmonious relationships with male *ahong* and men's mosques a necessity. But these relationships are negotiable, situating women's mosques in a social space inscribed by the dynamics of a realpolitik of interdependence (*duiying kongjian*) of women and men, characteristic of the survival strategies of central China's Hui Muslim community, and of women's own striving over many decades of a revolutionary twentieth century for greater degrees of independence (*duli*) from men's mosques, allowing for women-centered spaces for learning, worship, and social congregation, sustained by shared needs and close ties of affection.[44]

Religious life in a predominantly and punitively secularist society also requires spatial ownership through which to negotiate legal identity and social status. This goes some way to explain the survival to this day of gender segregation, which has allowed women to transform assigned spaces serving to conceal the bodies and voices of women into spaces that have over the years been invested with the strength of their occupants – spaces from where female *ahong* go out to engage with male counterparts and, beyond Muslim communities, with civic and local government

---

[44] Ibid.; Maria Jaschok and Jingjun Shui, in *Women, Religion, and Space in China: Islamic Mosques and Daoist Temples, Catholic Convents and Chinese Virgins* (New York: Routledge, 2011).

institutions. The strength of female leadership in Islam, noted by Jaschok and Shui,[45] has been mirrored in recent initiatives that have resulted, in the face of considerable opposition from within Islamic patriarchy, in the resurrection of a highly expressive gendered soundscape of Islamic chants and traditional Hui Muslim folk songs.[46]

If, as Wadud holds, 'the dominant attitude of the mosque is reflected in both its public demeanor and within the hegemony and authority maintained within it',[47] the gendered implications of this authority become evident in the rituals and practices of mosques in diaspora contexts. This points to the importance of comparative and cross-cultural investigations of the relationship between the spatial (Islamic) ordering of religious, gender, and social relationships and their impact on the social world of diaspora Muslim Women.[48]

THE PLACE OF MOSQUES IN THE HISTORY OF CHINESE HUI MUSLIM WOMEN

The diversity of Muslim culture and practice characterizes not only international Islam,[49] but also China's nationwide Muslim community. Whilst particularly in the borderland communities of concentrated Muslim populations more austere Islamic traditions of gender norms and practices prevail, as previously noted, that historically have never admitted the presence of women's mosques, other parts of China's

---

[45] Maria Jaschok and Shui Jingjun, 'Purity, Sexuality and Faith: Chinese Women *ahong* and Women's Mosques as Shelter and Strength', in *Sexuality in Muslim Contexts: Restrictions and Resistance*, ed. Anissa Hélie and Homa Hoodfar (London: Zed Books, 2012), 151–81; Jaschok, 'Sources of Authority'.

[46] Maria Jaschok, Shui Jingjun, and Ge Caixia, 'Equality, Voice, and a Chinese Hui Muslim Women's Songbook: Collaborative Ethnography and Hui Muslim Women's Expressive History of Faith', in *Ethnographies of Islam in China*, ed. Harris, Ha, and Jaschok, 180–203; Maria Jaschok, *Inside the Expressive Culture of Chinese Women's Mosques* (London: Routledge, 2025).

[47] Wadud, *Inside the Gender Jihad*, 174.

[48] Sylvia Frisk, *Submitting to God: Women and Islam in Urban Malaysia* (Copenhagen: NIAS, 2009); Talhami Ghada Hashem, *The Mobilization of Muslim Women in Egypt* (Gainesville: University Press of Florida, 1996); Yvonne Yazbeck Haddad, Jane I. Smith, and Kathleen M. Moore, *Muslim Women in America: The Challenge of Islamic Identity Today* (New York: Oxford University Press, 2006); Walid-Fazah and Nagel, eds., *Geographies of Muslim Women*; Carolyn Moxley Rouse, *Engaged Surrender: African American Women and Islam* (Berkeley: University of California Press, 2004).

[49] Elmastry, 'Women in Mosques'; N. Jeenah and S. Shaikh, eds., *Denying Women Access to the Main Space: A Betrayal of the Prophet* (Cape Town: Full Moon Press, 2000); Jane I. Smith, *Islam in America* (New York: Columbia University Press: 2009); Mattson, 'Women, Islam and Mosques'.

Muslim society feature a visible and fully legitimate tradition of women's mosques, albeit as an increasingly controversial part of organized Islam.⁵⁰

Research into the origin, evolution, and contemporary adaptations of female-led women's mosques in central China's Hui Muslim communities commenced in 1994, undertaken together with the Chinese Hui sociologist of religion Shui Jingjun.⁵¹ The history of women's mosques is long; its unique manifestation of independent institutions, locally referred to under various names, such as women's (Qur'anic) schools or women's mosques, *nüxue*, or *nüsi*, comes out of complex historical and socio-political negotiations over the nature of Muslim identity in the Chinese diaspora and over the means to keep faith alive and religio-ethnic identity intact. The incorporation of women into educational projects during the late Ming and early Qing Islamic renaissance (between the sixteenth and seventeenth centuries), inspired by Hui Muslim intellectuals and educationalists, was born of the need to bring religious knowledge into families and families into mosques.

Women as the primary educators of their children and the moral guardians of family life were seen as requiring a modicum of ritual and practical knowledge of Islam, and thus in need of rudimentary instruction in Muslim morality and its everyday observance. The subsequent growth and consolidation of women's own space of worship, education, and congregation were a direct consequence of women's value to their communities' preservation of the faith, which justified leaving home and domestic duties in a gender-segregated society for the purpose of religious instruction.

The expansion of mosques and educational sites for Muslim women was only halted with the religious persecutions of the 1950s, and hesitantly resumed in the course of less repressive government treatment of religions during the 1980s. The long period of persecution and the silencing of religious expression scars the memory still. Women's mosques have reopened, or, especially in the Muslim communities of central China, have been built anew, most especially since the late 1990s.⁵²

---

50   Jaschok, 'Sources of Authority'.
51   Jaschok and Shui, *The History of Women's Mosques*; Shui and Jaschok, *Zhongguo Qingzhen Nüsishi*, rev. ed. (Beijing: Sanlian Chubanshe, Chinese, 2002).
52   Although no statistics on women's mosques are available, in Muslim communities in the provinces of central China the norm is increasingly that, where men have their mosque, women too lay claim to one. In some communities, women's mosques outnumber the men's – Jaschok and Shui, *The History of Women's Mosques*. As noted above, the Chinese government has once more reverted to a restrictive, even repressive, treatment of religious communities.

Government policies have changed from outright repression to more indirect methods of control. The mandatory registration of all religious sites, which commenced in 1994, is marked by many female-led religious organizations as a turning-point in their quest for equality with men's mosques in law and political representation, because it has facilitated useful access to public resources and created opportunities for income-generating schemes. A younger generation of female *ahong*, on the whole better educated than their predecessors, furthermore contributed during a short period of expanding civil space to developments of women's mosques that allowed for their further growth in influence in the social, economic, and even political spheres of mainstream society (see below).

SUSTAINING PIETY: WOMEN'S MOSQUES IN TWO CONTEXTS

In order to understand the significance of the mosque in non-Muslim-majority sites, we must make sense of its location and interaction with the everyday environment.[53] What difference does the presence of a women's mosque make to women's faith and religiously informed lives in their daily traversing of spaces both religious and secular, both internal and external, and to the Muslim community?

By way of response, I am offering a study of contrast. The long history of female-led mosques in Zhengzhou, the provincial capital of Henan Province in central China, where improved education and material circumstances have enabled younger generations of female religious leaders to loosen the constraints on religious and social mobility under which female *ahong* and Muslim women had laboured, has led, as already intimated, to an extraordinary revival of the expressive culture of women's mosques and also to accusations, by opponents of women's forays into the public sphere, of the 'feminization' (*nüxinghua*) of Islamic life in central China. Before discussing the gendered reverberations of these developments, I want to give a brief impression of the impact of the absence of mosque life for women. Urban cosmopolitan Shanghai, where I conducted a series of fieldwork visits in 2015, was once a city that offered Muslim women their own places of worship, education, and celebration.

---

[53] Kim Knott, quoting D. Chidester and E. T. Linenthal, 'Introduction', in Chidester and Linenthal, eds., *American Sacred Space* (Bloomington: Indiana University Press, 1995), in *The Location of Religion*, 99.

Shanghai, a Cosmopolitan City
Both Shanghai and Zhengzhou have a history of women's mosques. In Shanghai, which had four women's mosques prior to the Cultural Revolution (1967–77), only one women's mosque, the Xiaotaoyuan Women's Mosque, was reopened in 1994, after much campaigning by the community of local Muslim women.[54] When I revisited the mosque in 2015, it had ceased to offer a spiritual and social home to women. Instead, I noted in my diary, the building presents itself to the visitor as well maintained and securely guarded; it has a modern façade and modern facilities, furnished with comfortable chairs and sofas to ensure comfort and a reassuring presentation of a benign state presence. But there is no woman *ahong*, and, during several visits paid to the mosque, there was scarcely a woman worshipper to be seen. The last woman *ahong* was not replaced. One of the most memorable meetings I had in Shanghai was with a group of older women, toothless with age, their tight, black silk headcoverings concealing their hair and necks.[55] Their venerable age did not prevent wordy expressions of nostalgia for 'the early years' when an *ahong* of great piety presided over the mosque. A young woman, who had, uninvited, joined our meeting, arrived from a nearby men's mosque. She disagreed, making the case for practices 'as in Saudi Arabia' and in line with 'a more authentic' Islam. In this 'official' rendering of the diasporic history of Hui Muslims, a two-part narrative became a story of Before and After reconnection with true Islam, with the symbolic divide between an aberrant past and a return to true Islam constituted by tightening prohibitions on the exercise of female religious authority and the continued legitimacy of female-led institutions of worship.

Thus, the Xiaotaoyuan Women's Mosque, which was the last remaining fully functioning women's mosque in downtown Shanghai, presided over by an assertive woman *ahong* until she was 'let go' in about 2005, was taken back into the authoritative fold of the neighboring men's mosque. Leading worship came to be the responsibility of the *ahong* from

---

[54] Jaschok and Shui, *The History of Women's Mosques*, 198–200; when Jaschok and Shui, in the course of an early extended visit in 1997, conducted interviews with religious leaders and representatives of the Shanghai Islamic Association, tensions over the status and doctrinal implications of the reopened women's mosque were already discernible. References to China's official gender policy (*nan-nü pingdeng*, gender equality) served to explain 'concessions', as male officials from the Islamic Association would have it, to such stubborn women. Their alleged ignorance of Islam was seen by them as perpetuating highly questionable (non-)Islamic practices.

[55] Based on interviews in Shanghai with *ahong* and local Muslims, April and November 2015; March and April 2016.

the neighboring men's mosque. Worship takes place in the men's mosque, my diary notes, as is the case with general education and Arabic language classes for women who congregate, once a week, in the men's mosque to be instructed by the *ahong*. There is no longer easy access to worship. The impact of urban city planning and modernization has added to the dispersal of what once was a tight-knit community. The spiritual centre of old, once of such symbolic and personal importance to women, has ceased to exist.

The sense of women dispossessed is overwhelming when visiting the site of the historic Women's Mosque in an old part of Shanghai, now with its limited opening hours (its time plan is based on the ordinary working hours of its staff, rather than on the discipline of prayer) and relegation to the status of a curious relic from the time when closed national borders and distance from the holy sites of Islam created conditions that resulted, so the leading local (male) *ahong* states, in regrettable and 'aberrant' Islamic practices. Younger Muslim women, after all, many of them working in central Shanghai, are also starting to desert the mosques of their mothers and grandmothers. In a trend even more notable in the case of young Muslim men, young women turn to other sources of authority and religious learning – to the charismatic presence of younger generations of male *ahong* from the frontier regions of northwest China's Muslim enclaves. Talked about as the phenomenon of 'greening' (*lühua*, a reference to the growing importance of *halal* strictures over the daily life of Muslim families), the influence of a more austere Islam over younger generations of women, as over men, is marked. Drawing worshippers away from traditional mosque sites, new sites of congregations can be found in public squares, under bridges and archways, wherever urban space permits the assembly of large crowds and long, eloquent sermons. These developments, because they affect younger women, compound the problems and accelerate a process by which women's mosques are assigned to the past and stories of women's unique history cease to be told.

Women's Mosques in Provincial Hui Muslim Communities

How does the situation of Muslim women in central China's Hui communities compare with their fellow believers in Shanghai who suffered the loss of female-led and -centred sites? More steeped in the past (after all, women's mosques originated in central China well over three centuries ago) and less exposed to the austere gender regimes of a more fundamentalist Islam, how differently have women negotiated their diasporic sensibility? What difference does the continuation of segregated Islamic organizations make to their power to bargain and to their engagement in political and social developments in Chinese society more widely?

Women's mosques in the provincial capital of Henan Province not only continue their institutional and cultural presence: in the case of a number of remarkable instances, because they are led by charismatic younger *ahong*, their influence is growing.[56] Of interest is both a reconnection with history, for so long interrupted by a political clampdown on all that revolutionary Maoism once considered fetters of superstition on the minds and bodies of women, and an increased willingness to contribute to the richness and heterogeneity (however received by the state and male-dominated Islamic authority) of current Muslim practices in China. Home is no longer confinement to the space of (often modest-sized) mosques, which left women disconnected from, and ignorant of, the wider *ummah*: home is expanding. Thus, the *ahong* of a major women's mosque can network with *ahong* and female teachers across the province of Henan. Her fellow *ahong* in a nearby township organizes most effectively all educational and cultural activities for those women who are without mosques of their own. Both *ahong* are part of associations of *ahong* exchanging teaching materials, updating on the most recent Arabic language-teaching textbooks, organizing gatherings – and in the process cementing solidarity. But home has also expanded beyond provincial and national borders – with pilgrimages on the rise, and opportunities for study abroad taken up by more young Muslim women. Linkages with Indonesian and Malaysian Muslim communities in particular have been successful in inspiring new pedagogies, new ideas of activism, and new cultural expressions and institutions. This has also meant that a number of young women are intent on study abroad. These transnational linkages have found their most eloquent, and contested, expression in the revival of a sonic culture resonant with the collective memory of women's faith and endurance.

The revival of the traditional oral transmission of learning and pleasure through *jingge* (Islamic chants) came late, in the 1990s, after a long period of ruptured memory and repressed longing for outlets of religious expression.[57] One of the crucial factors was the widely held prohibition

[56] At the time of writing, in 2023, whilst the authority of a younger generation of *ahong* continues to matter, the scope of their educational and social activities is more circumscribed and conducted with greater caution.
[57] Maria Jaschok and Shui Jingjun, 'Gender, Religion and Little Traditions: Henanese Women Singing *Minguo*', in *Women in China: The Republican Period in Historical*

of female sound and performance, considered by many male and female *ahong* of older generations as *xiuti*, immodest (*'awra*, in need of concealment). The revival of *jingge*, led mainly by women *ahong*, is thus not without opposition. However, even where these new developments are lamented as *haram* and as a break with women's past conduct, tacit support is growing, helped by enthusiasm for successful public *jingge* competitions in which any mosque may enter its chosen group of reciters. As some of the older women, somewhat conflicted in their views on the suitability of such performances, will readily admit, the competitions, or *zanzhu zansheng bisai*, the Islamic *zansheng* song competition, with contestants impressing with their distinct dress and intense performances, and with the excitement generated by receptive audiences and carefully composed panels of respected judges, are not to be missed.

This opportunity for performing popular Arabic or Chinese-language *jingge* (less often, chants from a Farsi tradition) has generated enthusiasm particularly among younger women for a new song repertoire, so as to compete with each other more effectively, in a spirit of friendly rivalry. The atmosphere of collectively felt religious intensity engendered on such occasions is singled out by advocates of the *jingge* revival as a most important means for deepening women's religiosity.

Female sound and sound-makers in Muslim communities in interior China are contributing to a resurgence of the oral traditions of women's mosque culture energized by selective absorption of religious chants from other Muslim cultures, such as the popular Malaysian *Nasyid* chants.[58] In its wake, we note an emerging (or re-emerging) heterogeneity of expressive Islamic culture that is shaped both by the gendered history of China's Islam and changing gender roles in contemporary society. Words and collective female sound in public spaces, performed in unison and for various, and mixed, audiences, are transcending the physical and mental confinement of the past.

It seems that the notion of 'home' has been expanding in a uniquely local and yet also utterly modern approach to Muslimness, female religiosity, and Chinese citizenship, accommodating itself most certainly

Perspective, ed. Mechthild Leutner and Nicola Spakowski, 242–81 (Munster: LIT Verlag, 2005); Jaschok, Jingjun, and Caixia, 'Equality, Voice, and a Chinese Hui Muslim Women's Songbook'; Jaschok, *Inside the Expressive Culture of Chinese Women's Mosques*.

[58] Tan Sooi Beng, 'Singing Islamic Modernity: Recreating Nasyid in Malaysia', *Kyoto Review of Southeast Asia* 8–9 (March 2007), https://kyotoreview.org/issue-8-9/singing-islamic-modernity-recreating-nasyid-in-malaysia/.

within the constraints of China's policy on religion and within an Islamic return to a more gender-segregated arrangement within the religious sphere, as practised in many Muslim communities elsewhere. But there is also a successful pursuit of and aspiration to the religious life in energetic and creative engagement with what might be described as a transnational network of solidarity rooted in local communities of support. Bypassing disapproving Islamic authority figures at home and allying with fellow believers in women's right to a public voice, often well beyond the territorial control by vested patriarchal interests, women *ahong* are exploring the potential benefits offered by a transnational Muslim community. It is thus that the diaspora of Chinese Hui Muslims is assuming varied, distinctive, and highly gendered characteristics. And in the process, it might appear, both 'home' and 'mosque' are reconfigured in ways that diversify Islam and diminish traditional sites of power whilst imbuing new spaces with the potency of invigorated faith and collective hope, giving women additional resources and a wider scope for activism.

To be observed by future scholarship are the wider tensions thus set up between the emergence of a lively, female-inspired Muslim culture in central China, with the religious mobilization of girls and women by strong women educators and orators on the one hand and, on the other, a nationwide, systematic Chinese government policy of the centralization of organized religion. Closer examination is needed to probe disparities notable not only in the findings of my own work that show us women ready to organize for an urgent cause on the one hand and, on the other, an outright absence of women's institutional presence in the religious sphere, or their minimal political representation in the public domain of society, as in so many a diasporic context. Observers have noted the changing trend from an earlier emphasis on models of multiculturalism to an increased preference for policies of 'unification'[59] under a Han Chinese banner. The concept of *jia* (family) has acquired prominence in propaganda, street posters, and public discourse, de-emphasizing diversity and foregrounding as a national priority strengthening the nation through 'Islam, the [Han] Chinese way' (*yiselanjiaode zhongguo lu*).

Our studies tell us of women's collective strength, of their capacity to formulate perspectives informed by individual and communal needs, and of their resourceful strategies for changes to benefit all, whilst

---

[59] James Leibold, 'Ethnic Policy in China: Is Reform Inevitable?', *Policy Studies* 68 (2013): 1–65.

retaining their deeply held religious convictions. In any outcome of current tensions in Chinese society over allegiance, identity, and citizenship, the role of women will be significant.

CONCLUSION: CHANGING GENDER REGIMES AND EXISTENTIAL DIASPORA

What do we take from the fact that in a cosmopolitan and seemingly world-open city such as Shanghai a tradition of female-led Islamic institutions has effectively been phased out of history, with a formerly active women's mosque near the old quarter of Shanghai turned into a contested monument to newly emerging fault-lines in the complex symbolic landscape of Chinese Islam?

With Islamic orthodoxy at home and abroad dictating strict lines of gender segregation, the international influence of a more austere Islam (as apparent in Shanghai as it is elsewhere), women continue to be marginalized in the public spaces of men's mosques and are assigned primary roles in the domestic, private sphere.[60] One might argue that the remaining Shanghai women's mosque was controversial because its line of segregation deviated from boundaries that were to keep women in their homes, offending international visitors from more austere Muslim contexts. It appears that threadbare historical justifications for the establishment of women's mosques within a context of growing Islamic orthodoxy, compounded by the impact of international Islamic circles, and a growing presence of austere Islam among northwest China's Islamic groups, have served to redefine women's space as properly 'at home'.

However, it would not be implausible to foresee as part of the Chinese government's tightening grip over Islam, and with it a trend towards more sinicization of religious expression, tacit official support for women's mosque institutions, particularly given the claims of women religious leaders that government insistence on male–female

---

[60] It is to be noted that, under current political restrictions, even where there is a history of women's mosques, some women prefer to return to the safety of the home, meeting in smaller groups. This also occurs where the leadership of a local women's mosque is seen as wedded to the past, not sufficiently relevant to younger generations of Muslim women; see Jaschok, *Inside the Expressive Culture of Chinese Women's Mosques*. Svetlana Peshkova argues, however, that 'home' deserves more theorization, offering during times of religious and political oppression 'an important center of religious practice and socio-political activism'. Svetlana Peshkova, 'Bringing the Mosque Home and Talking Politics: Women, Domestic Space, and the State in the Ferghana Valley (Uzbekistan)', *Contemporary Islam* 3, no. 3 (2009): 251–73.

equality as an achievement of Communist Party rule must be extended into the religious sphere.[61]

Where in central China women are retaining the tradition of their own (segregated) sites of female-led prayer, gender segregation has come, over centuries of occupation, to turn into something else. Far from merely 'conserving' tradition, beginning in the 1980s, shortly after the reopening of religious sites – when gender-segregated religious spaces were apparently on their way to oblivion – women's own mosques were opening themselves up to change, led by transformative leadership. And it is thus a tradition that can be held to serve women's claims to legitimacy and a strengthening of their bargaining power for an expansion of influence beyond the compound of a mosque.

In conclusion, a comparison of women's lives in the diverse Muslim communities of China (that is, a comparison of communities with a tradition of female-led religious organizations with those where this tradition is unknown or was not revived when religious sites reopened after 1978) suggests an important insight of pertinence to the situation of Muslim women internationally. Where women's mosques have survived and continue to grow, they constitute an important resource for women in times of multiple internal and international challenges. Women's capacity to negotiate discriminatory practices shows itself to be stronger when they are identified with an institution, legally registered, that has a recognized place in society. Through occupation of a social space invested with a history, tradition, and material infrastructure, through such legally registered and recognized sites, female leaderships marshal educational and social resources that enable them to engage with public institutions and withstand, where necessary, patriarchal, cultural, and political challenges in their quest for gender justice and salvation.

EPILOGUE

My chapter rests on research and fieldwork undertaken during the late 1990s and up to late 2017. I was able to conduct joint projects of investigation, together with my research partner, Shui Jingjun, and our research communities, which covered multifarious aspects of the history, evolution, sociology, and sensory anthropology of women's mosques under female *ahong* leadership in central China, predominantly Sunni Hui

---

[61] When in the late 1990s women's mosques in central China faced threats of abolition, largely the initiative of leading *ahong* from men's mosques, they turned to allies in local government to safeguard their rights as modern Chinese women. They won their case; see Jaschok and Shui, *The History of Women's Mosques*.

Muslim communities. Until a few years ago, it was possible to marshal fieldwork findings that highlighted the role of Chinese women *ahong* among those who were leading a resurgence of Islam in the country. These leading female religious have been, and are, rejecting the instrumentalization of religion for patriarchal justifications, instead claiming an equal right to participation in critical debates and learning. Moreover, they held, and hold, that women choosing to lead religiously informed lives are entitled to do so, and that it is their right as equal Chinese citizens to differ in their choice of religious conviction from their fellow secular Chinese, making their women's mosque, once a secluded space, a space of transformation 'from which to speak'.[62] What I am describing therefore reflects a time past, but not a time concluded or irrelevant. For history not to be misrepresented, records must continue to be written, kept, and made public where and when possible. The canon of scholarship, when it comes to the modern and contemporary history of Chinese women of religious identity, is all too limited, but their pertinence to historical memory is immeasurable.

SELECT BIBLIOGRAPHY

Beng, Tan Sooi. 'Singing Islamic Modernity: Recreating Nasyid in Malaysia'. *Kyoto Review of Southeast Asia* 8–9 (March 2007), https://kyotoreview.org/issue-8-9/singing-islamic-modernity-recreating-nasyid-in-malaysia/

Ha, Guangtian. *The Sound of Salvation: Voice, Gender, and the Sufi Mediascape in China*. New York: Columbia University Press, 2022.

Harris, Rachel. *Soundscapes of Uyghur Islam*. Bloomington: Indiana University Press, 2020.

Harris, Rachel and Jaschok, Maria. 'Introduction: Sounding Islam in China'. *Performing Islam* 3, nos. 1–2 (2014): 11–21.

Harris, Rachel, Guangtian Ha, and Jaschok, Maria, eds. *Ethnographies of Islam in China*. Honolulu: University of Hawai'i Press, 2021.

Hélie, Anissa and Hoodfar, Homa, eds. *Sexuality in Muslim Contexts: Restrictions and Resistance*. London: Zed Books, 2012.

Jaschok, Maria. *Inside the Expressive Culture of Chinese Women's Mosques*. London: Routledge, 2025.

  'Sources of Authority: Female *Ahong* and *Qingzhen Nüsi*'. In *Women, Leadership, and Mosques*, ed. Masooda Bano and Hilary Kalmbach, 37–58. Leiden: Brill, 2012.

Jaschok, Maria and Jingjun, Shui. *The History of Women's Mosques in Chinese Islam*. New York: Curzon/Routledge, 2000.

  Women, Religion, and Space in China: Islamic Mosques and Daoist Temples, Catholic Convents and Chinese Virgins. New York: Routledge, 2011.

---

[62] See Jaschok, *Inside the Expressive Culture of Chinese Women's Mosques*; Walid-Fazah, Ghazi, and Nagel, eds., *Geographies of Muslim Women*.

Jaschok, Maria, Shui Jingjun, and Caixia, Ge. 'Equality, Voice, and a Chinese Hui Muslim Women's Songbook: Collaborative Ethnography and Hui Muslim Women's Expressive History of Faith'. In *Ethnographies of Islam in China*, ed. Rachel Harris, Guangtian Ha, and Maria Jaschok, 180–203. Honolulu: University of Hawai'i Press, 2021.

Jeenah N. and Shaikh Shamima, eds. *Denying Women Access to the Main Space: A Betrayal of the Prophet*. Cape Town: Full Moon Press, 2000.

Li, Gang. 'Reasoning the Sharī'a and Constructing a Proper Muslim Woman: Reflections on the Issue of Chinese Muslim Women's Haircut in Republican China'. *Journal of Chinese Religions* 50, no. 2 (2022): 185–232.

Rosati, Francesca. 'Women's Qur'anic Schools in China's Little Mecca'. In *Ethnographies of Islam in China*, ed. Rachel Harris, Guangtian Ha, and Maria Jaschok, 155–79. Honolulu: University of Hawai'i Press, 2021.

Part III

Asserting Agency in Socio-Political Life

Marilyn Booth's *The Career and Communities of Zaynab Fawwaz: Feminist Thinking in Fin-de-Siècle Egypt* is a fascinating intellectual biography of Zaynab Fawwaz, an early advocate for women's rights in the Arab world, navigating the complex socio-political landscape of Ottoman Syria and Egypt from 1890 to 1910. Fawwaz, emerging from humble beginnings, passionately tackled such issues as social justice, girls' education, and the intricacies of marriage, divorce, and polygyny amidst the fervent discourse of nationalism, anti-imperialism, and feminism characterizing the period of al-Nahda, an Arab intellectual awakening. Her engagements in gender debates, notably through the press, challenged the entrenched male authority and patriarchal norms, and the nature- or religious scripture–based justifications for gender differentiation, while staunchly upholding an Islamic moral worldview.

In contrast, Zaynab al-Ghazali's activism presents an intriguing parallel. Emerging in Egyptian feminist and political circles towards the end of British colonial rule, al-Ghazali initially joined a feminist organization but quickly found its agenda lacking, leading her to establish the Muslim Women's Association, with a stronger focus on promoting Islamic teachings on gender norms. Despite an invitation from Hassan al-Banna, founder of the Muslim Brotherhood, to merge her organization with his, she maintained independence, eventually joining the movement on her own terms and rising to its senior ranks. Her imprisonment for alleged sedition against President Gamal Abd al-Nasser, her resilience under torture, and her subsequent work with *al-Da'wah* magazine underscores her unwavering commitment to Islam as a way of life. Publicly, al-Ghazali emphasized the pivotal role of mothers and wives in advancing the Islamic nation, while personally embodying feminist agency by fearlessly pursuing her vision for Egyptian women.

These narratives illuminate the varied paths of feminist activism in late nineteenth-century and early twentieth-century Egypt, revealing the distinct ways that Zaynab Fawwaz and Zaynab al-Ghazali influenced the conversation on women's rights. Both women, rooted in their Egyptian and Muslim identities, engaged boldly with societal norms, leveraging their understanding of Islamic teachings. Fawwaz leaned towards a Western feminist critique of patriarchy and advocated for equality, while al-Ghazali embraced Islamic complementarity. Despite their differing perspectives, both shared a strong feminist spirit, relentlessly pursuing the vision of female empowerment they believed in. Studied together, the two underscore the diversity and complexity of Muslim women's experiences, highlighting the non-monolithic nature of their identities and struggles.

PART III ASSERTING AGENCY IN SOCIO-POLITICAL LIFE   261

The chapters in this part underscore the notion that the experience of being a Muslim woman is diverse and shaped by various factors, including class, education, and social exposure. They contest the view that Islamic hierarchical structures are wholly incompatible with Western feminist values. They show how the adaptability found within Islamic legal reasoning has enabled Muslim women to exercise agency in socio-political and economic domains, mirroring the activism seen in Western feminism. Highlighting the dynamic roles of Muslim women across history, these chapters illustrate that they have always been proactive agents of change. The wives of the Prophet, discussed in Chapter 5, serve as early examples. Muslim women thus have adeptly navigated and influenced their socio-political environments, advocating for women's rights and challenging structural injustices with a vigor comparable to that of their Western counterparts. Through a rich mosaic of historical and contemporary examples, it becomes evident that Muslim women's agency, fuelled by their Islamic faith and feminist ideologies, plays a crucial role in the pursuit of social justice and gender equality.

In Chapter 11, D. Fairchild Ruggles shows how, historically, women in Muslim societies have made significant contributions as patrons of social and religious architecture, shaping urban environments through their endowments. While similar to men, in their influence, women's motivations were often distinct, rooted in their unique roles within patriarchal structures. Unlike men, who reinforced patrilineal lineages, women, often seen as movable and part of diplomatic exchanges through marriage, had their identities and contributions overlooked by traditional historiography. Despite this, Muslim women, unlike their Christian counterparts, were empowered by Islamic law to inherit and manage assets, enabling them to endow and build as acts of charity and familial prestige. Ruggles shows the ways Muslim women, including those in Muslim families who may not have converted to Islam, exerted their agency in the patronage of education, culture, the arts, and architecture. She explores the social and economic dynamics that enabled or constrained their public activities, questioning whether their architectural commissions were for personal expression or familial duty. Particularly, she scrutinizes women's patronage of tombs, which, despite being designed to stabilize identity, contrasts with the fluid identities of the women who commissioned them. The discussion also extends to mosques, madrasas, Qur'an schools, pavilions, hammams, and public fountains, showcasing the diversity of women's contributions to Islamic architectural heritage.

Through case studies, Ruggles reveals that women's architectural patronage often served familial interests, especially in securing their sons' positions. However, assessing women's agency in these endeavors is complex, as historical records predominantly frame their lives and actions within the contexts of their male relatives. Insights into their independent agency are most evident in the actions of widows such as Nur Jahan and Shajar al-Durr, whose widowhood afforded them greater freedom to engage in patronage without affecting the family lineage. The motivations behind women's architectural contributions varied widely, from strengthening their sons' futures to expressing political strategy, piety, romantic attachments, or personal ego. Their positions within the societal and familial hierarchy significantly influenced the nature and purpose of their patronage. For instance, architectural works could serve to enhance the prestige of their natal or marital families, act as a political statement, fulfill pious obligations, or serve as an expression of personal taste or ego. Examples include Durzan's Mosque of al-Qarafa in Cairo to bolster her son's position, Gawhar Shad's religious investments as political strategies, Nur Jahan's tomb for her parents driven by piety, and Shajar al-Durr's tomb for Sultan Salih, reflecting a mix of political and romantic motivations. We thus see that the architectural patronage by women in the Islamic world was multifaceted, driven by a complex interplay of personal, familial, and societal factors. Their contributions, while often overlooked, played a crucial role in shaping the Islamic architectural landscape, highlighting the need to recognize and appreciate the varied motivations and impacts of women's patronage across different contexts.

In the following chapter, Shahla Haeri examines the intricate position of Muslim women in political leadership through an Islamic feminist lens, addressing why the concept of female political authority is often met with contention, particularly from numerous Islamist factions opposed to women's leadership roles. Haeri embarks on this exploration by juxtaposing the varied depictions of women's political power found within Islamic texts – beginning with the Qur'an's viewpoint and moving to a hadith that seems to question the efficacy of female leaders. She endeavors to reconcile the Qur'an's affirmative outlook with the challenging hadith that declares, "Never will succeed such a nation as makes a woman their ruler." Haeri argues that this assertion is heavily influenced by patriarchal and politically charged interpretations of the scriptures.

Through an analysis of the Queen of Sheba's representation in the Qur'an, Haeri identifies a clear Qur'anic support for female political authority. She further profiles prominent women from both historical contexts and modern Muslim societies who have held significant power, undermining the argument that female leadership is without precedent. These figures, emerging from royal lineages or political families, illustrate that personal competence was equally as, if not more, important than familial background in establishing their positions of power. In concluding, Haeri scrutinizes the contemporary revival of the debated hadith, suggesting that opposition to women's political engagement, often veiled in religious rhetoric, actually originates from a broader reluctance towards gender equality and women's legal and political rights. This aversion is indicative of a larger confrontation with deep-seated patriarchal structures, fuelled by women's growing insistence on political participation and equitable representation.

In Chapter 13, Nelly van Doorn-Harder analyzes the intersection of Muslim women's social activism and the vernacularization of Islamic feminist debates in Indonesia, providing a complement to Nina Nurmila's insights from Chapter 9. This analysis reveals the coevolution of these two significant developments. Van Doorn-Harder outlines how women's socio-political activism in Indonesia has been shaped by the nation's colonial legacy, the quest for national independence, and the evolution of women's rights movements. Early pioneers like Raden Adjeng Kartini and Rahmah el-Yunusiyah were instrumental in championing women's education and rights in the early twentieth century, a period marked by rising literacy and Islamic consciousness fuelled by increased interactions with the Middle East and the proliferation of print media. The establishment of influential organizations such as Muhammadiyah and Nahdlatul Ulama, along with their women's divisions, Aisyiyah and Muslimat NU, represented pivotal moments in the advocacy for women's rights, blending religious and secular education, promoting women's participation in religious spaces, and addressing familial rights.

This historical backdrop has cultivated a dynamic arena of women's activism in Indonesia, advocating for the re-evaluation of traditional gender norms, especially regarding marital relations, and pushing for legal and political reforms to elevate women's status. This activism extends beyond enhancing women's conditions to seeking solutions for contemporary Islamic issues, proposing innovative forms of Muslim feminism that challenge and reinterpret traditional standards. Van Doorn-Harder delineates five stages of Indonesian women's rights activism: early twentieth-century initiatives focusing on education and the opposition to polygamy; advocacy for improved marriage rights; the independence movement; redefining women's societal roles; and the amalgamation of Islamic and feminist principles. This progression underscores the escalating impact of women's sociopolitical activism on shaping gender justice discussions and policies in Indonesia.

Moreover, van Doorn-Harder illustrates how Indonesian women activists have not only transformed national discourse but have also aligned with global movements advocating for women's fundamental human rights. The Indonesian Women's Ulama Congress (KUPI), with its sessions in 2017 and 2022, highlights a groundbreaking development where female Islamic scholars issued fatwas – a domain traditionally dominated by male scholars – demonstrating a collective capacity to challenge patriarchal norms and promote gender justice within an Islamic ethical framework. These efforts signify the profound influence of women's activism on the interpretation of Islamic teachings and the broader campaign for gender equality, signalling a shift towards more inclusive and equitable religious and societal standards.

In Chapter 14, Zuzanna Olszewska explores the impactful realm of poetry and written expression among Muslim women, demonstrating how these artistic avenues have bridged divides of literacy and class throughout history. Olszewska emphasizes poetry's role as a powerful platform for protest and dissent, allowing women, even within highly restrictive settings, to articulate their grievances and seek recognition while maintaining societal harmony. She posits that this form of expression not only highlights Muslim women's creative agency and linguistic prowess, but also their engaged role in reflecting upon and influencing their societal landscapes.

Olszewska contrasts the emphasis on historically celebrated elite female writers with the enduring oral traditions upheld by nonliterate Muslim women. These oral traditions, encompassing poems, songs, stories, and speeches, showcase a robust culture of verbal artistry that surpasses the confines of written documentation. Through reviewing anthropological and historical studies, Olszewska offers an exploration of the factors that have facilitated women's verbal expressions across various epochs and situations. Her approach uncovers the nuanced ways in which women navigate societal expectations of modesty and the delineation between public and private spheres, shaped by a complex interplay of influences, including ethnicity, immigration status, and socio-economic conditions.

Further enriching her narrative, Olszewska presents a case study of Afghan refugee poets in Iran, drawing from her ethnographic research between 2005 and 2010, as well as her continued interactions with Afghan poets in the diaspora. This case study underscores the profound effects of mass education, literacy, and modern influences on Muslim women's verbal art, through the experiences of two poets who are among the first literate members of their families. Despite their divergent views on religion – one disenchanted, the other devout – their poetry reveals a shared narrative of displacement, educational pursuit, and the enduring impact of oral traditions inherited from their foremothers. Their work, often focusing on domestic life and the specific adversities faced by refugee women, especially in caretaking roles, exemplifies the intricate and significant place of both oral and written expression in Muslim women's lives.

By placing their artistic endeavors within a larger socio-political and cultural framework, Olszewska illuminates the varied ways Muslim women utilize poetry and storytelling to express their identities, experiences, and dreams. This chapter not only deepens the understanding of the historical and current dynamics of women's verbal expression in the Muslim world, but also celebrates the persistent power and resilience of their voices.

The concluding chapter of the book delves into the interplay between religious devotion and feminist ambitions in Muslim communities, placing a spotlight on women engaging in contemporary spheres. Zilka Spahić Šiljak engages with the notion of "Feminist Spirituality," suggesting that spiritual experiences within a religious framework can embolden women to advance their feminist goals. This chapter explores the complex relationship between progressive Muslim women – who tend towards liberal viewpoints and distance themselves from conventional religious bodies – and their intertwining of religious identity with feminist principles. These women present a contrast to their Indonesian counterparts, who, while advocating for redefined domestic roles and combating gender-based violence, typically maintain traditional practices like wearing the hijab.

In the backdrop of post-socialist Bosnia, Spahić Šiljak focuses on women who have adopted socialist egalitarian values, along with a more lenient approach to gender segregation and dress norms. Her analysis, underpinned by in-depth interviews, sheds light on diverse perspectives. Echoing themes from other chapters in the collection, this study uncovers the complex relationships women forge with their faith within a single community. It underscores the influential role of Islamic spirituality, particularly Sufi traditions emphasizing love, care, and service, in empowering these women to pursue feminist endeavors in various domains, such as nongovernmental organizations, media, and academia. These individuals are notably critical of the institutionalization and politicization of religion and the restrictive norms imposed on them as women. Nevertheless, they find resonance with Sufi principles, which are deeply embedded in Bosnian Islam due to its Ottoman legacy. Sufi teachings, which capture the core of Islamic ethics, champion an equitable society for all, including women. This chapter thus reveals a layered identity landscape for women, interlaced with elements of religion, ethnicity, nationality, and personal preferences in thought and aesthetics.

Spahić Šiljak's analysis aligns with the broader narratives within the volume, illustrating that women's conditions in Muslim societies and their views on religion and feminism are shaped by a multiplicity of factors. These include local socio-economic and political contexts, as well as the unique historical development of Islamic teachings in different regions, highlighting that the interplay between religion and feminism in these communities is far from monolithic.

MASOODA BANO

11 Patrons of Art, Architecture, and the Urban Environment

D. FAIRCHILD RUGGLES

Historically, women have been active and significant patrons of social and religious institutions in Muslim societies, endowing key buildings and contributing to urban environments. But women's motivations for such patronage differed from those of men: to begin with, women and men had different responsibilities in the establishment and defense of patriarchy. Through a man's descent from his father and bequest to his son he established a patrilineal lineage that secured intergenerational stability. As in Europe, Muslim women were objects of exchange rather than stability because, unlike men, they did not generally remain in their father's house but were married off to another family for whom they produced the sons that would continue that family's lineage. Such a marriage might be a diplomatic opportunity. A woman from a noble family might bring her natal family's prestige with her into marriage, and through her offspring the two families would be united; nonetheless, the bloodline itself was traced through the father.[1] This way of ordering family and political relations emphasizes the male line to such an extent that modern historians often do not know the name of the mother of a sultan or caliph. Women were moveable, easily absorbed into the household of the husbands they married, especially if they bore a son to that family. In this sense, there is an odd disparity between the permanence of architecture and the moveability of women themselves.[2]

In at least one very significant way, Muslim women were different from Christian women, because Islamic law mandated that they inherit a portion of their father's and husband's assets. Moreover, wealth – whether gained through inheritance, business enterprises, or as a paid stipend from the royal coffers – belonged to the woman herself. Thus,

---

[1] Because of the widespread occurrence of polygamy, these were often not full cousins but rather the children of half-siblings.
[2] The transience of one such noble woman is traced by Antony Eastmond, *Tamta's World: The Life and Encounters of a Medieval Noblewoman from the Middle East to Mongolia* (Cambridge: Cambridge University Press, 2017).

women could use their economic and social resources to endow a foundation or to build a major monument, both as an act of charity for the common good and as a public sign that illuminated the beneficence of the family as a whole.

This chapter will examine some of the ways that Muslim women (and women in Muslim families who may not have converted to Islam) contributed to the patronage of education, culture, the arts, and the built environment, and will explain the degree to which they had agency to build in their time. It will examine the types of buildings patronized and whether the women were acting for themselves or on behalf of their families. The chapter will look at the social and economic forces that enabled each of the women patrons, as well as those forces that restricted their activities in the public sphere.

Gender and its mapping onto disparate human bodies have profound implications for culture, politics, and the patronage of art and architecture, but here I am focusing on women who were identified as such historically and how the sex of these individuals affected architecture.[3] A significant question to be addressed is: When elite women were sent forth to join the family of their husbands, for which context and on whose behalf did they commission works of architecture? Especially with regard to tombs, which commemorate the life of an individual or clan, did they build for their husbands, thus contributing to their marital family's expression of piety? Or did they focus their attention on themselves and their own offspring? Although women also built mosques, madrasas, Qur'an schools, pavilions, hammams (baths), and public fountains, their patronage of tombs is especially interesting since tombs seem designed to stabilize identity, not only for the here and now but for eternity. Yet this contradicts the fluid identities of the women who actually built them. These are the key questions that will be addressed in the following six profiles of women patrons and the buildings that they commissioned.

ARCHITECTURE AS AGENCY

Buildings are the material manifestation of human agency: built on site by an architect-engineer together with stone masons, carpenters, tile makers and a great many other forms of expert and ordinary labor;

---

[3] On the third gender, see Lucienne Thys-Şenocak, "Women in the City," in *A Companion to Early Modern Istanbul*, ed. Shirine Hamadeh and Çiğdem Kafescioğlu (Leiden: Brill, 2022), 86–113.

under the auspices and direction of a patron who usually provided funds to pay for the building; for the use of a community or a family, or a single person; and in service of an idea such as education, commemoration, or the expression and location of authority. There are a great many manuscript paintings and texts that tell us about privileged women enjoying the use of pavilions, baths, and palaces. Women of the lowest social echelons might be less likely to frequent such spaces but nonetheless contributed labor, as indicated by manuscript images that show them carrying construction materials and mixing mortar.[4] Those of the elite class provided funds and commissioned such buildings as mosques, tombs, *khanqahs* (Sufi hostels), and madrasas, reflecting religious piety and fulfilling the Islamic mandate of zakat (charity). But there is no evidence that they – or their elite male counterparts – served as architects. Thus, when we say that so-and-so built such-and-such a mosque, the implication is that the person commissioned and paid for it, not that she or he provided the architectural design. Nonetheless, patronage is a vital form of agency for both male patrons and female patrons, since without the funds and direction of the patron, major architectural monuments would not be built.

The mere fact that we are discussing architectural patronage circumscribes the pool of women within the highest social ranks. Large architectural works were made for women of considerable wealth and with sufficient social power to be able to obtain large tracts of land for their projects. Yet there were plenty of other more ordinary women who made an impact on their environments as owners of houses and land, and through other forms of material culture, such as textiles, objects, and household furnishings. These women appear in the hadith, in hagiographic and biographical texts, and in the legal literature (often as plaintiffs).[5]

As material categories, architecture and art are often catalogued together because both reflect the taste of the patron. But architecture's impact on the social sphere was different because, unlike art, it had a utilitarian purpose that determined the ability of people to pray, study, gather, and work in the building. In many ways, the building is inseparable from the institution it housed, as is reflected by the fact that both the physical building and its operational services were typically detailed in the *waqf* deed (deed of endowment) drawn up at the time of

---

[4] As for example, in the *Akbarnama* manuscript painting by the artist Tulsi, ca. 1590–5 CE, showing the construction of Fatehpur-Sikri (V&A, accession number IS.2:91–1896). https://collections.vam.ac.uk/item/O95 31/akbar-painting-tulsi/.

[5] Such cases of ordinary women are discussed in Manuela Marín, *Mujeres en al-Ándalus* (Madrid: Consejo Superior de Investigaciones Científicas, 2000).

the foundation.⁶ Whereas the faithful could pray anywhere and at any time, regardless of the spatial environment, for a community to gather as a congregation – as an identifiable social institution – a large open space was needed, that is, a mosque. And while a burial can take place in a cemetery or a domed mausoleum, the presence of the tomb's mihrab and the protective vault overhead facilitate visitation. Thus, architecture had a social impact.

While women were active and important patrons, their ability to commission works of art and architecture was inflected by their legal status, age, family connections, and personal wealth. Women, both freeborn and enslaved, could amass fortunes and play a key role in the transfer of property, the construction of family identity and genealogy, and the public display of piety through their activities and endowed foundations.⁷ They did not appear prominently in court chronicles and narrative histories – the textual records on which historians rely heavily – and yet they made a material impact on the built environment. Indeed, one can hardly imagine Istanbul without the mosque, tomb, and bath complexes commissioned by Ottoman women, or Cairo without the tombs and pious foundations of Fatimid and Ayyubid women.

The degree of a woman's agency depended considerably on her legal status as free or enslaved, marriage status, and social rank as the daughter of a powerful man or as the mother of sons. But rather than look at women as types, I wish to avoid the very generalizations that so often permeate our vision of women's lives and instead examine actual people to see how these strands of genealogy, legal status, rank, and wealth led to various kinds of agency vis-à-vis the built environment. The following examples are by no means comprehensive. They are selections that show the possibilities of and limits to female agency at various times in Islamic history.

DURZAN AND THE FATIMID MOSQUE OF AL-QARAFA

The first of our examples is a woman who is not well known in later history, because she was not written about in the chronicles and texts of the period in которой she lived. Durzan (d. AH 385/995 CE) was a concubine (and possibly, later, wife) of the Fatimid caliph al-Mu'izz

---

⁶ To see how a *waqf* was framed, see Amy Singer's analysis of the Jerusalem soup kitchen that was built and endowed by the Ottoman queen Hurrem, wife of Sultan Sulayman I, *Constructing Ottoman Beneficence* (Albany: SUNY, 2002).

⁷ D. Fairchild Ruggles, "Vision and Power: An Introduction," in *Women, Patronage, and Self-Representation in Islamic Societies*, ed. D. Fairchild Ruggles (Albany: SUNY Press, 2000), 1–15.

(r. AH 341–65/953–75 CE) and the mother of al-Mu'izz's successor, al-Aziz (r. AH 365–86/975–96 CE). Her biography is given in Delia Cortese and Simonetta Calderini's *Women and the Fatimids in the World of Islam*.[8] Fatimid royal wives received a stipend, as well as direct gifts from their husbands, members of the court wishing to curry favor, and political figures hoping for an entrée through them to the caliph. While free women did not inherit equally with their brothers, they nonetheless could acquire a lesser proportion of wealth through inheritance, as stipulated in the Qur'an. In addition to gold, jewelry, textiles, and slaves, many elite women also owned land and buildings which accrued rental income. Some became very rich, as for example a slave consort of one of al-Mu'izz's sons who had amassed 4 million dinars by the time of her death.[9] One of the daughters of al-Mu'izz, on her death, left 30 bundles of deeds to property, 400 bookcases, 400 gilded swords, jewels, and luxury cloth.[10] Such wealth must have reflected well on the court, a clear sign of Fatimid prosperity.[11] Durzan, too, must have gained great wealth because attributed to her in Cairo are a riverside pavilion (the Manazil al-Aziz), a mausoleum, a hammam, a garden, a well with a waterwheel (or some pumping device), the Mosque of al-Qarafa, and possibly the fountain in the center of Ibn Tulun Mosque.

Durzan's patronage seems to have begun or accelerated after the death of her husband, when she gained uniquely powerful status as the new sultan's mother. It was surely in this capacity that she built the Mosque of al-Qarafa (AH 366/976 CE), only the second congregational mosque to be constructed after the Fatimid conquest of Cairo. The mosque was named for the area where it was built, al-Qarafa, between the walled city of al-Qahira (from which modern Cairo gets its name) built by the Fatimids, and the older city of Fustat, which continued to flourish as a market area even after the administration moved to new quarters in al-Qahira. Little is known about the mosque's form because it burned down in the great fire of AH 564/1168–9 CE, which destroyed much of Fustat. However, Maqrizi

---

[8] Delia Cortese and Simonetta Calderini, *Women and the Fatimids in the World of Islam* (Edinburgh: Edinburgh University Press, 2006); see also Cortese and Calderini, "The Architectural Patronage of the Fāṭimid Queen-Mother Durzān (d. AH 385/995 CE): An Interdisciplinary Analysis of Literary Sources, Material Evidence and Historical Context," in *Material Evidence and Narrative Sources: Interdisciplinary Studies of the History of the Muslim Middle East*, ed. Daniella Talmon-Heller and Katia Cytryn-Silverman (Boston: Brill, 2014), 87–112.

[9] Calderini and Cortese, *Women and the Fatimids*, 151, citing al-Musabbiḥī, *Akhbār Miṣr*, vol. I, 105, and al-Maqrīzī, *Itti'āẓ*, vol. II, 173.

[10] Jonathan Bloom, "The Mosque of the al-Qarafa in Cairo," *Muqarnas* 4 (1987): 17.

[11] Calderini and Cortese, *Women and the Fatimids*, 152.

(who wrote the encyclopaedic *Khitat* in the first half of the fifteenth century and thus could not have seen the mosque himself) cited a Fatimid source which described it as following the style of the Mosque of al-Azhar in al-Qahira, and having marble columns, carved wall ornament, and colorful wall-painting rendered by painters from Basra.[12]

The building raises questions about patronage and the degree of a patron's agency. While Durzan clearly commissioned and paid for the mosque, did she exercise personal taste in its design? Calderini and Cortese, who have written extensively about the women of the Fatimid court, note that she seems to have acted through intermediary agents, first the vizier Ibn Killis (d. AH 378/989 CE or AH 380/991 CE), and secondly the *muhtasib* (inspector) al-Hasan (or al-Husayn) Abd al-Aziz al-Farisi, whom she appointed to supervise the construction of the mosque and other works.[13] The fact that the mosque was so close in style to the Mosque of al-Azhar suggests that the builders followed a Fatimid template. However, it would be incorrect to attribute any lack of design agency to Durzan's sex: both male and female patrons at all times in history have relied on intermediaries in the form of advisors, architects, masons, and painters.[14]

The second question concerns the motivation for architectural patronage. Given that she would rarely, if ever, have prayed in the mosque, how did its construction benefit her? Calderini and Cortese suggest that the scale and location of the mosque meant that it could serve as a political tool that Durzan could wield in support of her son.[15] They show that as patron of the mosque, she performed a public role of piety on his behalf and at the same time was able to use architecture to balance the values of the Shi'i Fatimid court in al-Qahira and the majority Sunni population of Fustat over whom the Fatimids ruled. The mosque that she built was located between those two urban nodes, which led the authors to conclude that she was "a mediating link between secular and religious arenas, between the private realm of the court and the public realities of Fustat, between female and male domains."[16]

[12] For a hypothetical reconstruction and a translation of the passage from Maqrizi, see Bloom, "The Mosque of the al-Qarafa in Cairo." Maqrizi's source was al-Qudai (died 1062 or 1065). On Maqrizi, see Nasser Rabat, "Khitat," in *Encyclopaedia of Islam*, 3rd ed., ed. Kate Fleet, Gudrun Krämer, Denis Matringe, et al. (Leiden: Brill, 2019).

[13] Calderini and Cortese, "The Architectural Patronage," 105.

[14] On this question of a patron's agency, see D. Fairchild Ruggles, *Tree of Pearls: The Extraordinary Architectural Patronage of the 13th-Century Egyptian Slave-Queen Shajar al-Durr* (New York: Oxford University Press, 2020), 143–144.

[15] Calderini and Cortese, "The Architectural Patronage," 87–112; also Yusuf Raghib, "Sur deux monuments funéraires du cimetière d'al-Qarāfa al-Kubrā au Caire," *Annales Islamologiques* 12 (1974): 67–83.

[16] Calderini and Cortese, "The Architectural Patronage," 110.

MAHPERI KHATUN AND THE SALJUQ MOSQUE–MAUSOLEUM COMPLEX

It is not always clear, when a work of architecture is built, whether the person who bears its name was the patron who commissioned the work or its recipient. Especially in the case of women, many scholars have assumed that the women acted on behalf of their families and may not have played an active role in the planning and design of the complex, serving more as pious representatives than active agents. Indeed, some women are not named by anything but their title or family role.[17] Hence the woman known as Malika Adiliyya, who became the second wife of the Anatolian Saljuq Kayqubad I (r. AH 617–34/1220–37 CE), was known as princess (*malika*) and by the name of her father, Adil I, who was the Ayyubid sultan of Egypt and the Jazira.[18] Her title alluded to that prestigious family line, but it was not a personal name so much as an indication of her role as a high-ranking daughter who was given in diplomatic marriage to cement an alliance.

Kayqubad's first wife, Mahperi Khatun, was also known by a sobriquet: Khatun meaning "lady," and Mahperi in Persian meaning "moon fairy." Although Mahperi seems to have been acquired by Kayqubad as either a slave or a wife in AH 618/1221 CE, when her city of Alanya (then known as Kalonoros) was conquered by Kayqubad, she too could claim a lineage through her Armenian father, who ruled Alanya in the early seventh/thirteenth century.[19] However, perhaps because her father was Christian, she did not carry his name but rather something more fanciful, the kind of name that was bestowed on the sultan's favorites. Mahperi Khatun either did not convert from Christianity to Islam or converted very late in life, perhaps after the death of her husband in AH 634/1237 CE when she gained a position of unique importance as the mother of the new sultan, or *valide sultan*. As such, Suzan Yalman

---

[17] Sara Wolper, "Princess Safwat al-Dunyā wa al-Dīn and the Production of Sufi Buildings and Hagiographies in Pre-Ottoman Anatolia," in *Women, Patronage, and Self-Representation*, ed. Ruggles, 35–52.

[18] Suzan Yalman, "The 'Dual Identity' of Mahperi Khatun: Piety, Patronage and Marriage across Frontiers in Seljuk Anatolia," in *Architecture and Landscape in Medieval Anatolia, 1100–1500*, ed. Patricia Blessing and Rachel Goshgarian (Edinburgh: Edinburgh University Press, 2017), 224–252.

[19] On Mahperi Khatun, see Antony Eastmond, "Gender and Patronage between Christianity and Islam in the Thirteenth Century," in *Change in the Byzantine World in the Twelfth and Thirteenth Centuries, 1. Uluslararası Sevgi Gönül Bizans Araştırmaları Sempozyumu / First International Sevgi Gönül Byzantine Studies Symposium, Vehbi Koç Vakfı*, ed. A. Ödekan, E. Akyürek, and N. Necipoğlu (Istanbul: Koç University Press, 2010), 78–88.

argues, she held "dual identity," thoroughly integrated into the household of her husband and then her son, yet retaining enough of her Christian identity that her son could boast of her religious freedom in a letter to Baldwin II, Latin emperor of Constantinople.[20]

Mahperi Khatun's architectural patronage occurred during the reign of her son, Kaykhusrau II (AH 634–44/1237–46 CE), the period when she had the greatest agency and power. Among her many architectural works, the mosque–tomb–madrasa–hammam complex that she built opposite the citadel of Kayseri has attracted the most attention from historians. The hammam probably preceded the complex, as it abuts awkwardly at the southwest corner of the mosque and has an entirely different orientation. Patricia Blessing speculates that the mosque, which is dated by inscription to AH 635/1238 CE, could have been undertaken as a gesture to celebrate Mahperi Khatun's conversion to Islam, but it is also possible that it was simply an expression of her new role as the *valide sultan* whose visible piety would reflect well on her family.[21] An inscription over the mosque's west portal praises her patronage of the mother of Kaykhusrau II, but does not give her name.

The hypostyle mosque attaches to a madrasa at the latter's southeast corner (Figure 1). But curiously, there is no direct access between the mosque and the madrasa, and even stranger, the patron's tomb serves as a kind of hinge between the two buildings. The extraordinary tomb stands in a small courtyard carved from the space of the mosque's prayer hall yet can be reached only from the madrasa. It rises above the walls of the mosque, a semiotic sign for the woman interred there. Inside there are cenotaphs for Mahperi Khatun, her daughter, and an unknown person. The inscription on the cenotaph marking Mahperi Khatun's place of burial extols her as both "Mary" and "Khadīja," which Yalman cites as references to her dual identity as Christian and Muslim:

> This is the tomb of the lady, the veiled, the fortunate, the happy, the martyr [al-shahīda], the ascetic, the obedient, the fighter, the promoter of faith, the chaste, the just, queen of the women in the world [al-malika al-nisā' fī'l-'ālam], the virtuous and clean, the Mary of her age [Maryam awāniha], the Khadija of her time [Khadīja zamānihā],

[20] Yalman, "The Dual Identity," borrowing the term from Rustam Shukurov, "Harem Christianity: The Byzantine Identity of Seljuk Princes," in *The Seljuks of Anatolia: Court and Society in the Medieval Middle East*, ed. A. C. S. Peacock and S. N. Yildiz (London: I. B. Tauris, 2012).

[21] Patricia Blessing, "Buildings of Commemoration in Medieval Anatolia: The Funerary Complexes of Ṣāḥib 'Aṭā Fakhr al-Dīn 'Alī and Māhperī Khātūn," *Al-Masāq* 27, no. 3 (2014): 225–252.

ART, ARCHITECTURE, AND THE URBAN ENVIRONMENT 275

FIGURE 1 Drawing of the mosque–tomb–madrasa–hammam complex of Mahperi Khatun in Kayseri. (Credit: Gabriel, *Monuments Turcs d'Anatolie*)

possessor of knowledge, almsgiver of wealth in thousands [ṣāḥibat al-marʿūfa al-mutaṣaddiqa bi'l-māl ulūf], purity of the world and religion [ṣafwat al-dunyā wa'l-dīn] Māhperī Khātūn, mother of the deceased and martyred sultan, Ghiyāth al-Dunyā wa'l-Dīn Kaykhusrau [Kaykhusrau II], the son of Kayqubād. May God have mercy on them, Amen.[22]

Here she is named, but again is identified as the mother of her (by now deceased) son. Given her prestigious position as *valide sultan* and her

---

[22] Yalman, "The Dual Identity," 231.

prolific patronage of the built environment, which included her own tomb, it is hard to see her taking anything other than an active role in the architecture that she commissioned. Nonetheless, the uncertainty with regard to her identity reflects the status of many women: emerging from their father's house to join that of their husbands, figures of diplomatic and cultural exchange.

SHAJAR AL-DURR AND THE AYYUBID AND MAMLUK TOMBS

Like Mahperi, Shajar al-Durr of Cairo also drew status from her son. Shajar al-Durr (d. AH 655/1257 CE) was a Qipcaq slave (*mamluk*) of the Ayyubid sultan Salih (AH 637–47/1240–9 CE), and became his wife after bearing him a son in AH 637/1240 CE. Indeed, her name, a slave moniker meaning "Tree of Pearls," may have been bestowed on her in that moment, as she bore the "pearl" that was the fruit of the Ayyubid family tree.[23] Although the son, Khalil, did not survive past infancy, Shajar al-Durr gained permanent status by virtue of having borne an heir for Salih, and thereafter he trusted her to act on his behalf when he went off to fight the Crusaders in Egypt's delta region. When he died there in AH 647/1249 CE, she again served as unofficial regent for several months until the sole surviving son (by a former wife) returned to Cairo. After the assassination of that son, Shajar al-Durr was unexpectedly raised to the throne (AH 647/1250 CE) and thus became the first of what would become a long line of Mamluk sultans (AH 648–922 CE/AH 1250–1517 CE).

That Shajar al-Durr ruled in her own right was confirmed by her name on the coinage that was issued during her reign and by the fact that she was officially named sultan in the *khutba* (weekly sermon) issued from the mosques. But when the news of her reign spread, the attacks came quickly. The Abbasid caliph in Baghdad reportedly sent a stinging letter in which he said: "If you lack men, let us know, and we can send you one."[24] The letter most likely entered the historic record well after the events themselves, but its expressed sentiment was very real, because contemporary observers reported that even the very *mamluks* and amirs who had appointed Shajar al-Durr had become worried about

---

[23] Ruggles, *Tree of Pearls*. I am grateful to William Granara and other members of the Harvard audience at the lecture that I gave on November 17, 2022 who proposed this explanation for Shajar al-Durr's name. Note that her name is spelled both as Shajar al-Durr and as Shajarat al-Durr in the primary sources.

[24] Ibid., 104, citing Maqrizi, Suluk, ed. Ziyada, I [part 2]: 368, Maqrizi, Khitat, III: 385; Suyuti Husn II: 46; Ibn Iyas, Bada'i', I: 287.

the wisdom of having set a woman on the throne.[25] As a result, she was forced to hand over the throne to a mid-level army general, and, probably for the sake of making the transfer appear legitimate, to marry him. In the marriage agreement she stipulated that he would divorce his current wife and take no other; and so, several years later, when he began to pursue a politically strategic marriage with the princess of a neighboring sultanate, she became enraged at the breach of contract and had him assassinated. Soon afterwards, the divorced first wife exacted her revenge on Shajar al-Durr, murdering her in the bathhouse of the Cairo Citadel.

In the year of her ascension and abdication, she built a tomb for her first husband, Salih, completing it in AH 648/1250 CE. It was added to one end of the madrasa that the sultan had founded in AH 639/1242 CE and that bore his name as the Madrasa al-Salihiyya (Figure 2). Shajar al-Durr also built a tomb for herself sometime between AH 648/1250 CE and her death in AH 655/1257 CE. Both mausolea are unusual for the way that they claim attention. If the conical roof of Mahperi Khatun's tomb in Kayseri rose above the height of the surrounding mosque walls, the mausoleum of Sultan Salih not only rose twice as high as the walls of the madrasa to which it was attached but also projected out into the street, which was the main avenue in the walled city of Cairo (Figure 3). The combination of prominent dome, height, and projection into the street was an innovative way of not only emphasizing the presence of the deceased sultan but placing him eternally at the center of the city. Reflecting the site's continuing political significance, the Madrasa al-Salihiyya served as the place for the swearing-in ceremony for manumitted *mamluks* for many years thereafter.

Shajar al-Durr's own tomb likewise celebrated the identity of the deceased but used a different strategy for doing so (Figure 4). It was located outside the walled city in an area that already held the tombs and shrines of important figures, many of them women. It probably belonged to a larger ensemble that may have included a mosque, but no traces of these other buildings remain today.[26] The mihrab of the mausoleum is filled with a rich red, gold, and black mosaic that represents a branch laden with luminous, white mother-of-pearl discs (Figure 5). On the one hand, the image echoes the paradisaic tree of life found in Islamic religious imagery and in mihrabs, but on

---

[25] Ruggles, *Tree of Pearls*, 104; Götz Schregle, *Die Sultanin von Ägypten: Saǧarat ad-Durr in der arabischen Geschichtsschreibung und Literatur* (Wiesbaden: O. Harrassowitz, 1961), 66.

[26] Doris Behrens-Abouseif, "The Lost Minaret of Shajar al-Durr at Her Complex," *Mitteilungen des deutschen archäologischen Instituts*, Abteilung Kairo, 39 (1983): 1–16.

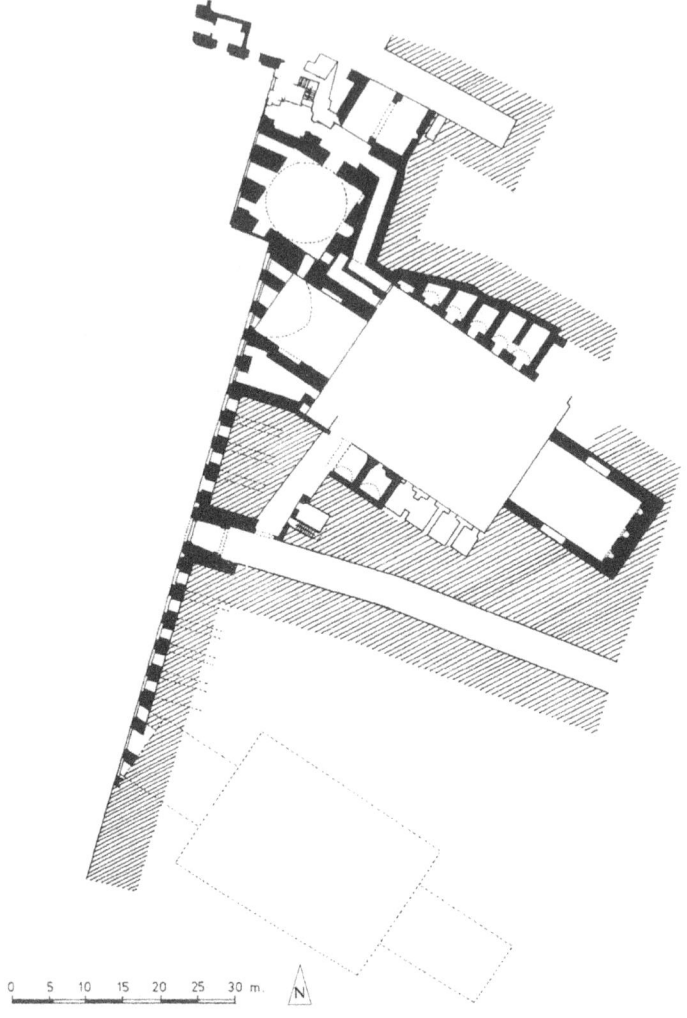

FIGURE 2 Plan of the madrasa and tomb of Sultan Salih in Cairo. (Source: drawn by Saeed Arida, reproduced courtesy of Nasser Rabbat)

the other hand, it was a bold reference to the sultan-queen as "Tree of Pearls." Carved into a wooden frieze than runs around the interior of the tomb, the inscriptions name her as "'Iṣmat al-Dunyā wa'l-Dīn, the mother of al-Malik al-Manṣūr Khalīl, of our lord the Sultan al-Malik al-Ṣāliḥ Najm al-Dīn Abū'l-Fatḥ Ayyūb, son of our lord the Sultan al-Malik al-Kāmil Nāṣir al-Dīn Abū'l-Ma'ālī Muḥammad ibn

FIGURE 3 Photo of the tomb of Sultan Salih. (Source: D. F. Ruggles)

Abū Bakr ibn Ayyūb," or, in brief, Shajar al-Durr, mother of Khalil, whose father was Sultan Salih.[27]

That Salih is named as the father of Khalil but not Shajar al-Durr's husband is not surprising in light of Muslim family alliances. Women typically commissioned mausolea to celebrate their sons or themselves, but rarely their husbands. This is because in a long life, a man or woman might have multiple or successive spouses, and those unions were contractual agreements that could be terminated, as in the case of Shajar al-Durr's second husband's divorce. But the birth of a child, and particularly

---

[27] Adapted from Bernard O'Kane, *The Monumental Inscriptions of Historic Cairo*, monument 169, https://islamicinscriptions.cultnat.org.

FIGURE 4 Photo of the tomb of Shajar al-Durr. (Credit: D. F. Ruggles, *Tree of Pearls*, p. 114)

a son, marked the beginning of a different kind of relationship, in which the woman became the mother of a potential heir. Shajar al-Durr, too, earned distinction as the mother of the (short-lived) heir, but unlike other women, she also held a key position in her own right in the dynastic lineage. This may explain why her architectural patronage began with a magnificent tomb that celebrated her husband, Salih – after all, it was through him that she ascended to the throne. But then, when she set about erecting a commemorative monument to herself, by which point she had married her second husband, the emphasis changed to her and her son.

FIGURE 5 Mosaic mihrab in the tomb of Shajar al-Durr. (Credit: D. F. Ruggles [not from *Tree of Pearls*])

A royal mother provided a kind of bridge – through the procreative ability of the female body – between one generation and the next. But instead of merely supplying the required son for the house of her Ayyubid husband, Shajar al-Durr became the *successor*, and ultimately the first in what became a long line of Mamluk rulers. Through the birth function, she achieved the transfer of power from father to son but also validated two distinct ways of governing: one based on the royal bloodline that required the existence, however brief, of her son, Khalil, and the other based on merit, which was a qualification held in her own right, whereby any capable former slave might rise to the throne.

GAWHAR SHAD AND TIMURID MOSQUE PATRONAGE

Because a woman could rise to the position of mother-of-the-ruler through giving birth, her parentage or lack of family ties were not an obstacle to her advance. Whether a trusted advisor or canny political operator, both of which describe Shajar al-Durr, an ambitious woman surely realized that power relied on two factors: bearing the son who would secure her position in the ruling family's lineage, and her relationships to other powerful actors in the court. As concubines, Durzan and Shajar al-Durr came to court with no genealogical capital and must have relied on charm, wit, beauty, and cultural refinement to attract the men who would become their consorts and eventually husbands. But a woman such as Mahperi Khatun came from a respectable lineage, and while it was a Christian rather than Muslim lineage, that very alterity proved to be useful to her family, as we have seen.

Gawhar Shad (b. ca. AH 780/1378 CE), whose name means "shining jewel," was likewise born into a prominent family as the daughter of one of the favorite emirs of Timur, founder of the Timurid dynasty. In ca. AH 795/1393 CE, she became the second wife to Shah Rukh, who would eventually become the Timurid emperor (r. AH 807–50/1405–47 CE), and with whom she had three sons – each an important arts patron or artist – and three daughters. Their son Ulugh Beg became ruler of Transoxiana (r. AH 850–3/1447–9 CE).

This was a brilliant period for the patronage of art and architecture in the Timurid empire, much of it commissioned by the women of the Timurid house. Gawhar Shad was a particularly prolific patron, much of her work centering in Herat and Mashhad. In the former, she was the patron of the Gawhar Shad musalla complex west of the city, consisting of a madrasa, mosque, and the patron's own tomb, built in the period AH 820–41/1417–38 CE and dated by a foundation inscription in the tomb. Of this site, only the tomb and one minaret survived destruction by the British army in the nineteenth century. In Mashhad the madrasa of the Gawhar Shad complex is in fragmentary state, but her mosque remains as a reminder of the former grandeur of the complex (Figure 6). It served as the congregational mosque for the tomb of 'Ali al-Reza (d. AH 203/818 CE) (the eighth imam of the Twelver Shi'a and thus one of the Prophet's descendants), which attracted many pilgrims to Mashhad. Inscriptions in the *qibla iwan* (or Persian *eyvan*, a barrel-vaulted arch facing the courtyard) as well as the *waqfiyya* (deed of endowment) name her as the mosque's founder. The architectural inscription names her architect as Qavam al-Din Shirazi (d. AH 841–2/1438 CE).[28]

Because the mosque was added onto the preexisting shrine of 'Ali al-Reza, it had to adapt to the latter's presence. Yet the planning was

---

[28] Lisa Golombek and Bernard O'Kane, *The Timurid Architecture of Iran and Turan*, 2 vols. (Princeton: Princeton University Press, 1988), vol. I, 328–331.

FIGURE 6 Courtyard façade of the Mosque of Gawhar Shad. (Credit: Goudarz.memar, Creative Commons license)

expertly contrived, and in some ways the mosque is a typical Timurid congregational mosque type, with a cruciform plan, four great *iwans* (vaulted spaces) marking the axes, laid out within a rectangular enclosure. However, two of its elements reveal that the architect was not following so much as leading design innovation. The first was the grand *qibla iwan* with its large dome that the architect ingeniously supported with transverse arches so as to open up the *iwan* as an airy continuous space. The second was the minarets. Rising directly from the ground, unlike in earlier mosques, the two cylindrical minarets appear not as appendages perched atop the mosque wall, but soaring towers that enhance the overall sense of verticality. The minarets and the courtyard façade were richly surfaced with blue glazed tile, contrasted with unglazed brick for visual emphasis, and bands of floral decoration and inscriptions in Kufic script.

Somewhat unusually for the Timurid period, copies of the mosque's original deed of endowment still exist, because Gawhar Shad had stipulated that the document be recopied regularly to ensure its preservation. Written in Persian and Arabic, it has been studied by Shivan Mahendrarajah, drawing upon a critical edition prepared by Mehdi Sayyidi.[29] The document begins with praise for Gawhar Shad's husband, Shah Rukh, and states that pious foundations are to the benefit of all. It proceeds to list the shops, houses, and a hammam that were set aside to provide rental income for the mosque (and also the Sunni shrine-complex of Ahmad-i Jam), as well as agricultural lands, their water rights and amenities such as mills and canals, and herds of sheep and oxen that were part of the agricultural property. Mahendrarajah has written that "Gawhar Shād's agro- and hydro-development initiatives inherent to the Gawhar Shād waqf are the continuation, in effect, of programs by the Ilkhanids and Timurids to restore irrigation systems and revivify agriculture in post-Mongol Persia."[30] While the patron's investments were designed as strategies to support the interests of the state, she also ensured that some spiritual and social benefit would accrue to herself: The *waqf* mandated that there should be Qur'an recitation twice weekly, each time preceded by praise for Gawhar Shad.[31]

Timurid patrons used architecture to communicate their support for both Sunni and Shi'i interests. Thus, when Gawhar Shad (and other Timurid patrons) added to the Imam 'Ali al-Reza shrine complex in Mashhad, she was acknowledging the importance of the site to the growing Shi'i population. Yet with her husband she also built a shrine in AH 829–32/1425–9 CE for the Sufi mystic saint Abd Allah Ansari on the outskirts of Herat at Gazur Gah, a site popular among Sunnis. In directing resources to both Shi'i and Sunni pilgrimage sites, and in visiting them with her husband and independently, she was showing respect for the interests of Iran's various religious constituencies.[32]

Gawhar Shah offers an example of a woman who did not limit her patronage to tombs that celebrated her family members but engaged in political patronage through the construction of mosques and madrasas. In this respect, she – as many others – used architecture to shape the political realm. When historians represent the lived space of women as restricted to the harem quarters, they overlook their very real and powerful effect on public space, where their patronage was not undertaken quietly, but proclaimed through the magnificence of the building and

---

[29] Shivan Mahendrarajah, "The Gawhar Shād Waqf Deed: Public Works and the Commonwealth," *Journal of the American Oriental Society* 138, no. 4 (2018): 821–857, drawing upon M. Sayyidi, *Masjid wa mawqūfāt-i Gawhar Shād* (Tehran: Bunyā d-i Pizhū hish wa Tawsi'a-yi Farhang-i Waqf, 2007), 100–102.
[30] Mahendrarajah, "The Gawhar Shād Waqf Deed," 854.
[31] Ibid., 850 (lines 198–199 of the *waqfiyya*).
[32] Ibid.

inscriptions, and the activities performed there, such as the regular invocation of Gawhar Shad's name, stipulated in the *waqfiyya* of her complex in Mashhad.

HADICE TURHAN SULTAN AND THE OTTOMAN MOSQUE

Ottoman women have been the topic of numerous studies, facilitated by the extensive records of the Ottoman empire. Ottoman archives have survived remarkably intact and include legal appeals, *waqf* documents, and letters where the voices and deeds of women are documented. Although women of the Ottoman court were not active patrons of books and other portable arts, they were important patrons of architecture.[33] They were diverse with respect to their origins, ethnicities, and languages spoken, and enjoyed wealth and power that increased according to higher social rank. The most powerful women came from outside the Ottoman house because, as Leslie Peirce has explained in her extensive studies, except for the very first generations the Ottomans chose to produce their future heirs with slave concubines rather than through formal diplomatic marriages.[34]

This was the story of Hadice Turhan Sultan (d. AH 1094/1683 CE). She was captured from Russia as a girl sometime in the 1630s and sent to the Ottoman palace as a slave to serve the current sultan's mother, Kosem Sultan. Chosen by Kosem to become the concubine of her son, Ibrahim, Turhan bore a son who became sultan in AH 1058/1648 CE, thus elevating Turhan to the supremely important position of *valide sultan*. Because her son was a child of six years at the time that he reached the throne as Mehmed IV (AH 1051–1104/1642–93 CE), Turhan served as his regent and remained politically powerful until her death. Her architectural works included a congregational mosque in Istanbul and two fortresses in the provinces, as well as additional works in Thrace, the Balkans, and Crete.[35]

Turhan's defensive works (begun in AH 1068/1658 CE) consist of two large fortresses. The Seddulbahir fortress stood on the European side of the Dardanelles straits, while the Kumkale fortress stood on the Asian

[33] Ülkü Bates, "The Architectural Patronage of Ottoman Women," *Asian Art* 6, no. 2 (spring 1993): 50–65.
[34] Leslie Peirce, "Gender and Sexual Propriety in Ottoman Royal Women's Patronage," in *Women, Patronage, and Self-Representation*, ed. Ruggles, 53–68; Leslie Peirce, *The Imperial Harem: Women and Sovereignty in the Ottoman Empire* (New York, Oxford: Oxford University Press, 1993).
[35] Lucienne Thys-Şenocak, *Ottoman Women Builders: The Architectural Patronage of Hadice Turhan Sultan* (Aldershot: Ashgate, 2006), 109–180.

side, straddling the entrance to the body of water and effectively choking off access to the straits. These forts were an important maritime defense against Venetian attacks and were praised in verse as "The lock of the sea of Istanbul, the sultan's holy barricade."[36] In building them, Turhan was following the example of the Ottoman emperor Mehmed II (AH 835–86/1432–81 CE), who had likewise built forts flanking the straits at the Gallipoli peninsula. Because Turhan's forts were not in Istanbul but far to the south, they adhered to the older tradition of the *valide sultan* embellishing the provinces, rather than the capital, with her architectural patronage. But in patronizing military architecture, Turhan was treading on ground that was a male prerogative among the Ottomans.

In the mosque complex that she built in the Eminönü district of Istanbul, her patronage again departed from traditional practice. The *külliye* (architectural complex) was built on foundations that had been laid by Safiye Sultan, beginning in AH 1006/1597 CE, but that had been left incomplete when Safiye was replaced as *valide sultan* in AH 1012/1603 CE and died a few years later. Turhan revived the project in AH 1073/1663 CE. The large *külliye* consisted of a pavilion, a tomb, a fountain, schools for teaching the Qur'an and hadith, and a large market, arrayed around the central congregational mosque (Figure 7). The mosque (which survives today, along with the tomb and pavilion) consists of an open prayer hall vaulted by a large dome buttressed by half-domes (Figure 8). Two slender minarets mark the corners of the wall that separates the prayer hall from the open courtyard. Entrance into the mosque can be had either through the courtyard or directly into the northeast side of the prayer hall.

In her study of the mosque, Lucienne Thys-Şenocak has analyzed the "weakness" that had long been attributed to its architectural layout.[37] Whereas classic Ottoman *külliyes* of the imperial period were symmetrical, with the mosque at the center and surrounded by secondary structures such as schools and madrasas, all adhering to a strictly orthogonal plan, Turhan's complex departed from this long-established norm. The Yeni Valide Mosque complex (as it is known today) has a correctly oriented mosque and a correctly oriented tomb, but the market (marked "D" on the plan), fountain, and royal pavilion (called the *hunkar kasrı*, marked "E") do not align with these; nor do they align with each other. (Urbanization projects in the mid twentieth century ran a street between

---

[36] Ibid., 112, citing Topkapı Palace Museum Archives E.2477.

[37] Ibid., 187–257; Thys-Şenocak, "The Yeni Valide Mosque Complex of Eminönü, Istanbul (1597–1665): Gender and Vision in Ottoman Architecture," in *Women, Patronage, and Self-Representation*, ed. Ruggles, 69–89.

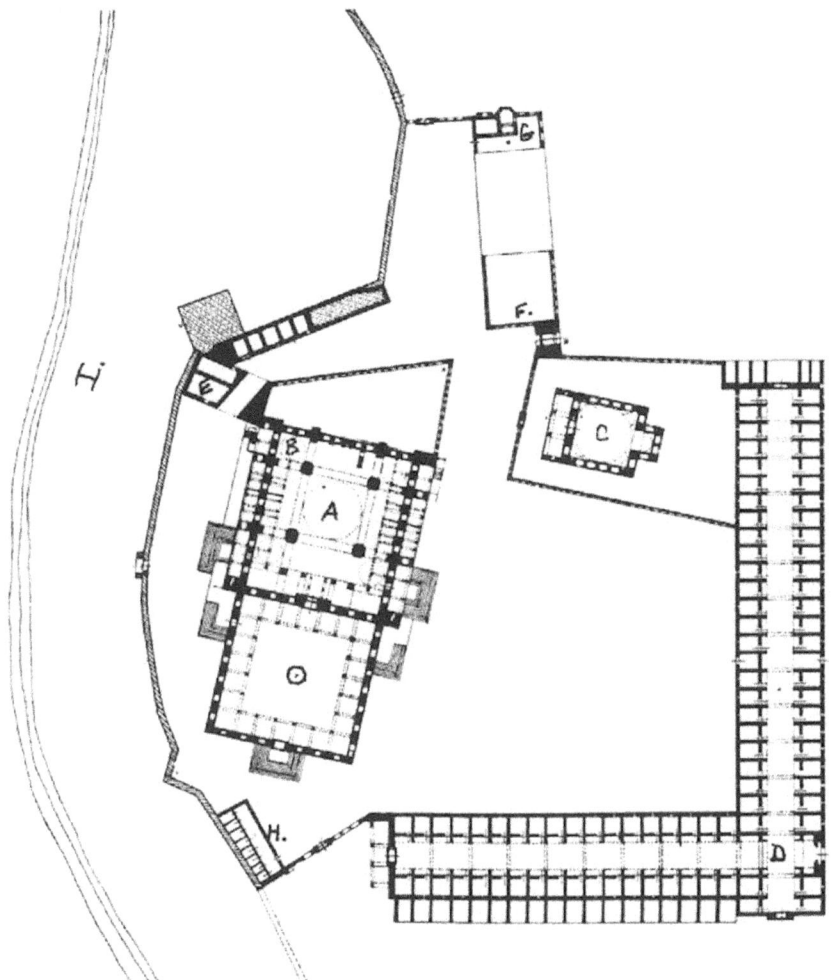

FIGURE 7 Yeni Valide Sultan Mosque, plan. (Credit: L. Thys-Şenocak)

the mosque and the market, destroying the integrity of the ensemble, but originally the various buildings were contained within a walled enclosure.) Thys-Şenocak shows that the pavilion, which is not a regular feature of an imperial Ottoman mosque, was the visual origin of the composition, in that it provided the place from which Turhan could survey the activities of the mosque complex without herself being seen. As the diagram shows, the pavilion enabled its occupant to see people entering the northeast entrance of the mosque, tomb, schools, and market, and also the waterfront entrance on the Golden Horn by which visitors could arrive by boat.

FIGURE 8 Yeni Valide Sultan Mosque. (Credit: Haluk Comertel, Creative Commons license)

She traces the pavilion's formal typology to the shoreline kiosks that lined the Bosphorus and were frequented by the women of the court, providing them with pleasant views, yet protecting them from exposure. This was not solely for the protection of their modesty: among the Ottoman elite neither men nor women subjected themselves to the public gaze, because to be unapproachable and unseen was a sign of elevated stature.[38] The pavilion performed the dual role of shielding Turhan herself from view, while at the same time affording surveillance of the *kulliye* that she had built. However, earlier architectural historians had dismissed the nonsymmetrical plan as irrational and chaotic, and regarded it as a reflection of the declining strength of the Ottoman state, which in turn was attributed to the destabilizing influence of powerful women. But, understood from the perspective of its patron and recognizing that men and women used such spaces very differently, the asymmetry makes sense. According to Thys-Şenocak: "With the skillful manipulation of the built environment, the *valide* extended the space and stage upon which she could exercise her authority and brought gender as a nuanced and

---

[38] Thys-Şenocak, *Ottoman Women Builders*, 101; Peirce, *The Imperial Harem*, 8.

important factor into the 'optical politics' of the Yeni Valide complex and the Ottoman architectural enterprise."[39]

NUR JAHAN AND THE MUGHAL TOMB

Many of the women discussed thus far accumulated power with age, particularly upon becoming widowed mothers of ruling sons. They were able to parlay their appeal as attractive young women to forge relationships with the sultan and *valide sultan*, negotiating family politics with skill as they rose in importance. Nur Jahan (ca. AH 985–1055/ca. 1577–1645 CE) similarly had the acumen and experience of an older woman, but when she married the Mughal emperor Jahangir (AH 977–1037/1569–1627 CE) in AH 1020/1611 CE, she was already thirty-four years old, a widow, and mother of a daughter from her previous marriage, and living at the Mughal court as a lady-in-waiting to one of the former emperor's widows.[40] Born Mihrunnisa, at the Mughal court she came to be called Nur Mahal, meaning "Light of the Palace," and later Nur Jahan, "Light of the World." With nineteen previous wives, Jahangir did not need to marry this older woman, and Nur Jahan bore him no children; instead, theirs was apparently a relationship based on trust and love.[41] From a noble family that had emigrated from Iran to India, Nur Jahan became unusually powerful both because the emperor relied so heavily on her and because she managed to thread members of her family into the Mughal court. Her father and brother rose to high positions in the Mughal government, providing support: her father, Ghiyath Beg (d. AH 1031/1622 CE), appointed as prime minister by Jahangir and acquiring the title of Itimad al-Dawla ("support of the state"), and her brother Asaf Khan (d. AH 1051/1641 CE), gaining the friendship of Jahangir and marrying his daughter to the future emperor Shah Jahan.

Nur Jahan was celebrated as a markswoman – highly unusual for women, yet significant in a culture where the royal hunt was an allegory for dominance and power – and was publicly acknowledged for her special role at Jahangir's side, accompanying him at the *jharoka* (royal window), minting coins, signing imperial orders, and engaging in

---

[39] Thys-Şenocak, "The Yeni Valide Mosque Complex of Eminönü," 86; she attributes the term "optical politics" to Gülru Necipoğlu, "Framing the Gaze in Ottoman, Safavid and Mughal Palaces," *Ars Orientalis* 23 (1993): 303–342.
[40] Ellison Banks Findly, *Nur Jahan: Empress of Mughal India* (New York: Oxford University Press, 1993), 32.
[41] There is no record of progeny. If there was any, they were daughters. Ibid., 18.

international trade and diplomacy.⁴² Ruby Lal, in her biography of Nur Jahan, writes: "The Mughal family into which Nūr married had a tradition of strong and prominent elder women – assertive royal wives, influential mothers and aunts whose opinions were valued. But no woman had ever openly and fully taken charge of the empire."⁴³ While there is no doubt that Nur Jahan exercised considerable political power and authority, Jahangir's own memoir, *The Jahangirnama*, confirms that the emperor never relinquished full control of his obligations, despite his failing health and opium addiction.⁴⁴

Nur Jahan was an important patron of poetry (and a poet herself), luxury textiles, gardens, and hostels for travelers, but her greatest accomplishment was the tomb that she built for her parents in Agra in the period AH 1031–7/1622–8 CE (Figure 9). The tomb of Itimad al-Dawla is important in the history of Mughal architecture because its white marble cladding and colored stone inlays were innovations that were realized on a larger, imperial scale in the Taj Mahal (built in Agra beginning in AH 1040/1631 CE). The tomb follows the plan of Mughal pleasure gardens that were arrayed along the riverbank across from the Agra fort, reached by boat for day outings. But while it has a waterfront pavilion that provided access from the river, its principal structure is the mausoleum, positioned in the center of the quadripartite gardened space. The nine-bay tomb, topped by an unusual vault that was neither a Persian-style dome nor a *bangla* (curved) roof, was the first to be made of white marble inlaid with colored stone to form images of plants, flower vases, and drinking vessels (Figure 10).⁴⁵ The interior had a marble-clad dado above which are painted images of drinking vessels alternating with bright red flowers. The floral imagery draws from two sources: one being European botanical prints that were circulating in the Mughal court, especially

---

⁴² Nisar Ahmed, "Empress Nūr Jahān and Her Coins," *Journal of the Uttar Pradesh Historical Society*, new series, 11–13 (1965): 27–39; A. I. Tirmizi, "A Rare Edict of Nur Jahan," *Indian Historical Records Commission: Proceedings* 35 (1960): 196–202.

⁴³ Ruby Lal, *Empress: The Astonishing Reign of Nur Jahan* (New York, London: W. W. Norton, 2018), 8.

⁴⁴ Corinne Lefèvre, "Recovering a Missing Voice from Mughal India: The Imperial Discourse of Jahāngīr (r. 1605–1627) in His Memoirs," *Journal of the Economic and Social History of the Orient* 50, no. 4 (2007): 452–489; *The Jahangirnama: Memoirs of Jahangir, Emperor of India*, trans. Wheeler Thackston (Washington, DC: Freer Gallery of Art; New York: Oxford University Press, 1999).

⁴⁵ Ebba Koch, "Notes on the Painted and Sculptured Decoration of Nur Jahan's Pavilions in the Ram Bagh (Bagh-i Nur Afshan) at Agra," in *Facets of Indian Art: A Symposium Held at the Victoria and Albert Museum on 26, 27, 28 April and 1 May 1982*, ed. R. Skelton, A. Topsfield, S. Strong, R. Crill, and G. Parlett (London: Victoria and Albert Museum, 1986): 51–65.

FIGURE 9 Photo of the tomb of Itimad al-Dawla in Agra. (Credit: D. F. Ruggles)

during Jahangir's reign, and the other being the embroidered and woven textiles that were of special interest to Nur Jahan. The inlay technique came from Italian *pietre dure* artisanry, introduced during the reign of Jahangir.[46]

White marble had previously been reserved for the tombs of saintly figures, such as that of Shaykh Salim Chisti (begun AH 988/ 1580 CE) at Fatehpur Sikri, but with the tomb of Itimad al-Dawla, and more importantly the Taj Mahal, it was now adopted for imperial tombs. This shift in the use of the lustrous material from pious to political settings was significant in that it tacitly transferred the aura of saintliness to political officials and emperors who were not otherwise known for their virtue or religious devotion. The white marble, colorful inlay, images of flowers, and waterfront location became distinctive elements of the imperial tomb, as seen in the

[46] William S. Meyer, Sir Richard Burton, James S. Cotton, and Sir Herbert H. Risley, *Imperial Gazetteer of India*, new ed., 26 vols. (Oxford: Clarendon Press, 1908–31), vol. II, 127; Ebba Koch, "Pietre Dure and Other Artistic Affinities between the Court of the Mughals and That of the Medici," in *A Mirror of Princes*, ed. Dalu Jones (Bombay: Marg, 1987), 29–56.

FIGURE 10 Inlaid stone panel at the tomb of Itimad al-Dawla. (Credit: D. F. Ruggles)

Taj Mahal (Figure 11), but it was an innovation that began earlier with work commissioned by Nur Jahan. Nur Jahan herself was interred after her death in a simple tomb near Lahore that she had commissioned, next to equally simple ones commemorating her deceased husband and her brother.

FIGURE 11 Taj Mahal façade, Agra. (Credit: Habeeb from Hyderabad, India, Creative Commons license)

CONCLUSION

In the preceding case studies, we have seen that women could be important and innovative patrons of architecture. A woman who gave birth to a son for her husband's family, particularly in the case of royal families, gained a permanent role in that new family through motherhood, and her architectural patronage often served the family's interests and especially the interests of her son. Yet, while the birth of a son consolidated a woman's social position in her new family, it does not reveal anything about her own desire to impact her immediate environment or the city in which she lived. It is often difficult for historians to assess the degree of agency exercised by women because their lives were contingent on the status of their fathers, consorts, or sons, and also because the entire concept of individual will is a very modern phenomenon. The best insight into their agency comes from mature widows, who were presumably past childbearing age, like Nur Jahan and Shajar al-Durr, and thus were less restricted in what they could do in large part because there was no fear of them polluting the family lineage. They were empowered by wealth and, in the case of free women, connections to their natal families. Women – particularly the *valide sultan* – were often tasked with representing the charitable face of the family by building mosques, tombs, and pious institutions, acts of patronage that were obligations rather than choices, and yet ones in which personal taste could be expressed.

There are clear differences in the reasons motivating architectural patronage among men and women. Yet the differences cannot entirely be ascribed to gender, or rather the fact of gender is not a unilateral explanation for what motivated women in the Islamic world to erect major works of architecture. No one would claim that male patrons all built architectural works for the same reason; likewise, a woman might be motivated by an array of reasons. She might use architecture to strengthen the position of her son and heir, as in Durzan's construction of the Mosque of al-Qarafa in Cairo, or she might understand architectural investments as political strategies, as in the case of Gawhar Shad's support for Sunni and Shi'i mosques and shrines in Mashhad. She might be driven by a sense of piety and fidelity, as in the tomb that Nur Jahan built for her parents in Agra, or a combination of political and romantic attachment, as in the case of the tomb that Shajar al-Durr built for Sultan Salih in Cairo. Some works of architecture may have reflected pure ego, as seems likely in the case of Shajar al-Durr's "tree of pearls" mosaic in the mihrab of her tomb. Finally, the position of the woman patron vis-à-vis the built environment could affect the work itself, as in the case of the Valide Sultan Mosque in Istanbul, where the architecture was skewed to accommodate the privileged view of the female patron.

SELECT BIBLIOGRAPHY

Arthur M. Sackler Gallery, Smithsonian Institution. Special issue: "Patronage by Women in Islamic Art." *Asian Art* (spring 1994).

Blessing, Patricia. "Buildings of Commemoration in Medieval Anatolia: The Funerary Complexes of Ṣāḥib 'Aṭā Fakhr al-Dīn 'Alī and Māhperī Khātūn." *Al-Masāq* 27, no. 3 (2014): 225–252.
Bloom, Jonathan. "The Mosque of the al-Qarafa in Cairo." *Muqarnas* 4 (1987): 7–20.
Cortese, Delia and Calderini, Simonetta. "The Architectural Patronage of the Fāṭimid Queen-Mother Durzān (d. 385/995): An Interdisciplinary Analysis of Literary Sources, Material Evidence and Historical Context." In *Material Evidence and Narrative Sources: Interdisciplinary Studies of the History of the Muslim Middle East*, ed. Daniella Talmon-Heller and Katia Cytryn-Silverman, 7–112. Leiden: Brill, 2014.
Eastmond, Antony. *Tamta's World: The Life and Encounters of a Medieval Noblewoman from the Middle East to Mongolia.* Cambridge: Cambridge University Press, 2017.
Findly, Ellison Banks. *Nur Jahan: Empress of Mughal India.* New York: Oxford University Press, 1993.
Hambly, Gavin, ed. *Women in the Medieval Islamic World.* New York: St. Martin's Press, 1998.
Lal, Ruby. *Empress: The Astonishing Resign of Nur Jahan.* New York, London: W. W. Norton, 2018.
Mahendrarajah, Shivan. "The Gawhar Shād Waqf Deed: Public Works and the Commonweal." *Journal of the American Oriental Society* 138, no. 4 (2018): 821–857.
Marín, Manuela. *Mujeres en al-Ándalus.* Madrid: Consejo Superior de Investigaciones Científicas, 2000.
Peirce, Leslie. *The Imperial Harem: Women and Sovereignty in the Ottoman Empire.* New York, Oxford: Oxford University Press, 1993.
Ruggles, D. Fairchild. *Tree of Pearls: The Extraordinary Architectural Patronage of the 13th-Century Egyptian Slave-Queen Shajar al-Durr.* New York: Oxford University Press, 2000.
Ruggles, D. Fairchild, ed. *Women, Patronage, and Self-Representation in Islamic Societies.* Albany: SUNY Press, 2000.
Thys-Şenocak, Lucienne. *Ottoman Women Builders: The Architectural Patronage of Hadice Turhan Sultan.* Aldershot: Ashgate, 2006.
Yalman, Suzan. "The 'Dual Identity' of Mahperi Khatun: Piety, Patronage and Marriage across Frontiers in Seljuk Anatolia." In *Architecture and Landscape in Medieval Anatolia, 1100–1500*, ed. Patricia Blessing and Rachel Goshgarian, 224–252. Edinburgh: Edinburgh University Press, 2017.

12 Women and Political Authority
SHAHLA HAERI

At the threshold of the twenty-first century, and when least expected, forty-seven Iranian women nominated themselves for president in 2001. At the time, not many women from the Global South were expressing interest in or campaigning to run for the office of president. Almost nothing was written about Iranian women presidential aspirants in the US media, nor was much attention paid them in their own country – except for some short bios and sporadic articles in more progressive newspapers, including an article by the leading women's monthly magazine *Zanan* (Women).[1] None of the applicants, predictably, was approved by the Guardian Council.[2] A gender-ambiguous term in article 115 of the constitution of the Islamic Republic of Iran provided the opportunity for women to challenge the exclusionary official reading of the constitution. The term *rijal* is a borrowed term from Arabic, meaning "men." Lacking gender preposition, in its Persian usage, the term means the "political elite." The women aspirants contended that gender should not be a barrier to the presidency because they are also a part of the political elite.

I had a chance to interview six of the women candidates in 2001 and created a video documentary titled *Mrs. President: Women and Political Leadership in Iran*.[3] With brave eloquence, the women expressed indignation regarding gender inequality, political deprivation, and social injustice. While underscoring their qualifications, they highlighted their deep disappointment with the state and the male political elite, and objected to women's vacillating status between subject and citizen

---

[1] *Zanan* magazine was censored in 2007 and forced to cease publication by President Mahmoud Ahmadinejad, who served as the sixth president of Iran from 2005 to 2013.
[2] The Guardian Council is a highly conservative all-male institution that must approve the "qualifications" of all candidates for national office before they can start campaigning.
[3] Shahla Haeri, *Mrs. President: Women and Political Leadership in Iran*, filmed in 2002. This video is distributed by Films for Humanities and Sciences: https://ffh.films.com/ecSearch.aspx?q=Shahla+Haeri.

in their society. One of the women contenders, a pharmacist, told me: "Presidency requires intelligence, wisdom, strategizing and consulting. It has nothing to do with the size of one's biceps, or physical strength. Both men and women are just as smart and intelligent. So, why can't women become the president of a country like the Islamic Republic of Iran?" When I asked another woman contender, a founder and principal of a private high school, what gave her the legitimacy to run for the office of president in the Islamic Republic of Iran, she said, without a pause: "Why not? We have in the Qur'an a country where a woman called the Queen of Sheba was ruling. This is very important for us." Repeating it emphatically, "this is very important for us!" "Historically," she continued, "women have played fundamental roles, *naqsh-i asli*, in the lives of male religious and political leaders. Take the role mothers and wives played in the lives of Muhammad, Jesus, and Moses." Yes, indeed! How clever she was, I thought – referencing the Qur'an – the highest source of authority and legitimacy for Muslims. Who could argue with her – who indeed in a society purportedly based on the Islamic law, shari'a. The women political candidates – and many more citizens – see no reason for which women should not or could not be president of Iran, or at least be given a chance to compete. In addition, for that they have the support of none other than the Qur'anic revelations of the Queen of Sheba (Q. 27:20–45).[4]

I begin this chapter from the beginning, from the Qur'an, the highest source of authority, legitimacy, and lawmaking for Muslims. Following the introduction, this chapter is divided into three parts. In part one, I briefly present my reading of the Qur'anic story of the Queen of Sheba while engaging with that of medieval interpretations of these revelations, in order to contextualize Muslim women's effort to secure legitimate political authority in modern times.[5] I juxtapose

---

[4]   This chapter is primarily based on my book, *The Unforgettable Queens of Islam: Succession, Authority, Gender* (Cambridge: Cambridge University Press 2020).

[5]   The two major primary sources used here are those of Abu Ishaq Ahmad Ibn Muhammed Ibn Ibrahim al-Tha'labi (d. 1035) and Abu Ja'far Muhammad ibn Jarir al-Tabari (838–923). (Dates in this chapter are CE.) William M. Brinner has translated and annotated Tha'labi's book *Ara'is al-Majalis fi Qisas al-Anbiya'* as *Lives of the Prophets: As Recounted by Abu Ishaq Ahmad Ibn Muhammed Ibn Ibrahim al-Thalabi*, 1st ed. (Leiden: Brill, 2002). All references to Tha'labi in this chapter are taken from Brinner's edition. Several scholars have translated different volumes of al-Tabari's monumental forty-volume *Ta'rikh al-Rusul wa'l Muluk* [The History of the Prophets and Kings]. William M. Brinner, trans., *The History of al-Tabari, Volume III: The Children of Israel* (Albany: State University of New York Press, 1991) is referenced in this chapter; see also Jacob Lassner, *Demonizing the Queen of Sheba: Boundaries of Gender and Culture in Postbiblical Judaism and Medieval Islam* (Chicago: University

these Qur'anic revelations with the following hadith (saying of the Prophet), "Never will succeed such a nation as makes a woman their ruler,"⁶ that is allegedly attributed to the Prophet Muhammad.⁷ How are we to interpret the differences between the Qur'an and the hadith, between these two supreme sources of authority regarding women and political authority in Islam, one supportive and the other opposing? It is at the intersection of these two supreme sources of authority and legitimacy that we need to locate opportunities for and obstacles to Muslim women's possibilities for political authority and power. In part two, I highlight a few cases of women who ruled the Muslim world and exercised a significant degree of power and authority in pre-modern and modern times in their respective societies. By way of some concluding remarks, in part three, I discuss some rationale and justifications for opposition to women's political visibility and authority. Counterintuitive though it may sound, it is in fact in modern times and in the aftermath of the emerging nationalism in much of the formerly colonized Muslim world that women have faced fierce political opposition – often couched in religious terms – to their agency in general and to their political visibility in particular. Such opposition, I argue, is in response to the growing organized mobilization of women and their demand for gender justice and legal/political rights in their contemporary societies. It is their collective agency and demand for having a seat at the proverbial political table that threaten the patriarchal apparatus.

---

of Chicago Press, 1993); Jamal J. Elias, "Prophecy, Power and Propriety: The Encounter of Solomon and the Queen of Sheba," *Journal of Qur'anic Studies* 11, no. 1 (2009): 57–74.

⁶ Variations on this hadith beginning with *la* ("no, not") instead of *lan* ("never") are also reported: Sahih al-Bukhari, "Afflictions and the End of the World," https://sunnah.com/bukhari/92.

⁷ Whether this is a "forged hadith" or whether the Prophet of Islam actually said it has been debated in modern times by scholars. See for example Jonathan A. C. Brown, ed., *Hadith: Muhammad's Legacy in the Medieval and Modern World* (Oxford: Oneworld Publications, 2018); Fatima Mernissi, *The Veil and the Male Elite: A Feminist Interpretation of Women's Rights in Islam* (Abingdon: Perseus Books, 1991), 58–61; Abu El Fadl Khaled, *Speaking in God's Name: Islamic Law, Authority and Women* (Oxford: Oneworld Publications, 2001); Mohammad Fadel, "Is Historicism a Viable Strategy for Islamic Law Reform? The Case of 'Never Shall a Folk Prosper Who Have Appointed a Woman to Rule Them'," *Islamic Law and Society* 18, no. 2 (2011): 131–176; Ibrahim Zakyi, "Reinstating the Queens: Reassessing the Hadith on Women's Political Leadership," *The American Journal of Islamic Social Sciences* 33, no. 2 (2016): v–x; Kaukab Siddique, *The Struggle of Muslim Women* (Delhi: Amer Society for Education, 1986).

THE QUEEN OF SHEBA AND THE "PROPHETIC" HADITH

The Judeo-Islamic story of the Queen of Sheba has captured the imaginations of many renowned artists, sculptors, architects, musicians, filmmakers, painters, and miniaturists throughout the ages in Eastern and Western cultures – and in some African cultures, particularly in Ethiopia.[8] While the Qur'an is silent on the queen's parentage, Muslim religious tradition has contrived a genealogy to account for this woman's fabulous and powerful reign. Without a hint of irony, they have posited that the Queen of Sheba is the child of a human father, a onetime king of Yemen, and a jinn mother, albeit a princess jinni – and hence not truly a human woman.[9] Infinite variations of the story of the Queen of Sheba's visit to the court of King Solomon have been told across different religious and cultural traditions.[10] In the Qur'an the queen is portrayed as a wise, just, and caring ruler to whom God has denied no bounty or riches. Above all, God has given the queen a Mighty Throne, *'arsh-i 'azim* (Q. 27:23). This legendary throne has received such prominence across cultures. Yet the impulse to conquer her "Garden" (her sovereign territory), deny her sovereignty, appropriate her authority, banish her from the public, restrict her mobility, and control her body remained constant.

Although popularly known as Bilqis,[11] the Queen of Sheba is left nameless in the Qur'an. Her namelessness is meaningful, I believe. Had the Queen of Sheba been named in the Qur'an, her case would have become specific to her and to that particular time only. The rationale behind it, in my view, is heuristic – one that renders female sovereignty a general principle, a rule that may be utilized by other women in other eras and in similar situations. In the Qur'an it is not her sovereignty and political authority that are at issue: it is her faith. The divine revelations have more to do with the sun-worshipping queen's subjective transformation from ignorance of Islam, *jahiliyya*, to attaining the enlightenment of the new faith. Her surrender is to Almighty God, and mediated by Solomon, not a submission to the patriarch's demand for sex and

---

[8] E. A. Wallis Budge, trans., *The Kebra Nagast: The Queen of Sheba and Her Only Son Menyelek* (London: Forgotten Books, 1932).
[9] A jinn is a supernatural creature mentioned in the Qur'an (*Sura al-Jinn* 72). Brinner, *Lives of the Prophets*, 523; Barbara Stowasser, *Women in the Qur'an, Traditions, and Interpretation* (New York: Oxford University Press 1994), 64.
[10] For a series of articles on the Queen of Sheba and her enduring transcultural presence, see James B. Pritchard, ed., *Solomon and Sheba* (London: Phaidon Press, 1974).
[11] Brinner, *Lives of the Prophets*, 519.

marriage, as written about copiously by medieval Muslim chroniclers and biographers.[12]

What we ought to understand in these divine revelations, I suggest, is what the Qur'an tells us about women and political authority, the queen's leadership and charisma, her wisdom and genuine concern for her people's lives, and her sustained diplomatic effort to negotiate peace with a much stronger and uncompromising adversary. I read this story as an example of commendable leadership, regardless of gender, as one that values negotiation over domination, life over death, and peace over war and destruction. The Qur'anic story begins with Solomon reviewing his extraordinary army. Not finding the hoopoe among the flock, he flies into a rage, vowing to punish the bird by having its feathers plucked or slaughtering it unless it has a good excuse (Q. 27:20–21).[13] Soon the hoopoe appears and tells Solomon all about the wondrous Queen of Sheba, her prosperous oasis, and her Mighty Throne, "the tools and equipment in her dominion."[14] The only problem, the hoopoe explains to an incredulous Solomon and his attending army, is that the queen and her followers worship the sun because Satan, *shaytan*, has deceived them by hiding knowledge of Allah from them (Q. 27:24–25). Solomon decides to determine the truth of the bird's eyewitness account for himself. He gives the hoopoe a letter, instructing it to take it to the queen and wait to see what answer she gives. The message to the queen is ominous: "Be ye not arrogant against me, but come to me in submission" (Q. 27:27–31). When the Queen receives the letter, she seeks her advisors' counsel (Q. 27:29–30). Acknowledging their leader's authority, they declare their willingness to fight on her behalf: "We possess force and we possess great might. The affair rests with you; we follow your command" (Q. 27:32–33). Mindful of the king's serious challenge to her sovereignty and her community, however, the caring and politically savvy queen cautions her counselors, "Kings, when they enter a city, disorder it and make the mighty ones of its inhabitants abased. That they will do," (Q. 27:34). Instead, the Queen of Sheba decides to send Solomon splendid gifts (Q. 27:35), in hopes that her peaceful gesture will serve as a prelude to ceasing or avoiding hostilities. Solomon, however, rejects the queen's gifts, stating that what God has given him far surpasses what God has given her (Q. 27:36). He then accuses the queen and her emissaries of

---

[12] Ibid., 534–536; Amina Wadud, *Qur'an and Woman: Rereading the Sacred Text from a Woman's Perspective* (New York: Oxford University Press, 1999), 40–42.

[13] I have consulted *Tanzil Quran Navigator*, https://tanzil.net/#27:23, accessing primarily Yusuf Ali's translation of the Qur'an.

[14] Brinner, *Lives of the Prophets*, 525.

being "vainglorious people, trying to outdo each other in things of this world" because they do not know anything else[15] – presumably meaning that they know nothing but power and greed. Solomon sends the queen's emissaries back with another threatening message, warning of his imminent attack and the expulsion of her and her people from their land, "abased and utterly humbled" (Q. 27:37). Certain of Solomon's military intention, the Queen of Sheba decides to embark on a journey herself to Jerusalem to meet with Solomon in hopes of averting the certain destruction of her community.

In the meantime, King Solomon, who had earlier rejected the queen's gifts and accused her of vaingloriousness, now wants her Mighty Throne – the seat of her sovereignty entrusted to her by God. The king was not wanting in mighty thrones – God had given him plenty of those. Still, Solomon covets the queen's Mighty Throne. Relying on his vast army of supernatural creatures, the warrior prophet–king asks his jinns and demons, "Which one of you can bring me her throne before they come to me in submission?" (Q. 27:38). A mighty creature from among the jinn offers to bring it to him before he can rise from his seat (Q. 27:39). But Solomon wants her throne in his possession even faster. One who has the knowledge of the Book[16] offers to bring the queen's throne to Solomon's court in the blink of an eye – and so he does[17] (Q. 27:40). Solomon then instructs his minions to disguise the throne in order to "see whether [the queen] is guided," that is, if she recognizes the "truth" (Q. 27:41).

Once the queen is in Solomon's presence, he asks her whether the Mighty Throne in his possession is hers. Seeing her throne at Solomon's court, the wise queen gives a measured response: "[It is] as though it were the very one," adding, "We were given the knowledge beforehand and we had submitted" (Q. 27:42). With the queen at the threshold of his palace and her throne in his possession, Solomon invites the Queen of Sheba to enter the palace, but not before subjecting her to another test. As the Queen of Sheba is about to cross the palace threshold, she perceives the entrance to the pavilion as "a spreading water" and so "uncover[s] her legs" – lifting up her skirt – to enter, only to recognize the "water" as slabs of smooth glass. Realizing her illusion, the queen says, "God, I have wronged myself [*zalamtu nafsi*] and surrender [*aslamtu*] with Solomon to God, the Lord of all Being" (Q. 27:44). Awakened to a new reality, the

---

[15] Ibid., 530.
[16] Ibid., 532; Roberto Tottoli, "Asaf b. Barakhyā," in *Encyclopaedia of Islam*, ed. Kate Fleet, Gudrun Krämer, Denis Matringe, et al. (Leiden: Koninklijke Brill NV, 2009).
[17] For justifications regarding Solomon's taking the queen's throne without her permission, see Brinner, *Lives of the Prophets*, 531; Stowasser, *Women in the Qur'an*, 65.

queen surrenders to God, and with that her story ends in the Qur'an. But not in the imagination of biographers and storytellers. Collapsing the queen's "surrender" to God with that of her submission to the patriarchal order, Muslim and Jewish sages brought the reign of her fabulous kingdom (queendom) to an end by placing it under the control and supervision of a husband, the great patriarch Solomon/Suleiman.[18] But, as was highlighted above, the Qur'anic revelations reveal a different reality.

In the Qur'anic revelations, the Queen of Sheba is not the daughter of a jinn princess, and nor is her sovereignty rejected by the rank and file – hence, she is not an impostor or a usurper of political authority. Besides, God gave the sun-worshipping queen a Mighty Throne that so powerfully confounded medieval Muslim sensibilities. The Queen of Sheba exhibited her leadership, and her love and compassion for her followers; and she negotiated peace and saved her people from certain destruction. At the center of the Qur'anic story is a drama of faith and paganism, a story in which neither the queen's autonomy nor her authority is at issue – her faith is. But in its medieval reconstructions and interpretations, the central issue of faith becomes secondary to political rivalry and the need for patriarchal conquest and domination.[19] The encounter between the king and the queen is interpreted as a drama of sexual politics, of domination and submission, of a zero-sum leadership competition. The queen had to be dethroned, her sovereignty usurped, and her authority transferred to a husband of sorts – patriarchal domination consolidated.[20]

By the Middle Ages the story of the Queen of Sheba had been incorporated into a rigid patriarchal sensibility and biases, and women were

---

[18] King Solomon asked his supernatural minions to remove the "unsightly hair." Obliging the king, his *afarit* made a depilatory paste to remove the queen's leg-hair, in Brinner, *Lives of the Prophets*, 535–537; Lassner, *Demonizing the Queen of Sheba*, 201. Accordingly, the removal of hair is a prelude to sexual coitus and marital relations. On the association of sex and hair, see Christian Bromberger, "Hair: From the West to the Middle East through the Mediterranean," *The Journal of American Folklore* 121, no. 482 (fall 2008): 379–399; Carol Delaney, "Untangling the Meanings of Hair in Turkish Society," *Anthropological Quarterly* 67, no. 4 (October 1994): 159–172; C. R. Hallpike, "Social Hair," *Man* 4, no. 2 (June 1969): 256–264; Edmund Leach, "Magical Hair," *Journal of the Royal Anthropological Institute of Great Britain and Ireland* 82, no. 2 (July–December 1958): 147–164; Shahla Haeri, *Law of Desire: Temporary Marriage in Shi'i Iran* (Syracuse, NY: Syracuse University Press 1989), 222, n. 23.

[19] See Wadud, *Qur'an and Woman*, 40–42; Stowasser, *Women in the Qur'an*, 65; Marilyn Booth, *Classes of Ladies of Cloistered Spaces: Writing Feminist History through Biography in Fin-de-Siècle Egypt* (Edinburgh: Edinburgh University Press, 2015), 140–141.

[20] Brinner, *Life of the Prophets*, 535–537; Lassner, *Demonizing the Queen of Sheba*, 201–203.

banished for the most part from the public domain. Throughout Islamic history, however, many women wielded power behind the throne, and several others have actually come to power and ruled as sultans, queens, prime ministers, and presidents, as I will discuss briefly in the following section. The Qur'anic story of the Queen of Sheba, a woman sovereign with political authority, was left in oblivion as the later hadith gained greater prominence.

The "Prophetic" Hadith

How and why did the following hadith, "Never will succeed such a nation as makes a woman their ruler," come about?[21] The military involvement of Aisha, Mother of the Faithful and beloved of Muhammad, in the battle of succession played a crucial role in polarizing the nascent Muslim community's sentiments during the reigns of the third and fourth caliphs.[22] Her dramatic loss at the Battle of the Camel, in which she led the opposition to the fourth caliph, Ali, allegedly occasioned the pronouncement of the above-mentioned hadith.[23] Neither Aisha herself nor her "soldiers/sons"[24] questioned her political legitimacy or the righteousness of her military objective – at least not until her defeat – as is made clear by the famed tenth-century chronicler and historian al-Tabari.[25] Aisha lost the battle not because she was a woman, or for want of a supportive political elite and soldiers/sons.[26] The fact is that she lost, and with that, the political legacy of her military misadventure and audacious political

---

[21] Tha'labi relates a hadith from Ibn Maymunah, tracing the chain of his transmissions back to Caliphs Ali and Abu Bakr, stating that when Bilqis was mentioned in the Prophet's presence, he said, "Never will succeed such a nation as makes a woman their ruler"; in Brinner, *Life of the Prophets*, 524. See also Abu El Fadl, *Speaking in God's Name*; Fadel, "Is Historicism a Viable Strategy"; Mernissi, *The Veil and the Male Elite*, 49–57; Siddique, *The Struggle of Muslim Women*, 57; Denise A. Spellberg, *Politics, Gender, and the Islamic Past: The Legacy of Aisha Bint Abi Bakr* (New York: Columbia University Press, 1994); Stowasser, *Women in the Qur'an*, 63–66.

[22] Nabia Abbott, *Aishah the Beloved of Mohammed* (Chicago: Chicago University Press; repr. London: Al-Saqi Books, 1942), 20–21, 136; Fatima Mernissi, *Hidden from History: The Forgotten Queens of Islam* (Lahore: ASR Publications, 1994), 66.

[23] Mernissi, *Hidden from History*.

[24] Adrian Brocket, trans., *The History of al-Tabari, Volume XVI: The Community Divided*, (Albany: State University of New York Press, 1997); Ashley Manjarrez Walker and Michael A. Sells, "The Wiles of Women and Performative Intertextuality: 'A'isha, the Hadith of the Slander, and the Sura of Yusuf," *Journal of Arabic Literature* 30, no. 1 (1999): 58.

[25] Stephen Humphreys, trans., *The History of al-Tabari, Volume XV: The Crisis of the Early Caliphate* (Albany: State University of New York Press, 1990); Brocket, *The History of al-Tabari*.

[26] Brocket, *The History of al-Tabari*, 46–47.

adventure against the reigning caliph, as argued by Spellberg, were ultimately "transformed into a convenient component of the medieval construct which defined all women as threats to the maintenance of Islamic political order."[27]

Reminiscent of the esteem the Queen of Sheba commanded as a sovereign, Aisha's gender did not seem odd to her followers or deter them from following her to the battlefield. The famed tenth-century historian al-Tabari discusses at length how Aisha, acting as a political leader, reached out to the public by sending forth messengers bearing letters to various notables from the expanding Muslim world or by speaking directly to the general public in the mosques.[28] Aisha's military adventure, thus, was not considered out of the ordinary by the rank and file – at least not by a good number of them.[29] This is not to say that her military leadership was not contested. Civil wars are always contested; some support it, some don't, and some want no part of it. Neither the political elite nor the public at large were unanimous in their response to Aisha's call to arms against the reigning caliph, nor did either group support the caliph. Aisha's gender was initially immaterial as the competition over succession to the caliphate was gathering force. In fact, Talha b. Ubaydallah (597–656) and Zubayr b. al-Awwam (594–656) – two of the Prophet's companions, and Aisha's brothers-in-law – both capitalized on Aisha's political authority, on their kinship ties to her, and on her genealogical pedigree and marital bonds in order to help them clinch the caliphate. Her gender became the most objectionable issue retroactively, however, in the revisionist medieval rewrites of the eighth and ninth centuries – given her spectacular loss in the battle for succession.[30] What is important to note, however, is the articulation of a Prophetic hadith at the moment the socio-political situation demanded it. The hadith highlights a situation of tradition-making, aptly characterized by Stowasser as "*sunna*-in-the-making."[31] In time, the hadith opposing women's leadership gained political capital and currency to the point of sidelining the authority of the Qur'anic revelations regarding the Queen of Sheba and her sovereignty. This hadith has been periodically invoked as a politically motivated religious justification for excluding women from the public domain and from assuming political authority in contemporary Muslim societies.[32]

[27] Spellberg, *Politics, Gender, and the Islamic Past*, 109.
[28] Brocket, *The History of al-Tabari*.
[29] Abbott, *Aishah the Beloved of Mohammed*.
[30] Ibid.; Mernissi, *Hidden from History*; Stowasser, *Women in the Qur'an*; Spellberg, *Politics, Gender, and the Islamic Past*.
[31] Stowasser, *Women in the Qur'an*, 115; *sunna* is the Prophetic tradition. See also Mernissi, *The Veil and the Male Elite*, 34.
[32] Mernissi, *The Veil and the Male Elite*; Fadl, *Speaking in God's Name*.

Whether or not it was the Prophet Muhammad himself who made such a pronouncement has been debated.[33] Nonetheless, it was almost 200 years after his death that this hadith was officially recorded by the famed hadith collector Imam Bukhari (d. 870 CE) despite the fact that it was a "singleton" and "weak," that is, not corroborated by other companions and associates of the Prophet.[34] The irony of it all is that Aisha is known to be a major contributor of hadith, particularly those having to do with Muhammad's private life and family.[35] She applied the principle of checking the hadith against the Qur'an conscientiously. This principle was later "formulated and agreed upon by all jurists," meaning that "if a hadith is contradicted by a Qur'anic verse, and there is no way of reconciling them, then the hadith will be 'left'."[36]

Why then was the hadith "Never will succeed such a nation as makes a woman their ruler" not ignored by the eminent medieval authorities, the exegetes, the jurists, and the religious scholars – those who have the knowledge of the book? Surely, they were not/are not unaware of the unquestioned authority of the Qur'an and the hierarchy of the sources of authority in the Islamic tradition.[37] The "Sunni exegetes," likewise argues Ismail Lala, have repeatedly asserted "the authority of the Qur'an to explain itself,"[38] but the early religious elites and scholars at times prioritized the hadith over the Qur'an: "the treatment that the Queen of Sheba receives by the exegetes reveals that, contrary to their assertions, they are influenced by and are products of their cultural and social milieu," departing noticeably from the plain reading of the text.[39]

---

[33] Fadl, *Speaking in God's Name*; Brown, ed., *Hadith*; Mernissi, *The Veil and the Male Elite*; Siddique, *The Struggle of Muslim Women*.

[34] Abbott, *Aishah the Beloved of Mohammed*.

[35] Muhammad Akram Nadvi, *Al-Muhaddithat: The Women Scholars in Islam*, 2nd rev. ed. (Oxford: Interface Publications, 2013). For differences between Sunnis' and Shi'is' hadith attributed to Aisha, see Spellberg, *Politics, Gender, and the Islamic Past*, 10–11.

[36] Nadvi, *Al-Muhaddithat*, 240.

[37] Riffat Hassan, similarly, admonishes medieval Muslim exegetes' interpretation of the Qur'anic story of creation. She highlights how the patriarchal predisposition persuaded Muslim scholars to knowingly misrepresent the evenhanded Qur'anic story of Adam and Eve by upholding its Biblical reconstruction in which Eve (not named in the Qur'an) is held responsible for the "original sin" by persuading Adam to eat the forbidden fruit and thus disobey God. "Made from Adam's Rib: The Woman's Creation Question," *Al-Mushir Theological Journal of the Christian Study Centre* (1985): 124–156.

[38] Lala Ismail, "The Queen of Sheba in the Sunni Exegetical Tradition," *Religions* 13, no. 233 (March 2022), 1–20, 1.

[39] Ibid.; Haeri, *Unforgettable Queens of Islam*, chapter 2.

WOMEN WHO RULED THE MUSLIM WORLD

The category of women who have come to power in the Muslim world is not monolithic, and neither are the structures of the political systems and the family dynamics under which they have assumed power, whether in medieval Egypt and Yemen or in modern Pakistan and Indonesia. Their paths to power depend on a multiplicity of factors, including ethnicity and social standing, kinship and marriage alliances, the presence or absence of politically viable male heirs, their own charisma, and the political authority of the ruling patriarch and his relationship with the religious establishment. In modern times, succession depends on the constitution and rule of law, elections and the ballot box. Viewing from historical and cross-cultural perspectives, we come to learn of a number of women political heads of state, particularly hailing from South and Southeast Asia. This should, perhaps, not come as a surprise, since the farther away societies are from the center of the Arab/Islamic world, the stronger the influence is of cultural traditions and local customs, 'urf and adat (indigenous norms and tradition), that pattern people's behavior and shape their sensibilities.[40] Specifically, a society's geographic location, ethnic identity, and political economy contribute significantly to the patterning of kinship relations, gender hierarchy, roles, and responsibilities.

As the political structure and administrative bureaucracies became more centralized in the Islamic caliphate in Baghdad, increasingly restrictive and misogynistic attitudes were expressed towards women's mobility, public visibility, and political authority. Comparing the representations of women companions of the Prophet in the biographies of Muslim chroniclers from the ninth to the fourteenth centuries, Asma Afsaruddin demonstrates the rise in patriarchal gender negativities.[41] In the further East and Southeast and Central Asia, however, gender relations and social attitudes towards women differed markedly. As those communities came under the control of Turco-Mongolian cultural domination, gender boundaries tended to be more fluid, particularly among the elite, who exerted authority and were accorded greater autonomy.[42] Women often shared political leadership with their husbands or were supported in leadership positions

---

[40] John Esposito, *The Oxford History of Islam* (Oxford: Oxford University Press, 1999), 424–425; Annemarie Schimmel, *Islam: An Introduction* (New York: State University of New York Press. 1992), 64.

[41] Asma Afsaruddin, "Early Women Exemplars and the Construction of Gendered Space," in *Harem Histories: Envisioning Places and Living Spaces*, ed. Marilyn Booth (Durham, NC: Duke University Press, 2010), 23–48.

[42] Joseph Fletcher, "Turco-Mongolian Monarchic Tradition in the Ottoman Empire," in *Harvard Ukrainian Studies, Part 1: Eucharisterion, Essays Presented to Omeljan*

by their fathers. Despite the increasing influence of Islam, Christianity, and Buddhism over the last four centuries in Southeast Asia, women's autonomy and authority have remained undiminished.[43] A. L. Khan describes the rulership of four successive generations of mothers, daughters, and sisters in the seventeenth-century Sultanate of Aceh, whose leadership was supported by both custom and Islam.[44] All four queens ruled "peacefully," and "it was not until the leadership of the fourth and last queen, Kamalat Syah, that pressures were brought to bear upon the state by a fatwa produced from the Shariff of Mecca stating that a woman cannot rule in Islam."[45] Shaharyar Khan, likewise, examines the political leadership of four successive generations of mothers and daughters in the nineteenth and early twentieth centuries in Bhopal, India.[46] Qudsiyya Begum, the first of the four, seized the opportunity to succeed her assassinated husband to become, at the age of nineteen, the regent of her infant daughter (r. 1819–37). Although pious, she abandoned veiling, arguing that veiling was not a sign of piety and virtue. Faced with opposition to her political leadership from her male relatives, who readily invoked the above-mentioned Prophetic hadith, she countered that the Prophet Muhammad's wife "was a great role model for women and even took part in battles."[47]

Yet, as far as the political leadership of women in the Middle Ages is concerned, the thirteenth century has been recorded as the most momentous period in the annals of the Islamic world. Three women in three different corners of the Muslim world took the reins of power.[48] Most notable among them was Razia Sultan, the only female ruler of the Delhi Mamluk Sultanate, who ruled from 1236 to 1240 (described below). Almost her contemporary, Shajarat al-Durr is another high-spirited Mamluk queen, who ruled Egypt in her own right for several months in 1250 before being ordered by the "short-sighted" caliph in Baghdad to forfeit the crown and marry.[49] Last is Abish Khatun (1263–89), the ninth

---

Pritsak on His Sixtieth Birthday by His Colleagues and Students (1979–80) (Cambridge, MA: Harvard Ukrainian Research Institute),236–251.
[43] Sher Banu A. L. Khan, "Rule behind the Silk Curtain: The Sultanahs of Aceh 1641–1699," PhD diss., Queen Mary College, University of London, 2009, 168.
[44] Ibid.
[45] Ibid., 167.
[46] Shaharyar M. Khan, *The Begums of Bhopal: A Dynasty of Women Rulers in Raj India* (London and New York: I. B. Tauris, 2000).
[47] Ibid.; Claudia Preckel, "Bhopāl," in *Encyclopaedia of Islam, Volume III: Brill Online*, ed. Fleet et al. (2011), https://doi.org/10.1163/1573-3912_ei3_COM_23872.
[48] Stanley Lane-Poole, *Medieval India under Mohammedan Rule, 712–1764* (New York: G. P. Putnam's Sons, 1903).
[49] Mernissi, *Hidden from History*, 28–29.

sovereign of the Persian dynasty of the Atabeks, also known as the Sulghurid.[50] As a child, Abish was sent to Shiraz, her native land, by her formidable mother during the troubled period of Mongol supremacy. Abish Khatun was caught in a revolt against the Il-Khans and was sent to jail in Tabriz (northwest Iran) in 1286–7, and was executed subsequently in 1289. Abish was twenty-six years old.[51] Indicative of their supreme position as sovereigns, all three queens had coins minted in their names and *khutbas* (official sermons) read in their honor. All three came to power, nominal though it was in the case of Abish, through dynastic ties and marriage alliances. I describe briefly a few examples of women rulers in medieval and modern Muslim societies.

One of the earliest Muslim women rulers with significant political acumen and power is Sayyida Hurra Queen Arwa (1047/8–1137/8) of the Ismaili Sulayhid dynasty in Yemen. The Sulayhid dynasty of Yemen was a satellite ally of the Fatimid Ismailis in Egypt, supporting and supported by the latter – the fates of the two states were intimately interconnected. Queen Arwa came to power through an accident of history, but she made history in taking the helm of the state and becoming a powerful local sovereign with long-term global consequences. Her sovereignty is unique in that she held both political and spiritual authority simultaneously. Queen Arwa, also known as the Little Queen of Sheba locally, was elevated to the status of *hujja*[52] by the Ismaili imam–caliph al-Mustansir (d. 1094). She is the only Muslim woman sovereign to hold both temporal and spiritual authority simultaneously. Ceremonial though her title of *hujja* might have been from the point of view of the male political elite,[53] the queen had no doubt about her own legitimacy and little hesitancy to use her authority as political situations demanded. She had de facto political authority for seventy-one years, though initially as a queen consort in collaboration with her husband, al-Mukarram bi Allah (1067–84), then as the queen regent of her son (1084–94), and finally as the "Great Queen of Arabia" – a sovereign in her own right until her death in 1138. As she gained more experience as sovereign, she was able to wield greater political leverage in her relationship with the

---

[50] Lane-Poole, *Medieval India*, 74.
[51] Nilgun Dalkeshen, "Gender Roles and Women's Status in Central Asia and Anatolia between the Thirteenth and Sixteenth Centuries," PhD diss., Middle East Technical University, Ankara, 2007, 174; B. Spuler, "Abeš Kātūn," *Encyclopaedia Iranica*, vol. I, fasc. 2, ed. Ehsan Yarshater (New York: Columbia University Press, 2011), 210.
[52] *Hujja* is the highest rank after the imam–caliph in the Ismaili Shi'i religiopolitical hierarchy.
[53] Samer Traboulsi, "The Queen Was Actually a Man: Arwā Bint Aḥmad and the Politics of Religion," *Arabica* 50, no. 1 (January 2003): 96–108.

increasingly younger and inexperienced Fatimid caliphs in Cairo. Unfazed by the social, political, and military roller-coaster of the Fatimid war of succession in Egypt and tribal infighting in Yemen, she performed a delicate balancing act of diplomatic deference and obedience to the Fatimid imams in Cairo while exercising authority and autonomy in Yemen.[54] She managed to keep the powerful and competing Yemenite tribal leaders in check, while delivering justice and ensuring the welfare of her people, who called her their "Mistress."[55]

Unlike Queen Arwa, who was accidently thrust into the political limelight, Razia Sultan of India (1236–40) actively vied for power, with the support of her royal father, Iltutmish.[56] Ascending to the throne in the aftermath of the disastrous but short reign of her brother, Razia Sultan brought peace and prosperity to her people, reduced the taxes on farmers, and included Hindus in her court, among other advancements she initiated in her people's lives.[57] She acted self-confidently, had a good sense of her own authority and independence, and felt secure in her relation with the public, from whom she drew affirmation and support. She tried hard to strike a balance of power and privilege among her father's Turkish slave–amirs who formed the military and political elite, while pursuing her own agenda of making a difference in the lives of the masses who had supported her sovereignty. However, her trust in the extent of her army's loyalty proved to be misplaced, and her belief in her own ability to keep them under control a miscalculation. Three years into her reign, she was accused of a moral lapse and alleged to have had improper relations with one of her loyal advisors. She was removed from power by her half-brothers[58] and killed by her brother's mercenaries.

With the post-Enlightenment institutionalization of authority in constitutions, political competition became "democratized." One of the first democratically elected Muslim women to the high office of prime minister was Benazir Bhutto of Pakistan (1953–2007). At thirty-five years of age, she was the first Muslim woman prime minister charged with the leadership of a modern Muslim society. She was the

[54] Husain F. Hamdani, "The Life and Times of Queen Saiyidah Arwā the Sulaihid of the Yemen," A Lecture at the Royal Central Asian Society, April 29, 1931, London: Royal Central Asian Society.
[55] Ibid.; Haeri, *Unforgettable Queens of Islam*, chapter 3.
[56] H. G. Raverty, trans., *Tabakat-i Nasiri: A General History of the Mohammedan Dynasties of Asia, Including Hindustan: From A.H. 194 (810 A.D.) to A.H. 658 (1260 A.D.)*, vol. I (New Delhi: Oriental Books [reprint. Corporation 1970]); Lane-Poole, *Medieval India*.
[57] Raverty, *Tabakat-i Nasiri*; Lane-Pool, *Medieval India*.
[58] Raverty, *Tabakat-i Nasiri*; Haeri, *Unforgettable Queens of Islam*, chapter 4.

daughter of Zulfikar Ali Bhutto, prime minister of Pakistan between 1973 and 1977.[59] Emerging from the trauma of witnessing her father subjected to a military execution, and herself imprisoned,[60] she dramatically rose to power. In her first term she was up against the entrenched male political elite and the army generals, the "deep state" or the "establishment," as it is known in Pakistan; her second term was marked by dynastic competition and the battle of succession between sister and brother – Benazir and Murtaza – that ultimately undid both her relationship with her brother and her administration. She was re-elected in 1993, despite fierce opposition from the religious establishment and the male political elite, including her own brother. Seeking a third term, in October 2007, an older and more experienced Benazir returned home to her "beloved Pakistan" from exile, determined to bring the country "back to democracy" and to act as a "catalyst for change."[61] It was not to be. On 27 December 2007, she was assassinated.

Another example of Muslim women exercising political authority is that of Megawati Sukarnoputri (1947–) of Indonesia, who was the first woman to become president of a Muslim-majority state. Daughter of Sukarno, Indonesia's first post-independence president and a national hero, Megawati, the "housewife," left the privacy of her home to occupy the presidential palace – the most public and visible place in her country. Her steep climb unsettled powerful men such as Suharto, the general who had overthrown her father in 1967, and confounded the male elite (some of whom were her father's friends), who perceived her active presence in politics and the public domain to be disruptive and subversive. Megawati found her political voice and galvanized the long-oppressed Indonesian people to support her to oust the strongman President Suharto (r. 1967–98), who had, for almost three decades, succeeded in vanquishing his rivals in the game of political succession.[62] Despite fierce objections to her rising political popularity and the invocation of the aforementioned Prophetic hadith,[63] by the time Megawati

[59] Charles Lindholm, *Charisma* (Boston: Blackwell, 1990), 7.
[60] Benazir Bhutto, *Daughter of the East* (London: Mandarin Paperbacks, 1989); *Reconciliation: Islam, Democracy, and the West* (New York: Harper Perennial, 2008).
[61] Bhutto, *Reconciliation*, 1–2.
[62] Clinton Bennett, *Muslim Women of Power: Gender, Politics and Culture in Islam* (New York: Continuum, 2010), chapter 6; Robert W. Hefner, *Civil Islam: Muslims and Democratization in Indonesia* (Princeton: Princeton University Press, 2000); Agnus McIntyre, *The Indonesian Presidency: The Shift from Personal toward Constitutional Rule* (Oxford: Rowman and Littlefield, 2005).
[63] Nelly van Doorn-Harder, "The Indonesian Islamic Debate on a Woman President," *Sojourn* 17, no. 2 (2002): 164–190.

Sukarnoputri won the presidency and was sworn in (2001), the rule of law and the constitution had prevailed. Similarly, in Bangladesh, Sheikh Hasina and Khaleda Zia (the daughter and the widow, respectively, of the founder and former presidents of Bangladesh) have dominated the political scene since the 1990s, alternately serving as prime minister and leader of the opposition, thus earning the label of the "battling Begums."[64] Both are leaders of their respective political parties, the Awami League and the Bangladesh Nationalist Party.

HADITH REMEMBERED?

Modern times have brought about significant shifts in women's knowledge and sensibilities regarding legal equality, gender justice, and political authority. Mobilizing their resources, Muslim women now demand equality and political representation. They are challenging the lopsided gender hierarchy, and the monopoly of male privileges and their domination of the political and spiritual domains. Simultaneously, women's awakening and political mobilization across the Muslim world have posed a serious threat to the male monopoly on sacred knowledge and political institutions. A growing number of Muslim women scholars (primarily outside of their own countries, often for fear of persecution) have brilliantly reinterpreted the Qur'an and rendered novel readings of the revelations.[65] Modernity has also triggered religious revivalism and an ideological reversion to an idealized past with a belief in an "immutable" tradition. With the emergence of religious radicalism in the Muslim world – indeed, in much of the modern world[66] – a backlash against the women's movement and its demands for gender justice, equality, and fair political representation has increased. The latter deploy religion to enforce traditional patriarchal gender hierarchy and thus safeguard male privileges and power. Against that background, the purported Prophetic hadith, cited above, has gained greater popularity among the religious *and* some political elites in Muslim societies.[67] The greater currency of this hadith in the modern era may seem surprising at

---

[64] Bennett, *Muslim Women of Power*, chapters 3 and 5.
[65] Prominent examples include Asma Afsaruddin, Leila Ahmed, Kecia Ali, Laleh Bakhtiar, Asma Barlas, Riffat Hassan, Mervat Hatem, Aziza Al-Hibri, Ayesha Hidayatullah, Amira Sonbol, D. Spellberg, Barbara Stowasser, and Amina Wadud.
[66] See the six volumes of the *Fundamentalism Project*, ed. Martin Marty and Scott Appleby (Chicago: University of Chicago Press, 1991–2004).
[67] Fadl, *Speaking in God's Name*; Brown, ed., *Hadith*; Fadel, "Is Historicism a Viable Strategy"; Mernissi, *The Veil and the Male Elite*; Siddique, *The Struggle of Muslim Women*.

first. But it makes sense, considering the growing awareness among Muslim women of a deep-rooted misogyny, women's being deprived of access to resources, and gender "apartheid" in some Muslim societies.[68]

Prior to the modern era and Muslim women's clamor for social and gender justice, the religious elite had little reason to invoke the hadith, 'especially when nothing practical seemed to turn on that interpretation.'[69] Muslim women's global mobilization and their demand for gender equality and political representation have threatened the foundations of belief in the "divinely" ordained patriarchal gender hierarchy, believed to be based on the "natural" differences between male and female, and the "inherent" intellectual inferiority of women. Currently, women's competition for power and political sway is all too real, infringing on the long-held "sacral" monopoly of male traditional domination and privileges – hence the greater political/religious push for the application of the Prophetic hadith to deny women political representation. Further, as more and more women from all over the world, including the Muslim world, demand the inclusion of their political rights in their constitutions, many once secular and presumably democratic male political elites have joined forces with religious elites to prevent women from assuming political leadership.[70]

The difference, briefly stated, has to do with women's organized mobilizations and their collective demand for legal equality and gender justice. Whereas in the medieval era one woman or another rose to power to become a political leader or ruler in one Muslim society or another, they did so through the structural support of their royal fathers, or (less frequently) their husbands. While these exceptional women had the political support needed to ascend to the throne after their fathers or husbands, they lacked the collective support of women's organizations and associations that are more representative of modernity and global institutional changes in gender relations, and collectively women's demands for political representation and equality.

Neither during the long reign of Queen Arwa in Yemen nor during the short sovereignty of Razia Sultan in India do we hear of any organized religious objections to their temporal authority. It is during the governments of Prime Minister Benazir Bhutto and President Megawati that the alleged Prophetic hadith was explicitly invoked by some religious

---

[68] Feriel Ben Mahmoud, *Feminism Inshallah: A History of Arab Feminism*, filmed in 2014. This video is distributed by Women Make Movies: www.wmm.com/catalog/film/feminism-inshallah-a-history-of-arab-feminism/.
[69] Fadel, "Is Historicism a Viable Strategy," 35.
[70] See Mernissi on Nawaz Sharif in Pakistan, in *Hidden from History*, 1–2; Seth Mydans, "Indonesia Gets a New Leader: Ex-Chief Balks," *New York Times*, July 24, 2001.

leaders[71] and supported by some among the political elites, in order to disqualify these two women from assuming the political leadership of their respective countries.[72] Pointing to "women's nature," the male political and religious elites upheld women's unsuitability for leadership, presumably based on the immutable "divine law," which in their understanding favors all men over all women.[73] As prime minister, Benazir Bhutto was challenged by Jamaat-i-Islami, a well-established religious party that invoked the alleged Prophetic hadith and objected to her leadership on the basis of her gender.[74] The Pakistani political elite, meanwhile, found it expedient to remain silent. Ultimately, Jamaat-i-Islami's suit was dismissed by the Lahore High Court. The fact that such institutional opposition was ineffectual – momentarily – in barring Benazir Bhutto in Pakistan and Megawati Sukarnoputri in Indonesia is not only indicative of the enduring power of dynastic ties, but also of the relative efficacy of the law, the constitution, and the power of the popular vote in these countries.

Like their medieval sisters, Benazir and Megawati enjoyed huge popular support, and their gender was no barrier to achieving political authority. Just as the Queen of Sheba was given all bounty and riches by none other than Almighty Allah, most notably, a Mighty Throne, the military leadership of Aisha, the beloved wife of the Prophet Muhammad, had the backing of the rank and file, in addition to that of many of the political elite. The Queen of Sheba's sovereignty and political authority lend legitimacy to Muslim women's demand for political participation and authority, as was underscored by one of the Iranian women contenders for the presidency in 2001, mentioned at the start of this chapter.

SELECT BIBLIOGRAPHY

Abu El Fadl, Khaled. *Speaking in God's Name: Islamic Law, Authority and Women*. Oxford: Oneworld, 2001.
Bennett, Clinton. *Muslim Women of Power: Gender, Politics and Culture in Islam*. New York: Continuum, 2010.

---

[71] Asma Jahangir, personal communication, February 2016; van Doorn-Harder, "The Indonesian Islamic Debate."
[72] Mernissi, *Hidden from History*, 1; Asma Jahangir, personal communication, February 2016.
[73] Asma Barlas, "Women's Reading of the Qur'an," in *The Cambridge Companion to the Qur'an*, ed. Jane McAuliffe (Cambridge: Cambridge University Press, 2006), 255–271.
[74] Asma Jahangir, personal communication, February 2016.

Bhutto, Benazir. *Reconciliation: Islam, Democracy, and the West*. New York: Harper Perennial, 2008.

Booth, Marilyn. *Classes of Ladies of Cloistered Spaces: Writing Feminist History through Biography in Fin-de-Siècle Egypt*. Edinburgh: Edinburgh University Press, 2015.

Brinner, William M., trans. *Lives of the Prophets: As Recounted by Abu Ishaq Ahmad Ibn Muhammed Ibn Ibrahim al-Thalabi*. 1st ed. Leiden: Brill, 2002.

Brocket, Adrian, trans. *The History of al-Tabari, Volume XVI: The Community Divided*. Albany: State University of New York Press, 1997.

Elias, Jamal J. "Prophecy, Power and Propriety: The Encounter of Solomon and the Queen of Sheba." *Journal of Qur'anic Studies* 11, no. 1 (2009): 57–74.

Fadel, Mohammad. "Is Historicism a Viable Strategy for Islamic Law Reform? The Case of 'Never Shall a Folk Prosper Who Have Appointed a Woman to Rule Them'." *Islamic Law and Society* 18, no. 2 (2011): 131–176.

Lassner, Jacob. *Demonizing the Queen of Sheba: Boundaries of Gender and Culture in Postbiblical Judaism and Medieval Islam*. Chicago: University of Chicago Press, 1993.

Mernissi, Fatima. *Hidden from History: Forgotten Queens of Islam*. Trans. Mary Jo Lakeland. Abingdon: Perseus Books, 1991.

Pritchard, James B., ed. *Solomon and Sheba*. London: Phaidon Press, 1974.

Spellberg, Denise A. *Politics, Gender, and the Islamic Past: The Legacy of Aisha bint Abi Bakr*. New York: Columbia University Press, 1994.

Stowasser, Barbara. *Women in the Qur'an, Traditions, and Interpretation*. New York: Oxford University Press, 1994.

al-Tha'labi, Abu Ishaq Ahmad Ibn Muhammed ibn Ibrahim. *'Ara'is al-majalis fi qisas al-anbiya* [Lives of the Prophets]. Trans. William M. Brinner. Leiden: Brill, 2002.

van Doorn-Harder, Nelly. "The Indonesian Islamic Debate on a Woman President." *Sojourn* 17, no. 2 (2002): 164–190.

Watt, Montgomery. "The Queen of Sheba in Islamic Tradition." In *Solomon and Sheba*, ed. James B. Pritchard, 85–103. London: Phaidon Press, 1974.

13 Women as Social Activists

NELLY VAN DOORN-HARDER

Muslim women's socio-political activism spans a vast array of endeavors, including grassroots organizing, social media campaigns, legal advocacy, and political movement involvement.[1] These women skillfully navigate the intricate landscapes of cultural, religious, and societal norms, often confronting resistance not only from broader societal biases but also from conservative factions within their own communities. Their activism has historical roots, drawing inspiration from significant figures like the Prophet Muhammad's wives and daughters, as explored in Chapter 5 in this volume, "Prophet's Wives: 'Mothers of the Believers'," by Mahjabeen Dhala. In modern times, their activism has been shaped by colonial legacies, national independence struggles, and the quest for women's rights within diverse cultural and legal contexts.[2]

One notable figure is Huda Sha'arawi of Egypt (1879–1947), who emerged as a pioneering feminist leader, founding the Egyptian Feminist Union in 1923.[3] Renowned for championing women's rights, particularly in education and the abolition of the harem system, her public removal of her face veil in 1923 became a powerful symbol of women's liberation in Egypt. Similarly, Begum Rokeya of British India (now Bangladesh) (1880–1932), an esteemed Bengali writer, educator, and social reformer, fought for gender equality and women's education,

---

[1] See, for example, the edited volume by Asma Afsaruddin, and especially chapters 15–28 in *The Oxford Handbook of Islam and Women* (Oxford: Oxford University Press, 2023).

[2] See, for example, Nicola Prat, *Embodying Geopolitics: Generations of Women's Activism in Egypt, Jordan, and Lebanon* (Berkeley: University of California Press, 2020).

[3] Notable is her memoir, Huda Sha'arawi, *Harem Years: The Memoirs of an Egyptian Feminist (1879–1924)*, trans. Margot Badran (New York: Feminist Press at the City University of New York, 1991); Amira Noshokaty, "March of Egyptian Women: Huda Sha'arawi," *AhramOnline*, March 16, 2023, https://english.ahram.org.eg/NewsContent/32/1169/491676/Heritage/Inspiring-Minds/March-of-women-Huda-Shaarawi-.aspx.

establishing Kolkata's first school for Muslim girls in 1911.[4] Her writings challenged patriarchal norms and envisioned a society where women enjoyed freedom and equality.

In the fields of education and legal reform, Muslim women have significantly contributed to expanding educational access and reforming family laws that discriminate against women. Malala Yousafzai from Pakistan, a global girls' education advocate, survived a Taliban attack and subsequently co-founded the Malala Fund, promoting global education for girls.[5] In 2014, she became the youngest Nobel Peace Prize laureate. Legal reformers like the Nobel laureate Shirin Ebadi from Iran and Asma Jahangir, a Pakistani human rights lawyer and social activist who co-founded and chaired the Human Rights Commission of Pakistan, have leveraged their legal acumen to safeguard women's rights, challenging laws and practices that marginalize women.[6] Tawakkol Karman, a young Yemeni journalist, politician, and human rights activist, shared the 2011 Nobel Peace Prize, recognized for her contributions to Yemen's pro-democracy and women's rights movements, especially during the Arab Spring.[7] Loujain al-Hathloul from Saudi Arabia has notably advocated for women's driving rights and the end of the male guardianship system, with these reforms now progressing in Saudi Arabia.[8] Nasrin Sotoudeh, an Iranian human rights lawyer, has represented jailed Iranian opposition activists and women arrested for defying the mandatory hijab, enduring multiple arrests for her activism and symbolizing resistance in Iran.[9]

[4] Mohammad A. Quayum, ed. and trans., *The Essential Rokeya: Selected Works of Rokeya Sakhawat Hossain 1880–1932* (Leiden: Brill, 2013).

[5] Malala Yousafzai, co-written with Christian Lamb, *I Am Malala: The Girl Who Stood up for Education and Was Shot by the Taliban* (London: Weidenfeld & Nicolson, 2013) and Yousafzai, *Malala: My Story of Standing up for Girls' Rights*, abridged ed. (Boston: Little, Brown, 2018).

[6] Ebadi Shirin, *Iran Awakening: A Memoir of Revolution and Hope* (New York: Random House, 2006); Asma Jahangir, "Speech by Ms Asma Jahangir," *Religion and Human Rights* 2, nos. 1–2 (2007): 37–43; Beena Sarwar, "A 'Human Rights Giant': Asma Jahangir (1952–2018)," *Economic and Political Weekly* 53, no. 12 (2018): 23–26.

[7] Kristian Coates Ulrichsen, "Karman, Tawakkol (1979–)," *A Dictionary of Politics in the Middle East* (Oxford: Oxford University Press, 2018); Tawakkol Karman, "Women and the Arab Spring," *UN Chronicle* 53, no. 5 (2017): 21–22; and "About: Nobel Peace Prize Laureate Tawakkol Karman," tawakkolkarman.net.

[8] "Statement on Imprisonment of Loujain Al-Hathloul," *Congressional Documents and Publications*, Washington: Federal Information & News Dispatch, LLC, 2020; Ruth Michaelson, "'What They Did to Me Was So Horrific': Brutal Silencing of a Saudi Feminist," *Guardian*, May 24, 2019, www.theguardian.com/global-development/201 9/may/24/what-they-did-to-me-was-so-horrific-brutal-silencing-of-a-saudi-feminist-l oujain-al-hathloul.

[9] Nasrin Sotoudeh, *Women, Life, Freedom: Our Fight for Human Rights and Equality in Iran* (Ithaca: Cornell University Press, 2023).

Grassroots and community activism examples include Kurdish women from Iran, Iraq, Syria, and Turkey who have been instrumental in advocating for Kurdish rights, gender equality, and combatting ISIS (Islamic State in Iraq and Syria). Their involvement in armed forces and political organizations has challenged traditional gender roles, underscoring their pivotal role in social activism. During the Arab Spring, women from Tunisia, Egypt, Libya, and Syria actively participated in protests, social media activism, and grassroots organizing, championing democracy, human rights, and social justice.

Muslim women's activism is thus far from uniform: it varies as much as the communities these women hail from. Their efforts may be driven by secular motives, religious beliefs, or a combination of both, encompassing a broad spectrum of strategies and objectives. Moreover, these women have adeptly utilized technological advancements to bolster their advocacy efforts. Social media has emerged as an essential tool for Muslim women activists, enabling them to connect, mobilize, and spread awareness about issues affecting their communities. These platforms offer a venue to express their views, share experiences, and counter stereotypes and misinformation regarding Islam and Muslim women, further facilitating their participation in global movements like #MeToo.[10]

Globally, Muslim women's activism extends to interfaith and intercultural dialogue, striving to foster understanding and combat the Islamophobia affecting their communities.[11] Figures like Linda Sarsour in the US have stood out in their fight against discriminatory policies targeting Muslims and in solidarity with movements like Black Lives Matter, showcasing the interconnection between various social justice efforts.[12] Muslim women are also increasingly visible in environmental preservation efforts, both locally and globally. Icons like Munira Ahmed have become symbols of resistance and diversity, actively championing environmental protection and social justice.[13] Similarly, activists like Hindou Oumarou Ibrahim from Chad and Dr. Fozia Tahir in Pakistan have made significant contributions to environmental conservation, focusing on the rights of indigenous communities and

---

[10] The work of Mona Eltahawy is one example, *The Seven Necessary Sins for Women and Girls* (Dublin: Tramp Press, 2021).

[11] For social media activism, see Faiza Hirji, "Claiming Our Space: Muslim Women, Activism, and Social Media," *Islamophobia Studies Journal* 6, no. 1 (2021): 78–92.

[12] Linda Sarsour, "Reflections of a Brooklyn-Based Arab American Activist," *Race/Ethnicity: Multidisciplinary Global Contexts* 4, no. 3 (2011): 351–359.

[13] Christina Cauterucci, "A Q-and-A with the Muslim Woman Whose Face Has Become a Symbol of Trump Resistance," *Slate*, January 25, 2017 https://slate.com/human-interest/2017/01/a-q-and-a-with-the-muslim-woman-whose-face-has-become-a-symbol-of-trump-resistance.html.

sustainable practices.[14] Organizations such as the Islamic Foundation for Ecology and Environmental Sciences (IFEES) and Green Muslims have been pioneers in Islamic environmentalism, with women playing pivotal roles in their initiatives, highlighting leadership in environmental stewardship.[15]

The impact of Muslim women's socio-political activism is multidimensional, leading to meaningful changes in laws and policies in certain contexts, fostering increased awareness and solidarity across various social justice movements, and contributing to the broader fight for gender equality within and beyond Muslim communities. Their activism helps us shift the narrative from viewing Muslim women as passive recipients of their circumstances to recognizing their agency and resilience.

In this chapter, I delve into the evolution of women's socio-political activism in Indonesia. I explore how today Indonesian women are active in social movements not only to improve the status of women but also to exert popular pressure on the state to deliver public goods. Through a case study of a women's rights movement in Indonesia with active networks across East Asian countries, the chapter demonstrates how significant political and economic developments directly influenced the trajectory of women's socio-political activism in Indonesia, yet the role of dynamic women activists who called for reforms has been central to bringing change.

THE CASE OF INDONESIA: DEFENDING WOMEN'S BASIC HUMAN RIGHTS

In Indonesia, activism for Muslim women's rights started to develop as early as the first decades of the twentieth century, when it acquired several unique traits that continue to influence these movements today.[16] During the late nineteenth and early twentieth centuries, pioneering women, such as the famous noblewoman Raden Adjeng Kartini (1879–1904) and Rahmah el-Joenesijjah (1900–69), promoted education for girls to advance their social and economic position. Raden Adjeng Kartini, who is now considered one of Indonesia's national heroes, was

---

[14] Hindou Oumarou Ibrahim, "The Climate Agreements: What We Have Achieved and the Gaps That Remain," in *Resilience through Knowledge Co-Production*, ed. Marie Roué (Cambridge: Cambridge University Press, 2022), 165–174; Fozia Tahir, "Significant Steps towards Sustainability in Pakistan," *TEDx Talk: Lahore*, March 2022, www.ted.com/talks/fozia_tahir_significant_steps_towards_sustainability_in_pakistan.

[15] "IFEES/EcoIslam," www.ifees.org.uk/; "Living the Environmental Spirit of Islam," www.greenmuslims.org/.

[16] Some of the information presented in this chapter necessarily overlaps with my chapter "Women's Religious and Social Activism in Southeast Asia," in *The Oxford Handbook of Islam and Women*, ed. Afsaruddin, 444–462.

the daughter of an influential Javanese regent who allowed his daughter to attend a Dutch-language primary school. This was during a time when the idea of women's education was considered unacceptable. During her short life, Kartini advocated for basic rights for women and education for girls. After her death in 1924, Dutch sympathizers proceeded to open several schools for girls in Kartini's name.[17] In 1923, on the island of Sumatra, in Padang Panjang, Rahmah el-Joenisijah opened the first Islamic school for girls, the Diniyah Putri.

These two women lived during a time when several developments were changing the frame of reference of the Indonesian people. Educational levels were rising since the Dutch colonial government, instead of exploiting the local population, allowed Indonesian children to attend Dutch schools. At the same time, Islamic awareness and empowerment rose with the expanding print culture and increased contacts with the Middle East after the opening of the Suez Canal in 1869. This shortcut to the heartland of Islam allowed more Indonesians to perform the Hajj to Mecca. Pilgrims often used the opportunity to engage in deeper studies of Islam. Upon their return they started to teach their new understanding of Islam, especially spreading ideas to reform what they considered forms of Indonesian Islam that were too closely connected to the many indigenous cultures.[18]

At the same time a sense of nationalism awoke, and during the early decades of the twentieth century, in response to the colonial bureaucratic system, voluntary organizations arose across the Archipelago. These included literary clubs, trade organizations, and educational and religious movements. In this spirit of renewing and reinventing, the Islamic reformist organization Muhammadiyah was founded in 1912. Its main agenda was to purify Islam of local practices and beliefs. In their interpretation of Islam, Muhammadiyah leaders relied on the original sources of the Qur'an and the hadith (sayings of the Prophet Muhammad). As a response to these modernist or reformist initiatives, the traditionalist Nahdlatul Ulama (NU) organization was founded in 1926. Its leaders aimed at representing the original form of Indonesian Islam as it had developed after Islam entered the Archipelago. While each of these organizations had its own agenda and members, both became vehicles to fight the Dutch (Christian) colonial power that had

---

[17] See Joost Cotee, trans., *Letters from Kartini: An Indonesian Feminist, 1900–1904* (Clayton, Victoria: Monash Asia Institute, 1992).

[18] For the role of Islam in developing Indonesian nationalism, see Michael Laffan, *Islamic Nationhood and Colonial Indonesia: The Ummah below the Winds* (London, New York: Routledge, 2003).

dominated the spice trade from the outer islands since the seventeenth century but become a real presence on the island of Java from 1830.

Women affiliated with the Muhammadiyah and NU organized their own groupings. The first was the Muhammadiyah-related Aisyiyah (founded in 1917), followed by the Muslimat NU (founded in 1946). While initially promoting arguments that sought to increase respect for women based on biological differences, activists mostly lobbied for access to education (religious and nonreligious), worship spaces for women, and the protection of women's rights within the family as wives, mothers, and daughters. These organizations were founded when Indonesia was still under Dutch colonial influence. As a result, after the end of the Second World War (1945), promoting the education of women also took on a nationalist character in the service of building a strong and independent Indonesian nation. Although Indonesian women continue to face patriarchal systems and misogyny, their rights were acknowledged in the preamble of the 1945 constitution, which acknowledges every person or citizen of the state and does not tolerate discrimination based on gender. Although currently around 87 percent of Indonesians are Muslim, they continue to adhere to a religiously neutral form of nationalism called Pancasila. This principle acknowledges the equality of all Indonesians and is based on the five principles of belief in one God, nationalism, humanitarianism, social justice, and democracy.

FIVE PHASES

In her book *A Genealogy of Islamic Feminism: Pattern and Change in Indonesia* (2018), Etin Anwar places the start of activism for women's rights at the beginning of the twentieth century, when Raden Adjeng Kartini corresponded with a Dutch acquaintance, bemoaning the lack of education for girls and the practice of polygamous marriages.[19] According to Anwar, this time represents the first phase of emerging feminist voices, which also can be called the "era of emancipation," and was followed by a second phase, when women started to advocate for stronger women's rights within the 1937 marriage law.[20] The third phase (1945) was marked by the fight for independence from the Dutch colonial power. At that time, government developmental policies mostly were designed to meet the needs of men.[21] During the fourth phase, women

---

[19] For the correspondence, see Cotee, trans., *Letters from Kartini*.
[20] Etin Anwar, *A Genealogy of Islamic Feminism: Pattern and Change in Indonesia* (Abingdon: Routledge, 2018), 20–21.
[21] Ibid., 21–22.

reconsidered not just their roles within marriage, but also their roles in society. This was the prelude to the fifth phase, when Islam and feminism converged, and women started to forge their own relationships to Islam and different expressions of Islamic feminism.[22]

In this chapter, I will first explain some of the foundational initiatives that Indonesian Muslim women as well as male leaders created during what Etin Anwar calls the "fifth phase." The focus of these activities was on basic human rights, the rights of women and children, and the strengthening of democracy. They mostly were undertaken during the 1980s–90s by nongovernmental organizations (NGOs) connected to established Muslim networks such as the Muhammadiyah and NU. According to Aihwa Ong, NGOs play critical roles as "key agents that translate human rights principles into ethical gender regimes that are acceptable in local contexts, the activities of NGOs – religious, feminist, political, humanitarian, and economic – expand civil society in Southeast Asia, bringing about new values of human justice and good in society around which gender issues crystallize."[23]

In my view this phase gave birth to a new movement that started with activism, study, and lobbying in preparation for the first KUPI congress (Kongres Ulama Perempuan Indonesia, the Indonesian Women's Ulama Congress, referred to as KUPI I), held in May 2017, followed by a second congress (KUPI II) held in November 2022.

In Indonesia, a watershed moment for activism for the rights of women was the 1995 Fourth World Conference on Women in Beijing that marked a turning point for the global agenda for gender equality. Indonesia was one of the 189 countries that adopted the conference's platform for action for the advancement of women and gender equality.[24] Furthermore, in Indonesia, historical moments such as the fall of President Suharto (1967–98) generated new forms of Muslim and other feminist activities. Suharto had been a dictator, and during his rule political activism as well as violent and extremist expressions of Islam were banned.[25]

---

[22] Ibid., 22–23.
[23] Aihwa Ong, "Translating Gender Justice in Southeast Asia: Situated Ethics, NGOs, and Bio-Welfare," *Journal of Women of the Middle East and the Islamic World* 9 (2011): 45.
[24] "World Conferences on Women," United Nations Women, www.unwomen.org/en/how-we-work/intergovernmental-support/world-conferences-on-women#mexico.
[25] For more about this period, see, among others, Robert W. Hefner, *Civil Islam: Muslims and Democratization in Indonesia* (Princeton: Princeton University Press, 2000) and Robert W. Hefner, "Islamization and Democratization in Indonesia," in *Islam in an Era of Nation-States*, ed. Robert W. Hefner and Patricia Horvatich (Honolulu: University of Hawaii Press, 1997), 75–128.

The time leading up to Suharto's stepping down was marked by severe political and economic unrest during which women fell victim to several incidents of extreme sexual violence.[26] Shortly afterwards, during the so-called era of *Reformasi*, the ensuing political ruptures allowed radical-minded Muslim groups to add their voices to the debates about the place of Islam in society and resulted in increased demands for the nationwide application of shari'a laws. Moral opinions about such issues as face-veiling changed, and new laws were created that directly affected women's role and status.[27]

The violence against women, in combination with the call for the nationwide application of Islamic laws, prompted Muslim and non-Muslim activists to launch new initiatives to protect women. For example, they pushed the government to create an organization that would defend basic women's rights. As a result, in 1998, Komnas Perempuan (Komisi Nasional anti Kekerasaan terhadap Perempuan, the National Commission against Violence against Women) was officially founded by presidential decree to serve as one of Indonesia's three National Organizations for Human Rights. Strictly speaking, Komnas Perempuan is not an Islamic organization but serves all women in culturally and religiously plural Indonesia. Such issues as domestic violence concern women of all religious backgrounds. Even one of their main programs, abolishing child marriage, is not just a Muslim concern, since there are several areas in Indonesia where it is engrained in local cultures and practiced by non-Muslims as well.

Another development during what Etin Anwar has called the "fifth phase" was that education for girls started to mature to the point where it allowed them to continue at university level. Organizations such as the Muhammadiyah-related Aisyiyah had long focused on creating networks of educational institutions for girls. While offering mixed curricula of religious and nonreligious subjects, these schools trained many future members of the current cohorts of female specialists of Islam. At the same time, increasing numbers of women started to study at the various NU *pesantren*, the Islamic boarding schools that form the backbone of the NU interpretation of Islam. Until the 1950s, few women attended these schools, where students engage in intensive studies of the Qur'an,

---

[26] For examples of this violence, see Himawan, Eunike Mutiara, Annie Pohlman, and Winnifred Louis, "Revisiting the May 1998 Riots in Indonesia: Civilians and Their Untold Memories," *Journal of Current Southeast Asian Affairs* 41, no. 2 (August 2022), 169–330.

[27] Eva F. Nisa, *Face-Veiled Women in Contemporary Indonesia* (New York: Routledge, 2023).

hadith, *fiqh*, and their interpretations. However, once women started to graduate from the *pesantren*, many continued on to obtain degrees in Islamic Studies at one of the many Islamic universities and institutes for higher Islamic education.[28] Together with women graduating from religious schools within the Muhammadiyah network, these educational opportunities allowed for a new cohort of Muslim activists to grow and take on various positions within society.

By the 1980s, NU activists (in cooperation with intellectuals from other Islamic organizations) started to launch NGOs such as LP3ES (Institute for Economic and Social Research, Education, and Information), and LSP (Institute for Development Studies). NU involvement within the NGO world especially took off towards the middle of the 1990s, when national NU chair Abdurrahman Wahid (1984–99), who later briefly served as Indonesia's president (1999–2001), spearheaded several community development projects that focused on educating *pesantren* leaders and students in order to transform the traditional educational models and to train leaders who could be instrumental in social change.[29] For the NU, these schools provided a rigorous spiritual, religious, and secular formation that traditionally has been the backbone of strong NU leadership.[30] One such project was P3M, the Association for the Development of Pesantren and Society (Perhimpunan Pengembangan Pesantren dan Masyarakat), in 1983. P3M worked on creating awareness about such issues as Islam and democracy and women's reproductive rights, and raising levels of gender awareness among teachers and students in the *pesantren*. In retrospect, many consider the P3M educational activities foundational to changing views on gender bias within the holy texts among the traditional male and female *pesantren* leaders. Especially its so-called *Fiqhunnisa* program, which in 1995 started to offer workshops on the interpretation and analysis of the traditional *fiqh* or Islamic jurisprudence texts, opened the eyes of Muslim leaders within NU circles to matters of gender equality and how the male-

---

[28] Eka Srimulyani's *Women from Traditional Islamic Educational Institutions in Indonesia: Negotiating Public Spaces* (Amsterdam: University of Amsterdam Press, 2012) provides several interesting cases of women students and leaders in the *pesantren*.

[29] Pieternella van Doorn-Harder, *Women Shaping Islam: Reading the Qur'an in Indonesia* (Urbana and Chicago: University of Illinois Press, 2006), 34, 189. Also see Martin van Bruinessen, "Overview of Muslim Organizations, Associations and Movements in Indonesia," in *Contemporary Developments in Indonesian Islam: Explaining the Conservative Turn*, ed. Martin van Bruinessen (Singapore: ISEAS, 2013), 45–49.

[30] van Doorn-Harder, *Women Shaping Islam*, 189–202.

biased lens had contributed to misogynistic interpretations of the Qur'an and the hadith.[31]

The 1995 Beijing Fourth World Conference on Women also inspired a new generation of activists to translate the conference's recommendations into Islamic-based projects that strengthened women's basic rights, for example where it concerned reproductive rights. As women pursued higher degrees in Islamic Studies, large Islamic universities launched Women's Studies Centers where scholars studied the writings of Islamic feminist and human rights activists, such as Amina Wadud, Riffat Hassan, Ali Asghar Engineer, and Abdullahi Ahmed An-Naim. By the early 1990s, these initiatives generated new forms of Islamic feminist activism which promoted gender equality not just based on their readings of the Qur'an but also through referencing human rights discourses.[32] Indonesian Muslim feminists firmly believe that this type of feminism is compatible with Islam and must be reflected in everyday life.[33] The term "Islamic feminism" in this context covers a range of frames of reference and methodologies. However, those identifying with this movement are united in their support of reinterpreting the Qur'an and deploying "the tenets of Islam as a discursive reference for promoting gender equality and for eliminating oppression."[34] While this movement includes women as well as men, some propose that the term "Islamic feminist" should not be used to refer to male proponents of gender justice; "Muslim feminists" should be used instead, due to the reality that men do not experience what women do.[35]

During the 1990s, alumni from these various projects and institutes started to create agencies focusing solely on women's issues. For example, Rifka Annisa (1993) was set up to assist victims of domestic violence.[36] Over the years, this NGO expanded its services to include rehabilitation of the male perpetrators.[37] To cooperate closely with religious leaders, teachers, and government officials, former P3M activists established Rahima, the Center for Education and Information on Islam

[31] "Sejara Kupi," Kupipedia.id, https://kupipedia.id/index.php/Sejarah_KUPI. Please note that this reference, like those to some of the primary documents cited in this chapter, is in Indonesian and not available in English.
[32] For a detailed study of the various movements in Indonesia, see Anwar, *A Genealogy of Islamic Feminism*.
[33] Ibid., 188.
[34] Ibid., 14.
[35] Ibid., 15.
[36] "Rifka Annisa," https://rifka-annisa.org/en/.
[37] "Counseling for Men," Rifka Annisa, https://rifka-annisa.org/en/services/counseling-for-men.

and Women's Rights Issues. This center also became one of the international partners of the Sisters in Islam (SIS).[38] Around the same time (2000), two NGOs were launched that focused solely on the *pesantren* world. Puan Amal Hayati (established under the patronage of Abdurrahman Wahid's wife, Sinta Nuriyah) sought to empower women students and teachers at the *pesantren*. After KUPI II (November 23–26, 2022) issued legal advice against female genital mutilation (FGM), by 2023 this project had spearheaded a nationwide drive to curtail or prevent the practice.[39] In 2001, prominent religious leader and feminist Kyai Husein Muhammad set up the Fahmina project at his *pesantren* in Cirebon to empower women in the *pesantren* environment.[40] Among other things, researchers focused on analyzing gender discourse in the hadith, which resulted in such publications as *Hadith and Gender Justice* (2007) by Fahmina co-founder Faqihuddin Abdul Kodir.[41] And finally, in 2005, Muslim feminist Lies Marcoes-Natsir, who had coordinated the P3M programs on women's reproductive rights, went on to create the influential NU-related NGO called Rumah KitaB (Rumah Kita Bersama, meaning "our common home").[42] This NGO had as its goal the transformation of Indonesia's Muslim society by addressing the religious paradigms, moral and ethical norms, values, and teachings that have shaped current ways of thinking.[43]

The idea behind such projects was that, to advocate reforms and changes in laws, it was not enough to foster cooperation among Muslim groups, but that there should also be strong relationships between NGOs and Muslim intellectuals and scholars. Furthermore, Muslim women needed to be "actively engaged with the project of interpretation of texts and laws."[44]

---

[38] "About Rahima," https://swararahima.com/en/about-rahima/. As stakeholders, the website mentions: *pesantren*, faith-based organizations, different levels of Islamic school ranging from middle school to university, research centers, media outlets, governmental agencies, domestic and international donors, embassies, and the corporate world.

[39] For a description of the various projects that Puan Amal Hayati works on, see its website: www.puanamalhayati.org/en.

[40] See the website "Fahmina," https://fahmina.or.id/.

[41] Faqihuddin Abdul Kodir, *Hadith and Gender Justice: Understanding the Prophetic Traditions* (Cirebon: Fahmina Institute, 2007).

[42] See the website "Rumah KitaB," https://rumahkitab.com/en/.

[43] For more details about the Rumah KitaB vision and goals, see the website "Rumah KitaB."

[44] Norani Othman, "Muslim Women and the Challenge of Islamic Fundamentalism/Extremism: An Overview of Southeast Asian Muslim Women's Struggle for Human Rights and Gender Equality," *Women's Studies International Forum* 29 (2006): 339.

THE SIXTH PHASE: PREPARING FOR KUPI I AND II

Muslim text-based activism emerged in specific social, political, and economic contexts. These women activists continue to belong to groups that represent a wide spectrum of Islamic interpretations, with varying ideas about hotly debated issues such as marital rape, polygyny, and child marriage. Some advocate for the application of certain shari'a laws, while others fight against it. Many Muslim women's organizations do not strive for a level of gender equity but prefer forms of complementarity. The KUPI I congress (2017) showed that many of them read the sacred texts through the lens of universal human rights. What connects these groups is that they propose "critical re-examination and reinterpretation of Islamic texts so that an Islamic tradition advocating women's rights, human rights, democracy, and modernity can be invoked."[45] In their view, the interpretation of religious texts and the process of the codification of laws have been dominated by male jurists and scholars.[46] Central to the methodologies of Islamic feminists is the exercise of *ijtihad* (independent reasoning) when reading and interpreting religious texts.[47] This method offers Indonesian Muslim women "strategic access to participate in religious discourse."[48] Participation is not just academic, however: in many cases, activists seek to change national laws, mostly where it concerns personal-status laws, in order to strengthen the rights of women and children. Furthermore, women-centered interpretations of religious texts aim to participate in the construction of Islamic jurisprudence (*fiqh*), the body of legal literature that is based on certain readings of the Qur'an and the hadith and transmits specific rules concerning women's rights and duties.

As becomes clear, different forms of Muslim activism in Indonesia intersect and overlap. Female and male religious leaders connect between intellectual and religious movements, and bring theory into

---

[45] Zainah Anwar, "What Islam? Whose Islam? Sisters in Islam and the Struggle for Women's Rights," in *The Politics of Multiculturalism: Pluralism and Citizenship in Malaysia, Singapore, and Indonesia*, ed. Robert W. Hefner (Honolulu: University of Hawaii Press, 2001), 228.

[46] Cecilia Ng, Maznah Mohamad, and Tan Beng Hui, *Feminism and the Women's Movement in Malaysia* (London, New York: Routledge, 2006), 98.

[47] Yasmin Moll, "Islamic Feminism between Interpretive Freedom and Legal Codification: The Case of Sisters in Islam in Malaysia," in *Contesting Feminisms: Gender and Islam in Asia*, ed. Huma Ahmed-Ghosh (New York: SUNY Press, 2015), 163.

[48] Azza Basarudin, "In Search of Faithful Citizens in Postcolonial Malaysia: Islamic Ethics, Muslim Activism, and Feminist Politics," in *Women and Islam*, ed. Zayn R. Kassam (Oxford: Praeger, 2010), 117.

conversation with societal practices, including the government and national laws. Furthermore, they forge ties between global movements and local practices. An example of this reality is the organization of the Fatayat NU, the NU branch for younger women that became a type of NGO by focusing on issues of women's rights and health.[49] Highly trained women scholars of Islam started to teach about issues of gender and feminism as conceptual tools for women to understand their circumstances.[50] Quite a few active Fatayat members had been previously or were concurrently involved in Rahima, Lakpesdam, or other NGOs. At the same time, the Fatayat and other similar organizations provided one of the main platforms through which Muslim feminist ideas could percolate down to the grassroots level.

Reinterpretation of the Qur'an and hadith, paired with analysis of the commentary literature and jurisprudence derived from these texts that affect women's lives, resulted in numerous publications, most of them in Indonesian. Among others, the Fatayat have dealt with issues related to *fiqh* and abortion;[51] Fahmina has developed juridical interpretations to stop human trafficking;[52] and Rumah KitaB has published several books about child marriage.[53] These works are widely disseminated via discussions with advanced students at the *pesantren*, workshops for religious leaders and teachers, and groups of women who lead Qur'an study circles for women (*pengajian*).

Several feminist activists have gone on to earn PhD degrees at Indonesian and international universities. Siti Musdah Mulia was the first Islamic feminist to earn a PhD at an Indonesian, Islamic, state university (1997). In 2001, the Indonesian government launched the National Action

---

[49] For an analysis of the activism of the Fatayat NU, see chapters 1 and 3 in Rachel Rinaldo, *Mobilizing Piety: Islam and Feminism in Indonesia* (Oxford, New York: Oxford University Press, 2013).

[50] Anwar, *A Genealogy of Islamic Feminism*, 189.

[51] Maria Ulfah Anshor, *Fikih Aborsi: Wacana Pengauatan Hak Reproduksi Perempuan* (Jakarta: Kompas, 2006).

[52] Faqihuddin Abdul Kodir, Abd Moqsith Ghazali, Imam Nakha'i, KH Hussein Muhammad, and Marzuki Wahid, *Fiqh Anti-Trafficking: Jawaban atas Berbagai Kasus Kejahatan Perdagangan Manusia dalam Perspektif Hukum Islam* (Cirebon: Fahmina Institute, 2006).

[53] Mukti Ali, Roland Gunawan, Jamaluddin Mohammad, and Ahmad Hilmi, *Aku, Kamu, End: Membaca ulang teks keagamaan kawin anak* [Re-reading Religious Texts about Child Marriage] (Jakarta: Rumah KitaB, 2015); Mukti Ali, Roland Gunawan, Ahmad Hilmi, and Jamaluddin Mohammad, eds., *Fikh Kawin Anak: Mebaca Ulang Teks Keagamaan Perkawinan Usia Anak-Anak* (Jakarta: Rumah KitaB, 2015); Roland Gunawan and Nur Hayati Aida, eds., *Fikih Perwalian, Membaca Ulang Hak Perwalian untuk Perlindungan Perempuan dari Kawin Paksa dan Kawin Anak* (Jakarta: Rumah KitaB, 2019).

Plan to combat violence against women and created a committee to review the marriage section of the Islamic legal Code (1974) with Siti Musdah Mulia as chair. The current legal code is highly gender-biased, defining the role of the husband as "the head of the family" and that of the wife as "homemaker."[54] Under Mulia's guidance, the committee designed a Counter Legal Draft (2004), based on the principle that women are full equals within marriage, and prohibiting child marriage and polygyny.[55] According to committee member Kyai Husein Muhammad, the Counter Legal Draft has been one of the greatest contributions to the development of the feminist movement in Indonesia.[56] One of Siti Musdah Mulia's latest works, called *Ensiklopedia Muslimah Reformis: Pokok-pokok Pemikiran Untuk Reinterpretasi dan Aksi* [The Reformist Muslim Woman's Encyclopaedia: Essential Ideas for Reinterpretation and Action], provides legal, theoretical, and religious foundations for Islamic feminism. In seventeen entries, totalling 865 pages, Mulia covers such topics as gender equality, education, justice, and religious pluralism, explaining how a Muslim feminist activist can combine faith and spirituality with activism.[57]

Other feminist scholars include Nina Nurmila, who published an in-depth study about Qur'anic hermeneutics and the practice of polygyny,[58] and Eva Nisa, who has published widely on a range of topics concerning the status of women in Islam.[59] In fact, the movement of Islamic feminism is so well established in Indonesia that Indonesian feminist scholar

---

[54] Siti Musdah Mulia and Mark E. Cammack, "Toward a Just Marriage Law: Empowering Indonesian Women through a Counter Legal Draft to the Indonesian Compilation of Islamic Law," in *Islamic Law in Contemporary Indonesia: Ideas and Institutions*, ed. R. Michael Feener and Mark E. Cammack (Cambridge, MA: Harvard University Press, 2007), 139.

[55] Mulia and Cammack, "Toward a Just Marriage Law," 140. Also see Musdah Mulia's book in Indonesian about the Counter Legal Draft: *Posisi Perempuan Dalam Undang-Undang Perkawinan: Indonesia dan Kompilasi Hukum Islam* [The Position of Women in the Marriage Laws: Indonesia, and the Compilation of Islamic Law] (Jakarta: LKAJ, Ministry for Religious Affairs, 2001).

[56] Sebastian Partogi, "Musdah Mulia: Injecting Spirituality into Human Rights Activism," *Jakarta Post*, February 18, 2021, https://muslimahreformis.org/beranda/post_profil_musdah/musdah-mulia-injecting-spirituality-into-human-rights-activism/.

[57] Siti Musdah Mulia, *Ensiklopedia Muslimah Reformis: Pokok-pokok Pemikiran Untuk Reinterpretasi dan Aksi* [The Reformist Muslim Woman's Encyclopaedia: Essential Ideas for Reinterpretation and Action] (Jakarta: Mizan Publishers, 2020). In the following Youtube presentations, she explains her core ideas: www.youtube.com/watch?v=5Dtc4ILr44s (www.youtube.com/watch?v=Z17RUPyzkck, "Muslimah Reformis: Jejak Perempuan Inspirasional, Prof. Musdah Mulia" [Reformist Muslim Women: Traces of an Inspirational Woman, Prof. Musdah Mulia]).

[58] Nina Nurmila, *Women, Islam and Everyday Life* (New York: Routledge, 2009).

[59] For a list of publications, see "Dr. Eva Nisa," Australian National University, https://researchers.anu.edu.au/researchers/nisa-e#related_websites.

Etin Anwar could frame and analyze it in her groundbreaking 2018 study that I previously mentioned called *A Genealogy of Islamic Feminism: Pattern and Change in Indonesia*.[60]

A unique aspect of activism for women's rights is that it intersects with national governmental goals on crucial topics. Komnas Perempuan (National Commission against Violence against Women) is an example of such cooperation.[61] It is government-sponsored and was launched in 1998 after the collapse of the oppressive Suharto regime. Its mandate is to report gender-based human rights abuses and create awareness among the Indonesian public. Komnas Perempuan is a multilevel organization; its partners (called *mitra*) operate on the national, provincial, county, and local level, and represent a large spectrum of organizations advocating for and protecting women's rights. Several of its commissioners have been and still are active in, for example, the Fatayat NU, Aisyiyah, and Fahmina. Its agenda emerges from the activities of the NGOs, and it supports, for example, anti-polygyny and anti-child-marriage initiatives. In 2019, for example, two years after KUPI I, Komnas Perempuan's activities resulted in changing the minimum marriage age in the Marriage Law to nineteen years old for women and men.[62]

Given the need to articulate women's agency and feminist solidarity as interconnected across national borders and cultures,[63] international cooperation between activist groups increased around the end of the twentieth century, when NGOs such as the Malaysian SIS[64] joined meetings organized by Indonesian activists. These forms of collaboration laid the foundation for international platforms, such as the online network of Musawah,[65] which was launched in Malaysia in 2009, and the KUPI I congress that was held in May 2017, in a *pesantren* in Cirebon, the town that also houses the center of Fahmina's activities. One of the main reasons for the KUPI initiative was to formulate an alternative interpretation of Islam that could counter the evergrowing number of ultraconservative, male-oriented interpretations of Islam in Indonesia. In my view, this first KUPI congress embodies the expression of the sixth phase of Muslim women's activism in Indonesia; Muslim scholars and activists started to combine discourses

---

[60] Anwar, *A Genealogy of Islamic Feminism*.
[61] See the website of "Komnas Perempuan," www.komnasperempuan.go.id/.
[62] Adelia Putri, "Indonesian Court Says No to Raising Minimum Marrying Age for Girls," *Asia Pacific*, June 19, 2015, www.rappler.com/world/regions/asia-pacific/indonesia/96905-indonesian-court-rejects-judicial-review-marrying-age.
[63] See Chandra Mohanty, *Feminism without Borders: Decolonizing Theory, Practising Solidarity* (Durham, NC: Duke University Press, 2003).
[64] "Homepage," Sisters in Islam, https://sistersinislam.org/.
[65] "Home," Musawah, www.musawah.org/.

based on the holy texts of the Qur'an and hadith with basic human rights for women.

Different religious leaders support the programs I have described so far. They each have their own priorities, structure, and constituencies. Many of them emerged from the NU educational networks; a lesser number are associated with organizations such as the Muhammadiyah, although individual Muhammadiyah members are active in several NGOs. If we look at the names of the board and founding members of the different initiatives, we see several recurring, for example, those of Dawam Rahardjo, Kyai Husein Muhammad, Sinta Nuriyah (former first lady and founder of Puan Hayati), Kamala Chandrakirana, Masrucha (who, in 1991, among others founded Yayasan Kesejahteraan Fatayat [YKF], the Fatayat Welfare Project, which aims to improve women's health), and Maria Ulfah Ansor (former national chair of the Fatayat NU). All these activists had spent most of their lives fighting for the promotion of social justice and basic human rights.[66]

What seems like an alphabet soup of names shows the intricate connections between the various Muslim organizations and the manifold Muslim initiatives to defend women's basic rights. They also are the knowledge brokers who connect the large and complex organizations, with their sprawling, nationwide programs, to the NGOs. For example, by virtue of his position as a *kyai*, the head of a *pesantren*, Kyai Husein Muhammad also is an esteemed member of the NU. According to an article analyzing his gendered interpretation of the Qur'an, "The importance of Kyai Husein's works and activism, however, has to be seen in the context of his position as an Indonesian *kyai* (a religious leader) of [an] Islamic boarding school (*pesantren*), which are usually regarded as the preserver and maintainer of Islamic traditions."[67]

THE CULMINATION OF SMALL STEPS: THE KUPI CONGRESSES

According to Kamala Chandrakirana (co-founder and first chair of Komnas Perempuan), the KUPI congresses were the culmination of small steps that Muslim leaders and activists have taken since the 1980s.[68] In my view, the

[66] For an in-depth history of some of the Muhammadiyah and NU projects, see my book *Women Shaping Islam*, especially chapters 4 and 7 about the Islam-based activism that a younger generation developed within these organizations.

[67] Yusuf Rahman, "Feminist *Kyai*, K. H. Husein Muhammad: The Feminist Interpretation on Gendered Verses and the Qur'ān-based Activism," *Al-Jāmi'ah: Journal of Islamic Studies* 55, no. 2 (2017): 293–326, 295, available at: https://repository.uinjkt.ac.id/dspace/bitstream/123456789/70385/1/Artikel.pdf.

[68] Interview with Kamala Chandrakirana, Jakarta, June 5, 2023.

2017 conference was the culmination of more than thirty years of targeted education and awareness-building to create spaces and mechanisms for the inclusion of female scholars in the production of religious knowledge in Indonesia. Based on their specific interpretations of the holy texts, the women participating in the conferences and the organizations carrying it also joined hands to formulate text-based responses to the ever-growing influence of growing religious conservatism within Indonesian society.

The Rahima initiative also had the goal of creating a new cohort of women Muslim scholars of Islam ('ulama'). Its founders were Muslim leaders connected to the P3M programs on women (in particular, the *Fiqhunnisa* program) that focused on building awareness about women's rights in Islam.[69] In her PhD dissertation, "Women Issuing Fatwas: Female Islamic Scholars and Community-Based Authority in Java, Indonesia," Nor Ismah, a graduate of this program herself, explains the intensive study program that Rahima established in 2001 to train future women 'ulama', or specialists of Islam.[70] Only women with advanced knowledge of Islamic texts could join this program. Among others, they focused on studying the so-called *kitab kuning*, the traditional texts used in the *pesantren* that convey centuries-old interpretations of the Qur'an and the hadith. These texts used to be the purview of male scholars of Islam alone. In fact, in some *pesantren*, women were specifically forbidden to engage with them. Rahima required that women participating in the workshops not only studied the textual sources of the Qur'an, hadith, and the *kitab kuning*, but also studied more contemporary interpretations of the Qur'an. Furthermore, holy texts were read within the context of national and international laws, using the lens of women's experiences. Guided by Kyai Husein Muhammad, the women studied the classical Islamic texts in the fields of jurisprudence (*fiqh*), Qur'anic exegesis (*tafsir*), the hadith, and Sufi texts, using the analytical lens of gender.[71]

I am explaining this at great length since the P3M program allowed Rahima to create part of the new generation of Muslim women scholars who could participate in the first KUPI congress that became "a meeting space for Indonesian Women Ulama from various educational and organizational backgrounds that is non-partisan, inclusive, participatory,

---

[69] See Rahima's website: https://swararahima.com/en/.
[70] Nor Ismah, "Women Issuing Fatwas: Female Islamic Scholars and Community-Based Authority in Java, Indonesia," PhD diss., Leiden University, 2023, 79.
[71] Ibid., 79.

across organizations, across generations, across social and educational backgrounds."[72]

In 2017, Rahima was one of the three main KUPI constituents, as was the Fahmina Institute, which provided the theological guidance in producing Islamic knowledge via the lens of women's realities. Rahima represented the grassroots of the *pesantren* world and Muslim women leaders who were teaching at the grassroots. Fahmina, while well-known through its publications and workshops, has its headquarters in Cirebon, a town with dozens of *pesantren* but far removed from the centers of political and economic power in the big cities of Jakarta, Bandung, and Surabaya. To connect with these centers of power, those envisioning KUPI decided to include Alimat: a network of Muslim women leaders who have been involved in local and national politics, and have experience at the national level. This network focuses on family law, in particular marriage law, and represented twelve Indonesian Muslim organizations advocating for women's rights during the launching of the Musawah network in 2009.[73] Several of the Musawah members were among the 519 women 'ulama' core participants in the 2017 KUPI congress, and 131 core observers. Most of them were Indonesian; however, some of the women 'ulama' and core observers came from thirteen other countries. Furthermore, there were people of various backgrounds who attended one or other of the many events, such as, for example, the international conference. The total tally of participants was estimated to be around 1,500.[74]

The inclusion of the Musawah (meaning "equality") is an important move, since the organization reflects KUPI's ultimate goals. Musawah, a transnational initiative, was launched and coordinated by the SIS in Kuala Lumpur with the goal of realizing equality between women and

---

[72] "5 Crucial Issues of the Second Indonesian Women's Ulama Congress (KUPI), Encouraging Justice," November 23, 2022, https://kupi.or.id/5-isu-krusial-kongres-ulama-perempuan-indonesia-kupi-ii-dorong-keadilan/.

[73] According the KUPI website, https://kupipedia.id/index.php/Alimat, explaining the Alimat organization, its leaders represent twelve large Indonesian Muslim organizations: Komnas Perempuan, Fatayat NU, Aisyiyah, Nashiyatul Aisyiyah, the Fahmina Institute, Gerakan Perempuan Pembela Buruh Migran (GPPBM, the organization for women migrants), Rahima, Pemberdayaan Perempuan Kepala Keluarga (Pekka, the organization for the empowerment of women heads of families), Koalisi Perempuan Indonesia (KPI, the Indonesian Women's Coalition), LAKPESDAM NU, Pusat Studi Wanita UIN Sunan Kalijaga Yogyakarta (the Center for Women's Studies at the Islamic State University of Sunan Kalijaga in Yogyakarta), Pusat Studi Gender (PSG) STAIN Pekalongan (the Center for Women's Studies at the Higher Institute for Islamic Studies in Pekalongan), and the Universitas Pancasila.

[74] For a general description of the conference on Kupipedia, see: https://kupipedia.id/index.php/KUPI.

men by reforming Muslim family laws. It was founded during a 2009 international meeting in Kuala Lumpur. Its network consists of scholars, activists, lawyers, and policymakers in forty-seven countries who cooperate in order to realize the Musawah framework of action that holds "the principles of Islam to be a source of justice, equality, fairness and dignity for all human beings,"[75] and that equality and justice within the family and family laws and practices are necessary and possible in Muslim countries and communities. While its agenda is large and ambitious, the organization's focus on issues related to child marriage, polygyny, and male guardianship (*qawama* and *wilaya*), intersects with Indonesian feminist priorities and some of the KUPI outcomes.[76] At the end of the first KUPI congress, the women 'ulama' issued several religious recommendations, or fatwas. One of them advised a total ban on child marriage.

KUPI I AND II

According to one of the main organizers, Dr. Nur Rofiah, KUPI I was "a universal declaration of equality, a manifesto that women have the same spiritual and mental potentials as men."[77] Over the course of three days, the participants discussed Islamic teachings that touch on Islamic extremism, violence against women, and environmental problems. The main goal was to "build long-term perspectives on women's rights that are currently being ignored."[78] The theme of the second conference, held in a *pesantren* in Jepara (November 23–26, 2022), was "Reaffirming the Role of Women Ulama for a Just Civilization."[79] This time, the number of groups supporting the conference had increased and included *pesantren*-based Puan Amal Hayati and AMAN (the Asian Muslim Action Network), which focuses on peace education for women at the grassroots.[80] Also the audience had become more diverse, with participants hailing from thirty countries. The wealth of articles written after the first conference shows the high level of interest within the circles

[75] "Musawah Framework for Action, English version," www.musawah.org/resources/musawah-framework-for-action/.
[76] Anwar, "Sisters in Islam," 121.
[77] Dr. Nur Rofiah, Jakarta, interview with author, July 6, 2018.
[78] Dr. Nur Rofiah, Jakarta, interview with author, July 6, 2018. "Discussion: Wilayah (Guardianship) and Qiwamah (Protection) of Females," Rumah KitaB, Unpublished Activity Report, 2018. Eva F. Nisa, "Muslim Women in Contemporary Indonesia: Online Conflicting Narratives behind the Women's Ulama Congress," *Asian Studies Review* 43, no. 3 (2019): 434–454.
[79] For the agenda of KUPI II, see https://kupi.or.id/.
[80] See the AMAN website, www.amanindonesia.org.

of Muslim leaders who are interested in adapting their religious interpretative framework to contemporary thoughts and requirements.

After the first conference in 2017, the organizers and participants actively started to teach and develop their ideas and writings via books and articles and also on TV, radio, social media, and other electronic networks, with the goal of stimulating discussion about their religious and legal methodologies. One of the most controversial moves had been the formulation of fatwas, an exercise that traditionally had been within the purview of male 'ulama' only. This bold action sent shock waves through more conservative Muslims in Indonesia. The fatwas of the first conference called for a prohibition on and end to the practice of forced or child marriage, domestic violence, and other forms of sexual violence, and the curtailment of environmental destruction.[81] During the second conference (2022), the earlier fatwas were further refined. The role of waste production and management was added to the theme of environmental destruction, as was the elaboration on forced marriage to the one on child marriage. A new fatwa promoted the protection of women and the possibility to have an abortion in the case of rape. Whereas, in Indonesia, abortion is legal in the case of rape or medical emergency, in reality it is difficult for victims to find the help they need. Two more fatwas suggested a total ban on FGM, and supported the role of women in protecting the country from the risks of religious extremism.[82]

The KUPI approach to decision-making is based on a communal process that consists of several religious consultations (*musyawarah keagamaan*) and discussion groups (*halaqa*) that are held over the course of several months leading up to and during the conference. Guiding the decisions that come out of these consultations and discussions are the sources of the Qur'an, the hadith, Qur'anic exegesis (*tafsir*), and the Indonesian constitution. KUPI religious decision-making is furthermore based on two innovative Islamic ways of reasoning. Fahmina scholar Faqihuddin Abdul Kodir developed the hermeneutical methodology of

---

[81] Kupipedia section "fatwa," https://kupipedia.id/index.php/Fatwa. "Discussion: Wilayah (Guardianship) and Qiwamah (Protection) of Females," Rumah KitaB, Unpublished Activity Report, 2018. Eva F. Nisa, "Muslim Women in Contemporary Indonesia: Online Conflicting Narratives behind the Women's Ulama Congress," *Asian Studies Review* 43, no. 3 (2019): 434–454.

[82] KUPI, *Hasil Musyawarah Keagamaan Kongres Ulama Perempuan Indonesia (KUPI) Ke-2. Pondok Pesantren Hasyim Asy'ari Bangsri, Jepara, Jawa Tengah. 24–26 November 2022 M/ 30 R. Akhir – 2 Jumadal Ula 1444H* [Results of Religious Deliberations of the Second KUPI Congress] (Jakarta: KUPI, 2022). For a detailed description of the process of religious deliberation leading up to the formulation of the fatwas, see Ismah, *Women Issuing Fatwas*, 152–156.

the so-called reciprocal reading of the holy texts of the Qur'an and hadith (*Qirā'ah Mubādalah*). This methodology is based on the idea that these texts traditionally have been "interpreted only for men or only for women."[83] However, according to Abdul Kodir, the one who is interpreting should "adopt interpretive lenses that unearth principles which can lead to equal cooperative relationships between men and women in all spaces, both within the family and in society."[84] This method is grounded in the three ethical concepts of the unicity of God (*tawhid*), human dignity (*karama*), and collective well-being (*maslaha*).[85] Nur Rofiah uses this method of interpretation to map out the Qur'anic trajectory towards *haqiqi* justice, or real and authentic justice, for women.[86] This type of justice takes into account the full range of human experience, including experiences that men will never have, such as menstruation, pregnancy, and giving birth.[87] According to Rofiah, this approach serves not just to strengthen women's basic human rights but also benefits the Indonesian nation: "when we improve the rights of women and women's issues are no longer being ignored, we not only look at our holy texts with fresh eyes, but we strengthen the policies about these issues and strengthen our nation."[88]

KUPI I and II built on earlier research and activism provided by such organizations as Musawah, Rumah KitaB, Komnas Perempuan, and Fahmina. For example, concerning the practice of child marriage, some of the foundational arguments were developed through the work of Komnas Perempuan and Rumah KitaB.[89] In order to strengthen activism against child marriage, these two organizations had also focused on the role of the girl's *wali* (guardian). Basically, marriage is a contract where the woman's *wali* transfers her to the protection of the husband. Rumah KitaB addressed the reality of this inequality by studying various parts of Islamic family law, looking at such issues as lineage, sustenance, dowry, the head of the family, polygyny, the *mahram* (a woman's male companion when she moves in public spaces), and the unequal valuation of male and female

---

[83] Faqihuddin Abdul Kodir, "*Qirā'a Mubādala*: Reciprocal Reading of Hadith on Marital Relationships," in *Justice and Beauty in Muslim Marriage: Towards Egalitarian Ethics and Laws*, ed. Ziba Mir-Hosseini, Mulki al-Sharmani, Jana Rumminger, and Sarah Marsso (London: Oneworld Publications, 2022), 181–182.

[84] Abdul Kodir, *Qirā'a Mubādala*, 187.

[85] Nur Rofiah, "Reading the Qur'an through Women's Experience," in *Justice and Beauty in Muslim Marriage*, ed. Mir-Hosseini et al., 57–84, 61.

[86] Ibid., 62.

[87] Ibid.

[88] Dr. Nur Rofiah, Jakarta, interview with author, July 6, 2018.

[89] Nisa, "Muslim Women in Contemporary Indonesia."

lives. While re-reading religious texts and pairing them with international human rights values, Rumah KitaB also appealed to the Indonesian legal establishment. Like KUPI, Rumah KitaB argued that women and men are equal at the spiritual level and have similar rights and obligations.[90]

Following these forms of earlier activism that had been going on for decades, the KUPI supporters, backed by such organizations as Komnas Perempuan, started to lobby for a new national law changing the minimum marriage age from sixteen to nineteen years old. The government had been fully committed to ending the practice of child marriage.[91] After issuing a fatwa laying out the religious arguments against child marriage, the women intensified their lobbying, and in 2019, by law, the marriage age was raised to nineteen years for both spouses. Although this new law seemed a big win, much resistance against it came from conservative Muslim circles and from areas where the practice of early marriage was rooted in local cultures. One of the main conservative arguments was that child marriage prevents sex before marriage and helps preserve the good name of the family.[92] The second KUPI congress addressed the issue again, this time by adding the concept of forced marriage. Following the fatwa against sexual violence, in 2022 a law was passed providing protection to victims of sexual violence, including those within a marriage.[93]

CONCLUSION

In Indonesia, vibrant groups advocating for the rights of Muslim women are creating new models and repertoires of Muslim feminism. They propose new interpretations of the holy texts that traditionally have governed the rights and duties of women, and translate their new findings into social, cultural, legal, and political agendas. While focusing on the plight of women, in fact they contribute to changing the face of Islam itself. The events of KUPI I and II show that Indonesian Muslim activists are connecting globally with like-minded groups addressing women's basic human rights. In Indonesia, while facing strong forces of resistance, locally and

---

[90] "Discussion: Wilayah (Guardianship) and Qiwamah (Protection) of Females," Rumah KitaB, Unpublished Activity Report, 2018.
[91] See the website of Global Human Rights Defense: www.ghrd.org/wp-content/uploads/2024/03/Child-Marriage-in-Indonesia-October-2022.pdf.
[92] Nancy Hefner Smith, *Islamizing Intimacies: Youth, Sexuality, and Gender in Contemporary Indonesia* (Honolulu: University of Hawai'i Press, 2019), 121–123.
[93] "KUPI and the Women's Ulama Movement in Indonesia," https://kupi.or.id/kupi-dan-gerakan-ulama-perempuan-di-indonesia/; Srimulyani, *Women from Traditional Islamic Educational Institutions*; van Bruinessen, ed., *Contemporary Developments in Indonesian Islam*; van Doorn-Harder, *Women Shaping Islam*.

globally, women's religious activism and teachings, emboldened by a register of activist and interpretative agendas, no longer remain confined to informal platforms such as women's Qur'an study groups and other gatherings. They are now reaching wider audiences. As a result, these activist interventions in traditional religious practices and interpretations can no longer be ignored, as, slowly but steadily, they are making inroads into public conversations across Indonesia.

SELECT BIBLIOGRAPHY

Abdul Kodir, Faqihuddin. *Hadith and Gender Justice: Understanding the Prophetic Traditions*. Cirebon: Fahmina Institute, 2007.
   "*Qirā'a Mubādala*: Reciprocal Reading of Hadith on Marital Relationships." In *Justice and Beauty in Muslim Marriage: Towards Egalitarian Ethics and Laws*, ed. Ziba Mir-Hosseini, Mulki al-Sharmani, Jana Rumminger, and Sarah Marsso, 181–212. London: Oneworld Publications, 2022.
Anwar, Etin. *A Genealogy of Islamic Feminism: Pattern and Change in Indonesia*. Oxford: Routledge, 2018.
Cotee, Joost, trans. *Letters from Kartini: An Indonesian Feminist (1900–1904)*. Clayton, Victoria: Monash Asia Institute, 1992.
Ismah, Nor. "Women Issuing Fatwas: Female Islamic Scholars and Community-Based Authority in Java, Indonesia." PhD diss., Leiden University, 2023.
Mulia, Siti Musdah, with Cammack Mark E. "Toward a Just Marriage Law: Empowering Indonesian Women through a Counter Legal Draft to the Indonesian Compilation of Islamic Law." In *Islamic Law in Contemporary Indonesia: Ideas and Institutions*, ed. R. Michael Feener and Mark E. Cammack. Cambridge, MA: Harvard University Press, 2007.
Nisa, Eva F. *Face-Veiled Women in Contemporary Indonesia*. New York: Routledge, 2023.
   "Muslim Women in Contemporary Indonesia: Online Conflicting Narratives behind the Women's Ulama Congress." *Asian Studies Review* 43, no. 3 (2019): 434–454.
Nurmila, Nina. *Women, Islam and Everyday Life: Renegotiating Polygamy in Indonesia*. New York: Routledge, 2009.
Rinaldo, Rachel. *Mobilizing Piety: Islam and Feminism in Indonesia*. Oxford, New York: Oxford University Press, 2013.
Rofiah, Nur. "Reading the Qur'an through Women's Experience." In *Justice and Beauty in Muslim Marriage: Towards Egalitarian Ethics and Laws*, ed. Ziba Mir-Hosseini, Mulki al-Sharmani, Jana Rumminger, and Sarah Marsso, 57–84. London: Oneworld Publications, 2022.
Smith Hefner, Nancy. *Islamizing Intimacies: Youth, Sexuality, and Gender in Contemporary Indonesia*. Honolulu: University of Hawai'i Press, 2019.

14 Poets and Writers

ZUZANNA OLSZEWSKA

> *It is not unknown to the learned and to artists that those are wise who do everything they can to leave a trace of their being on the pages of time. Day by day, that trace is covered by the dust of oblivion and the duration of time eliminates its form from memories. Therefore, it is necessary to build a work – a monument – that causes the name to endure after the body decays.*
>
> Jahan Malek Khatun, fourteenth-century Persian poet[1]

*

> *Our voices can no longer be hidden. Today it is no longer like it used to be. Now we can say, 'This is me, this is us.' We can show our existence to the world.*
>
> Gazin, contemporary Kurdish poet and singer[2]

*

> *I love writing before sunrise. I usually wake up one hour before, I pray, and then I write. You know, when I connect with writing, I don't want it to stop. There is something very intimate and sweet in writing. The feeling of having found myself. Life, life, for me, this is life!*
>
> Intisar Rabi, contemporary Egyptian novelist[3]

*

With these words, three Muslim women describe what writing and creative verbal expression mean to them. Their perspectives span seven centuries, three different languages and several literary genres,

---

[1] Rebecca R. Gould and Kayvan Tahmasebian, 'Writing Poetry in 14th-Century Iran: Jahan Malek Khatun and Women's Writing in the Islamic World', *Global Literary Theory*, last modified 6 July 2021, https://globallit.hcommons.org/2021/07/06/writing-poetry-in-14th-century-iran-jahan-malek-khatun-and-womens-writing-in-the-islamic-world/.

[2] Marlene Schäfers, *Voices That Matter: Kurdish Women at the Limits of Representation in Contemporary Turkey* (Chicago: University of Chicago Press, 2023), 1.

[3] Giedrė Šabasevičiūtė, 'Women Writing in Cairo: Midlife, Self-Care, and the Informal World of Literature', *Journal of Middle East Women's Studies* 19, no. 3 (2023): 317.

but make clear the strength of their motivation, albeit with different emphases: whether the importance of leaving a lasting mark on the pages of history, speaking up on behalf of one's gender or community, or the sheer pleasure and intimacy of gaining a better knowledge of oneself and of life through practising one's craft.

What insight do we gain from writing about Muslim women *writers*? We do so to direct attention to the imaginative worlds, creative agency, and verbal virtuosity of Muslim women. We acknowledge their ability to document, and participate and intervene actively in their social worlds. These are important and laudable objectives of feminist enquiry, for it is a commonplace that women in the Islamicate world live in a 'cultural context that idealizes women's anonymity',[4] in which women's public speech is linked with immodesty, impropriety, and disorder, and where 'private life, family life, inner feelings and thoughts' are sacrosanct.[5] In the past few decades there has been a veritable boom in feminist scholarship that seeks to recover these voices, 'however muted or enigmatic or coded they may be'.[6] This is a growing literature that I can only hope to survey with the broadest brushstrokes here.

But in focusing on *writers* we quickly confront a serious problem with this formulation: in much of the Muslim world for much of its history, literacy was restricted, and literate traditions were dominated by men and a small number of high-status, often aristocratic, women. Jahan Malik Khatun, a fourteenth-century Persian princess, acknowledged this in the source of her quotation above (her preface to her *divan* or book of collected poems), in which she situated herself within a long line of 'great noblewomen and distinguished ladies, among both Arabs and Iranians' who had gained renown in the art of poetry.[7] Focusing on writers limits us to this handful of elite women who have survived in written records from the past, with the addition of perhaps just a century or so of widening participation in written literature by more recent women.

And yet anthropologists and folklorists have also amassed a substantial literature demonstrating the rich verbal expression of non-literate Muslim women through participation in oral traditions,

---

[4] Siobhan Lambert-Hurley, *Elusive Lives: Gender, Autobiography, and the Self in Muslim South Asia* (Stanford: Stanford University Press, 2018), 7.
[5] Margot Badran, preface to Huda Sha'arawi, *Harem Years: The Memoirs of an Egyptian Feminist (1879–1924)*, trans. Margot Badran (London: Virago, 1986), 1.
[6] Lambert-Hurley, *Elusive Lives*, 2.
[7] Gould and Tahmasebian, 'Writing Poetry in 14th-Century Iran'. See also Dominic P. Brookshaw, 'Odes of a Poet-Princess: The Ghazals of Jahān-Malik Khātūn', *Iran* 43 (2005): 173–95.

whether as composers or transmitters of poems, songs, stories, or orations. We know from those that were written down in the past that women have been cherished participants in oral traditions since the dawn of the faith itself.[8] Thus, conceptually it is important to avoid the pitfall of a Eurocentric (or perhaps modern-centric, or phallocentric) category of literature that privileges writing and reading; I favour instead the category of *texts*, whether oral or written, as proposed by Karin Barber for an anthropological approach to literature.[9] This perspective allows us to give non-literate Muslim women who were powerful oral poets, orators, and storytellers credit where it is due, and to emphasize how women's texts have circulated in both the oral and written domains in the Islamicate world, frequently moving between the two.

Is the phrase *Muslim women authors* any better, then? This has the advantage of spanning the domains of orality and literacy, perhaps, but continues to pose problems when we realize that the concept of authorship and the category of the author are themselves socio-historically contingent and constructed, as Foucault was one of the first to note.[10] Oral literature often circulates anonymously by design, and attributions, where they exist, may be to a persona or pseudonym that does not exist in reality – or was designed to obscure a true identity. Women's *voices*, then? Although I do use this term in this chapter, anthropologist Marlene Schäfers reminds us that we must likewise problematize and contextualize it, arguing that the concept of 'voice', including whose voices deserve to be heard and how, has its own politics in any particular time and place that must be reckoned with.[11] The idea of a voice as an authentic and transparent expression of an inner self and its actual biographical experience that deserves to be heard by all is one that has gained prominence in recent times and particularly in liberal political regimes – a move that has been located in history and termed the 'ultimate unveiling' in the case of Muslim women by a number of authors[12] – but not necessarily in others.

---

[8] Marlé Hammond, 'Literature: 9th to 15th Century', in *Encyclopedia of Women and Islamic Cultures*, vol. I, ed. Suad Joseph (Leiden: Brill, 2003), 42–50.

[9] Karin Barber, *The Anthropology of Texts, Persons and Publics: Oral and Written Culture in Africa and Beyond* (Cambridge: Cambridge University Press, 2007).

[10] Michel Foucault, 'What Is an Author?', in Michel Foucault and Paul Rabinow, *Aesthetics, Method, and Epistemology: Essential Works of Foucault 1954–1984*, Vol. II, ed. James D. Faubion, trans. Robert Hurley (London: Penguin Classics, 2020), 205–22.

[11] Schäfers, *Voices That Matter*.

[12] See, e.g., Lambert-Hurley, *Elusive Lives*, 7, 189–94, for a discussion of the metaphorical and literal similarities between writing (especially autobiographical writing) and

In this contribution, then, I am concerned with Muslim women's verbal expression, whether oral or written, across a range of eras and contexts. Having thus expanded my terms of reference to a range impossible to do justice to in a short companion piece such as this, I wish to focus back in on a select number of themes. I attempt to combine the insights of anthropological and historical scholarship on women's expression, paying particular attention to the *conditions of possibility* for diverse kinds of women's verbal creativity and 'voice'. A combination of ethnographic and historical studies allows us insights into the micro- and macro-politics of expression that shed light on how women have negotiated norms and conventions of female modesty and propriety, public and private (both religious and cultural), for the purpose of the composition and circulation of texts. Although these norms have undergone numerous historical transformations and vary even today across Muslim societies, they still require negotiation – particularly in the everyday lives of poets and writers.

A final note of caution must be sounded regarding the need for an intersectional and contextually nuanced perspective on Muslim women's verbal expression. The constraints and possibilities open to them may at times have been shaped more forcefully by, or in tandem with, factors other than religion or gender, for example ethnic-minority or immigrant status, language, class, or colonial subjection. The worlds of non-literate women have held very different creative possibilities from those of literate, educated, middle-class women, and the scales at which they have operated have also varied – ranging from face-to-face local audiences to national or international, mass-mediated publics. The conditions for the expression of aristocratic women have been different from those of courtesans. It is impossible in this short chapter to comprehensively survey all the literature on Muslim women's verbal expression from the dawn of the faith to the present while adequately capturing this nuance; I shall not attempt to do so. I thus restrict my geographical focus to Anglophone scholarship on the Arabic- and Persian-speaking worlds (with a detour into Kurdish), as well as to South Asia, because these are the regions with whose writing and ethnography I have the greatest familiarity. I also present an extended case study from my own ethnography of Afghan women's poetry.

physical unveiling/breaking of *purdah* practices through analogous examples from South Asia, Egypt, and Iran. See also Farzaneh Milani, *Veils and Words: The Emerging Voices of Iranian Women Writers* (Syracuse, NY: Syracuse University Press, 1992).

In this chapter, with this caveat in mind, I wish to put paid to the myth that Islamicate cultures somehow (or straightforwardly) silence women, but rather invite us to see Muslim women's expression as vibrant and dynamic, strongly attuned to particular contexts, audiences, and genres, and attentive to the possibilities and moral hazards of numerous communication technologies, including oral transmission, manuscripts, print, and – most recently – the internet and social media.

MUSLIM WOMEN'S ORAL TEXTS

Oral literature – both prose and poetry, spanning a wide variety of genres and many languages and dialects – has been present across the Islamic world since the dawn of the religion. It was vital, of course, to the emergence of Islam itself. As Tahera Qutbuddin has demonstrated, 'the first generations of Muslims and their forebears in the Arabian Peninsula assiduously cultivated the art of the eloquently, metaphorically, rhythmically, appositely, mnemonically spoken word'[13] – and to a great extent this remains the case today. Along with the Qur'an itself and poetry, the oration was a major genre that commanded great respect and was highly politically efficacious, and orality was the medium in which governance, diplomacy, philosophy, and theology were conducted. Such texts often circulated orally at first before being compiled and written down in later centuries.

Even after writing became more prominent, however, for much of the history of Islam literacy has been heavily restricted, particularly among women. Oral literature is by its nature portable and has accompanied nomadic pastoralists, migrants, traders, soldiers, and pilgrims on their journeys. Oral literature differs from writing in that the composition and recitation of poetry are the prerogative of all, not merely an elite few who have had access to a formal education, although some talented individuals, women as well as men, often do specialize in this art and gain renown and admiration. In this section I survey some of the key literature on Muslim women's oral texts in the past and present, focusing on the social and political efficacy of women's speech and what it reveals about the gendered nature of expression.

Numerous studies from across the Islamicate world attest to the fact that the written and oral traditions have often intermingled and nourished each other, and it is common now for scholars to describe an oral–literate 'nexus' or 'continuum' rather than an evolutionary transition

---

[13] Tahera Qutbuddin, *Arabic Oration: Art and Function* (Leiden: Brill, 2019), 1.

between the two.¹⁴ For example, Mills, through a meticulous study of the oral performances of traditional Persian-language folk-tales (*afsanah*) and their relationships with written texts in Afghanistan, found 'a long-standing symbiotic relationship in Persian between oral and literary narrative traditions [with] a sustained, mutual cross-fertilization of oral and literary traditions' that had endured both in Iran and Afghanistan at least until the 1970s.¹⁵ The presence of schools and structures of Islamic learning played an important role in promoting this cross-fertilization due to the practices used in Islamic pedagogy, which often privileged the use of mnemonic techniques alongside reading and writing.

Qutbuddin's magisterial study of the art of oration (*khatabah*) in the early Islamic period of the first to second centuries AH (seventh to eighth centuries AD) devotes a chapter to women's orations. She acknowledges that since orations were usually delivered by those in positions of authority, orations composed and delivered by women are an anomaly in this tradition, or at least in the surviving written records of it – but they do exist. Those that have been preserved in written anthologies from later centuries stand out for two reasons, she argues: their authority derives from their kinship to men who were important leaders, and their public speech often arises in cases of injustice or great trauma in order to seek redress for it. Thus, we have records of orations by the Prophet Muhammad's daughter, Fatimah al-Zahra, the daughters of the first three Sunni caliphs, Aisha bint Abi Bakr, Hafsah bint Umar, and Aisha bint Uthman (the first two of whom were also wives of the Prophet), the Prophet's granddaughters, Umm Kulthum bint Ali and Zaynab bint Ali, and several other notable women. Their themes and occasions ranged from eulogies for their fathers or husbands, to rallying tribesmen to fight in various battles, to the orations in captivity of Umm Kulthum and Zaynab following the Battle of Karbala and the killing of their brother, Husayn, and other male kin by the Umayyads. These women's oratorical style and structure were similar to those of men, and their skill in the use of rhetorical techniques was no less than that of men. Qutbuddin suggests that while neither men nor women were formally trained in oratory, they would have learned the same techniques from listening to the

---

¹⁴ See, e.g., Julia Rubanovich, ed., *Orality and Textuality in the Iranian World* (Leiden: Brill, 2015).

¹⁵ Margaret Mills, 'Gender and Verbal Performance Style in Afghanistan', in *Gender, Genre and Power in South Asian Expressive Traditions*, ed. Arjun Appadurai, Frank Korom, and Margaret Mills (Philadelphia: Pennsylvania University Press, 1991), 57.

public speeches of others: women were known to be often included in the audiences of male orators.[16]

But ethnographers of contemporary oral poetic practice in the Arabian Peninsula give us an insight into an even deeper intertwining of rhetorical and poetic skill with everyday life, regardless of gender. Caton, for example, stresses that in highland Yemen both tribesmen and tribeswomen regularly participate in genres of sung oral poetry, including improvised challenge-and-retort routines used for dispute resolution or public celebrations like weddings.[17] They are thus trained from a young age in the mnemonic techniques, stock phrases, proverbs, and rhetorical strategies required for public speech, and these may be deployed across genres when needed. If this was also true in the early Islamic period, can we know for certain whether only women in positions of authority by virtue of their powerful male kin were permitted to 'break the silence'[18] in order to deliver public oratory at all, or if only these women's orations were deemed significant and worthy enough to be memorialized for later generations, at first through oral circulation and later through anthologization?

Lila Abu-Lughod's celebrated ethnography *Veiled Sentiments: Honor and Poetry in a Bedouin Society* offers another deep insight into women's oral poetry among a Bedouin group in Egypt.[19] Although the Awlad Ali Bedouin have a deeply entrenched ideology of honour and modesty, in which women and other dependants must exercise sexual modesty and restraint, this does not equate to the complete silencing of women. They have a genre of 'little song' (*ghinnawa*) – a short poem in the form of a couplet that allows the reciter (usually a woman or young man) to express deeply personal emotions and values that appear to contradict the dominant norms of modesty, and may even celebrate romantic love and sentiments of weakness. But crucially, this genre of poetry is not recited in public, but for audiences of social equals: 'Poetry indexes social distinctions by following the lines of social cleavage. It usually does not cross the boundaries created by differential power and status, including those associated with gender.'[20] Indeed, Abu-Lughod was warned not to share the women's poetry she collected with men.

---

[16] Qutbuddin, *Arabic Oration*, 383–5.
[17] Steven C. Caton, *'Peaks of Yemen I Summon': Poetry as Cultural Practice in a North Yemeni Tribe* (Berkeley: University of California Press, 1990). See also W. Flagg Miller, 'Public Words and Body Politics: Reflections on the Strategies of Women Poets in Rural Yemen', *Journal of Women's History* 14, no. 1 (2002): 94–122.
[18] Qutbuddin, *Arabic Oration*, 384.
[19] Lila Abu-Lughod, *Veiled Sentiments: Honor and Poetry in a Bedouin Society* (Berkeley: University of California Press, 1986).
[20] Ibid., 234.

This boundary allows the reciter to express sentiments that are not otherwise expressible in public discourse, further bolstered by the formulas and conventions of poetry that set it apart from other discourse and offer protection to the author: 'Inherently ambiguous, formulaic poems protect the anonymity of the poet, of the addressee, and of the subject.'[21]

Abu-Lughod goes so far as to see the discourse of poetry as a second ideology in Bedouin culture which provides models and a language for alternative kinds of experience. It allows for the possibility of creativity, defiance, and intimacy within a limiting system of morality.[22] But she argues that we should not see the *ghinnawa* simply as a form of women's resistance: paradoxically, the sentiments of weakness skilfully expressed in poetry serve to strengthen the normative ideology of honour, because the verbal virtuosity and self-mastery in the face of profound passions that it demonstrates all contribute to the honour of the poet.

Interestingly, Abu-Lughod's findings concerning the relationship between tribal ideology, poetry, and gender were anticipated a few years earlier in an entirely different region and language by Inger Boesen, who documented an oral-poetic genre that is almost exclusively the preserve of Pashtun women, the *landay*.[23] Landays are short, two-line poems on a variety of themes. They are always sung and are accompanied by a tambourine, and are never performed in the presence of men. Boesen found that in the pre-war period in Afghanistan, rural Pashtun women shared the ideology of an honour-bound society founded upon the premise of control of women by men, but they expressed their divergent views in the form of oral poetry. In some respects the 'alternative conscience' they revealed reflected the 'general dilemma inherent in the relation between ideology and individual practice', but in this case, there was also a specific dilemma: 'that of being both Pakhtun and women'.[24] Women's poetry thus often dealt with themes of illicit love, a woman's only recourse in the case of an unhappy marriage, for which she must risk

---

[21] Ibid., 239.
[22] Ibid., 259.
[23] Inger W. Boesen, 'Conflicts of Solidarity in Pakhtun Women's Lives', in *Women and Islamic Societies: Social Attitudes and Historical Perspectives*, ed. Bo Utas (London: Curzon Press, 1983). See also Sayd Bahodine Majrouh, *Songs of Love and War: Afghan Women's Poetry* (New York: Other Press, 2003). Majrouh's volume dates to the anti-Soviet resistance of the 1980s, when he collected close to 100 *landays* of exile in the Afghan refugee communities of Peshawar, in which women pined for lovers fighting in the homeland, ridiculed men who did not wish to fight in the jihad and praised those who did, and rhetorically offered sexual reward to those who proved most courageous.
[24] Boesen, 'Conflicts of Solidarity', 107.

her life. Boesen argues that this is 'a clear illustration of the conflicting values existing in Pakhtun society: the set of values embodied in the *Pakhtunwali* [the Pakhtun moral code] based on honour, self-control, and male control; and its opposite, romantic and passionate love breaking the rules of society'.[25] These themes are not uniquely Pashtun, however, as the women's couplets collected by Mousavi in an ethnography of the Hazara ethnic group of Afghanistan similarly speak unabashedly of illicit relations with a beloved who is preferable to the (often elderly and ridiculed) husband.[26]

Schäfers' ethnography of contemporary Kurdish women's oral poetry and songs in Turkey interrogates the political contexts that provide the conditions of possibility for women's expression in a time of conflict and rapid social change.[27] She argues that voice itself should not be taken for granted. The idea of raising one's voice and self-expression as congruent with one's authentic self may be something we take as a given, but this idea itself is shaped by specific socio-historical forces. Schäfers shows that where new vocal practices arise, they produce new selves and practices of social relations.

She focuses on the *dengbej*, a kind of Kurdish performer who is at once a poet and singer, historian and storyteller, and her ethnography is based on her time with an association of women *dengbej* in the city of Wan in eastern Turkey. They perform 'different forms of sung narrative, including epic tales of war and battle, stories of tragic love and courageous deeds, and personal accounts of painful experience'.[28] In contemporary Kurdish society, forms of expression and appropriate settings for it are highly gendered, and it is seen as immodest and improper for a woman to sing in public. The reason for this, according to Schäfers, is that it is the *audibility* of women's voices, rather than the content of their speech, that is disruptive for the gendered Kurdish social order. Voice, for the female *dengbej*, is a form of social action and is relational: it is the way to lament the suffering and loss of loved ones under Turkish colonialism.

But what happens when these women encounter liberal discourses foregrounding the need to 'give voice' both to women and to minorities? Here, the idea of voice was held up as 'a powerful index of emancipation and empowerment. In a context rife with political subjection and gendered

[25] Ibid., 119.
[26] Sayed Askar Mousavi, *The Hazaras of Afghanistan: An Historical, Cultural, Economic and Political Study* (Richmond, UK: Curzon Press, 1998), 84–5.
[27] Schäfers, *Voices That Matter*.
[28] Ibid., 3.

disciplining, it held outstanding liberatory potential. Freely circulating voices signalled free subjects.'[29] But, eager as the *dengbej* were to have their voices heard (as demonstrated by Gazin in the chapter epigraph), the process could also be fraught with risk and contradiction, and was not always empowering. When they were invited to Istanbul to perform at an event for a Turkish audience, for example, their performances were heavily regulated by the organizers, showing that voices and the way they sound have their own politics, and the liberal politics of representation, too, requires voices to sound a particular way in order to be heard. Schäfers thus argues that we should not evaluate liberal pluralism on how well it gives voice to the disenfranchised but attend to how liberal regimes themselves shape and foster particular kinds of voices.[30]

The examples from the Awlad Ali and Afghanistan show that women's oral expression, often designed to be performed for women-only audiences, is highly context-specific and operates through mastery of genres that afford protection through anonymity. Rather than seeing anonymity as oppressive, it is precisely what gives these genres and their practitioners their extraordinary power to 'say the unsayable'. And it is perhaps not far-fetched to say that this everyday training in verbal skill in women-only spaces gives women the eloquence to intervene also in the public/male domain in times of great need. But we must be cautious about assuming too simple an equation between the erosion of boundaries between male and female spaces or publics in more recent times, and women's 'empowerment'. The Kurdish example demonstrates that the power structures that now legitimate the audibility of certain voices in public, including those of women, ultimately still shape what those voices can say, and how they will be heard.

MUSLIM WOMEN AS WRITERS

Marlé Hammond argues that women's literature has thrived in the Islamicate world from as early as the ninth century CE, but it may not always be readily discerned as such; what has come down to us is usually packaged within texts that were written or framed by men, and few book-length works attributed to women survive.[31] Thus, scholars have required additional methodological and analytical creativity, including

---

[29] Ibid.
[30] Ibid., 24.
[31] Hammond, 'Literature', 42. See also Marlé Hammond, *Beyond Elegy: Classical Arabic Women's Poetry in Context* (Oxford: Oxford University Press for the British Academy, 2010).

at times a modified understanding of authorship, to extract and understand it from the framing texts, such as biographical compendia (*tazkirahs*) and prose texts written by men that include women's voices, often in the form of poetic quotations. Although there is evidence that women continued to be highly regarded as composers of oral texts in the medieval period, and increasingly wrote both poetry and prose, and that some even worked as scribes and scholars, it was their poetry that was best preserved in written form from this period – almost exclusively in anthologies compiled by men.[32]

In the Persianate world, such anthologies retain traces of some extraordinary moments in women's literary history, including the flourishing female literary cultures in royal courts like those of the Timurids in Herat (fourteenth to sixteenth centuries CE) and the Qajars in Tehran (eighteenth to twentieth centuries), as well as a broader-based literary culture that expanded outside court circles from the eighteenth century onwards.[33] Yet, as Sunil Sharma has shown, numerous forces, whether political or idiosyncratic to a particular compiler, conspired to keep women in the margins of *tazkirahs*.[34]

A handful of women were able to exert some authorial and editorial control in the early modern period, although this was often 'literary agency by proxy'[35] through male relatives. Zia' al-Saltanah (1799–1873), daughter of the Qajar king Fath Ali Shah, who was highly educated and very influential in the court as private secretary to her father, commissioned a *tazkirah* from her brother, Mahmud Mirza, a scholar and patron of the arts.[36] She seems to have had some influence on the choice of poets (including herself), and poems by other women praising her are also included in the volume, but despite her own high level of learning she exercised this agency through her brother, the compiler. As Brookshaw writes, 'women's poetry (especially that penned by royal women) was still

---

[32] Ibid., 42.
[33] Sunil Sharma, 'From 'Ā'esha to Nur Jahan: The Shaping of a Classical Persian Poetic Canon of Women', *Journal of Persianate Studies* 2, no. 2 (2009): 149, 151. See also Maria Szuppe, 'The "Jewels of Wonder": Learned Ladies and Princess Politicians in the Provinces of Early Safavid Iran', in *Women in the Medieval Islamic World: Power, Patronage, and Piety*, ed. Gavin R. G. Hambly (New York: St Martin's Press, 1999), 325–45.
[34] Sharma, 'From 'Ā'esha to Nur Jahan'.
[35] Dominic Parviz Brookshaw, 'Qajar Confection: The Production and Dissemination of Women's Poetry in Early Nineteenth-Century Iran', *Middle Eastern Literatures* 17 (2014): 113–146, 123. See also Dominic P. Brookshaw, 'Women in Praise of Women: Female Poets and Female Patrons in Qajar Iran', *Iranian Studies* 46, no. 1 (2013): 17–48.
[36] Brookshaw, 'Qajar Confection', 122.

considered to be private in some respects, and ... there was a certain degree of anxiety over its dissemination'.[37] Another example from this period, but from colonial India, of a woman exercising her own authorial capacity to write a book remains unusual: Bibi Hashmat al-Dawla was the consort of a British official in India (whose Persian title she adopted), and it is probably thanks to this that she attained the high level of education in Persian that she did, and also why her text (a compilation of vernacular Indian stories that she collected) survived in colonial archives.[38]

Another interesting way that women poets exercised their literary agency was in their choice of *takhallus* or pen name. Although *takhallus* were also used by men, whose real names were usually known in parallel, in the case of women, there was a striking pattern: names like Effat or Esmat (both meaning 'chastity'), Mahjubah ('the veiled/modest one'), Masturah, Makhfi, or Nahani (all meaning 'the hidden one') were used as pen names of women poets across the Persianate world, as if the *takhallus* could function as a symbolic veil, allowing their words to circulate while preserving their privacy. In these ways, certain female poets and writers, often of already privileged backgrounds, could create, leave traces in the world, and hope for a wider dissemination of their work, without violating the norms of seclusion.

This situation changed radically in the late nineteenth and early twentieth centuries, when modernizing movements both in literature and in politics championed women's right to public participation. This moment has been studied extensively in the Iranian context by Farzaneh Milani: 'Significantly, the movement to unveil in Iran is associated with women's attempt to break into print as writers.'[39] She describes the public unveiling of Tahereh Qorratolayn, a Babi leader who was also an accomplished poet, in 1848 as a watershed moment in this regard, culminating in a dramatic transformation: 'in less than 150 years [women] have desegregated a predominantly all-male tradition. They have reappraised cultural norms and patterns on a very intimate level.'[40] Women began to publish under their own full names and across the same range of genres as men. In concluding her book with Tahereh Saffarzadeh, a poet from the post-revolutionary period who voluntarily took up the veil again, Milani

---

[37] Ibid., 121.
[38] Zahra Shah, 'Negotiating Female Authorship in Eighteenth-Century India: Gender and Multilingualism in a Persian Text', *Journal of the Royal Asiatic Society* 29, no. 3 (2019): 447–66.
[39] Milani, *Veils and Words*, 7.
[40] Ibid., 72.

acknowledges that the veil can now also be a tool for facilitating women's access to public life and is no longer at odds with public expression.[41]

Two contemporary ethnographies of writers and their milieus in Egypt demonstrate the ongoing importance of the negotiation of boundaries of public and private expression.[42] They focus in particular on writing as a project of self-making. They highlight the diverse cultural institutions and the different but sometimes overlapping literary milieus they produce, in which women have increasingly been active, and give particular attention to writers in categories of literary practice that have been neglected by left-liberal international observers. These are middle-class, not cosmopolitan, women who abide by norms of modest behaviour in their everyday lives but who still find great joy and freedom in writing and literary conviviality. Both ethnographies draw inspiration from Foucault's notions of 'care of the self', describing writing as a 'technology of the self' that allows women to create literary personae for themselves and bring about changes in their lives. Although all authors need to find a way to balance the personal and literary parts of their lives, this is harder to achieve for women, and some take radical measures: Schielke and Shehata describe one woman who wrote about 'sex, desire, and discontent', yet wore a face veil to her meeting with them and kept her writing and her personal life strictly separated, telling no one in her workplace about it.[43] This suggests that despite the pervasive force of literary modernism in the Islamicate world, it has not been totalizing, and Muslim women writers continue to grapple with norms of privacy and modesty.[44]

CASE STUDY: CONTEMPORARY AFGHAN WOMEN POETS

I present here a case study drawn from my ethnography of Afghan refugee poets in Iran based on fieldwork performed over several periods between 2005 and 2010, and subsequent ethnography, much of it digital, with Afghan poets in the worldwide diaspora until the present day.[45] This case

---

[41] Ibid., 153.
[42] Šabasevičiūtė, 'Women Writing in Cairo'; Samuli Schielke and Mukhtar S. Shehata, *Shared Margins: An Ethnography with Writers in Alexandria after the Revolution* (Berlin: De Gruyter, 2021).
[43] Schielke and Shehata, *Shared Margins*, 78.
[44] I have explored a similar dynamic among Afghan women poets in Zuzanna Olszewska, 'Claiming an Individual Name: Revisiting the Personhood Debate with Afghan Poets in Iran', in *The Scandal of Continuity in Middle East Anthropology: Form, Duration, Difference*, ed. Judith Scheele and Andrew Shryock (Bloomington: Indiana University Press, 2019), 163–86.
[45] See Zuzanna Olszewska, *The Pearl of Dari: Poetry and Personhood among Young Afghans in Iran* (Bloomington: Indiana University Press, 2015). Afghan refugees in

study allows me to illuminate the effects of the advent of mass education and literacy on Muslim women's verbal expression, given that many of the poets I discuss were from the first literate generation in their families. Also of great importance in post-revolutionary Iran were other features of modernity, including reworkings of Islam itself and discourses on the legitimacy of women's public expression of their voices and inner experiences. I explore the lives of two poets and a poem by each: one by a poet who has become disillusioned with her faith, and another who has embraced it as a strong element of her identity.

As the wars in Afghanistan that began in 1979 passed through successive stages and years of exile turned into decades, new literary cultures emerged in relation to political and cultural developments in diverse diasporic communities. Most notably, widespread access to education for both boys and girls in many refugee communities brought about a revolution of literacy and the broadening of writing, readership, and publication – first in print, and later online. There have been at least three distinct moments in refugee poetic production, in response to wider socio-political transformations: the war and the resistance poetry of the 1980s; the post-ideological poetry of the 1990s onwards; and what might be termed the social-media poetry of the 2010s onwards, which embraces both earlier strands in a literary moment that continues to be experimental and eclectic. During my fieldwork, young women, buoyed by their education and protected by the Islamization of the public sphere in the Islamic Republic, comprised at least half of the regular participants in refugee literary associations. They wrote short stories and poetry on a wide range of themes – social and anti-war critique, love, women's everyday lives and domesticity, the hardships of exile and poverty, and poems of exilic longing for the homeland. They have also edited, compiled, and critiqued the poetry of other women.

The following poem, posted on Facebook on 27 February 2021, is one example (my translation):

> I used to think
> love's fragrant lips
> the firm arms of faith
> and the homeland's warm embrace
> would save me.

Iran have had access to good-quality public education in unprecedented numbers, raising literacy rates most strikingly among women. At the same time, they continue to face legal discrimination and social prejudice, poverty, heavy restrictions on employment (educated refugees cannot work legally in their professions), and the constant threat of deportation.

Now
I am grateful to love
for finding better prey
taking its teeth off my throat
and allowing me
to breathe in the scent of the pine trees.

However hard I tried
I couldn't find a place in the arms of faith
The harem was big
I was wild
and I couldn't wait my turn
for lovemaking.
I was afraid of being stoned.
I broke the locks
and fled.

But my homeland
is still my mother
who sold all her wedding gold
to buy me a plane ticket
so I could go
and stay alive.

One day
without love
without faith
just
for my mother's sake
I will return.

The poem's author was Mahbouba Ibrahimi, an Afghan poet and filmmaker who now lives in a village north of Uppsala in Sweden. Born in Kandahar in 1975 as a member of that city's Shi'i, Hazara minority, she grew up and was educated in Iran. I first interviewed her in 2005, when she was one of the key poets and activists of an Afghan literary association in Tehran, together with her then husband, also a poet. The family repatriated to Kabul in 2007, where I met them again, but soon re-migrated to Sweden to seek a better future for their young children. Although now separated from her husband and geographically isolated in rural Sweden from most of her compatriots, Ibrahimi is active on Facebook and Instagram, and regularly shares her new work there, helping her stay connected to transnational networks of Afghan writers and intellectuals.

She has published three books of her poetry, one in Iran and two in Afghanistan, and still aspires to print rather than online publication as the pinnacle of literary durability and success.

The poem, in blank verse, reflects Ibrahimi's disillusionment with the three former cornerstones of her identity – love, her faith, and her homeland, although she reaffirms her love for her mother and gratitude for her sacrifices. Written in blank verse without rhyme or metre, the poem relies on striking images and wordplay for its poetic effect: here, the use of the harem and lovemaking as metaphors for religion are particularly bold, as is the inversion of the typically positive associations of love, usually a cherished feature of the Persian poetic tradition. The homeland may now be a hostile place for her, but as in many of her other poems, Ibrahimi clings to a hope of return, if only for her mother's sake.

The poem resonated with many of Ibrahimi's Persian-speaking friends (it received 258 like/love reactions and 101 comments, and was shared 7 times). In style and content, it was similar to many other poems in blank verse expressing gendered social critiques that I heard and collected during my initial fieldwork in Iran, owing a great deal to their illustrious precursor Forugh Farrokhzad (1934–67), a beloved Iranian modernist poet whose frankly confessional lyrics continued to be published after the Islamic Revolution.[46] One poet commented: 'What a great sorrow your poem had, my Mahbouba. It pierced me to the core of my soul.' But if this poem's values are congruent with Western liberal sentiments of individual autonomy and its genre familiar as a confessional lyric in blank verse, we should not make the mistake of neglecting those that are not.

Later that year, in December 2021, another of my Afghan poet friends shared a rather different social media post, a video of herself reciting a poem at a formal poetry event. She stands at a lectern speaking into a microphone in measured, rhythmic tones in a voice that, while clear, appears from time to time to tremble with emotion, and she moves her hand to emphasize certain words. Banners display the name of the event: an international women's poetry congress on the theme of 'Ashura' hosted by the foundation that runs the Holy Shrine of Imam Reza in Mashhad, Iran. She is appropriately dressed for the event with a black *chador* (a head-to-toe veil that does not cover the face) and headscarf, but a hint of red embroidery is just visible between the folds

---

[46] See Dominic P. Brookshaw and Nasrin Rahimieh, eds., *Forugh Farrokhzad, Poet of Modern Iran: Iconic Woman and Feminine Pioneer of New Persian Poetry* (London: I. B. Tauris, 2021).

of the *chador*. Murmurs of appreciation are heard periodically from the audience.

This video was posted on Instagram by Zahra Hosseinzadeh, (@zahra_hosainzade), one of the best-known female poets from the Afghan refugee community in Iran, with over 24,000 followers on the platform. It begins (my translation):

> I have seen nothing but sorrow;[47] please step into my heart.
> Your veil brings healing, place it upon my head for eternity.
>
> Although I've been struck by many slingshot stones,
> take these two eastern eyes as defenders of your shrine.
>
> We Hazaras don't consider our heads our own.
> I am blood without a homeland, dip your pen in my veins.
>
> The shreds of my faith fell into the hands of the Kufans;
> Deliver a sermon,[48] my Lady, put oppression to the sword.

This poem, a *ghazal* in honour of Sayyida Zaynab bint Ali, granddaughter of the Prophet Muhammad, is a play on the story of the Battle of Karbala as the paradigmatic account of oppression for Shi'i Muslims, here linked to the plight of the Hazara ethnic group. The narrator of the poem seeks the protection of Zaynab for her people, among the most persecuted groups in Afghanistan due to their Shi'i faith – a group who experience so much violence and suffering that they do not even expect to keep their heads, and whose members have scattered in exile like 'blood without a homeland'. In return she promises 'these two eastern eyes' as protectors of the shrine of Zaynab, a reference to the 'almond-shaped' eyes of many Hazaras that highlight their physical difference from the majority of Iranians (and other Afghans).

Born in 1979 to a family of landless Hazara farmers in Ghor Province, Afghanistan, Hosseinzadeh's life is a striking example of the social advancement made possible for Afghans by migration to Iran. She is a pious Shi'i Muslim who has a degree in Islamic Studies from a university in Mashhad, and is a teacher and one of the key poets and literary activists in the Durr-i

---

[47] This phrase, given in the original Arabic in the poem, is a reference to Sayyida Zaynab's retort to her Umayyad captors' taunts after her brother Imam Hussein's defeat and murder at the Battle of Karbala, when she said that, despite the tragedy, she had seen nothing but beauty from Allah: *mā ra'aitu illā jamīlā*. Here the author has substituted 'sorrow' for 'beauty'. The other images in the poem also allude to the captives' suffering at the hands of the Umayyads.

[48] Note that this is a reference to the same oration by Zaynab in Umayyad captivity that is discussed by Qutbuddin in *Arabic Oration*.

Dari Cultural Institute in Mashhad, a leading Afghan cultural institution in Iran. She takes great care in her self-presentation both in real life and in the virtual space: she flawlessly wears the kind of hijab that indexes piety and commitment to the Islamic regime in Iran, a black *chador* in addition to an overcoat, and a headscarf fully covering her hair. Yet her pride in her Hazara identity is also evident in the brightly coloured scarves and traditional patterns or embroidered dresses she frequently wears under her *chador* – or without the *chador* in many of her Instagram posts. She has published three books of poems, won numerous prizes in Afghan refugee literary festivals, and has even been invited to participate in a poetry evening held by Iran's Supreme Leader Ali Khamenei. She has an unusual talent for writing metric and rhyming verse, and uses the *ghazal* form with particular skill. When I first met her during my fieldwork from 2005 to 2010 her poetry was neither overtly political nor ideological, although she considered herself a Muslim feminist, and often portrayed the injustices and indignities suffered particularly by refugee women. The focus on Hazara identity by 2017 seemed new to me but coincided with a growth in Hazara ethnic consciousness and activism in the global diaspora.

This poem is in the genre known as *ghazal-i naw*, the new *ghazal*: meeting the requirements of rhyme and meter of the classical form, but with more contemporary, conversational language influenced by modernist developments in Persian literature. The *ghazal* has traditionally been associated with love (whether earthly or divine), as well as its mystical elaborations. Its rhythmic nature and deeply emotional tone made it very appropriate to be read aloud at a congress on the theme of 'Ashura', an occasion for public displays of mourning in Shi'i culture.[49] Both men and women write in this form, but it is the most common of the 'neoclassical' genres (which also include the *masnavi* and the *qasidah*) for women to write in, and as a genre with strict formal requirements that require great skill to navigate, it allows women who excel in it to win great acclaim.

Although their 'personas' and religious leanings differ, the contrast I have hinted at between Ibrahimi and Hosseinzadeh belies a great many similarities. They were both Hazara refugees educated to degree level in Iran as the first literate women in their families, and they were both highly respected, published, and award-winning figures and organizers in the same Afghan refugee literary milieu. Both spoke of the powerful, formative effect on them of the oral poetry and tales told by their

---

[49] Indeed, the audience's vocalizations and the conventional recitation style suggest the ongoing importance of the recitation and hearing of poetry in Iran.

mothers and grandmothers. The contrasting genres of the poems here are also misleading, as Ibrahimi, too, was a skilled composer of *ghazals* and Hosseinzadeh sometimes wrote blank verse; they used both of these to discuss domesticity and the trials large and small of refugee women's everyday lives, especially in their roles as carers for children or disabled family members. It is a testament to the extraordinary space created for women's poetry by Afghan refugee literary organizations in Iran that it allowed for this range of themes, perspectives, and styles to be fostered. The biggest difference was that Hosseinzadeh's religious piety and the strategies of personal and poetic expression that she chooses are 'safer' in the context of the Islamic Republic, and have allowed her a degree of social and cultural capital that she would not otherwise have been able to attain – and which led Ibrahimi, who considered them out of reach, to leave the country. Despite this and perhaps most importantly, they are friends, and they remain in touch: the admiring comment under Ibrahimi's poem on Facebook that I quoted above was by Hosseinzadeh.

CONCLUSION

Although I have crossed a wide range of time periods, localities, languages, and literary genres from the Islamicate world in this chapter, a common theme has emerged: women's capacity for verbal expression has always been highly contextual, and inextricably regulated by power and ideology. Until recently, and in some cases still, women's expression was relational: either restricted to women's publics, or reaching into the male public domain through the proxy of men; this was true of both oral and written texts but particularly so in the written domain, tended more assiduously by male gatekeepers. As Hammond has put it, 'Historically, women ... had considerable power to compose texts, but they had less power to frame these texts for posterity in their own names.'[50]

But we should be extremely cautious about attributing these facts solely to *Islam* or even to local iterations of patriarchy. After all, similar problems have been noted in the history and canonization processes of women's participation in literature and other arts in Europe and elsewhere. It is now increasingly well-established that even in times and places when women equalled or outperformed men in literary or other artistic pursuits, they would not necessarily be remembered for it: women made up the majority of writers and readers of English literature in the eighteenth century, for example, but were 'edged out' of the

---

[50] Hammond, 'Literature'.

literary marketplace and written out of the canon itself when the 'high culture novel' and the 'Great Literary Tradition' emerged and came to be dominated by men.[51] Other processes that edged women out of literary canons have been documented for a variety of reasons not related to religion in the Persian and Chinese traditions, in which the compilers of anthologies were in the past exclusively male.[52] Today, other forms of selectivity are brought to bear: less than one-third of literary works translated into English are by women.[53] It would appear that gender inequality in literary gatekeeping practices – criticism, anthologization, canonization, publishing, translation – is a universal problem, obscuring women's actual literary output in any time and place and misleading later readers about their nature in the past.

What, then, of Jahan Malik Khatun's desire to create a literary 'monument' to herself, to withstand the 'dust of oblivion'? To a very regrettable extent, she, too, has been 'edged out' of the Persian canon, despite having left behind a vast corpus of poetry in a *divan* published in her own name with her own introductory framing (the only female poet to do so in the medieval period). She is considered by scholars to be equal in talent to her great contemporary, Hafez, a poet of national importance in Iran and a household name, yet the first critical edition of her work was not published in Tehran until 1995, and her work has been little studied.[54] Yet it is a testament precisely to her ingenuity and prolific output that her self-built monument has endured, and interest in it is growing today. I believe it to be our duty as feminist scholars and curious readers to seek out such studies and undertake more of them, and to shift our assumptions about Muslim women's expressive capacities in the past and present.

To do so would be to fulfill Mahbouba Ibrahimi's wish when I first interviewed her in Tehran almost two decades ago: 'We hope to introduce ourselves to the world – to countries which only see the face of poverty of Afghanistan ... however, from the cultural perspective, we are a rich people. We want to promote the face that is not seen in the world, to translate our work.' May she succeed.

---

[51] Gaye Tuchman and Nina E. Fortin, 'Fame and Misfortune: Edging Women out of the Great Literary Tradition', *American Journal of Sociology* 90, no. 1 (1984): 72–96.
[52] See Sharma, 'From 'Ā'esha to Nur Jahan'; Grace S. Fong, 'Gender and the Failure of Canonization: Anthologizing Women's Poetry in the Late Ming', *Chinese Literature: Essays, Articles, Reviews* 26 (2004): 129–49.
[53] Women in Translation Project, http://womenintranslation.org.
[54] Brookshaw, 'Odes of a Poet-Princess', 176.

SELECT BIBLIOGRAPHY

Abu-Lughod, Lila. *Veiled Sentiments: Honor and Poetry in a Bedouin Society.* Berkeley: University of California Press, 1986.

Brookshaw, Dominic Parviz. 'Odes of a Poet-Princess: The Ghazals of Jahān-Malik Khātūn'. *Iran* 43 (2005): 173–95.

 'Qajar Confection: The Production and Dissemination of Women's Poetry in Early Nineteenth-Century Iran'. *Middle Eastern Literatures* 17 (2014): 113–146, 123.

Brookshaw, Dominic P. and Rahimieh, Nasrin, eds. *Forugh Farrokhzad, Poet of Modern Iran: Iconic Woman and Feminine Pioneer of New Persian Poetry.* London: I. B. Tauris, 2021.

Hammond, Marlé. *Beyond Elegy: Classical Arabic Women's Poetry in Context.* Oxford: Oxford University Press for the British Academy, 2010.

Lambert-Hurley, Siobhan. *Elusive Lives: Gender, Autobiography, and the Self in Muslim South Asia.* Stanford: Stanford University Press, 2018.

Milani, Farzaneh. *Veils and Words: The Emerging Voices of Iranian Women Writers.* Syracuse, NY: Syracuse University Press, 1992.

Mills, Margaret A. 'Gender and Verbal Performance Style in Afghanistan'. In *Gender, Genre and Power in South Asian Expressive Traditions*, ed. Arjun Appadurai, Frank Korom, and Margaret Mills, 56–77. Philadelphia: Pennsylvania University Press, 1991.

Olszewska, Zuzanna. *The Pearl of Dari: Poetry and Personhood among Young Afghans in Iran.* Bloomington: Indiana University Press, 2015.

Qutbuddin, Tahera. *Arabic Oration: Art and Function.* Leiden: Brill, 2019.

Šabasevičiūtė, Giedrė. 'Women Writing in Cairo: Midlife, Self-Care, and the Informal World of Literature'. *Journal of Middle East Women's Studies* 19, no. 3 (2023): 317–36.

Schäfers, Marlene. *Voices That Matter: Kurdish Women at the Limits of Representation in Contemporary Turkey.* Chicago: University of Chicago Press, 2023.

Shah, Zahra. 'Negotiating Female Authorship in Eighteenth-Century India: Gender and Multilingualism in a Persian Text'. *Journal of the Royal Asiatic Society* 29, no. 3 (2019): 447–66.

Sharma, Sunil. 'From 'Ā'esha to Nur Jahān: The Shaping of a Classical Persian Poetic Canon of Women'. *Journal of Persianate Studies* 2, no. 2 (2009): 148–64.

Szuppe, Maria. 'The "Jewels of Wonder": Learned Ladies and Princess Politicians in the Provinces of Early Safavid Iran'. In *Women in the Medieval Islamic World: Power, Patronage, and Piety*, ed. Gavin R. G. Hambly, 325–45. New York: St Martin's Press, 1999.

15 'Feminist Spirituality' as Lived Religion
ZILKA SPAHIĆ ŠILJAK

Religion and spirituality vary in their focus; religion is centered on adhering to organized doctrines and participating in communal rituals, while spirituality prioritizes a personal connection with the transcendent, fostering individual paths to truth, love, and peace. "Spirituality," derived from the Latin for "breath," revitalizes the soul in its pursuit of these ideals.[1] However, as noted by some scholars,[2] personal spirituality does not exist in isolation, detached from formal religious teachings and rituals. Initially, the second wave of feminism (emerging in the 1960s–80s) largely ignored the role of religion and spirituality, viewing them through a lens of oppression and patriarchy.[3] Iconic works by radical feminists and theologians such as *The Church and the Second Sex* (1968) and *Beyond God the Father* (1973) criticized Christian theology as inherently patriarchal.[4] Over time, a distinct strand of scholarship has emerged within sociology that advocates for the recognition of a spiritually oriented feminist perspective. This perspective recognizes that spirituality can be important to feminist experience, whereby one might opt not to adhere to institutionalized religion yet remain guided by its overarching spiritual message.[5] Such a framework emphasizes the relational nature of religion, spirituality, and feminist struggle.

---

[1] Leo Booth, *Spirituality and Recovery: A Classic Introduction to the Difference between Spirituality and Religion in the Process of Healing*, 4th ed. (Deerfield Beach, FL: Health Communications Inc., 2012), 20.

[2] Meredith B. McGuire, *Lived Religion: Faith and Practice in Everyday Life* (Oxford: Oxford University Press, 2008); Elizabeth Shakman Hurd, *Beyond Religious Freedom: The New Global Politics of Religion* (Princeton: Princeton University Press, 2015).

[3] Simone de Beauvoir, *The Second Sex*, trans. Constance Borde and Sheila Malovany-Chevallier (Random House: Alfred A. Knopf, 2009 [1949]).

[4] Mary Daly, *The Church and the Second Sex* (New York: Harper and Row, 1968); *Beyond God the Father* (Boston: Beacon Press, 1973).

[5] Kristin Aunne, "Feminist Spirituality as Lived Religion: How UK Feminists Forge Religio-spiritual Lives," in *Secular Societies, Spiritual Selves?: The Gendered Triangle of Religion, Secularity and Spirituality*, ed. Anna Fedele and Kim E. Knibbe (London, New York: Routledge, 2020), 39–57, 32.

Building on my previous work on feminist and Muslim identities in the post-socialist context of the Balkans[6] and the work on feminist spiritualities that focuses on studying lived religio-spiritual lives,[7] in this chapter I examine intersections of the lived religious, spiritual, and feminist experiences of Muslim women in Bosnia and Herzegovina (BiH). Issues that I explored in detail with my respondents are: 1) family upbringing and religious practices; 2) their perceptions of religiosity, spirituality, and feminism; 3) the texts, messages, and principles from Islamic tradition that are important to them; 4) their levels and methods of religious practice; 5) how they integrate religion and/or spirituality into their activism; 6) how they reconcile feminism with religion; and 7) how they navigate between private and public expressions of their faith.

The chapter demonstrates how their feminist agency is influenced by their individualized mixing of Islamic religio-spiritual practices, as well as the socialist and post-socialist secular principles, with a focus on the equality and nondiscrimination that came to shape Bosnian society. A defining aspect of their religio-spiritual and feminist identities is their choice to distance themselves fully or partially from institutionalized religion, focusing instead on a relational and practical application of the ethical teachings from their faith. Their feminist activism is enriched by Sufi cosmology, a fundamental element of Bosnian religious heritage, embraced by Muslims since the Ottoman era.[8] We thus see how Islamic divine principles of *tawhid* (unity) and *taqwa* (God-conscious piety), as discussed by Muslim feminists such as Riffat Hassan[9] and Amina Wadud,[10] are critical to shaping Bosnian women's aspirations, as well as strategies for advancing feminist ideals.

---

[6] In this chapter, I leverage years of my research on the subject referenced on numerous occasions in this chapter and complement it with recent data collected during fieldwork involving women from various professional sectors, including secular and faith-based NGOs, universities, media, and art institutions in Sarajevo, Tuzla, Mostar, and Zenica. Through focus group discussions and in-depth interviews, I delve into themes that shed light on how their daily experiences in a post-socialist society and religious beliefs shape their activism.

[7] Gerda Lerner, *The Creation of Feminist Consciousness from the Middle Ages to the Eighteenth Century* (Oxford: Oxford University Press, 1993); Anne Carr, "On Feminist Spirituality," in *Women's Spirituality: Resources for Christian Development*, 2nd ed., ed. Joann Wolski Conn (New York: Paulist Press, 1996), 49–58; Aunne, "Feminist Spirituality."

[8] Ines Aščerić-Tod, *Derwishes and Islam in Bosnia: Sufi Dimensions to the Formation of Bosnian Muslim Society* (Leiden, Boston: Brill, 2015).

[9] Riffat Hassan, "Equal before Allah? Women–Men Equality in Islamic Tradition," *Harvard Divinity Bulletin* 17, no. 2 (1987): 2–20.

[10] Amina Wadud, *Qur'an and Woman: Rereading the Sacred Text from a Woman's Perspective* (New York: Oxford University Press, 1999), xii, 3, 36–37.

The chapter initiates its discussion by setting the historical backdrop of BiH. It then elucidates how, even within a post-socialist framework, Islamic religious and spiritual beliefs and experiences significantly influence the agency of Bosnian women. This influence extends to those who maintain a secular perspective, are critical of institutionalized religion, and exhibit a relaxed approach towards fulfilling their ritual obligations.

CONTEXT OF BOSNIA AND HERZEGOVINA

The religio-spiritual life of Bosnian women cannot be understood properly without contextualizing the impact of both socialist and post-socialist secularization processes in BiH. BiH was part of the Socialist Federal Republic of Yugoslavia from 1945 to 1991. Yugoslavia was a socialist welfare state founded on three main principles: self-management, non-alignment, and brotherhood and unity.[11] Growing industrialization and urbanization went hand in hand with the emancipation of women. State policies supported obligatory primary education, created employment opportunities, and encouraged engagement in politics. Gender equality was included in the constitution because the state wanted women to contribute to socio-economic progress and societal development.[12] Women had access to free healthcare and education, and paid maternity leave and childcare. Reproductive rights were guaranteed, and the rapid expansion of employment led to greater economic independence for women. However, as Marina Blagojević finds: "the communist-style modernization was mostly reduced to modernization in the public sphere, while the private sphere depended heavily on the exploitation of women's resources through unpaid domestic labor, which was supported by patriarchal values."[13] Thus, the socialist secularist formation had its limitations, with guaranteed equality in public life while the private sphere

---

[11] Sabina Ramet, ed., *Gender Politics in the Western Balkans: Women in Society in Yugoslavia and the Yugoslav Successor States* (Philadelphia: Pennsylvania State University Press, 1999).

[12] Gorana Mlinarević, "Socio-political Conditions in BiH and Kosovo," in *Contesting Female, Feminist and Muslim Identities: Post-Socialist Contexts of Bosnia and Herzegovina and Kosovo*, ed. Zilka Spahić Šiljak (Sarajevo: Center for Interdisciplinary Postgraduate Studies of the University of Sarajevo, 2012), 88–98.

[13] Marina Blagojević, "Mapping Misogyny in the Balkans: Local/Global Hybrids in Culture and Media," in *Transformationen von Geschlechterordnungen in Wissenschaft und anderen sozialen Instituten: Internationale Frauen- und Genderforschung in Niedersachsen*, vol. II, ed. Waltraud Ernst and Ulrike Bohle (Munster: LIT Verlag), 74–95, 64.

"remained deeply shaped by traditional gender roles."[14] Although gender equality was part of the socialist system, feminism was viewed as a "bourgeois" import from the West, which contrasted with communist ideology. However, as the second wave of feminism was flourishing in Western Europe and North America, in the late 1970s women in academia in BiH started publishing and organizing lectures and workshops as a reaction to state-controlled gender politics.[15]

Religion was suppressed in the first period of Yugoslavia (1945–53), when shari'a courts and the veiling of women were banned and Islamic primary schools were shut down.[16] In addition, all Sufi *tekkes* (dervish lodges) were closed down.[17] Harsh state measures in that period were intended to suppress any opposition, and "religious authorities were seen as especially dangerous because they could provide an alternative ideology that might endanger the fragile, post-revolutionary socialist political and economic system."[18] When the Law on the Legal Status of Religious Communities was enacted in 1953, church–state separation was confirmed, and religion was designated a private matter. Yugoslav participation in the non-alignment movement under Tito's leadership enabled the Islamic Community[19] to establish better communication with the state, which was keen to demonstrate to Islamic countries that Muslims had freedom in Yugoslavia. Significant developments in church–state relations happened between 1965 and 1971; this period "was characterized by the proliferation of religious publications, opening of new theological schools, and freedom of clerics to travel abroad."[20]

BiH comprises three major religious groups: Muslims, Orthodox Christians, and Catholics. Muslims did not have the right to an ethnic designation, unlike Orthodox Christians, who are ethnically Serbs, and Catholics, who are ethnically Croats. In 1968 the Communist government in BiH decided that Muslims should be recognized as a separate

---

[14] Zilka Spahić Šiljak, "Women, Religion and Politics," in *Religion, the Secular and the Politics of Sexual Difference*, ed. Linell E. Cady and Tracy Fessenden (New York: Columbia University Press), 121–136, 121.

[15] Ana Dević, "Redefining the Public–Private Boundary: Nationalism and Women's Activism in Former Yugoslavia," *Anthropology of East Europe Review* 15, no. 2 (1997): 45–61, 45.

[16] Noel Malcolm, *Bosnia: A Short History* (London: Pen Books, 2002).

[17] Sead Fetahagić, "Islam in Socialism and Post-socialism," in *Contesting Female, Feminist and Muslim Identities*, ed. Šiljak, 112–126, 112–113.

[18] Ibid., 113.

[19] "Islamic Community" refers to the official Islamic regulatory body in BiH, which was established under the rule of the Habsburg Empire.

[20] Ibid., 114.

ethnic group. They were recognized as a "member of the Islamic Religious Community," which is a national-level body overseeing the working of mosques and Islamic teachings, and their ethnic designation became "Muslim" as a distinct ethnic/national group.[21] Only in 1993 during the war (1992–5) did the Congress of Bosnian Intellectuals decide to revive the old ethnic name "Bosniac" from the medieval period instead of "Muslim," which is a more religious designation.

The newly established democratic government, according to the post-war Dayton Peace Agreement (1995), consisted of these three major ethnic/religious groups and a small percentage of minorities. During this period, the ethno-national political and religious elites advocated for a re-traditionalization of gender roles, glorifying family values and the responsibility of women in the new nation-state building as reproducers of the nation. Women almost disappeared from politics after the first democratic elections in 1990.[22] In the transition from socialism to democracy and self-management to the open-market capitalist system, women gained more civil and political freedom but lost social and economic security, which affected their employment and engagement in public life. Thanks to the activism of civil society organizations and the feminist movement, women regained a greater share of political representation, and today in the House of Representatives of the Parliamentary Assembly of BiH, 16–17 percent of seats are held by women.[23] Women have also played an important role in peace and reconciliation and transitional justice,[24] with an emphasis on eradicating gender-based violence and on economic and political empowerment; they have also engaged in the ecological movement, with an eco-feminist agenda building local networks to protect the environment from corporate companies. In this complex historical context, marked by dramatic changes in the socio-political realities, what values and ideals inform Bosnian women's struggle for equality?

---

[21] Malcolm, *Bosnia*.
[22] Zilka Spahić Šiljak, *Women, Religion and Politics: Impact Analysis of Interpretative Religious Heritage of Judaism, Christianity and Islam on the Engagement of Women in Public Life and Politics* (Sarajevo: IMIC-CIPS-TPO, 2010).
[23] Zilka Spahić Šiljak and Đipa Dino, *Gender Equality Barometer of Bosnia and Herzegovina* (Sarajevo: United Nations Development Programme, 2024).
[24] Elissa Helms, *Innocence and Victimhood: Gender, Nation, and Women's Activism in Postwar Bosnia-Herzegovina* (Madison: Wisconsin University Press, 2013); Zilka Spahić Šiljak, *Shining Humanity: Life Stories of Women of Bosnia and Herzegovina* (Newcastle: Cambridge Scholars Publishing, 2014).

RELATIONAL ASPECT OF FEMINIST SPIRITUALITY

In my research, I have found spirituality to be a key dimension in understanding Bosnian women's feminist agency. In Sufi cosmology, developing relations with God requires a right relation to oneself, to other human beings, and to the whole of nature. Feminist spirituality is relational. I have found the religio-spiritual, lived experiences of my respondents to be deeply embedded in their relationships with God, people, and nature, which is in line with the *tawhidic* (unity) principle.

These women had their first relationship with religion and God in their childhoods, when their grandparents (usually their grandmothers) taught them some prayers and imparted basic Islamic teachings. Previous research on lived Islam in BiH also confirms that religious socialization occurred through elderly family members,[25] who knew that their own children had to adjust to the socialist reality in public life. They therefore focused on transmitting religious knowledge to their grandchildren. In the words of two of my respondents:

> All that I have learned about religion, I've researched on my own, having, of course, that Islamic background. My grandfathers and grandmothers were devout believers, and somehow we respected that traditional model. We knew how Eid was celebrated, how religious holidays were observed. (Aida, poetess, Tešanj)

> My mom's mom, when I stayed over ... prayed sometimes ... and when she lay down and I slept with my mother, she always recited to me in my ear, and those were some of my first encounters with faith. (Iman, actress, Zenica)

Primary socialization in religion came through stories, prayers, and the *adab* (good manners) that help a person to cultivate an ethical self.[26] Being a good person, not causing harm, showing empathy, and demonstrating solidarity were the key messages these women received from their grandparents. They discuss these values not only as religious but as broader social principles inherent in human nature.

These women underline how important it is for them to be ethical human beings who do not just preach about Islam, but cultivate it through actions and manners. These values were an important part of their activism

---

[25] Zora Kostadinova, "Becoming a Good Person: Islam, the Self, and the Ethical Imagination among Naqshbandi Muslims in Postwar Sarajevo," PhD diss., University College London, 2023.

[26] Zora Kostadinova, "Edep: Ethical Imagination and the Sunna of the Prophet Muhammad," *Contemporary Islam*, December (2023), on open access.

and helped them to become moral human beings who not only master theories on ethics, but also act on the moral obligation to be responsible. The highest level of that responsibility is summarized in the "golden rule" often quoted as the cornerstone of their religio-spiritual life:

> The fundamental principle that arises from my faith is that I do not do to others what I would not want done to me. (Dina, activist, Sarajevo)

Their relationship with God evolved over time, and, depending on circumstances, it was either silenced or contested. These women experienced changes in their religio-spiritual lives, with periods when they drifted away from religion before returning to it. For many, the war or the death of beloved family members marked a turning point, prompting them to seriously reconsider their faith and the meaning of life. Some found that their work environment left little room for religio-spiritual practices, while others sought peace in different religious and spiritual traditions.

> However, after the war, of course, life goes on, I moved into the media, you see, religiosity in such an environment loses its importance ... Of course, it never left my soul, but you change your environment when you're not daily with people who love and practice [religion], so the intensity of that diminishes. (Biba, university teacher, Sarajevo)

> During that period [during the war], I was religious, and then came a phase of questioning everything. A new environment emerged where ... I stepped out of my comfort zone, and a billion questions arose. I never doubted the existence of God, but the way I practice, is it right? Is it good for me? That was the most painful period for me. (Myra, actress, Sarajevo)

These women also express resentment towards practicing believers who fulfill all the formal duties of religion, and at the same time religion is not reflected in their manners and deeds, or they misuse it for the purposes of day-to-day politics. The women were of the view that religion is now present in public life much more than in the socialist era; people talk about their religiosity and judge others, including women who do not wear hijab, but don't follow ethical values. One of my respondents noted:

> I don't live the life of a practitioner every day. I strive to be a good human being, someone people can rely on, not to lie, not to steal, not to do what everyone else around us does, and then go to the mosque and think that's good. (Zehra, activist, Tuzla)

Most of these women do not distinguish between religion and spirituality, because for them the two are interconnected, although they acknowledge that some people can be spiritual and not religious, and vice versa. Faith in God is crucial, but the way they relate to it and how they live their faith can vary considerably. The majority of my respondents emphasized the three key principles of Islam: *tawhid* (unity), *taqwa* (God-conscious piety), and *tawakkul* (relying on God). The importance of these concepts in deepening faith was noted by two of my respondents in these words:

> I don't just believe in God. I trust God. I believe that what He tells us in the Qur'an, or what He has sent to us in various ways and continues to send us through His signs, and one of those signs is the Qur'an ... I believe that there are things that will reach us, whether we want them to or not. There are things that will pass us by, whether we want them to or not ... So, I believe that there is a greater plan, beyond me. (Ilma, faith-based activist, Sarajevo)

> If I'm in a certain dilemma, when I completely surrender to Him, and when, for example, lately I've been doing that and practicing, it's really a big challenge ... when I completely surrender to Him and say: "Dear Allah, I have given my all completely, it's in Your trust, You lead it further as You think it should be. This is from me, what I could do and what I have done." And somehow, I deeply believe ... that this is absolutely Allah's decree. Whatever will happen. And there, I don't have any kind of dilemma, whether I should have done this, whether I should have done that, whether it was wise or not, no, not at all. (Dina, activist, Sarajevo)

A few of them emphasize how it is central to Islamic faith to be aware of God's presence in every moment, believing that everything happens for a reason, and to cultivate gratitude for God's protection and mercy.

For some women, conversation with God is helpful, soothing, and liberating from constant worries and fear, and attempts to control life. That relationship is cultivated through paintings or acting, as some women artists explain the interconnectedness of everything and the role of human beings as the masterpiece of creation. The conversation with God can also take the form of arguing with God when these women seek solutions for self-healing and repairing their relations with others. These moments help them to cultivate gratitude, which is often mentioned in all the interviews:

> I don't know about others, but I, for example, argue with God and talk to God every day. It's a kind of dialogue I have every day ... because I become grateful. (Sena, activist, Sarajevo)

One of the issues that informs the spirituality of some Muslim women is experience of gender-based violence during the war. Sexual violence was a tool of war in the Balkans, and thousands of women were raped. One of the activists emphasized how it changed the course of her life and the way she perceives the world. She was of the view that people who have not experienced sexual violence have different religio-spiritual perceptions. As she explained, the locus of her action is shaped by the experience of the violence she, and the other women she works with, experienced:

> One of the very important aspects in defining my spirituality, and I believe in defining the spirituality of women from this region, is the violence we have experienced in our lives. I don't know if I would be like this if I hadn't been exposed to war, if I hadn't survived war, and if I hadn't seen the consequences of violence in its cruelest form ... I could have been a completely different person if what happened hadn't happened. (Sena, activist, Sarajevo)

Rumi's poetry and his emphasis on the ultimate divine Love that embraces everyone is the best channel for some women to explain Islam to people, especially today, with rising Islamophobia and portrayals of Muslims as terrorists and backward, as highlighted by one of my respondents.[27] For her, there is no intermediate between God and a human being, and that direct connection to God is something she cherishes and celebrates as a unique opportunity for every person:

> I have brought many women and people closer to Islam precisely because I have shown them my love and shattered those taboos, or rather, those opinions and stereotypes that I must primarily wear a headscarf, pray five times a day, respect everything ... It's easiest for me to bring them closer through the philosophy of Rumi ... People who have great resistance to religions ... resistance to Islam, often equate it with terrorism, which is terrible ... and that's why it's easiest for me when I talk to people, I talk through Rumi's poetry because that way I can bring them closer to that language of love. (Ziba, journalist, Sarajevo)

---

[27] Rumi was a thirteenth-century Persian poet, mystic, and Sufi master whose profound works on love, spirituality, and unity continue to inspire people worldwide.

The relational aspect of feminist spirituality is reflected in the respondents' feminist activism. They have careers as university teachers, journalists, and artists, but they are also socially engaged. They create a web of networks, they educate, organize support groups, they protest injustice and inequality, they help those who are marginalized, and they advocate for their rights. They find compatibility between Islam and feminism, and they do not make compromises between feminism and religion. For them, both are important and can be easily reconciled:

> To me, that's not reconcilable, it's just the same to me ... Simply put, to me, Dear God created men and women as equal beings, from the same substance, with the same intention, and only makes distinctions based on how we are towards Him, towards other people ... So, that is the most basic form of feminism, recognizing women as equal people. (Ilma, faith-based activist, Sarajevo)

However, they struggle with a patriarchy that resists feminism as something opposed to traditional values (family, marriage, sexuality, reproductive rights). These women blame both men and women in BiH society who defend patriarchal values in order to keep the status quo, and who lack the courage to take on the responsibility to make change. Their feminism was initially informed by socialist ideals focused on securing social and economic rights and security, but it has slowly transformed into a feminism that is focused equally on civil, political, and economic rights. Whenever I have explored with my respondents the question of how religion and spirituality affect their activism and how feminism informs their spiritual path, I have found they explain how the two are inevitably connected.

> I view feminism ... it's all that is not sexism, it's the fight for equal rights for women and men. It's not the desire for women to have better rights, greater rights, but simply the fight for equality ... and we are all equal before God. (Delila, university teacher, Tuzla)

Among my respondents, women want to connect their feminism and religio-spiritual life, but they face challenges, because gender roles still operate in binary forms, and if women demonstrate a spiritual side, they are portrayed as emotional and not capable of being in decision-making positions in politics:

> A woman is treated exclusively as an emotional being. If she seeks spirituality, it's not considered strong enough to make political

decisions, to be economically independent, and I see cynicism and a kind of exclusivity... legal equality is there, which is emphasized, I think there is not enough space for a multitude of different concepts of religiosity and spirituality. (Biba, university teacher, Sarajevo)

FEMINIST SPIRITUALITY AS PRACTICE

The greatest level of spirituality for some women is actions, good deeds, and kindness, in accordance with the Qur'anic principle (Q. 2:148) of competing in good deeds. Practicing *adab*[28] and living the religio-spiritual life through giving and showing solidarity with good causes are core values informing the activism of these women.[29] One of the faith-based activists explained why doing is the "real" sacrifice for her:

> Sometimes I meditate, sometimes I have... admiration for God, the connection with nature is always important, but what truly fulfills me and where I see the meaning of it is... if I do something. So, for me, it's about action... where I then see the meaning... to truly sacrifice, not to complain, not to pity myself on that path. (Fatma, faith-based activist, Sarajevo)

Prayers and meditations are an important part of life, and all the women interviewed pray either in the form of obligatory prayers (*salat*) in the Arabic language, or their own prayers in their mother-tongue, Bosnian language. The most common prayer is *Bism Allah al-Rahman al-Rahim* (In the Name of Allah, Most Gracious, Most Merciful), and these women start the day and their activities with this sentence, which is a constant reminder of God's presence:

> Literally in everyday life... when I step out onto the street... I start with "bismillah," when I go to sleep, I recite it, I think it's very, very important to me... and I still believe that there's no need for me to express it visibly, but it's something that makes me stronger in what I do. (Nuna, journalist, Sarajevo)

Those who pray regularly discuss how these prayers help them to function and calm down during the day, and that they experience relief and catharsis through prayer:

> Namaz (daily prayer) is my daily routine, and as the years go by, I completely thank God to help disconnect. It really agrees with me,

---

[28] Kostadinova, "Edep."
[29] Aunne, *Feminist Spirituality as Lived Religion*, 52.

and it's my routine that really helps me function better. (Delila, university teacher, Tuzla)

Somehow you always feel somewhat lighter, cleansed when you perform prayer or give charity. (Iman, actress, Zenica)

One woman described daily prayers as a tool that helps deepen her relationship with God. For this reason, she sometimes attends her local mosque, where imams welcome everyone, both women and men, to recite the Qur'an together or to sing *mawlid* songs in celebration of the Prophet's birthday or on other occasions. She observed differences between the main city mosques and local ones. In the big city mosques, men dominate, and all the rituals are conducted exclusively by men. In contrast, local mosques, especially in suburban and rural areas, embrace practices that are more gender-inclusive, allowing women to participate in reciting the Qur'an and singing spiritual songs during the celebration of religious holidays or family-related rituals:

> It's important for me to perform those rituals. I mentioned these because they deepen my relationship with God. I love going to the mosque, it's very dear to me, and I make an effort to make space in my life to attend prayers at the mosque... even when it's hectic, for example, I regularly attend the *muqabala* [face-to-face meeting to discuss] during Ramadan every day, because the *muqabala* is after the afternoon prayer, because I find it beautiful, because we all learn together... and the imam allows us all to learn, that's nice, it's a nice feeling, I attend the *mawlid* [events celebrating the birth anniversary of the Prophet], and we all learn together. (Ilma, faith-based activist)

The above-mentioned *muqabala* is a ritual practice organized usually during Ramadan time, when in many mosques believers gather to recite portions of the Qur'anic text, and before Eid (*Bayram*) they finish the reading and organize *khatma-i-dua* (final prayer) to mark the end of the month-long ritual. In addition to the Ramadan *muqabala*, the women interviewed mentioned other types of prayer, including online *muqabala* they organize with groups of friends and acquaintances. Women who want to learn to recite the Qur'an in Arabic participate in special circles that help them to master the Arabic alphabet and the reading rules (*tajwid*):

> Well, um, I've been attending an online *muqabala* for some time now ... it's a women's *muqabala*, and it's something that really agrees with me, it happens twice a week. (Dina, activist, Sarajevo)

Some women mentioned online spiritual practices in which they participate twice a month, and they include *dhikr* (remembrance) with God's beautiful names, sending blessings on the Prophet Muhammad (*salawat*), and reciting some chapters from the Qur'an, such as the *Sura Yasin* and some other, shorter chapters, as well as singing religious songs and reading Rumi's poetry.

Some women developed their own routine of meditative practices that are deeply rooted in Sufism and the concept of Divine Love that is for them overarching and the greatest power in the universe. Reading Sufi literature, specifically Rumi's poetry, visiting shrines, listening to the recitation of the Qur'an, and finding connections with nature is individually tailored spiritual practice:

> Whenever it's Ramadan, I have the Qur'an recorded ... on my phone and laptop, then, a few days before Ramadan, I play it for twenty-four hours, it brings a nice harmony into my home ... when, for example, I travel somewhere, then I put on headphones, listen from my phone ... That voice, that prayer is a kind of sedative and calming agent and meditation, and so on. The basis for me is Islam. I really love Rumi, I've been to Konya [Turkey] four times already, I'll go again ... it's a special experience and I don't flaunt it in front of anyone, I don't think it's an advantage or a flaw, but I love it, I feel good about it. (Zehra, activist, Tuzla)

> When I need to clear my mind and when I feel exhausted, I go for a walk in the mountains or around the river. Trees and water make me calm, and I enjoy being in nature, which is also a revelation of God. (Fatma, faith-based activist, Sarajevo)

DE-INSTITUTIONALIZED FEMINIST SPIRITUALITIES

Feminist spirituality as lived religio-spiritual experiences of my respondents is thus de-institutionalized. It means that the majority of them, although fully or partially observant in religion, do not declare any belonging to the Islamic Community. Some even pay annual membership, but they do not actively participate in their activities. They go to mosque only in cases of death rituals (*janazah*) or to attend some other family rituals, and they do not uncritically follow the mainstream interpretations of Islam but have their own individualized understanding of faith. Grace Davie's thesis "believing without belonging" is applicable, but, as Davie warns, these two categories "are not to be considered too rigidly," because the whole idea of "believing without belonging" is "to capture a mood, to suggest an area of enquiry, a way of looking at the problem, not to describe a detailed set of characteristics."[30]

Unlike in some Western European contexts, traditional religion in BiH has not been in decline, but has revived since the late 1980s, and flourished with ethno-national and ethno-religious political structures in power. Formal identification with religion in BiH is over 85 per cent.[31] However, it is hard to measure someone's religiosity or spirituality, especially if people keep their religion private. The majority of the women from among my respondents do not attend mosque services, and they do not express their personal religious views in public. Their religio-spiritual life is private, except for a minority who wear hijab.

The de-institutionalization of religio-spiritual life started during the socialist period. The majority of Muslim families, specifically in urban areas, accepted the socialist fashion of life as workers and respected members of the working class. Those who held important positions in the society were expected to leave off religion, including attending services in mosques. One of the women recalled what happened to her father, who was the CEO of a big company in their city:

> I remember well the moment when my mom told me that my dad no longer works in that job, that he's not in a managerial position any more ... It was only, for example, about ten years ago when I found out from my brother that he was dismissed because he went to his father's funeral. (Jasmina, journalist, Sarajevo)

Religion was not prohibited, and from the 1970s all religious communities and churches could organize their educational and other activities,[32] but it was not popular or in line with Communist ideology to be a practicing believer. Religion was perceived as something backward and an obstacle to internalizing brotherhood and an ideology of unity. Families who were better educated cultivated secular humanist values.

In many families Islam was not observed, except for celebrating holidays, giving children Muslim names, giving *sadaqat al-fitr* (almsgiving

---

[30] Grace Davie, *Religion in Britain since 1945: Believing without Belonging* (Blackwell: Oxford, 1994), 93.

[31] Dino Abazović, "Religious Nationalism in the Western Balkans," in *Religion and Neo-nationalism in Europe*, ed. Florian Höhne and Torsten Meireis (Baden-Baden: Nomos Verlagsgesellschaft, 2020), 321–332; Hans-Dieter Klingemann, WV4World Values Survey, "Bosnia and Herzegovina Crossings by Sex and Age," www.nomos-el ibrary.de/10.5771/9783748905059/religion-and-neo-nationalism-in-europe?page=1.

[32] S. Sead Fetahagić, "Islam in Socialism and Post-Socialism", in *Contesting Female, Feminist and Muslim Identities*, ed. Šiljak, 111–125.

during Ramadan), and not eating pork. Alcohol was acceptable, and it had been culturally justified since Ottoman times, and hence many Muslims drank alcohol, stopping only during the month of Ramadan. Disassociation from the institution of the Islamic Community continued after the war in BiH, because these socially engaged women who rediscovered Islam as adults in that period have not accepted the politicization of religion, conservativism, the retraditionalization of gender roles, interference in reproductive rights, and the commercialization of religion:

> I would like religious institutions not to deeply involve themselves in politics in terms of managing political processes. (Biba, university teacher, Sarajevo)

The politicization of religion is not a new phenomenon, but in the Balkans in the 1990s, after the collapse of socialism, religious institutions started to play a crucial role in identity politics and nation-state building. They imposed themselves "as moral guardians of the nations (each religious tradition), as educators (by becoming a part of regular schooling), and a mobilizing agency for all the different kinds of political goals."[33] Due to the overwhelming politicization of religion during and after the war, many socially engaged activists find it disturbing and divisive when religious communities engage in day-to-day politics:

> I believe that religion must be completely separated from sociopolitical governance ... not to involve itself in everyday political events ... and religious institutions must be more open to the communities surrounding them, and in the context of Bosnia and Herzegovina, which has certain values that can be transferred to other communities, that interreligious dialogue must exist and be nurtured. (Sena, activist, Sarajevo)

However, some activists rationalize the overlapping of ethnic and religious identities, and the emphasis on religion, particularly among Bosniaks/Muslims who experienced genocide in Srebrenica and who were the biggest victims of the war (1992–5). They found refuge in religion and used it as a coping and defense mechanism in the postwar recovery. These people have been facing a denial of crimes against them and a struggle for their ethnic and religious rights in the places where they returned to their pre-war homes, and religion

---

[33] Gorana Ognjenović and Jasna Jozelić, *Politicization of Religion, the Power of Symbolism: The Case of Former Yugoslavia and Its Successor States* (New York: Palgrave Macmillan, 2014), xviii.

happens to help them to persevere despite all the hardships they have been through:

> Religion was the Bosniaks' only lifeline in every respect. I really understand those people ... no one directly from my family suffered during the war, and that's rare luck. (Zehra, activist, Tuzla)

Another reason for the disassociation from the Islamic Community is the misuse of religion and religious sentiments to cover up corruption, lack of expertise, and arrogance, which many of the women interviewed found very disturbing. A journalist activist who has received awards for her groundbreaking stories on corruption in state institutions disclosed that she was disappointed when she learned how religious institutions were also engaged in corruption. Many of these women argued that religious institutions are run by people who lack expertise, knowledge, and credibility, and send the wrong message to the public and to believers:

> Here, religion is misunderstood, and I believe that at this moment, everyone is exploiting religion ... Behind religion are ... ignorant individuals, criminals, so religion has become everything it shouldn't be in our ... truly failed society. (Jasmina, journalist, Sarajevo)

Conservativism is another reason for these women's decision to disassociate from organized religion, referring to the changes they have seen when they compare the pre-war socialist and post-socialist periods. For them, the rigid interpretations of their faith represent its politicization. They also thought that popular online preachers who studied in Saudi Arabi and brought back modernist, conservative interpretations of Islam have had an impact on society. For them, conservativism is closely connected to a re-traditionalization of gender roles,[34] justifying the subordination of women to men based on an idealized, patriarchal cosmology of gender relations.[35]

The women were highly vocal in their criticism of the use of religion to discriminate against, exclude, and patronize women:

> However, as soon as I step out of that bubble a bit, there's this imposition of how you should live, who you should live with, how

---

[34] Danijela Majstorović, "What It Means to Be a Bosnian Woman," in *Living with Patriarchy: Discursive Constructions of Gendered Subjects across Cultures*, ed. Danijela Majstorović and Inger Lassen (Philadelphia: John Benjamins, 2011), 81–109; Spahić Šiljak, "Women, Religion and Politics"; Spahić Šiljak and Đipa, *Gender Equality Barometer*.

[35] Ayesha S. Chaudhry, *Domestic Violence and the Islamic Tradition: Ethics, Law, and the Muslim Discourse on Gender* (Oxford: Oxford University Press, 2013).

you should dress, how you shouldn't dress, whether it's for you, whether it's not for you ... And that comes from these religious circles, but I don't think they're religious, I think it comes from ignorance, from not knowing about true religion and spirituality. (Anita, activist, Sarajevo)

I don't practice religion in the designated places for it, not in mosques or places of worship, but I'm focused on myself and my home because I don't trust what I hear from them, they in no way affirm the position of women or encourage women to emancipate in any way and stand shoulder to shoulder with them. (Aida, poetess, Tešanj)

One of the faith-based activists was of the view that the main reason patriarchal interpretations of Islam are still in force and that it is hard to make changes in the mainstream teachings that affect the new generation through Islamic religious education in public schools is because of the financial and symbolic capital[36] invested in the hierarchical and patriarchal structures of the Islamic Community. Noting that it is not profitable for those at the top to change the narrative and advocate for change, she commented:

I think there are too many people invested in the existing interpretations and they're not willing to depart from those interpretations ... and they'll lose the capital they've built, which suits them. So, when someone says, "Look, it's not like that any more," one house of cards falls, one structure within which someone earns on that structure ... but I think there are from symbolic capital to ... various kinds of financial capital, material capital, from that someone lives, has a position ... has a reputation ... they won't be called any more to speak, won't make money from it any more if we now introduce an alternative interpretation, alternative understanding, broader and different. (Ilma, faith-based activist, Sarajevo)

Reproductive rights are also part of the re-traditionalization trends, because nationalist and religious communities are critical of socialism for disrupting the traditional family order. These groups maintain that if the nation is to survive, women must resume their traditional roles as "keepers of the private sphere."[37] Debates in the

---

[36] Pierre Bourdieu, *Masculine Domination*, trans. Richard Nice (Palo Alto: Stanford University Press, 2002).

[37] Spahić Šiljak, "Women, Religion and Politics," 121–136, 125.

BiH parliament about in vitro fertilization and other artificial reproductive techniques have faced resistance from the religious communities and included discussions about reproductive rights that were guaranteed in the Constitution of Yugoslavia of 1974. These women want to keep the rights they have acquired, and criticize any interference from religious communities in these matters:

> And I am appalled by the fact that some cantons, you know, when asked about practices of abortion from an institutional position, respond that it is religiously prohibited. I am not interested in that because our system is secular, our healthcare is comprehensive ... So, religious beliefs must not be obstacles for all others and different ones, all others who want their legal rights to be respected. (Sena, activist, Sarajevo)

Finally, all the women interviewed mentioned that they were not comfortable with the commercialization of faith in the media and in public places.[38] For them, religion is something intimate and beautiful, and should not be commercialized and sold like any other product. All of them emphasized that there is too much formal religiosity in public, such as *iftar* dinners (opening the fast during Ramadan) in sports arenas or in the main squares, or the commercializing of fasting in the media. Such activities, in the view of these women, reduce one of the key principles of the faith to food and music, whereas fasting should be about solidarity, humility, and cultivating the soul to be in a state of *taqwa* and equilibrium, which is critical to Islam:

> First, faith is a private matter, and then faith should not be turned into a spectacle in the public sphere and made a circus out of, because I believe that in everything, including demonstrating faith or religiosity in the public space ... that moderation in everything is important. (Delila, university teacher, Tuzla)

> I am somewhat in favor of a civil state, secular, where one does not wave it around in public life like a flag, giving me the permission not to do something in its name, or God forbid, to do something in its name. (Myra, actress, Sarajevo)

---

[38] Belma Buljubašić, "Analiza jednog intervjua: Estradizacija religije u političke svrhe" [An Analysis of an Interview: Commercializing Religion for Political Purposes], *Analiziraj.ba*, April 15, 2022, https://analiziraj.ba/analiza-jednog-intervjua-estradizacija-religije-u-politicke-svrhe/.

One the visible signs of religion is the hijab, which is a very controversial issue in public life, and there is a ban on women wearing hijab if they work in state, judicial, or military institutions. An increasing number of Muslim women have started to wear hijab, during and after the war. My respondents were of the view that freedom of religion should be defended, and no one has the right to impose or forbid a certain dress code; however, some of them disclosed an uneasiness about an overemphasis on hijab and judgemental attitiudes towards those women who do not wear it:

> Unfortunately, there has been a sudden surge in the expression of religion, and it has even been trivialized to some extent. We cannot deny anyone the right to feel as they want to feel and express their religiosity ... I am against prohibitions such as not wearing head coverings; you don't have the right to demand that. But there must be some social measure ... I respect everyone ... women who have chosen to be covered ... but I don't like it when they start waving that around and expect to have more rights or expect something more just because they have made that choice. (Zehra, activist, Tuzla)

My respondents who do wear hijab, such as faith-based activists and one who is a university teacher, although they were against the politicization and commercialization of religion, do not find any problem with wearing hijab in public institutions. In their understanding, it does not violate the principles of secularism, if those who wear it respect their civil rights and responsibilities:

> So basically, I am who I am, I live as I live, and I exist as a citizen of this country. I have a contract with this state, I have a passport, I must respect certain obligations, and I have certain rights and responsibilities, and that's how I exist. If I don't bother anyone else, I really don't see any problem with existing the way I do. (Ilma, faith-based activist, Sarajevo)

All of my respondents expressed criticism of the politicization of religion and its superficial, commercialized application. For them, freedom of religious expression, especially through wearing the hijab as a visible symbol of faith, is entirely justified. The majority, however, believed that religion should remain a private matter, with one's religious and spiritual life manifesting itself through actions, behavior, and responsible citizenship.

CONCLUSION

Through my engagement with Muslim women active in feminist movements in Bosnia and Herzegovina (BiH), I have endeavored to illustrate the nature of feminist spirituality as a practiced religion within the post-socialist landscape of BiH. This spirituality, either wholly or partly distanced from institutionalized religion, is characterized by its relational aspect and its focus on the practical application of Islam's ethical teachings. Central to this spirituality are the principles of *tawhid* (the oneness of God), *taqwa* (God-conscious piety), and *tawakkul* (relying on God). For these women, feminism and Islam are complementary, yet they challenge the socially conservative or strict interpretations of Islam propagated by traditional institutions that curtail women's autonomy. They argue that such interpretations contravene the spiritual principles of Islam listed above.

The war between 1991 and 1995, or the loss of loved ones, was a pivotal moment for these women, leading them to re-evaluate their faith and purpose in life. Their religious and spiritual lives have been influenced by a combination of socialist and post-socialist secular education, their activism, and their feminist beliefs. Additionally, their primary religious socialization, along with the heritage of the Sufi interpretations of Islam, has shaped their activism and professional lives. As a result, the agency of Muslim women in BiH is formed by their responses to discrimination in both secular and religious contexts, fostering a feminist spirituality characterized by solidarity, a dedication to goodness, and a commitment to combating all forms of discrimination. This approach mirrors the broader feminist movement's diverse tactics in striving for gender equality and empowerment.

SELECT BIBLIOGRAPHY

Abazović, Dino. "Religious Nationalism in the Western Balkans." In *Religion and Neo-nationalism in Europe*, ed. Florian Höhne and Torsten Meireis, 321–332. Baden-Baden: Nomos Verlagsgesellschaft, 2020.

Ašćerić-Tod, Ines. *Derwishes and Islam in Bosnia: Sufi Dimensions to the Formation of Bosnian Muslim Society*. Leiden, Boston: Brill, 2015.

Aunne, Kristin. "Feminist Spirituality as Lived Religion: How UK Feminists Forge Religio-spiritual Lives." In *Secular Societies, Spiritual Selves?: The Gendered Triangle of Religion, Secularity and Spirituality*, ed. Anna Fedele and Kim E. Knibbe, 39–57. London, New York: Routledge, 2020.

Lerner, Gerda. *The Creation of Feminist Consciousness from the Middle Ages to the Eighteenth Century*. Oxford: Oxford University Press, 1993.

Majstorović, Danijela and Lassen, Inger, eds. *Living with Patriarchy: Discursive Constructions of Gendered Subjects across Cultures*. Amsterdam: John Benjamins, 2011.
Malcolm, Noel. *Bosnia: A Short History*. London: Pen Books, 2002.
McGuire, Meredith B. *Lived Religion: Faith and Practice in Everyday Life*. Oxford: Oxford University Press, 2008.
Ognjenović, Gorana and Jozelić, Jasna. *Politicization of Religion, the Power of Symbolism: The Case of Former Yugoslavia and Its Successor States*. New York: Palgrave Macmillan, 2014.
Ramet, Sabina, ed. *Gender Politics in the Western Balkans: Women in Society in Yugoslavia and the Yugoslav Successor States*. Philadelphia: Penn State University Press, 1999.
Redfern, Catherine and Aunne, Kristin. *Reclaiming the F Word*. London, New York: Zed Books, 2013.
Shakman Hurd, Elizabeth. *Beyond Religious Freedom: The New Global Politics of Religion*. Princeton: Princeton University Press, 2015.
Spahić Šiljak, Zilka. *Women, Religion and Politics: Impact Analysis of Interpretative Religious Heritage of Judaism, Christianity and Islam on the Engagement of Women in Public Life and Politics*. Sarajevo: IMIC-CIPS-TPO, 2010.
    "Women, Religion and Politics." In *Religion, the Secular, and the Politics of Sexual Difference*, ed. Linell E. Cady and Tracy Fessenden, 121–136. New York: Columbia University Press, 2013.
Spahić Šiljak, Zilka, ed. *Contesting Female, Feminist and Muslim Identities in Bosnia and Herzegovina and Kosovo*. Sarajevo: Center for Interdisciplinary Postgraduate Studies of the University of Sarajevo, 2012.
Spahić Šiljak, Zilka and Dino, Đipa. *Gender Equality Barometer of Bosnia and Herzegovina*. Sarajevo: United Nations Development Programme, 2024.

Volume Bibliography

Abazović, Dino. "Religious Nationalism in the Western Balkans." In *Religion and Neo-nationalism in Europe*, ed. Florian Höhne and Torsten Meireis, 321–332. Baden-Baden: Nomos Verlagsgesellschaft, 2020.

Abdul Kodir, Faqihuddin. *Hadith and Gender Justice: Understanding the Prophetic Traditions*. Cirebon: Fahmina Institute, 2007.

——— "*Qirā'ah Mubādalah*: Reciprocal Reading of Hadith on Marital Relationships." In *Justice and Beauty in Muslim Marriage: Towards Egalitarian Ethics and Laws*, ed. Ziba Mir-Hosseini, Mulki al-Sharmani, Jana Rumminger, and Sarah Marsso, 181–212. London: Oneworld Publications, 2022.

Abdul Rahman, Aisha. "The Islamic Conception of Women's Liberation." *Al-Raida* (1970): 37–43.

Abu El Fadl, Khaled. *Speaking in God's Name: Islamic Law, Authority and Women*. Oxford: Oneworld, 2001.

Abu-Lughod, Lila. *Do Muslim Women Need Saving?* Cambridge, MA: Harvard University Press, 2013.

——— "Do Muslim Women Really Need Saving? Anthropological Reflections on Cultural Relativism and Its Others." *American Anthropologist* 104, no. 3 (2002): 783–790.

——— *Veiled Sentiments: Honor and Poetry in a Bedouin Society*. Berkeley: University of California Press, 1986.

Ahmad, Attiya. "Explanation Is Not the Point: Domestic Work, Islamic *Da'wa* and Becoming Muslim in Kuwait." *The Asia Pacific Journal of Anthropology* 11, nos. 3–4 (2010): 293–310.

Akhtar, Sabeena, ed. *Cut from the Same Cloth*. London: Unbound, 2020.

Ali, Kecia. *Sexual Ethics and Islam: Feminist Reflections on Qur'an, Hadith, and Jurisprudence*. Oxford: Oneworld Publications, 2006.

Amin, Yasmin. "Umm Salama: A Female Authority Legitimating the Authorities." In *Female Religious Authority in Shi'i Islam: Past and Present*, ed. Mirjam Künkler and Devin J. Stewart, 47–77. Edinburgh: Edinburgh University Press, 2021.

Anwar, Etin. *A Genealogy of Islamic Feminism: Pattern and Change in Indonesia*. Oxford: Routledge, 2018.

Armstrong, Karen. *Muhammad: A Prophet for Our Time*. San Francisco: HarperOne, 2007.

Arthur M. Sackler Gallery, Smithsonian Institution. Special issue: "Patronage by Women in Islamic Art." *Asian Art* (spring 1994).

Ašćerić-Tod, Ines. *Derwishes and Islam in Bosnia: Sufi Dimensions to the Formation of Bosnian Muslim Society*. Leiden, Boston: Brill, 2015.
Ascha, Ghassan. "The 'Mothers of the Believers': Stereotypes of the Prophet Muhammad's Wives." In *Female Stereotypes in Religious Traditions*, ed. Ria Kloppenborg and Wouter J. Hanegraaff, 89–107. Leiden: Brill, 1995.
Ashraf, Hasan. *The Prophet's Marriage to Zaynab bint Jahsh: A Reexamination from a Historiographic Perspective*, Yaqeen Institute. March 2, 2023. https://yaqeeninstitute.org/read/paper/the-prophets-marriage-to-zaynab-bint-jahsh
Aunne, Kristin. "Feminist Spirituality as Lived Religion: How UK Feminists Forge Religio-spiritual Lives." In *Secular Societies, Spiritual Selves?: The Gendered Triangle of Religion, Secularity and Spirituality*, ed. Anna Fedele and Kim E. Knibbe, 39–57. London, New York: Routledge, 2020.
Avishai, Orit. "'Doing Religion' in a Secular World: Women in Conservative Religions and the Question of Agency." *Gender & Society* 22 (2008): 409–433.
Ayyad, Essam S. "The 'House of the Prophet' or the 'Mosque of the Prophet'?" *Journal of Islamic Studies* 24, no. 3 (2013): 273–344.
el-Badawi, Emran Iqbal. *Queens and Prophets: How Arabian Noblewomen and Holy Men Shaped Paganism, Christianity, and Islam*. London: Oneworld, 2022.
Badran, Margot. "Political Islam and Gender." In *The Oxford Handbook of Islam and Politics*, ed. John L. Esposito and Emad el-Din Shahin, 112–124. Oxford: Oxford University Press, 2013.
Bano, Masooda. *Female Islamic Education Movements: The Re-democratisation of Islamic Knowledge*. Cambridge: Cambridge University Press, 2017.
    The Revival of Islamic Rationalism: Logic, Metaphysics and Mysticism in Modern Muslim Societies. Cambridge: Cambridge University Press, 2019.
Bano, Masooda and Kalmbach, Hilary E., eds. *Women, Leadership, and Mosques: Changes in Contemporary Islamic Authority*. Leiden, Boston: Brill, 2012.
Bardan, Margot. *Feminism in Islam: Secular and Religious Convergences*. Oxford: Oneworld Publications, 2009.
Barlas, Asma. *Believing Women in Islam: Unreading Patriarchal Interpretations of the Qur'an*. Austin, TX: University of Texas Press, 2002.
Bauer, Karen. *Gender Hierarchy in the Qur'an: Medieval Interpretations, Modern Responses*. Cambridge: Cambridge University Press, 2015.
Bauer, Karen and Hamza, Feras. "Qur'anic Morality as Qur'anic Law (What Is Qur'anic Law?)" Forthcoming in *Regulative Verses of the Qur'an: From Historical Trends to Contemporary Trajectories*, ed. Karen Bauer, Mohammed Fatemi, Robert Gleave, and Devin Stewart.
    Women, Households, and the Hereafter in the Qur'an: A Patronage of Piety. Oxford: Oxford University Press, 2023.
Beng, Tan Sooi. "Singing Islamic Modernity: Recreating Nasyid in Malaysia." *Kyoto Review of Southeast Asia* 8–9 (March 2007), https://kyotoreview.org/issue-8-9/singing-islamic-modernity-recreating-nasyid-in-malaysia/.
Bennett, Clinton. *Muslim Women of Power: Gender, Politics and Culture in Islam*. New York: Continuum, 2010.
Bhutto, Benazir. *Reconciliation: Islam, Democracy, and the West*. New York: Harper Perennial, 2008.
Biagini, Erika. "The Egyptian Muslim Sisterhood between Violence, Activism and Leadership." *Mediterranean Politics* 22, no. 1 (2017): 35–53.

"Islamist Women's Activism under Morsi's Government (2011–2013): Political Inclusion, Gender and Discourse." *Égypte/Monde arabe* 21 (2020): 37–55.

Bint al-Shati, *Wives of the Prophet*. Trans. Matti Moosa. New Jersey: Gorgias Press, 2006.

Blessing, Patricia. "Buildings of Commemoration in Medieval Anatolia: The Funerary Complexes of Ṣāḥib 'Aṭā Fakhr al-Dīn 'Alī and Māhperī Khātūn." *Al-Masāq* 27, no. 3 (2014): 225–252.

Bloom, Jonathan. "The Mosque of Qarafa in Cairo." *Muqarnas* 4 (1987): 7–20.

Bonci, Alessandra. "*Ilmi* Salafi Women in Tunisia after the Revolution: What Kind of Quietism?," *Contemporary Islam* 17, no. 2 (2023): 243–262.

Booth, Marilyn. *The Career and Communities of Zaynab Fawwaz: Feminist Thinking in Fin-de-Siècle Egypt*. New York: Oxford University Press, 2021.

Classes of Ladies of Cloistered Spaces: Writing Feminist History through Biography in Fin-de-Siècle Egypt. Edinburgh: Edinburgh University Press, 2015.

Brant, Jennifer. "Aboriginal Mothering: Honouring the Past, Nurturing the Future." In *Mothers, Mothering and Motherhood across Cultural Differences: A Reader*, ed. Andrea O'Reilly, 7–40. Bradford: Demeter Press, 2014.

Brocket, Adrian, trans. *The History of al-Tabari, Volume XVI: The Community Divided*. Albany: State University of New York Press, 1997.

Brookshaw, Dominic Parviz. "Odes of a Poet-Princess: The Ghazals of Jahān-Malik Khātūn." *Iran* 43 (2005): 173–195.

"Qajar Confection: The Production and Dissemination of Women's Poetry in Early Nineteenth-Century Iran." *Middle Eastern Literatures* 17 (2014): 113–146.

Brookshaw, Dominic P. and Rahimieh, Nasrin, eds. *Forugh Farrokhzad, Poet of Modern Iran: Iconic Woman and Feminine Pioneer of New Persian Poetry*. London: I. B. Tauris, 2021.

Brown, Jonathan A. C. *Muhammad: A Very Short Introduction*. Oxford, New York: Oxford University Press, 2011.

Bullock, Katherine. *Rethinking Muslim Women and the Veil: Challenging Historical and Modern Stereotypes*. 2nd ed. London: International Institute of Islamic Thought, 2007.

Chaudhry, Ayesha S. *Domestic Violence and the Islamic Tradition: Ethics, Law, and the Muslim Discourse on Gender*. Oxford: Oxford University Press, 2013.

Clark, Janine. "The Conditions of Islamist Moderation: Unpacking Cross-Ideological Cooperation in Jordan." *International Journal of Middle East Studies* 38, no. 4 (2006): 539–560.

Clohessy, Christopher Paul. *Angels Hastening: The Karbala Dreams*. New Jersey: Gorgias Press, 2021.

Cook, Michael. *Commanding Right and Forbidding Wrong in Islamic Thought*. Cambridge: Cambridge University Press, 2000.

Cortese, Delia and Calderini, Simonetta. "The Architectural Patronage of the Fāṭimid Queen-Mother Durzān (d. 385/995): An Interdisciplinary Analysis of Literary Sources, Material Evidence and Historical Context." In *Material Evidence and Narrative Sources: Interdisciplinary Studies of the History of* the *Muslim Middle East*, ed. Daniella Talmon-Heller and Katia Cytryn-Silverman, 7–112. Leiden: Brill, 2014.

Cotee, Joost, trans. *Letters from Kartini: An Indonesian Feminist (1900–1904)*. Clayton, Victoria: Monash Asia Institute, 1992.

Davitashvili, Ana. "The Inner-Qur'ānic Development of the Images of Women in Paradise: From the *ḥūr ʿīn* to Believing Women." *Journal of the International Qur'anic Studies Association* 7 (2022): 27–54.

de Cillis, Maria. *Free Will and Predestination in Islamic Thought: Theoretical Compromises in the Work of Avicenna, al-Ghazālī and Ibn ʿArabī*. Abingdon: Routledge, 2013.

de Koning, M. J. M. *Changing Worldviews and Friendship: An Exploration of the Life Stories of Two Female Salafists in the Netherlands*. Oxford: Oxford University Press, 2009.

Dhala, Mahjabeen. *Feminist Theology and Social Justice in Islam: A Study on the Sermon of Fatima*. Cambridge: Cambridge University Press, 2024.

Dutton, Yasin. "Conversion to Islam: The Qur'anic Paradigm." In *Religious Conversion. Contemporary Practices and Controversies*, ed. Christopher Lamb and Darroll Bryant, 151–166. London: Cassell, 1999.

Eastmond, Antony. *Tamta's World: The Life and Encounters of a Medieval Noblewoman from the Middle East to Mongolia*. Cambridge: Cambridge University Press, 2017.

Elias, Jamal J. "Prophecy, Power and Propriety: The Encounter of Solomon and the Queen of Sheba." *Journal of Qur'anic Studies* 11, no. 1 (2009): 57–74.

Engineer, Asghar Ali. *The Rights of Women in Islam*. London: C. Hurst & Co., 1992.

Esholdt, Henriette Frees. "The Attractions of Salafi–Jihadism as a Gendered Counterculture: Propaganda Narratives from the Swedish Online 'Sisters in Deen'." In *Salafi–Jihadism and Digital Media*, ed. Magnus Ranstorp, Linda Ahlerup, and Filip Ahlin, 66–91. London: Routledge, 2022.

Fadel, Mohammad. "Is Historicism a Viable Strategy for Islamic Law Reform? The Case of 'Never Shall a Folk Prosper Who Have Appointed a Woman to Rule Them'." *Islamic Law and Society* 18, no. 2 (2011): 131–176.

Findly, Ellison Banks. *Nur Jahan: Empress of Mughal India*. New York: Oxford University Press, 1993.

Gabbay, Alyssa. "Heiress to the Prophet: Fatima's Khutba as an Early Case of Female Religious Authority in Islam." In *Female Religious Authority in Shiʻi Islam: Past and Present*, ed. Mirjam Künkler and Devin J. Stewart, 78–104. Edinburgh: Edinburgh University Press, 2021.

Geissinger, Aisha. *Gender and Muslim Constructions of Exegetical Authority: A Rereading of the Classical Genre of Qur'an Commentary*. Leiden: Brill, 2015.

al-Ghazālī, Abū Ḥāmid. *The Book of Prophetic Ethics and the Courtesies of Living*. Trans. Adi Setia. Louisville: Fons Vitae, 2019.

Ha, Guangtian. *The Sound of Salvation: Voice, Gender, and the Sufi Mediascape in China*. New York: Columbia University Press, 2022.

Hallaq, Wael. *Authority, Continuity, and Change in Islamic Law*. Cambridge: Cambridge University Press, 2004.

Hambly, Gavin, ed. *Women in the Medieval Islamic World*. New York: St. Martin's Press, 1998.

Hammond, Marlé. *Beyond Elegy: Classical Arabic Women's Poetry in Context*. Oxford: Oxford University Press for the British Academy, 2010.

Hanafi, Sari and Tomeh, Azzam. "Gender Equality in the Inheritance Debate in Tunisia and the Formation of Non-Authoritarian Reasoning." *Journal of Islamic Ethics* 3 (2019): 207–232.

Hanif, Sohail. "A Theory of Early Classical Ḥanafism: Authority, Rationality and Tradition in the *Hidāyah* of Burhān al-Dīn 'Alī ibn Abī Bakr al-Marghīnānī (d. 593/1197)." D.Phil. diss., University of Oxford, 2017.

Harris, Rachel, *Soundscapes of Uyghur Islam*. Bloomington: Indiana University Press, 2020.

Harris, Rachel and Jaschok, Maria. "Introduction: Sounding Islam in China." *Performing Islam* 3, nos. 1–2 (2014): 11–21.

Harris, Rachel, Guangtian Ha, and Jaschok, Maria, eds. *Ethnographies of Islam in China*. Honolulu: University of Hawai'i Press, 2021.

Haylamaz, Resit and Harpci, Fatih. *The Sultan of Hearts: Prophet Muhammad*. Clifton, NJ: Tughra Books, 2020.

Hélie, Anissa and Hoodfar, Homa, eds. *Sexuality in Muslim Contexts: Restrictions and Resistance*. London: Zed Books, 2012.

Hibri, Azizah al-. *Women and Islam*. Oxford, Sydney: Pergamon Press, 1982.

Hidayatullah, Aysha. *Feminist Edges of the Qur'an*. Oxford: Oxford University Press, 2014.

Horii, Satoe. "Reconsideration of Legal Devices (*Ḥiyal*) in Islamic Jurisprudence: The Hanafis and Their 'Exits' (*Makhārij*)." *Islamic Law and Society* 9, no. 3 (2002): 312–357.

Ibn Hishām, 'Abd al-Malik. *The Life of Muhammad*. Trans. Alfred Guillaume. Karachi: Oxford University Press, 2011.

Ibn Musa al-Yahsubi, Qadi 'Iyad. *Muhammad, Messenger of Allah: Ash-Shifa of Qadi 'Iyad*. Trans. Aisha Bewley. Bolton: Madinah Press, 2014.

Ibn Sayyid an-Nās, Abū'l-Fatḥ Muḥammad. *Nūr al-'Uyūn: The Light of the Eyes*. London: Turath Publishing, 2016.

Ibrahim, Celene. "Introduction." *Journal of Feminist Studies in Religion* 39, no. 2 (2023): 57.

"Of Poets and Jesters: Methodologies and Reception Politics in Qur'anic Studies." *Journal of Feminist Studies in Religion* 39, no. 2 (2023): 79–81.

Women and Gender in the Qur'an. Oxford: Oxford University Press, 2020.

Inge, Anabel. *The Making of a Salafi Muslim Woman: Paths to Conversion*. Oxford: Oxford University Press, 2016.

Ismah, Nor. "Women Issuing Fatwas: Female Islamic Scholars and Community-Based Authority in Java, Indonesia." Ph.D. diss., Leiden University, 2023.

Jacobsen, Sara Jul. "Calling on Women." *Perspectives on Terrorism* 13, no. 4 (2019): 14–26.

Jaschok, Maria. *Inside the Expressive Culture of Chinese Women's Mosques*. London: Routledge, 2025.

"Sources of Authority: Female *Ahong* and *Qingzhen Nüsi*." In *Women, Leadership, and Mosques*, ed. Masooda Bano and Hilary Kalmbach, 37–58. Leiden: Brill, 2012.

Jaschok, Maria and Jingjun, Shui. *The History of Women's Mosques in Chinese Islam*. New York: Curzon/Routledge, 2000.

Women, Religion, and Space in China: Islamic Mosques and Daoist Temples, Catholic Convents and Chinese Virgins. New York: Routledge, 2011.
Jaschok, Maria, Shui, Jingjun, and Caixia, Ge. "Equality, Voice, and a Chinese Hui Muslim Women's Songbook: Collaborative Ethnography and Hui Muslim Women's Expressive History of Faith." In *Ethnographies of Islam in China*, ed. Rachel Harris, Guangtian Ha, and Maria Jaschok. Honolulu: University of Hawai'i Press, 2021.
Jawad, Haifaa. *The Rights of Women in Islam: An Authentic Approach*. London: Palgrave Macmillan, 1998.
Jeenah N. and Shaikh S., eds. *Denying Women Access to the Main Space: A Betrayal of the Prophet*. Cape Town: Full Moon Press, 2000.
Johansen, Baber. *Contingency in a Sacred Law: Legal and Ethical Norms in the Muslim Fiqh*. Leiden: Brill, 1999.
Jørgensen, Kathrine Elmose and Frees Esholdt, Henriette. "'She Is a Woman, She Is an Unbeliever – You Should Not Meet with Her': An Ethnographic Account of Accessing Salafi–Jihadist Environments as Non-Muslim Female Researchers." *Journal of Qualitative Criminal Justice and Criminology* 10, no. 3 (2021): 1.
Jouili, Jeanette. "Beyond Emancipation: Subjectivities and Ethics among Women in Europe's Islamic Revival Communities." *Feminist Review* 98 (2011): 47–64.
Karam, Azza M. *Women, Islamism and the State: Contemporary Feminisms in Egypt*. New York: St. Martin's Press, 1998.
Karaman, Nuray and Christian, Michelle. "'Should I Wear a Headscarf to Be a Good Muslim Woman?': Situated Meanings of the Hijab among Muslim College Women in America." *Sociological Inquiry* 92, no. 1 (2022): 225–243.
Karima, Marzuqa "On the Hermeneutics of the Qur'ānic Verse of *khimār*." *Medium*. Last modified August 23, 2021. https://medium.com/@marzuqa.karima/on-the-hermeneutics-of-the-qur%CA%BE%C4%81nic-verse-of-khim%C4%81r-73f7a43665f1
Katz, Marion. *Wives and Work: Islamic Law and Ethics before Modernity*. New York: Columbia University Press, 2022.
Khalidi, Tarif. *Images of Muhammad: Narratives of the Prophet in Islam across the Centuries*. New York, London: Doubleday, 2009.
Khelghat-Doost, Hamoon. "The Strategic Logic of Women in Jihadi Organizations." *Studies in Conflict and Terrorism* 42, no. 10 (2019): 853–877.
Kolman, Iris. *Gender Activism in Salafism: A Case Study of Salafi Women in Tunis*. Oxford: Oxford University Press, 2017.
Künkler, Mirjam and Stewart, Devin J., eds. *Female Religious Authority in Shi'i Islam: Past and Present*. Edinburgh: Edinburgh University Press, 2021.
Lal, Ruby. *Empress: The Astonishing Reign of Nur Jahan*. New York, London: W. W. Norton, 2018.
Lambert-Hurley, Siobhan. *Elusive Lives: Gender, Autobiography, and the Self in Muslim South Asia*. Stanford: Stanford University Press, 2018.
Lassner, Jacob. *Demonizing the Queen of Sheba: Boundaries of Gender and Culture in Postbiblical Judaism and Medieval Islam*. Chicago: University of Chicago Press, 1993.
le Renard, Amélie. *A Society of Young Women: Opportunities of Place, Power, and Reform in Saudi Arabia*. Stanford: Stanford University Press, 2014.
Lerner, Gerda. *The Creation of Feminist Consciousness from the Middle Ages to the Eighteenth Century*. Oxford: Oxford University Press, 1993.
Li, Gang. "Reasoning the Sharī'a and Constructing a Proper Muslim Woman: Reflections on the Issue of Chinese Muslim Women's Haircut in Republican China." *Journal of Chinese Religions* 50, no. 2 (2022): 185–232.

Lings, Martin. *Muhammad: His Life Based on the Earliest Sources*. Rochester: Inner Traditions, 2006.
Mahendrarajah, Shivan. "The Gawhar Shād Waqf Deed: Public Works and the Commonweal." *Journal of the American Oriental Society* 138, no. 4 (2018): 821–857.
Mahmood, Saba. "Feminist Theory, Embodiment, and the Docile Agent: Some Reflections on the Egyptian Islamic Revival." *Cultural Anthropology* 16, no. 2 (2001): 202–236.
  The Politics of Piety: The Islamic Revival and the Feminist Subject. Princeton: Princeton University Press, 2005.
Majstorović, Danijela and Lassen, Inger, eds. *Living with Patriarchy: Discursive Constructions of Gendered Subjects across Cultures*. Amsterdam: John Benjamins, 2011.
Makboul, Laila. "Beyond Preaching Women: Saudi *Dāʿiyāt* and Their Engagement in the Public Sphere." *Die Welt des Islams* 57, nos. 3–4 (2017): 303–328.
Malcolm, Noel. *Bosnia: A Short History*. London: Pen Books, 2002.
Marín, Manuela. *Mujeres en al-Ándalus*. Madrid: Consejo Superior de Investigaciones Científicas, 2000.
McGinty, Anna Mansson. *Becoming Muslim: Western Women's Conversions to Islam*. New York: Palgrave Macmillan, 2006.
McGuire, Meredith B. *Lived Religion: Faith and Practice in Everyday Life*. Oxford: Oxford University Press, 2008.
Medina, Jameelah. "This Battlefield Called My Body: Warring over the Muslim Female." *Religions (Basel, Switzerland)* 5, no. 3 (2014): 876–885.
Mernissi, Fatima. *Beyond the Veil: Male–Female Dynamics in a Modern Muslim Society*. Bloomington: Indiana University Press, 1975.
  Dreams of Trespass: Tales of a Harem Girlhood. Reading, MA: Addison-Wesley, 1994.
  The Forgotten Queens of Islam. Cambridge: Polity Press, 1993.
  Hidden from History: Forgotten Queens of Islam. Trans. Mary Jo Lakeland. Abingdon: Perseus Books, 1991.
  Women and Islam: An Historical and Theological Enquiry. Oxford: Blackwell, 1991.
Mhajne, Anwar and Brandt, Rasmus. "Rights, Democracy, and Islamist Women's Activism in Tunisia and Egypt." *Politics and Religion* 14, no. 4 (2020): 577–608.
Milani, Farzaneh. *Veils and Words: The Emerging Voices of Iranian Women Writers*. Syracuse, NY: Syracuse University Press, 1992.
Mills, Margaret A. "Gender and Verbal Performance Style in Afghanistan." In *Gender, Genre and Power in South Asian Expressive Traditions*, ed. Arjun Appadurai, Frank Korom, and Margaret Mills, 56–77. Philadelphia: Pennsylvania University Press, 1991.
Moors, Annelies and Vroon-Najem, Vanessa. "When Islamic Marriage Travels to the Netherlands: Convert Muslim Women (Re)Signifying the Marriage Guardian and the Dower." In *Muslim Marriage and Non-Marriage: Where Religion and Politics Meet Intimate Life*, ed. Julie McBrien and Annelies Moors, 223–247. Leuven: Leuven University Press, 2023.

Mubarak, Hadia. "Classical Qur'anic Exegesis and Women." In *The Routledge Handbook of Islam and Gender*, ed. Justine Howe, 23–42. Milton: Taylor & Francis Group, 2020.

Mulia, Siti Musdah (with Cammack, Mark E.). "Toward a Just Marriage Law: Empowering Indonesian Women through a Counter Legal Draft to the Indonesian Compilation of Islamic Law." In *Islamic Law in Contemporary Indonesia: Ideas and Institutions*, ed. R. Michael Feener and Mark E. Cammack. Cambridge, MA: Harvard University Press, 2007.

Nadwi, Abul Hasan Ali. *Prophet of Mercy* [Nabiyy-i Rahmat]. London: Turath Publishing, 2014.

Nielsen, Richard A. "Women's Authority in Patriarchal Social Movements: The Case of Female Salafi Preachers." *American Journal of Political Science* 64, no. 1 (2020): 52–66.

Nieuwkerk, Karin van, ed. *Women Embracing Islam: Gender and Conversion in the West*. Austin, TX: University of Texas Press, 2006.

Nisa, Eva F. *Face-Veiled Women in Contemporary Indonesia*. New York: Routledge, 2023.

"Muslim Women in Contemporary Indonesia: Online Conflicting Narratives behind the Women's Ulama Congress." *Asian Studies Review* 43, no. 3 (2019): 434–454.

"Women and Islamic Movements." In *Handbook of Islamic Sects and Movements*, ed. Muhammad Afzal Upal and Carole M. Cusack, 151–75. Leiden: Brill, 2021.

Nurmila, Nina. "The Influence of Muslim Global Feminism on Indonesian Muslim Feminist Discourse." *Al-Jami'ah: Journal of Islamic Studies* 49, no. 1 (2011): 33–64.

"Qur'ān: Modern Interpretations: Indonesia." In *Encyclopaedia of Women and Islamic Cultures*, gen. ed. Suad Joseph. Netherlands: Brill Online, 2012: https://referenceworks.brill.com/display/db/ewio.

"The Spread of Muslim Feminist Ideas in Indonesia: Before and after the Digital Era." *Al-Jami'ah Journal of Islamic Studies* 59, no. 1 (2021): 97–126.

Women, Islam and Everyday Life: Renegotiating Polygamy in Indonesia. London, New York: Routledge, 2009.

Ognjenović, Gorana and Jozelić, Jasna. *Politicization of Religion, the Power of Symbolism: The Case of Former Yugoslavia and Its Successor States*. New York: Palgrave Macmillan, 2014.

Olszewska, Zuzanna. *The Pearl of Dari: Poetry and Personhood among Young Afghans in Iran*. Bloomington: Indiana University Press, 2015.

O'Reilly, Andrea. "African-American Mothering: 'Home Is Where the Revolution Is'." In *Mothers, Mothering and Motherhood across Cultural Differences*, ed. Andrea O'Reilly, 93–118. Bradford: Demeter Press, 2014.

Özyürek, Esra. *Being German, Becoming Muslim: Race, Religion, and Conversion in the New Europe*. Princeton: Princeton University Press, 2014.

Pappano, Margaret Aziza and Olwan, Dana M. *Muslim Mothering: Local and Global Histories, Theories, and Practices*. Bradford: Demeter Press, 2016.

Pearson, Elizabeth and Winterbotham, Emily. "Women, Gender and Daesh Radicalisation: A Milieu Approach." *The RUSI Journal* 162, no. 3 (2017): 60–72.

Peirce, Leslie. *The Imperial Harem: Women and Sovereignty in the Ottoman Empire*. New York, Oxford: Oxford University Press, 1993.

Philbrick-Yadav, Stacey. "Segmented Publics and Islamist Women in Yemen: Rethinking Space and Activism." *Journal of Middle East Women's Studies* 6, no. 2 (2010): 1–30.
Pritchard, James B., ed. *Solomon and Sheba*. London: Phaidon Press, 1974.
Qutb, Muhammad Ali. *Women around the Messenger*. Trans. Abdur-Rafi' Adewale Imam. Riyadh: International Islamic Publishing House, 2007.
Qutbuddin, Tahera. *Arabic Oration: Art and Function*. Leiden: Brill, 2019.
Rahman, Fazlur. *Islam and Modernity: Transformation of an Intellectual Tradition*. Chicago: University of Chicago Press, 1982.
  Major Themes of the Qur'an. Chicago: University of Chicago Press, 1980; repr. with an intro. by Ibrahim Moosa, 2009.
Ramet, Sabina, ed. *Gender Politics in the Western Balkans: Women in Society in Yugoslavia and the Yugoslav Successor States*. Philadelphia: Penn State University Press, 1999.
Rapoport, Yossef. *Marriage, Money and Divorce in Medieval Islamic Society*. Cambridge: Cambridge University Press, 2005.
Redfern, Catherine and Aunne, Kristin. *Reclaiming the F Word*. London, New York: Zed Books, 2013.
Rinaldo, Rachel. *Mobilizing Piety: Islam and Feminism in Indonesia*. Oxford, New York: Oxford University Press, 2013.
Roded, Ruth. "Bint al-Shati's 'Wives of the Prophet': Feminist or Feminine?" *British Journal of Middle Eastern Studies* 33, no. 1 (May 2006): 51–66.
Rofiah, Nur. "Reading the Qur'an through Women's Experience." In *Justice and Beauty in Muslim Marriage: Towards Egalitarian Ethics and Laws*, ed. Ziba Mir-Hosseini, Mulki al-Sharmani, Jana Rumminger, and Sarah Marsso, 57–84. London: Oneworld Publications, 2022.
Rogozen-Soltar, Mikaela. "Striving toward Piety: Gendered Conversion to Islam in Catholic-Secular Spain." *Current Anthropology* 61, no. 2 (2020): 141–167.
Rosati, Francesca. "Women's Qur'anic Schools in China's Little Mecca." In *Ethnographies of Islam in China*, ed. Rachel Harris, Guangtian Ha, and Maria Jaschok. Honolulu: University of Hawai'i Press, 2021.
Ruby, Tabassum F. "Listening to the Voices of Hijab." *Women's Studies International Forum* 29, no. 1 (2006): 54–66.
Ruggles, D. Fairchild. *Tree of Pearls: The Extraordinary Architectural Patronage of the 13th-Century Egyptian Slave-Queen Shajar al-Durr*. New York: Oxford University Press, 2000.
Ruggles, D. Fairchild, ed. *Women, Patronage, and Self-Representation in Islamic Societies*. Albany: SUNY Press, 2000.
Šabasevičiūtė, Giedrė. "Women Writing in Cairo: Midlife, Self-Care, and the Informal World of Literature." *Journal of Middle East Women's Studies* 19, no. 3 (2023): 317–336.
Safi, Omid. *Memories of Muhammad: Why the Prophet Matters*. New York: HarperCollins, 2010.
Said, Edward. *Orientalism*. London: Penguin Books, 2003.
Salime, Zakia. *Between Feminism and Islam: Human Rights and Sharia Law in Morocco*. Minneapolis: University of Minnesota Press, 2012.

Schäfers, Marlene. *Voices That Matter: Kurdish Women at the Limits of Representation in Contemporary Turkey*. Chicago: University of Chicago Press, 2023.
Schimmel, Annemarie. *And Muhammad Is His Messenger: The Veneration of the Prophet in Islamic Piety*. Chapel Hill: University of North Carolina Press, 1985.
"Women in Mystical Islam." *Women's Studies International Forum, Special Issue: Women and Islam* 5, no. 2 (January 1982): 145–151.
Schmid, Nora K. "Lot's Wife: Late Antique Paradigms of Sense and the Qurʾān." In *Qurʾānic Studies Today*, ed. Angelika Neuwirth and Michael Sells, 52–81. Abingdon: Routledge, 2016.
Schwedler, Jillian. "Islamists in Power? Inclusion, Moderation, and the Arab Uprisings." *Middle East Development Journal* 5, no. 1 (2013): 1–18.
Sehlikoglu, Sertac. "Revisited: Muslim Women's Agency and Feminist Anthropology of the Middle East." *Contemporary Islam* 12 (2018): 73–92.
Shah, Zahra. "Negotiating Female Authorship in Eighteenth-Century India: Gender and Multilingualism in a Persian Text." *Journal of the Royal Asiatic Society* 29, no. 3 (2019): 447–466.
Shakman Hurd, Elizabeth. *Beyond Religious Freedom: The New Global Politics of Religion*. Princeton: Princeton University Press, 2015.
Sharma, Sunil. "From ʾĀʾesha to Nur Jahān: The Shaping of a Classical Persian Poetic Canon of Women." *Journal of Persianate Studies* 2, no. 2 (2009): 148–164.
Siraj, Asifa. "Meanings of Modesty and the Hijab amongst Muslim Women in Glasgow, Scotland." *Gender, Place and Culture: A Journal of Feminist Geography* 18, no. 6 (2011): 716–731.
Sirajuddin, ʿAbdallah. *Our Master Muhammad, The Messenger of Allah*. Trans. Khalid Williams. 2 vols. Rotterdam: Sunni Publications, 2008.
Sirri, Lana. *Islamic Feminism Discourses on Gender and Sexuality in Contemporary Islam*. London: Routledge, 2022.
Smith Hefner, Nancy. *Islamizing Intimacies: Youth, Sexuality, and Gender in Contemporary Indonesia*. Honolulu: University of Hawaiʿi Press, 2019.
Spahić Šiljak, Zilka, *Women, Religion and Politics: Impact Analysis of Interpretative Religious Heritage of Judaism, Christianity and Islam on the Engagement of Women in Public Life and Politics*. Sarajevo: IMIC-CIPS-TPO, 2010.
"Women, Religion and Politics." In *Religion, the Secular, and the Politics of Sexual Difference*, ed. Linell E. Cady and Tracy Fessenden, 121–136. New York: Columbia University Press, 2013.
Spahić Šiljak, Zilka, ed. *Contesting, Female, Feminist and Muslim Identities in Bosnia and Herzegovina and Kosovo*. Sarajevo: Center for Interdisciplinary Postgraduate Studies of the University of Sarajevo, 2012.
Spahić Šiljak, Zilka and Dino, Đipa. *Gender Equality Barometer of Bosnia and Herzegovina*. Sarajevo: United Nations Development Programme, 2024.
Spellberg, Denise A. *Politics, Gender, and the Islamic Past: The Legacy of Aisha bint Abi Bakr*. New York: Columbia University Press, 1994.
Spiker, Hasan. *Hierarchy and Freedom: An Examination of Some Classical Metaphysical and Post-Enlightenment Accounts of Human Autonomy*. Dublin: New Andalus Press, 2023.

Stewart, Devin J. "Understanding the Quran in English: Notes on Translation, Form, and Prophetic Typology." In *Diversity in Language: Contrastive Studies in Arabic and English Theoretical and Applied Linguistics*, ed. Zeinab M. Ibrahim, Sabiha T. Aydelott, and Nagwa Kassabgy, 31–48. Cairo: American University in Cairo Press, 2000.

Stowasser, Barbara. "The Mothers of the Believers in the 'Hadith'." *The Muslim World (Hartford)* 82, no. 1–2 (1992): 1–36.

——. *Women in the Quran: Traditions, and Interpretation*. New York: Oxford University Press, 1994.

Szuppe, Maria. "The 'Jewels of Wonder': Learned Ladies and Princess Politicians in the Provinces of Early Safavid Iran." In *Women in the Medieval Islamic World: Power, Patronage, and Piety*, ed. Gavin R. G. Hambly, 325–345. New York: St. Martin's Press, 1999.

Tadros, Mariz. *The Muslim Brotherhood in Contemporary Egypt: Democracy Redefined or Confined?* New York: Routledge, 2012.

Tajali, Mona. *Women's Political Representation in Iran and Turkey: Demanding a Seat at the Table*. Edinburgh: Edinburgh University Press, 2022.

Tarlo, Emma. *Visibly Muslim: Fashion, Politics, Faith*. New York: Berg, 2010.

al-Tha'labi. *Lives of the Prophets: As Recounted by Abu Ishaq Ahmad Ibn Muhammed Ibn Ibrahim al-Thalabi*. Trans. William M. Brinner. 1st ed. Leiden: Brill, 2002.

Thimm, Viola. *(Re-)Claiming Bodies through Fashion and Style: Gendered Configurations in Muslim Contexts*. Cham, Switzerland: Springer International Publishing AG, 2021.

Thys-Şenocak, Lucienne. *Ottoman Women Builders: The Architectural Patronage of Hadice Turhan Sultan*. Aldershot: Ashgate, 2006.

at-Tirmidhī, Muḥammad ibn 'Īsā. *A Portrait of the Prophet: As Seen by His Contemporaries*. Trans. Muhtar Holland. Louisville: Fons Vitae, 2017.

Tønnessen, Liv. "Ansar al-Sunna and Women's Agency in Sudan: A Salafi Approach to Empowerment through Gender Segregation." *Frontiers: A Journal of Women Studies* 37, no. 3 (2016): 92–124.

Tottoli, Roberto. *Biblical Prophets in the Qur'ān and Muslim Literature*. Richmond: Routledge Curzon, 2002.

Tucker, Judith E. *Women, Family, and Gender in Islamic Law*. Themes in Islamic Law. Cambridge: Cambridge University Press, 2008.

van Doorn-Harder, Nelly. "The Indonesian Islamic Debate on a Woman President." *Sojourn* 17, no. 2 (2002): 164–190.

Vroon-Najem, Vanessa. "Muslim Converts in the Netherlands and the Quest for a 'Culture-Free' Islam." *Archives de Sciences Sociales des Religions* 186 (2019): 33–51.

Wadud, Amina. *Qur'an and Woman*. Kuala Lumpur: Fajar Bakti SDN BHD, 1992.

——. *Qur'an and Woman: Rereading the Sacred Text from a Woman's Perspective*. New York: Oxford University Press, 1999.

Watt, Montgomery. "The Queen of Sheba in Islamic Tradition." In *Solomon and Sheba*, ed. James B. Pritchard, 85–103. London: Phaidon Press, 1974.

Wickham, Carrie Roosefsky. *The Muslim Brotherhood: Evolution of an Islamist Movement*. Princeton: Princeton University Press, 2013.

Yalman, Suzan. "The 'Dual Identity' of Mahperi Khatun: Piety, Patronage and Marriage across Frontiers in Seljuk Anatolia." In *Architecture and Landscape in Medieval Anatolia, 1100–1500*, ed. Patricia Blessing and Rachel Goshgarian, 224–252. Edinburgh: Edinburgh University Press, 2017.

Yamani, Muhammad Abduh. *Our Lady Fāṭima al-Zahrā'*. Trans. Khalid Williams. Alburtis, PA: Ihya Publishing, 2024.

Youssef, Maro. "Strategic Choices: How Conservative Women Activists Remained Active throughout Tunisia's Democratic Transition." *Sociological Forum* 37, no. 3 (2022): 836–855.

Zebiri, Kate. *British Muslim Converts: Choosing Alternative Lives*. Oxford: Oneworld Publications, 2008.

Zellentin, Holger Michael. *Law beyond Israel: From the Bible to the Qur'an*. Oxford: Oxford University Press, 2022.

The Qur'ān's Legal Culture: The Didascalia Apostolorum as a Point of Departure. Tübingen: Mohr Siebeck, 2013.

Zempi, Irene. "'It's a Part of Me, I Feel Naked without It': Choice, Agency and Identity for Muslim Women Who Wear the Niqab." *Ethnic and Racial Studies* 39, no. 10 (2016): 1738–1754.

Index

INTRODUCTORY NOTE

References such as '178–9' indicate (not necessarily continuous) discussion of a topic across a range of pages. Wherever possible in the case of topics with many references, these have either been divided into subtopics or only the most significant discussions of the topic are listed. Because the entire work is about 'women' and 'Islam', the use of these terms (and certain others which occur constantly throughout the book) as an entry point has been restricted. Information will be found under the corresponding detailed topics. Cross-references in a form such as 'mosques, *see also individual mosque*' direct the reader to headings in a particular class (e.g. in this case 'al-Qarafa Mosque') rather than a specific *'individual mosques'* entry.

abaya, 1, 103
Abd al-Rahman b. Awf, 117
Abdel Aal, Soad, 191
Abdul Kodir, Faqihuddin, 224, 226–8, 232, 335
Abdul Rahman, Aisha, 87
Abish Khatun, 307–8
ablution, ritual, 91, 113
abortion, 327, 334, 376
Abraham, 45–6, 107, 205, 223
Abu al-Ala al-Mawdudi, 97, 100
Abu Ali al-Daqqaq, 110
Abu Bakr, 139, 140–1
Abu Bakra, 217
Abu Hanifa, 15, 73, 77–8
Abu Huraira, 91
Abu-Lughod, Lila, 1, 19, 344–5
Abu Yusuf, 77–8
abuse, 52–3, 55, 87, 103, 108, 223, 329
Aceh, 307
activism, 21, 125, 263–4, 360, 368–9, 378
  feminist, 260, 360, 368

  mothering, 139–42
  political, 24, 176–8, 180, 189, 321
  social, 27, 139, 141, 142, 263, 315–37
  socio-political, 263–4, 315, 318
activists, 26–7, 169, 188, 229, 323–4, 329–30, 365–7, 370–1, 373–5, 376–7
  faith-based, 366, 368–70, 371, 375, 377
  Islamist, 187, 189
actresses, 364, 365, 370, 376
Adam, 37, 45–6, 48, 53, 96, 108–10
Adil I, 273
adultery, 50, 90–1, 98, 217
advocacy, 26, 178, 263, 317
  campaigns, 190
  legal, 171, 315
affection, 18, 57–8, 208, 240, 245
Afghan poets, 265, 350–6
Afghanistan, 1, 343, 345–6, 347, 351, 353–4, 357
Afghans, 352, 354–5
Afsaruddin, Asma, 306

afterlife, 35, 41, 44, 53–4, 57, 60, 61–2, 113, 203, 206–7
age, 16, 38, 98–9, 192, 217, 249, 289, 299, 307, 309
  minimum, 191–2
agency, 5–6, 19, 88–9, 128–30, 151–3, 160–2, 164–8, 170–1, 196–7
  architecture as, 268–92
  of believing women, 16–23
  creative, 264, 339
  expressions of, 6, 19, 197
  female, 3, 146, 152–3, 159, 161, 169–71, 174, 184–8, 196–8, 262
  human, 3, 196, 268
  moral, 35, 43–5, 46, 47, 58–61
  pietistic, 85, 93, 101
  political, 163, 174, 178, 180, 189
  relational, 234, 236, 238
  social, 43, 58–9, 61
Agra, 290–2, 294
Ahmad, Attiya, 210
Ahmad-i Jam, 284
ahong, 23, 239–40, 244–5, 249–50, 251
  female, 235, 238, 245, 248, 252
  male, 238, 250
al-Ahzab, 50
Aisha bint Abi Bakr, 18, 24, 29, 38–9, 90, 99, 107, 111–15, 126, 217, 303–5, 343
Aisha bint Uthman, 343
Aisyiyah, 263, 320, 322, 329
alcohol, 99, 201–3, 204–5, 373
Ali, Kecia, 7–8, 89, 110
Alimat, 226, 228, 229, 232, 332
Allah, 86, 90–1, 92–3, 97–9, 128–9, 130–2, 135, 136–7, 219–20, 225
  see also God.
  signs of, 130, 133
Allah's Messenger, 91, 92
alms, 43, 92, 200, 226, 372
Amin, Yasmin, 139–40
angels, 93, 140, 142, 200
anonymity, 339, 345, 347
anthologies, 102, 343, 348, 357
Anwar, Etin, 320–1, 322
Anwar, Zainah, 215, 232
Apostle of Allah, 128–9, 130–3, 135–6
Arab Spring, 157, 175, 178, 316–17

Arabia, 138, 237, 308
  early Islamic, 58
  pre-Islamic, 138
  seventh-century, 41–2, 48, 52, 55, 58, 134–5
Archangel Gabriel, 111–13, 116, 121, 275
architects, 269, 272, 282–3, 299
architectural patronage, 26, 262, 269, 272–4, 280, 286, 293–4
architectural works, 262, 269, 273–4, 285, 294
architecture, as agency, 268–92
Argumen Kesetaraan Jender, 225
art, 3, 18, 26–7, 261, 268, 269–70, 282, 342–3, 348, 356
artists, 216, 282, 299, 338, 368
Asma bint Umays, 141–2
audiences, 5, 11, 42, 53, 98, 252, 333, 337, 344, 347
authenticity, 7, 101, 137, 163, 165, 169, 216–17
authority, 127, 140, 158, 227, 246, 288–90, 298–9, 302, 304–7, 308–9
  spiritual, 127, 308
autonomy, 1, 22, 35, 146, 153, 161, 210, 239, 306, 309
Awami League, 311
ayat, 133–4
Ayubi, Zahra, 9, 13
Ayyubid and Mamluk tombs, 276–81
al-Azhar, 103, 272

Baghdad, 276, 306–7
balance, 20, 146, 176, 272, 309, 350, 376
baligh, 192
Balkans, 285, 360, 367, 373
Balqis, 182
Bangladesh, 21, 311, 315
al-Banna, Hassan, 176, 179, 260
Barber, Karin, 340
Barlas, Asma, 6, 149, 214–16, 221–4, 232
beauty, 38, 49, 100, 102, 106, 109, 118, 230, 282
Bedouin, 117, 344–5
Begam of Bhopal, 26, *see also* Sultan Jahan

Beijing Fourth World Conference on Women, 324
beliefs, 34, 44, 58, 85–7, 158, 175, 200, 203, 311–12, 319–20
beliefs, Salafi, 154, 170
believers, 14, 34, 42–3, 44–5, 47–9, 51, 57, 58–62, 86, 88–9, 97, 99–100, 104, 106, 108, 124, 128, 130, 133, 228, 239, 240–1, 315, 365, 372, 374
   female, 7, 47, 61, 104
   male, 60, 61, 126
   mothers of, 7, 16, 34, 39, 89, 99–100, 126–7, 128, 142, 315
believing community, 60–1
believing households, 57, 59
Benazir Bhutto, 309–10, 312–13
bequests, 81–2, 267
Beyond the Veil, 6
Bhopal, 26, 307
biases, 65, 125, 158, 302
BiH (Bosnia and Herzegovina), 360–3, 364, 368, 372–3, 376, 378
   and feminist spirituality, 361–3
Bint al-Shati, 87–8, 137
biographers, 116, 121, 300, 302
biological differences, 5, 34, 174–5, 320
Blagojević, Marina, 361
Boesen, Inger, 345–6
Bonci, Alessandra, 20, 152, 169
Book of Maintenance, 66
Booth, Marilyn, 14, 260
Bosnia, 265, 360–1, 373, 378
Bosnia and Herzegovina, *see* BiH.
Bosnian Islam, 28, 266
Bosnian women, 361, 363
boundaries, 10, 15, 19, 48, 170, 190, 254, 344–5, 347, 350
boyfriends, 201, 212
boys, 67, 88, 117, 351
Brandt, R., 21, 188
Brant, Jennifer, 126
breastfeeding, 56, 228
bridal payments, 53–4, 58, 59–60
brothers, 73–4, 97, 116, 128, 207, 271, 289, 292, 309–10, 348

Cairo, 217, 262, 270–1, 276–7, 294, 309
Calderini, S., 272

caliphate, 25–6, 304
caliphs, 139, 140, 142, 181, 217, 267, 271, 303–4
Camel, Battle of the, 24, 121, 217, 303
candidates, 177, 180
care of the vulnerable, 42, 53
Career and Communities of Zaynab Fawwaz, 13, 260
case studies, 76–7, 102, 174, 184, 262, 264–5, 318, 350
centrality, 77, 106, 242–3
CFCM (Conseil Français du Culte Musulman), 103
chador, 354–5
charisma, 300, 306
charity, 38, 44, 93–4, 113, 120, 129, 187, 261, 268, 269
chastity, 58–9, 90, 97, 132, 137, 220, 223, 274
childcare, 36, 67, 361
child marriage, 27, 326, 327, 333–6
children, 42, 53–4, 66–8, 69–72, 73, 75, 81, 116–17, 168–9, 182–3, 230
   maintenance/support, 71–2, 75
   young, 67, 70, 111, 118, 352
China, 2, 29, 150
   central, 23, 150, 234–5, 237–8, 247–8, 250, 253, 255
   changing gender regimes and existential diaspora, 254–5
   Communist Party rule, 244, 255
   Henan Province, 150, 251
   mosques and 'home' in diasporic contexts, 240–2
   piety as diasporic, relational construct, 236–40
   place of mosques in history of Chinese Hui Muslim women, 246–8
   provincial Hui Muslim communities, 250–4
   religious life, 245, 253
   religious piety of Chinese Hui Muslim women, 243–6
   Shanghai, 249–50, 254
   sustaining piety, 248–54
   women's mosques, 150, 234–66
Chinese Communist Party, 150, 238, 244, 255

Chinese Hui Muslim women, 235–6, 243–8
Chinese Muslims, 29, 150, 235, 238, 240, 244
chivalrous prophet, 110–12
choices
  deliberate, 3, 29, 160
  informed, 200, 204
  moral, 43–5, 59, 62
Christianity, 12, 108, 202, 273, 307
Christians, 42, 108, 362
churches, 62, 209, 359, 372
Cirebon, 226, 325, 329, 332
cities, 25, 248, 271, 273, 277, 282, 294, 300, 332, 346
  walled, 271, 277
citizens, 296–7, 320, 377
class, 4, 72, 193, 261, 264, 341, 372
Clohessy, Christopher, 139–40
closeness to God, 44, 46, 50
clothes, 48, 119–20
COLIBE (Committee on Individual Liberties and Equality), 80
comfort, 23, 47, 57–8, 112, 228, 249
commands, Qur'anic, 48, 52, 98
commitments, 25, 29, 37–8, 136, 168, 232, 240, 355, 378
Committee on Individual Liberties and Equality, *see* COLIBE
communal identity, 43, 47–51, 243
communist ideology, 362, 372
communities, 7, 10, 13–14, 22, 24, 29, 38, 48, 51–2, 57, 59, 60, 62, 79, 93–4, 96–7, 108, 110, 116, 118–19, 126, 149, 150, 172, 181, 196, 198, 243, 247, 249, 255, 260, 266, 269, 270, 300–1, 306, 315, 317, 333, 339, 373
  believing, 60–1
  Muslim, 2, 13, 24–5, 37, 49, 93–4, 125, 146, 217, 252–3
  religious, 11, 107, 158, 362, 372–3, 375–6
companions, 78, 88, 93, 110, 112, 118, 120–1, 201, 305
compassion, 35, 38, 106, 117, 120, 302
complementarity, 34, 88, 147–8, 185, 190, 191–2, 326

gender, 147, 150, 174–83, 186, 188, 245
  principle, 147, 174, 180
complexity, 3, 13, 15, 20–1, 24, 35, 39, 239, 241, 260
conceptions, 15, 64–5, 197, 366
conceptualization, 9, 197, 241
conduct, ethical, 9, 35, 38
conflict, 4, 20, 27, 55, 64, 88, 206, 346
congregation, 117, 234, 239, 245, 247, 250, 270
congregational prayer, 92, 181
consent, 57, 89, 92, 95, 177, 191–2, 230
conservativism, 373, 374
consorts, 282, 294, 349
constitutions, 80, 175–7, 296, 306, 309–11, 312–13, 320, 361
contradictions, 34, 165–6, 243, 347
control over women?, 43, 58–61
conversion, 22, 112, 148, 162–4, 195–212, 237
  and changes in daily life, 197, 198, 203–7
  and ethnography, 198–9
  existential reorientation, 198, 199–203, 206
  and sisters in Islam, 207–11
  women's, 148, 195, 196–7, 200, 212
corruption, 79, 115, 374
Cortese, D., 272
Conseil Français du Culte Musulman (CFCM), 103
couples, 55, 57, 93, 135
courtesies, 114–16, 122
creator, 45, 89, 102, 134
crimes of honour, 50
cultural norms, 134, 138
cultural traditions, 103, 161, 243, 299, 306
cultures, 12, 39, 89, 103, 107, 126, 162, 198, 219, 221, 235, 239, 241, 261, 268, 289, 299, 319, 329

Daesh, 156, 158, 165
daily life, 39, 148, 160, 202, 210, 250
  changes in, 197, 198, 203–7
daily prayers, 68, 200, 369–70
damnation, 42, 44–5, 47

daughters, 24–5, 68–9, 72, 73, 75, 115–16, 270–1, 289, 307, 319–20
Davie, Grace, 371
de-institutionalized feminist spiritualities, 371–7
De Koning, M. J. M., 163, 166–7
death, 24, 50, 112, 116–17, 202, 271, 273, 292, 300, 308
debt, 70–1, 76
decorum, 35, 42–3, 46, 47–50, 51
  sexual, 49–50
deeds, 41, 47, 86, 203, 221, 271, 285, 346, 365
deeds, good, 44, 61, 86, 207, 228, 369
deeds of endowment, 269, 282–3
democracy, 317, 320–1, 323, 326, 363
Deobandi mosques, 161, 169
dependence, 235, 238–9, 378
dependants, 47, 52, 66, 83, 344
descendants, 73, 148, 196, 237
deterrent, 90, 92–3, 97
dhu al-rahim, 72
diaspora, 234, 237, 238, 240–1, 253, 265
diet, 204–6
differences, biological, 5, 34, 174–5, 320
discourses, 1, 8, 9–10, 14, 149, 168, 210, 214, 329, 345
discrimination, 15, 103, 190, 320, 378
disillusionment, 353
distancing, 91–2, 100
diversity, 1, 3–4, 20, 24, 89, 168, 179, 193, 228, 260–1
divine names, 109–10, 113
divine revelations, 125, 128, 134, 199, 299–300
divorce, 7–8, 48, 51–3, 55, 56, 67, 71, 87, 115, 135–6, 228
divorce, Qur'an's verses on, 55
doctrines, 10, 23, 74, 109, 130, 167, 170–1, 202
  Islamic, 38, 108, 124, 125, 179
  mystical, 109–10
domestic violence, 322, 324, 334
domination, 42, 300, 302, 311
double movement method, 230
dowry, 53, 57, 92, 335
dress, 98, 114, 163, 179, 204–7, 375

Durzan, 270–2
Dutch converts, 21–2, 198, 209
Dutch language, 212, 319
Dutchness, 149, 198, 204
duties, 36, 57–8, 65–9, 71–2, 78–9, 82–3, 103, 136, 167, 326
  domestic, 67, 247
  financial, 66, 69, 77, 79, 114
  protective, 36, 66

earth, 37, 111–12, 182, 221, 225
education, 24–6, 181, 209–10, 248–50, 260–1, 268–9, 315–16, 319–20, 322–3, 351
  women's, 26, 263, 315, 319
egalitarianism, 14, 41, 223–4
Egypt, 13, 21, 147–8, 159, 160, 176–8, 185, 308–9, 315–17, 344
Egypt, Fin-de-Siècle, 13, 260
elections, 180, 183–4, 306
elite women, 133, 268, 271, 339
elites, 9, 20, 269, 306, 342
  male political, 296, 308–10
  political, 296, 304, 309, 311–13
emancipation, 14, 346, 361
emissaries, 107, 110, 113, 114, 116–17, 118–19, 300–1
emotions, 27, 117, 136, 163, 165, 240, 353
emperors, 289–91
employment, 102, 197, 361, 363
empowerment, 2, 38, 95, 134, 146–7, 153, 165, 260, 346–7
  narratives, 163, 171
  social, 58, 121
endowments, 25, 261, 269, 282–3
engagement, 3, 7, 64–5, 147, 150, 215, 245, 260, 363, 378
Engineer, Asghar Ali, 149, 214–16, 220–1, 224, 232
Ennahda, 147, 174
Ensiklopedia Muslimah Reformis, 328
equal responsibility, 89–92, 104
equality, 9, 34, 65, 80–2, 149–50, 175–6, 190, 311–12, 332–3, 363
  see also Musawah
  gender, 4–5, 9, 21, 88, 159, 263–4, 315–17, 321, 323, 361–2

male–female, 243, 244, 254
social, 54, 58
spiritual, 35, 37, 43, 47, 61
equity, 21, 34, 88, 148, 176, 183, 190, 191–2, 220, 326
error, 44–6, 50, 88, 107, 135, 136
estates, 79, see also inheritance
ethical conduct, 9, 35, 38
ethical teachings, 26, 108, 360, 378
ethics, 9, 13, 93, 106, 113, 124, 125, 133, 167, 220, 365
    marriage, 13
    sexual, 7, 37, 43, 47–8, 89, 95
ethnic background, 198–9, 208–9
ethnicity, 204, 221, 264, 266, 285, 306
ethnography, 19, 341, 346, 350
    and conversion, 198–9
Europe, 2, 12, 25, 28, 153, 158, 162–3, 210, 211, 267
Eve, 37, 45–6, 48, 96
everyday life, 20, 28, 98, 146, 324, 344, 369
ex-wives, maintenance, 71
exclusion, 27, 183, 189, 228, 237–8, 241
exegetes, 126, 131, 133–5, 217, 305
exile, 237, 310, 351, 354
existential reorientation, 198, 199–203, 206
expectations, societal, 20, 102, 166, 264

Facebook, 351–2, 356
Fadak, 141
Al Fadl bin Abbas, 91
Fahmina, 226, 327–9, 332, 335
Fahmina, Institute, 332
fairness, 15, 34, 81–2, 333
faith, 2–3, 5–6, 11–12, 23, 199–200, 302, 351–4, 360, 364–6, 376
faith, Islamic, 11, 238, 243, 366
faith-based activists, 366, 368–70, 371, 375, 377
families, 54–5, 67–8, 70, 113–14, 136, 175–8, 190–1, 226–7, 267–9, 335–6
families, Muslim, 149, 215, 226, 232, 250, 261, 268, 372
family laws, 316, 332–3
family life, 5, 38, 62, 177, 224, 247, 339

of Muhammad, 113–15
family members, 18, 79, 125, 161, 166, 284, 365
fasting, 43–4, 47, 92, 200–1, 203, 206, 376
Fatayat, 228, 327–30
fate, 41, 44, 200
fathers, 67–9, 71–3, 75, 116, 141–2, 267, 273, 279–81, 289, 310
    see also parents
    royal, 309, 312
Fatima, Prophet's daughter, 139, 141–2
Fatima al-Fihri, 25
Fatimids, 270–2, 309
fatwas, 88, 103, 192, 264, 307, 333–4, 336
Fayumi, Badriyah, 224, 229
fear, 53, 94, 135, 137, 207, 231, 235, 294, 311, 366
female agency, 3, 146, 152–3, 159, 161, 169–71, 174, 184–8, 196–8, 262
female agency, Salafi, 166–70
female *ahong*, 235, 238, 245, 248, 252, 253
female believers, 7, 47, 61, 104
female characters, 44–5, 46–7
female empowerment, 164–5, 260
female genital mutilation (FGM), 325, 334
female Islamists, 148, 175–6, 178, 181–2, 188–91
female leadership, 182, 189, 232, 246, 263, 304
female patrons, 269, 272, 294
female piety, 19, 126, 134, 158, 234
female poets, 349, 354, 357
female religious leaders, 150, 244, 248
female respondents, 163–4
female Salafis, 146–7, 152, 155–8, 160–1, 163, 167–70
female slaves, see slave women.
feminism, 88, 102–3, 266, 321, 324, 327, 359–60, 362, 368, 378
    Islamic, 2, 4–5, 6–8, 10–11, 12–14, 214–32, 320–1, 324, 326–9
    Western, 2, 5, 10, 18–19, 21, 34, 36, 159, 193, 260–1
feminist scholarship, 30, 196, 339

feminist scholarship, Islamic, 2, 6–8, 10, 12–14, 149
feminist spirituality, 27, 265, 359–78
and Bosnia and Herzegovina, 361–3
de-institutionalized, 371–7
as practice, 369–71
relational aspects, 364–9
feminists, 9, 157, 321, 325, 360
activism, 260, 360, 368
Islamic, 4–5, 6, 10, 215, 216, 232, 324, 326
Muslim, 15, 215, 324–7, 355, 360
FGM (female genital mutilation), 325, 334
fieldwork, 17, 25, 198–9, 248, 255, 350–1, 355, 360
financial duties, 66, 69, 77, 79, 114
financial maintenance, 36, 64, 65, 68
financial responsibilities, 15, 36, 64, 74, 79, 111–12
financial rights, 48, 52–4, 68
findings, 22, 79, 163, 166, 168–9, 206, 253, 300, 352, 376
fiqh, 15–16, 50, 58, 85, 91, 226, 323, 326–7, 331
followers, 66, 107, 121, 162, 302–4, 354
food, 70, 111–12, 118, 204–5, 210, 376
forced marriages, 161, 334, 336
forgiveness, 45, 50
fornication, 37, 50–1, 89–92
forums, 207–8, 212
frameworks, 3, 12, 15, 25, 28, 82, 127, 160, 167, 197, 219, 229, 359
patriarchal, 11, 94
France, 103, 164, 210, 216, 225
free women, 57, 59, 271, 294
freedom, 12, 14, 21, 65, 98, 103, 200, 262, 350, 362
friendship, 201, 208, 289
Fustat, 271–2
futuwwa, 110–12

Gabriel, Archangel, 111–13, 116, 121, 275
gardens, 45, 271, 290, 299
garments, 57, 96, 99, 219
Gawhar Shad, 262, 281–5
gaze, 49, 90, 91, 97, 100, 102, 125, 133

Gazin, 338
Geissenger, Aisha, 133
gender, 8–9, 34–5, 44–5, 50, 65–9, 77–9, 88, 224–8, 312–13, 344–5
complementarity, 147, 150, 174–83, 186, 188, 245
differentiation, 215, 260
discourses, 21, 204, 325
dogmas, 188–90
dynamics, 8, 24, 34, 150
equality, 4–5, 9, 21, 88, 159, 263–4, 315–17, 321, 323, 361–2
equity, *see* equity.
hierarchy, 15, 39, 66, 167, 306
identification, 77–8
ideology, 147, 164, 174–5, 185
justice, 9, 175, 226, 255, 264, 298, 311–12, 324–5
segregation, 163, 165, 178–80, 188, 239, 245, 254–5, 265
and the soul, 86–9
training sessions, 149, 214–15
gender-based violence, 265, 363, 367
Gender Hierarchy in the Qur'an, 14–15
gender mixing, 179
dangers, 178–9
gender norms, 5, 10, 13, 15, 20–1, 22–3, 34, 35, 147, 188
Islamic, 2, 14–16, 21, 34, 39
traditional, 23, 263
gender roles, 9, 21, 27, 36, 147, 363, 368, 373, 374
traditional, 158, 165, 317, 362
genealogy, 270, 299
Genealogy of Islamic Feminism, 320, 329
generations, 107, 119, 133, 150, 164, 193, 214, 240, 244, 252
genitals, 77, *see also* private parts
genres, 65, 68, 338, 342, 344, 347, 349, 353, 355–6
Germany, 151, 161–2, 164
al-Ghazali, Abu Hamid, 9, 92
al-Ghazali, Zaynab, 26, 135–8, 260
ghazals, 354, 355–6
Ghiyath al-Din Kaykhusraw II, 26
gifts, 54, 81, 300
lifetime, 81

girls, 26, 67–8, 113, 253, 260, 316, 318–19, 320, 322, 351
Global South, 126, 153–5, 170, 296
God
  see also Allah and *Introductory Note.*
  closeness to, 44, 46, 50
  emissary of, 106, 108
  remembrance of, 38, 44, 113
God-consciousness, 28, 96–7, 378
God's command, 44, 46–7, 49, 60, 100
good deeds, 44, 61, 86, 207, 228, 369
government, 312, 322, 327, 336
granddaughters, 68, 354
grandfathers, 38, 69, 73–4, 116–17, 364
grandmothers, 69, 250, 356, 364
grandparents, 72, 75, 364
grandsons, 69, 73, 117, 139
grants, 41, 54, 60, 91
grassroots, 26, 315–17, 332, 333
gratitude, 47, 221, 228, 353, 366
greetings, 46, 112, 121
growth, 2, 12, 22, 27, 89, 95, 247, 355
guardians, 60, 78, 136, 176, 191, 335
  male, 22, 176–7, 191, 230–1, 333

Habib, Belkhouja, 82
Hadice Turhan Sultan, 285–9
hadith, 7–8, 91–3, 99–101, 139–41, 216–17, 222, 226–8, 303–5, 325–7, 331
  literature, 127, 139
  'Prophetic', 303–5, 307, 310, 312–13
  scholars, 18, 133, 134, 142
  tradition, 24, 38, 96, 107
Hafsah bint Umar, 343
hair, 95, 99, 204, 223, 249, 355
Hajj, 91, 133, 240, 319
hammams, 261, 268, 271, 274, 284
Hanafi school, 8, 15, 34, 35–6, 64, 75, 78, 81–2, 98, 229
hardships, 45, 46–7, 161, 351, 374
harmony, 80, 81, 88, 178, 220, 371
al-Hasan, 139, 272
Hasina, Sheikh, 311
Hassan, Riffat, 214, 324, 360
haya, 19, 37, 96–7
Hazaras, 346, 354–5

headscarves, *see also* hijab; veiling, 353–5, 367
health, 205, 229, 290, 327
hearts, 43, 76, 91, 112, 116–17, 131–2, 135, 136, 354
heaven, 112, 182, 203, 207, 221
heirs, 276, 280, 285, 294, *see also* inheritance
Herat, 282, 284, 348
hermaphrodite, 77
Herzegovina and Bosnia, *see* BiH
hierarchy, 9, 15, 34, 62, 64–6, 85, 305
  gender, 15, 39, 66, 167, 306
  social, 36, 43, 47, 58
hijab, 1, 5, 37, 100–1, 103, 179, 204, 212, 265, 355, 372, 377
  see also veil.
  ban, 102
  wearing, 100, 195, 365, 377
hikma, 134
His Apostle, 129, 130, 133, 135, 136
Holy Qur'an, *see* Qur'an
holy texts, 128, 134, 169, 197, 218, 323, 326, 331, 335–6, 356
homelands, 241, 351–4
honorable words, 130–1
honour, 308, 344–5
  crimes of, 50
  of women, 122
household morality, 43, 51–8
households, 42, 47, 51–3, 57–8, 60–1, 62, 111–14, 116, 267, 274
houses, 49, 51–2, 56, 112, 114, 130–2, 138, 140, 182, 329
Hui Muslims, 23, 234–5, 238, 244, 247, 249
Hui Muslims, Chinese, 235–6, 240, 243, 246, 253
hujja, 308
human agency, 3, 196, 268
human beings, 219, 333, 364, 366
human rights, 27, 103, 215
  fundamental, 149, 264
  Indonesia, 318–36
  international, 187, 190, 192
humans, 44, 47, 53, 86, 142
husbands, 7–8, 18, 43, 45, 47, 50, 54–8, 59–61, 67, 69–73, 76–7, 79, 82,

87–8, 93, 97, 106, 111–12, 114–15, 119–20, 134, 191, 200–1, 205, 210, 219–20, 223, 225, 227–8, 238, 267–8, 271, 273–6, 279–82, 284, 302, 306, 312, 328, 335, 343, 346, 352
Husein Muhammad, Kyai, 224, 232, 325, 330–1
al-Hussain, 139–40

Ibn Arabi, 109
Ibn Kathir, 87, 90, 99, 124
Ibrahimi, Mahbouba, 352–3, 355–6, 357
ICRS (Indonesian Consortium for Religious Studies), 226
'idda, 55, 71, 76
'ideal' in Islam, 106–10
identification of gender, 77–8
identity, 126, 129, 241, 260–1, 276, 277, 340, 351, 353
 communal, 43, 47–51, 243
 new, 22, 165, 205, 212
ideologies, 159–61, 167, 184–6, 193, 344–5, 356
 gender, 147, 164, 174–5, 185
IFEES (Islamic Foundation for Ecology and Environmental Sciences), 318
ignorance, 99, 108, 130, 299, 375
imams, 10, 139–40, 208, 282, 370
impiety, 43, 53
imprisonment, 74, 82, 260
independence, 150, 245, 309, 320
India, 2, 26, 29, 211, 220, 289, 307, 309, 312, 349
Indonesia, 10, 23, 27, 29, 149, 163–4, 196, 214–15, 224–5, 231–2, 263–4, 306, 310, 313, 318, 320–2, 328–31, 334, 336–7
 KUPI, *see* KUPI.
 social activism, 318–36
Indonesian Consortium for Religious Studies (ICRS), 226
Indonesian feminist re-reading of the Qur'an, 224–31
Indonesian Muslims, 224, 321, 324, 326

Indonesian Women's Ulama Congress, *see* KUPI
inequalities, 9–10, 44, 65, 69, 335, 368
informal networks, 180, 188–9
inheritance, 15, 48, 58, 64–83, 141–2, 271
 divisions, 64, 68, 73–6, 79, 81–3
 identification of gender, 77–8
 modern reflections, 78–82
 rights, 37, 139, 142
 rules, 36, 64–5, 68, 74, 75–6, 81
inheritors, *see also* heirs
injunctions, 18, 68, 75, 133, 134
injustice, 99, 108, 231, 343, 355
insaf, 176, 183, 190
inscriptions, 274, 282–5
Instagram, 352–4
institutes, 179, 323–4
institutionalized religion, 28, 359–61, 378
institutions, 16, 37, 92, 94, 215, 237, 251, 255, 269, 373
 political, 184, 311
 public, 255, 377
 religious, 65, 267, 373–4
interdependence, 150, 238, 245
interlocutors, 196, 198–9, 204, 206, 209, 210–11
International Qur'anic Studies Association (IQSA), 11
interpretations, 4, 14, 18, 20, 21–2, 23–4, 27, 62, 93, 99, 125, 146, 148, 152, 169, 174, 176–9, 191, 206, 217, 219–20, 222, 231–2, 234–7, 242, 264, 302, 312, 323, 325–6, 331, 335, 337, 374–5, 378
 of Islam, 148, 319, 322
 of Islamic law, 37, 86, 103
 new, 182, 191–2, 336
 oppressive, 221–2
interviews, 175, 181, 191–2, 237, 244, 265, 296, 360, 366
intimacy, 8, 14, 37, 119, 339, 345
IQSA (International Qur'anic Studies Association), 11
Iran, 187, 264, 284, 289, 296–7, 316–17, 343, 349, 350–7
Iranians, 179, 316, 339, 354

Iraq, 139–40, 317
ISIS, 152, 164
Islamic Community, 362, 371–3, 374–5
Islamic faith, 11, 238, 243, 366
Islamic feminism, 2, 4–5, 6–8, 10–11, 12–14, 214–32, 320–1, 324, 326–9
  reinterpreting the Qur'an, hadith and *tafsir*, 216–24
Islamic Foundation for Ecology and Environmental Sciences (IFEES), 318
Islamic gender norms, 2, 14–16, 21, 34, 39
Islamic inheritance, *see* inheritance.
Islamic jurisprudence, 8, 20, 24, 80, 197, 326
Islamic law, 8, 34, 36, 50, 58, 64, 65–8, 76–7, 81–2, 297
Islamic literature, 3, 16–17, 23, 34, 39, 150
Islamic movements, 14, 155, 175, 176–80, 186–8, 189, 193
  political, 174, 184, 187–8
Islamic Republic of Iran, *see* Iran.
Islamic teachings, 5, 18–19, 25, 146, 222, 260, 264, 266, 333, 363
  classical, 5, 23, 25
Islamic tradition, 7, 8, 29, 35, 45, 93, 109, 129, 136, 360
Islamist movements, 148, 174, 176, 179, 181, 184, 190
Islamists, 147, 174–7, 179, 183–4, 188–90, 192
  female, 148, 175–6, 178, 181–2, 188–91
Islamiyya schools, 16–17, 25
IslamQA, 88
Ismail, Nurjannah, 224
Ismailis, 308
Istanbul, 270, 285–6, 294, 347
Itimad al-Dawla, tomb of, 290–1

Jahan Malik Khatun, 338–9, 357
Jahangir, 289–91
jahiliyya, 99, 108, 299
Jakarta, 224, 332
Jamaat-i-Islami, 21, 313
Java, 320, 331

jealousy, 111, 132, 134
Jesus, 47, 91, 107, 112, 297
jilbab, 95, 97
Jordan, 184, 225
Joseph, 45–6, 49–50
journalists, 367–9, 372, 374
joy, 37, 92
jurisprudence, 7, 15, 90, 93, 327, 331
jurisprudence, Islamic, 8, 20, 24, 80, 197, 326
jurists, 75–6, 78, 98, 305
  Hanafi, 75, 78
  legal, 8, 34
  Muslim, 65, 75, 76, 94
justice, 38, 106, 142–3, 149, 183, 191–2, 220, 228–9, 230–2, 333
  gender, 9, 175, 226, 255, 264, 298, 311–12, 324–5
  substantive, 228

Kamala Chandrakirana, 330
Karbala, 139–40, 343, 354
Kaykhusrau II, 274–5
Kayqubad I, 273
Kayseri, 274, 277
Khadija bint Khuwaylid, 18, 29, 111–13, 124–6, 127, 135, 139, 274
Khaleda Zia, 311
Khalil, 276, 279
Khan, A. L., 307
Khan, Mariam, 93, 102
khuntha, 77–8
khutbas, 276, 308
kindness, 38, 115, 122, 227, 229, 369
kinship, 42, 91, 236, 306, 343
Kitab al-Nafaqat, 66, 69
knowledge, 25–6, 128, 135, 149, 171, 212, 216, 235, 300, 301
Kolman, I., 163–4, 167
Komnas Perempuan, 322, 329, 330, 335–6
Küng, H., 108
KUPI (Indonesian Women's Ulama Congress), 215, 226, 229, 264, 321, 325–6, 329, 330–6
  conferences, 330
Kurdish, 341, 347
Kuwait, 177–9, 210–11

Lal, Ruby, 290
languages, 60, 102, 166, 209, 216, 219, 285, 341–2, 345, 356
law, 35, 48, 60–1, 66–8, 76–8, 80–3, 103, 191–2, 325–6, 336
   Hanafi, *see* Hanafi school
   Qur'anic, 48
   schools of, 36, 80, 81, 98
   shari'a, *see shari'a*
   Sunni, 90, 93
leaders, 7, 18, 65, 176, 178, 183, 226, 229, 311, 319, 321
   Muslim, 323, 331, 334
   political, 4, 27, 141, 297, 304, 312
leadership, 21, 38–9, 177–9, 214, 234, 302, 307, 309, 313, 323
   female, 182, 189, 232, 246, 263, 304
lecturers, 182, 215, 226
lectures, 196, 198, 203, 207–8, 212, 362
legal change, 79–81
legal jurists, 8, 34
legal status, 56, 244, 270, 362
legitimacy, 13, 235, 239, 249, 255, 297–8, 308, 313, 351
letters, 274, 276, 285, 300, 304
liberation, 163, 197, 210, 224
lifestyles, 20, 129, 133, 157, 171
lifetime gifts, 81
lineage, 37, 54, 91, 273, 282, 335
literacy, 263, 264–5, 339–40, 342, 351
literary genres, 338, 356
literature, 22, 64, 128, 146, 153, 171, 174, 184–8, 193, 339–41
literature, Islamic, 3, 16–17, 23, 34, 39, 150
lived religion, 166, 359–78
local contexts, 27, 162, 167, 321
logic, 15, 34, 48, 94, 99, 158
Lot, 47
love, 13, 101, 111, 114, 116–17, 219, 223, 289, 351–3, 367
lovemaking, 352–3

al-mabadi, 227–8
madhhabs, 15, 64, 91
Madrasa al-Salihiyya, 277
madrasas, 20, 261, 268–9, 274, 277, 282, 284, 286

Mahendrarajah, Shivan, 283
Mahmood, Saba, 17, 19, 146, 160, 196
Mahmud al-Mawsili, 69, 74
Mahperi Khatun, 26, 273–6, 277, 282
maintenance, 36, 51, 56, 66–8, 70–6, 79, 91, 191, 304
   children, 71–2, 75
   ex-wives, 71
   financial, 36, 64, 65, 68
   parents, 72, 75
   payments, 70–1, 74–6, 82–3
   relatives, 72, 75
   rules, 69–74, 79, 83
   system, 74–6
   widows, 71
   wives, 70–1, 74
makruf, 229–30
Malaysia, 217, 225, 329
male *ahong*, 238, 245, 250
male believers, 60, 61, 126
male–female equality, 243, 244, 254
male guardians, 22, 176–7, 191, 230–1, 333
male political elite, 296, 308–10
male relatives, 72, 262, 307, 348
Malika Adiliyya, 273
Maliki school, 8, 16, 98, 168
Manazil al-Aziz, 271
marital relationships, *see also* divorce; marriage, 219–20, 228
market, 286–7
marriage, 7–8, 51–3, 54–61, 76–7, 79, 92–4, 135–8, 191–2, 229–30, 335–6
   alliances, 306, 308
   child, 27, 326, 327, 333–6
   contracts, 191
   ethics, 13
   forced, 161, 334, 336
   Islamic, 77, 209, 223–4
   law, 230, 320, 329, 332
   minimum age, 22, 148, 191–2, 329, 336
   multiple, 54
   polygamous, 220, 229–30, 231, 320
   Prophet's, 132, 135, 136, 138
   and sex positivity, 92–5
Mary, 44, 46–7, 112, 274
Mashhad, 282, 284–5, 294, 353–5

mass education, 265, 351
masters, 8, 18, 78, 107, 225, 370
maternal uncles, 74
maturity, 192, 230
mausoleum, 271, 277, 290
Mecca, 112, 121, 133, 200, 238, 307, 319
media, 158, 195, 263, 266, 360, 365, 376
  social, 94, 156, 208–9, 317, 334, 342
Medina, 52, 110, 116, 117, 129, 139, 210
meetings, 92, 196, 198–9, 203, 207–9, 211, 249, 329, 350, 355
Megawati Sukarnoputri, 285, 310, 313
Mehmed II, 286
Mehmed IV, 285
mercy, 57, 113–14, 117, 122, 183, 219, 223, 275, 366
Mernissi, Fatima, 6, 12, 25, 39, 139, 141–2, 149, 214, 216–17, 224, 232, 243
messengers, 60, 107–9, 110–11, 119–20, 129, 142, 304
metaphysics, 9, 106, 113
methodologies, 6, 12, 30, 222–3, 324, 326, 335
Mhajne, A., 21, 188
military, 121, 182, 183, 303, 309
minarets, 282–3
minimum marriage age, 22, 148, 191–2, 329, 336
Mir Hussaini, Ziba, 232
modern Muslim societies, 6, 263, 308, 309
modern readers, 48, 58, 60
modern times, 96, 297–8, 306, 311, 315
modernity, 19, 26, 65, 107, 311–12, 326, 351
modesty, 35, 37, 46, 47–9, 96–7, 158, 160, 218, 344, 350
monasteries, 62
monotheism, 86, 229
monuments, 268, 338, 357
moon, 45–6
moral agency, 35, 43–5, 46, 47, 58–61
moral choices, 43–5, 59, 62
moral foundations, 228–9
moral perfection, 166

moral protection, 60, 62
moral trajectory, 41, 44, 47
moral worldview, Qur'anic, 43–7, 58
morality, 42, 43, 48, 55, 158, 160, 217, 220, 345
  household, 43, 51–8
  sexual, 42, 50, 201
Morocco, 25, 179
Moses, 45–6, 107, 111, 297
mosques, 150, 208, 268–70, 271–6, 282–4, 286–7
  see also individual mosques
  Deobandi, 161, 169
  and 'home' in diasporic contexts, 240–2
  Salafi, 161–2, 166
  Timurid mosque patronage, 281–5
  women's, *see* women's mosques in China.
motherhood, 22, 125–6, 178, 293
mothering, 124, 126–7, 130
  activism, 139–42
  and agency, 127–30
  non-normative, 39, 125, 143
  normative, 126
  Qur'anic pietistic paradigm, 130–4
  social reform, 135–8
mothers, 68–9, 71–3, 112–13, 126–8, 142, 151, 270–1, 273–5, 278–80, 289–90
  see also parents
  of believers, 7, 16, 34, 39, 89, 99–100, 126–7, 128, 142, 315
  biological, 124, 128, 132
  under the gaze of classical and contemporary scholarship, 125–7
movements, 93, 147, 153–4, 174–5, 185–6, 188–9, 193, 317–18, 324, 349
  Islamic, 14, 155, 175, 176–80, 186–8, 189, 193
  Islamist, 148, 174, 176, 179, 181, 184, 190
  political Islam, 20, 147, 174, 184, 187–8, 193
  Salafi, 22, 147, 152, 154, 158, 160
mu'amalat, 80
Mughal court, 289, 290
Mughal Tomb, 289–92

Muhammad, 7, 16, 24, 38–9, 135, 297–8, 303–5, 313–15, 319
  as chivalrous prophet, 110–12
  and honour of women, 122
  as ideal community leader, 117–21
  ideal father, 115–17
  ideal husband and family life, 113–15
  as ideal man, 106–22
  marriage, 132, 135, 136, 138
  wives, 18, 29, 34, 38–9, 60–1, 124–50, 217
Muhammadiyah, 263, 319–21, 330
muhsinun, 46
al-Mujadila, 59
al-Mukarram bi Allah, 308
mukhtasar, 69, 74
Mulia, Siti Musdah, 327–8
Murad, Abdul Hakim, 88, 100
Musawah, 215, 226, 232, 329, 332, 335, *see also* equality
Muslim Brotherhood, 147, 177, 180–1, 183, 185, 189, 260
Muslim Brotherhood, Egypt, 176–8, 185
Muslim identities, 124, 243, 247, 260, 360
Muslim societies, modern, 6, 263, 308, 309
Muslimat NU, 263, 320
Muslims, *see also* Introductory Note
Muslims, Hui, 23, 234–5, 238, 244, 247, 249
mystical doctrines, 109–10

nafaqa, 36, 65, 69, 191
Nahdlatul Ulama, 263, 319
nakedness, 45, 48, 96
Nana Asma'u, 25
narration, 72, 73, 75, 116, 118, 139, 142
narratives, 13, 43, 134, 138–9, 142, 164, 169, 260
nationalism, 260, 320
negotiations, 146, 150, 153–5, 234, 341, 350
Netherlands, 148, 161, 164, 195–6, 198–200, 204, 207–9, 225

networks, 17, 25, 163, 169, 212, 322, 332–3, 368
  informal, 180, 188–9
New York, 218, 221
NGOs (non-governmental organizations), 266, 321, 324–7, 329–30
niqab, 98, 101, 151, 165, 166, 171
al-Nisa', 53
Noah, 46–7
Nobel Peace Prize, 316
noble family, 267, 289
non-governmental organizations, *see* NGOs
non-normative mothering, 39, 125, 143
norms, 7, 25, 34, 129, 134, 138, 186, 205–6, 219–20, 349–50
  gender, 5, 10, 13, 15, 20–1, 22–3, 34, 35, 147, 188
  social, 102, 135, 229
  societal, 8, 39, 136, 148, 260, 315
al-Nur, 50, 51, 90
Nur Jahan, 262, 289–92, 294
nüsi, 235, 247

obedience, 44, 46–7, 48, 60, 86–7, 102–4, 191–2, 219, 225, 309
obligations, 7, 87, 99, 103, 130, 174, 175–6, 290, 294, 336
Olszewska, Zuzanna, 27, 264–5, 338
oppression, 46, 95, 170, 190, 195, 324, 354, 359
oral literature, 340, 342
oral poetry, 27, 344–6, 355
oral texts, 342–7, 348
oral traditions, 124, 252, 264–5, 339–40, 342
orations, 340, 342–3
O'Reilly, Andrea, 125, 126
orphans, 38, 42, 52, 53–4, 118, 220, 230–1
Ottomans, 270, 285–9
Özyürek, Esra, 161–2

pagan women, 49
pagans, 42, 49, 57
painters, 272, 299
Pakistan, 17, 309–10, 313, 316–17

Paradise, 86, 96, 112, 113, 116, 118–19, 142, 199, 207, 228
parents, 42, 70–2, 75, 163, 166, 205, 210–11, 262, 290, 294
  maintenance/support, 72, 75
  unconverted, 205, 206
parliaments, 24, 80, 177, 179–81, 191, 363
participation, 7, 137, 159, 161, 164, 171, 178, 256, 326, 339
  political, 174, 184, 188, 263, 313
parties, political, 147, 175, 181, 183–4, 193
passive Salafi women, 156–9
passive victimhood, 151–3, 157, 170
paternal uncles, 73–4
patriarchal frameworks, 11, 94
patriarchal norms, 126, 260, 264, 316
patriarchal structures, 157, 186, 261, 375
patriarchy, 126, 159, 160, 223, 260, 267, 356, 359, 368
patronage, 42, 52, 262, 267–9, 272, 274, 284, 286, 294, 325
  architectural, 26, 262, 269, 272–4, 280, 286, 293–4
patrons, 4, 27, 42–3, 62, 261, 269, 272–3, 282, 294, 348
pavilions, 261, 268–9, 286–8, 301
payments
  bridal, 53–4, 58, 59–60
  maintenance, 70–1, 74–6, 82–3
peace, 46, 92–3, 112, 121, 229, 300, 309, 359, 363, 365
Pearson, E., 159, 164–5
perceptions, 3, 36, 100, 146, 157, 201, 204, 212, 360
permanent separation, 55–6, 61
Persian, 283, 296, 343, 349, 353
Persianate world, 348–9
personal convictions, 19, 37, 196, 204
perspectives, 3, 7, 13, 34, 48, 58, 88, 126, 182–3, 223–4
  philo-Salafi, 146, 152, 159–61, 165
pesantren, 322–5, 327, 329–32, 333
pietistic agency, 85, 93, 101

piety, 19, 39–43, 47, 51, 62, 125–6, 129–30, 234–6, 239–40, 262, 268–70
  as diasporic, relational construct, 236–40
  female, 19, 126, 134, 158, 234
  God-conscious, 360, 376
  quotidian, 42, 51–8, 62
  religious, 235–6, 239, 243, 269, 356
platforms, 92, 149, 217, 317, 354
Plato, 38, 106
plight, 129, 223, 336, 354
plotlines, 44–5
poems, 264, 340, 348, 351–6
poetry, 26, 264–5, 290, 339, 342, 344–5, 348, 351–3, 355, 357
  oral, 27, 344–6, 355
poets, 25, 27, 265, 290, 338–57
  Afghan, 265, 350–6
  female, 349, 354, 357
political activism, 24, 176–8, 180, 189, 321
political agency, 163, 174, 178, 180, 189
political authority, 7, 141, 217, 262, 296–313
  and 'Prophetic' hadith, 299, 303–5, 307, 310, 311–13
  Queen of Sheba, 297–303, 304, 305, 313
  women who ruled in Muslim world, 306–11
political contexts, 163–5, 193, 266, 346
political debates, 158, 182–3
political elites, 296, 304, 309, 311–13
  male, 296, 308–10
political institutions, 184, 311
political Islam
  and gender complementarity, 175–83
  joining, 174–93
  movements, 20, 147, 174, 184, 187–8, 193
  Sudan, 189–92
  women's agency and mobilization, 185–9
  women's inclusion/exclusion, 184–5
political issues, 183

political leaders, 4, 27, 141, 297, 304, 312
political leadership, 27, 193, 262, 307, 312–13
political participation, 174, 184, 188, 263, 313
political parties, 147, 175, 181, 183–4, 193
political power, 42, 262, 290
political pragmatism, 184, 193
political representation, 187, 248, 311–12, 363
political rights, 177, 179–82, 183, 187, 190, 263, 312
political strategies, 157, 193, 262, 294
political structures, 177, 188, 306
politicization of religion, 266, 373, 377
politics, 38–9, 159, 176–8, 180–4, 191–3, 195, 221, 310, 361, 363
polygamous marriages, 220, 229–30, 231, 320
polygamy, 27, 54, 94, 214, 224, 230–2, 263
polygyny, 94, 149, 223–4, 260, 326, 328, 333, 335
possessions, 51, 97, 230–1, 301
power, 52–4, 107, 281–2, 289, 298, 301, 306, 307–10, 311–13, 356
pragmatism, political, 184, 193
prayers, 8, 47, 78, 113, 119, 130–1, 182, 203, 364, 369–71
    daily, 68, 200, 369–70
preachers, 18, 106
pregnancy, 56, 71, 77, 228, 335
presidency, 177, 296–7, 311, 313
prevention, 48, 157
pride, 111, 138, 166, 183, 244, 355
prime ministers, 289, 303, 309, 311, 313
prioritizations, 88, 97, 100, 104
privacy, 52, 310, 349–50
private parts, *see also* genitals
private sphere, 51–2, 163, 176, 254, 264, 361, 375
privileges, 41, 100, 127, 130, 133–4, 197, 309, 312, 340
programmes, 118, 208, 284, 325, 330–1

prohibitions, 37, 52, 89, 128, 146, 205, 217, 230–1, 249, 251, 377
property, 27, 52–4, 270–1
Prophet. *see* Muhammad
'Prophetic' hadith, 299, 303–5, 307, 310, 311–13
propriety, 49–50, 341
    sexual, 49–51
protection, 35, 42, 45, 51–2, 53–4, 55, 92, 94–5, 158, 335–6
    of women, 42, 50, 62, 334
protective duties, 36, 66
protectors, 42, 53, 62, 164, 225–6, 354
protests, 88, 95, 102–3, 264, 317
proximity, 118–19, 134, 139
PSGA (Pusat Studi Gender dan Anak), 149, 215
puberty, 67, 192
public domain, 157, 206, 253, 303, 304, 310
public life, 176–7, 181, 350, 361–4, 365, 376–7
public spaces, 178–9, 252, 254, 284, 335, 376
public speech, 339, 343–4
public sphere, 4, 154, 164, 175, 178, 234, 248, 268, 351, 361
punishments, 50, 90, 107, 129, 167, 228
Pusat Studi Gender dan Anak (PSGA), 149, 215

qadi, 74, 83
al-Qahira, 271–2
al-Qarafa Mosque, 262, 270–2, 294
al-Qarawiyyin University, 25
Qashawa, Suad Abu, 181, 190
Qatar, 151, 170
al-qawa'id, 227–8
qawama, 22, 176, 190–1
Qirā'ah Mubādalah, 226–7, 335
Qubasiyyat, 17
Qudsiyya Begum, 307
Queen Arwa, 308–9, 312
Queen of Sheba, 45–6, 297–303, 304, 305, 313
quotidian piety, 42, 51–8, 62

Qur'an, 34–5, 107–8, 140, 209, 217–19, 220–3, 226, 228, 232, 297–300, 335, 370
  and *hadith*, 2, 4, 7, 34, 327, 330
  Indonesian feminist re-reading, 224–31
  rulings, 48–9
  text, 62
  women in, 41–62
Qur'anic commands, 48, 52, 98
Qur'anic exegesis, 7–8, 124, 228, 334
Qur'anic law, 48
Qur'anic moral worldview, 43–7, 58
Qur'anic revelations, 218, 222–3, 297–8, 302, 304
Qur'anic stories, 49, 297, 300, 302–3
Qur'anic verses, 15, 35–6, 44, 86–7, 134, 141, 217, 219–21, 223–4, 230

Rabi, Intisar, 338
race, 102, 115, 221
Rahima, 226, 228, 324, 327, 331–2
Rahman, Fazlur, 218, 230
Ramadan, 200, 205, 208, 211, 370, 371–3, 376
rape, 90, 334
rationale, 4–5, 157–8, 298–9
Razia Sultana, 307, 309, 312
reciters, 252, 344–5
recognition, 13, 103, 264, 359
reforms, 80, 82, 134, 148, 159, 189, 192, 316, 318–19, 325
  social, 25, 125–6, 135, 136–7, 138
rejection, 4, 65, 157, 159, 161
relationships, 55–6, 89, 219–20, 239–40, 245–6, 280–2, 289, 308, 364–5, 370
relatives, 54, 68, 72, 75–6, 82–3
  blood, 73, 75
  maintenance/support, 72, 75
  male, 72, 262, 307, 348
religio-spiritual life, 365, 366, 368, 372
religiosity, 11, 360, 365, 369, 372, 376–7
religious authorities, 139, 155, 239, 362
religious backgrounds, 162, 209, 322
religious beliefs, 317, 360, 376

religious communities, 11, 107, 158, 362, 372–3, 375–6
religious devotion, 4, 265, 291
religious elites, 312, 363
religious institutions, 65, 267, 373–4
religious knowledge, 235, 247, 331
religious leaders, 239, 244, 254, 312, 324–5, 327, 330
religious piety, 235–6, 239, 269, 356
  of Chinese Hui Muslim women, 243–6
religious sites, 248, 255
religious sphere, 182, 253–5
religious texts, 149, 224, 226, 232, 326
remarriage, 127–8, 130
remembrance of God, 38, 44, 113
repentance, 44–5, 50, 97
representation, 29, 177, 187, 306, 347
  political, 187, 248, 311–12, 363
reproductive rights, 323–4, 325, 361, 368, 373, 375–6
research, 17, 19–20, 146, 160, 166, 171–2, 187–8, 198–201, 202–3, 211–12
residence, 70–1, 140
resilience, 11, 23, 240, 260, 265, 318
resistance, 19, 160, 166, 170, 197, 219, 315, 317, 336, 376
resources, 3, 94, 110, 125, 134, 253, 284, 311–12
  material, 150, 244
  social, 235, 239, 255, 268
respondents, 13, 154, 168, 210, 360, 364, 365–6, 367–8, 371–2, 377
responsibilities, 46, 71, 77, 87, 92–3, 100–1, 224, 227–8, 363, 377
  equal, 89, 92, 104
  social, 76, 87, 100, 227
  towards wives, 56
restraint, sexual, 5, 16, 22, 96
restrictions, 49, 81, 127, 130, 178–9, 188, 205, 230
  on sexual liberty, 36–7, 85, 89–95, 96, 104
revelation, 111–13, 115, 118–20, 125, 134, 219, 221, 229–31, 297, 311
  Qur'anic, 218, 222–3, 297–8, 302, 304
  time of, 222–3, 230–1

rewards, 44, 60, 61, 113, 167, 228
rich women, 66, 70, 72, 74, 82
Rifka Annisa, 324
rights, 5, 26, 36, 52-3, 54-5, 58, 65-6, 77, 78-9, 83, 87, 89-90, 92-3, 129, 142, 174, 175-6, 190, 210, 220, 224, 231, 263, 316-17, 319-20, 324, 330, 336, 368, 377
   human, 27, 103, 215, 317, 318, 321, 322, 326, 330, 335-6
   inheritance, 37, 139, 142
   political, 177, 179-82, 183, 187, 190, 263, 312
   reproductive, 323-4, 325, 361, 368, 373, 375-6
   women, 8, 184-5, 192-5, 209-10, 260-1, 315, 320-1, 326-7, 331, 332-3
rijal, 225-6
risks, 14, 79, 94, 98, 168, 334, 345, 347
ritual ablution, 91, 113
rituals, 134, 199, 241, 246-7, 359, 370
Rofiah, Nur, 224, 228-9, 333-5
role models, 129-30, 134
roles
   active, 178, 181, 273, 276
   complementary, 21, 175
   gender, *see* gender roles
   societal, 35, 221, 227, 264
   traditional, 39, 143, 158, 165, 317, 362, 375
romantic attachments, 262, 294
royal fathers, 309, 312
rules of inheritance, 36, 64-5, 68, 74, 75-6, 81
rules of maintenance, 69-74, 79, 83
rulings, 4, 20, 47, 50, 54, 80, 94, 99, 297
rulings, Qur'an, 48-9
Rumah KitaB, 325, 327, 335-6
Rumi, 367, 371
Russia, 2, 29, 285

sacred texts, 128, 134, 169, 197, 218, 326
sacrifice, 46, 101, 163, 353, 369
Salafi activists, female, 155, 172
Salafi beliefs, 154, 170

Salafi-jihadi groups, 155, 158
Salafi mosques, 161-2, 166
Salafi movements, 22, 147, 152, 154, 158, 160
Salafi perspectives, internal, 153, 159, 160-1, 166-7
Salafi-phobia, 152-3, 156-9
Salafi women, 20, 22, 146-7, 151-61, 162-72
   lack of research on, 154-6
   passive, 156-9
   reasons for appeal to some women, 161-5
Salafism, 13, 20, 22, 146-7
   becoming Salafi, 151-72
   contradictions, pragmatism and compromises, 165-6
   female Salafi agency, 166-70
   lack of research on Salafi women, 154-6
   philo-Salafi research perspectives, 159-61
   Salafi-phobia and passive Salafi women, 152-3, 156-9
Saljuq mosque-mausoleum complex, 273-6
salvation, 37, 42, 44-5, 46, 48, 53, 85, 161, 240, 255
Sarajevo, 360, 365-9, 370-7
Satan, 45, 51, 300
Saudi Arabia, 4, 156, 161-2, 225, 316
Sawda, 115
scholars, 6-7, 12-15, 29, 81, 215-16, 217, 220, 224, 325-6, 347-8
   classical, 15-16, 34
   hadith, 18, 133, 134, 142
   international, 149, 214
   male, 264, 331
   Muslim, 38, 99, 106, 192, 199, 215
   respected, 15, 34
scholarship, 1, 2, 6, 10-11, 12-13, 152, 177, 186, 214-15, 359
schools, 26, 36, 88, 103, 109, 166, 179, 286-7, 319, 322-3
schools, Hanafi, 8, 15, 34, 35-6, 64, 75, 78, 81-2, 98, 229
scriptures, 107, 111, 241, 262
seclusion, 96, 179, 218, 349

secularism, 102, 236, 377
security, 95, 121, 153, 155, 229, 368
  agencies, 157–8
Seedat, Fatima, 93
segregation, gender, 163, 165, 178–80,
  188, 239, 245, 254–5, 265
self, 9, 92, 163, 167, 364, 366
separation, 8, 55–6, 71
  act of, 56
  period of, 55–6
  permanent, 55–6, 61
sermons, 12, 117, 122, 141, 276, 354
servants, 52, 70, 110, 114, 117, 225, 228
sex positivity and marriage, 92–5
sexual ethics, 7, 37, 43, 47–8, 89, 95
sexual liberty, 5, 22
  restrictions on, 36–7, 85, 89–95,
    96, 104
sexual morality, 42, 50, 201
sexual propriety, 49–51
sexual restraint, 5, 16, 22, 96
sexual restrictions, 36–7, 85, 95–6, 104
sexual transgressions, 56
sexual violence, 334, 336, 367
sexuality, 8, 29, 37, 85, 89, 93, 102,
  158, 368
shahada, 199–200, 201, 203, 208, 211
Shah Rukh, 282–4
Shahih Bukhari, 216–17
Shajar al-Durr, 262, 276–81, 282, 294
Shanghai, 249–50, 254
shari'a, 74, 81, 148, 192, 226, 229,
  322, 326
Shaykh Salim Chisti, 291
Sheba, Queen of, 45–6, 297–303, 304,
  305, 313
Shi'i, 24, 29, 39, 124, 139–41
Shi'i, *tafsir*, 86–7
shrines, 277, 284, 294, 354, 371
sins, 53, 87, 90–1, 92, 100–1, 202, 203
sira, 7–8, 16, 34, 87, 124, 125
SIS, *see* Sisters in Islam.
sisterhood, 149, 207–9, 212
sisters, 69, 73, 112, 116, 128, 198, 199,
  207–9, 212, 307
Sisters in Islam (SIS), 198, 217, 232,
  325, 329, 332

slander, 47, 50–1
slave concubinage, 53
slave women, 52, 54, 57, 58–9
slaves, 8, 9, 51–2, 54, 57, 65, 90, 271,
  273, 285
social activism, 27, 139, 141, 142, 263,
  315–37
social activism, Indonesia, 318–36
social agency, 43, 58–9, 61
social empowerment, 58, 121
social equality, 54, 58
social hierarchy, 36, 43, 47, 58
social imagination, 76
social justice, 8, 14, 26, 124, 260–1,
  317, 320, 330
social life, 24, 179, 227, 236
social media, 94, 156, 208–9, 317,
  334, 342
social milieu, 41, 159, 305
social mobility, 95, 150, 248
social norms, 102, 135, 229
social realities, 20–1, 106, 228–9
social reform, 25, 125–6
  mothering, 135–8
social reformers, 25, 26, 315
social resources, 235, 239, 255, 268
social responsibilities, 76, 87, 100, 227
social spaces, 159, 234, 241–3, 245, 255
social standings, 35, 70, 306
social status, 42, 44, 47, 50, 52, 57, 138,
  141, 244, 245
socialism, 363, 373, 375
societal expectations, 20, 102, 166, 264
societal norms, 8, 39, 136, 148, 260, 315
societal roles, 35, 221, 227, 264
societies
  Muslim, 2, 3, 6, 29, 34, 124, 216,
    266–7, 311–12, 341
  non-Muslim, 150, 241–3, 245
socio-political activism, 263–4,
  315, 318
sociology, 80, 255, 359
Sokoto Caliphate, 25–6
solidarity, 203, 245, 253, 317–18, 364,
  369, 376, 378
Solomon, King, 299–301
songs, 91, 264, 340, 346

sons, 28, 46, 69, 72–3, 75, 81, 97, 115, 136, 139–40, 170, 262, 267, 270, 272–6, 278–82, 285, 293–4, 308
  adopted, 135–8
soul, 37, 44, 47, 90, 142, 221, 353, 359
  and gender, 86–9
Southeast Asia, 224, 306–7, 321
sovereignty, 299–301, 302, 304, 308–9
speech, 114, 130–1, 264, 346
spiritual authority, 127, 308
spiritual equality, 35, 37, 43–7, 61
spiritual trajectory, 35, 45, 47
spirituality, 8, 102, 127, 129, 328
  feminist, 27, 265, 359–78
spouses, 37, 57, 114, 212, 226, 228, 238, 279, 336
stars, 45–6
status
  legal, 56, 244, 270, 362
  social, 42, 44, 47, 50, 52, 57, 138, 141, 244, 245
step-mothers, 72
stereotypes, 186, 203, 367
stipends, 139, 142, 267, 271
stories, 37, 44–7, 50, 138, 211, 235, 249, 250, 299–300, 302
Stowasser, B., 133, 304
strategies, political, 157, 193, 262, 294
stresses, 153–4, 164, 167, 344
students, 3, 73, 103, 110, 114, 215, 225, 322–3
study circles, 17–18, 20, 169
styles, 12, 28, 98, 131, 204, 272, 353, 356
Suad al-Fatih al-Badawi, 176, 181
Subhan, Zaitunah, 224
succession, 139, 303–6, 309, 310
Sudan, 22, 147–8, 163–4, 174–7, 178–80, 182–3, 189–92
Sufi tradition, 28, 265
Sufism, 8, 168, 371
Suharto, President, 310, 321, 329
sultan, 267, 277, 285, 289, 303
Sultan Jahan, 26
Sultan Salih, 276–9
sun, 45–6, 300
sunna, 91, 98, 124, 125, 133, 167, 199
Sunni Islam, 29, 96, 181

Sunni law, 90, 93
Sunni traditions, 29, 126, 139
Sunnis, 29, 86, 284
suras, 50, 53, 60
surrender, 70, 299, 301–2, 366
survival, 129, 150, 189, 237, 245
Sweden, 352
Syah, Kamalat, 307
symbols, 37, 186, 204, 317, 377
Syria, 17–18, 226, 317

al-Tabari, 97, 128, 131–2, 136–8, 141, 217, 303
Tadros, M., 185
tafsir, 7–8, 87, 90, 216, 331, 334
Taj Mahal, 290–2
talaq, 55, 79
Tantawi, Muhammad Sayyid, 103
taqwa, 28, 207, 360, 366, 376, 378
Tarlo, E., 204, 206
tawhid, 161, 229, 335, 360, 366, 378
teachers, 25, 103, 106, 172, 323–5, 327, 354
  university, 365, 368–70, 373, 376–7
teachings, 13, 17, 38, 64, 107–8, 117–18, 210, 325, 332, 337
  ethical, 26, 108, 360, 378
Tehran, 348, 352, 357
temporality, 170–1
temptation, 44, 49, 100
tensions, 20, 36, 82, 162, 166, 177, 195, 204–5, 211–12, 242, 253
Tešanj, 364, 375
testimony, 114, 118–19, 141
texts, 5–7, 13–14, 43–4, 46, 219, 222–3, 226–7, 331, 340–2, 347–9
  holy/sacred, 27, 128, 134, 169, 197, 218, 323, 326, 331, 335–6, 343, 356
  oral, 342–7, 348
theophanies, 109
throne, 122, 276–7, 280–1, 285, 301–3, 309, 312
Thys-Şenocak, Lucienne, 286–7
time of revelation, 222–3, 230–1
Timurids, 281–5, 348
tombs, 261, 268–70, 274–6, 282, 284, 286–7, 290–4
tombs, Ayyubid and Mamluk, 276–81

tradition, oral, 124, 252, 264–5, 339–40, 342
traditional roles, 39, 143, 158, 165, 317, 362, 375
traditions, 7, 15–16, 23–4, 29, 126, 140, 162, 169, 254–5, 304–6
  cultural, 103, 161, 243, 299, 306
trajectories, 109, 153, 188, 201, 318
  spiritual, 35, 45, 47
trajectory, moral, 41, 44, 47
translations, 77, 149, 214, 224, 351, 354, 357
transmitters, 239, 243, 340
'Tree of Pearls', 276, 278
trust, 98, 240, 289, 309, 366, 375
Tunisia, 20–1, 25, 80, 147, 163–4, 169, 174, 175, 187, 317
al-Turabi, Hasan, 181–2
Turkey, 187, 225, 228, 317, 346, 371
Tuzla, 360, 365, 368, 370, 371, 374, 376–7
Twelver Shi'ism, 92

Uhud, Battle of, 112, 121, 230
UK, *see* United Kingdom
ulama, 331, 332–3
Umar, Nasaruddin, 132–3, 140, 224–6
Umm Ayman, 141–2
Umm Kulthum, 343
Umm Salama, 24, 29, 39, 126, 139–42
Umm Zar', 115
ummah, 150, 198, 207, 212, 251
unbelievers, 43, 59–61, 166
uncles, 74, 111, 128
unconverted parents, 205, 206
United Kingdom, 20, 157, 161, 164, 168–9
United States, 171, 217, 317
unity, 360–1, 364, 366
universities, 25, 221, 225, 354, 360
university teachers, 365, 368–70, 373, 376–7
Usman dan Fodio, 25
Uthman, Caliph al-Rashidun, 96, 116, 140

vagina, 77–8
valide sultan, 273–5, 285–6, 289, 294

Valide Sultan Mosque, 287, 294
values, 5, 21, 26, 124, 151, 218, 243, 325, 344–6, 363–4
veil, 220, 315, 349–50, *see also* hijab
veiling, 8, 37, 85, 95–104, 206
verbal expressions, 264–5, 339, 341, 351, 356
verbal virtuosity, 339, 345
vernacular literature/scholarship, 16–17, 23, 34, 150
vernacularization, 236, 263
verses, 34–5, 41, 44, 52–5, 80, 86–7, 90, 94, 97–9, 114, 127–32, 134–8, 221, 222–3, 225, 227, 228–31, 286
victimhood, passive, 151–3, 157, 170
victims, 160, 232, 322, 324, 334, 336, 373
violence, 159, 232, 322, 329, 333, 354, 367
  domestic, 322, 324, 334
  gender-based, 265, 363, 367
virtuosity, verbal, 339, 345
visitors, 117, 132, 201, 207, 249, 287
voices, 1, 112, 119, 188, 197, 245, 285, 338–41, 346–7, 351
volunteers, 149, 198–9, 201, 207, 212
vulnerable individuals, 51–3
vulnerable orphaned girls, 230–1

Wadud, Amina, 6, 10, 149, 214–16, 217–22, 224, 232, 241, 246, 324, 360
Wahhabi tradition, 146, 152
waiting period, 56, 71, 76
waqfiyya, 282–5
wars, 66, 178, 300, 346, 351, 363, 365, 367, 373–4, 377–8
wasiyya, 81–2
wealth, 44, 69–70, 74–6, 79, 114, 230–1, 269–71, 285, 294, 333
Western feminism, 2, 5, 10, 18–19, 21, 34, 36, 102, 159, 193, 260–1
Wickham, C. R., 159, 185
widows, 94, 118, 128, 262, 289, 311
  maintenance, 69, 71, 74, 79, 83
  mature, 294
Winterbotham, E., 159, 164

wisdom, 38, 114, 130, 133–4, 277, 297, 300
witnesses, 50–1, 56, 92, 128, 217
wives, 8, 16, 18, 20, 22, 38–9, 43, 45, 47, 49–50, 52, 54–8, 59–61, 66, 69–72, 73, 74, 76–7, 82, 87–8, 90, 93–4, 97, 111–12, 114, 119–20, 124–6, 127–9, 130–2, 135–7, 138, 141–2, 179, 191, 210, 214, 219–20, 223–4, 227–8, 229–32, 238, 243, 260–1, 270, 273, 276–7, 282, 297, 307, 313, 320, 325, 328, 343
  maintenance, 70–1
  mothering, activism, 139–42
  mothering, and agency, 127–30
  mothering, Qur'anic pietistic paradigm, 130–4
  mothering, social reform, 135–8
  mothers under the gaze of classical and contemporary scholarship, 125–7
  multiple, 53, 231
  Prophet's, 18, 29, 34, 38–9, 60–1, 124–50, 217
  see also individual names
wombs, 53, 122
women, see Introductory Note
women activists, 164, 174, 179, 217, 326
women *ahong*, see female *ahong*
women poets, 349
women poets, Afghan, 350–6
women's mosques in China, 150, 234–66
  mosques and 'home' in diasporic contexts, 240–2
  place in history of Chinese Hui Muslim women, 246–8
  provincial Hui Muslim communities, 250–4
  Shanghai, 249–50, 254
  sustaining piety, 248–54
women's rights, 8, 184–5, 192–5, 209–10, 260–1, 315, 320–1, 326–7, 331, 332–3
workshops, 149, 207, 212, 323, 327, 331–2, 362
World Cup, 151, 170
worship, 62, 86, 88–9, 92, 98, 103, 235, 237, 245, 248–50
writers, 4, 13, 27, 101, 214, 216, 338–57
  see also individual names
  Muslim women as, 347–50
wudu, 91–2

Xiaotaoyuan Women's Mosque, 249

Yemen, 184, 299, 306, 308–9, 312
young children, 67, 70, 111, 118, 352
young women, 158, 203, 208–9, 251, 289, 351
Yugoslavia, 361–2, 376
Yusuf Ali, Abdullah, 225

Zahra Hosseinzadeh, 354–6
Zaid, 135–8
Zainah Anwar, 215, 232
Zaynab bint Ali, 343, 354
Zaynab bint Jahsh, 39, 132, 135, 137–8
Zaynab Fawwaz, 13–14, 26, 260
Zenica, 360, 364, 370
Zhengzhou, 150, 248–9
Zina, 37, 50, 89–91, 97, 100
Zulaykha, 45–6, 49–50

CAMBRIDGE COMPANIONS TO ... *(continued from page ii)*

THE CISTERIAN ORDER Edited by Mette Birkedal Bruun
CLASSICAL ISLAMIC THEOLOGY Edited by Tim Winter
THE COUNCIL OF NICAEA Edited by Young Richard Kim
JONATHAN EDWARDS Edited by Stephen J. Stein
EVANGELICAL THEOLOGY Edited by Timothy Larsen and Daniel J. Treier
FEMINIST THEOLOGY Edited by Susan Frank Parsons
FRANCIS OF ASSISI Edited by Michael J. P. Robson
GENESIS Edited by Bill T. Arnold
THE GOSPELS Edited by Stephen C. Barton
THE GOSPELS, 2nd edition Edited by Stephen C. Barton and Todd Brewer
THE HEBREW BIBLE/OLD TESTAMENT Edited by Stephen B. Chapman and Marvin A. Sweeney
HEBREW BIBLE AND ETHICS Edited by C. L. Crouch
THE JESUITS Edited by Thomas Worcester
JESUS Edited by Markus Bockmuehl
JUDAISM AND LAW Edited by Christine Hayes
LAW IN THE HEBREW BIBLE Edited by Bruce Wells
C. S. LEWIS Edited by Robert MacSwain and Michael Ward
LIBERATION THEOLOGY Edited by Chris Rowland
MARTIN LUTHER Edited by Donald K. McKim
MEDIEVAL JEWISH PHILOSOPHY Edited by Daniel H. Frank and Oliver Leaman
MODERN JEWISH PHILOSOPHY Edited by Michael L. Morgan and Peter Eli Gordon
MUHAMMAD Edited by Jonathan E. Brockup
THE NEW CAMBRIDGE COMPANION TO BIBLICAL INTERPRETATION Edited by Ian Boxhall and Bradley C. Gregory
THE NEW CAMBRIDGE COMPANION TO CHRISTIAN DOCTRINE Edited by Michael Allen
THE NEW CAMBRIDGE COMPANION TO JESUS Edited by Markus Bockmuehl
THE NEW CAMBRIDGE COMPANION TO ST. PAUL Edited by Bruce W. Longenecker
NEW RELIGIOUS MOVEMENTS Edited by Olav Hammer and Mikael Rothstein
NEW TESTAMENT Edited by Patrick Gray
PENTECOSTALISM Edited by Cecil M. Robeck, Jr and Amos Yong
POSTMODERN THEOLOGY Edited by Kevin J. Vanhoozer
THE PROBLEM OF EVIL Edited by Chad Meister and Paul K. Moser
PURITANISM Edited by John Coffey and Paul C. H. Lim
QUAKERISM Edited by Stephen W. Angell and Pink Dandelion
THE QUR'AN Edited by Jane Dammen McAuliffe
KARL RAHNER Edited by Declan Marmion and Mary E. Hines
JOSEPH RATZINGER Edited by Daniel Cardó and Uwe Michael Lang
REFORMATION THEOLOGY Edited by David Bagchi and David C. Steinmetz
REFORMED THEOLOGY Edited by Paul T. Nimmo and David A. S. Fergusson
RELIGION AND ARTIFICIAL INTELLIGENCE Edited by Beth Singler and Fraser Watts
RELIGION AND TERRORISM Edited by James R. Lewis
RELIGIOUS EXPERIENCE Edited by Paul K. Moser and Chad Meister
RELIGIOUS STUDIES Edited by Robert A. Orsi

FRIEDRICH SCHLEIERMACHER Edited by Jacqueline Mariña
SCIENCE AND RELIGION Edited by Peter Harrison
ST. PAUL Edited by James D. G. Dunn
SUFISM Edited by Lloyd Ridgeon
THE SUMMA THEOLOGIAE Edited by Philip McCosker and Denys Turner
THE TALMUD AND RABBINIC LITERATURE Edited by Charlotte E. Fonrobert and Martin S. Jaffee
THE TRINITY Edited by Peter C. Phan
HANS URS VON BALTHASAR Edited by Edward T. Oakes and David Moss
VATICAN II Edited by Richard R. Gaillardetz
JOHN WESLEY Edited by Randy L. Maddox and Jason E. Vickers
WOMEN AND ISLAM Edited by Masooda Bano

For EU product safety concerns, contact us at Calle de José Abascal, 56–1°,
28003 Madrid, Spain or eugpsr@cambridge.org.

www.ingramcontent.com/pod-product-compliance
Ingram Content Group UK Ltd.
Pitfield, Milton Keynes, MK11 3LW, UK
UKHW030805150425
457293UK00016B/261